Introducing
# CULTURAL STUDIES

# Introducing
# CULTURAL STUDIES

## Second edition

**Brian Longhurst**
*University of Salford*

**Greg Smith**
*University of Salford*

**Gaynor Bagnall**
*University of Salford*

**Gary Crawford**
*University of Salford*

**Miles Ogborn**
*Queen Mary, University of London*

*with*

**Elaine Baldwin**
*University of Salford*

**Scott McCracken**
*University of Keele*

PEARSON
Longman

Harlow, England • London • New York • Boston • San Francisco • Toronto • Sydney • Singapore • Hong Kong
Tokyo • Seoul • Taipei • New Delhi • Cape Town • Madrid • Mexico City • Amsterdam • Munich • Paris • Milan

**Pearson Education Limited**
Edinburgh Gate
Harlow
Essex CM20 2JE
England

and Associated Companies throughout the world

*Visit us on the World Wide Web at:*
www.pearsoned.co.uk

Prentice Hall Europe
First published 1999 by Prentice Hall Europe

ISBN: 978-1-4058-5843-4

**British Library Cataloguing-in-Publication Data**
A catalogue record for this book is available from the British Library

**Library of Congress Cataloging-in-Publication Data**
Introducing cultural studies / Brian Longhurst . . . [et al.]. -- 2nd ed.
    p. cm.
  Includes bibliographical references and index.
  ISBN 978-1-4058-5843-4 (alk. paper)
1.   Culture--Study and teaching. I. Longhurst, Brian, 1956–
  HM623.I685 2008
  306--dc22
                                    2007047293

10 9 8 7 6 5 4 3 2 1
11 10 09 08

Typeset in 9.75pt Minion by 3
Printed by Ashford Colour Press Ltd, Gosport

# Contents

Contents

## Part 2  CULTURAL STUDIES

Contents

Contents

# Key influence boxes

# Defining concept boxes

# Preface: a user's guide

We think that cultural studies is one of the most stimulating areas of activity in intellectual life. It is also something that is studied at different levels, forming an important part of the profile of many university courses. There are many books on cultural studies. However, as we have found in our own teaching, there are relatively few introductions to the field that seek to offer an overview and exploration of some of the most important avenues of research in the field – hence this book, which deliberately and very consciously sets out to be a textbook for students who are studying cultural studies as part of a university course.

In seeking to write an introduction we have not attempted to be completely comprehensive. We think that we cover the most important aspects of cultural studies, but ultimately this can only be our interpretation of the field, written from particular standpoints. We have organized the substantially revised second edition of the book into ten chapters divided into two parts. Part 1, on cultural theory, contains four chapters. In the first we introduce some different meanings of the concept of culture and the issues arising from these meanings. This leads us to point to the importance of cultural studies as an activity that produces knowledge that separate disciplines cannot. Our own disciplinary training and affiliations vary, taking in anthropology, sociology, geography and English, and we continue to work in universities, which are organized to reflect disciplinary concentrations. However, we would all attest to the ways in which our contacts with cultural studies have changed the ways in which we think, teach and research.

In Chapter 2 we examine some important aspects of communication and representation, introducing critical issues of language and meaning. This is followed by a chapter concerned with multiple

dimensions and theories of power and inequality, which looks at these issues in the context of globalization. Chapter 4, which is completely new for this edition, addresses how culture is researched and how cultural studies knowledge is produced. Together the four chapters in Part 1 address important general issues and debates in cultural studies and provide a map around them. In these chapters, and in the rest of the book, we are particularly concerned with the division of culture along the lines of class, race and gender.

Part 2 of the book contains six chapters which examine in some detail different dimensions of culture. One of the most significant areas of debate across the humanities and social sciences is over how to understand the nature and importance of space. Indeed, we would argue that cultural studies has been an important impetus behind these debates. We reflect these concerns in Chapter 5, which points to the ways in which culture cannot be understood without significant attention to space, place and social change. Of course these academic developments are contextualised by the increased pace of contemporary life and the ease of communication and travel which are producing new experiences of space, mobility and cultural interaction.

Another important dimension of culture and its study has been a redefinition of politics. Often arising from the new social movements of the 1960s and after, there is now an understanding of the way in which politics, as activity concerned with power, is all around us. In Chapter 6 we address a number of issues raised by this expansion and change in the meaning of politics. Chapter 7, which is also completely new, considers the increasingly important changes brought about in everyday life by consumption and technological changes, including discussion of new media and new interactive forms of technologically facilitated social networking.

Despite the increasing significance of virtual existence, another significant area of concern in contemporary life remains the body. We are all aware of the state of our bodies and the forms of treatment for them when they are not functioning adequately. Moreover there is increased debate around new technologies of healing and body alteration. Again, cultural studies has been in the vanguard of consideration of some of these issues – a concern reflected in the subject matter of Chapter 8.

Culture can often be seen as all-encompassing in that many things and activities are seen to be part of a 'culture'. However, cultures are also divided along the lines of class, race, gender and age and, as we have suggested, by space and time. One important way of discussing and characterising such divisions is through the concept of subculture. Chapter 9 is devoted to this area. In particular, it examines work on youth subcultures, where much important work has been done in cultural studies.

The final chapter of the book returns to some of the issues of representation outlined in Part 1. Using ideas about technological change and broad shifts in culture, we address important developments in visual culture. Part of our concern here is to locate forms of visual representation and the visual aspects of everyday interaction historically and spatially.

That is the outline of the structure and content of our book. We expect that you will read those chapters that most interest you or will be of most use at any one time for a particular purpose. To facilitate the use of the book, we have further divided all the chapters into sections. You will find extensive cross-referencing between chapters and sections, but it is also important that you use the Table of Contents and the Index for these purposes as well. The sections of chapters can be read on their own, but you will also find that they fit into an argument that is developed through a chapter.

We have included other types of devices to convey our ideas: figures, diagrams, cartoons, photographs of buildings, monuments or paintings discussed in the text and tables. We have also included three types of box: Key Influences, Defining Concepts and Extracts. You will find concepts and people who are boxed highlighted in bold in the text, for example **Donna Haraway**. Defining Concept boxes provide an overview to help generate a basic understanding. Extract boxes include material that is often then discussed in the text, but which we think also repays more detailed study on your part. Key Influence boxes address the most salient aspects of the life and work of some of the major thinkers in cultural studies. We have tried in these to include three different types of writer: first, those who have been particularly important in the development of cultural studies (examples include Richard Hoggart, E.P. Thompson and Raymond Williams); second, those authors who historically initiated important general approaches that have subsequently been developed or become influential in cultural studies (examples here are Karl Marx, Michel Foucault, Max Weber and C.L.R. James); finally, there are those who were and are part of the redevelopment of cultural studies as it has become more attentive to issues of gender, 'race', postcolonialism, cultural hybridity and so on, such as Judith Butler, Angela McRobbie, Paul Gilroy and Edward Said.

This approach means that the majority of our Key Influence boxes represent white men, some of whom are long dead. This in itself reflects the development of the field and the power struggles that shape it. We wish that the situation were otherwise. However, it is perhaps of some significance that even many of these white men were marginal to mainstream academic life. We are also conscious of some of the names that are missing (for example Derrida, Lyotard, Jameson), which may mean little to you at the moment, but which you will come across in this book and others you read. However, we have tried to box those people whose ideas are most used in the book, reflecting the sense that this is our version of cultural studies.

All the Key Influence and Defining Concept boxes contain further reading that can be used to deepen the understanding of the concepts, approaches and people they contain. We have also included a guide to further reading and a guide to Internet resources at the end of each chapter.

# Acknowledgements

All books are the products of a number of influences. Textbooks are even more so. Many people over more years than we would care to remember have affected this book. We would like to begin by acknowledging this general debt. We are also particularly grateful to the anonymous reviewers for their helpful comments.

Gaynor Bagnall would like to thank Graham, Claire and Jack for their support and enthusiasm for all things cultural.

Garry Crawford would like to thank his friends and family for being there, and most importantly Victoria Gosling for her continued support.

Brian Longhurst would like to thank the students who have worked with him on the material in this book. His biggest debt is to Liz for all her support. James and Tim are always there and his parents can't be thanked enough.

Miles Ogborn would like to thank the students on GEG247 Society, Culture and Space at QMUL who road-tested the material for Chapter 5 and have shown what works and what does not.

Greg Smith would like to thank Julie Jones for instructive discussions about a range of topics covered in this book. Particular thanks are due to Juli Weir for permission to use her excellent photograph in Chapter 8.

The authorial team who produced this edition of the book were Brian Longhurst, Greg Smith, Gaynor Bagnall, Garry Crawford and Miles Ogborn. We would like to record our special thanks to two authors for the first edition, Elaine Baldwin and Scott McCracken, who were not able to participate in the second.

## Publisher's acknowledgements

We are grateful to the following for permission to reproduce copyright material:

### Illustrations

Figure 1.1, Indian woman taking photograph in Peacock Court, © Martin Harvey/Corbis; Figure 2.3, 'Communication between men and women', from J. Fleming, *Never Give Up* (1992), with permission of the author, Jacky Fleming; Figure 2.4, from S. Hall (1980), 'Encoding/decoding', in S. Hall, D. Hobson, A. Lowe, P. Willis (eds), *Culture, Media, Language: Working Papers in Cultural Studies*, 1972–79, p.130, with permission of Cengage Learning Services; Figure 3.2, 'World debt cartoon', from the *Observer*, © Chris Riddell; Figures 5.2 and 5.4, Thomas Gainsborough, 'Mr and Mrs Andrews', and John Constable, 'The Hay-Wain', The National Gallery, London; Figure 5.3, Yinka Shonibare, 'Mr and Mrs Andrews Without Their Heads', The National Gallery of Canada; Figure 5.5, Paul Henry, 'The Potato Diggers', The National Gallery of Ireland; Figure 5.6, reprinted by permission of *Foreign Affairs*, 72(3), copyright 1993 by the Council on Foreign Relations, Inc.; Figure 5.7, PRM 1981.12.1 Yoruba carving, 1930s, Pitt Rivers Museum, Oxford; Figure 5.8, from G. Gómez-Peña (2000), *Dangerous Border Crossings: The Artist Talks Back*; 'Cyber-Vato', with permission of Cengage Learning Services;

Figure 5.9, 'European gun with inlaid shell decoration from the Western solomon Island', The Australian Museum; Figure 5.10, 'Joseph Banks with part of his collection of Pacific objects', with permission of the National Maritime Museum; Figures 6.1, 6.2, Corbis and 6.9 and 6.10, ©Reuters/CORBIS; Figure 6.3, © The Press Association; Figure 6.8, 'The toppling of the Verdôme Column (1871)', Musée Carnavalet, Paris; Figure 9.1 from S. Cohen (1973), *Folk Devils and Moral Panics: The Creation of Mods and Rockers*, p. 199, with permission of Cengage Learning Services; Figure 9.2, from J. Clarke, S. Hall, J. Jefferson, B. Roberts (1976), 'Subcultures, cultures and class', *Resistance through Rituals: Youth Subcultures in Post-war Britain*, p. 34, with permission of Cengage Learning Services; Box 9.3, a young Teddy boy, a skinhead and a mod on his scooter, © Getty Images; Figure 10.3, reproduced with permission from Macdonald, K.M., 'Building respectability', in *Sociology*, 23, p.62, copyright © SAGE Publications 1989, by permission of Sage Publications Ltd; Table 10.3, reproduced with permission from J. Urry, 'The tourist gaze and the environment', in *Theory Culture and Society*, 9(3), p.22, copyright © Sage Publications 1989, by permission of Sage Publications Ltd; Table 10.4, from D. Harvey (1990), 'Fordist modernity v. flexible postmodernity, or the interpretation of opposed tendencies in capitalist society as a whole', in *The Condition of Postmodernity*, pp. 340–1, with permission of Blackwell Publishing.

## Text

Oxford University Press, 'Social Class and Linguistic Development: A Theory of Social Learning', from *Education: Culture, Economy and Society*, edited by A. H. Halsey, J. Floud and C. A. Anderson; Cambridge University Press, 'Classes, status groups and parties', from *Max Weber: Selections in Translation*, edited by W. G. Runchiman, translated by E. Matthews (1978); Curtis Brown Group Ltd, London, on behalf of David Lodge and Random House Group Ltd, *Nice Work* by David Lodge, © David Lodge 1988, published by Secker and Warburg; Ashgate Publishing Ltd, Aldershot, for *Learning to Labour* by Paul Willis (1977); Taylor and Francis Group for 'Bureaucracy' by Max Weber, from *Max Weber: Essays in Sociology*, edited by H. H. Gerth and C. Wright Mills, published by Routledge and Kegan Paul, and for 'Subcultures, cultures and class' by J. Clarke, S. Hall, T. Jefferson and B. Roberts, from *Resistance through Rituals: Youth Subcultures in Post-war Britain*, edited by S. Hall and T. Jefferson, published by Taylor and Francis Books UK; Guardian News and Media Limited for the article 'Symbolic in more ways than one' by Brian Whitaker from the *Guardian*, 10 April 2003, © Guardian News and Media Limited 2003; Springer Science and Business Media for 'Throwing like a girl: a phenomenology of feminine body comportment, motility and spatiality', by Iris Marian Young, *Human Studies*, 3(1), pp. 137–56 (December 1980); Verso for *All That is Solid Melts into Air: The Experience of Modernity* by M. Berman; Georges Borchardt, Inc., Editions Gallimard and Penguin Group (UK) for *Discipline and Punish: The Birth of the Prison* by Michel Foucault, English Translation © 1977 by Alan Sheridan (New York: Pantheon), originally published in French as *Surveiller et Punir: Naissance de la prison* © 1975 Editions Gaillimard, © 1975 Allen Lane; Blackwell Publishing Limited for *Folk Devils and Moral Panics: The Creation of the Mods and Rockers* by Stanley Cohen, and *The Condition of Post Modernity* by D. Harvey; Palgrave Macmillan for *Black Culture, White Youth: The Reggae Tradition from JA to UK* by S. Jones (1988); The MIT Press for *The Image of the City* by Kevin Lynch © Massachusetts Institute of Technology (1960), pp. 46–8; and Sage Publications Ltd for 'The Tourist Gaze and the Environment' by J. Urry, *Theory, Culture and Society*, 9(3) (1992), © Sage Publications 1992.

In some instances we have been unable to trace the owners of copyright material, and we would appreciate any information that would enable us to do so.

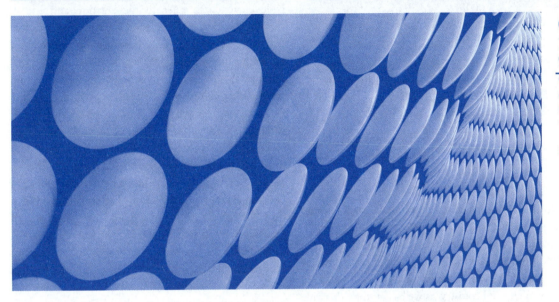

Chapter 1

# Culture and cultural studies

## 1.0 Introduction

Cultural studies is a new way of engaging in the study of culture. In the past many academic subjects – including anthropology, history, literary studies, human geography and sociology – have brought their own disciplinary concerns to the study of culture. However, in recent decades there has been a renewed interest in the study of culture that has crossed disciplinary boundaries. The resulting activity, cultural studies, has emerged as an intriguing and exciting area of intellectual inquiry that has already shed important new light on the character of human cultures and which promises to continue so to do. While there is little doubt that cultural studies is coming to be widely recognised as an important and distinctive field of study, it does seem to encompass a potentially enormous area. This is because the term 'culture' has a complex history and range of usages, which have provided a legitimate focus of inquiry for several academic

disciplines. In order to begin to delimit the field that this textbook considers, we have divided this chapter into four main sections:

1.1 A discussion of some principal *definitions* of culture.

1.2 An introduction to the *core issues* raised by the definitions and study of culture.

1.3 A review of some leading *theoretical accounts* that address these core issues.

1.4 An outline of *our view* of the developing field of cultural studies.

In introducing our book in this way, we hope to show the complexity of the central notion of culture and thereby to define some important issues in the field of cultural studies.

1

### Learning objectives

► To understand different definitions of the concept of culture.
► To identify the principal issues in the study of culture.
► To learn about some of the leading theoretical perspectives in cultural studies.

## 1.1 What is culture?

The term 'culture' has a complex history and diverse range of meanings in contemporary discourse. Culture can refer to Shakespeare or Superman comics, opera or football, who does the washing-up at home or how the office of the President of the United States of America is organised. Culture is found in your local street, in your own city and country, as well as on the other side of the world. Small children, teenagers, adults and older people all have their own cultures; but they may also share a wider culture with others.

Given the evident breadth of the term, it is essential to begin by trying to define what culture is. Culture is a word that has grown over the centuries to reach its present broad meaning. One of the founders of cultural studies in Britain, **Raymond Williams** (p. 3), has traced the development of the concept and provided an influential ordering of its modern uses. Outside the natural sciences, the term 'culture' is chiefly used in three relatively distinct senses to refer to: the arts and artistic activity; the learned, primarily symbolic features of a particular way of life; and a process of development.

## Culture with a big 'C'

In everyday talk, culture is believed to consist of the 'works and practices of intellectual and especially artistic activity', thus culture is the word that describes 'music, literature, painting and sculpture, theatre and film' (Williams, 1983b: 90). Culture in this sense is widely believed to concern 'refined' pursuits in which the 'cultured' person engages.

## Culture as a 'way of life'

In the human sciences the word 'culture' has achieved wide currency to refer to the creation and use of **symbols** (p. 214) which distinguish 'a particular way of life, whether of a people, a period or a group, or humanity in general' (Williams, 1983b: 90). Only humans, it is often argued, are capable of creating and transmitting culture and we are able to do this because we create and use symbols. Humans possess a symbolising capacity which is the basis of our cultural being.

What, then, is a symbol? It is when people agree that some word or drawing or gesture will stand for either an idea (for example, a person, like a pilot), or an object (a box, for example), or a feeling (like contempt). When this has been done, then a symbol conveying a shared idea has been created. These shared ideas are symbolically mediated or expressed: for example, by a word in the case of 'pilot', by a drawing to convey the idea of a box or by a gesture to convey contempt. It is these meanings that make up a culture. A symbol defines what something means, although a single symbol may have many meanings. For example, a flag may stand for a material entity like a country and an abstract value such as patriotism. To study culture is thus to ask what is the meaning of a style of dress, a code of manners, a place, a language, a norm of conduct, a system of belief, an architectural style, and so on. Language, both spoken and written, is obviously a vast repository of symbols. But symbols can take numerous forms: flags, hairstyles, road signs, smiles, BMWs, business suits – the list is endless.

Given the way that we have discussed culture so far, it might be thought that culture is everything and everywhere. Indeed, some approaches to the study of culture take such a position, especially, for instance, those coming at the topic from a more anthropological point of view. Thus, the nineteenth-century anthropologist Edward Tylor (1871: 1) famously defined culture as 'that complex whole which includes knowledge, belief, art, morals, law, custom, and any other capabilities and habits acquired by man [sic] as a member of society'. This definition underlines the pervasiveness of culture in social life. It also emphasises that culture is a product of humans living together and that it is learned. A similar idea informs the definition offered by the American poet and critic T.S. Eliot:

## Key influence 1.1

### Raymond Williams (1921–88)

Raymond Williams was a Welsh cultural analyst and literary critic. His 'serious' attention to 'ordinary culture' was a key influence on the development of the idea of cultural studies, of which he is normally seen as a founding figure.

Born into a Welsh working-class family, Williams studied at Cambridge before serving as a tank commander in the Second World War. He returned to Cambridge after the war to complete his degree. He taught for the Workers' Educational Association during the 1950s, before returning to Cambridge to take up a lectureship in 1961. He was appointed Professor of Drama in 1974.

Williams's earliest work addressed questions of textual analysis and drama and can be seen as reasonably conventional in approach, if not emphasis. His influence was enhanced and reputation made by two key books: *Culture and Society* (1958) and *The Long Revolution* (1961). The former re-examined a range of authors to chart the nature of the formation of culture as a response to the development of industrialism. The latter pointed to the democratic potential of the 'long revolution' in culture. Williams distanced himself from the elitist and conservative perspectives of F.R. Leavis and T.S. Eliot in arguing for both socialist transformation and cultural democracy. Williams emphasised these themes in *Communications* (1962) which also contained some proto-typical media analysis. Television was the subject of the later *Television: Technology and Cultural Form* (1974) which introduced the concept of 'flow'. From the 1960s on, Williams's work became more influenced by Marxism, resulting in *Marxism and Literature* (1977) and *Culture* (1981). His *The Country and the City* (1973a) greatly influenced subsequent interdisciplinary work on space and place. His vast corpus of work (including over 30 books) also addressed drama, cultural theory, the environment, the English novel, the development of language, leftist politics and, in the period before his death, Welshness. He was also a prolific novelist.

The impact of Williams's rather dense and 'difficult' writings was often in terms of his overall approach, cultural materialism, and emphasis rather than in the detail of his analyses. His lifelong commitment to socialism, combined with the desire for cultural communication and democracy, was greatly attractive to a generation of leftists. His current status is enhanced by the use of his concept of structure of feeling to study various phenomena from literary texts to urban ways of life.

#### Further reading

Williams wrote a vast amount, so much so that his identity has been seen as that of 'writer'. The first reference is a revealing set of interviews, which combine the life and work.

Williams, R. (1979) *Politics and Letters: Interviews with New Left Review*, London: New Left Books.

Eldridge, J. and Eldridge, L. (1994) *Raymond Williams: Making Connections*, London: Routledge.

Inglis, F. (1995) *Raymond Williams*, London: Routledge.

Milner, A. (2002) *Re-imagining Cultural Studies: The Promise of Cultural Materialism*, London: Sage.

---

Culture ... includes all the characteristic activities and interests of a people. Derby Day, Henley Regatta, Cowes, the 12th of August, a cup final, the dog races, the pin table, the dart board, Wensleydale cheese, boiled cabbage cut into sections, beetroot in vinegar, nineteenth century Gothic churches, and the music of Elgar.

(Eliot, 1948, quoted in Williams 1963[1958]: 230)

Other approaches have tended to argue that some areas of social life are more properly thought of as political or economic than cultural and thus can in some fashion be separated from culture. Thus, those who would define culture in the sense of 'arts and artistic activity' would tend to exclude some institutions and phenomena that others who accept the definition of 'way of life' would see as part of culture. There is little consensus on this matter but it is clear that it will be an issue in this book.

Culture in the sense of way of life, however, must be distinguished from the neighbouring concept of society. In speaking of society we refer to the pattern of social interactions and relationships between individuals and groups. Often a society will occupy a territory, be capable of reproducing itself and share a culture. But for many large-scale, modern societies it may make more sense to say that several cultures coexist (not always harmoniously) within the society.

## Process and development

The earliest uses of the word 'culture' in the late Middle Ages refer to the tending or cultivation of crops and animals (hence agriculture); a little later the same sense was transferred to describe the cultivation of people's minds. This dimension of the word 'culture' draws attention to its subsequent use to describe the development of the individual's capacities and it has been extended to embrace the idea that cultivation is itself a general, social and historical process (Williams, 1983b: 90–1).

The different senses in which the concept of culture can be used are illustrated in the following examples. A play by Shakespeare might be said to be a distinct piece of cultural work (sense: culture with a big 'C'), to be a product of a particular (English) way of life (sense: culture as a way of life) and to represent a certain stage of cultural development (sense: culture as process and development). Rock 'n' roll may be analysed by the skills of its performers (culture with a big C); by its association with youth culture in the late 1950s and early 1960s (culture as a way of life); and as a musical form, looking for its origins in other styles of music and also seeing its influence on later musical forms (culture as a process and development).

In this book we shall consider all three of these different senses of culture. However, it is important to note that these definitions and their use raise a number of complex issues and problems for the analysis of culture which we introduce in the next part of the chapter.

## 1.2 Issues and problems in the study of culture

The three senses of culture identified in the previous part of this chapter have tended to be studied from different points of view. Hence, artistic or intellectual activity has commonly been the province of the humanities scholar. Ways of life have been examined by the anthropologist or the sociologist, while the development of culture might seem to be the province of the historian using historical documents and methods. These disciplines have tended to approach culture in different ways and from different perspectives. However, as we shall demonstrate in this chapter, the special merit of a distinct cultural studies approach is that it facilitates the identification of a set of core issues and problems that no one discipline or approach can solve on its own. Let us explain what we mean through the identification and exemplification of these core questions. As you will see, they both start and finish with the issue of the relationship between the personal and the cultural.

## How do people become part of a culture?

Culture is not something that we simply absorb – it is learned. In anthropology this process is referred to as acculturation or enculturation. In psychology it is described as conditioning. Sociologists have tended to use the term 'socialisation' to describe the process by which we become social and cultural beings. The sociologist Anthony Giddens (2006:163) describes socialisation as the process whereby, through contact with other human beings, 'the helpless infant gradually becomes a self-aware, knowledgeable human being, skilled in the ways of the culture in which he or she was born'. Sociologists have distinguished two stages of socialisation. Primary socialisation usually takes place within a family, or family-like grouping, and lasts from birth until the child participates in larger and more diverse groupings beyond the family, usually beginning with school in Western societies. Primary socialisation involves such elements as the acquisition of language and a gendered **identity** (p. 142). Secondary socialisation refers to all the subsequent influences that an individual experiences in a lifetime. Psychology and its subdisciplines like **psychoanalysis** (p. 5) pay particular attention to childhood and the conditioning that relates to the acquisition of a gender and a sexuality. Gender refers to the social roles that different societies define as masculine or feminine. Sexuality refers to the desires and sexual orientation of a particular individual. The founder of psychoanalysis, Sigmund Freud, argued that masculinity and femininity and the choice of a sexual object are not directly related to biology, but are a result of conditioning. Feminists have used Freud's theories to oppose the idea that men are naturally superior, even though Freud himself was not

## Defining concept 1.1

### Psychoanalysis

Psychoanalysis is the name given to the method developed by Sigmund Freud (1856–1939). Freud himself used his interpretative technique to analyse literature and art. Psychoanalytic theory has subsequently developed into a number of different schools, some of which have influenced **feminist** (p. 82), **postcolonial** (p. 143), **Marxist** (p. 65) and **postmodernist** (p. 295) cultural criticism. Critics who have used psychoanalytic ideas include members of the **Frankfurt School** (p. 75), **Julia Kristeva** (p. 149) and **Judith Butler** (p. 148).

Freud's method of interpretation is first developed in *The Interpretation of Dreams* (1900). He describes how symbols in dreams represent condensed or displaced meanings that, when interpreted, reveal the dreamer's unconscious fears and desires. In *The Psychopathology of Everyday Life* (1901), he showed how slips of the tongue and the inability to remember words are also symptoms of unconscious mental processes. Condensation, displacement and 'symptomatic' methods of interpretation have been deployed by critics to decode cultural texts. Psychoanalysis has been particularly influential in film criticism. Freud developed a tripartite theory of the mind: the id or unconscious; the ego, which adjusts the mind to external reality; and the super-ego, which incorporates a moral sense of society's expectations. Perhaps his most important work was on a theory of sexuality. The psycho-

analytic concept of sexuality posits a complex understanding of desire. The fixed binarism of masculine/feminine given by earlier biologistic theories of sexual difference tended to assume an equally fixed desire by men for women and by women for men. In psychoanalysis, there is no presupposition that sexual desire is limited to heterosexual relations. Rather, the adaptable nature of desire is stressed and an important role is given to fantasy in the choice of sexual object. Freud's work was still partially attached to a theory of biological development.

The influential psychoanalytic critic, Jacques Lacan, argued that the unconscious is structured like language. In other words, culture rather than biology is the important factor. Lacan's work has been important for feminist critics, who have developed an analysis of gender difference using Freud's Oedipus complex. According to feminist psychoanalytic criticism, the context in which feminine sexuality develops is different to that of masculine sexuality. Men and women enter into different relationships with the symbolic order through the Oedipus complex. The Oedipus complex arises through the primary identification of both boys and girls with their mother. Paradoxically, it is the mother who first occupies the 'phallic' position of authority. The discovery that the mother does not hold as powerful a position in society as the father (it is the father who symbolises the phallus) creates the crisis

through which the boy and the girl receive a gendered identity. The boy accepts his 'inferior phallic powers', sometimes known as 'the castration complex', but with the promise that he will later occupy as powerful a position in relation to women as his father does. The girl learns of her subordinate position in relation to the symbolic order, her castration complex, but for her, there is no promise of full entry to the symbolic order; consequently her feeling of lack persists as a sense of exclusion (Mitchell, 1984: 230).

In cultural studies the theory of the unconscious has allowed a more subtle understanding of the relationship between **power** (p. 64) and the formation of subjectivity. While psychoanalysis has been found wanting in that it suggests but does not actually show how the social relates to the psychic, that suggestion has been the starting point for some of the most fascinating investigations in cultural studies.

### Further reading

Mitchell, J. (1984) *Women: The Longest Revolution, Essays in Feminism, Literature and Psychoanalysis*, London: Virago.

Thwaites, T. (2007) *Reading Freud: Psychoanalysis and Cultural Theory*, London: Sage.

Weedon, C., Tolson, A. and Mort, F. (1980) 'Theories of language and subjectivity', in *Culture, Media, Language*, London: Unwin Hyman.

particularly sympathetic to **feminism** (p. 82). The concepts of acculturation and enculturation, conditioning and socialisation draw attention to the many and various social arrangements that play a part in the ways in which humans learn about meaning.

## How does cultural studies interpret what things mean?

Anthropology and some forms of sociology see meaningful action, the understandings that persons attribute to their behaviour and to their thoughts and feelings, as cultural. This approach to culture refers to the shared understandings of individuals and groupings in society (or to the way of life sense of culture – see above). Some sociologists, for example Berger and Luckmann (1966), stress that human knowledge of the world is socially constructed, that is, we apprehend our world through our social locations and our interactions with other people. If it is the case that our understanding is structured by our social locations, then our views of the world may be partial. This view suggests that there is a real world but we can only view it from certain angles. Thus, our knowledge of the world is inevitably perspectival. The perspectival view of the world complements the issue of cultural relativism (see section 3.4). It emphasises the way that social roles and relationships shape the way we see and give meaning to the world, whereas cultural relativism stresses the way that habitual, taken-for-granted ways of thought, as expressed in speech and language, direct our understandings. An example of perspectival knowledge is the differing accounts of the dissolution of a marriage given by those involved and affected by it. The explanation given for the break-up of a marriage by one partner will rarely coincide with the explanation given by the other (Hart, 1976).

The sociology of knowledge, as this approach to understanding is known, suggests that the sense that we make of the world can be made intelligible through the examination of our social location. For example, it is sometimes proposed that one's view of the world is linked to class position, so that working-class people will have a different view of the world from upper-class people. Sociologists of knowledge do not propose that our beliefs can always be reduced to, or simply read off

from, our social location, but they do suggest that these world-views are cultural, and that culture has to be studied in relation to society. Moreover, the interpretation of culture in relation to social location introduces further issues of evidence and relativism. If knowledge is socially constructed, can there be such a thing as 'true' knowledge? If perceptions and beliefs are always relative to social location, then why should we believe any particular view, even the view of the person asserting this statement, since it too will be influenced by the person's location? In seeking to interpret a way of life of a different society or a different group in our own society, why should we believe one interpretation rather than any other? If we are to begin to adjudicate or evaluate different interpretations then we will need to consider the types of evidence offered for the particular interpretation. Interpretation of meaning is therefore a core issue in cultural studies, and it relates to how we understand the relationship between the past and the present.

## How does cultural studies understand the past?

One hears much talk in England of the traditional nature of culture (see Box 1.1); England is seen by some to have a culture that stretches back over a thousand years. Within this context, culture in English studies has often been conceived in terms of influence and tradition. For T.S. Eliot (1932: 15), for example, 'no poet, no artist of any art, has his complete meaning alone. His significance, his appreciation is the appreciation of his relation to the dead poets and artists'. More recently, English studies has begun to question the values of the canon, that is, those written texts selected as of literary value and as required reading in schools and universities. Texts that have been previously neglected have been introduced into school and university syllabuses. More women's writing, writing by minority groups in British society, non-British writing and popular fiction have been included in the canon. For example, the poems of Derek Walcott (St Kitts, Caribbean), the novels of Chinua Achebe (Nigeria) and those of Alice Walker (USA) are now regarded as deserving literary consideration. English studies has widened its outlook beyond the influence of other poets and writers to look

## Box 1.1

### Tradition and traditional

Derived from the Latin verb *tradere* meaning to pass on or to give down. Commonly used in cultural studies to refer to elements of culture that are transmitted (e.g. language) or to a body of collective wisdom (e.g. folk tales). As an adjective (traditional) it implies continuity and consistency. Traditions and traditional practices may be seen positively or negatively. Where the past is venerated, traditions may be seen as a source of legitimacy and value; in revolutionary situations the past may be viewed with contempt and seen as a brake upon progress.

The term 'tradition' has a number of different meanings, all of which are central to how culture is understood. It can mean knowledge or customs handed down from generation to generation. In this sense the idea, for example, of a national tradition can have a positive sense as a marker of the age and deep-rooted nature of a national culture. On the other hand, the adjective 'traditional' is often used in a negative or pejorative sense from within cultures like those of North America or Western Europe which describe themselves as modern. Here 'traditional', when used

to describe non-European cultures and societies, can mean 'backward' or 'underdeveloped', terms that assume that all societies must modernise in the same way and in the same direction. Cultural studies is always critical of this kind of imposition of the standards of one culture upon another to define it as in some way inferior. 'Traditional' can also refer to social roles in society which are often taken for granted, but which might be questioned in cultural studies: for example, what it is to be a mother or a father.

at social and historical factors affecting the production of texts. It is now common for critics to look at, for example, the position of women in the nineteenth century when considering the novels of the period. Critics like **Edward Said** (p. 115) and Gayatri Spivak have also looked at the history of European imperialism and asked how that history manifests itself in literature.

This particular example from the discipline of English shows that traditions are not neutral and objective, somehow waiting to be discovered, but are culturally constructed. In being constructed and reconstructed some things are included and others excluded. This reflects, according to many writers, patterns of the distribution of **power** (p. 64) in society. Let us attempt to clarify some of these points through another example.

The kilt and Highland dress are presented, both in Scotland and outside, as Scottish traditional costume. This garb is one of the most recognisable and visible components of Scottish culture and is worn by Scottish people at a variety of special occasions. It is thus presented to the non-Scots world as a component of Scottishness – the attributes of a particular place. It also functions in this manner for many Scots who

consider the wearing of the tartan to be a method of identification with their cultural heritage. However, it appears that the kilt as a traditional cultural form has been constructed and repackaged to meet some historically specific needs. David McCrone (1992: 184) has suggested that 'a form of dress and design which had some real but haphazard significance in the Highlands of Scotland was taken over by a lowland population anxious to claim some distinctive aspect of culture at a time – the late nineteenth century – when its economic, social and cultural identity was ebbing away'. Thus a widely accepted and representative cultural form is shown to have been far from universal but rather associated with a particular group at a specific moment in time. Furthermore, this means that the meaning of the kilt is constantly changing within Scottish society. For example, in the 1950s wearing a kilt was thought effeminate by certain sections of the younger generation; however, since the recent increase in Scottish nationalism the kilt has come back into fashion, and is often worn at occasions such as weddings.

# Can other cultures be understood?

An issue of reliability of evidence is also raised through this example as it may be difficult to know precisely who wore the kilt and when. Further, it raises the problem of what has been termed 'historical relativism'. What this draws attention to is the extent to which we, as contemporaries of the first decade of the twentieth-first century, dwell in a world that is sufficiently different from the worlds in which our predecessors lived that it may be very difficult for us to understand those worlds in the same way that they did. How well can we understand what was in the middle-class, lowland Scots person's mind when he or she adapted and adopted Highland dress? There are some similarities between the issues raised under this heading and others thought more often to be associated with cultural relativism, which we discuss next.

Further to the difficulty of studying culture across history, there is the parallel problem of interpretation of cultures from different parts of the world or in different sections of our own society. To what extent is it possible for us to understand the cultures of other peoples in the way they do themselves? Will our understanding inevitably be mediated via the distorting prism of our own cultural understandings? These problems have always confronted anthropologists in their attempts to interpret the other worlds of non-European societies. Is it possible to convey adequately the evident seriousness that the Azande accord to the consultation of oracles (see Box 1.2) or the conceptions of time held by Trobriand Islanders (see Box 1.3), in texts designed for consumption by Western audiences who hold very different temporal conceptions and ideas about magic and witchcraft? Novelists, sociologists and journalists also face this problem in describing the ways of life of different groups in their own society. Many quite serious

## Box 1.2

### Azande

The Azande, an African people, live around the Nile–Congo divide. The classic work on their belief systems is *Witchcraft, Oracles and Magic among the Azande* by E.E. Evans-Pritchard, published in 1937. The Azande believe that many of the misfortunes that befall them are caused by witchcraft (*mangu*). *Mangu* is inherited; the Azande believe that it has the form of a blackish swelling in the intestines, and it is this substance that, when activated, causes harm to others. Even though individuals may have inherited *mangu* they do not necessarily cause harm to others because it is only bad, anti-social feelings that set off witchcraft. As long as a person remains good tempered they will not cause witchcraft. Since witchcraft is the product of bad feelings, then a person who suffers a misfortune suspects those who do not like her or him and who have reason

to wish harm. The first suspects are therefore one's enemies. There are five oracles that a Zande (singular of Azande) may consult in order to have the witch named. After an oracle has named the witch, the person identified is told that the oracle has named them and she or he is asked to withdraw the witchcraft. Usually named people protest their innocence and state that they meant no harm; if they did cause witchcraft it was unintentional. Evans-Pritchard states that Azande do not believe that witchcraft causes all misfortunes and individuals cannot blame their own moral failings upon it. Azande say that witchcraft never caused anyone to commit adultery. Witchcraft is not the only system of explanation among the Azande; they do recognise technical explanations for events: for example, a man is injured because a house collapses, but witchcraft attempts to

answer the question of why *this* house collapsed. All systems of explanation involve the 'how' of events and the 'why' of events; the house collapses because the wooden supports are rotten – this is the technical 'how' of explanation – but why did it collapse at a particular time and on a particular man?

The 'why' of explanation deals with what Evans-Pritchard calls the singularity of events: 'why me?', 'why now?' Religious explanations offer the answer that it was the will of God; scientific explanations speak of coincidences in time and space; agnostics may see the answer in chance; the Azande know that it is witchcraft. Evans-Pritchard comments that while he lived among the Azande he found witchcraft as satisfactory a form of explanation for events in his own life as any other.

## Box 1.3

### Trobriand Islanders

The Trobriand Islands are politically part of Papua New Guinea. The best-known works on the Trobriand Islands are by Malinowski but E.R. Leach has written on Trobriand ideas of time in 'Primitive calendars' (*Oceania* 20 (1950)), and this, along with other work, is discussed in *Empires of Time: Calendars, Clocks and Cultures* by Anthony Aveni, 1990.

The Trobriand calendar is guided by the moon: there are twelve or thirteen lunar cycles but only ten cycles are in the calendar; the remaining cycles are 'free time' outside the calendar. The primary event of the Trobriand calendar is the appearance of a worm which appears for three or four nights once a year to spawn on the surface of the water. There is a festival (*Milamak*) in this month which inaugurates the planting season. The worm does not appear at exactly the same time every year and planting does not take place at exactly the same time every year so there is sometimes a mismatch between worm and planting. This situation is exacerbated because the Trobriand Islands are a chain and the worm appears at the southern extremity of the chain, so news of its appearance takes time to communicate. The consequence is that the festivals, and so the calendar, vary greatly in the time of their celebration from island to island. When the discrepancies are felt to be too great to be manageable there is a realignment and the calendar is altered to achieve consistency.

Trobriand reckoning of time is cyclical, associated with the agricultural year. Lunar cycles that are not connected to this activity are not recognised so there is time out of the calendar; a difficult notion to grasp in modern industrial societies where time is believed to be a natural and inevitable constraint upon activity. The Trobriand language has no tenses; time is not a linear progression that, once passed, cannot be regained; in the Trobriand system, time returns. Trobriand ideas of the nature of existence are not set in time but in patterns; it is order and patterned regularity that locates events and things, not time.

practical difficulties can arise from this problem. For example, one influential study of conversation (Tannen, 1990) suggests that the many misunderstandings that occur between men and women arise because what we are dealing with is an everyday version of the difficulties of cross-cultural communication. In the USA 'women speak and hear a language of connection and intimacy while men speak and hear a language of status and independence' (Tannen, 1990: 42). Differing conversational practices are employed by men and women. Tannen observes that in discussing a problem, women will offer reassurance whereas men will seek a solution. Women tend to engage in 'rapport-talk' while men are more at home lecturing and explaining. Men tend to be poorer listeners than women. According to Tannen, women engage in more eye contact and less interruption than men in conversation. Her argument is that men and women employ distinct conversational styles that she labels 'genderlects'. These styles are sufficiently different from each other that the talk between men and women might be appropriately regarded as a form of cross-cultural communication (see Chapter 2).

Hollis and Lukes (1982) include both historical and cultural relativism under the broad heading of 'perceptual relativism' and argue that there are two different dimensions to be examined. First, there is the degree to which seeing or perception is relative; that is, when we look at something or seek to understand it, do we actually see the same thing as another person looking at it? Second, there is the extent to which perception and understanding rely on language. These questions about perception remind us that, as students of culture, we must constantly think about who we are – where we come from and what our 'position' is – in order to understand who and what we are studying.

## How can we understand the relationships between cultures?

This question of position raises another problem in terms of how we understand the relationships between cultures. One conventional way of understanding this is to see cultures as mutually exclusive blocs that may interface, intersect, and interact along a boundary or 'zone of contact'. For example, it would be possible to consider the interactions between the Trobriand Islanders or the Azande and the Europeans who arrived as part of the process of **colonialism** (p. 143) (including, of course, the anthropologists who studied them and wrote about them). This way of thinking about culture often describes these relationships in terms of 'destruction' of cultures or their 'disappearance' as one culture 'replaces' or 'corrupts' another. A good example would be the fears of Americanisation as McDonald's hamburgers, Coca-Cola and Levis' jeans spread to Europe, Asia and Africa through processes of **globalisation** (p. 125).

However, this point of view is limited in certain ways. First, it is impossible to divide the world up into these exclusive cultural territories. As we have pointed out, culture is also a matter of age, gender, class, status – so that any such cultural bloc, defined in terms of nation, tribe or society, will be made up of many cultures. This means that we will also be positioned in relation to not just one culture but to many. Second, culture does not operate simply in terms of more powerful cultures destroying weaker ones. Since culture is a never-ending process of socially made meaning, cultures adapt, change and mutate into new forms. For example, the Trobriand Islanders took up the English game of cricket, but they did so in terms of their own war-making practices. So cricket did not simply replace other Trobriand games, it was made into a new **hybrid** (p. 126) cultural form that was neither English cricket nor Trobriand warfare. Finally, it might be useful to think about the relationships between cultures in terms of a series of overlapping webs or networks rather than as a patchwork of cultural 'territories' (see, for example, Chapter 9). This would mean that understanding the meaning of any cultural form would not simply locate it within a culture but would look at it in terms of how it fitted into the intersection between different cultural networks. For example, Coca-Cola has taken on different meanings in different parts of the world: signifying **neo-colonial** (p. 143) oppression in India (and being banned for some time), while it suggests freedom and personal autonomy to British–Asian young people in London. Its meanings cannot be controlled by the Coca-Cola company, although they try

through their advertising campaigns. Neither do their meanings simply involve the extension of an 'American' culture. Instead these meanings depend upon the location of the product in a complex network of relationships that shape its significance and value to differently positioned consumers.

## Why are some cultures and cultural forms valued more highly than others?

In English studies, literature has traditionally been seen as part of high culture (sense: arts and artistic activity). Certain literary texts have been selected as worthy of study, for example the novels of Charles Dickens or the plays of Shakespeare. This process of selection has meant the simultaneous exclusion of other texts, defined as non-literary. It has also led to an emphasis on writing, to the detriment of other, more modern forms of cultural activity, for example film and television. In a further step such forms of literature or high culture are regarded by some to be culture itself. Other excluded forms of writing or texts are defined as simply rubbish, trash or, in another often derogatory phrase, as mass culture. This entails a judgement of value, which is often assumed to be self-evident. Thus some forms of culture are to be valued and protected and others written off as worthless and indeed positively dangerous. However, as we have already seen, such canons or traditions are themselves constructed. Furthermore, as Hawkins (1990) has maintained, things that are thought to be high culture and those defined as mass culture often share similar themes and a particular text can be seen as high culture at one point in time and popular or mass culture at another. The example of opera may be used to illustrate this point. In Italy opera is a popular and widely recognised cultural form, singers are well known and performances draw big audiences who are knowledgeable and critical. In contrast, opera in Britain is regarded as an elite taste and research shows that typically audiences for opera are older and are drawn from higher social classes than other forms of entertainment. Yet in 1990, following the use of *Nessun Dorma* from the opera *Turandot*, sung by Pavarotti, to introduce the BBC television coverage of the 1990 World Cup Finals, opera rocketed in public popularity in Britain. In addition to increased audiences at live performances in opera houses, there were large-scale commercial promotions of concerts of music from opera in public parks and arenas. Television, video and compact disc sales of opera increased enormously and an album, *In Concert*, sung by Carreras, Domingo and Pavarotti, was top of the music charts in 1990. The example illustrates the point that it is often empirically difficult to assign cultural practices to neat conceptual divisions.

The question of boundaries between levels of culture and the justification for them is an area of central concern for cultural studies. Pierre Bourdieu (1984) (see Defining Concept 9.1, p. 259) has maintained that the boundaries between popular and high art are actually in the process of dissolving. Whether or not one accepts this view, it is clear that the study of boundaries and margins may be very revealing about cherished values which are maintained within boundaries. The relationships between cultural systems are a fruitful area for the study of the processes of boundary maintenance and boundary change, linked as these topics are to issues of cultural change and cultural continuity (sense: culture as a process of development).

Within social anthropology there is an established practice of demonstrating the value and viability of cultures that are often regarded by the relevant authorities as poor and impoverished or as anachronisms and, as such, ripe for planned intervention to bring about change. Studies by Baxter (1991) and Rigby (1985) have argued that nomadic pastoralism, that is a way of life in which people move with animals and in which animal products are the staple diet, is a wholly rational and efficient use of resources. Such peoples are able to live in inhospitable areas where cultivation is not possible and enjoy a rich cultural, social and political life. Despite this evidence there is pressure from development planners to enforce change through land policies that compel pastoralists to give up their traditional way of life and become settled cultivators or wage labourers. Similarly, Judith Okely in her study of gypsies (1983) has shown the complex richness of gypsy cultural beliefs and practices, identifying a set of core principles around which gypsy life is articulated and which gives meaning to all activities. Gypsies, like pastoralists, are under pressure to settle down and to conform to prevailing ideas about a proper and fitting way of life. Both these examples draw attention to the issues of power and inequality in cultural and social life to which we turn in the next section of the chapter.

## What is the relationship between culture and power?

Implicit in our discussions so far has been the issue of **power** (p. 64). Since it is a product of interaction, culture is also a part of the social world and, as such, is shaped by the significant lines of force that operate in a social world. All societies are organised politically and economically. Power and authority are distributed within them, and all societies have means for allocating scarce resources. These arrangements produce particular social formations. The interests of dominant groups in societies, which seek to explain and validate their positions in particular structures, affect cultures.

One of the ways in which groups do this is through the construction of traditions and their promulgation through the population. Thus it might be argued that the idea of a tradition of British Parliamentary democracy excludes other ideas of democracy and social organisation that are against the interests of the powerful. Likewise, tradition in English literature excludes and marginalises other voices. The definition of trash or mass culture might be seen to negate forms of culture that are actually enjoyed by oppressed groups.

However, another way of looking at this suggests that such mass or popular forms are actually used by those in power to drug or indoctrinate subordinate groups. Forms of popular culture can in this view be seen to be like propaganda. For example, one commentary on modern culture, that of the **Frankfurt School** (p. 75) of critical theory, argues that the culture industries engender passivity and conformity among their mass audiences. For example, in this type of analysis the relationship between a big band leader and his fans could be seen to mirror the relationship between the totalitarian leader and his followers. Both fans and followers release their tensions by taking part in **ritual** (p. 214) acts of submission and conformity (Adorno, 1967: 119–32).

Whatever view is adopted, it is clear that power and culture are inextricably linked and that the analysis of culture cannot be divorced from politics and power relations. Indeed, we would argue that this is a very important reason for studying culture and for taking culture seriously. However, the precise way in which forms of culture connect to power remains a complex issue requiring careful investigation.

## How is 'culture as power' negotiated and resisted?

Given the interests of different groups in society, it is inevitable that cultural attitudes will always be in conflict. Thus, the process of negotiation is endemic to societies and cultural **resistances** (p. 170) occur in many areas of life. Four key areas of struggle and negotiation that have concerned cultural studies are around gender, 'race', class and age (for more on these categories see pp. 18–19 and Chapter 3). These concepts define social relationships which are often fraught. To take one area as an example, the concept of gender encompasses both how masculinity and femininity are defined (see pp. 4–6) and how men and women relate to one another. Gender definitions are points of struggle in many societies since what it is to be a man and what it is to be a woman are never fixed. Indeed, these definitions themselves are, in part, the product of a power struggle between men and women.

Feminist writers have been most influential in gender studies. Feminist discussion of gender might be divided broadly into three arguments: for equality, for commonality or universality, and for difference. The argument for *equality* emphasises the political idea of rights. Equality between men and women is defined by abstract rights, to which both sexes are entitled. Inequality can be defined by women's lack of rights, for example to vote or to equal pay. Negotiation here is around the concept of women's rights. The argument for *commonality or universality* stresses that although women may belong to very different social, geographical and cultural groups they share common or universal interests because of their gender. Negotiation here is around the fundamental inequality of women because of their subordination in all societies. The argument for *difference* is more complicated; it rejects both ideas of simple equality and universality. Instead, it maintains that differences between men and women and between different groups of women mean that a concept of gender can never be abstracted out of a particular situation. Negotiation, therefore, while not denying inequality, will be around the specificity of differences. Critics of gender divisions struggle to redefine cultural constructions of gender. Women's movements, but also campaigns for lesbian and gay rights, seek to redraw the cultural boundaries of men's and women's experience. Such political movements are often drawn into conflict with the law and social and political institutions like religious organisations and political parties that do not wish the cultural support for their dominance to be eroded or destroyed. In these examples it can be seen that the wider frameworks of society (power and authority structures) influence and impose themselves on cultural belief and practice to affect outcomes. We have already introduced a number of other areas where culture can in some sort of way be held to be connected to relationships and patterns of power.

## How does culture shape who we are?

The above examples demonstrate that struggle and negotiation are often around questions of cultural **identity** (p. 142). An example that gives the question of identity more prominence is the way in which the origins of English studies in the nineteenth century were closely linked to the growth of universal education. As a discipline English was, in the view of many commentators, designed to give schoolchildren a sense of a national culture (Batsleer *et al.*, 1985, as discussed in Ashcroft *et al.*, 1989). Literary texts were used to instil this sense. Consequently, although English literature was often presented as a proper study in itself, the way it was taught was often designed, consciously or unconsciously, to encourage a particular national identity, a sense of what it meant to be British. In teaching this sense of British identity, other national cultures or identities within Britain were either treated uncritically as part of English culture, or were left out of the canon.

Another effect of this process, which some writers have detected, was to infuse a pride in the British

## Box 1.4

### Conrad on Africa

The prehistoric man was cursing us, praying to us, welcoming us – who could tell? We were cut off from the comprehension of our surroundings; we glided past like phantoms, wondering and secretly appalled, as sane men would be before an enthusiastic outbreak in a madhouse. We could not understand because we were too far and could not remember because we were travelling in the night of first ages, of those ages that are gone, leaving hardly a sign – and no memories.

The earth seemed unearthly. We are accustomed to look upon the shackled form of a conquered monster, but there – there you could look at a thing monstrous and free. It was unearthly, and the men were – No, they were not inhuman. Well, you know, that was the worst of it – this suspicion of their not being inhuman. It would come slowly to one. They howled and leaped, and spun, and made horrid faces; but what thrilled you was the thought of their humanity – like yours – the thought of your

remote kinship with this wild and passionate uproar. Ugly. Yes, it was ugly enough; but if you were man enough you would admit to yourself that there was in you just the faintest trace of a response to the terrible frankness of that noise, a dim suspicion of there being a meaning in it which you – you so remote from the night of first ages – could comprehend.
Joseph Conrad, *Heart of Darkness* (1898); quoted in Chinua Achebe (1988: 6)

Empire. For example, the Nigerian writer and critic Chinua Achebe has criticised the way that the novel *Heart of Darkness* by Joseph Conrad is still often presented as a great example of English culture. The novel describes a nightmarish encounter with Africa from the European point of view (see Box 1.4). However, Achebe has demonstrated that the representation of African culture that it contains is partial, based on little knowledge and is thus grossly distorted. Consequently, to read the novel as an English or even a European (Conrad was Polish in origin) work of art is to receive a very one-sided view of European imperialism in Africa. Through such processes an English national identity was constructed which involved constructing African identities in particular ways: as irrational and savage 'others'.

Identities are very often connected to place both locally and more widely. We may feel that we identify with a particular local area, a city, a region and a country and that the extent to which we place emphasis on one of these may depend on a context, for example, who we are talking to at any particular time. However, it is clearly the case that these identities can cause conflict and disagreement and that important issues in the study of culture concern the way in which such identi-

ties are constructed and how they reflect and inflect particular distributions of power.

## Summary examples

In order to examine some of the ideas contained in section 1.2, two short examples are given below: the family and Shakespeare.

### Example 1: The family

An examination of family life reveals some of the issues that we have identified in the study of culture. For instance, within a family adults have great power over the lives of children because human infants are dependent on adults for their survival for relatively long periods of time. One way of understanding family life is to examine relationships and processes in terms of dominant and subordinate cultures. This approach has been used extensively by many feminist writers who have used the concept of patriarchy to refer to the assemblage of cultural and material power that men enjoy *vis-à-vis* women and children (Campbell, 1988; Pateman, 1989). The period of dependence of children varies from culture to culture, both historically and contemporaneously, and a number of writers have

13

commented that the Western notion of childhood is a relatively recent concept (Aries, 1962; Walvin, 1982). Further, in many parts of the contemporary world it is a mistake to think of the lives of children in terms of childhood as it is understood in the West; this period of growth and learning is seen quite differently from that in Western societies. Caldwell (1982), writing of India, remarks that in Indian rural society there is the cultural belief and practice that wealth flows from children to parents as well as from parents to children. He comments that, typically in Western society, resources flow in a one-way direction from parents to children and parents do not expect young children to contribute to the material wellbeing of the family of origin. However, in many parts of the world children are valued, at least in part, for the contributions that they make to the domestic economies of family and household; there is what Caldwell calls a 'reciprocal flow' of goods and services between parents and even quite young children. For example, toddlers can join in gathering firewood and this is a valuable contribution in economies where this is the only fuel available for cooking and boiling water. This cultural view of children is significant in understanding responses to family planning projects. Caldwell argues that all too often Western cultural assumptions about family life and desirable family size direct the policy and goals of these projects. Looking beyond the English family to families in other parts of the world reminds us of the heterogeneity and diversity of culture and alerts us to the dangers for understanding in assuming that cultures and cultural meanings are the same the world over.

Indeed, even in Western societies there is much cultural diversity. Novels and academic studies point to the effects of class and power on family life. In the recent past criticisms have been levelled against some traditional reading for children because it portrays a middle-class view of family structures and relationships which is far removed from the experiences of many children. Accusations of sexism and racism in literature for children have also been made. These criticisms again draw our attention to the relationships between general, diffuse cultures and local, particular cultures. Although we may identify an English culture as distinct from, say, a French culture, it cannot be assumed that all English families have identical cul-

tures. This opens up the challenging issue of how particular local cultures relate to the broader, more general ones of which they may be thought to be a constituent part.

It is also clear that family structures and organisation change over time, not just chronological, historical time, but also structural time, that is as relationships between family members change as a consequence of age and maturation. In all societies, as children grow to adulthood the power of other adults over them diminishes. This occurs both as a result of physiological change (children no longer depend on their parents for food) and also as a result of cultural expectations about the roles of parents and children. These cultural expectations may be gendered; for example, the English idiom that describes adult children as 'being tied to their mother's apron strings' can be read as a general disapproval of adults who do not leave the immediate sphere of their mother. Yet this idiom is overwhelmingly applied to adult male children and thus expresses a view about the proper, expected relationships between adult males and their mothers. Men are expected to be free from the close influence of their mothers, whereas there is often felt to be an identity between adult women and their mothers. Variables such as the sex of children, the number of children and the age of the parents when children are born, all affect the course of family life. In Victorian England, when family size was bigger and life expectancy less than now, some parents had dependent children for all their lives – there was no time in which all their children had grown up and left home. These demographic and social factors greatly influence the course of family life and demonstrate not only the heterogeneity of culture but also the malleability of culture. All cultures are reproduced in specific circumstances; ideas and values are interpreted and understood in the light of local conditions. This last point brings us back to the issues of judgement and relativism in the understanding of cultural practice that we raised earlier in this section. A cultural approach to a common institution, in this case the family, demonstrates the power of cultural studies to generate a wide range and number of potential areas of investigation. Some of these have been alluded to in this example but you will be able to identify more.

## Example 2: Shakespeare

The study of Shakespeare has always been central to English studies and to some constructions of English **identity** (p. 142). Traditionally, in English studies, Shakespeare's plays and Shakespeare's language have been presented as the essence of Englishness. They have been made to serve as the defining features of a homogenous and unchanging culture. Subsequent authors have often been judged in terms of how they fit into that tradition. Because of this connection between Shakespeare and national identity the position of these plays in schools has become an important issue. The argument is sometimes put forward that children must read Shakespeare in order to learn English and Englishness. Shakespeare's plays become valued over and above other forms of cultural production. As a result the teaching of Shakespeare, and English history, was also a part of **colonialism**'s cultural project (p. 143).

However, cultural studies asks rather different questions about Shakespeare. Instead of taking Shakespeare's position for granted, it asks what the social position of the theatre was in Elizabethan times. Further, it asks how plays were written and produced in the sixteenth and seventeenth centuries. Evidence that shows a high degree of collaboration between playwrights and adaptation of plays on the stage changes the conception of Shakespeare as individual genius. He appears as part of a wider culture. Shakespeare is then placed historically rather than his plays being seen as 'timeless' or 'eternal'. The question of the audience is addressed both in the sixteenth and seventeenth centuries and now. This gives a sense of who the plays were intended for and how they have been received, further challenging the conception that his work is universal: that is, for everyone, all of the time. We might ask what groups of schoolchildren make of Shakespeare's plays depending on class, race and gender, or whether they have seen the plays in the theatre or in versions made for the cinema.

The timeless nature of Shakespeare can also be challenged by studies that show that the texts have been altered considerably over the years and that he was not always considered as important as he is now. Cultural studies looks at the changing conceptions of Englishness – and its relationships to the rest of the world – that caused Shakespeare to be rediscovered in the eighteenth century as the national poet. This extends from studying different versions of the plays to

---

## Box 1.5

### Troilus and Cressida

But when the planets
In evil mixture to disorder wander,
What plagues and what portents, what mutiny!
What raging of the sea, shaking of earth!
Commotion in the winds! frights, changes, horrors
Divert and crack, rend and deracinate
The unity and married calm of states
Quite from their fixure! Oh when degree is shak'd,

Which is the ladder of all high designs,
The enterprise is sick. How could communities,
Degrees in schools, and brotherhoods in cities,
Peaceful commerce from dividable shores,
The primogenity and due of birth,
Prerogative of age, crowns, sceptres, laurels,
But that degree stand in authentic place?
Take but degree away, untune that string,

And hark what discord follows.
Each thing meets
In mere oppugnacy: the bounded waters
Should lift their bosoms higher than the shores,
And make a sop of all this solid globe;
Strength should be lord of imbecility,
And the rude son should strike his father dead
    Troilus and Cressida I.iii.94–115

looking at the tourist industry in Stratford-upon-Avon. It can also involve studying the versions of Shakespeare that are produced in other parts of the world. These do not simply show the imposition of English cultural meanings, but the complex processes of negotiation within networks of cultural interaction which mean that Shakespearean history plays were vehicles for discussing political authority in the Soviet Union, and which recently brought a Zulu version of *Macbeth* from post-apartheid South Africa to the reconstruction of Shakespeare's Globe Theatre in London.

All of these processes of questioning and negotiation are of course political. They show that the interpretation of Shakespeare is a matter of power. This argument is developed by Margot Heinemann (1985) in her essay 'How Brecht read Shakespeare'. She gave the example of Nigel Lawson, Chancellor of the Exchequer in the late 1980s, who quoted from Shakespeare's play *Troilus and Cressida* (1601–2). Lawson used the quotation 'Take but degree away, untune that string/And hark what discord follows' to

argue that Shakespeare was a Tory. However, as Heinemann pointed out, the character who makes the speech, Ulysses, is in fact a wily, cunning politician, who is using the threat of social disorder to attain his own ends (see Box 1.5).

All of these questions and issues derive from adopting a rather different approach to the study of culture to that represented by English studies in its more conventional guises. They are the sorts of questions posed by those adopting a cultural studies perspective and are shaped by the core issues that we have identified. However, they also involve asking questions which lead us on to examining the theoretical perspectives used within cultural studies: what is the relationship between the social position of the audience (for example, race, class and gender) and the interpretation of the text? How can we understand the ways in which the meanings of Englishness (and their link to Shakespeare) and the meanings of Frenchness become defined as opposites? What ideas and methods can we use to interpret plays in their historical context or the

**Figure 1.1** The rapid pace of social change raises issues of difference, identity and the impacts of technology and globalisation. These provide leading questions for contemporary cultural studies. (Indian woman taking photograph in Peacock Court.) (Source: ©Martin Harvey/Corbis.)

contemporary meanings of Shakespeare within schools? In the next section we examine some of the most influential ways of theorising culture.

## 1.3 Theorising culture

This section introduces theories of culture which attempt to address the issues and problems set out above and to unite them within frameworks of expla-

nation. The bringing together of diverse issues and problems into a single form necessarily involves a process of abstraction. Theorists move away from the detail of particular instances and look for connections in terms of general principles or concepts. For the student, this means that theories are often difficult to grasp at first sight, couched as they are in abstract language. It may help you to think of issues and problems we have just introduced as the building blocks of theories. But there is no escaping the fact that the

---

### Defining concept 1.2

#### Structuralism and poststructuralism

Structuralism was an intellectual approach and movement which was very influential in the social sciences and the arts in the 1960s and 1970s. The basic idea of structuralism is that a phenomenon under study should be seen as consisting of a system of structures. This system and the relationship between the different elements are more important than the individual elements that make up the system.

The Swiss linguist de Saussure is regarded as the founder of structuralism. In his study of language, he drew attention to the structures (langue) that underpin the variation of everyday speech and writing (parole) and analysed the sign as consisting of a signified (concept) and signifier (word or sound), founding **semiotics** (p. 29) as the science of the study of signs. The emphasis on the structure to be found below or behind everyday interaction, or the variety of literary texts, was taken up by a number of (mainly French) writers working in different areas of the social sciences and humanities. Examples include: Lévi-Strauss (anthropology) in studies of kinship, myth and totemism; Lacan (psychoanalysis) who re-worked Freud,

arguing that the unconsciousness is structured like a language; **Barthes** (p. 96) (literary studies), who examined the myths of bourgeois societies and texts; **Foucault** (p. 20) (history and philosophy) who pointed to the way that underlying epistemes determine what can be thought in his archaeological method; and Althusser (philosophy), who drew on Lacan's re-working of Freud in a re-reading of **Marx** (p. 66) which emphasised the role of underlying modes of production in the determination of the course of history. Debate around Lacan was influential on the work in feminism of writers like **Kristeva** (p. 149) and Irigaray.

Poststructualism developed partly out of critique of the binary divisions so often characteristic of structuralism. So, for example, it criticised the idea that there is actually a distinct structure underlying texts or speech, blurring such distinctions. Moreover, it is critical of some of the scientific pretensions of structuralism. Structuralism tended to work on the premise that the truth or the real structure could be found. Poststructuralism is more concerned with the way in which versions of truth are produced in texts and

through interpretation, which is always in dispute and can never be resolved. Poststructuralism therefore tends to be more playful in practice if not outcome. The work of Derrida and Baudrillard exhibits some of these poststructuralist ideas. Derrida shows how texts subvert themselves from within and Baudrillard explodes the neat oppositions of sign and signifier, use and exchange value.

Examples of structuralist and poststructuralist analyses can be found in cultural studies. More formal structuralist analyses have sought to find the hidden meanings of folk tales (Propp), James Bond (Eco), the Western film (Wright) and romantic fiction (Radway). Poststructuralist influence is more diffuse, but can be found especially in more literary forms of cultural studies, where the complexities of texts and their multiple meanings are interpreted.

#### Further reading

Hawkes, T. (1991) *Structuralism and Semiotics*, London: Routledge.

Wright, W. (1975) *Sixguns and Society*, Berkeley, CA: University of California Press.

---

language of theory is abstract, and you may well find it difficult on first reading.

In this section we wish to outline the main features of some leading theoretical approaches in cultural studies. Broadly – and this is a caricature that can be filled out by looking at examples in the rest of the book – we start with functionalist and **structuralist** (p. 17) forms of understanding which suggest clearly defined, and often rather rigid, relationships between culture and social structure. From these we move on to theoretical approaches, which sometimes might still be called structuralist and are often influenced by **Karl Marx** (p. 66), that place emphasis on the understanding of culture and meaning through thinking about their relationships to political economy (for example, class structures, modes of production, etc.) and their importance within conflicts between differently positioned social groups. Finally we stress what are often called **poststructuralist** (p. 17) or **postmodern** (p. 295) theoretical approaches which retain a concern with politics (and some concern for economics) in explaining culture (see Chapter 6), but use a much more flexible sense of how cultures and meanings are made.

## Culture and social structure

Sociologists often use the term 'social structure' to describe 'the enduring, orderly and patterned relationships between elements of a society' (Abercrombie *et al.*, 1984: 198). Society is often considered to be ordered, patterned and enduring because of the structures that underlie it. Just as a tall building is held together by the girders underneath the stone and glass exterior, so too society is held together by its distinct configuration of institutions (political, economic, kinship and so forth)

One influential version of this way of thinking can be seen in the work of the American sociologist Talcott Parsons. Parsons treats culture as necessary for the proper functioning of society. In general terms culture – that is, values, norms and symbols – provide the linchpin of Parsons's solution to the problem of social order. This problem is an analytical issue concerning the sources of the enduring quality of social life – how is the regularity, persistence, relative stability and pre-

dictability of social life achieved? Parsons maintains that culture is the central element of an adequate solution to this problem because it provides values, the shared ideas about what is desirable in society (perhaps values like material prosperity, individual freedom and social justice), and norms, the acceptable means of obtaining these things (for example, the idea that honest endeavour is the way to success). Culture also provides language and other symbolic systems essential to social life. Parsons further maintains that culture is internalised by personalities and that individual motivation thus has cultural origins. Moreover two of society's basic features, its economy and its political system, are maintained by culture. Hence there is an important sense in which culture 'oils the wheels' of society. In the functionalist view of Parsons, society, culture and the individual are separate but interrelated, each interpenetrating the other. Culture occupies a central place because on the one hand it is internalised by individuals and on the other it is institutionalised in the stable patterns of action that make up major economic, political and kinship structures of the society.

## Social structure and social conflict: class, gender and 'race'

The separation of culture and social structure is not limited to functionalist theorists. It appears also in the work of theorists who argued that conflict is at the core of society and who understand culture in terms of the structured relationships of politics and economics (or political economy). **Karl Marx** (p. 66), the nineteenth-century philosopher and revolutionary, and the social theorist **Max Weber** (p. 158) treated beliefs, values and behaviour as products of social and economic inequalities and power relationships. Although Marx's ideas are very complex, some of his followers have argued that those who hold the means of production in society will control its ideas and values. The ruling ideas of a society (its forms of law, politics, religion, etc.) will be those of the dominant class. These ideas will be used to manage and perpetuate an unequal and unjust system. In this scheme, culture serves as a prop to the social structure, legitimising the existing order of things.

## Box 1.6

### Subordination and patriarchy

*Subordination of women:* a phrase used to describe the generalised situation whereby men as a group have more social and economic power than women, including power over women (Pearson, 1992). Men are dominant in society and masculinity signifies dominance over femininity in terms of ideas.

*Patriarchy:* originally an anthropological term that describes a social system in which authority is invested in the male head of the household (the patriarch) and other male elders in the kinship group. Older men are entitled to exercise socially sanctioned authority over other members of the household or kinship group,

both women and younger men (Pearson, 1992).

Patriarchy has been criticised by some feminists as too all-embracing a term to describe the different forms of male dominance in different societies.

**Feminist** (p. 82) theorists have also seen culture as a product of social conflict; but whereas Marxists see social conflict as between classes, feminists see gender relations as just as important. Two key terms in feminist theory are 'subordination' and 'patriarchy' (see Box 1.6). Both these terms describe how men have more social and economic power than women. Feminist theory focuses on the political and economic inequalities between men and women. However, because women have often been excluded from the mainstream of political and economic life, feminists have also emphasised the importance of studying culture as the place in which inequality is reproduced. Because it is within culture that gender is formed, feminists have studied culture in order to examine the ways in which cultural expectations and assumptions about sex have fed the idea that gender inequality is natural.

Culture and conflict are also linked in the study of 'race' and racism. The concept of 'race' is often put in inverted commas because 'race', like gender, is also a social rather than a biological category. Although people are often differently defined by 'racial' characteristics, there are always as many differences within a defined 'racial' group as between 'racial' groups (Fields, 1990: 97). Fryer (1984) has argued that racial prejudice is cultural in the sense that it is the articulation of popular beliefs held by a people about others who are felt to be different from themselves. Racism, however, articulates cultural difference with structured inequality, using perceptions of these differences to validate oppression. The argument is that cultural

domination is an essential element of economic and political control. Just as feminists contend that the cultural roles assigned to women (gendered roles) serve to account for their separate and unequal relationship with men, so critics of racism argue that prejudicial values and attitudes towards colonised peoples developed as European imperialists slaughtered them, took their lands and destroyed their cultures (Richards, 1990).

## Culture in its own right and as a force for change

However, culture need not be seen as dependent upon and derivative of the economic or any other dimension of social structure. The celebrated case here is **Max Weber**'s (p. 158) account of the part played by the Protestant ethic in explaining the origins of modern capitalism. Weber argues that the beliefs of the early Protestant sects played a key causal role in the establishment of the 'spirit' or culture of capitalism, and thereby contributed to development of the capitalist economic system. Many of the early Protestant groups subscribed to the teachings of Calvin's doctrine of predestination that maintained that the believer's eternal salvation was determined at birth and that no amount of good works could alter God's decision. This placed a tremendous psychological burden on believers who had no way of knowing whether they numbered among the Elect (those who achieve eternal salvation in the life hereafter). The practical solution offered by the Protestant religion to the anxiety thus generated lay in the notion of vocation: the believer was instructed to work long and hard in an occupation in order to attest his/her confidence and conviction that Elect status was assured. Later, the doctrine was relaxed so that systematic labour within a vocation and the material prosperity that accompanied it came to be seen as a sign of Election. The consequences of these beliefs and related restrictions on consumption and indulgence was (a) to introduce a new goal-orientated attitude towards economic activity to replace the diffuse attitudes that had persisted through the Middle Ages, and (b) to facilitate the process of capital accumulation. Weber of course was well aware that a number of factors other than the cultural contributed to a phenomenon as complex as capitalism (Collins, 1980).

## Key influence 1.2

### Michel Foucault (1926–84)

Michel Foucault was a French philosopher and historian – indeed these two categories or identities become blurred together in his writing and thought – who has had a dramatic and far-reaching impact on cultural studies through his work on the connections between **power** (p. 64), knowledge and subjectivity.

Foucault's varied career took him through several disciplines – including philosophy and psychology – and various countries – he worked in France, Sweden, Poland, Tunisia and Germany before taking up a position at France's premier academic institution, the Collège de France, in 1970. Significantly, his job in Paris was, at his suggestion, a professorship in History of Systems of Thought and in this we can trace the themes of much of the work that he undertook from the 1950s through into the 1980s.

Foucault's early work traced changing modes of thought in relation to 'psychological' knowledges. His book *Madness and Civilisation* (1961) traced the relationship between madness and reason; reading the changing reactions to madness, and the incarceration of the mad, in terms of thinking about rationality as they changed from the medieval period, through the Enlightenment's Age of Reason, and into the nineteenth century. The issues that it raised were explored in varied and changing ways in his subsequent work. Careful attention to the changing patterns of knowledge produced *The Birth of the Clinic* (originally published in French in 1963), *The Order of Things* (French original 1966) and *The Archaeology of Knowledge* (French original 1969). Indeed, he used the term 'archaeologies' to describe all these projects. The connections between knowledge and power which the treatment of the insane had revealed were further explored in relation to other marginalised groups in his *Discipline and Punish: The Birth of the Prison* (originally published in French in 1975), his edited editions of the lives of the murderer Pierre Rivière (1975) and the hermaphrodite Herculine Barbin (1978), and his three books on *The History of Sexuality* (originally published in French: Volume I 1976, Volumes II and III 1984). In all of these studies – which he called genealogies – he used theories of **discourse** (p. 21) to trace the changing ways in which power and knowledge are connected in the production of subjectivities and **identities** (p. 142).

Foucault's impact has been academic. He has changed the ways in which we think about power, knowledge and subjectivity, encouraging us to look at the ways in which they are connected and the ways in which they change from context to context. In emphasising that 'Nothing is fundamental. That is what is interesting in the analysis of society', he has encouraged us to think about the ways in which things – power relations, ways of thinking, and ways of understanding ourselves and others – could be different. This means that his influence has also been political. His attention to the forms of power which shape institutions and subjectivities has been influential in, for example, campaigns over prisoners' rights and gay rights.

#### Further reading

Foucault, M. (1980) *Power/Knowledge: Selected Interviews and Other Writings 1972–1977*, ed. Colin Gordon, Brighton: Harvester Press.

Kritzman, L.D. (ed.) (1988) *Michel Foucault: Politics, Philosophy, Culture. Interviews and Other Writings 1977–1984*, London: Routledge.

Rabinow, P. (ed.) (1984) *The Foucault Reader*, Harmondsworth: Penguin.

## Defining concept 1.3

### Discourse

Discourse is a way of thinking about the relationship between **power** (p. 64), knowledge and language. In part it is an attempt to avoid some of the difficulties involved in using the concept of **ideology** (p. 35). It is a way of understanding most associated with the work of the French philosopher and historian **Michel Foucault** (p. 20).

For Foucault a 'discourse' is what we might call 'a system that defines the possibilities for knowledge' or 'a framework for understanding the world' or 'a field of knowledge'. A discourse exists as a set of 'rules' (formal or informal, acknowledged or unacknowledged) which determine the sorts of statements that can be made (i.e. the 'moon is made of blue cheese' is not a statement that can be made within a scientific discourse, but it can within a poetic one). These 'rules' determine what the criteria for truth are, what sorts of things can be talked about, and what sorts of things can be said about them. One example that Foucault uses which can help us here is the imaginary Chinese encyclopaedia about which the Argentinian writer Jorge Luis Borges has written a short story. Foucault uses this to challenge our ideas about the inherent truthfulness and rationality of our own classification systems and scientific discourses. In the encyclopaedia:

[A]nimals are divided into: (a)

belonging to the Emperor, (b) embalmed, (c) tame, (d) sucking pigs, (e) sirens, (f) fabulous, (g) stray dogs, (h) included in the present classification, (i) frenzied, (j) innumerable, (k) drawn with a very fine camelhair brush, (l) *et cetera*, (m) having just broken the water pitcher, (n) that from a long way off look like flies.

(Foucault, 1970: xv)

Foucault's aim is to problematise the relationship between words and things. He suggests that there are lots of ways in which the world can be described and defined and that we have no sure grounds to choose one over the others. In turn this also means that he is dedicated to recovering those ways of knowing that have been displaced and forgotten.

Discourse is also about the relationship between power and knowledge. Foucault (1980) argues that we have to understand power as something productive. For example, it is not in catching a criminal that power lies but in producing the notion of 'the criminal' in the first place. As he says: 'There is no power relation without the correlative constitution of a field of knowledge, nor any knowledge that does not presuppose and constitute at the same time power relations' (Foucault, 1977: 27). To continue the example, it is the body of knowledge – the discourse – that

we call 'criminology' that produces 'the criminal' (and, in the past, now forgotten figures like 'the homicidal monomaniac') as an object of knowledge, and suggests ways of dealing with him or her. The criminal, the criminologist, the policeman and the prison are all created together 'in discourse'.

This does not mean that the world is just words and images. Foucault is keen to talk about the institutions and practices that are vital to the working of discourse. If we think about medical discourse we soon realise that the forms of knowledge and language that make it up are inseparable from the actual places where these discourses are produced (the clinic, the hospital, the surgery) and all the trappings of the medical environment (white coats, stethoscopes, nurses' uniforms) (see Prior, 1988).

### Further reading

Foucault, M. (1980) *Power/Knowledge: Selected Interviews and Other Writings 1972–1977*, ed. Colin Gordon, Brighton: Harvester.

Purvis, T. and Hunt, A. (1993) 'Discourse, ideology, discourse, ideology, discourse, ideology . . .', *British Journal of Sociology*, 44, 473–99.

His intention was to show how ideas can be 'effective forces' (Weber, 1930: 183) in the historical development of societies. Culture (here in the form of religious ideas) can shape as well as be shaped by social structure.

A more interwoven view of the relationship between culture and society is shown in the work of Mary Douglas and **Michel Foucault** (p. 20). They both stress in their writings that our understanding of particular objects relates as much to the way we think about those objects as to any qualities those objects may have in themselves. There is a reciprocal relationship between thought and the object(s) of thought: a two-way process where objects have qualities that make an impression upon us, but that impression is influenced by the ways in which we have been conditioned to think about that object. Thought and object are, then, inseparably linked but this does not mean that we always think in the same way about things and that ideas never change. It does mean that change is the outcome of reciprocal relationships, not a uni-directional causality from structure to culture. This means that culture may influence structure, as well as structure influencing culture. The recognition that culture is a force for change (not simply the object of change) leads to the belief that culture can be examined as a system in its own right. For example, in *Purity and Danger* Mary Douglas (1966) argues that ideas about dirt and hygiene in society have a force and a compulsion, not simply because they can be related to the material world through ideas about contamination, germs and illness, but because they are part of a wider cosmology or world-view. Dirt and hygiene are understood within a culture not just in terms of their relation to disease, but also in terms of ideas of morality, for example moral purity versus immoral filth. Thus, a cultural understanding of dirt will have to take into account the meaning of dirt in more than just a medical sense. It will have to understand dirt's place historically, within a specific culture. The ordering and classifying of events which result from ideas about the world gives meaning to behaviour. The state of being dirty is thus as much the product of ideas as it is of the material world.

In turn, Foucault argues that social groups, identities and positions – like classes, genders, races and sexualities – do not pre-exist and somehow determine their own and other cultural meanings. They are produced within **discourses** (p. 21) which define what they are and how they operate. So, for Foucault, even though there have always been men who have sex with men, there was no 'homosexual' identity, and no 'homosexual sex' before that identity and the figure of the 'homosexual' were defined in medical, psychological and literary texts at the end of the nineteenth century. That those discourses about homosexuality both produced moves to regulate male sexuality – and therefore defined more clearly a group of homosexual men – and provided the basis for positive identification with that term on the part of some of those men, meant that 'homosexuality' came to have a significant place within the social structure. In Foucault's version of things there is no determinate relationship between social structure and culture. Instead there is a flexible set of relationships between **power** (p. 64), discourse and what exists in the world.

In considering theoretical accounts of the relation of culture and social structure we have demonstrated the rigid determinism of the functionalists; the strong connections between cultural struggles and the social relations of class, race and gender made by Marxists and feminists; and the importance of culture in reciprocally shaping social structures and social positions and identities argued by Foucault. These introductory remarks will be taken further in subsequent chapters that examine the issue they raise in more detail

## 1.4 Conclusion

What, then, is cultural studies? Throughout this chapter we have stressed the linkages between something that we have called cultural studies and the disciplines of sociology, history, geography, English and anthropology. We have discussed a set of central concerns for these disciplines, arguing that, given their common interests in culture, there are issues and problems that they all must address. These central concerns we call the core issues and problems in the study of culture. The shared interest in the topic of culture and the recognition of common themes brought practitioners from different disciplines together in the belief that it is through cooperation and collaboration that understanding and explanation will develop most powerfully. This clustering of different disciplinary perspectives around a common object of study offers the possibility of the development of a distinctive area of study characterised by new methods of analysis. It is this configuration of collaborating disciplines around the topic of culture that we see constituting both the substance and the methods of cultural studies. The arena in which this takes place can be labelled an 'interdiscursive space', capturing the fluidity and focus that characterise cultural studies and contrasting the emergent, innovatory themes in substance and method that arise out of collaboration with the traditional themes of single disciplines. The metaphor of space also draws attention to the permeable nature of cultural studies: there are no fixed boundaries and no fortress walls; theories and themes are drawn in from disciplines and may flow back in a transformed state to influence thinking there.

Richard Johnson (1986) has pointed out the dangers of academic codification in regard to cultural studies, suggesting that its strength lies in its openness and hence its capacity for transformation and growth. He argues that cultural studies mirrors the complexity and polysemic qualities of the object of its study, culture. The power of culture arises from its diffuseness: the term is used where imprecision matters, where rigidity would destroy what it seeks to understand. Consciousness and subjectivity are key terms in Johnson's portrayal of cultural studies. Consciousness is used in the Marxist sense of knowledge and also in a reflexive sense to give the idea of productive activity. Subjectivity is used to refer to the construction of individuals by culture. Combining these two concepts leads Johnson (1986) to describe the project of cultural studies as being to 'abstract, describe and reconstitute in concrete studies the social forms through which human beings 'live', become conscious, sustain themselves subjectively'.

This project has been interpreted in cultural studies in terms of three main models of research: (a) production-based studies; (b) text-based studies; (c) studies of lived cultures. As you can see, there is a close correspondence here with the three senses of culture that we elaborated earlier in this chapter. Each one of these areas has a different focus; the first draws attention to processes involved in and struggles over the production of cultural items; the second investigates the forms of cultural product; the third is concerned with how experience is represented. Johnson points to the necessarily incompleteness of these ventures; like the wider arena in which they operate, they are fed by interactive communication. Each one gives to and takes from the others.

In summary, we suggest approaching cultural studies as an area of activity that grows from interaction and collaboration to produce issues and themes that are new and challenging. Cultural studies is not an island in a sea of disciplines but a current that washes the shores of other disciplines to create new and changing formations.

## Recap

➤ In cultural studies the concept of culture has a range of meanings which includes both high art and everyday life.

➤ Cultural studies advocates an interdisciplinary approach to the study of culture.

➤ While cultural studies is eclectic in its use of theory, using both structuralist and more flexible approaches, it advocates those that stress the overlapping, hybrid nature of cultures, seeing cultures as networks rather than patchworks.

## Further reading

Although they are not always easy reading, the best place to begin exploring the issues raised in this chapter is to look at the acknowledged early 'classics' of cultural studies: Richard Hoggart's *The Uses of Literacy* (1958), Raymond Williams' *Culture and Society 1780–1950* (1963) and E.P. Thompson's *The Making of the English Working Class* (1968). Each of these works has had a profound influence over the subsequent development of cultural studies. Important stocktakings of the field's development are Cary Nelson and Lawrence Grossberg's *Marxism and the Interpretation of Culture* (1988) and the substantial collection edited by Grossberg, Cary Nelson and Paula Treicher, *Cultural Studies* (1992). John Storey's *Cultural Theory and Popular Culture: An Introduction* (2006) connects debates about popular culture to the concerns of cultural studies. Richard Johnson's 'What is cultural studies anyway?' (1986) critically charts the possibilities of three models of cultural studies (production-based studies, text-based studies and studies of lived cultures). Some of these ideas feed into a recent collaborative work by Johnson, Deborah Chambers, Parvati Raghuram and Estella Tincknell (2004) *The Practice of Cultural Studies*. Distinctive takes on the topic matter of cultural studies are provided in David Inglis and John Hughson *Confronting Culture* (2003) and by

Angela McRobbie in *The Uses of Cultural Studies* (2005). A good guide to key concepts in cultural studies is provided by Tony Bennett, Lawrence Grossberg and Meaghan Morris (2005). For original recent work in cultural studies, the reader may wish to consult the following journals: *Cultural Studies*, *New Formations* and *Social Text*. You will probably need access to a university library to read these periodicals.

# Culture, communication and representation

## 2.0 Introduction

Chapter 1 presented an introduction to the ideas of culture and structure. Here in Chapter 2, we develop these discussions in relation to key debates and theories on communication and representation.

Communication is the process of making meaning. It is how one individual (or a word, object, sign, gesture or similar) conveys meaning to another individual – be that meaning intentional or not. Significantly, this process of communication also involves **representation** (p. 43), in that meaning is *represented* through objects or actions. For example, certain letters written on a page may spell the word 'cat' and those three small shapes (letters) placed together convey the meaning, and therefore represent, the idea of a cat. However, what is significant about the study of communication and representation for cultural studies, is the suggestion that it is through language and communication that we define and shape our social and cultural world. It is through language and communication that we

make sense of our world, and convey these meanings to others, through which we develop shared meanings and shared cultures, which shape our understanding and interpretation of our whole social world.

This idea of 'making meanings' is considered in the first of three main sections within this chapter. This first main section (*the organisation of meaning*) begins by considering how meanings can be defined by the nature or form of communication, and in particular, considers *spoken, written and visual texts*. Within this section we present an introduction to the ideas of semiotics and the Sapir-Whorf hypothesis (the former discussed in more detail later in Chapter 4), which suggest that language is a structured system that shapes our cultures. This idea is developed further in the discussion that follows of *structuralism and the order of meaning*. The ideas that meanings are 'rigid' is challenged in the following discussion of *hermeneutics and interpretation*. Next, this section considers the role of the *political economy, ideology and meaning*, which suggests that meanings are defined through (dominant) ideologies. This section concludes with discussions of *poststructuralism and the patterns of meaning* and *postmodernism and semiotics*, which both question the idea of meanings as structured and as shaped along social 'group' lines.

In the second main section of this chapter we move on to consider *language, representation, power and inequality* in more detail. This begins with a consideration of *language and power*, before considering the way language has been used in relation to *class, race and ethnicity* and *gender*.

The third and final main section of this chapter focuses more specifically on forms of *mass communication and representation*, and more specifically the *mass media and representation*. In this, we consider three examples of mass media representations – of *race and ethnicity*, *gender* and *celebrity*. This section, and chapter, then concludes with a consideration of *audiences and reception*. Within this discussion we focus on the important and influential work of **Stuart Hall** (p. 55) on encoding/decoding, before finally finishing off with a consideration of how this work is located with Abercrombie and Longhurst's (1998) theorisation of paradigms of audience research.

## Learning objectives

➤ To understand the complexity of processes of communication and representation.

➤ To understand how language, communication and representation shape our social world and cultures.

➤ To reflect on the powerful role language plays in shaping our understanding of social factors such as class, gender and ethnicity.

➤ And also to understand how social and cultural 'groupings' such as ethnicity, gender and celebrity are presented and understood through and via the mass media.

# 2.1 The organisation of meaning

**Raymond Williams** (p. 3) argues that the patterning of meaning is a crucial starting point for cultural analysis:

> [I]t is with the discovery of patterns of a characteristic kind that any useful cultural analysis begins, and it is with the relationships between these patterns, which sometimes reveal unexpected identities and correspondences in hitherto separately considered activities, sometimes again reveal discontinuities of an unexpected kind, that general cultural analysis is concerned.
>
> (Williams, 1965: 47)

However, there are many different ways in which this search for patterns of meaning can proceed. In particular, this section begins by considering how meaning can be shaped by the form of communication used, this is then followed by discussions of communication and meaning, structuralism and meaning, hermeneutics and interpretation, the political economy and ideology, poststructuralism, and postmodernism.

## Spoken, written and visual texts

A 'text', quite simply, is any cultural item that can be 'read' or interpreted. These can be (semi)permanent, such as books, letters or television shows, or can be more temporal such as someone speaking or watching a live football match. In particular, the 'openness' and degree of meaning that can be read into a text is a crucial consideration of poststructuralism (and this is considered further, later in this chapter). However, here we wish to highlight how the nature or form of a text can significantly contribute to the meaning derived from it. In particular, this can be summed by Marshall McLuhan's famous dictum that 'the medium is the message'. By this McLuhan (1964) is suggesting that too often we focus on the content of a message, but overlook its context, form or the medium through which it is delivered – and it is these which are crucial in determining what the content (message) is.

A significant contributor to the meaning of a text is the form that this takes; such as spoken, written or visual texts. Of course, to some degree this is a false distinction, as forms of communication often blur with each other. For instance a person talking (speech), will often use their hands, face and body to gesture (visual) and might also be wearing a t-shirt with writing on, which will also convey (written) meaning. However, it is important to realise that meaning is conveyed differently depending on the form of the medium or message carrier.

Spoken language first developed as sounds made to accompany gestures, which through use, developed into more elaborate codes (Newsom, 2007: 57). However, the development of spoken language should not be seen as a natural uncontested process of evolution. The history of any language is a history of contest, conflict and struggle. For instance, the 'English' language is in origin an Anglo-Frisian (i.e. Germanic) language first brought to Great Britain probably in the fifth century. This 'imported' language combined with Celtic dialectics to form 'old English', which over the centuries was adapted and changed, primarily due to successive invasion, such as from (Norse) Vikings and (Franco) Normans – each bringing, and at times imposing, their own languages.

What we have come to view as 'Standard British English' developed primarily as a merchant dialect in England in the Middle Ages. With the continued growth in importance of merchants, trade and business this dialect was increasingly used in the development of institutions, such as the law, government and financial institutions, facilitating the spread of this dialect and its common acceptance (Schirato and Yell 2000). This then becomes accepted as the 'correct' way to speak, with all other dialects being rejected, and viewed as 'incorrect' if not 'vulgar' (Schirato and Yell 2000). Then (just as invaders had done in Britain) the rise of the British Empire from the fifteenth century onwards sees the imposition of this language on many nations around the world; who in turn have added to the use and development of this.

Still today *how* we speak is very important. For instance, in the UK there continues to be an emphasis of speaking 'correctly' (what is sometimes referred to as 'The Queen's English'), and Shnukal (1983, cited in

Schirato and Yell, 2000) suggests that this prioritisation of one form of dialect, and seeing all other as 'bastardised' or 'ungrammatical', is a form of linguistic racism – a point developed further, later in this chapter (p. 46).

Spoken language also has complexities in meanings beyond the actual words spoken themselves. For instance, the meaning of spoken words can be greatly influenced by tone, pitch, speed and volume – and this is sometimes referred as 'paralanguage' (Schirato and Yell, 2000). Speech will also often be punctuated by the use of noises or what Goffman (1981) referred to as 'response cries' such as 'ouch' (to being hit) or 'oops' (to a minor accident). Speech, and the meanings associated with it, are also frequently accompanied by non-verbal forms of communication, such as facial expression or gestures, and these have a very important role in communication and can significantly alter the meaning of what is being spoken. Also, for many, such as some who are hearing impaired, non-verbal gestures constitute the main form of communication, but even here, non-verbal communication (such as sign language) can be manipulated in subtle ways to convey different meanings and emotions.

Goffman (1959) also highlights how social interaction between people is shaped by their social status; such as people's behaviour and speech patterns may alter if the are talking to someone perceived to be more or less powerful than themselves. For Goffman social interaction was a social performance similar to acting on a stage, where people will also carefully consider how they are perceived by others and alter their behaviour and what they say accordingly – and Goffman refers to this as 'impression management'.

Turning to written language, it is evident that this first developed as symbolic, usually artistic, representations (such as cave paintings and later hieroglyphics) of aspects of the world, but did not relate directly to spoken words. The earliest written language that was also spoken was probably Sanskrit, which was first used in India in the fourth and fifth centuries BC (Newsom, 2007). Writing can be understood as a technology, which allows communication at distance. However, written language often lacks the same ability to convey the subtle meanings and variations that can be conveyed through paralanguage. To convey subtle meanings, written language must rely on emphasis and punctuation, such as exclamation or question marks, or even emoticons (also known as 'smileys'), which are particularly common in Internet chat-rooms/messaging and emails, and use punctuations to represent faces and emotions such as :-) (smile) :-(( (sad/sulk) ;-) (wink) :-o (shock) :-P (tongue poking).

Written language is a form of communication that negates some of the unequal power relations associated with speech. For instance, it is often easier to tell a powerful person something in a letter than face-to-face. However, written words still involve some of the social conventions and role taking associated with speech. For instance, a letter writer will write in a very different style if they were writing to their mother, lover or boss. Written language styles also differ in various forms of document. For instance, legal, academic or scientific documents, comic books, novels, love letters and newspapers, may all be written in the same language, but will often use very different writing styles and techniques – and these will often be shaped by the **ideologies** (p. 35) or **discourses** (p. 21) of both the writer and the conventions associated with that type of document/publication. Though all texts (including written words) are open to multiple readings/interpretations by their audiences, it is evident that most texts will have a 'preferred reading' – in other words a 'dominant' meaning, which was intended by the author.

Communication can also take the form of visual communication. A full discussion of visual culture is provided later (in Chapter 10), but it is important to acknowledge here the powerful role of visual representations (such as painting, photographs and television) as a form of communication. Visual representations, often give the impression of being neutral (after all, many would argue that 'seeing is believing') and lacking in the ideology or discourses associated with spoken or written language. However, visual imagery is just as prone to, and shaped by, ideologies and discourses as written or spoken texts. For instance, paintings will be painted to portray particular meanings or sentiments, and will focus on particular subjects (and not others). Similarly, photographs only show particular angles or perspectives, they are frequently 'posed', if not 'set-up', they can then be edited, re-shot, touched up, and certain shots excluded in preference to

others. And this is particularly the case in the mass media, which is in the business of image 'creation' (rather than presentation). Hence, it is important that visual images are seen as a **representation** (p. 43), and not *presentation*, of the world – and this point is taken up later in this chapter.

# Communication and meaning

As already suggested the term communication refers to the process of making meaning. For instance, at its simplest, an individual speaks a word, which is heard and interpreted by a second person and this conveys a meaning to the listener. Similarly, an individual may wear a t-shirt or a hat, which conveys meaning to an observer – for example, that the wearer is the supporter of a particular sport team – or the meaning conveyed may be unintentional, such as the receiver of the message may think that the person in the hat or t-shirt looks silly or unfashionable.

However, this was not the original use of the term 'communication'. Gunther Kress (1988) in *Communication and Culture* suggests that the term communication came into popular usage first in the nineteenth century to refer to physical means of connection, such as railroads, roads and shipping. However, it was with the development of new technologies, such as the telegram, and later the radio and telephone, that the term 'communication' became more commonly used to refer to the delivery of information, rather than physical objects.

The origins of the term communication (as a simple process of passing on an object) strongly influenced early considerations of the communications process. In particular, one of the earliest studies of telecommunications was conducted by Claude Elwood Shannon who worked for the Bell telephone corporation in America in the 1940s. Shannon developed a mathematical model of communication that was concerned with the most effective way of transmitting information, which attempted to eliminate any disruption of the original message. This disruption in the transfer of a message Shannon referred to as 'noise'. Therefore, this early study of communication processes was primarily concerned with the transmission and reception of a

# Defining concept 2.1

## Semiology and semiotics

The study (or science) of 'signs' is known in Europe as 'semiology' (a term coined by Ferdinand de Saussure (1857–1913), a Swiss linguist) and in North America as 'semiotics' (a name devised by C.S. Peirce (1839–1914) for his independently developed philosophical system that shared many common premises with de Saussure's).

The simplest way to define what a sign is, is to consider the components or parts that make it up. At its simplest a *sign* consists of two components. First, there is a spoken, written, or visual symbol (such as a word, a road sign or an advertisement) – this is known as the *signifier*. Second, associated with this symbol will be a certain concept or idea – this is the *signified*. For example, the word 'cat' (the signifier) along with our understanding of what a cat is (a small furry domestic animal – this is the signified) together provides us with an understanding or meaning of a 'cat'. This then is the sign – the sum of both the word and the meaning we attach to it.

One of the key suggestions of de Saussure is that the relationship between a sign and its meaning is *arbitrary*. That is to say, that meaning is not straightforward. For example there is no reason why the three letters that make up the word 'cat' should mean a small furry domestic animal. These three letters could just as easily have been used to refer to what we call a 'dog' or a 'fish' or a 'banana'.

De Saussure's most influential ideas were set out in lectures given between 1907 and 1911 and published posthumously in 1916 as *Cours de Linguistique Général*, edited from de Saussure's papers and his students' notes. De Saussure emphasised that what a sign stands for is simply a matter of cultural convention, of how things are done in a given culture. This can clearly be seen in the way different people attach different meanings to a word or the way people use different words to refer to the same object/thing. For instance, the word 'pig' could refer to a farmyard animal. However, in a different context, or to a different person, a 'pig' could refer to a greedy person or even a police officer. Likewise to a French speaking person the farmyard animal in question is not called a 'pig' at all, but rather a 'porc'. This is also the case for all signs and symbols. For instance, many Western cultures see black as a colour for mourning and funerals; however, in many Asian nations it is white (and not black) that is associated with death (Newsom, 2007).

If the sign is arbitrary, then its meaning can only be established by considering its relation to other signs. It is thus necessary to look for the connections and differences between signs. These are classified in two broad ways:

➤ Syntagmatically – the linear or sequential relations between signs (thus traditional English meals consist of a starter, followed by a main course and a dessert).

➤ Paradigmatically – the 'vertical' relations, the particular combination of signs (thus soup or melon but not apple pie for starters).

Semiologists also speak of different levels of signification. The skilled semiologist can proceed from the level of denotation, the obvious meaning of the sign (e.g. a photograph of a cowboy smoking a Marlboro cigarette), to the connotation of the sign, its taken-for-granted meaning (e.g. that smoking Marlboro is something that tough 'real' men do.)

In this way the ideological functions of signs can be exposed. Certain cultural forms can be seen as myths which serve to render specific (often bourgeois) values as natural, universal and eternal.

A further influential distinction suggested by de Saussure is between language as a patterned system (langue) and language as embodied in actual speech (parole) – and in particular, de Saussure himself concentrated most of his studies on language systems (langue), which are relatively stable, unlike spoken language (parole) that are much more fluid and dynamic. This is because de Saussure located the study of language as part of a larger science devoted to 'the study of the life of signs within society'. In particular, semiologists maintain that it is possible to discern certain logics or structures or codes, which underpin the multiplicity of cultural life as we experience it – and in particular semiology is associated with **structuralism** (p. 17).

De Saussure's ideas have been developed effectively in the broader sphere of culture by **Roland Barthes** (p. 96). His writings explicate the latent meanings (the myths and codes) that inform such diverse cultural phenomena as guide books, steak and chips, electoral photography, all-in wrestling, margarine, and the Eiffel Tower. A good example of Barthes use of semiology is his analysis of a cover photograph on the French magazine, *Paris Match* (p. 31).

## Defining concept 2.1 (continued)

**Further reading**

Barthes, R. (1973) *Mythologies*, St
Albans: Paladin.

Gottdeiner, M. (1995) *Postmodern
Semiotics*, Oxford: Blackwell.

message or information. This model therefore presents a very straightforward and simplistic understanding of communication, which at its simplest involves a three-stage process of 'sender – message – receiver'. First, there is an individual (the sender) who composes a message (such as a letter or a spoken sentence or phrase), this is then delivered to and received by another individual (the receiver).

What this model fails to recognise or consider, is the social context of message creation, conveyance and reception. For instance, the process of communication does not simply involve a message, which is clearly intended by the sender and likewise clearly understood in the same way by the receiver. The meaning of a message will be determined by many different social factors, such as the contexts of the message, the form it takes, the power relations between the 'sender' and 'receiver' and the process of interpretation and re-interpretation undertaken by the receiver. All of these (and more) are what helps create the meaning of a message and also form important constituent parts of the communication process, and cannot therefore be simply dismissed as 'noise' that needs to be overcome. In particular, **semiotics** (or semiology as it is also known), which is the study (or science) of 'signs', shows us that 'meaning' is not straightforward or 'natural'; but rather that there is an arbitrary relationship between a signifier (word, symbol or similar) and the meaning that this carries (the signified).

Therefore, there is no natural commonsensical reason why we attach certain meaning to words or symbols. Furthermore, de Saussure suggests that the semiotic systems (such as language) we use are not made *by* 'the world', but rather it is semiotic systems that *make* the world (Schirato and Yell, 2000). That is to

say, it is not simply the existence of pigs or cats that makes us form words to describe these, but rather the words and signs we develop, and the meaning we attach to these, that shape our understanding of the world.

This can be clearly illustrated by Benjamin Lee Whorf's work on the language system of the Hopi, a Native American people. Unlike mainstream American culture which expresses the understanding of time in spatial metaphors, for example, one may say 'it is a *long time* since . . .' or 'it will happen in a *short time*', the Hopi expressed events as happenings taking place in a state of *being*, a condition that does not lend itself to being categorised in the same way as mainstream American notions of time. Similarly the tenses of the Hopi language did not correspond with American customary notions of past, present and future.

Whorf's work is built upon the earlier work on linguistics of Edward Sapir who suggested that there develops in all languages specialised and elaborated lexicons dedicated to the description and understanding of important features of social and cultural life. Whorf's work on the Hopi, together with Sapir's earlier analysis, contributed to the formulation of the Sapir–Whorf hypothesis that states that language creates mental categories through which humans make sense of the world. The proposition is that the world is filtered through the conceptual grids produced by language and the routine and regular use of particular languages produces habitual thought patterns, which are culturally specific. It is these culturally specific thought patterns that Sapir and Whorf refer to as *thought worlds*. Whorf expresses the idea in the following way:

> We dissect nature along lines laid down by our
> native languages. The categories and types that we

# Box 2.1

## Semiotics of colonialism

**Figure 2.1** Cover of *Paris Match*.

One of the best-known examples of semiotic analysis can be found in Roland Barthes' (1915–80) analysis of a photograph from the magazine *Paris Match* (1976). This photograph was published at the time when France was embroiled in the conflict over the decolonisation of Algeria. As will be seen, this context of conflict over empire is very significant to the meaning and analysis of the photograph. Barthes says: 'I am at the barber's, and a copy of *Paris-Match* is offered to me' (1976: 116). He continues, 'On the cover, a young Negro in a French uniform is saluting, with his eyes uplifted, probably fixed on the fold of the tricolour. All this is the

*meaning* of the picture.' Barthes has identified the denotative meaning of the photograph. Having done this, Barthes develops his analysis. He says:

> But, whether naively or not, I see very well what it signifies to me: that France is a great Empire, that all her sons, without any colour discrimination, faithfully serve under her flag, and that there is no better answer to the detractors of an alleged colonialism than the zeal shown by this Negro in serving his so-called oppressors.
>
> (1976: 116)

After identifying these connotations of the photograph, Barthes locates his discussion within the language of semiotics:

> I am therefore again faced with a greater semiological system: there is a signifier, itself already formed within a previous system (a black soldier is giving the French salute); there is a signified (it is here a purposeful mixture of Frenchness and militariness); and finally a presence of the signified through the signifier.

The discussion of these photographs has introduced several important points about semiotics which can be summarised as follows:

1 Any image or text can be said to contain different layers or levels of meaning. In particular there is a distinction between *denotative* and *connotative* levels.

2 The nature of such meanings will depend on the context in which they are contained, or the surrounding circumstances. Meaning is *relational*.

3 Some of the levels of meaning or *codes* are relatively neutral, or objective, whereas others will be saturated with social meanings or discourses.

4 The recognition and elucidation of these different meanings involves analysis or *decoding* which often depends on the nature of the knowledge and experience brought to the analysis.

Using the language of semiotics, the photographs considered here are acting as signs. The sign consists of two elements: the signifier and the signified. The signifier is a sound,

## Box 2.1 (continued)

printed word or image, and the signified is a mental concept.

The semiotic approach, which was developed from the study of language by de Saussure, has been applied widely. Thus, **Barthes** (p. 96) argues (1976: 113):

> take a black pebble: I can make it signify in several ways, it is a

mere signifier; but if I weigh it with a definite signified (a death sentence, for instance, in an anonymous vote), it will become a sign.

Barthes shows how different levels of meaning are associated. This is shown in Figure 2.2.

This demonstrates the relationship

between the denotative or connotative levels of meaning. Barthes also writes here about the distinction between language and myth. For Barthes, myths shore up existing structures of power, which favour the bourgeois class. Myths make what is historical or changeable appear to be natural and static and are thus ideological. Thus, the myth constructed in part by the photograph of the young black man in uniform would seek to represent the Algerian conflict in such a way as to prevent change and decolonialisation.

### Further reading

Barthes, R. (1973) *Mythologies*, St Albans: Paladin.

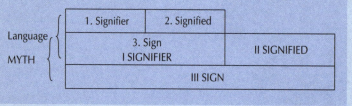

**Figure 2.2** Language and myth. (Source: Barthes, 1976.)

isolate from the world of phenomena we do not find there because they stare every observer in the face; on the contrary, the world is presented in a kaleidoscopic flux of impressions which has to be organized by our minds and this means largely by the linguistic systems in our minds. We cut nature up, organize it into concepts, and ascribe significances as we do, largely because we are parties to an agreement to organize it in this way – an agreement that holds through our speech community and is codified in the patterns of our language. The agreement is, of course, an implicit and unstated one. *But its terms are absolutely obligatory*; we cannot talk at all except by subscribing to the organization and classification of data which the agreement decrees.

(Carroll, 1956: 212–14, in Black, 1972: 97)

Therefore, for linguistic theories, such as semiotics and the Sapir–Whorf hypothesis, language is seen as a structural system, which is both stable and provides a

useful tool for understanding the social world in which these are used. Therefore linguists such as Saussure provides the basis of **structuralism** (p. 17) – the idea that there are structures to be found below or behind everyday interaction.

## Structuralism and the order of meaning

Structuralists see culture as an ordered system or structure. Culture is presented as a system of coded meanings that are produced and reproduced through social interaction. Their interest is in how participants through interaction learn and use the codes of communication. A number of perspectives have been brought to this issue.

Certain theories of linguistics, for example those of Ferdinand de Saussure and Noam Chomsky, state that there is a universal structuring principle in all human language: that of binary oppositions. Binary oppositions consist of two opposing terms; for example, black and white, man and woman, high and low. Lévi-Strauss (1966) argues that these oppositions are not amenable to direct observation or analysis. Instead, they operate at a level that is not conscious, a level sometimes described as that of deep structure. The study of culture, according to structuralists, consists of an examination of cultural forms. These cultural forms are the result of the human mind being brought to bear on particular environments. Lévi-Strauss argues that the resultant cultural forms all exhibit the same pattern, that of binary oppositions. The content of particular cultures may be different but this is the result of different environments. What is significant is not the different contents, but the identical patterning of cultural forms. Working from the assumption that cultural forms consist of identical patterns, Lévi-Strauss says that individuals have an innate biological capacity, what he calls a 'bio-grammar', which they use to 'decode' or interpret codes of cultural information. Codes are cultural in the sense that they are the expression of a people's shared conventions at a particular time. Acculturated members of a society know the codes for their society. Codes are culturally specific, but the ability to decode is universal and innate.

This means that everyone makes sense of the world at two distinct levels, which take place simultaneously. The first is at the level of deep structure where the binary oppositions operate. The second is at the surface level of contemporaneous activity where knowledge of a cultural code allows sorting and classifying to operate and meaning to emerge. Lévi-Strauss likens this thinking to what we engage in when we listen to music. We hear both the melody and the harmony, but in order to achieve an understanding of the music we have to integrate them. It is the whole that gives us the message, and so it is both surface and deep structure that gives us our understanding of cultural messages. Lévi-Strauss worked out these ideas through the analysis of myth, which he argues is one of the clearest forms of cultural expression of a society's view of itself.

Mary Douglas (1966) and Edmund Leach (1970) adopt a similar stance to that of Lévi-Strauss towards cultural understanding and the reception of cultural messages. They both agree that meaning arises out of patterning and order, but they differ from Lévi-Strauss in locating the source of order in the social world and not in physiology. It is the social and cultural contexts and the agreed meanings of shared experience through interaction that allocate and set meanings. Leach, for example, illustrates his case with colour classifications. In English culture there are customary associations made between colours and fact and feeling – thus red is the colour of danger, red is also associated with pomp, it is the colour of the British Labour Party and it is a term used to describe members of the Communist Party. A native user of English is aware of some if not all of the repertoire of available meanings and on hearing the word 'red' will decide, according to context, which meaning is appropriate. This will be the meaning that makes sense to the hearer and gives a message. This sociocultural explanation of culture and communication also pays attention to other features of conventional cultural systems, such as gesture, dress, physical appearance, volume and tone of communication. The standardised meanings that cluster around each cultural item provide support and evidence for situationally preferred readings.

## Hermeneutics and interpretation

Another significant tradition in the social sciences concerned with meaning and interpretation is hermeneutics. Derived initially from debates in German-speaking countries over the interpretation of the Bible, this approach has become increasingly concerned with wider issues of interpretation and with philosophical debates over the connections between meaning and existence. Hermeneutics argues that it is impossible to divorce the meaning of a text from the cultural context of its interpreter. In order to interpret any text the interpreter necessarily and unavoidably brings to the text certain prior understandings or fore-understandings from their own culture. The interpreter's fore-understandings facilitate the process of interpretation and are themselves worked upon (i.e. confirmed, modified, refuted, amended, etc.) in the course of interpretation. This conversation-like process is sometimes described by the term 'the hermeneutic circle' (Gadamer, 1975: 235–45). Advocates of the hermeneutic circle maintain that interpretation is not a simple one-way transmission of ideas from text to reader but it is rather an interactive process in which the reader's fore-understandings are required for any further understanding of the text to be possible. Thus, when we read Shakespeare's *Hamlet* (1600–1), or watch a performance of it, we bring to bear our present-day cultural understandings about familial relations, jealousy and revenge, sexual propriety, etc., and these understandings are elaborated and modified in consequence of our reading of this play. The notion of the hermeneutic circle has fed into many theories of culture in the social sciences and humanities. One of its central implications is to underscore the absence of any privileged or objective position for the interpretation of cultural phenomena – knowledge of a culture, to paraphrase the American sociologist Harold Garfinkel, is always knowledge 'from within' a culture.

One example of the development of a sociological approach to interpretation influenced by the hermeneutic tradition can be found in the work of the Hungarian sociologist of knowledge Karl Mannheim. Mannheim argues that a cultural act or text contains three levels of meaning: objective, expressive and documentary. Mannheim uses the hypothetical example of a friend giving alms to a beggar to bring out the differences between these three layers of meaning. The first level is the objective meaning of the act or product inheres in the act itself, and in this example it is assistance. The second level, expressive meaning, involves the consideration of what an actor intended or wishes to express by any particular act. Mannheim's friend may have been wishing to convey sympathy to the beggar through his act. The third layer of meaning is the most important for Mannheim as it links the act to wider contexts. The act can function as a document of the friend's personality and could be seen to document hypocrisy if, for example, the friend was a multi-millionaire who made his money by making the beggar redundant from a job in the first place. However, to formulate this interpretation we have to know the wider context of the act, for example, that its author was exceptionally wealthy. This connection to wider contexts establishes, in this case, links between the act and the political economy within which it takes place. In the next section we discuss political economy and the importance of **ideology** (p. 35) as a way of understanding patterns of meaning.

The importance of social context in determining meaning is also illustrated by several other sociologists, including, most notably the work of **Erving Goffman** and **Pierre Bourdieu** (see below). Goffman (1974) highlights how our social experiences are interpreted and understood through 'frames' of reference. Frames are basically cognitive tools that we subconsciously construct to help us make sense of a social situation. For instance, if we see an individual standing on a street corner playing a guitar, with an open guitar case in front of them full of money, we apply our existing frame to this to make sense of this. This allows us to understand that the individual is 'busking' and therefore (if we feel so inclined) we could put money in their case, rather than that this person is giving away free money, and we should reach down and take some. However, as with the hermeneutic circle, these frames are formed on the basis of interaction, and hence have both structure and flexibility.

Goffman also discusses at length the use of frame narratives. Narratives refer to the structured meanings within a story, which have a sense of sequence and causality. For instance, take our busker. By playing a guitar on the street corner, they want (and often get) people to place money in their guitar case. This then tells a structured mini-story (a narrative) where events progress and cause others to occur. Though not considered by Goffman, it is also important to recognise that narratives are also strongly influenced by **ideologies** (p. 35). For instance, narratives will have an 'expected' sequence of events based upon commonsensical ideas of what 'should' happen. For instance, most romance novels or film narratives prescribe to a heterosexual ideology, where the viewer expects the story to follow an excepted 'boy-meets-girl' story and structure (Schirato and Yell, 2000).

The nature of narratives is also shaped by genre. Genres are types or forms of communication practice (Schirato and Yell, 2000). For instance, a face-to-face argument between two people, or a romance novel, or a newspaper article on poverty – these different genres all have different types (and expected) narrative structures and frames.

Pierre Bourdieu (1984) also contributes to our

understanding of social interactions and the meanings of communication through his discussion of 'fields' and 'habitus'. Fields for Bourdieu are the constituent parts of a society or 'social space' – and some examples discussed by Bourdieu include the contemporary fields of art, politics, sport and economics. Society, for Bourdieu, consists of multiple interrelated fields, where each of these will have its own habitus.

Habitus is similar to what other authors have described as the 'culture' of a particular group or society. However, key to Bourdieu's understanding of habitus is that this is embodied. Jenkins (1992: 74) writes that *habitus* is Latin to mean 'a habitual or typical condition, state or appearance, particularly of the body'. Bourdieu maintains much of the original meaning of this word, and particular emphasis is placed upon the embodiment of habitus. This Jenkins (1992: 74) argues is manifested in three ways: First, habitus only exists 'inside the heads of actors' – for instance, ways of behaving and modes of practice are learnt and internalised by social actors. Second, habitus only exists through the practice and actions of social actors – their ways of talking, moving, acting and behaviour. Third, the 'practical taxonomies' actors use to make sense of the world are all rooted in the body – such as male/female, hot/cold, up/down are all linked to our senses and physically located in relationship to our bodies.

This Bourdieu links to the term 'hexis', which refers to individuals' deportment, their stance, grace and gestures. Though habitus is located within the body it is not a form of innate human behaviour but rather a way of behaving and understanding the world that is taught to us through social interaction. Unlike theories of socialisation, for Bourdieu habitus is achieved primarily through instruction, rather than experience.

For instance, in respect to art, the 'sophisticated' observer has been taught the mechanisms and language for decoding the symbolic meaning of the art form through their social network, education and interaction with others. This therefore, is crucial in our understanding of why certain social groups (such as social classes) possess the skills to 'understand' and interpret art, and others do not. However, it is also important to recognise that habitus is not a set inflexible frame, which people simply learn and remains static throughout their lives. As Bourdieu and Wacquant (1992: 133) suggest in relation to the concept of habitus:

> Habitus is not the fate that some people read into it. Being the product of history, it is an open system of dispositions that is constantly subjected to experiences, and therefore constantly affected by them in a way that either reinforces or modifies its structure.

Hence, for both Bourdieu and Goffman meanings are shaped by existing frames of reference that social actors possess. However, these frames do not simply 'appear' ready-formed within individual heads, but rather it is important to recognise the role of **ideology** (see below) and the political economy in shaping these.

## Defining concept 2.2

### Ideology

Theories of ideology are an attempt to understand ideas in terms of **power** (p. 64). This has been most fully developed within **Marxist** (p. 65) theory (see Williams, 1977) and what follows is a consideration of that tradition and critiques of it. **Raymond Williams** (p. 3) (1977) stresses the various meanings that the term 'ideology' can have from explicitly acknowledged political ideologies to more subconscious 'common-sensical meanings' or 'taken-for-granted beliefs'. He identifies two components to Marxist understandings of ideology:

➤ Ideology as the ideas of a particular social group.

➤ Ideology as a system of illusory beliefs.

#### Ideologies as the ideas of a social group

This is the argument that social groups (and within Marxism the debate has revolved mainly around social classes) have particular beliefs associated with them. One source of this is **Karl Marx** (p. 66) and Fredrich Engels's *The German Ideology*. In this critique of idealism (a way of thinking

## Defining concept 2.2 (continued)

that identifies ideas as the main properties of a society) they asserted that ideas were not independent. Instead ideologies come from social classes in their social relations with each other. Or, as Janet Wolff says, 'the ideas and beliefs people have are systematically related to their actual and material conditions of existence' (Wolff, 1981: 50).

Ideas, or ideologies, are seen to be rooted in the material conditions of the everyday life of classes (including their relations with other classes). Yet these classes are not equal; some ideas dominate because of the unequal material social relations of a class-based society. Marx sums this up in a famous phrase: 'The ideas of the ruling class are in every epoch the ruling ideas, i.e. the class which is the ruling *material* force of society, is at the same time its ruling *intellectual* force' (Marx and Engels, 1968: 64). Indeed, these ideas are part of their rule. They serve to legitimate their domination (for example, the Swedish ruling classes legitimating capitalist modernisation with ideologies of both progress and tradition – see p. 112) and to reproduce the unequal social relations from which they benefit (there are a whole series of arguments about how education is part of the reproduction of class relations, for example, Althusser, 1971; and Willis, 1977).

Generally, then, ideology (the realm of ideas) is seen to be shaped by something 'deeper' – the social (or class) relations within which people live their lives or even the economic organisation of society (or 'mode of production') which shapes those class relations. There is, however, a recognition that ideologies have real consequences. They operate as 'maps of meaning', used to interpret and define what is going on. That they

work better for some groups than others is the second component of Marxist theories that Williams identifies.

### Ideology as a system of illusory beliefs

This is the suggestion that, because of their origins as part of unequal social relations, ideologies are a distorted representation of the truth. This relies on the points set out above to argue that there are sets of ideas appropriate to each class, generated by their position within exploitative social relations, but that people may have adopted other ideas via education, the media, entertainment and so on. Since a true class consciousness with an objective material basis is being claimed here, then people who do not think that way are said to have 'false consciousness'. There is a sense that they have been hoodwinked. Their real interests are concealed from them and the real interests of the exploitative classes are also concealed (for example, nationalism which serves the political, military and economic interests of ruling classes might be said to be false consciousness for a working class that 'should' think of itself not as divided but as internationally united).

There are a series of problems with these ways of thinking. First, 'false consciousness' is always something that someone else has, not oneself. It has a tendency to define people as 'cultural dupes' who can be led out of their ignorance by a right-thinking vanguard or the visionary theorist who knows the 'Truth'. Second, can classes and ideas be matched as neatly as this way of thinking suggests? Can we allocate ideologies to social groups in this way? Third, can the world be understood in terms of

class alone? If not, do the forms of analysis (often rooted in understanding economic relationships) set out above work for social groups defined in terms of gender, race, sexuality or age?

In response to these problems the 1970s and 1980s saw the development of more and more elaborate and difficult theoretical work on the relationships between ideas and power (see Althusser, 1971; Thompson, 1984). The main path that this took was through understanding language, thinking about ideas not as something 'free-floating' but as existing as words spoken or written. It also meant a move away from only studying class.

This work has stressed that ideology is about the relationship between language and power. Instead of thinking about ideas being fixed to particular social groups or about them being untrue there is a sense that meanings are not fixed, that they arise in language, in communication and representation. This means thinking about many competing ideologies, not one dominant one, and about a whole range of social groups. The connection to power lies in the ways in which meanings present the world to the advantage or disadvantage of particular social groups, and the ways in which those groups can attempt to fix or challenge those meanings. For example, a set of widespread ideas about nature, motherhood and domesticity which served to legitimate women's dependence within the home benefited and were reproduced by men, but have in many ways been effectively challenged by women. As Thompson says: 'To study ideology, I propose, is to study the ways in which meaning (or signification) serves to

## Defining concept 2.2 (continued)

sustain relations of domination' (Thompson, 1984: 4).

This way of thinking is very close to other theoretical concepts that look at the relations between meaning and power (for example, **discourse** – p. 21) and has raised the question of whether we still need the concept of ideology. Those arguing against using it suggest that it still brings with it the problems of believing in something called 'the truth', and of being too rooted in economic class relations (Foucault, 1980). Those who want to retain it claim that it brings a necessary critical edge to making judgements about the power relations involved in statements (Eagleton, 1991; Purvis and Hunt, 1993).

### Further reading

Eagleton, T. (1991) *Ideology: An Introduction*, London: Verso.

Thompson, J. (1984) *Studies in the Theory of Ideology*, Cambridge: Polity.

Williams, R. (1977) *Marxism and Literature*, Oxford: Oxford University Press.

# Political economy, ideology and meaning

An interest in political economy means an interest in issues of power and inequality that are associated with the allocation of resources and the formation of wealth. The ideas of political economy have had a widespread value and application in social science and in disciplines such as history and English studies because they have proved fruitful in the investigation of patterns of meaning. To relate political economy to culture is to prompt some of the following questions. What are the connections between ownership and control of the media and cultural transmission? What is the role of the economic infrastructure in the dissemination of ideas? What are the links between technology transfer and the transfer of knowledge? In all these areas of investigation a relationship is sought between politics, economics and culture.

An example of this approach would be an analysis of newspaper content to see if a connection can be established between the ownership and control of the newspaper and the type and nature of news printed. In simple terms, it suggests considering the extent to which the owner's views and interests are reflected in the content of the newspaper. Newspaper coverage of the news has been found to be overwhelmingly pro-capitalist, pro-*status quo* in character. The question then becomes: how is this coincidence with owner's interests to be explained? One explanation points to the concentration of ownership and control of British newspapers (for instance, the Australian businessman Rupert Murdoch owns and controls *The Sun*, *News of the World* and *The Times* newspapers in the UK). Newspaper proprietors have mutual interests in other financial and industrial undertakings (for instance, Murdoch also owns numerous other businesses and media networks the world over, including *BSkyB* television and the *Fox* network), and also have an upbringing and lifestyle in common; in short, they have shared economic interests and a shared culture. Thus it is hardly surprising that the press's coverage is biased in favour of the interests and values of private enterprise.

An alternative explanation draws attention to some different features of the political economy of newspaper production. Here emphasis is placed on the prevailing logic of the market in which newspapers are presently produced. The commercial survival of newspapers depends upon advertising revenue which in turn generates a pressure to maintain a newspaper's circulation. To retain a large readership, newspapers give people what they are believed to want – human interest stories, crime, sex, sport and scandal. Entertaining the readership comes to take precedence over providing information about significant world events and educating the public in the ways of responsible citizenship. Material documenting cultural difference and ideological diversity tends to get squeezed out of newspapers, leaving only a relatively narrow middle ground.

A more sophisticated way of connecting the concerns of political economy and questions of cultural meaning are through the concept of **ideology** (p. 35). Ideologies can be of various sorts. **Antonio Gramsci** (see below) divided up ideologies into three categories. The first is that of common sense. Common-sense ideas are those we all take for granted. Common-sense ideas and values are part of everyday life. They form the bedrock of our understanding of the world; but when examined closely they may appear to be either contradictory or very superficial. An example of a common-sense ideology is given in the phrase 'Boys are better at football than girls'. This expresses a widely held idea, commonly held to be true. A closer examination of this 'truth', however, might question its validity by asking 'Are boys encouraged to be more physically active than girls?' or 'Are girls allowed to participate in football or are they excluded at home, at school, or at club level?' If the answer to these questions is yes, then the common-sense idea that boys are better at football than girls is shown to be true only because of particular circumstances.

Gramsci's second category of ideology is that of a particular philosophy. This means not so much the thought of a particular philosopher but of a particular group of people in society who put forward a reasonably coherent set of ideas. These people Gramsci calls intellectuals; and he includes both traditional intellectuals such as priests, and intellectuals who emerge from social movements, like trade unionists or political

---

## Key influence 2.1

### Antonio Gramsci (1891–1937)

Antonio Gramsci was an Italian political activist and writer who was influential in the development of **Marxist** (p. 65) cultural theory. He aimed to develop concepts that would enable the understanding and transformation of twentieth-century political and economic structures and social and cultural relations. He is best known for his work on the idea of **hegemony** (p. 73).

Gramsci was born in Sardinia and was educated in Turin where he joined the Italian Socialist Party, and worked as a journalist. In 1921 he was a founder member of the Italian Communist Party (PCI) and, after a visit to Moscow, was elected to the Italian Parliament. He later became leader of the PCI and, in 1926, was sentenced to 20 years' imprisonment by Mussolini's Fascist government. At his trial the official prosecutor demanded of the judge that 'We must stop this brain working for 20 years!' However, during his imprisonment Gramsci wrote his most famous works, published as *Selections from*

*Prison Notebooks* (1971), which combined studies of politics, philosophy, history, literature and culture. He died shortly after being released from prison.

Gramsci is important to cultural studies because of his attempts to develop the connections between class relations, culture and **power** (p. 64) without reducing issues of culture and meaning to a superstructure determined by an 'economic base'. His concept of hegemony aimed at understanding how dominant classes could organise their rule through consent when their political and economic power was not in the interest of those they subordinated. However, this was not a static situation within which the ideas of the powerful went unchallenged. Gramsci used the metaphor of a 'war of manoeuvre' to suggest that political struggles were continually being fought in a whole variety of arenas: political, economic and cultural. In turn this meant conceptualising the role of the intellectuals who were part

of fighting these 'wars'. Through his notion of the 'organic intellectual' he argued that everyone who used ideas was an intellectual (it was not just a label for a small professional group) and that these 'thinkers' and their ideas were organically tied to particular class interests. It can be argued that it is Gramsci's ideas that form the basis of the notion of 'cultural politics', due to the ways in which they were taken up and reworked by those working in the Birmingham **Centre for Contemporary Cultural Studies** (p. 241) in the 1970s.

#### Further reading

Gramsci, A. (1971) *Selections from Prison Notebooks*, London: Lawrence and Wishart.

Gramsci, A. (1985) *Selections from Cultural Writings*, London: Lawrence and Wishart.

Joll, J. (1977) *Gramsci*, London: Fontana.

activists. Thus, examples of ideologies that are philosophies are Roman Catholic teachings or the ecological ideas of Greenpeace or the beliefs of Right to Life anti-abortionist groups. Gramsci's third category is that of a dominant or **hegemonic** (p. 73) ideology, that is one that has a leading role in society. An example of a hegemonic ideology in a particular society might be the dominance of one person's ideas, for example in a dictatorship. Or it might be the description of a society as capitalist or individualistic, whereby ideas (or ideologies) like 'the primacy of monetary profit' or 'the survival of the fittest' are the dominant ideas.

An understanding of how these three different categories of ideology may interrelate can be gained by thinking about the ideology of racism. In the first category, 'common-sense' racism might consist of phrases like 'The English are cold', or 'Black people are natural athletes'. These phrases express everyday prejudices as common sense. They do not, on their own, express anything more than the individual prejudice of the speaker. If, however, these common-sense ideas become part of a coherent system, then they enter Gramsci's second category of a philosophy. Nineteenth-century anthropologists classified the 'races' of humanity, placing Europeans at the top of a purportedly evolutionary ladder with Orientals and Africans coming further down; this is plainly an example of a racist philosophy. The Nazi and Fascist beliefs about Aryan racial superiority are of the same type. Racism becomes a dominant or hegemonic ideology when it is used within a particular society to legitimate the social divisions and organisation of that society. So, for example, the use of racist ideas to justify the European colonisation of India and Africa or to exclude black people from housing or particular jobs is an example of a hegemonic ideology. In practice, these three categories are often combined. Thus, a common-sense racist remark is often made in the context of an accepted knowledge of available racist philosophies and of racism as a hegemonic ideology – and the relationship between power and language is considered in more detail later in the chapter (p. 44).

# Poststructuralism and the patterns of meaning

Thinking through the concept of ideology means considering a whole range of social groups and their relationship to ideas and cultural meanings. In the structuralist version these meanings are strictly patterned according to specific structures and systems such as binary opposition. In the political economy view there are more or less strong links between the different groups and the ideas and meanings that they hold. Poststructuralism has questioned the nature of the connections that are made in both of these other theoretical approaches.

First, it questions what are seen as the rigidities of structuralist systems of thought. Instead of binary oppositions it suggests that there are much more complicated and ever-changing systems of meaning that need to be understood in their particular contexts. Thus, the meanings that things have are not fixed – they are fluid and changing. As in our Shakespeare example, the meanings of the plays are not defined by fixed systems of signs – for example, thinking about the relationships between harmony and disharmony or order and disorder in the comedies – but are dependent on the contexts in which they are written, enacted, consumed and interpreted. Thus Shakespeare's understandings of race and money (such as in a play like *The Merchant of Venice*) can be interpreted in terms of contemporary **discourses** (p. 21) of economics and morality. This need not be based upon direct knowledge that Shakespeare had, but a set of interlocking cultural codes. As Stephen Greenblatt argues, dealing with the correspondences between medical texts and Shakespeare's texts:

[T]he state of Shakespeare's knowledge of medical science is not the important issue here. The relation I wish to establish between medical and theatrical practice is not one of cause and effect or source and literary realization. We are dealing rather with a shared code, a set of interlocking tropes and similitudes that function not only as the objects but as the conditions of representation.

(Greenblatt, 1988: 86)

It is not, therefore, the systems and structures of meaning that are important but the ways in which more diffuse patterns of meanings intersect in particular situations.

Second, poststructuralists question the solidity of the relationships that the political economy approach argues exist between economic relationships and cultural meanings. Instead of asserting that there are ideologies appropriate to classes, they argue that the relationships are both contingent and contextual. Again, classes, genders and races are, in part, formed through the ideas, ideologies and discourses that are used about them and that they use in their struggles; and these will differ depending on the time, the place, the nature of the struggle, and the history of that struggle. Thus the patterns of meaning cannot be traced back to underlying political and economic structures; they are related to them but in ways that are ever-changing and which must be explored and interpreted by the cultural analyst. Thus, Shakespeare does not always define Englishness for a certain class, but is taken up in that way in particular battles over education, status and **cultural capital** (p. 259). All of this puts much more of a burden on our own interpretations of culture.

A central element of poststructuralist thought is the idea that culture – in all its forms – is a 'text' which can be 'read'. This theoretical move towards 'textuality' shifts the focus of the study of culture. What is studied is not so much cultural forms or representation as the text itself. Whereas before it has been assumed that it might be possible to gain knowledge by the study of cultural form, poststructuralist theorists (**Barthes** (p. 96), **Foucault** (p. 20) and Jacques Derrida) have questioned the search for meaning and coherence.

Semiology suggests that all cultural products should be seen as 'texts'. However, unlike de Saussure and other structuralists would have us believe, the meaning of these texts is not set. For instance, for de Saussure meaning was seen as intentional. De Saussure saw signs as consisting of specific (and to some degree independent) components that were 'put together' by someone. Therefore, de Saussure prioritises the importance of the sender of a message, and the act of sending as a conscious decision. However, not all meanings are intended. Poststructuralism highlights how meanings are not always intended, and that texts are *polysemic* (open to multiple readings).

Jacques Derrida has argued that the texts that make up culture can never be pinned down. Instead of yielding meaning and knowledge to the student of culture, they defer it. The task of students of culture is not, therefore, to look for explanations, but to 'deconstruct' meaning in culture. Students of culture should not look for systems, structures and ideologies but should look at the gaps, discontinuities and inconsistencies in texts. Followers of this approach contend that there is always partiality and subjectivity in understanding; culture consists of multiple realities that are never understood in their entirety either by the sender or the receiver of information. Texts are always subject to interpretation, doubt and dispute, whatever the attempts of authors to exercise control. As Schirato and Yell write:

> texts circulate widely within a variety of contexts and situation types. They last of a time and then disappear from circulation, perhaps to reappear later in a different form. Riddles, jokes, fashions, limericks, songs, advertising, slogans and jingles, memorable lines from movies, characteristic sayings of public figures, whole texts and fragment of texts of all kinds are used and re-used within cultures.
>
> (Schirato and Yell, 2000: 52)

Though texts circulate, and may have a life beyond their original context, all texts carry with them elements of their previous context(s). This means that texts do not exist in isolation, but always refer or relate to other texts. Hence, it is argued by Bakhtin that all texts are simply a composite of 'where they have been' and other texts that they relate, so therefore no text can claim 'originality'.

The 'Bakhtin School', and particularly V.N. Volosinov, argues that the sign (see **semiology** – p. 29) is a site of social contestation. This means that different groups within society struggle, argue and dispute over the meanings of different signs. Volosinov argues, that unlike de Saussure suggests there can never be perfect autonomous semiotic system, as semiotic systems are constantly in use, and therefore constantly being contested and therefore changing.

In *Marxism and the Philosophy of Language* (1973) Volosinov argues that it is class conflict that conditions the struggle over signs. Bakhtin's idea that any text contains 'multiple voices' within it has been developed by **Julia Kristeva**'s (p. 149) influential concept of 'intertextuality'. This idea concerns the relation of a given text to other texts. Any text, it is argued, can be analysed in terms of the other texts that it has absorbed and transformed. Thus intertextuality embraces various forms of textual borrowing and echoing, such as allusion, parody, pastiche and quotation. The concept allows us to appreciate how a science fiction movie like *Blade Runner* draws on 1940s 'hard-boiled' detective stories and *film noir* as intertexts (*The Maltese Falcon*, *The Big Sleep*, etc.). What we see in *Blade Runner* is the incorporation and transformation of these intertexts in a futuristic setting (the movie is set in 2019). Most of the action takes place in shadowy rooms or after dark in poorly lit public places; the film's hero makes a living out of a technologically advanced parody of the classic gumshoe role; the heroine dresses in 1940s retro style; like many *film noir* movies, the development of the plot is at times opaque and, also like many movies of this genre, in the original version of *Blade Runner* the hero provides 'voice-over' to link scenes. By deconstructing *Blade Runner* in terms of its intertexts it becomes possible to realise one poststructuralist premise, 'the death of the author'. What this means is that the author's intentions are adjudged irrelevant to the interpretations of the text; the text is a separate and autonomous entity. Thus, instead of studying the influences on the author and the sources s/he drew upon in authoring the text (a notoriously contentious interpretive strategy), the interpreter is left instead to consider the intertexts figuring in a given text.

## Postmodernism and semiotics

The philosophic origins of **postmodern** (p. 295) thought can be traced back to the philosophy of Nietzsche and Heidegger. These philosophers, and in particular Nietzsche, question the ideas of the Enlightenment that there exists one 'true' reality, which is delivered to us by science and rationality. Nietzsche suggested that all social reality was a product of language and thought, and not objective truths or realities.

These ideas were then developed further by postmodern writers such as Jean-Francois Lyotard and **Jean Baudrillard** (p. 299). Lyotard is often viewed as one of the 'founding fathers' of postmodern social theory. Like many postmodernists, Lyotard's philosophical origins can be seen in his disillusionment with traditional **Marxist** (p. 65) theory. Lyotard rejects the idea that Marxism offers the only objective knowledge of society, and rejects the idea that society is based around technologies of production (as Marx would have us believe). Instead Lyotard suggests that social life revolves around language and **discourse** (p. 21). In particular, he highlights the changing nature of narrative in social life.

Lyotard suggests that in pre-industrial times, myths and stories had a religious quality and assisted in the reproduction of the social order. With the Enlightenment came a new set of narratives, which emphasised progress and reason, knowledge and technology. These provided social life with an order and regularity. However, he suggests we have now moved into a postmodern era, where science, technology and computers have developed to such as point that the principle force within our society has become knowledge. Knowledge becomes more widespread and accessible, hence, there is a decline in belief of one truth or one knowledge.

Lyotard refers to this as the decline in grand narratives or metanarratives. He suggests that knowledge has always been made up of different, and at times incompatible perspectives or views, but these were often hidden within modernism and scientific positivism, which claimed to provide one absolute truth. However, most people no longer believe that there is one truth that is delivered to us by science and rationality. Nor do they believe that there is one theory, which can explain all aspects of our social lives. As a result, knowledge and societies fragment. As Lyotard writes:

> The social bond is linguistics, but it is not woven with a single thread ... nobody speaks all those languages, they have no universal metalanguage ... the goal of emancipation has nothing to do with science ...
>
> (Lyotard, 1984: 40–41)

Hence, what defines our postmodern social lives is language and linguistic, but there exists no one true meaning, no one true reality. There is no truth, but only truths.

Postmodern knowledge comes by 'putting into question existing paradigms, by inventing new ones, rather than assenting to universal truth or in agreeing to a consensus' (Best and Kellner, 1991: 166), and draws on the work of poststructuralist such as Derrida. Derrida (1978) suggest that the relationship between the signifier and the sign (see **semiology** – p. 29) is now *completely arbitrary* and lacks any connection at all. The signifier (the concept or idea) has no link to the real world or to an object (the signified), but exists on its own. Signs therefore become free floating, without any link or relationship to an underlying reality. All that exists is a concept, or 'image', without any basis or link to reality.

In particular, these are ideas developed further by Jean Baudrillard (p. 299). Baudrillard, following Derrida, also sees signs as becoming free-floating, disconnected from reality. In particular, Baudrillard suggests that society has become overrun by simulacra. This is an 'image' or representation of a person or thing, which lacks the substance or qualities of the original. Baudrillard argues that these *simulacra* 'are so omnipresent that it is henceforth impossible to distinguish the real from simulacra' (Best and Kellner, 1991: 101).

Baudrillard links this to ideas of *hyperreality*. Hyperreality is 'the blurring of distinctions between the real in the unreal and which the prefix 'hyper' signifies more real than real whereby the real is produced according to a model' (Best and Kellner, 1991: 119). For postmodernists there is no longer an underlying reality, which has an existence apart from the simulations and simulacra. The only reality is a reality created by signs (which have no depth or relation to real objects). What we consider to be social reality is indefinitely reproducible and extendable, with the copy indistinguishable from the original, or perhaps seeming more real than the original.

For instance, Baudrillard suggests that Disneyland is presented to America (and the rest of the world) as an 'unreal' fantasy land – but this conceals that fact that all of America *is* Disneyland, it is all a hyperreal theme park. However, Disneyland does not hide social reality, in the sense that Marx argues that social reality is hidden from people, but rather Disneyland conceals that fact that there is nothing to conceal, nothing to hide, because America is a superficial hyperreal nation, where there is no depth. Everything appears on the surface (Inglis and Hughson, 2003).

Baudrillard also uses the term *implosion* to refer to the process whereby simulation and reality collapse in on each other and become the same, so that there is no longer any distinction between the two. This is:

> A process of social entropy leading to a collapse of boundaries, including the implosion of meaning in the media and the implosion of media messages and the social in the masses. . . . The dissemination of media messages and semiurgy saturates the social field, and meaning and messages flatten each other out in a neutralized flow of information, entertainment, advertising, and politics.
>
> (Best and Kellner, 1991: 121).

All the different parts of the social world implode, leaving no separation between formerly distinctive parts of society – politics and sports become entertainment, or the latter become the former. For instance, with the O. J. Simpson or Michael Jackson trials it becomes difficult to separate entertainment, legal issues, private, public and the social reality – all imploded together and all that is left is a depthless spectacle. The public become mesmerised by the spectacular. Reality and meaning no longer matter or even exist – just the spectacle. Therefore for postmodernists (like Baudrillard) there is no social world, or individuals, just an all consuming mass wrapped up in the consumption of signs and spectacles.

## 2.2 Language, representation, power and inequality

Representation and communication of cultural meaning takes place through language because of two sets of standardisations: the customary meanings attached to words and the customary ways of speaking in given social and cultural settings. In both instances membership of the language community may be tested or decided according to the familiarity of a language user with the conventions of use. Language is seen as *problematic*, and this approach owes much to the development of social and cultural theorising which stresses the partial and contested nature of social life; such theorising is often labelled as **postmodern** (p. 295) but it also characterises much feminist analysis, as well as race, ethnic and class analyses.

A key source for them is the work of the Russian Marxist analyst of language V.N. Volosinov (1973).

Volosinov argues that language has to be understood in social context and in social activity. It is this stress on social activity that is perhaps of central importance to subsequent developments. As **Raymond Williams** (p. 3) argues:

We then find not a reified 'language' and 'society' but an active *social language*. Nor (to glance back at positivist and orthodox materialist theory) is this language a simple 'reflection' or 'expression' of

## Defining concept 2.3

### Representation and realism

Raymond Williams (1983b: 296) points to two meanings of 'represent' that have developed through history. A representation, he suggests, can mean either 'a symbol or image, or the process of presenting to the eye or the mind'. The meaning of symbol or image is particularly important. A representation re-presents or stands for something else. As Williams explains, this meaning is complicated by the development of the idea of an 'accurate reproduction'. Hence, a photograph represents that which was arranged before the camera, but is also often thought to be an accurate reproduction of it. We are familiar with the common phrase 'the camera never lies'. However, we should also be aware that photographs may be cropped or doctored to produce a particular meaning.

Realism in art or culture seems to be simply captured in the idea that it attempts 'to show things as they really are' (Lovell, 1980). However, such simplicity is illusory and realism has been hotly debated. Berger (1972) points to the way in which realism in art develops at a particular historical moment. Likewise Watt (1963) illuminates the beginnings of the realist novel, which used real names for characters and was set in

recognisable places and so on. Some versions of realism attempt to capture the details of everyday life in all its aspects. This approach was labelled naturalism in the nineteenth century. The novels of Zola are held to be an important example. Other forms of realism have worked through the practice of typicality. It does not matter, it may be suggested, that all life is not shown (indeed, how could it be?) as long as recognisable types are used for characters and events. However, some **Marxist** (p. 65) approaches to realism often criticise these ideas, as they suggest that there is some deeper truth or reality to be known, which will not be captured by conventional realist depiction. Somewhat paradoxically, the attempt to capture this reality is often through avant-garde methods. Debates between the Marxist critics Lukács and Brecht pointed up some of these issues, as did the later work of MacCabe. The latter used a very wide definition of realism, which he then criticised as being unable to capture the real.

Despite the difficulties involved in defining realism, the term is much used in everyday discussions about fiction. Being authentic or real is often seen as praiseworthy and being

melodramatic a criticism. However, such simplifications evade the difficulties surrounding the terms. For example, soap operas are often criticised for their inadequate representation of the real: too much happens, they do not contain enough ethnic minorities, whole rich families share one house and so on. They are not empirically or objectively real. However, as Ang (1985) in her discussion of viewers' reactions to the American soap Dallas shows, these representations may convey ideas and feelings that viewers feel to be subjectively real or important. They may be emotionally realist. Criticising or praising realism is not to be done lightly without a clear definition of the meaning of the term.

### Further reading

Lovell, T. (1980) *Pictures of Reality: Aesthetics, Politics and Pleasure*, London: BFI.

Hill, J. (1986) *Sex, Class and Realism: British Cinema 1956–1963*, London: BFI.

Williams, R. (1983b) *Keywords: A Vocabulary of Culture and Society*, London: Fontana.

'material reality'. What we have, rather, is a grasping of this reality through language, which as practical consciousness is saturated by and saturates all social activity, including productive activity. And, since this grasping is social and continuous (as distinct from the abstract encounters of 'man' and 'his world', or 'consciousness' and 'reality', or 'language' and 'material existence'), it occurs within an active and changing society.

(Williams, 1977: 37)

Williams took these ideas very seriously in his own work – so much so that he devoted extensive sections of many of his own books to the consideration of the history and development in social context of important concepts. The zenith of this work came in his book *Keywords* (Williams, 1983b), which appears to be a dictionary, but is actually an investigation of the contested meaning and social import of some terms and concepts that Williams takes to be central in contemporary social and political struggles. As Eagleton (1983: 117) argues, concerning Volosinov but which could equally be applied to Williams, 'It was not simply a matter of asking "what the sign meant", but of investigating its varied history, as conflicting social groups, classes, individuals and discourses sought to appropriate it and imbue it with their own meanings'.

## Language and power

*Cultural politics* (see Chapter 6, p. 141) introduces the dimension of inequalities in **power** (p. 64) and authority in cultural forms and the *contested* nature of cultural practice; it is these concerns that drive the analysis of language when it is linked with the domains of class, race or gender. Thus, as will be suggested below, language has become increasingly politicised and implicated in social struggles. Consequently, argument has moved from seeing language as a neutral instrument for objectively representing and communicating the views of a uniform grouping to seeing language as a politically and culturally charged medium over which groups wrestle for control.

Benedict Anderson (1991) drew attention to the role of print languages in enabling the rise and spread of nationalism. At present, it is sufficient to single out that thread of Anderson's argument that says that the invention of print language gave a 'new fixity' to language and created languages of power; particular forms of language became dominant. Spoken languages that were close in form and vocabulary to printed language were the most prestigious (Anderson, 1991: 44–5). In this way written language came to be viewed as more 'correct' than spoken language and oral communication was, and often still is, evaluated socially according to its degree of resemblance to written language (Street, 1993; Leech *et al.*, 1982). In this process of evaluation, ways of speaking such as dialect (local language), accent, choice of words and use of grammar were all assessed and ranked against the social conventions of language as typified in written language (Street, 1993; Labov, 1973). These rankings were extended to other areas of social experience and, through the overlaying of social action by cultural ways of speaking, became a symbolic representation of ways of life – a situation summed up by Pulgram in the following way:

> We can recognise a person by his speech quite apart from the intelligence or intelligibility of his utterance. The mere physical features of his speech, conditioned automatically and by habits, suffice for identification. If, in addition, what he says and how he says it, in other words his style, provide further clues all the better. The what and how are socially conditioned, however, by the speaker's education, surroundings, profession, etc. Directors and actors of radio plays who cannot convey any part of the contents of the performance visually are very skilful in the art of voice characterisation. Even the psyche; the temperament of a person finds expression in his speech, to say nothing of his temporary moods and every hearer makes a certain value judgement of a speaker simply on the basis of 'what he talks like'.
>
> (Pulgram, 1954, in Street, 1993)

A cultural studies approach reminds us that what is being described is not simply **difference** (p. 121) but hierarchies of prestige which are often also hierarchies of **power** (p. 64). Street (1993) alerts us to the resonances of words: he argues that the use of the word 'one' as in 'one knows' implies status; the use of the word 'we' can express solidarity but when used by a doctor, as in 'and how are we feeling today?', it can imply power and status (Street, 1993: 71).

The specialised lexicons and forms of speech that characterise certain social groupings serve to facilitate communication among those who belong to the group but exclude those who are outside and cannot speak the language. It is debatable whether specialised lexicons (semantic domains) can be ranked in terms of functional use – some being more useful than others; but what is certain is that it is possible to rank the social groupings who use particular semantic domains, so, for example, the professional language of doctors and lawyers is more prestigious than that of youth groups (see below). Language as a communicative form which represents, constructs and reproduces social and cultural inequality is the focus of the next sections.

## Language and class

The work of the sociologist Basil Bernstein (1924–2000) is an influential example of research linking social class, language and speech. Educational policies and practices in Britain and the USA in the 1960s were much affected in their design and implementation by his explanations of the educational failure of young people. In essence, Bernstein argued that his researches showed that lower-class members of English society spoke a language that was *restricted* in comparison with the *elaborated* code of the middle classes. This restricted code handicapped them in their quest for social and economic betterment because schools, which were seen by Bernstein as the chief agency for social mobility, required the use of elaborated codes. Elaborated codes were necessary for the intellectual activity of learning and for the social and political purposes of receiving favourable recognition from teachers. See Box 2.2.

Bernstein revised the characteristics of restricted and elaborated codes a number of times in the light of empirical and theoretical work and eventually abandoned them. It is important to note that the changing configurations reveal the difficulties of identifying a set of inherent characteristics of cultural forms, especially when, as in this case, they are linked in opposition to each other.

Bernstein's depiction of the relationship between language and class is reminiscent of the Sapir–Whorf hypothesis; indeed it is possible to recast Bernstein's analysis in terms of lower- and middle-class groups occupying different 'thought worlds'. Both hypotheses give weight to the effects of socialisation in establishing taken-for-granted ways of seeing the world that form the texture of thought for group members. And in both cases ways of thinking are a response to socioeconomic environments. Bernstein's work is distinctive in that it is looking at language use within an apparently homogeneous language group, whereas Sapir's and Whorf's studies relate to quite different and distinct language groups; the most startling difference for our purposes is Bernstein's linking of speech and language with the structured inequalities of the English class system. For Bernstein, class-based language is not simple variation but reflects the hierarchies of the English class system with the consequence that some languages are socially and culturally dominant. Success comes to those who speak the dominant language and use its skills. Bernstein argues that formal or elaborated language is better than public or restricted language because it is constituted through the operation of logic and abstract thought – qualities that are functionally necessary for learning. Lower-class language is more context bound and encourages the assertion of uniformity, not the appreciation of difference. In this sense lower-class language is a less competent form than middle-class language and its speakers and users are not able to benefit from education which requires discrimination and logic. Bernstein's analysis suggests that the class base of English society is perpetuated and made visible through language; language both **represents** (p. 43) and *constitutes* the class system.

New emphases in cultural and social theory, more empirical studies and changes in policy making and implementation have called into question many of the conclusions of Bernstein's work. Compensatory education was recommended for children who had allegedly suffered linguistic deprivation, a condition said to be rooted in the home life of the child and in particular in the mother–child relationship. Such policies have now been switched to working with schools to enable them to be more accommodating to all children, not just those with favoured cultural characteristics.

## Box 2.2

### Speech codes

Restricted or public speech codes are characterised by the following:

1 Short, grammatically simple, often unfinished sentences with a poor syntactical form (stressing the active voice).

2 Simple and repetitive use of conjunctions (so, because, then).

3 Little use of subordinate clauses to break down the initial categories of the dominant subject.

4 Inability to hold a formal subject through a speech sequence: thus a dislocated informational content is facilitated.

5 Rigid and limited use of adjectives and adverbs.

6 Infrequent use of impersonal pronouns as subjects of conditional clauses.

7 Frequent use of statements where the reason and conclusion are confounded to produce a categoric statement.

8 Using a large number of statements/phrases that signal a requirement for the previous speech sequence to be reinforced: Wouldn't it? You see? You know? etc. This process is termed sympathetic circularity.

9 Individual selection from a group of idiomatic phrases or sequence will frequently occur.

10 The individual qualification is implicit in the sentence organisation: it is a language of implicit meaning.

Elaborated or formal speech codes are characterised by the following:

1 Accurate grammatical order and syntax regulate what is said.

2 Logical modifications and stress are mediated through a grammatically complex sentence construction, especially through the use of a range of conjunctions and subordinate clauses.

3 Frequent use of prepositions that indicate logical relationships as well as prepositions that indicate temporal and spatial contiguity.

4 Frequent use of the personal pronoun 'I'.

5 A discriminative selection from a range of adjectives and adverbs.

6 Individual qualification which is verbally mediated through the structure and relationships within and between sentences.

7 Expressive symbolism which discriminates between meanings within speech sequences rather than reinforcing dominant words or phrases, or accompanying the sequence in a diffuse, generalised manner.

8 Language use which points to the possibilities inherent in a conceptual hierarchy for the organising of experience.

(Bernstein, 1961: 169f., in Dittmar, 1976).

---

This switch has been prompted by empirical and theoretical work that has shown that all languages are characterised by the capacity for logical argument and abstract thought; the privileging of one form of language against others is a *political* and not a linguistic act. Consequently the reasons that children fail must be sought in the realms of social and political economy. It is in these areas that the work of Bernstein remains influential, as his linking of social structure with language opened up a wider investigation into ideas of dominant cultures and their formation, transmission and maintenance. By drawing attention to the social and political dimensions of cultural forms Bernstein rebutted the contention that language is simply a technical device for the representation and communication of culture.

## Language, race and ethnicity

In 1966 Bereiter and Engelmann applied Bernstein's theories to the language of black children in the USA and concluded that 'the poor intellectual ability of Black lower class children is reflected in their inadequate speech' (Dittmar, 1976: 80) and the children showed 'a total lack of ability to use language as a device for acquiring and processing information. Language for them is unwieldy and not very useful' (Bereiter and Engelmann, 1966: 39, in Dittmar, 1976: 81). These conclusions were challenged by Labov (1972b) from the findings of a number of studies that he conducted on the use of non-standard English by black youths. His work demonstrated that the language of black youth (Black English Vernacular or BEV) was different from that of middle-class speech forms; however, to describe BEV as a poor language was simply middle-class ideology. Labov criticised the data collection methods of Bereiter and Engelmann's study on two counts: (a) the data did not describe natural black language use despite purporting to do so – in fact the material gathered was a set of responses to issues set by the researchers; (b) the interviewer in the study was a white adult – Labov contends that such a person would be seen by black youth as an authority figure, a representative of a dominant other culture, to whom they would not speak freely and openly. Although the criticism is a methodological one, it is another reminder that language and language use are political and that it is important to treat critically any claims that language speaks for everyone, everywhere, at all times.

The fabrication of language as a natural, politically neutral device which 'tells things as they are' is one of the means by which language and truth are associated. There is in English culture a widespread belief that nature and the natural are truthful and reliable since they are apparently outside the realm of human manipulation; language is, as we have seen, felt to be part of nature as it is so instinctive and taken for granted. It is a short step from these assumptions to see language as truth. This discourse about language offers the opportunity to know truth through language. In this reasoning language is extremely powerful for it both constitutes truth and guarantees truth. In this formulation, questions about language use and 'who speaks for whom?' are matters of great significance for whoever gives the account is able to pronounce the truth of things. Speakers and writers of non-standard language may suffer the fate of others claiming to speak for them or of their own accounts of their situation being declared untrue or unworthy of attention. Such practices have marked the discipline of literary criticism where, for example, writings from former colonial countries written in the metropolitan language have been declared not to be literature – due to two reasons: (a) local variants of the metropolitan language are not legitimate for the writing of literature; (b) writing about colonial or postcolonial society from the experiences of native peoples is not a legitimate

subject for literature. This example serves as another illustration of language as 'the medium through which a hierarchical structure of power is perpetuated and the medium through which conceptions of 'truth', 'order', and 'reality' become established' (Ashcroft *et al.*, 1989).

In the face of the imperialising cultural power of metropolitan language the writers and speakers of local variations of the language are encouraged by their compatriots to treat the language as if it was their own. They are urged to shrug off the metropolitan meanings and associations of the language and to appropriate it for their own use and by these actions 'make language "bear the burden" of one's own cultural experience' (Ashcroft *et al.*, 1989: 38) in order to 'convey in a language that is not one's own the spirit that is one's own' (Rao, 1938: vii, in Ashcroft *et al.*, 1989: 39). An example of this can be seen in the extract from the poem 'Inglan is a Bitch' by the black British poet Linton Kwesi Johnson (see Box 2.13).

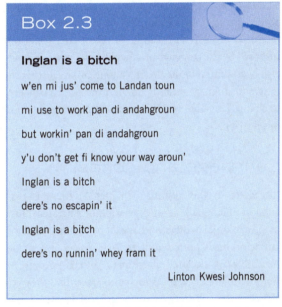

### Box 2.3

**Inglan is a bitch**

w'en mi jus' come to Landan toun

mi use to work pan di andahgroun

but workin' pan di andahgroun

y'u don't get fi know your way aroun'

Inglan is a bitch

dere's no escapin' it

Inglan is a bitch

dere's no runnin' whey fram it

Linton Kwesi Johnson

The work of Edward Said (1993) covers the same territory of cultural imperialism as cited above albeit with a perspective that illuminates how writers from metropolitan countries have, through their language, created an image of 'other societies' that is a product of language. His argument is that, alongside the devaluing of local culture and cultural products of 'other societies', a parallel process has taken place in which metropolitan versions of these societies have been configured. These versions are in accord with the imaginings of metropolitan society, not with the experienced realities of native social actors. The example serves as a further illustration of the power of language to constitute the object of regard and simultaneously affirm the truth of that regard.

The force of the comments about the political use of language moves the discussion away from language as a technical instrument communicating politically neutral information to one that stresses that language takes its meaning from the social settings in which it operates. When it is used by the powerful it may be a subtle instrument of oppression, the more so because of its apparently neutral and natural attributes. In these circumstances it is no surprise that aspirant national groups seek to recreate or revivify local languages to symbolise their identity and carry the weight of their political ambition. The revival of Hebrew in the creation of the nation-state of Israel is one example; language as a political issue in Canada, Spain, France and Wales are other examples. In all these cases the intent is to rid themselves of **identities** (p. 142) imposed by the language of others. Such processes have also been central to the debates about 'political correctness' and language recently. So there has been a concern to change language use to eliminate oppressive uses and implications.

## Language and gender

Elsewhere in this volume (Chapter 1) there is discussion of language as an expression of patriarchy. Just as postcolonial writers and speakers of non-standard language have protested that their voices are made inaudible or declared illegitimate by the power of dominant language, so women also assert that they are voiceless in language. As in the case of language and class discussed earlier in this chapter, the consideration of language and gender serves as a reminder that a language is not necessarily one's own even if one is a native speaker. The meaning and the power of language is determined by social practice; even a native speaker may be mute or dumb in certain settings. The suggestion is that this is the fate of women language users.

In this respect, Edwin Ardener (1974) suggested that 'women are often more "inarticulate" than men' by which he meant that the arenas of public discourse are typically dominated by men and the language of public discourse is 'encoded' with male meanings (Ardener, 1974: viii). The implication of this for women is that they must struggle to be heard and that they must learn male language.

Robin Lakoff (1975) is an influential early writer in the discussion of women and language; her book *Language and Women's Place*, which was based on the observation of her own and her friends' language use, set an agenda for the discussion of the topic, arguing that women's language is characteristically weak in form (not in content) and that this fits well with women's subordinate position *vis-à-vis* men. The characterisation of women's language as weak rests on Lakoff's assertion that women's speech has more 'tag' forms than men's speech. A typical example of a tag form is the statement 'It's a nice day, isn't it?'; in this example 'isn't it?' is the tag. The speaker is not seeking information but confirmation; there is the desire to achieve consensus with the hearer and the hearer is invited to participate in the statement and share the belief. Lakoff's contention is that women's speech is weaker than men's, less decisive and functionally less useful. Labov (1966), in his research on language and class, noted a gendered difference in language use which suggested that women were more deferential and less assertive than men. He found that lower middle-class women used fewer stigmatised forms than men of the same social class. The picture that emerges from this writing is one of highly gendered speech: men are said to use competitive, aggressive speech while women's speech is cooperative. Deborah Tannen (1990) argues that characteristics of the two forms of speech are so distinct that talk between men and women really represents a form of cross-cultural communication. In the language of the Sapir–Whorf hypothesis men and women inhabit different thought worlds. The characteristics of male and female talk (Tannen 1990) are as follows:

| Male Talk | Female Talk |
| --- | --- |
| Hierarchies | Network |
| Independence | Intimacy |

| | |
|---|---|
| Information | Sharing |
| Attention | Symmetry |
| Big talk | Small talk |
| Superiority | Inferiority |
| Powerful | Powerless |

The issue of cross-cultural communication between men and women is addressed in the cartoon by Jacky Fleming in Figure 2.3.

Deborah Tannen's work introduces the consideration of an important issue in the study of language, communication and representation. The discussion of language using a sociolinguistic model has alerted us to how language is embedded in social practice and has drawn attention to the ways in which language is suffused with the significant structuring principles of society.

Although Tannen's findings are broadly consistent with those of Ardener and Lakoff, her interpretation stresses cultural difference (p. 121) rather than super- and subordination. She does not see women's language as inferior to men's as, for her, the two languages are directed towards the creation of different **discourses** (p. 21) about the world. This difference does not imply that women's talk is trivial or less functionally useful than men's; indeed she would argue that women's talk has many positive virtues, stressing, as it does, inclusion rather than exclusion and cooperation rather than competition.

The possibility of interpreting gendered speech as difference rather than hierarchy reminds us that language is expressive and hence open to interpretation. Any discussion of language as a meaningful system must take account of the intentions of those who utter language and those who hear the utterances.

## 2.3 Mass communication and representation

Up to this point, this chapter has been primarily (though not exclusively) concerned with interpersonal communication and representation. This section relates more specifically to forms of mass communication – though obviously many issues already discussed, for example representation and ideology, relate to both interpersonal and mass communication.

The term 'mass communication' is generally used in academic studies to refer to the study of the mass media. The advent of mass media, and mass communication, is tied in with the history of printing. Block printing probably dates back to as early as the seventh century AD in China, but did not become commonplace in Europe until the fourteenth century. The advent of

**Figure 2.3** Communication between men and women. (Source: Fleming, 1992.)

'mass media' is usually attributed to what are referred to as 'popular prints', which became popular in Europe from the fifteenth century onwards. These were commonly produced by woodcut printing, which were then crudely coloured by hand.

The mechanical printing press, invented by German goldsmith Johannes Gutenberg in 1447, greatly increased printing capabilities, speed and reduced costs, and would subsequently lead to the production of the first newspaper in Strasbourg, Germany, in the early seventeenth century. Throughout the seventeenth century there were many types of publications featuring 'news' stories, but across Europe in this period there starts to develop more regular and periodical publications, which we associate with contemporary newspapers.

The development of the mass media is then greatly enhanced by several key inventions in the nineteenth century, such as photography, the telephone, phonograph, cinematography, the wireless telegram and loudspeakers. Shortly after, the early twentieth century brings radio and talking film and television, and the importance of the mass media in our society begins to increase to the levels of saturation (seeping into every corner of our lives) that it has reached today.

This section, continuing the chapter's overall theme, deals specifically with the issue of mass media representations, and specifically those of ethnicity, gender and celebrity. It then concludes with a discussion of audiences and reception and in particular highlights the important work of Stuart Hall on encoding and decoding.

# The mass media and representation

As suggested earlier, it is important that we do not see visual imagery and the mass media as simply a window on the world, showing us 'truth' and 'reality'. What the mass media gives us is a selected view of the world, which is always given to us from a certain perspective and angle. Hence, the mass media does not present the world, but rather gives a **representation** (p. 43) of it. Furthermore, there can never be an unbiased, objective representation of the world, as all representations come from humans and hence come from a particular position or viewpoint (O'Shaughnessy and Sadler 1999). In particular, here we now turn to the issues of media representation of race/ethnicity, gender and celebrity as illustrations of this (though equally we could have considered other representations such as of age, disability, religion, nationality, sexuality, politics, sport, crime, plus numerous other social 'groups' or phenomenon).

## Mass media representations of race and ethnicity

It is often assumed by the mass media that ethnic or 'racial' groups are fundamentally different, with 'black' and 'white' frequently set up as binary opposites. For example, films such as the *Indiana Jones* series portray a white male hero adventuring in 'uncivilised' lands populated by non-white dangerous and animal-like savages. Frequently films that cover Britain's colonial history (such as *Zulu* or even *Carry On up the Khyber*) or any number of 'cowboy' films represent these as stories of native (non-white) 'savages' attacking the civilised (white) 'settlers'. This association of 'colour' with good and evil even continues over to the dress of characters in many 'cowboy' films, where the hero would frequently wear a white hat, compared with the black hat of the villain. Hence, many film narratives perpetuate these ideas of fundamental white and non-white difference:

| White | Non-White |
|---|---|
| Civilised | Primitive |
| Sophisticated | Savage |
| Rational | Irrational |
| Scientific | Magical |
| Good | Evil |
|  | (O'Shaughnessy 1999: 237) |

Stereotyped ways of portraying black and minority ethnic people in the mass media today may be less obvious, but are still apparent. For instance, non-white people continue to be stereotyped as 'deviant' and threatening by the mass media (Cole and Denny, 1994: 129). For instance, television shows, films, and popular music frequently portray black men as 'gangsters' or thugs, and black women as sexualised and permissive, or generate **moral panics** (p. 238) around issues such as 'immigration' or 'multiculturalism' in Britain.

Van Dijk (1991) carried out an investigation into racism in the printed press and examined 2700 news articles on ethnic issues. Unsurprisingly his study suggested that the mass media is primarily run and produced by white people, who convey through this, dominant (often racist) ideological attitudes. However he suggests that racist views, such as not allowing immigrants into the country are constructed as 'not being prejudiced', but rather just 'common sense' (see **ideology** p. 35).

Though certain black celebrities (such as film or sport stars) are sometimes elevated and promoted by the mass media, these individuals can lose their 'privileged status' and be 're-raced' when associated with deviance. For instance, O.J. Simpson's 'race' was not an issue while he was a successful American football player and film star, but became important in the way the national and international press treated him after he was accused of murder – such as accusing him of trying to 'play the race card' to gain sympathy during his trial. Furthermore, it is significant how the Olympic sprinter Ben Johnson was hailed as a Canadian hero when he won the gold medal in the 1988 Olympic Games until he tested positive for 'performance enhancing' drug use and was re-raced by the Canadian press as a 'Jamaican immigrant' (Davis and Harris, 1998).

Today, images of black people are often used in advertising, film and music to represent something as 'cool', or part of 'street' or 'urban' culture. Though some could argue that through this, black culture is being portrayed in a more positive light, this is still a very

## Box 2.4

### The invisible man

This woman is looking at a man (who may coincide with the reader: he is drawn in): her words are in reply to his 'what will you drink?' Her dress is unbuttoned provocatively, indicating beyond doubt that the invisible character is male; the final factor is the chess set visible behind her, implying a second person, an intimacy, yet defining her intellectual quality in relation to the man, as does her decided preference for a certain drink. The message is that she is at home in a man's world, yet is sexy; and not in a passive way, as is shown by her unbuttoning of her dress. Women (in media) are 'entirely constituted by the gaze of man'. This woman is alone, is decisive and intellectual: 'Femininity is pure, free, powerful; but man is everywhere around, he presses on all sides, he makes everything exist; he is in all eternity the creative absence. . . .' The man in this picture is nowhere and everywhere, a pervasive presence defining and determining everything, and in whose terms the woman must define herself. She is doomed to see herself through his eyes, describe herself in his language.

(Williamson 1978: 80)

stereotypical and one-dimensional view of black people, and one that still carries many negative connotations and connections.

## Mass media representations of gender

Tuchman (1981) referred to the 'symbolic annihilation of women' in popular culture – that is to say, either an absence, marginalisation or stereotyping of women in many aspects of popular culture, such as the mass media. Though, of course, there is some evidence of women taking more active and prominent roles within the mass media – for example, journalists, television presenters and movie or digital game action heroes, such as *Lara Croft* (in both games and films) – women continue to be largely portrayed in the mass media as sexual objects, and/or fulfilling their traditional roles as wives, mothers and partners. This is clearly visible in the way women are objectified in men's magazines and advertising, but also in other aspects of popular culture, such as in song lyrics. A good illustration of this is the song 'Wives and Lovers', written by Burt Bacharach in the 1960s, which suggests a wife's primary role is to remain 'pretty' and take care of her man to ensure his fidelity. Of course, it could be argued that this song is now quite dated, but very similar sentiments are expressed in the Destiny's Child song 'Cater 2 U', from their 2004 album *Destiny Fulfilled*, which similarly suggests a woman's role is to 'keep her self up' and 'keep it tight', and 'cater to' their man by providing him with his dinner, a foot rub, a manicure, fetching his slippers, and much more, all on demand.

Tuchman (1981) suggests that the mass media reflects society, not as it really is, but rather how it would like to see itself. For instance, today two-parent headed households with two or three children are in the minority in Britain, but still, this is how the mass media tends to represent 'typical' British family life. Likewise, women are frequently portrayed in very traditional, or trivialised, roles.

This is even evident in the ways in which women are represented in the media in traditional 'male' domains, such as sport. For example, van Zoonen (1994) argues that in sport photography male athletes are always portrayed in active roles, their bodies hard and tough, never passive and never yielding to the viewer. Though

the rise in popularity of exercise and sport for women in recent years has increased the portrayal of women in the mass media in more active performing roles, Leath and Lumpkin (1992) suggests that women are still most likely to be depicted in the mass media in 'posed' rather than 'athletic' shots.

Hargreaves (1994) even goes as far to suggest that the portrayal of women in active sporting poses only further extends the male objectification of the female body – as these are still sexualised images. For example, how *The Sun* newspaper in 2003 printed a picture of tennis player Anna Kournikova every day (in its 'Kourni-corner') throughout that year's Wimbledon tennis tournament – irrespective of whether she played that day or not.

Even though we are now seeing situations where men, and in particular male athletes, are portrayed in the mass media in sexualised ways, Whelehan (2000: 131) argues that men remain represented in dominant strong roles, and more importantly, this does 'nothing to affect our perceptions of these men as people, or prompt us to question their fitness for work, their sexual propriety or anything else' – unlike women, men never become truly *objectified*.

## Mass media representation of celebrity

Rojek (2001: 10) defines celebrity as 'the attraction of glamorous or notorious status to an individual within the public sphere'. By this he means that people gain celebrity status for either 'glamorous' reasons, such as super-models, footballers and pop stars, or for more 'notorious' reasons, such as serial killers or people who have committed 'lewd acts'.

Rojek suggest that although the idea of 'fame' may be historic (having existed for maybe thousands of years, in the form of monarchy and ancient 'heroes') 'celebrity' is very much a contemporary phenomenon. Rojek (2001) suggests that the rise in social importance of celebrities has occurred due to three main and interrelated historical processes:

1 The democratisation of society – which has increased our freedom of choice and allowed 'ordinary' people to rise to the status of celebrity.

2 The decline in organised religion – where in a

secular society celebrity culture replaces religious icons and role models.

3 The commodification of everyday life – where almost everything in life becomes commodified and purchasable, such as magazines which sell us insights into how to dress like celebrities, or celebrities themselves who sell us clothing ranges, perfumes or underwear bearing their names; such as *Glow* perfume by J-Lo or *Lovely* underwear by Kylie.

In particular, it is suggested that where 'fame' was once based upon success or achievement, contemporary celebrity is primarily a media creation or a 'cultural fabrication' (Rojek, 2001). As Schickel (1985: 47) argues, from the 1920s onwards:

reward began to detach itself from effort and from intrinsic merit, when the old reasonable correlation between what (and how) one did and what one received for doing it became tenuous (and, in the upper reaches of show biz, invisible).

Furthermore, Boorstin (1992: 57–61) draws a distinction between the historical 'hero' and contemporary 'celebrity':

The celebrity is a person who is known for his well-knownness ... The hero was distinguished by his achievement; the celebrity by his image or trademark. The hero created himself; the celebrity is created by the media. The hero is a big man [sic]; the celebrity is a big name.

Echoing the sentiments of Schickel (1985) and Boorstin (1992), as well as Monaco (1978) and numerous others, Rojek (2001) therefore distinguishes between three 'types' of celebrity:

1 Ascribed celebrity – which is celebrity status that typically follows bloodline and biological dissent. The foundation of this celebrity is predetermined and something born into; for example, monarchy.

2 Achieved celebrity – derives from the (perceived) accomplishments of an individual in open competition. In the public realm these celebrities are recognised as individuals with rare talent. For example, early sporting stars such as Jesse Owen.

3 Attributed celebrity – result of the representation of an individual as noteworthy or exceptional by cultural producers (such as the mass media), regardless of an individual's actual talent or skill.

Achieved celebrity pre-dates the rise of the mass-media, and whilst those who were marked out for their significant achievements were widely known and talked about, key elements of their private self were secret from public view. By contrast the contemporary 'achieved' celebrity is ever present and open to digestion through various arms of the mass media, and as such, become much dependent upon their 'public' face.

The contemporary celebrity is therefore closely associated with the mass media and a **postmodern** (p. 295) era, where depth or meaning are no longer important, and increasingly what is important is surface and image. It does not really matter what David Beckham or Brad Pitt are *really* like – all that matters is their media and celebrity images, which become disconnected from any sense of reality. For instance, in his book on David Beckman, Ellis Cashmore (2002) utilises the work of Andy Warhol, and in particular his repetition of images of stars such as Marilyn Monroe and Elvis Presley, to highlight the way in which contemporary celebrities are produced and reproduced like any other consumer commodity by the mass media. And as Cashmore (2002: 192) writes, David Beckham is 'as much a [media] construction as Bob the Builder or Tony Soprano – a product of imagination and industry, rather than exploits'.

However, the mass media created 'celebrity' can be very short-lived. Rojek (2001) suggests that the term celebrity is linked to the Latin word *celere*, which means 'swift', and therefore in doing so highlights the precarious nature of celebrities. In particular, he identifies what he refers to as 'celetoids', who are individuals who command media attention for only a very short period of time. Examples include lottery winners, stalkers, streakers or kiss-and-tellers. In particular, celetoids are often constructed around sexual scandal, such as Monica Lewinsky, who had an affair with the (then) US president Bill Clinton. The celetoid receives their moment of fame and then disappears from public consciousness rapidly, although they can achieve a degree of longevity – such as Monica Lewinsky who in the period after her affair, launched her own brand of handbags and appeared on several chat and 'reality' television shows, and gave numerous interviews to newspapers and magazines.

Similarly, just as celebrity fades, so too can media and public adulation be transformed into revulsion. Many celebrities have seen their celebrity 'glamorous' status pulled from under them, and replaced with one of shame and 'notoriety'. This is particularly common in sport, where very easily, failures, or off-field behaviour can turn stars into villains overnight. A good example being the life and changing (media) fortunes of the one time professional footballer Paul 'Gazza' Gascoigne. Gascoigne's career and life has continuously been the focus of British tabloid journalism for well over a decade.

His life has been recounted like that of a soap character, featuring the highs of his success (and England's *almost* success) at the 1990 football World Cup finals, which ended (literally) in tears for Gascoigne, to the lows of his struggles with his weight and depression and admission of abuse toward his wife (see Giulianotti and Gerrad 2001). Though undoubtedly Paul Gascoigne was a footballer of great talent, it was his tears in 1990, not his talent, which made him a celebrity, and this is a celebrity that was maintained by continued media interest in his private life, long after his professional career had ended.

# Audiences and reception

This chapter has highlighted the processes of communications and representation as involving complex patterns of interaction and interpretation between the sender and receiver of a 'message'. The relationship between message or textual production and its reception should be understood as a complex cycle, rather than a unidirectional process. However, it is still frequently the case that the production (or 'encoding' processes) of a text or message are given precedence in many studies of communication and the mass media, at the expense of reception (or 'decoding' processes). However, an important contribution to our understanding of both these encoding and decoding processes is the work of Stuart Hall (p. 55).

## Stuart Hall: encoding, decoding and ideology

Work on the media developed and operationalised some of the key debates on **ideology**. In particular the research carried out at the Birmingham **Centre for Contemporary Cultural Studies** (p. 241) was hugely influential. The cornerstone of this was the work of Stuart Hall.

In 'Encoding/decoding', Hall (1980) argues that television programmes, and by implication all other forms of text, should be understood as 'meaningful **discourse**' (p. 21). In the language of **structuralism** (p. 17) and

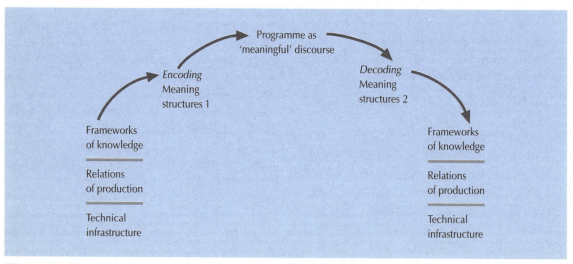

**Figure 2.4** Encoding and decoding. (Source: Hall, 1980: 130.)

# Key influence 2.2

## Stuart Hall (1932–)

Stuart Hall is a Jamaican-born intellectual and political activist who can in many senses be seen as the crucial figure in the development of contemporary cultural studies through his own work, his stimulation of others and his continued attention to the interconnections between politics and the pursuit of knowledge.

Born into a middle-class family, Hall left Jamaica in 1951 to study at Oxford. He was active in left politics and became the first editor of New Left Review in 1960. In 1964 he was appointed as deputy director (to Richard Hoggart) of the newly created **Centre for Contemporary Cultural Studies** (p. 241). He subsequently became director, before taking the Chair of Sociology at the Open University in 1979.

Hall's early engagement with the New Left stimulated his interest in popular culture and he published an important text with Paddy Whannel, The Popular Arts (1964). This interest continued in a number of papers on diverse topics in the area of media and communication, including news photographs, the magazine Picture Post, and news and current affairs television. His ongoing concern with issues of race was combined with this emphasis in the influential (collectively authored) Policing the Crisis (1978). He wrote on subcultures specifically on hippies, but most importantly in the key collective text Resistance through Rituals (1976). His theoretical interests were developed in papers on ideology, which were influenced by both Althusser and **Gramsci** (p. 38). He was one of the first leftist analysts to confront Thatcherism and from 1979 on developed an analysis and critique based in a Gramscian approach. This resulted in the concept of 'authoritarian populism', The Politics of Thatcherism (1983) and New Times (1989), both edited with Martin Jacques. Confronting **postmodernism** (p. 295) led Hall to increased concern with issues around 'race' and **'identity'** (p. 142) in the 1990s, when he also continued to reflect on the development of 'cultural studies'.

The impact of Hall's own work, centred on the interconnections between **ideology** (p. 35), identity, culture and politics, on cultural studies cannot be overestimated. He remains at the cutting edge of developments, continuing to argue for the relevance of a sophisticated Marxism to the understanding of contemporary social formations, as well as a force for social change. Moreover, especially during his time at the Centre for Contemporary Cultural Studies in Birmingham, he influenced a generation of researchers who were themselves to become some of the leading writers in the field. His commitment to collective work is reflected in his joint authorship and editorship of many volumes.

### Further reading

Morley, D. and Chen, K.-H. (eds) (1996) Stuart Hall: Critical Dialogues in Cultural Studies, London: Routledge.

Hall, S. and Jefferson, T. (eds) (1976) Resistance through Rituals: Youth Subcultures in Post-war Britain, London: Hutchinson.

Hall, S., Critcher, C., Jefferson, T., Clarke, J. and Roberts, B. (1978) Policing the Crisis: Mugging, the State and Law and Order, London: Macmillan.

---

semiotics (p. 29) introduced earlier in this chapter, they consist of codes. To achieve this status they must be encoded by those involved in their production, and be capable of being decoded by the audiences who watch them. They are social phenomena subject to struggle and change. These relationships are summarised by Hall in the diagram reproduced in Figure 2.4.

Hall argues that the television text, or sign, is very complex; furthermore that it can be decoded in different ways by the audience. Hall identifies three positions 'from which decodings of a televisual discourse may be constructed' (1980: 136). These he calls the 'dominant-hegemonic', the 'negotiated' and the 'oppositional' (1980: 136–8). In the dominant-**hegemonic** position (p. 73) the logic of the television programme is gone along with.

When the viewer takes the connoted meaning from, say, a television newscast or current affairs programme full and straight, and decodes the message in terms of the references code in which it has been encoded, we might say that the viewer is *operating inside the dominant code.*

(Hall, 1980: 136)

The negotiated code may also operate within this framework, but will allow for disagreements within it. Thus, on the basis of experience, for example, there may be specific challenges to aspects of the dominant frame.

> Decoding within the *negotiated version* contains a mixture of adaptive and oppositional elements: it acknowledges the legitimacy of the hegemonic definitions to make grand significations (abstract), while, at a more restricted, situational (situated) level, it makes its own ground rules – it operates with exceptions to the rule.
>
> (Hall, 1980: 137)

In the oppositional position the dominant framework is directly resisted, in a 'globally contrary way' (Hall, 1980: 137–8).

These potential positions were empirically considered by Morley (1980). Reiterating the influence of the sociologist Frank Parkin (1973) on his and Hall's position, Morley found evidence for the existence of the different positions among social groups to which he showed examples of the British current affairs magazine programme *Nationwide* (see further Abercrombie, 1996; Abercrombie and Longhurst, 1998).

## Audiences

The work of Stuart Hall on encoding/decoding was (and continues to be) significant for the study of audiences. Prior to the work of Hall and his colleagues at the University of Birmingham, audience members were frequently cast as 'passive dopes' (Garfinkel 1967) who passively absorbed messages communicated to them by the mass media. This is the attitude towards audiences that appears to be conveyed by **Frankfurt School** writers such as Theodor Adorno (p. 75), and it is also the attitude of many (even contemporary) psychological studies of audiences, such as the perceived 'effect' of media violence on individuals (p. 193).

This perspective of audience members as passive recipients of mass media 'messages' (Abercrombie and Longhurst (1998)) refers to as the *Behavioural Paradigm* of audience research. However, they suggest that the influential work of authors such as Stuart Hall led to a recognition that audiences are not passive, but can actively 'decode' and engage with texts. This then leads to the development of a new paradigm in audience research, which they call the *Incorporation/Resistance Paradigm*.

In this model audiences are seen as more active in their consumption, where the messages conveyed by the mass media are reinterpreted or even rejected (resisted) by audience members (see **resistance** p. 170). Put simply, they suggest that the focus of this paradigm is on 'whether audience members were incorporated into dominant ideology by their participation in media activity, or whether to the contrary, they are resistant to that incorporation' (1998: 15).

However, Abercrombie and Longhurst (1998) argue that there are a number of weaknesses with this paradigm. These include, most notably, that the power an audience has to resist or reinterpret the messages the mass media conveys to them is often overstated within this paradigm, and second, that there exists little empirical evident to support this paradigmal framework – on the contrary, as audiences becoming more skilled in their media use, their responses and actions are less likely to conform to this simple model.

In particular, Abercrombie and Longhurst (1998) argue there is now occurring a shift towards a new paradigm, and this they refer to as the *Spectacle/Performance Paradigm*. They suggest that within an increasingly spectacular and performative (**postmodern** – p. 295) society individuals become part of a 'diffused audience'. That is to say, we draw on the mass media as a resource and use this in our everyday social performances, rendering us (and others) both performances, and audiences to others' performances, in our everyday lives.

The Incorporation/Resistance Paradigm therefore recognises audiences as not the passive product of production/text process, while more contemporary debates (within a Spectacle/Performance Paradigm) allow us to break down the boundaries between production/text/consumption, and see audiences as both consumers and producers of texts and performances.

## 2.4 Conclusion

In this chapter we have considered the social and cultural importance of communication and representation. In particular, we have highlighted that unlike early theorisations of communication, such as that offered by Claude Elwood Shannon, communication is not a simple straightforward process of a sender constructing a message and sending it to a receiver, who understands the message in exactly the way it was intended. Communication is rather, an extremely complex process. In particular, we have illustrated how the form of a message (or 'text'), such as being spoken, written or visual, can shape its meaning. Through a discussion of meanings and semiotics, we have also shown how the meanings attached to signs (such as words) are arbitrary, and hence language and meaning is not a straightforward and simple association. However, it is argued that the association between a sign and its meaning is a structured one, and this is illustrated with the work authors such as de Saussure, Chomsky and Lévi-Strauss, and also the ideological nature of meaning. This, however, is challenged by hermeneutics, poststructuralism and postmodernism, which emphasise the more subjective and/or fluid nature of meanings in contemporary society.

This chapter also highlights the importance of recognising the complexities involved in processes of representation, and also the power relations intrinsic to this. In particular, it considers the role language plays in structuring gender, race and ethnicity and social class. Finally, in this chapter we have consider mass media representations of gender, race and ethnicity, and celebrity, and again highlighted the important role that meanings represented through the mass media can have in shaping our understanding of cultural forms and 'groupings'. But here we also highlight the important work of Stuart Hall, which makes us aware that mass media 'messages' need not always be accepted or encountered in the way they were intended, and that audiences have the ability to 'decode' and reinterpret 'texts'.

### Recap

➤ Communication and representation are a complex process and cycle of making meanings, interpretation and re-interpretation.

➤ Communication and representation are not neutral, but rather can be value-laden.

➤ That it is through language and communication that we make sense of our world, and through this, help shape our world.

## Further reading

An excellent short introduction to issues of language and representation, especially as discussed in the structuralist and semiotic viewpoints, can be found in Terence Hawkes, *Structuralism and Semiotics* (1977). The classic study which applies these to advertising is Judith Williamson *Decoding Advertisements: Ideology and Meaning in Advertising* (1978), which might be used to prompt analyses of your own. Connections between representation and power (especially of class and gender) are economically and influentially dealt with by John Berger in *Ways of Seeing* (1972). John Fiske and John Hartley, *Reading Television* (1978) apply semiotics to television; Fiske's *Television Culture* (1987) develops the argument and approach. And a good introduction to the Mass Media is O'Shaughnessy and Sadler's *Media and Society: An Introduction* (1999).

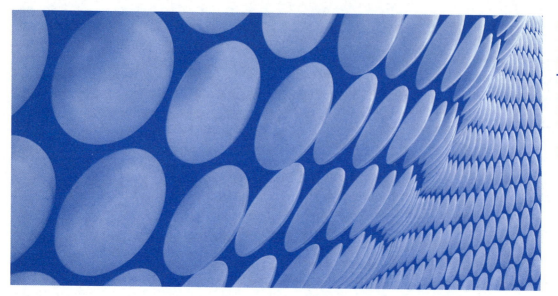

# Chapter 3

# Culture, power, globalisation and inequality

## 3.0 Introduction

Globalisation, is the buzzword that has been coined to describe the spread of economies, cultures and power across national borders. It is a highly contested term that is both used and misused. Indeed as Dicken (2007) suggests it has become a convenient term used to collect together all the 'goods' and 'bads' facing contemporary societies. However, it is true to say that there is an increasingly global scale to the complex geography of production, distribution and consumption of the things that we use in our daily lives (Dicken, 2007). We shall suggest that the globalisation of capitalist economies and a westernised consumer culture has had a significant impact on contemporary societies. We will see that in many ways culture is the most visible manifestation of this globalisation. However, we also want to suggest that the globalisation of capitalism leads to an unequal distribution of income and wealth between and within societies.

The development and global expansion of a world capitalist system of production has generated increasing disparities of wealth, income and life chances within and between the populations of the world's nation-states. The pursuit of capitalist goals is contrary to social, economic and political egalitarianism; capitalism produces inequality. It is also becoming more and more apparent that the sources and manifestations of this inequality are not simply produced by the globalisation of market logics and mechanisms. The cultural dimension is increasingly significant.

This chapter begins with a discussion of globalisation and the cultural and economic effects it produces. We examine a range of approaches to the study of globalisation taken by writers in and around cultural studies. We shall suggest that the pessimism that often frames the debate around the globalisation of culture is not always well founded. However, we shall see that inequalities are inherent to a global capitalist system of economic production. Second, we develop this idea and examine the relationship between culture, power and inequality, looking at explanations of the origins of inequality in capitalist societies. Third, the chapter considers how and why inequality is maintained in capitalist societies with particular reference to the role of culture. Fourth, it looks at systems of inequality that are commonly seen to be rooted and expressed in non-economic values, namely race, ethnicity, age and gender. This will allow us to examine the principal sources and characteristics of inequality (class, status and caste), the ways that inequality is made acceptable to people, that is how it comes to be seen as legitimate, and some of the leading cultural consequences of inequality. In the concluding section we shall examine the idea that different kinds of inequality interact to produce multiple disadvantages.

## Learning objectives

➤ To understand the social, economic and cultural significance of globalisation.

➤ To recognize the main structural sources of social inequality.

➤ To appreciate the various conceptions of the part played by culture in legitimating inequality.

➤ To learn about the leading cultural manifestations of inequality.

➤ To grasp some of the ways in which cultural power is displayed.

## 3.1 Understanding globalisation

Globalisation is a term that tries to capture the rapid social change that is occurring simultaneously across a number of dimensions, including the economy, politics, communications and culture (Tomlinson, 1999, 2006). Theorists of globalisation emphasise that we inhabit a world where there are global economies, a global media, a world characterised by virtual communication, institutional deregulation, and the movement of capital, information and people at great speed across large distances (Savage *et al.*, 2005). Where social and cultural life can no longer be seen as firmly located in particular places with clear boundaries (Abercrombie *et al.*, 2000).

## Globalisation: cultural and economic change

We can think of globalisation in two senses as a process and as an outcome, in both these senses globalisation leads to cultural and economic change. Firstly, it is a process over time that is compressing the distances between people and places and which increases the sense that we live in a single world. Secondly, it is suggested that the outcome of globalisation is that we live in a world criss-crossed by global processes, where individual places, groups of people and societies have lost their significance and power and where there is interdependency, culturally, politically, economically and militarily (Abercrombie *et al.*, 2000).

New forms of global communications, such as the development of international travel via mass jet transportation, or high-speed trains, and the increased prevalence of mobile phones, the internet, fax and satellite communications play a key role in the development of globalisation. It is suggested that such developments reduce the distance between places and people, as they reduce the time taken to move people, images or information. They lead to a re-drawing of the categories of time and space, and a compressing of distance: we are seen to inhabit a 'small world' where there is an increasing sense of global interdependence (Abercrombie *et al.*, 2000). These technological developments are seen to be sweeping away cultural boundaries and creating the possibility, even the likelihood of a global culture (GPF, 2007).

Another key aspect of globalisation is that there are huge flows of money between different foreign exchange markets, leading to an internationalisation of economies, and a sense of economic interdependence. Companies, such as Microsoft, Nike, McDonalds, Virgin, or Sony adopt global strategies, and have an annual turnover greater than whole national economies. An extensive range of products are available worldwide, such as the *iPod* or *Coca Cola*. There is growth in scale of the import and export of goods and services as the barriers to international trade are

59

reduced and the capitalist system expands on a world-wide scale.

Large corporations also control the world's mass media, leading to a uniformity of programmes based on a large international market, and reducing the impact of local programmes and identities. We begin to inhabit a world of media sameness and again there is the suggestion that this leads to a homogenised global culture. The proliferation of 'reality television' across the globe is symptomatic of this. International companies such as Endemol N.V, market themselves as 'global leaders' aiming to promote their 'premium entertainment concepts' or brands such as 'Big Brother' across the globe (www.endemoluk.com). Global entertainment companies have the capacity to shape people's perceptions and dreams wherever they may live. The culture, norms and values promoted tend to support Western ideals of capitalism and consumer culture.

The extent and effects of globalisation are difficult to measure, but the World Bank suggests that the scope and pace of change can be monitored along four key channels: trade in goods and services; financial flows; the movement of people; and the diffusion of technology and knowledge. The following data from the 2007 edition of the World Bank's annual publication, *World Development Indicators* go some way to illustrating the scale and the growth of globalisation over the past 20–30 years.

➤ Exports and imports of goods and services exceeded $26 trillion in 2005, or 58 per cent of total global output, up from 44 per cent in 1980.

➤ Gross private capital flows across national borders exceeded 32 per cent of global output in 2005, up from 9 per cent in 1980.

➤ People have become more mobile. More than 800 million people travelled to foreign destinations in 2005, nearly triple the number in 1980. Some 190 million people are estimated to reside outside their land of birth, nearly double the 1980 level.

➤ Technology and knowledge are diffusing at unprecedented speed across countries. International phone traffic, measured in minutes, increased more than fourfold between 1995 and 2005 (World Bank, 2007).

## Theorising about globalisation

Globalisation theory emerged from the late 1980s onwards as commentators tried to make sense of the rapid social change they were observing. Early globalisation theory was a response to the new forms of capitalist power and dominance that were being identified (Robertson, 1992). The collapse of most state socialist regimes, as well as the weakening power of labour movements and socialist politics within many capitalist nations removed the main political alternative to capitalism (Bauman 1987). Economic restructuring, state deregulation, the power of large transnational corporations, and the proliferation of new technologies facilitating the mobility of goods, capital, people and symbols, led to a new sense of global connectivity (Savage *et al.*, 2005). As Tomlinson (1999) has outlined, at the heart of globalisation is a process of accelerating 'connectivity', a rapidly developing and increasingly dense network of interconnections and interdependencies that characterise modern social life (Tomlinson, 2006).

Commentators have tried to connect this process to historical and social change indicating that we have entered a 'global age', one that marks the end of modernity (Albrow, 1996). Consequently, a new kind of consumerist post-modern aesthetic and intensified forms of individualised identities were heralded as indications of new social relations generated by global flows (see Harvey, 1990; Jameson 1991; Lash and Urry, 1987; Bauman, 1987). By the early 1990s it was possible to conceive of one world organised around common capitalist parameters, for the first time since the First World War (Fukuyama, 1992). Roland Robertson (1992) developed the first major account of globalisation as the rise of a 'global awareness'. He argued that globalisation was making the world a 'single place' which was leading to 'the compression of the world and the intensification of consciousness of the world as a whole' (1992: 8).

The move towards the characterisation of the world as a single place went alongside a fear of the decline in importance of the local. As communication was no longer confined to the boundaries of particular places, practices became increasingly detached from their local settings. An important impetus here was the way that new media technologies could be seen to play a crucial role in time–space distanciation. Early globalisation theorists' response to this was rather pessimistic. Giddens (1991) argued that new forms of media generated 'no sense of place', with people defining their salient relationships not in terms of face-to-face contacts but in terms of media characters and celebrities. Concern was expressed over the spread of a global culture that would homogenise cultural experience, destroy local identities and localities, and lead to a loss of community and 'face-to-face' interaction (Savage *et al.*, 2005). There was anxiety that local cultures would be taken over by a global consumer culture, and that consumer values would overwhelm people's sense of community and social solidarity. However, for some there was also the hope that a common culture would lead to greater shared values and political unity. This early period of classic globalisation theory was, however, short-lived.

By the early 1990s any simple hopes for a new world order were dissipated behind growing national and cultural conflicts (Savage *et al.*, 2005). It became clear that major global tensions, between religious blocs and between national and ethnic groups, only served to highlight the significance of boundaries. It was clear that the world was not a single unified place, politically, economically or culturally. Globalisation was and is an uneven process: it does not spread to all corners of the globe. For example, the developing world is not able to participate in global communications or the global economy to the same extent as the developed world (Massey, 1994).

A different approach to globalisation and spatial change emerged by the mid 1990s, and can be found in the later work of Robertson (1995), in the writings of Lash and Urry (1994), Massey (1994), Appadurai (1996) and Castells (1996, 1997). These writers did not emphasise the erosion of place but rather focused on new forms of connection and mobility, of global flows between places, and their potential to rework social relationships and to reconstruct localism. As Beck says (2002: 23), 'you cannot even think about globalisation without referring to specific locations and places'. A key point made by these writers was that the local is not transcended by globalisation, but rather that the local is to be understood through the lens of global relationships (Savage *et al.*, 2005). Globalisation, therefore, produces new forms of localisation in a dialectical relationship that Robertson (1995) popularised as 'glocalisation', where 'globalisation' has involved the reconstruction of 'home', 'community' and 'locality'. As Urry states 'the global and local are inextricably and irreversibly bound together through a dynamic

**Figure 3.1** The McTurco.

relationship' (2003: 84) so that people dwell 'in and through being at home and away, through the dialectic of roots and routes' (Urry 2000: 132–3). Hence, whilst, there is evidence of the spread of a westernised or Americanised consumer culture, this does not necessarily translate into a uniform global culture, rather it can lead to the appearance of new cultural forms, for example Disneyland Paris, or the transformation of traditional cultural expressions such as Turkish McDonald's restaurants serving their customers a 'McTurco' (see Figure 3.1) a type of Turkish kebab. However, this does not mean that globalisation is unproblematic. As we shall see in the next section inequalities are an inherent part of the global capitalist system.

## Globalisation and inequality

Globalisation leads to an unequal distribution of income and wealth. The development and global expansion of a world capitalist system of production has generated increasing disparities of wealth, income and life chances within and between the populations of the world's nation-states. In 1996 the Organization for Economic Cooperation and Development (OECD) complimented the British government on its economic success in controlling inflation and reducing unemployment in the British economy but warned that there might be a high price to pay in terms of social disharmony and civil unrest because the policies of sound economics had produced a big gap in incomes and wealth in British society. By 2006 the OECD was warning that exceptionally strong labour force growth, driven by high immigration and rising workforce participation was outstripping employment growth, pushing the UK unemployment rate up and contributing to a high rate of child poverty and joblessness. Similar warnings have been given about the relationships between the industrially developed and economically advanced nations of the world and areas of the former communist world and countries of the so-called developing or Third World. This is a political term which is used to describe poor countries in Africa, Latin America and parts of Asia, many of which were former colonies of European states. In all cases the warning is that there are dangers to social cohesion and

political stability as a result of the operation and continuing expansion of the capitalist system.

If we consider the global economic differences between societies, it is evident that the contrasts are very marked in scale and continuing to grow. Economists speak of these increasing differences in the wealth of the developed and developing world societies as the 'development gap'. One way of measuring the development gap is to compare the gross national income per head of the population (GNI per capita). This is the total value of goods and services produced annually in a nation divided by its population. In 2005 the World Bank's 'high income' nations – mainly in North America, Europe, Australasia and parts of the Middle and Far East – made up 16 per cent of the world's population yet had an average GNI per capita well over 20 times higher than the average for the rest of the world (World Bank, 2007).

A key area of concern is Third World debt, which has long been recognised as a major obstacle to human development, education, health and economic recovery and growth. Many other problems arise because of the enormous debt that Third World countries owe to rich countries: it is estimated that about 11 million children die each year around the world, due to conditions of poverty and debt. The developing world now spends $13 on debt repayment for every $1 it receives in grants. In 1970, the world's poorest countries (roughly 60 countries classified as low-income by the World Bank) owed $25 billion in debt: by 2002, this was $523 billion. For Africa, in 1970, it was just under $11 billion and by 2002 it was $295 billion. These countries have paid back $550 billion in principal and interest over the last three decades, on $540 billion of loans and they still continue to pay (**http://news.bbc.co.uk**). The G8 Summit (the periodic meeting of the eight most industrialised nations in the world to discuss and draw up global economic policies) in July 2005 promised debt relief and a doubling of aid for some poor countries in Africa. However, to date, whilst there has been some reduction in debt, the World Bank (2007) notes that 'donor nations are falling behind in fulfilling their promises' (see the satirical cartoon in Figure 3.2).

Debt has impeded sustainable human development, security and political or economic stability in the developing world. It leads to an unequal distribution of

**Figure 3.2** World debt. (Source: the *Observer*, 17 May 1998, © Chris Riddell.)

power and wealth throughout the globe. It is partly in response to such inequalities that we have seen the development of the anti-globalisation movement which is both a political and cultural response to the effects of globalisation. This is a diverse new social movement (NSM) or collection of social movements (see also Chapter 6 for discussion of NSMs) who oppose certain aspects of globalisation, such as the political and economic power of large corporations and industrial nations, or the environmental impacts. They campaign for human rights and the dissolution or reform of the capitalist system. The movement is made up of different groups and organisations, with different viewpoints, strategies and tactics but who come together to demonstrate at international events. This has led to anti-globalisation demonstrations and mobilisations against organisations such as the World Trade Organization, International Monetary Fund and the World Bank. The anti-globalisation movement is against neo-liberalism, United States imperialism and domination by US-based transnational corporations (Epstein, 2001). They have been involved in a variety of peaceful and violent marches, demonstrations and street protests. They have employed civil disobedience and used a strategy of confrontation against, amongst

others, the WTO in Seattle in 1999, and the G8 summit meetings in Genoa in 2001 and Germany in 2007.

Of course what these data about inequalities between societies overlook are the very considerable differences in income, wealth and associated life chances that individuals may experience *within* any given society. Even in a rich society such as the USA, the poor encounter real deprivation. Nevertheless, the differences between rich and poor societies in a global perspective are striking, for example, in 2005 life expectancy at birth varied from

**Figure 3.3** Anti-globalisation civil disobedience.

## Defining concept 3.1

### Power

Power has come to be one of the crucial concepts in cultural studies. Interpretations of culture that draw upon ideas of 'cultural politics' argue that everything is political and, as a result that power is everywhere (see Chapter 6). For example, it is used in this book to understand relations of class, race, gender and age; to interpret the body and representations of people and places; and to make sense of our understandings of time and space. As **Michel Foucault** (p. 20), one of the theorists responsible for extending the use of ideas of power, put it: 'Power is everywhere; not because it embraces everything, but because it comes from everywhere.' To understand what he meant by this, and its implications, we need to look more closely at how power has been understood.

In a classic essay originally written in 1974, and updated and reissued in 2004, Steven Lukes argued that there are three views of power. The 'one-dimensional view' is that it means that person A can get person B to do something that they would not otherwise do. The 'two-dimensional view' is that group A has power to the extent that they can define not just the outcomes but the 'rules of the game' to their advantage. The 'three-dimensional view' is where the powerful have power to the extent that they can prevent people, to whatever degree, from having grievances by shaping their perceptions, cognitions and preferences in such a way that they accept their role in the existing order of things either because they can see or imagine no alternative to it, or because they see it as natural and unchangeable, or because they value it as divinely ordained and beneficial (Lukes, 1974, 2004). This third view has many similarities to that which is put forward in the notions of **ideology** (p. 35) and **hegemony** (p. 73), and it helps us to understand the importance of the ways in which the unequal distribution of power is made to seem appropriate – the way it is given legitimation.

The challenge that is offered to these views of power is that they are essentially negative. They all involve trying to understand how people are prevented from doing what they want, defining the 'rules of the game' as they want, or thinking their own thoughts. Instead of this Foucault suggests that power is productive. Power lies in the creation of **discourses** (p. 21), institutions, objects and **identities** (p. 142); power is all about making and remaking the world in a particular way. Thus, in his analysis, power produces classifications of knowledge which define our understanding of the relationship between people and nature; power produces bodies that can be made even more productive in factories and prisons; and power produces sexuality as the site that tells us most about ourselves. Power is not about saying 'no'; it is about producing things, identities and ideas.

Taking these views together, what we have are multiple forms of power. In each case, rather than trying to track down who finally holds 'power' and what that power is in the sort of abstract language that Lukes uses, we can try to understand how the relations of power work. There are plenty of examples in this book – such as analyses of orientalism, monuments or the body – where we have tried to offer this sort of interpretation. What we find is that power works in many different ways because, as Foucault says, 'power comes from everywhere'; it is part of all relationships. Yet this is not a matter of reducing the world to a grey arena in which we are all totally dominated and controlled by capitalism or patriarchy or 'the system'. There are always **resistances** (p. 170) (which we need to think about not as qualitatively different from power but as forms of 'counter-power') which – together with the fact that the forces they oppose are often in conflict – produce a vibrant world of many contending people, institutions and discourses engaged in never-ending contests over resources, meanings, spaces, identities, positions and representations.

### Further reading

Clegg, S.R. (1989) *Frameworks of Power*, London: Sage.

Lukes, S. (ed.) (1986) *Power*, Oxford: Blackwell.

Lukes, S (2004) *Power: A Radical View*, Basingstoke: Palgrave Macmillan

75 years in 'high income' nations to 59 years in 'low income' nations (World Bank, 2007). These differences remain an underlying source of tension and instability in the contemporary world.

# 3.2 Theorising about culture, power and inequality

We have suggested that globalisation and the expansion of the global capitalist system leads to an unequal distribution of power, income and wealth within and between societies. In this section we shall look at how theorists have tried to explain this and we show how culture contributes to the production and maintenance of inequalities and power relations in the contemporary world. We begin with the work of Karl Marx.

## Marx and Marxism

Much contemporary theorising about culture, power and inequality derives from **Marx's** theories (Marx and Engels, 1967; McLellan, 2000) and Marxian analyses and models of the social and economic processes of class formation in capitalist society. As Raymond Williams (1983a: 16) has noted, Marxism has made an influential contribution to modern cultural thought, even though Marx himself never developed a fully systematic theory of culture. Marx outlines a historical progression from societies that he saw as exhibiting primitive communism through feudal society and into various forms of capitalist society, leading eventually to a revolution in which the agencies of the state would be overthrown and a socialist society emerge. There are a number of features of Marxian analyses that are significant for consideration of the connections between culture and inequality: the underlying economic structure of class inequality; Marx's emphasis on the opposed and antagonistic relationship between the classes; and the connection between power and culture.

It is economic relationships that underpin inequality for Marx; in all known societies (save the early state of primitive communism) there has always been the basic and fundamental contradiction that some members of society have owned and controlled the means of pro-

duction, a characteristic that has given them power over the remaining members of society who, in order to make a livelihood, participate in production on terms and conditions set by these owners. For Marx, inequality in capitalist society hinges on whether one is an owner of the means of production or an owner of one's labour. As capitalism develops, the class structure simplifies around two main classes, proletariat and bourgeoisie. The relationship between these classes is asymmetrical: there is an unequal distribution of power between them. In the context of the underlying economic relationship this asymmetrical relationship is an antagonistic one as the owners of the means of production increasingly seek to exploit the providers of labour. It is this antagonism and contradiction at the heart of society that acts as the dynamic that propels society on to new forms of exploitation. As it is inherent in capitalism to expand and to destroy all other forms of production, the relationship between the principal classes, the bourgeoisie (the owners of the means of production, those with power and money) and the proletariat (the owners only of their labour, and so lacking in power and money), becomes ever sharper and more antagonistic until eventually the proletariat rises up in revolution and overthrows the bourgeoisie.

For Marx, inequality in society is grounded in antagonistically related social classes. Marx addresses the question of how and why it is possible for the bourgeoisie to maintain its position of dominance for protracted periods, given the fact that it is a minority in society and given the level of oppression and hardship experienced by the masses, the proletariat. Part of the answer is that the bourgeoisie, through its economic power, also exercises political power and so shapes and controls the agencies of the state. Effective control of the state apparatus also gives it a monopoly on the use of force. Another aspect of its power to shape and control the state is the cultural control exercised by the bourgeoisie. Marx sees the bourgeoisie spreading and implementing beliefs and values that sustain the unequal system of relationships by legitimising it through reference to non-economic domains of social experience. An example of this is the realm of spirituality and religious belief. Marx sees the particular beliefs of organised religion as buttresses for an unequal, unjust society. Religion, in his celebrated

## Key influence 3.1

### E.P. Thompson (1924–93)

Edward Palmer (E.P.) Thompson was a very influential English Marxist historian and political activist. His education at Cambridge was interrupted by war service in Italy, but he returned to finish his degree and then took up a position as extra-mural lecturer at Leeds University (1948–65). He was also a Reader at the Centre for the Study of Social History at the University of Warwick, where he influenced a whole generation of social historians. As well as writing on history and theory, he was an active campaigner for nuclear disarmament and a novelist.

E.P. Thompson's most influential work is probably *The Making of the English Working Class* (1968). This social and political history of the working class in the English industrial revolution attempted to present a 'history from below', one written from the perspective of an increasingly proletarianised and politicised working class. It sought, as he put it, 'to rescue the poor stockinger from the enormous condescension of posterity' and to present a history in which the working class were active in their own 'making'. In doing so he offered a challenge to Marxist interpretations of history which saw the history of capitalism as foretold by the inevitable movements of modes of production and social formations. This attention to agency – the power of people to shape history – was stated in opposition to the structuralist theories of Louis Althusser in Thompson's caustic attack entitled *The Poverty of Theory* (1978). It also offered an understanding of class and power which saw them not only as economic relationships but also as social and cultural ones. This led to studies of law and custom that considered class relations in eighteenth- and nineteenth-century Britain in terms of the ways in which classes defined themselves and were brought into conflict over questions of criminality and customary rights (see *Whigs and Hunters* (1975); *Albion's Fatal Tree* (1975) and *Customs in Common* (1991)).

Thompson has been criticised for failing to pay sufficient attention to issues of gender and race in the 'making of the English working class', and the role of agency and culture in the history of capitalism is still a matter of ongoing debate. However, his impact on cultural studies has been to stress the importance of theoretically informed histories, especially 'histories from below', and his attention to the active role of culture in the making of class relations is important.

#### Further reading

Kaye, H.J. and McClelland, K. (eds) (1990) *E.P. Thompson: Critical Perspectives*, Oxford: Polity Press.

Thompson, E.P. (1991) *The Making of the English Working Class*, Harmondsworth: Penguin (orig. 1963, Allan Lane).

## Key influence 3.2

### Karl Marx (1818–83)

Marx's work has been widely influential in the social sciences, arts and humanities. He did not write much about culture itself, but Marxist cultural critics have developed his ideas and those of his collaborator, Friedrich Engels, on alienation, ideology, history and value.

Marx was born in Trier, Prussia, in 1818 to a Jewish family which later converted to Christianity. He studied law at Bonn and Berlin. In 1842 he became editor of the *Rheinische Zeitung*, and in this year he also met his lifelong collaborator Friedrich Engels. In the 1840s Marx began to study French utopian socialism. Combining socialist ideas and an interpretation of Hegel's philosophy, he developed a theory of consciousness as a product of human labour. In the writings later collected as the *Economic and Philosophical Manuscripts*, he argued that capitalism is the last in a series of modes of production that alienate workers from their labour. Earlier modes of production include primitive communism, the slave mode of production (employed in ancient Greece and

## Key influence 3.2 (continued)

Rome), and feudalism. In 1846 he published *The German Ideology* with Engels, in which they argued that: 'The ideas of the ruling class are, in every epoch, the ruling ideas.' *The Communist Manifesto* (1848) proposed that all history is the history of class struggle, and predicted the victory of the new industrial working class, the proletariat, over capitalist society. The demise of capitalism would lead to socialism and ultimately a higher form of communism, where alienation would be at an end. Marx's radical political views meant that he ran into trouble with first the Prussian, then the French and then the Belgian authorities. He and his family were eventually exiled to England. Here Marx worked on his most ambitious project, *Capital*, a detailed analysis of the development and workings of capitalist political economy. At the centre of the three volumes of *Capital* (only one of which was published before Marx's death) lies his account of the commodity. He

noted a contradiction within capitalism between the market value (exchange value) of a particular product and its value as an item that somebody might actually use (use value). Capitalism holds the market value of goods and people to be worth more than the people themselves. In effect, both goods and people are commodified: they become no more than their exchange value. The capitalist allocation of goods by their market value leads to inequalities of wealth between rich and poor and large-scale wastage of resources.

In cultural studies it has been Western Marxism, and especially the work of Georg Lukács, the **Frankfurt School** (p. 75) and **Gramsci** (p. 38) that has had most influence. Marx's theory of alienation has had a profound impact. Marxist cultural theorists view culture in relation to the mode of production, as a historical product of human labour rather than representing timeless human values. Marxist critics have

understood art both as an expression of human alienation and as having the utopian potential to imagine an unalienated world. Marxist-informed theories of ideology have allowed critics to interpret cultural artifacts in relation to social structure. An understanding of cultural production in relation to political economy has been a vital part of studies of the culture industry and mass media.

### Further reading

McLellan, D. (ed) (2000) *Karl Marx: Selected Writings,* Oxford: Oxford University Press.

McLellan, D. (2006) *Karl Marx; A Biography,* Basingstoke: Palgrave Macmillan.

McLellan, D (2007) *Marxism after Marx,* Basingstoke: Palgrave Macmillan.

Singer, P. (2000) *Marx: A Very Short Introduction,* Oxford: Oxford Paperbacks.

---

phrase, is the opiate of the masses. Thus Marx presents culture as ideology, as a partial, biased prop for the bourgeoisie, which is fashioned by it in its own interests. Culture as ideology blunts the understanding of the proletariat: it is the instrument of its deception, occluding its true interests. Culture in this sense stands as somehow opposed to the truth of things.

This is an important aspect of Marx's and Marxist thought and one that reverberates in wider discussions of culture, many of which are discussed in this book. The proposal is that culture is partial, often promoting

a 'false consciousness' of the world and thereby acting as an instrument of oppression. Marx sees all the agencies of the state operating within cultural values that serve the interests of the bourgeoisie. The bourgeoisie has power, through its power it has knowledge and through its power and knowledge it creates the dominant culture. Marxist thought draws attention to the connections between power, knowledge and culture and proposes a systematic relationship in which cultural beliefs and practices are a cultural code for relationships of power.

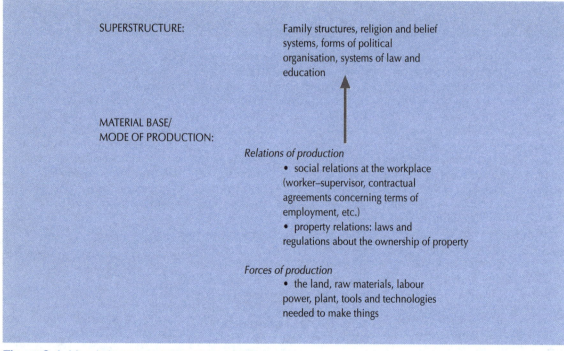

SUPERSTRUCTURE: Family structures, religion and belief systems, forms of political organisation, systems of law and education

MATERIAL BASE/
MODE OF PRODUCTION:

*Relations of production*
• social relations at the workplace (worker–supervisor, contractual agreements concerning terms of employment, etc.)
• property relations: laws and regulations about the ownership of property

*Forces of production*
• the land, raw materials, labour power, plant, tools and technologies needed to make things

**Figure 3.4** Marx's base–superstructure model.

Marx's favoured method for conceptualising these connections is the base-superstructure metaphor (see Figure 3.4). The formula that Marx proposes is that the economic (or material) base of a society determines the broad character of its superstructure. In other words, if we wish to understand the principal features of the superstructure (i.e. culture – including the legal institutions, political organisations and belief systems) of a society then we must carefully analyse the forces of production (productive technologies, institutionalised

---

## Box 3.1

### Marx and Engels on 'ruling ideas'

The ideas of the ruling class are in every epoch the ruling ideas: i.e. the class which is the ruling *material* force in society is at the same time its ruling *intellectual* force. The class which has the means of material production at its disposal, has control at the same time over the means of mental production, so that thereby, generally speaking, the ideas of those who lack the means of mental production are subject to it. The ruling ideas are nothing more than the ideal expression of the dominant material relationships, the dominant material relationships grasped as ideas; hence of the relationships which make the one class the ruling one, therefore, the ideas of its dominance. The individuals composing the ruling class possess among other things consciousness, and therefore think. In so far, therefore, as they rule as a class and determine the extent and compass of an epoch, it is self-evident that they do this in its whole range, hence among other things rule also as thinkers, as producers of ideas, and regulate the production and distribution of the ideas of their age: thus their ideas are the ruling ideas of the epoch. For instance, in an age and in a country where royal power, aristocracy, and bourgeoisie are contending for mastery and where, therefore, mastery is shared, the doctrine of separation of powers proves to be the dominant idea and is expressed as an 'eternal law'.

(Marx and Engels, 1968)

property relations) and the social relations of production consequent upon these productive forces. In a famous passage Marx and Engels (1968: 61) contend that 'the ideas of the ruling class are in every epoch the ruling ideas' (see Box 3.1).

When nineteenth-century capitalist England is analysed in these terms, it is no surprise to find that the state is the 'executive committee of the bourgeoisie' (Marx and Engels, 1967), that the laws and courts consistently favour the interests of capital (those with power and money) as against those of organised labour, and that Christian doctrine as institutionalised in the established Church endorses the existing ordering of society and preaches the virtues of humility to the poor. Although Marx is sometimes equivocal about how strict a relation of determination obtains between base and superstructure, the broad thesis that he advances is that forms of consciousness crystallise into cultural forms and practices which are to be understood as originating socially. The social relationships that provide the touchstone for understanding cultural forms and practices are those predicated on the mode of production.

At first sight this formulation seems to allocate a secondary role to culture as a mere reflection of the material base of a society. Indeed, even Engels, whom many regard as a simplifier of Marx's ideas, baulks at the implications of this position. It is a view that gives culture no significant role in social change; for example, it denies the potentially revolutionary effects of art forms such as theatre and novels in transforming people's perception of the world and thus their action within it. The debate focuses around the determining power of the material base and the degree of autonomy to be given to the superstructure. Williams (1973b: 4) suggests that Marx 'uses the notion of determination and conditioning not in the narrow sense but in a much looser sense of setting limits, exerting pressure and closing off options'. He goes on to argue that Marx did not see either base or superstructure as fixed entities but as dynamic and shifting relationships, and this therefore precludes any simple formulaic conception of the relationship between the two. If determination is to be understood as setting limits, exerting pressure and closing off options, then what we have instead is an agenda for empirical inquiry. This is precisely the view

taken by versions of cultural Marxism (e.g. Jameson, 1991), where the base-superstructure metaphor becomes simply a problem to guide inquiry, not a solution. Historically, the significant challenge to Marxian conceptions originates in the thought of **Max Weber** (1864–1920).

# Weber, status and inequality

Max Weber (1978) proposed a complex approach to inequality which expressly takes account of non-economic dimensions of ranking and inequality. Against Marx, Weber maintains that the operation of **power** (p. 64) in societies is yet more fundamental than their economic basis. Power is defined as the capacity of individuals or groups to realise their will, even in the face of the opposition of others. This yields three categories fundamental to the analysis of inequality: *class*, *status* and *party*. Inequality may be located in economically defined classes (here Weber emphasises market capacity in contrast to Marx's stress on property) but could also be founded in status groups (organised around notions of prestige and honour) and political parties and groupings. In this elaboration he sought to refine the measurement of inequality and to show the potential singularity of his criteria as well as their connectedness. For example, power is often linked to class-based wealth but it can be separated in situations where power is linked to knowledge. Status refers to style of life. It also refers to social esteem, the respect and admiration accorded a person according to their social position (see Box 3.2), and this can be local rather than structural and take account of interpersonal subjectivities. Marx's stress on structural relationships and on the duplicitous nature of culture tends to be replaced by a view of classes as ranked hierarchies of fixed groupings through which individuals may be mobile. While the categories are fixed and classes are bounded, individuals may, nonetheless, change their class position. Furthermore, Weber's discussion emphasises how both class and status distinctions can affect people's *life chances*, that is, the chances that an individual has to share in the economic and cultural goods of a society. Material and cultural goods are often asymmetrically distributed and class and status rankings will ensure that people will have

## Box 3.2

### Weber on status

In modern 'democratic' society ... all explicitly regulated status privileges for individuals are done away with. [In some of the smaller Swiss cities] only families belonging to broadly similar taxation groups dance with each other... But status is not necessarily connected with a 'class situation': normally it stands rather in glaring contradiction to the pretensions of naked property ownership ... The 'equality' of status of the American 'gentleman' finds expression in the fact that ... it would be considered the height of bad taste – wherever the old tradition prevails – for even the richest 'chief' to treat his 'clerk' as in any way at all of unequal rank, even in the evening in the club, over billiards or at the card table. It would be unacceptable to treat him with that kind of condescending affability which marks a difference in position, and which the German chief can never avoid entirely – one of the most important reasons why German club-life has never managed to seem so attractive there as the American club.

In content, social status is normally expressed above all in the imputation of a specifically regulated style of life to everyone who wishes to belong to the circle. This goes together with a restriction of 'social' intercourse – that is, intercourse that does not serve any economic, commercial or other 'practical' purposes – including especially normal intermarriage, to the circle of status equals ... [In the USA] one example of this is that only those who reside in a certain street ('The Street') are regarded as belonging to 'society' and as fit for social intercourse, and are accordingly visited and invited... For the rest, social 'status' is usurped by certain families who have resided in a certain area for a long time (and who are, naturally, correspondingly well-to-do), such as the 'FFV' or 'first families of Virginia', or the descendants, real or alleged, of the 'Indian princess' Pocahontas or the Pilgrim Fathers, or the Knickerbockers, or the members of some extremely exclusive sect, or all kinds of circles of associates who mark themselves off by some criterion or other. In this case it is a matter of a purely conventional social differentiation based essentially on usurpation (although this is admittedly the normal origin of almost all social 'status'). But it is a short step from this to the legal validation of privilege (and lack of privilege), and this step is usually easy to take as soon as a certain arrangement of the social order has become effectively 'settled' and has acquired stability as a result of the stabilisation of economic power. Where the consequences are followed through to the limit, the status group develops into a closed *caste*. That is, distinction of status is guaranteed not only by convention and law, but also by ritual sanction to such an extent that all physical contact with a member of a caste regarded as 'inferior' is held to be ritually polluting for members of the superior caste, a stain which must be religiously expiated. The individual castes, indeed, in part develop quite separate cults and gods.

(Weber, 1978: 49–50)

differential access to these goods. These features of Weber's thought are important to bear in mind when considering non-class based systems of inequality.

This approach allows for the consideration of systems of inequality other than class. There are ranked societies where there is unequal access to positions of status and prestige and these are not necessarily linked to economic wealth. An example is found in those traditional African societies where the chiefs did not live at a higher standard of living than their subjects and where economies were redistributive, that is the chief received tribute which he then gave back to his followers as a mark of his status and largesse. The position of many European noble families is a contemporary example of ranked society: access to claim a title is limited, usually to family members, and many of these titled families are no longer wealthy and have no power by virtue of their nobility in their societies. Within families there are usually ranked orders, sometimes of generations, sometimes of generation and gender. Once one starts to look and notice, it is clear that notions of rank and inequality are pervasive in English society. In England accent still serves as a telling sign of status. Other features of speech patterns also express status rankings. Studies of who interrupts whom have found that parents interrupt children, men interrupt women, doctors are not to be interrupted by patients. All these are illustrations of the pervasive nature of hierarchy and status-based inequality in day-to-day living in which a socially adept member of society must be well versed.

## Caste societies

Comparisons are often drawn between caste and class societies. These comparisons sometimes draw attention to the apparent similarities of the structured system of groups and the fixed relationships between constituent groups. However, it is misleading to link the two systems in this way since to do so is to focus upon structure at the cost of overlooking culture. Class inequality is based on economic criteria and culturally it is open to an individual to achieve their own class position. Individual class mobility is possible in class systems, and indeed this is the ethos of most industrial class systems in the contemporary world. Caste systems are based on religious and ritual criteria. Castes cannot be understood in secular terms of inferiority and superiority for the principle that ranks the parts in the whole is religious (Dumont, 1970). In Hindu India there are four categories (varnas) which are distinguished from one another by degrees of **ritual** purity (p. 214) as established in the Sanskrit texts. These varnas are: Brahmins, who are the priests and scholars; Kshatriyas, who are the rulers, the warriors and the landowners; Vaisyas, who are the entrepreneurial middle classes; Sudras, who are the cultivators, workers and traders. The Harijans, or untouchables, perform the most menial tasks. In theory they lie outside the caste system because they are ritually impure. Although these broad varnas are associated with occupation, in practice within a village there will be a number of occupations associated with a particular varna, so although the system is clear and unambiguous in principle, empirically there may be variety and complexity.

A person's caste membership is ascribed; this ascription is given religiously and is dependent upon the individual's conduct in their past life. Reincarnation is a central doctrine of Hindu belief, so to be given a favourable caste position one must lead a good life according to caste values and conventions, and fulfill caste expectations. If one fails to meet caste expecta-

tions then in reincarnation one will come back as a member of a lower caste or even in non-human form. The insistence upon living according to caste expectations places great value on maintaining caste boundaries, since contact with lower castes may be polluting and one may only carry out those tasks that are fit for one's own caste. The consequence of this is that there is a high degree of social segregation between castes but, of necessity, there is a high degree of economic interdependence as castes rely on others to perform tasks for them which they themselves are forbidden to carry out.

An important aspect of the maintenance of group boundaries is that marriage is endogamous, that is, individuals must marry within their own caste. This is an important difference from class societies where marriage is not formally circumscribed between classes, and can be an acceptable means of achieving social mobility.

The variety of occupational ranking and the diversity within villages means that in practice the significant groupings of caste in day-to-day relationships are the *jati*, endogamous groups of kin who are associated with certain occupations. These local subgroups of caste often compete with one another for ranking in the caste system and it is not unusual for a local *jati* to seek to improve their caste ranking by adopting the manner and practices of a higher-ranking group. It may take time for these aspirations to be met and their claims to be realised but movement is possible within the caste system and boundaries are more permeable than might at first seem possible. However it would be a mistake to assume that the possibility of mobility raises again the possibility of comparison with class systems. The mobility issue in the caste system is that the claim of the *jati*, the whole group, must be recognised, not just the claim of a single individual. Adrian Meyer (1960) observed that in one village in South India which he studied there were 23 castes which grouped themselves according to the use of the same smoking pipe, the provision of ordinary food for common meals and the provision of food for feasts. The higher castes in the village would share the pipe with almost all castes except four; between 12 and 16 castes would smoke together, although in some cases a different cloth must be placed between the pipe and the lips of the smoker. Meyer writes that castes that enjoyed power in the village were not fussy about what they ate and with whom they ate. It was the middle range of castes who were very fussy so that if, for example, they were invited to a feast by a more powerful group, they would insist on having their food served raw and carrying it home to cook. The untouchables – the outcasts – are literally outside the caste system altogether. Caste discrimination is not allowed in modern India, but in practice the diversity of groupings and the complexity of relationships make such a ruling difficult to enforce. There are other examples of religious ranking and hierarchies that you may wish to explore, for example Drid Williams' (1975) study of Christian nuns where she found that for nuns what mattered and what came first was the issue of nearness or distance from God. The hierarchies of the convent were hierarchies of spirituality, not power.

## 3.3 Legitimating inequality

Whenever the topic of inequality is addressed, the question that sooner or later must be asked is: why do people allow such manifest inequalities, disadvantages and injustices to remain as an acceptable part of their lives? Weber's answer is that people believe in certain legitimate forms of authority – an ordering of the world which they accept as 'right', as justifiable and reasonable. Three bases of legitimate authority are identified: *traditional* ('accept this, because it is what our people have always done'), *charismatic* ('accept this, because of the leader or prophet's exceptional powers which can transform your life'), or *legal-rational* ('accept this, because this is what is specified in the laws and rules governing our society'). These forms of legitimacy show how cultural power is institutionalised and given moral grounding. They provide the bases on which people may tolerate inequality and subordination, if not actually embrace it. A somewhat different range of solutions to this problem gives more explicit attention to the cultural dimension. We consider next: Gramsci on hegemony; the Frankfurt School's development of the theory of ideology; and Bourdieu's theory of the habitus.

## Ideology as common sense: hegemony

One development of Marx's thinking about ideology which has proved influential and productive in cultural studies is the concept of **hegemony** (p. 73), advanced by the Italian Marxist Antonio **Gramsci** (1891–1937) (p. 38). He wanted to explain how, despite manifest evidence of inequality, capitalist ruling classes continue to rule. Only part of the explanation, Gramsci believed, was due to ruling-class control of the means of coercion in society (the military and police). Underlying repressive state power lay hegemony, 'a special kind of power – the power to frame alternatives and contain opportunities, *to win and shape consent*, so that the granting of legitimacy to the dominant classes appears not only ' "spontaneous" but natural and normal' (Clarke *et al.*, 1976: 38). Hegemony is about what passes as the common-sensical, unquestioned backdrop of reflection on the workings of society. Consequently, the terrain on which hegemony 'is won or lost is the terrain of superstructures'. The central institutions of capitalist society – its courts and schools, its churches and mass media – are framed by ideas and beliefs that promote ruling-class interests. The pervasiveness of hegemony is described by writers from the Birmingham School thus:

> A hegemonic cultural order tries to *frame* all competing definitions of the world within its *range*. It provides the horizon of thought and action within which conflicts are fought through, appropriated (i.e. experienced), obscured (i.e. concealed as 'national interest' which should unite all conflicting parties) or contained (i.e. settled to the profit of the ruling class). A hegemonic order prescribes, not the specific content of ideas, but the *limits* within which ideas and conflicts move and are resolved.
>
> (Clarke *et al.*, 1976: 39)

The notion of hegemony is related to the concept of ideology but can be distinguished from it:

> Hegemony works through ideology, but it does not consist of false ideas, perceptions, definitions. It works *primarily* by inserting the subordinate class into the key institutions and structures which

## Defining concept 3.2

### Hegemony

The concept of hegemony is used as a way of thinking through the relationships between culture and **power** (p. 64). It was developed within the work of the Italian activist and Marxist theorist **Antonio Gramsci** (p. 38). His concern was to understand how social groups organise their rule and, more pressingly for him, why there had been no proletarian revolution. His conclusion was that rule involves both domination (the coercive use or threat of force via the military and the police) and hegemony (the organisation of consent based upon establishing the legitimacy of leadership and developing shared ideas, values, beliefs and meanings – a shared culture). Rule for Gramsci was hegemony armoured with coercion (Gramsci, 1971; see also Williams, 1977, Bennett *et al.*, 1981, and Jones, 2006).

In his theoretical and political work Gramsci's aim was to show how this consent (hegemony) had two characteristics. First, that it was class based and class biased. He wanted to show that culture is saturated with class power. As 'hegemony', shared values, shared meanings and shared beliefs are seen to act in the interests of the dominant (or hegemonic) class. The examples that Gramsci uses are ideas like religion in Italy and Fordism in America which promote certain values and forms of conduct over others, e.g. the work ethic. He connects both with the economic and political development of class-divided societies. Second, hegemony does not just happen; it is something that has to be organised. This also carries the positive political message that the situation can be altered. In many way this goes beyond **Marxist** (p. 65)

theories of **ideology** (p. 35). It rejects the notion that ideas are firmly rooted in class positions and sees them as 'material forces' which can organise groups, shape terrains of encounter and debate, and define positions to be attacked or defended. It also has a rather deeper notion of culture and meaning which sees them as basic to the formation of all social relations rather than as something 'added on', the icing on the economic cake. Here classes are defined as much culturally as economically.

There are several problems that must be noted. First, just as for ideology, Gramsci's concentration on class makes the concept of hegemony problematic. Any suggestion that people have singular **identities** (p. 142) and interests and that there is a singular political project is not useful when trying to deal with the multiplicity of interrelated identities and power relations within which we all live. These singular class identities also carry with them the unhelpful notion of 'false consciousness'. The question is whether we can extend the term to use it to talk about race, gender and sexuality. Second, the tendency to use the notion of 'hegemony' to imply the existence of one dominant, totalising culture of power must be avoided. Gramsci certainly did not mean the concept to be a rigid, static, uniform and abstract one. Partly, this means talking about counter-hegemonies and a whole series of competing alternative hegemonies. It also means recognising that hegemonies are constructed: they are forms of rule that social groups try to put together. We might think of them as ongoing 'projects' of legitimating leadership and negotiating consent through a whole series

of channels. Here is Gramsci on American Fordism:

> Recall here the experiments conducted by Ford and the economies made by his firm through direct management of transport and distribution of the product. These economies affected production costs and permitted higher wages and lower selling prices. Since these preliminary conditions existed, already rendered rational by historical evolution, it was relatively easy to rationalise production and labour by a skilful combination of force (destruction of working-class trade unionism on a territorial basis) and persuasion (high wages, various social benefits, extremely subtle ideological and political propaganda) and thus succeed in making the whole life of the nation revolve around production. Hegemony here is born in the factory and requires for its exercise only a minute quantity of professional political and ideological intermediaries.
>
> (Gramsci, 1971: 285)

These 'projects' are about the organisation of ruling groups, the creation of alliances ('hegemonic blocs') and the forging of collective identities (perhaps via religion, politics or culture). They are also about the organisation of power-laden relations with others in order to create a managed consent. This is all to be understood as a continual process with a whole variety of different social groups involved. In order to understand this we can use another, related Gramscian term: 'war of manoeuvre'. This means seeing society as both a real and an ideological battlefield

## Defining concept 3.2 (continued)

where everyone is trying to establish what side they are on, who are enemies, who are allies, what position they are in, what the terrain looks like, how the battle is progressing, and what weapons they should use. It is a constant ongoing struggle within which ideas, beliefs, values and meanings are among the weapons. However, what is important is not any

innate characteristics of these weapons but whether they are effectively deployed. This sense of hegemony as a process of active organisation is a useful one which is not restricted to understanding class relations.

### Further reading

Gramsci, A. (1971) *Selections from the Prison Notebooks*, London: Lawrence & Wishart.

Jones, S. (2006) *Antonio Gramsci*, London: Routledge

Williams, R. (1977) *Marxism and Literature*, Oxford: Oxford University Press.

support the power and social authority of the dominant order. It is, above all, in these structures and relations that a subordinate class *lives its subordination*.

(Clarke *et al.*, 1976: 39)

Gramsci believed that capitalism could not be overcome until the working class developed its own counter-hegemony which successfully challenged the existing ruling-class cultural hegemony.

Existing power relations and inequalities are thus stabilised through cultural hegemony. The concept has been influential in cultural studies since the 1970s because it offered a more complex analysis of ruling-class domination than older models of ideological domination. The Birmingham School linked the concept of hegemony to Althusser's notion of ISAs (ideological state apparatuses – schools, churches, media, etc., which support state ideology) to present a more complex analysis of how class domination worked. Hegemony emphasises that the ruling class was itself composed of different fractions, that class rule also required the winning of the consent of the subordinate class, and that it facilitated the empirical exploration of the institutions through which cultural hegemony works such as youth subcultures (Hall and Jefferson, 1976), schools (Willis, 1978) and broadcast news (Glasgow University Media Group, 1976). Importantly, the notion of hegemony is amenable to historical analysis since it is not a 'given' of any particular class or organisation but is something that has to be worked for and sustained. So it can be argued, for

example, that hegemonic cultural domination was a more significant source of working-class subordination in Britain in the 1950s than in the 1930s. That stabilisation was obtained in the 1930s by market effects (unemployment as an instrument of labour discipline), whereas in the prosperous 1950s working-class consent was obtained through the hegemonic domination of an ideology of affluence.

## Ideology as incorporation: the Frankfurt School

Members of the **Frankfurt School** (p. 75), in particular Theodor Adorno and Max Horkheimer (in *Dialectic of Enlightenment*, 1972) developed an analysis of the part played by the superstructure in accounting for the failure of the revolutionary social change that Marx had predicted. They focused on the role played by mass culture, or what they preferred to call the 'culture industry' (to distance themselves from the – erroneous – idea that mass culture is a spontaneously erupting popular culture) in securing the incorporation of the working class into capitalist society.

Through radio, TV, movies and forms of popular music like jazz, the expanding culture industries were disseminating ruling-class ideologies with greater effectiveness than Marx could have envisaged. The further development of consumer society in the twentieth century powerfully aided the process of working-class incorporation by promoting new myths of classlessness, and wedded the working class even more tightly to acquisitive and property-owning beliefs. Even oppositional and critical forms of culture can be marketed (consider Andy Warhol, the Sex Pistols, Damian Hirst). The development of the culture industries, one part of the superstructure, seemed destined to subvert the social changes that Marx saw as originating in society's material base. Other Frankfurt School theorists, notably Marcuse, condemned the 'one-dimensionality' of the society that the culture industries were shaping with increasing success. Unfortunately, the force of the Frankfurt School's critique was weakened by their apparently elitist dismissal of forms of popular culture.

The celebrated – some might say notorious – example of the Frankfurt School's dismissive approach to popular culture is Theodor Adorno's (1903–69) analysis of popular music. Writing in the late 1930s and early 1940s Adorno proposed that the industrialisation of musical production and the commercialisation of musical consumption had a baleful influence on musical form. Popular music had become standardised: 'all aspects of musical form – Adorno instances overall structure (the thirty-two-bar chorus), melodic range, song-types and harmonic progressions – depend upon pre-existing formulae and norms, which have the status

## Key influence 3.3

### The Frankfurt School

The Frankfurt School describes the social and cultural theorists who worked for, or were connected with, the Frankfurt Institute for Social Research. Their method, known as 'critical theory', has influenced the study of mass culture and elements of feminist, postmodernist and post-colonial theory.

The Institute was founded in 1923. At its inception, it was very much a product of the cultural freedom and political struggles of the German Weimar Republic (1918–33). Key members of the Institute were Max Horkheimer, Theodor Adorno and Herbert Marcuse. **Walter Benjamin** (p. 274) was an important associate. Along with **Gramsci**'s (p. 38) writings, critical theory forms the main body of Western (as opposed to Soviet-influenced) **Marxism** (p. 65). Influenced by the ideas of **Marx** (p. 66) and Freud, it resists systematic, universal explanations of cultural and social phenomena. In 1933 the Nazis' rise to power forced the Institute into exile in Germany. Many of the members were Jewish and faced death if they stayed. Horkheimer, Adorno and Ernst Bloch all went to

the USA. Post-Weimar, the School began its critiques of the Fascist system from which they fled and the new experience of North American mass culture: for example, Adorno's well-known critique of popular music. This culminated in Adorno and Horkheimer's best-known work, *The Dialectic of the Enlightenment* (1972, orig. 1944) which contains seminal chapters on the origins of **modernity** (p. 295), mass culture and anti-Semitism. After the war, the Institute returned to Germany. Adorno contributed works of philosophy, *Negative Dialectics* (1973) and *Aesthetic Theory* (1984). Hannah Arendt continued the critique of authoritarian regimes in *The Origins of Totalitarianism* (1958). Ernst Bloch and Herbert Marcuse explored the utopian dimension of critical theory in *The Principle of Hope* (1986, orig. 1959) and *Eros and Civilization* (1955). The political events of the 1960s led to a revival of interest in the School's work. Its recognised heir is Jürgen Habermas. True to its impulse, in his *The Philosophical Discourse of Modernity* (1987), he criticises both members

of the School and poststructuralist thought.

The key to understanding critical theory is the recognition that it is not a unified body of thought. Rather, it defines itself 'negatively' against other theoretical systems. Each strand criticises and debates in a polemical style. Each thinker is best understood in his or her relation to other thinkers. For example, Adorno's apparent resistance to utopian solutions is best understood in relation to the more overt utopianism of Bloch and Benjamin. It is this tradition of critique and debate that is the School's most important legacy.

### Further reading

Crossley, N (2005) *Key Concepts in Critical Social Theory*, London: Sage

Jay, M. (1996) *The Dialectical Imagination: A History of the Frankfurt School and the Institute of Social Research 1923–1950*, California: University of California Press.

Held, D. (1980) *Introduction to Critical Theory*, London: Hutchinson.

virtually of rules, are familiar to listeners and hence are entirely predictable' (Middleton, 1990: 45). Popular music has become standardised into particular types (country & western, heavy metal, pop, etc.) and within each type particular formulas develop. Adorno contrasted popular with 'serious' music which was not standardised but distinctive and original. Beethoven's work was Adorno's exemplar of serious music. Not only were popular and serious music different in form, they encouraged different responses from listeners. Serious music made challenging demands on the listener while popular music made little – popular music had become just another stultifying element of mass culture. Adorno maintained that:

> Music for entertainment … seems to complement the reduction of people to silence, the dying out of speech as expression, the inability to communicate at all. It inhabits the pockets of silence that develop between people moulded by anxiety, work and undemanding docility. … It is perceived purely as background. If nobody can any longer speak, then certainly nobody can any longer listen. … Today … [the] power of the banal extends over the whole society.
>
> (Adorno, quoted in Middleton, 1990: 34)

Adorno's searing critique of popular music places it alongside film, cheap holidays and comic books as a method of incorporating the working class. But it is an analysis that has a number of flaws (see Longhurst, 2007a: 6–11) The popular/serious distinction introduces a value judgement before the analysis has begun. The scope of Adorno's theory (all popular music under capitalism) seems far too broad and Adorno does not appear to appreciate how that scope might be constrained by his own social and historical location. Some types of music (jazz, blues, rap) might have non-standard structures or might express resistance to dominant ideologies. The development of new musical technologies might also work against the tendencies that Adorno noted in popular music. Thus critics suggest that the claims of the theory exceed what can be reasonably sustained. As a critique of Tin Pan Alley in the 1930s and 1940s Adorno made some sense, but the application of his ideas to the proliferation of popular musical styles since then tells only a small part of the story.

The contribution of the Frankfurt School was to indicate the enormous expansion of the culture industries and their increasing influence in modern capitalism. Leo Lowenthal (1961) captured this change well in his study of the biographical articles appearing in popular US magazines between 1890 and 1940. He found that in the earlier period it was predominantly 'captains of industry and finance' who were profiled. This gave way in the later period to a preponderance of interviews with movie stars and singers. There had been a shift from the 'idols of production' to the 'idols of consumption' – the culture's heroes were now firmly located in superstructural occupations, not the material base. Unlike the economism of earlier Marxian traditions, the Frankfurt School attributes a significant role to the domain of culture in analysing relations of culture and power.

## Habitus

The work of Pierre Bourdieu (Robbins, 1991, 1999) stresses the learned, unquestioned, taken-for-granted aspect of cultural behaviour. He puts forward the notion of **habitus**, the cultural framework wherein and whereby the habitual aspects of everyday social thought and action operate. People's perceptions, thoughts, tastes and so forth are shaped by their habitus. These principles are symbolically mediated in action and are learned through experience. However, the power of the dominant classes ensures that their cultural habitus is preferred over others. Schooling is a process in which dominant class power works symbolically to legitimate the kinds of accomplishment that will count as knowledgeable and worthy and to relegate features of the habitus of working-class pupils as evidence of failure. In effect, one cultural system of **symbolism** (p. 214) and meaning is imposed on that of another social group – a process termed 'symbolic violence' (Bourdieu and Passeron, 1990).

Bourdieu is especially interested in the ways in which particular groups (classes) in society mark their identity, the symbolic ways in which they express values and seek to maintain boundaries between themselves and other groups. He describes this as the process of 'distinction' (Bourdieu, 1984). Again there is a stress that culture is deceptive. While novelty and creativity is acknowledged, the emphasis lies on the ways in which what is learned and practised is an affirmation of an existing set of hierarchically organised systems of relations. Bourdieu's position has been described thus:

> To a very large extent we do not choose our identity. We receive the cultural identity which has been handed down to us from previous generations. . . . We adhere to groups, whether clubs or political or religious organisations, and we adopt the identifying images of social groups, whether in hair-style or clothing, so as to confirm our social identity. For the same reason, we take steps to distinguish ourselves from those who belong to different groups. Our tastes and our lifestyles have no intrinsic value but serve to maintain the coherence of the group to which we belong.
>
> (Robbins, 1991: 174)

Bourdieu's focus on distinctions between groups rather than on the whole system of which they are a constitutive part contrasts with the Marxian and the dominant ideology approach. Bourdieu sees cultural striving for individual expression as a sham but in many ways he has a more organic approach to the issue of inequality than Marx, Gramsci or the Frankfurt School.

These debates around hegemony, incorporation and habitus show how misleading it is to think of culture as a mere superstructural 'effect' determined by the material base. In the views of the theorists reviewed in this section, culture plays a part in legitimising and naturalising many forms of inequality. The extent to which dominant ideologies are themselves guarantors of social order has been questioned by some sociologists. Abercrombie et al. (1980) propose that the dominant ideology only brings coherence to the dominant class, not to the society as a whole. Subordinate classes are incorporated by political and economic control, not ideological dominance. A different approach is taken by other theorists who argue that the cultural dimension is a significant source of inequality. We next consider a selection of studies that examine this idea.

# 3.4 Culture and the production and reproduction of inequality

In this section we explore the relevance of the explanations of inequality discussed above by means of a review of some cultural manifestations of inequality. We shall look at studies that focus on the key variables of class, ethnicity, gender and age as sources of cultural inequality.

## Class

The notion that cultural differences follow class lines has a long history. Weber's concept of status includes the notion of style of life and opens the way for considering overlaps and disparities between class and status. The early classics of cultural studies, notably Hoggart (1958) and Thompson (1968) were very much concerned with the shaping, characteristics and development of working-class culture. In more recent work on youth subcultures the notion of class cultures is also prominent (see Chapter 9). Cultural commentary has long addressed the lifestyles of the rich as well as the poor. Those living at the extremes of society, it is sometimes felt, are perhaps very different in their ways of life from the broad mass in the middle. In this section the issue of class, culture and inequality is approached by means of a survey of explanations of the lifestyles of the poor: we shall consider in turn the culture of poverty thesis, the cycle of deprivation theory and the putative emergence of an underclass.

The culture of poverty thesis was popularised in the 1950s and 1960s by the American anthropologist Oscar Lewis's studies of the poor in Mexico, Puerto Rica and the USA. He sought to understand how it was that poverty seemed to reproduce itself across generations: how poor people appeared to produce more poor people. His explanation concentrated on the distinctive cultural features shared by the so-called undeserving or disreputable poor. Lewis (1961, 1966) proposes that the poor have a distinctive subcultural lifestyle which, like any culture, is a design for living that provides a structure and rationale enabling the poor to go on with their lives. Controversially, he suggests that this way of life is passed down across the generations through the medium of the family. At the centre of this theory is the identification of about seventy traits said to characterise the culture of poverty. They include the following:

➤ The poor are not integrated into the major institutions of the society and remain fearful of them.

➤ There is a low level of community organisation or identification with place in slum neighbourhoods.

➤ Families display the following features:

– absence of a lengthy childhood phase of the life-cycle

– early initiation into sex

– free unions or consensual marriages

– high incidence of abandoned wives and children

– female-centred households

– predisposition to authoritarianism and frequent use of violence as a way of resolving conflict

– competition for household maternal affection

– sibling rivalry.

## Key influence 3.4

### Richard Hoggart (1918–)

Best known for his singular 1957 study of working-class culture, *The Uses of Literacy* was written when he worked in adult education at the University of Hull. Subtitled 'aspects of working-class life with special reference to publications and entertainments', the book focuses on how working-class culture has been affected by mass publications in the decades leading up to the mid-century. The impact of *Uses* stems from its literary critic's dissection of popular publications by an author who imaginatively draws upon his experiences of being brought up as an orphan in the Chapeltown and Hunslet working-class districts of Leeds. '*Uses*' portrays northern working-class life with a striking evocativeness, particularity and vividness. It also marks a significant intervention into debates about the cultural value of the mass media and emergent forms of popular culture.

*The Uses of Literacy* contains two parts. The first examines the remains of an 'older order' of working-class life, a collection of cultural attitudes and beliefs. Hoggart describes the binding influences of home, parents and neighbourhood; the organisation of the world into 'us' and 'them'; the

focus on the personal and the concrete rather than the general and the abstract; the attractions of the immediate, the present and the cheerful. The second part of *Uses* considers some of the ways in which the old order is 'yielding place to the new'. Hoggart critiques the personalisation, oversimplification and pandering to base motives of much popular journalism and questions the real worth of 'spicy' magazines and sex-and-violence novels. (In places Hoggart's critique seems dated, as in his denunciation of the 'juke-box boys who while away their evenings in milk-bars'.) His general argument is that the older culture 'of the people' is under siege from a 'new mass culture' that 'is in some important ways less healthy than the often crude culture it is replacing' (*Uses*, 1958: 24). While *The Uses of Literacy* heralds a new sensitivity to the nuances of working-class culture in literary and ethnographic terms, it also participates in an older tradition of judging its worth. In *Uses*, as in much of his writing, Hoggart displays a sharp appreciation of the subtleties of everyday language as a finely culturally differentiated communicative medium.

Hoggart's other principal contribution to cultural studies was to found the **Centre for Contemporary Cultural Studies** (p. 241) in 1964 shortly after he became Professor of English at the University of Birmingham (**Stuart Hall** (p. 55) was the Centre's first research fellow). He became an assistant director-general of UNESCO in 1970, gave the Reith Lectures in 1971 (published as *Only Connect*, 1972) and later played a leading role in the British Arts Council. His long career as a writer, teacher and public servant is reviewed in three absorbing volumes of autobiography.

### Further reading

Hoggart, R. (1988) *A Local Habitation*, London: Chatto & Windus.

Hoggart, R. (1990) *A Sort of Clowning*, London: Chatto & Windus.

Hoggart, R. (1992) *An Imagined Life*, London: Chatto & Windus.

Hoggart, R (2006) *Mass Media in a Mass Society: Myth and Reality*, London: Continuum International Publishing Group Ltd.

Lewis argues that the culture of poverty only emerges in specific historical and social contexts, namely the early free enterprise phase of class-stratified individualistic capitalist society. Excluded are pre-literate societies where poverty is no bar to social integration and the lower castes of India (because caste membership is a source of integration). The culture of poverty is regarded as a creative, adaptive response on the part of the poor to their material deprivation. An implication of the culture of poverty thesis is that the poor will always be with us as long as their culture is.

The theory has been roundly criticised (see Valentine, 1968). Although Lewis recognises the fundamentally material origins of poverty, he does not attempt to assess the relative importance of social and economic compared to cultural factors. He assumes that the culture of poverty will override other cultural traditions, such as those that new immigrants bring with them. He agrees that not all the poor participate in the culture of poverty but he fails to specify fully the criteria of inclusion. It seems plausible that chronically poor people will lead distinctive styles of life, but these cannot be explained in purely cultural terms.

This was also the conclusion arrived at by social scientists in the 1970s charged with investigating the 'cycle

of deprivation'. The idea came to public attention in a speech made by Sir Keith Joseph, the Secretary of State for Social Services, in 1972. He asked, 'Why is it that, in spite of long periods of full employment and relative prosperity and the improvement in community services since the Second World War, deprivation and problems of maladjustment so conspicuously persist?' His reply was to posit a 'cycle of deprivation' (see Figure 3.5).

In Sir Keith's view, parents who were themselves deprived in one or more ways in childhood went on to become the parents of another generation of deprived children. This political initiative was recast in social scientific terms as an investigation of the intergenerational continuities in 'disadvantage', a more inclusive term than deprivation. It also conceded that factors other than family and culture might cause disadvantage, such as social group membership, ethnic discrimination or residence in a particular locality. The outcome of this research was to build a more comprehensive picture of the multiple disadvantages faced especially by members of the lowest social classes (see Rutter and Madge, 1976).

Blaming the poor for their circumstances is still a popular activity for cultural commentators. It some-

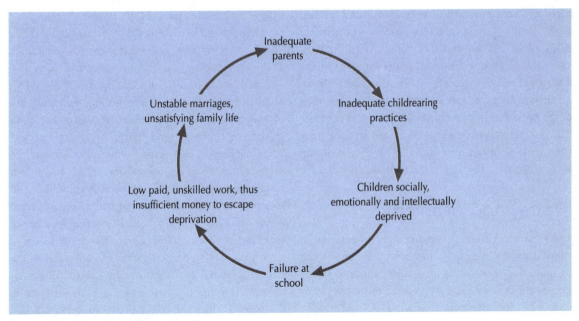

**Figure 3.5** The cycle of deprivation.

times surfaces in debates about the 'underclass'. Beginning with Marx's comments about the lumpen proletariat, class analysts have long recognised the existence of a class beneath the established working class. Attempts have been made to identify this class in structural terms, that is, in terms of the conditions of life encountered by people in particular circumstances. For example, in the UK the underclass is often felt to comprise groups such as the long-term unemployed, single-parent families and elderly pensioners. In the USA it is often associated with poor black residents of inner-city ghettos. Structural explanations of the underclass are usually advanced by academic sociologists who emphasise that these groups of people have most to lose from processes of continuous industrial restructuring and its impact on the patterning of work. But other commentators, notably the influential New Right theorist Charles Murray, have seen this phenomenon in primarily cultural (and by extension highly moralistic) terms. Murray focuses on the significance of illegitimacy, marital breakdown, inadequate patterns of childrearing and criminality among the poor (for a review of the debates about the underclass in the USA see Wilson, 1993; for the UK, see Lister, 1996). Correspondingly, the solutions advanced for the problems of the underclass differ. Structural explanations emphasise that underclass problems are rooted in the social and economic structures of societies. Culturalist accounts of the underclass seek changes to the moral fabric of individuals and their family circumstances. The debate between these two understandings of the underclass reruns elements of a much older cultural distinction between the 'deserving' and 'undeserving poor'. An assertion of cultural difference is a response that is apparently only acceptable in the first case. (See Skeggs, 1997 for a discussion of the relationship between gender, class and 'respectability'.)

## 'Race' and ethnicity

The term 'race' is often placed in inverted commas in cultural studies to signal its historical dubiousness and its questionable status as an analytic concept. In the nineteenth century there were numerous attempts by European investigators to classify people according to racial groups ('white', 'yellow', 'black') and ascribe

unchanging characteristics to them. These attempts to legitimate sets of stable racial differences scientifically are now widely regarded as spurious (Miles, 1989). However, race is an everyday concept that people routinely employ to categorise themselves and others.

Irrespective of the scientific utility of the term, race is widely believed to serve as a potent marker of cultural difference. These differences, whether they are believed to be grounded in culture or biology, are often manifest in expressions of racism, the discrimination against others on the basis of their membership of a perceived 'racial' group. Racism, when it is practised by an individual towards another person, is often termed 'racial prejudice'. However, racism can also take institutional form, as when a political policy takes it for granted that immigration is a problem, or when schools systematically understate the contribution of ethnic minorities to the development of art and science and teach history that fosters a negative perception of Africa or Asia. Institutional racism may be more deeply taken for granted and thus harder to dislodge than a prejudicial attitude.

Sometimes the terms 'ethnicity' and 'ethnic groups' are employed in an attempt to put some distance between the historically racist implications of 'race' and to emphasise that it is cultural and not biological difference that is the key distinction. Writers within cultural studies have tended to avoid the anodyne terminology of 'ethnicity' and headed straight for the freighted term 'race' in an attempt to grasp the real-world significances of this dimension of cultural difference and inequality. One early study in this tradition, by Hall *et al.* (1978), examined the moral panic surrounding the emergence of 'mugging' as a social problem. 'Mugging' was not a legal term ('robbery' and 'larceny from the person' being the English legal terms) but it quickly came into popular and media discourse from 1972. The category was imported from the USA and, translated into British society, it came to stand for a particular kind of perpetrator – a young, black male, usually acting with one or more accomplices. Hall *et al.* trace the development of a moral panic that bears some resemblances in form to the earlier moral panics surrounding 1960s youth subcultures (see the discussion of mods and rockers in Chapter 9). The myth of the black mugger condensed many exaggerated fears about youth, crime and personal safety, race and immigration. Hall *et al.* see mugging as an 'ideological conductor' of the 'crisis of hegemony of early 1970s Britain'. They show how the moral panic over mugging, a social constructed deviant behaviour, nevertheless articulated deeper concerns about British society. The exaggerated response to the 'problem' of mugging is indicative of a drift towards more authoritarian state interventions.

The theme of racial issues sparking a hegemonic crisis in Britain where established understandings about the ordering of ethnic groups come to be challenged is taken up in *The Empire Strikes Back* (Centre for Contemporary Cultural Studies, 1982). This is the work of seven members of the Birmingham centre who set out to analyse race and racism during the 1970s from a vantage committed to black resistance. They emphasise the need to locate racism not in individual psyches but in large-scale social processes. They draw particular attention to the change in Britain's international position since the end of the Second World War. They suggest that the prominence of 'race' as an issue in the 1970s is connected to the decline of Britain's position as a major trading nation. It is in the context of these changes that immigration policies, ethnic bases of competition in housing and labour markets, etc., must be set. In the crisis of hegemony facing British capitalism, the **Centre for Contemporary Cultural Studies** (CCCS) (p. 241) collective maintains, the British state is moving in authoritarian directions (which were shortly to become even more pronounced as Thatcherism became established). At the level of lived experience this issues forth in forms of popular authoritarianism of which racism is the most conspicuous example. Racism, then, cannot be understood as a simple ideological phenomenon. To appreciate its force requires a detailed and specific analysis of changes in the British state and Britain's dominant and working classes.

*The Empire Strikes Back* sparked a good deal of controversy when it appeared, not least because of its criticisms of the 'race relations industry' which they saw as just one more instrument of control over black working-class communities. They are especially critical of those studies that account for black disadvantage in terms of fractured nuclear families that fail to provide adequate material and emotional support to children.

Such studies 'pathologise' black subcultures. The CCCS collective are hesistant about offering recommendations beyond a general endorsement of black **resistance** (p. 170). In the analysis of cultural forms, this emphasis on a complex Marxism in which close historical analysis of political and economic circumstances is combined with a commitment to black struggles has been taken forward most notably in the work of **Paul Gilroy** (p. 131).

Another part of the larger picture in which 'race' and racism is located is the history and consequences of **colonialism** (p. 143). Many influential conceptions of racial difference have their origin in the colonial encounters of European powers with the societies that they sought to dominate. Cultural analysts such as **Edward Said** (p. 115) Gayatri Spivak, and Frantz Fanon have focused on colonial texts to consider what they tell us about oppressor and oppressed. Said's (1978) monumental study, *Orientalism* (p. 115) shows how European writing, from the nineteenth century onward, constructed a conception of the 'Orient' (the Middle East in particular) as exotic, glamorous and dangerous. This fictional, simplified framework nevertheless served to act as a potent cultural grid through which the cultures of the East were apprehended. Gayatri Spivak (1987) is more concerned with issues of power and representation. In a world dominated by Western discourses, how can the 'subaltern' status of Third World voices achieve parity in dialogue with those of the West? The work of Frantz Fanon (1968) is concerned with language as an index of power, and the objectification of the black body through literary and other representations. Said, Spivak and Fanon deepen our understanding of racial difference by using the tools of literary and cultural analysis to problematise the representations of the 'other' contained in Western texts

## Gender

Discussions about relationships between men and women mirror many of the arguments that have been discussed above. It is often remarked that, whatever the nature and type of relationships between men and women in whatever part of the world, there is inequality, men are the dominant sex and are regarded as superior to women. It is suggested that there is a

## Defining concept 3.3

### Feminism

Feminism describes both the broad movement that has campaigned against the political and social inequalities between men and women and the school of academic criticism that takes gender inequality as its object of study. Feminists all critique the subordination of women to men, but they differ widely in their strategies for empowering women. Feminist accounts of the role of culture in gender inequality have been central to the development of cultural studies.

A crude periodisation of feminism might identify three phases: first-wave, second-wave and postmodern feminism. First-wave feminism describes the women's movement of the late nineteenth and early twentieth century. While it contained many different political strands, first-wave feminists generally accepted a fundamental, natural difference between men and women, but argued for their political equality. The best-known campaign of first-wave feminism was for women's suffrage. Second-wave feminism describes the women's movement from the 1960s on. This period has seen an enormous growth in feminist scholarship, which has employed various forms of understanding inequality. An early concept used was patriarchy. This was originally an anthropological term which describes a social system in which older men are entitled to exercise socially sanctioned authority over other members of the household or kinship group, both women and younger men. However, this term has been criticised subsequently, because it does not discriminate between the different forms of inequality manifested in different cultures. An alternative concept, proposed by Gayle Rubin, was the sex/gender system. This makes use of an important distinction between sex and gender where sex describes biological or natural differences, while gender describes the social roles of masculinity and femininity. Rubin argued that different societies assign different kinds of roles based on biological differences. The object of feminist inquiry should then be the kinds of cultural expectations that these roles presume.

Research into gender identity has taken many different paths in the investigation of how gender is socially constructed. One influential strand has been poststructuralist, psychoanalytic feminism. This argues that gender identity is constructed through language. In Western culture, language is phallocentric, or male centred. Because they are excluded from full access to language, women are refused entrance to a masculine symbolic order. However, psychoanalytic accounts have been criticised for universalising male dominance. More recently, postmodernist feminism has queried the sex/gender distinction. Judith Butler has suggested that it is a mistake to assume that there is a foundational, natural sex upon which gender identity is constructed. Instead, she argues that sex itself is socially constructed. A useful metaphor is employed by Linda Nicholson, we use the body as a coat rack to hang our cultural assumptions about sexual differences. For example, women's bodies are soft, passive and yielding, men's are hard, active and forceful. Butler's argument usefully problematises the idea that sex comes first and that gender is somehow created from it. While no one argues that there are not physical differences between men and women, Butler directs the spotlight back onto the question of how culture interprets those differences. As white academic feminism has been challenged by the diverse strands of the women's movement worldwide, the question of cultural difference and the relationships between gender, 'race', sexuality and class have moved to centre-stage in feminist theory. However, there is a continuing and productive tension between this emphasis on difference and feminists' desire to assert a collective identity to combat the abiding social inequalities between men and women.

### Further reading

Haraway, D. (1991) 'Gender for Marxist dictionary', in D. Haraway, Simians, Cyborgs and Women: The Reinvention of Nature, London: Free Association Books.

Haraway, D. (2003) The Haraway Reader, London: Routledge

Nicholson, L. (1995) 'Interpreting gender', in L. Nicholson and S. Seidman (eds) Social Postmodernism, Cambridge: Cambridge University Press.

natural hierarchy between men and women, a natural inequality. Support for this inequality is often drawn from historical evidence and from comparison with the animal world (the science of ethology, popularised by the works of Desmond Morris). It seems that it is impossible to think about gender without thinking about hierarchy (Moore, 1993). One suggestion about the seemingly inevitable connection between male superiority and female inferiority is that this thinking is congruent with other patterns of thought in Western society, namely the hierarchical relation between nature and culture. Moore (1993), Ortner (1974) and Strathern (1981) have all drawn attention to the association of female with nature and male with culture; female with the private and the domestic and male with the public and the collectivity. They argue that, in societies where culture is seen as preferable and superior to nature and where the public always encompasses the private, then it is inevitable that gender relations will be apprehended in hierarchical terms.

The argument is similar to the discussion of caste and class above. It is necessary to understand that cultures may be organised differently and experienced differently from those in the West and that it is important not to fall into the trap of thinking 'that all societies struggle with the same givens of nature, so that all social formations appear equivalently and thus holistically organized to the same ends' (Strathern, 1988: 342–3). A general theme of women anthropologists writing about issues of gender and inequality (and some men, notably Ardener, 1974, and Errington and Gewertz, 1987) is that much of the writing on non-Western societies is formulated in terms of Western assumptions about persons and relationships; there is a Western folk model which sees social life in dichotomous terms and this is imposed onto the substance of other lives and other arrangements. In making this line of argument – namely that the dichotomies are a feature of anthropological discourse, not the social and symbolic systems of the societies studied by the anthropologist – the reasoning is similar to that made in discussions about writing culture. Errington and Gewertz (1987), who studied the Chambri people of Papua New Guinea (a people made famous by Margaret Mead and Reo Fortune as the Tchambuli), write that in her wish to explore variations in culture

and personality, Mead, paradoxically, underestimated the extent to which cultures differ from one another. In a complex argument they contrast Western views of persons as distinct and competent individuals with private subjective selves and unique dispositions with the Chambri view that persons are constituted by social relationships. Individuals are not bounded entities who possess certain characteristics as they are said to be in the West (and note the value-laden term 'possess' – denoting a materialist view of persons) but persons who share and who are part of others through their relationships and are multiply constituted (see also Strathern, 1988). Errington and Gewertz (1987) argue that women among the Chambri are very different from women in the Western world and gender concepts have a different meaning.

The caution against assuming universal patterns of superiority and inferiority has a validity beyond that of the discussion of gender and has particular importance for discussions about the ways in which people are multiply constituted in Western society through race, ethnicity, class, age and gender. All these are attributes of personhood and the task for the analyst is to see how these different attributes constitute the person rather than assuming that these categories of difference simply attach to the person (Strathern, 1988). The reflexive process with regard to Western ideas of personhood and gender has been taken further by some to question the distinction between sex and gender (Collier and Yanagisako, 1987; see also Chapter 8). Collier and Yanagisako take from Foucault (1984b) the idea that sex is an effect rather than an origin; just as it has been argued above that gender is the product of discursive practices, so also is sex.

> The notion of 'sex' made it possible to group together, in an artificial unity, anatomical elements, biological functions, conducts, sensations, and pleasures and it enabled one to make use of this fictitious unity as a causal principle, an omnipresent meaning: sex was thus able to function as a unique signifier and as a universal signifier.
>
> (Foucault, 1984b: 154)

This does not mean that anatomical differences are not noted but these are not necessarily the basis of a binary sex classification (Moore, 1993). Notwithstanding the suggestion that perhaps sexual differences are culturally constructed, there seems to be general agreement among commentators about the cultural constructs of gender in Western society (Strathern, 1988; Moore, 1993; Butler, 1990; Tcherkezoff, 1993).

Taking up the issues of knowledge and the power to impose particular knowledge constructs on society as a whole, which were considered earlier in this chapter, feminists have developed the idea of patriarchy. This is a male-dominated social system in which society is seen as male-dominated, identified or centred. The argument is that society is based on convention, a convention in which men are prominent – men have certain interests in the framing of cultural conventions which give them power and exclude women from power. Strathern (1988) states that women experience a double arbitrariness: the Western dichotomous model creates opposed categories so women are what men are not, and since it is men who decide who men are, then women are doubly excluded. These feminist arguments rest on the cultural conventions about the nature of persons in Western society, the idea of duality and dichotomy and the connectedness of these ideas to the domains of the individual and society and to men and women/male and female in Western society. Strathern argues that there is in Western society a social contract view of society – culture is collective – held in common and so individuals willingly subordinate themselves to it (Strathern, 1988). This masks the reality that culture is 'authored' – 'it is patriarchy that produces cultures' (Strathern, 1988: 323).

These views have also been given voice in discussions about women's participation in science (Harding, 1991), where it is said that the idea of woman the 'knower' is a contradiction in terms. Harding points to the male domination in scientific fields. The production of scientific knowledge tends to be the province of those who have male characteristics and since it is predominantly men who have male characteristics so women are excluded (Harding, 1991: 48). Dale Spender (1982), writing about women in education, makes a similar cultural argument: that women cannot have a voice as producers of art and knowledge because they are not men. Spender cites the marginalisation of many

women in the field of literature and women's rights, for example, Aphra Benn, Mary Wollstonecroft, Catherine Macauley (see also Chapter 6).

While feminism has served to refocus attention on the nature and sources of women's subordination it has also, obliquely, stimulated interest in the characteristics of masculinity and the sources of male domination. There is what is sometimes termed 'hegemonic masculinity' (Connell, 1987) (see also p. 218), the ideal form of being a man: a configuration of courage, physical strength and toughness that is endlessly paraded in the mass media (see also Chapter 8). One codification of the US version is offered by Brannon (1976):

➤ 'no sissy stuff' – the avoidance of all feminine behaviours and traits

➤ 'the big wheel' – the acquisition of success, status and breadwinning competence

➤ 'the sturdy oak' – strength, confidence and independence

➤ 'give 'em hell' – aggression, violence and daring

In recent times masculinity itself has, in some quarters at least, become another contested terrain. The pervasiveness of hegemonic masculinity has been empirically questioned and it is suggested that there are in fact multiple discourses of masculinity rather than a single ideal (Edley and Wetherall, 1996), a situation that has led some commentators to speak in the plural of 'masculinities' (Hearn, 1996). Masculinity or masculinities are undoubtedly real but whether the concept on its own has much efficacy in explaining the gendered basis of domination seems open to question.

## Age

Age and the ageing process are, like gender and the body (see Chapter 8), apparently natural processes. Yet it will come as no surprise that within this chapter, as in the book as a whole, the argument will be made that what seems straightforwardly natural is highly cultural and culturally specific, with the added twist that the cultural ordering locates age in the biological world. Culture naturalises age, as it also naturalises gender, race, ethnicity – all those aspects of human experience that seem to be rooted in biology. Age is a cultural construct symbolically located in a biological metaphor (Spencer, 1990). The apparently natural process of the person's passage from birth to death in chronological time is ordered, sometimes controlled, but always shaped by cultural ideas of what is appropriate and conventional behaviour at certain ages.

Age has different meanings among different peoples not only for the individual but for all those with whom the individual is associated; a change of status for an individual involves others in new roles and relationships. Also as with gender (see above), theorising about the significance of age must give regard to, and account for, the ways in which age is mediated by class, gender, race, ethnicity and all other culturally significant variables at particular moments and contexts. A small example to make the point is that most people who live in British society treat age as if it was a linear process in which one is born and one passes through measured time until one's death. However, there are those in British society who believe in reincarnation and so the ageing process is for them a circular and not a linear journey, and they look forward to a rebirth – equally for those who believe in the resurrection of the spirit and/or operate with a different sense of time than those who believe that death is the end of being.

In fact something that seems so taken for granted and unremarkable empirically turns out to be an important principle of social organisation and marker of social differentiation. It is arguable that age and gender are the most important shapers of social experience for individuals. For example, if we look at how people spend their leisure time we see that the type of leisure people engage in is related to their age. Research has shown that the range and frequency of participation in out-of-home leisure declines with age, so that 42 per cent of 16–24 year olds spend their free time mainly at home compared to 67 per cent of over 60 year olds (Martin and Mason, 1998: Roberts, 1999). It seems that in all societies people are treated differently on the basis of age. It is possible to speak of age roles, the clusters of expectations that accrue to certain chronological and structural age bands. Most societies have conventions about the age at which it is suitable for individuals to marry (this may be gendered), to engage in sexual relations, and in British society there are a set of age-determined laws regarding employment and retirement.

The significance of age is not just a matter for the individual; it is a relational matter touching on how one behaves to others. The ideas about the relationship are incorporated into social expectations, often into scientific, 'natural' ideas about how children should develop and how they should behave to others. The disciplines of child psychology and developmental psychology and the psychology of ageing rest on models of 'normal' (cultural) expectations. In the individual life course the experience and practice of age roles is common within the domestic life-cycle. Most people grow up in the company of others and learn the age-appropriate behaviour for their sex, class, race or ethnic group and according to scientific and medical knowledge.

Historical evidence shows that our ideas of age-appropriate behaviour have changed considerably in the recent past in Western society. Aries (1962) has written that the idea of childhood is a recent one, and Mayhew's (1968) survey of the London labouring classes in the middle of the nineteenth century showed clearly the class-based experience of childhood. Mayhew declared himself appalled by the lack of childhood for these children, noting how they looked older than their years and finding that children as young as six or seven years old were making a living for themselves independently on the streets of London. Reports in the contemporary world often speak of the high incidence of child labour in developing world countries where children are seen as a resource to make a contribution to household economies. Caldwell (1982) points out that the flow of resources from parents to children in affluent Western societies is unidirectional, whereas in developing world countries resources flow both ways when children start to make a contribution to the household.

In some societies the transition to new status roles based upon age is highly ritualised. Such highly ritualised movements are named rites of passage. The seminal work on rites of passage was carried out by van Gennep (1960) who established a common threefold pattern in such rites: the phase of separation (when the initiate leaves old associations and relationships); the liminal (limbo) phase; and the phase of incorporation into the new status. It is possible to identify several rites of passage in modern society. Weddings and funerals are both loosely associated with age but not necessarily so. There are a few rites of passage that are tightly linked to age and to major shifts in life courses. The commonest example in Western society is that of the bar mitzvah for young Jewish boys (and bat mitzvah for girls) which takes place around the age of thirteen when boys become ritually full adult members of the religious community. The best-known ceremonies of status change are to be found in African societies, for example among the Masai and the Hazda people. Young men, when they are initiated into the status of warriors, become the herders of cattle and serve in this role for several years until a new cohort of young men are initiated. Rites of passage often involve scarification or other forms of bodily mutilation so that there is a permanent, visible sign of changed status. Sociologists have taken these ideas further, advancing the idea that 'status passage' (Glaser and Strauss, 1971) is a very common feature of modern societies. For example, occupational life is increasingly frequently thought of in 'career' terms and the status passages associated with promotion, retirement and so forth are important ceremonial occasions in organisational cultures.

All this may yield the misleading impression that status passages are pre-programmed by the culture and unproblematically experienced by the passagee. Often there is considerable individual diversity of experience in negotiating status passages, even among persons in broadly similar situations. Consider the transition from school to work. Although it is becoming increasingly less common for this transition to be made at the age of sixteen, until the mid–1970s this was a standard trajectory for very many British schoolchildren (as late as 1976 only 25 per cent of pupils stayed on beyond their sixteenth year). Almost a quarter of school-leavers entered the labour market with no educational qualifications. Many ended up in poorly paid occupations. Of course, the process is not random: this is an important moment of social and cultural reproduction. As Paul Willis pointedly puts it:

> The difficult thing to explain about how middle class kids get middle class jobs is why others let them. The difficult thing to explain about how working class kids get working class jobs is why they let themselves.

> (Willis, 1977: 1)

The conventional sociological wisdom invokes a description of class culture that suggests that working-class children are enmeshed in cultural notions such as a lack of deferred gratification, weak or absent future orientations and the like. For Willis such explanations are doubly inadequate, for they fail to suggest where these attitudes originate (1977: 141) and they work with a notion of culture as something passively absorbed by the children rather than as at least in part actively constructed, a 'product of collective human praxis' (Willis, 1977: 4).

The core of Willis's explanation turns on his interpretation of the 'lads' counter-school culture. His ethnography of school-leavers in their final year at school distinguishes the 'lads' from the more conventional pupils (the 'ear 'oles'). The lad's culture is sexist and racist, as well as anti-school and anti-conventional morality. Most of the lads will end up with unskilled, heavy labouring jobs that pay reasonably well early on but which will soon take their toll on their health. Ironically, this is a future that the lads choose and willingly embrace.

Willis documents the features of the lads counter-school culture – drinking and smoking, sticking up for their mates, 'dossing, blagging and wagging', 'having a laff' and so on. He goes on to argue that the counter-school culture is both ideological in character and a rational response to the realities of their situation. The lads culture is ideological because it facilitates their smooth transition into dead-end work. As an ideology the culture masks the reality of the lads' situation and effectively dupes them into accepting the worst jobs going. But the counter-school culture is also a considered, rational response. The lads positively value manual work which they regard as masculine, an activity infused with machismo. Moreover they do not much care what work they do providing that it is a manual job (white-collar work they define as effeminate). In their indifference to occupational choice the lads effectively reaffirm their conviction that all jobs are essentially the same. And this, for Willis, represents a penetration of the real conditions of their existence as a class – it is a profound expression of the reality of their situation. As capitalism advances, labour becomes more abstract and thus it matters less and less what occupation you work in so long as you work. In this sense the lads counter-school culture is a rational assessment of the reality of their situation in the labour markets of advanced capitalism.

There has been criticism of the emphasis on age as an indicator of a person's social role or influence upon their social experience. It is suggested that in a post-industrial society that is characterised by de-standardisation and flexibility. There is a less secure work life, families are more diverse and less stable, and major life events are no longer so closely linked to age. There is a greater variety within all age groups and it is difficult to generalise about the circumstances and behaviour of people at any life stage. For example, women aged 25–40 may still be traditional housewives, in full-time employment, or single and childless. Young adults by the age of 25 may have established themselves in careers and good jobs, may have poor jobs, may be unemployed or on various schemes, or may be full-time students (Roberts, 1999). This is not to suggest that age has become socially meaningless, it is still a basis for social discrimination, and people's behaviour early in life still has important implications for their future.

## Structural and local conceptions of power

To conclude this section we can make two general observations about the workings of culture, power and inequality. These concern power as a local phenomenon and the interrelations of systems of domination and disadvantage.

All the theories reviewed above tend to take an objectivist, structural view of power and inequality. They decode the cultural to reveal the true nature of the relationships involved and, as has been argued, much of that revelation has turned on power and its manifestations. Often that power seems to be encompassing in form, lodged in the class structure or ethnic hierarchy or institutionalised arrangements between men and women. But, as Foucault reminded us, power is also something diffused throughout the working of a society. So power is also local and can be understood contextually rather than structurally – a recommendation for a hermeneutic approach to understanding culture, power and inequality.

This can be illustrated by two studies of power and control in work organisations: Malcolm Young's study of the police (1991) and Sallie Westwood's study of Asian women garment workers (1984). In both cases control was in the hands of men, and in the case of the factory the control was experienced through the discipline of the operation of a capitalistic enterprise. The firm was, Westwood says, a reputable and paternalistic firm, which stressed good time-keeping and maximising output. There were separate canteens for management (all men) and workers (mainly women) and there were considerable differences in pay and conditions, with the management receiving company cars and allowances. Westwood describes how the women developed a 'shopfloor culture of resistance and celebration'. Elaborate rituals were engaged in to celebrate the events of the women's lives (weddings, engagements) and the women used company time and resources for their own affairs. The shopfloor culture was one that emphasised friendship and solidarity. The playful antics of the women can be regarded as rituals of resistance which served to emphasise 'sisterhood and strength against the patriarchy and gender inequalities of the company' (Westwood,1984: 2).

The women police officers described by Young had scant opportunity to develop a counter-culture to the heavily masculine ethos of the police force. There were fewer women and they tended to be more isolated. Additionally they were not seen as legitimate members of the force by the policemen. Young describes (1991: 219, 242, 233) the ways in which the women were marginalised and denigrated by the men, given abusive and humiliating names, and repeatedly subject to sexual innuendo in an organisation that was dedicated to a traditional masculine ethos and imagery. Young remarks that the state of the institutional mind kept women in narrowly defined roles and subject to the formal and informal domination of men.

In this last illustration the power exercised was in terms of gender hierarchies, a reminder that modern societies are subject to many systems of domination, not simply that of class, which nevertheless tends to be the predominant typifying feature of modern industrialised society. Power also worked in a capillary fashion, in that it was evident in everyday acts and their implications and consequences. If there are different hierarchies through which power is 'exercised', or different forms of power through which domination works, how are these systems of domination interrelated?

This is sometimes formulated as: how do race, gender, age and class disadvantages relate to each other? Note that the very way that the question is formulated disposes us towards a structural rather than Foucauldian conception of power. Within the frame set by a structural approach there is, as we saw in considering the cycle of deprivation, substantial evidence that economic and cultural factors can overlap or interact to produce multiple disadvantage. Being a black woman can increase the likelihood of the person being found in an underclass location. A poor black woman is likely to face disadvantages that those situated higher up class, racial and gender hierarchies will not. These are well-supported facts. There is a risk, however, of running away with such geometrical metaphors of overlapping disadvantageous categories of class, race, gender and age. These factors certainly describe the broad patterning of disadvantage and the oppressions (racism, sexism, class oppression, etc.) that result. Whether they illuminate the particularities of people's ordinary cultural experience is more open to question, as in everyday life we are all gendered, raced, classed and aged and these categories may have variable relevance to how we are treated in particular instances in everyday life (see West and Fenstermaker, 1995). For instance, we may sometimes feel ourselves to be badly treated by a shop assistant. Is this because of our race or class or gender or age? In actual instances the answer can be very variable for any given person, so it can be very difficult to pin down which particular source of disadvantage is operating. This difficulty does not deny the reality and force of these disadvantages. But it does serve to further underline Foucault's fundamental point about the omnipresence of power and resistance: dominations of class or race or gender are never complete or total and can be challenged in the conduct of our everyday lives.

## 3.5 Conclusion

News broadcasts daily provide us with information about the effects of globalisation and the cultural differences between people. The inequalities premised on these differences are the basis of many social conflicts. Witness, for example, the long-running conflicts in the Basque region, central Africa, and the Middle East, or the violent anti-globalisation demonstrations that have accompanied the annual summit meetings of the G8.

In this chapter we have reviewed explanations of the origin of inequality in capitalist societies and considered some of the leading theoretical ideas. Concepts such as hegemony, incorporation and habitus have been used to explain how inequality is justified and rendered acceptable. The chapter has also focused on the ways that these inequalities are made manifest through characteristic cultures of class, ethnicity, gender and age. The concepts, theories and studies reviewed above show some of the many ways in which all cultures are 'structured in dominance'. This work might also help to suggest ways in which strategies of resistance to systems of dominance might be organised.

> ## Recap
>
> This chapter has:
> - considered the cultural and economic effects of globalisation;
> - reviewed the principal structural sources of inequality;
> - surveyed explanations of the role of culture in legitimating forms of inequality;
> - examined how class, race, gender and age inequalities are culturally produced and reproduced.

# Further reading

A helpful survey of the base-superstructure debate and beyond can be found in Jorge Larrain's *The Concept of Ideology* (1979). Some of the ramifications of the dominant ideology debate are explored in Nicholas Abercrombie, Stephen Hill and Bryan S. Turner (eds) *Dominant Ideologies* (1990). Ruth Lister's collection *Charles Murray and the Underclass: The Developing Debate* (1996) contains short, lively contributions about the concept and reality of the underclass. On race and ethnicity, *The Empire Strikes Back* (1982), collectively authored by members of the Birmingham Centre for Contemporary Cultural Studies, is still an engaging read. There is a video of an illustrated lecture by Stuart Hall (1997) entitled 'Race as a floating signifier' available from Media Education Foundation, **www.mediaed.org/**, or you can view an extract from the Lecture on You Tube **www.youtube.com/ watch?v=bMo2uiRAf30**. Judith Butler's *Gender Trouble: Feminism and the Subversion of Identity* (2006) has been influential in shaping recent debates on gender. A good resource for exploring the complex issues involved in the globalisation process is *The globalisation Reader* (2003), edited by Frank J. Lechner and John Boli. See also the Globalisation Website: **www.sociology.emory.edu/globalization/**

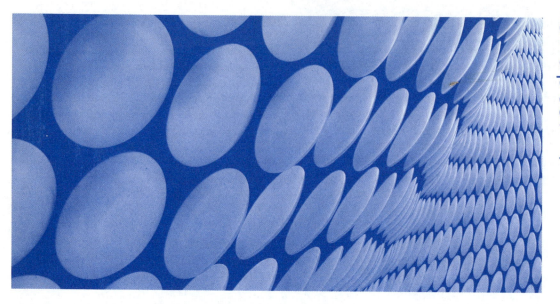

# Researching culture

## 4.0 Introduction

This chapter concentrates not on theories or analytic standpoints but on methods of research, that is how knowledge is produced in cultural studies. The term research originates from the French 'rechercher', meaning to search for the facts, to investigate something thoroughly. Researchers in cultural studies have used a wide array of methods drawn from the humanities and social sciences, and especially those methods that prize interpretation. Whether cultural studies has any distinctive methods of its own is a moot point. For example, Jim McGuigan (1997: 1) observes that 'still it remains difficult to see quite what cultural studies amounts to methodologically'. Often, the metaphor of bricolage is employed to describe the eclectic, topic and problem-driven approach of cultural studies. What seems to matter most is the selection of methods that treat culture seriously as a topic in its own right, not as a mere 'effect' (Alasuutari, 1995).

In many quarters of cultural studies what is known

as methodological pluralism prevails. This is the idea that different methods of investigation can illuminate different aspects of culture, and that methods have to be appropriate to the research question posed. For example, questions about just how common are particular kinds of images in 'lad's mags' can be best addressed by using a method like content analysis, which allows the researcher to carefully measure the incidence and prevalence of specific features of texts. But if the research question seeks to discover say, the ways in which male–female relationships are portrayed in a magazine's editorial column, then a semiotic approach may be more helpful. Pluralism means that we cannot speak of any single method as *the* method of cultural studies. There are 'cultural methodologies' (McGuigan, 1997) but no one cultural methodology.

All research involves an initial stage of planning. This is often called the research design stage. It involves making key decisions about what you want to find out (your research question or problem), how you will obtain facts or evidence that will provide an answer to your research question (methods of data collection), and how that evidence will be analysed (methods of data analysis).

In this chapter we will provide a brief overview of some of the leading methods of data collection and analysis used in cultural studies. Much work in cultural studies focuses on the analysis of texts and lived experience. A good deal of culture is textually mediated through advertisements, magazines, films, computer games, music and the like. We will begin by considering first content and thematic analysis, and then semiotics. Each of these methods facilitates the analysis of cultural texts. But culture is not merely textual. It is also lived through our day-to-day experiences. Accordingly, the chapter will then look at the use by cultural studies of ethnographic methods to study culture as a lived, ordinary experience, beginning with a famed study of the lived experience of school leavers (Willis 1977), before coming full circle to a consideration of the methods used to study how audiences experience cultural texts (Radway, 1987).

## Learning objectives

➤ To, understand the differing objectives of the leading methods for producing knowledge in cultural studies.

➤ To, appreciate the range of theoretical and practical issues generated by the use of these methods.

➤ To, acquire a knowledge of the processes through which investigations of texts and lived experience in cultural studies are accomplished.

# 4.1 Content and thematic analysis

'Content analysis' is a term which covers a range of ways of analysing the written and visual elements of texts. It can be quantitative or qualitative in character. The quantitative version emerged in the early twentieth century. One of its best known exponents was Bernard Berelson, who in 1952 published *Content Analysis in*

*Communication Research.* Or it can be used in a more qualitative manner to refer to any attempt to identify recurrent ideas or themes in a document or collection of documents.

For Berelson, content analysis is 'a research technique for the objective, systematic and quantitative description of the manifest content of communication' (1952: 18). The definition is worth unpacking. Communication is considered to consist of a flow of messages from a transmitter to a receiver; thus, from an author to a readership, from a television programme to its audience, or from a photograph to its viewer. It is the 'manifest' – that is, the obvious, palpable, self-evident-features of the message – that are of relevance to content analysis, not its latent or hidden dimensions. Thus content analysis is primarily limited to what is expressly communicated by some document rather than the motives animating the construction of the document or the responses that persons make to it (Berelson, 1952: 16).

The method claims to offer an 'objective,' 'systematic,' and 'quantitative' (Berelson, 1952: 16–17) analysis of documentary content. The objectivity of content analysis resides in the devising of precisely and clearly defined categories to apply to the material analysed. The idea is that different analysts using the same categories and rules of application would obtain identical results from their analysis of any given body of data. This is the key to the reliability of the method. The rules of application serve to minimise the influence of the individual analyst's disposition and preconceptions. The requirement that content analysis is systematic means that *all* the material relevant to the investigation must be analysed, not just a selection designed to support a preferred hypothesis. Content analysis is often regarded as primarily a quantitative technique because it aims to establish the frequency with which certain categories or themes appear in the material investigated. This quantitative dimension is facilitated by assigning numerical values to category or theme and is a basic characteristic of the method. Of course, some kinds of content analysis have a qualitative orientation. These are also considered below.

# Quantitative content analysis: gangsta rap lyrics

Use of the method of content analysis involves six basic steps: (1) selecting a topic and determining a research problem; (2) selecting a documentary source; (3) devising a set of analytic categories; (4) formulating an explicit set of instructions for using the categories to code the material; (5) establishing a principled basis for sampling the documents; and (6) counting the frequency of a given category or theme in the documents sampled (Ball and Smith 1992). We can understand how content analysis is done by looking at how these steps are applied in Edward Armstrong's (2001) study of gangsta rap lyrics.

## Selecting a topic and determining a research problem

In cultural studies inquiry begins with the selection of a topic for investigation and the determination of a 'research problem'. Armstrong's research question is to describe the nature and extent of violent and misogynist messages in rap music. While it is possible to interpret rap music as part of an oppositional culture committed to social critique, such views overlook the presence of a lyrical content that portrays violence against women as a normal and acceptable fact of life. Armstrong's task is primarily descriptive: he seeks to ascertain the extent of such imagery in rap music.

## Selecting a documentary source

The next step in content analysis involves the identification of a collection of documents relevant to the research problem. Armstrong (2001: 98) suggests that rap lyrics are well-suited to content analysis because they are in first-person accounts that avoid metaphor and word play and favour the direct communication of meaning. Rappers are committed to speaking straightforwardly: manifest content is what rap is about. Armstrong draws upon the lyrics of 490 songs made by 13 popular and well-regarded rap artists between the years 1987 and 1993.

## Devising a set of categories

The categories into which the content is to be coded are plainly central parts of the analytical process. As Berelson observed, 'Content analysis stands or falls by its categories ... since the categories contain the substance of the investigation, a content analysis can be no better than its system of categories' (1952: 147). The categories chosen must reflect and be sensitive to the research problem. Armstrong's categories concentrate on criminal offences directed against women: assault, forcible rape, murder, and a combined rape and murder category. Further requirements are that categories are mutually exclusive and exhaustive of the content under consideration. It is important that any element of the content is coded under one and only one category and that the category system is sufficiently comprehensive to provide space for every relevant aspect of content. Armstrong's four categories meet these requirements.

## Formulating an explicit set of coding rules

Any given instance of content has to be coded, that is, allocated to one (and only one) category. Sometimes, however, a given item of content may be ambiguous and fall between two or more categories, and for that reason, it is essential that categories are sufficiently explicit to provide coders with clear instructions about how to deal with the problematic item. Armstrong does not report any difficulties in coding lyrics into his four categories.

## Sampling the documents

Some selection of the material to be analysed is usually necessary in order to ensure that a properly representative sample is obtained. Armstrong chooses to analyse the work of rap's 'ruling class' in its foundational period, before it began to diversify and fragment. While there is an arbitrary element to selection of the 13 artists, the 490 songs represent to totality of their published output in the 1987–93 period.

## Counting the frequencies of the categories

A count must be made of how often the categories appear in the content under investigation. The information thus obtained can be readily presented in tables or graphs. Armstrong (2001: 126) tabulates his findings, which are presented as whole numbers and percentages. Overall, 22 per cent of the 490 songs have violent and misogynist lyrics. Assault, followed by murder, are the commonest forms of violence and misogyny depicted. In strictly quantitative content analysis, the provision of examples of the data is deemed superfluous. What matters is the tabular and graphical representation of the research findings, which indicate the patterns relevant to the research question. Much large-scale content analysis readily lends itself to cross-tabulation and significance testing. Armstrong does not go this far in his study. Instead, he argues that once the categorisation process is complete, the interesting step is not statistical analysis but consideration of the meanings of the lyrics. Thus Armstrong (2001: 100–4) gives attention to exactly how his categories of assault, rape, murder and rape, and murder are depicted in the lyrics. This part of Armstrong's study moves towards a more qualitative thematic analysis.

Of course, gangsta rap has been and continues to be an enormously controversial cultural phenomenon. On the one hand, some see it as a cause of social problems, as providing a source of and legitimation for the growing violence in urban neighbourhoods. On the other, its supporters argue that its messages need to be decoded and are not as unambiguous as they seem to critics from the outside. The point of Armstrong's study is to establish the factual basis of claims about the violence and misogyny of gangsta rap lyrics. Statistics always have to be interpreted so it could be suggested that 'only' 22 per cent deal with violent and misogynist themes, therefore 78 per cent do not. Also, Armstrong's analysis gives lie to some common misconceptions that the more shocking a rapper is, the more successful he will be. Armstrong show that those artists who score highest on violence and misogyny are the least commercially successful. Or at least they were, in 1987–93. Armstrong ends with a quick comparison of this period with the lyrics of Eminem's successful albums. This suggests that in more recent years a 'hard' image is coming to be more commercially successful than was the case in the earlier period.

Certain shortcomings are associated with quantitative content analysis as a method of analysis. These centre on issues of manifest and latent content, data fragmentation and decontextualisation. For cultural studies, these issues set limits on the usefulness of the method. Berelson (1952) sought to restrict content analysis to what is manifestly apparent in the communicative message, excluding implicit or latent meanings from the coding operation. Content analysis also depends upon a communicative message – song lyrics, for example, being fragmented for purposes of coding. What can be lost is the latent meaning of a message that may only become apparent when the fuller context of the message is taken into account. So content analysis risks fragmenting and decontextualising its topic matter, losing the sense that is given it by the local circumstances in which it appears. Armstrong's study at least partially escapes these criticisms. He is able to maintain that many rap lyrics have a literalness that makes it unnecessary to seek for subtler decodings. He also focuses not simply on the presence or absence of certain words and images in the lyrics but places these terms in the bleak contexts in which they occur as representations of acts of violence.

## Thematic analysis

Thematic analysis or qualitative content analysis stands closer to the traditional methods of the humanities. It involves close scrutiny of texts in order to ascertain key ideas or themes. Thematic analysis is broadly what Siegfried Kracauer meant when he defined qualitative content analysis as: 'the selection and rational organization of such categories as condense the substantive meanings of the given text, with a view to testing pertinent assumptions and hypotheses. These categories *may* or *may not* invite frequency counts' (1952: 638). Kracauer argued that the quantitative dependence upon pre-established categories applied to manifest elements of the content of communication can easily result in the inadequate treatment of the significance of key words or phrases. Qualitative analysis, in contrast, is appropriately equipped to pick up such nuances. Note how far Kracauer's recommendations depart from

Berelson's: there is no requirement to treat only manifest content, but equally there are no clear, replicable procedures presented whereby the substantive meanings of a given text can be condensed. Much, then, is left to the ingenuity of the individual analyst. Nor are frequency counts barred from qualitative content analysis, but this point simply sidesteps the problem: under what circumstances is a count to be preferred over a qualitative appraisal of communication content?

Erving Goffman's (1979) book *Gender Advertisements* offers a pictorial variation of thematic analysis. He takes a constructionist stance towards gender that anticipates the later and better known ideas of Judith Butler. His focus in this book is on 'gender displays', the nonverbal ways through which we exude 'femininity' or 'masculinity'. For Goffman how we sit, stand, hold hands, cuddle, tilt our heads, lower our bodies, etc. all speak of our gendered natures. There is a (culturally variable but socially sanctioned) feminine way to sit, just as there is a (culturally variable but socially sanctioned) masculine way to stand. His argument is that these gender displays are cultural practices that are socially learned. His book offers an analysis of some practices of gender display using a collection of more than 500 images, mostly drawn from newspaper and magazine adverts.

The pictures are grouped under six broad themes, with sub-themes developed as and when Goffman's analysis suggests it appropriate. The main features of gender displays are:

➤ *relative size*: men are typically depicted as bigger than women;

➤ *function ranking*: if men and women are depicted together engaged in a task, the man will likely be in charge;

➤ *the feminine touch*: men grasp objects, women gently touch or stroke them;

➤ *the family*: family photographs often depict the man at the head of the family in a protective and authoritative role;

➤ *the ritualisation of subordination*: the various forms of bending and lowering of the body through which people, and especially women, display their subordinate status;

➤ *licensed withdrawal*: the various ways in which people remove themselves from full involvement in the situation through forms of reserve, gazing vacantly into the distance, nuzzling and cuddling another, that are typically done by women.

Overall, Goffman suggests that the 'parent–child complex' serves as a model for the gender displays of adult men and women. His analysis of these themes is conducted in words and pictures. He presents a short written description of a theme or sub-theme then follows it with a series of pictures that illustrate it. For example, in the section of the ritualization of subordination, Goffman presents a series of advertising pictures where women are playfully being 'attacked' by men – being pulled down the beach into the sea, having water thrown over them, being lifted off the ground. He precedes the series of pictures with the comment:

Adults play mock assault games with children, games such as chase-and-capture and grab-and-squeeze. The child is playfully treated like a prey under attack by a predator. Certain materials (pillows, sprays of water, light beach balls) provide missiles that can strike but not hurt. Other materials provide a medium into which the captured body can be thrown safely – beds, snow banks, pools, arms. Now it turns out that men play these games with women, the latter collaborating through a display of attempts to escape and through cries of alarm, fear, and appeasement. (Figure-dancing provides occasion for an institutionalized example, the partners who are swung off their feet never being men.) Of course, underneath this show a man may be engaged in a deeper one, the suggestion of what he could do if he got serious about it. In part because mock assault is 'fun' and more likely in holiday scenes than in work scenes, it is much represented in advertisements.

(Goffman, 1979: text preceding pictures 235–43)

The juxtaposition of written text and pictorial display allows the reader to develop a subtle understanding of features of gender display through the interaction between the written text and pictorial sequence, each elaborating the other. Goffman's book can be read as an example of a thematic analysis of gender displays. Goffman maintains that advertising photographs are not, of course, 'real life', but that they offer an exaggerated and stylised representation of what we do in ordinary everyday life. As such, advertisements provide a strategic research site for the student of gender display. In Goffman's hands they provide a magnifying glass for what we routinely undertake when performing gender.

## 4.2 Semiotics as a method of analysis

Semiotic approaches noticeably contrast with quantitative content analyses. Content analysis is based upon traditional social scientific preoccupations such as clearly defined concepts, testable hypotheses and representative samples. These ideas are not prominent in semiotics. It is much more interested in how cultural knowledge figures in the interpretation of cultural features. It is a method that has proved effective in the

humanities as well as in cultural studies. From a semiotic point of view, content analysis seems to fragment the cultural phenomena it investigates when it categorises elements or features of texts. In seeking to quantitatively describe these features, it loses sight of the text as a unified package – of the overall meaning of a song or an image as it might be heard or viewed. Semiotic analyses offer an opposing approach centred on the close study of individual cases taken as a whole. The aim is to provide an analysis that attuned to what is communicated by the text in its entirety. In this respect semiotic analysis has a rigour of its own: but differences remain. As we shall see, semiotic analyses often concentrate on only one or two texts, or bigger collections of texts that have not been assembled by a systematic sampling procedure.

Much recent writing on the communication and representation of meaning, as other chapters in this book suggest, has been influenced by **structuralism** (p. 17) and **semiotics** (or **semiology** – p. 29). One important source of structuralism was the theories of the Swiss linguist Ferdinand de Saussure (1857–1913),

**Figure 4.1** A sign is always a thing plus meaning.

whose ideas were developed in the 1960s by influential writers such as Althusser, **Barthes** (p. 96), Chomsky, Foucault (p. 20), Lacan and Lévi-Strauss. Keat and Urry (1975: 124–6) identify the main features of structuralism as follows:

1 Systems must be studied as a set of interrelated elements. Individual elements should not be seen in isolation. For example, in a set of traffic lights, green only means go because red means stop.

2 An attempt to discover the structure that lies behind or beneath what is directly knowable.

3 The suggestion that the structure behind the directly visible and the directly visible itself are both products of structural properties of the mind.

4 The proposal that the methods of linguistics can be applied to other social and human sciences.

5 Culture can be analysed in terms of binary oppositions: for example, between good and bad or hot and cold.

6 The adoption of a distinction between synchronic (static) and diachronic (changing) analyses.

7 The attempt to identify similar structures in different aspects of social life.

## Key influence 4.1

### Roland Barthes (1915–80)

Roland Barthes was a French literary critic and cultural analyst. His development of **structuralist** and **poststructuralist** (p. 17) ideas in the context of writing on aspects of everyday life was particularly influential in the early development of cultural studies.

Barthes' early life was dogged by tuberculosis. He taught in French lycées and abroad before being appointed to the Ecole Pratique des Hautes Etudes in 1962. He was appointed to a Chair at the Collège de France (Paris) in 1976. He died after being knocked over by a truck outside the Collège.

Barthes' early work concerned the nature of language and representation from a **structuralist** (p. 17) point of view. Examples of his general approach can be found in *Writing Degree Zero* (1953) and *Elements of Semiology* (1964). He worked on the formal properties of literary texts and carried out influential specific analyses such as *S/Z* (1970), which addresses the structure of a novella by Balzac. His identification of proairetic, hermeneutic, semic, sym-bolic and referential codes was innovative and consequential. Barthes was also concerned to apply the ideas of semiology to aspects of everyday life. He wrote a regular newspaper column in the 1950s that covered topics such as margarine, the brain of Einstein and wrestling from this point of view. These short analyses were collected in *Mythologies* (1957): a best selling text which encapsulates some of the key aspects of decodings based in a cultural studies approach. Barthes sought to dig below the surface of the everyday for deeper meanings and to show how those meanings were implicated in relations of **power** (p. 64) and structures of domination. He mounted an attack on the role of such seemingly innocent representations and activities in the **ideological** (p. 35) dominance of the bourgeois class. He also examined fashion in *The Fashion System* (1967). The sometimes playful nature of Barthes' analyses became more prominent in his later work which, under the influence of **poststructuralism** (p. 17), is less concerned with the methodical mapping of codes and meanings and more with the interrogation of pleasure and the self. Examples of this can be found in *The Pleasure of the Text* (1973), *Camera Lucida* (1980) and *Roland Barthes on Roland Barthes* (1975).

Barthes' attention to everyday life and popular texts from an academic point of view was groundbreaking. It is likely that his later work would have developed further in parallel with the **postmodernist** (p. 295) emphases on **identity** (p. 142) and pleasure. He remains, however, one of the seminal figures of postwar French thought, who influenced a variety of disciplines in the humanities and the social sciences.

#### Further reading

*Mythologies* is a great place to start reading Barthes.

Barthes, R. (1973) *Mythologies*, St Albans: Paladin.

Culler, J. (1983) *Barthes*, London: Fontana.

Sontag, S. (ed.) (1982) *A Barthes Reader*, London: Cape.

Roland Barthes adopted many of these features of structuralism in his influential analyses. Barthes followed de Saussure's preoccupation with the nature of signs. De Saussure was well-aware of the wide scope of semiology, which he defined as 'the science that studies the life of signs within society' (de Saussure,1966:16). However, his own work concentrated on language. Barthes' accomplishment was to provide a wide array of worked examples of how the whole of culture, not just language, could be analysed semiologically. In a sense, Barthes encashed de Saussure's promise, taking semiology out of linguistics and into cultural studies.

Chapter 2 (p. 32) has introduced some of the key components of Barthes' ideas about semiotics. (Barthes preferred the term semiology but for the sake of consistency in this chapter we will speak of semiotics.) The discussion here will concentrate on areas where Barthes has been particularly important, the semiotic analysis of photography and advertising. The aim is to show how semiotic concepts are mobilised to facilitate the analysis and understanding of images.

Photographs were a class of signs that long fascinated Barthes. In his 1961 essay, 'The photographic message' (Barthes, 1977) the press photograph is examined. The photograph in a newspaper when treated as a sign seems to occupy the realm of 'pure denotation'. It appears as a literal representation of a factual state of affairs, depicting the actuality of a flood victim's plight or a wounded soldier's suffering or a politician making a speech. The press photograph is denotative in that it directly indicates what there is in the world. In this sense, states Barthes, it seems to be a 'message without a code'. But the press photo is always surrounded by written text such as a caption and a news story and such written texts follow certain codes for reporting diplomatic manoeuvring, disasters, political conflicts and so on. The written text is widely acknowledged to be a source of connotation. So the two messages co-exist: one without a code and one with one. This is what Barthes calls 'the photographic paradox'.

But Barthes then goes on to suggest that this is not a true paradox. This is because a photograph is a message without a code only in respect of its referent, that is to *what* it points to in the world. *How* the photograph is taken is the source of the photograph's connotation. Photographs have to be taken in some way, in some

style or other. Barthes resolves the photographic paradox by identifying six 'connotation procedures' that show how photographs are not simple denotative signs depicting brute, natural fact. Through connotation procedures photographers can alter reality or their images of reality. The three procedures that can modify the reality shown in a photograph are *trick effects* (for example, unlikely photos that put together people who have never actually met); decisions about *pose*; and the manipulation of *objects* in the scene photographed. Three connotation procedures concern what the photographer does with the image: *photogenia* is the selective use of lighting, exposure, cropping, etc. to produce a particular effect; *aestheticism* is the attempt to introduce artistic elements into the production of the photograph by, for example, modelling a photograph after a well-known painting; and *syntax*, which is the photograph's placement in a sequence of other photographs. The message conveyed by the photograph is no less connotative and therefore contestable as a representation of reality than is a written text.

Barthes turned his attention to advertising images in his 1964 paper, 'Rhetoric of the image'. Here he dissects a Panzani advertisement (see overleaf) depicting a string bag containing Panzani spaghetti, tomato sauce and grated cheese along with fresh vegetables.

In speaking of an image's 'rhetoric', Barthes is asking how this image works as an advertisement. Specifically, he wants to know how it works to provoke desire in the viewer and persuade them to buy Panzani products. Barthes locates the question in a broader concern with how an image signifies, i.e. how it is constructed in order to convey a range of meanings (wholesomeness, freshness, 'Italianicity').

Barthes suggests that to understand the advertisement it is important to recognise that both the verbal and visual elements operate at denotative and connotative levels. The verbal part – the labels bearing the name Panzani and the caption at the bottom of the image – are denotative in that they describe what the products are and who makes them. But there is also a connotational level: the name Panzani just sounds Italian. Likewise, the visual element has a denotational component. What we 'see' when we look at the image is a string shopping bag containing vegetables and Panzani products. It also carries a rich range of connotations.

PATES · SAUCE · PARMESAN
A L'ITALIENNE DE LUXE

**Figure 4.2** Panzani.

The signifier of the string bag, for example, suggests 'return from the market' which in turn implies 'freshness of the products' destined for 'home preparation'. The varied collection of objects in the bag conveys the idea of a 'carefully balanced dish' in which an equivalence can be drawn between the natural produce (onions, tomatoes, etc.) and the Panzani products, even though the latter are manufactured (Barthes 1977: 34–35). The advertisement tells us that we are looking at the constituents of a complete and wholesome meal. By analyzing what is signified by the various signifiers in the advertisement Barthes is able to build up a convincing analysis of how this message is achieved.

## Semiotics of advertising

A number of writers have drawn attention to the way in which advertisements deploy particular representations of gender relations. Feminist writers have suggested that they often contain grossly caricatured or stereotyped representations of women. Yet they also portray a glossy, attractive world that many readers find appealing. This is the contradiction that drives Judith Williamson's (1978) semiotically-inspired *Decoding Advertisements*. Williamson asks how advertisements work and analyses a large number of advertising images in semiotic terms. She breaks down advertisements into their constituent parts – their signifiers – and asks what they mean and how they are related. For example, she takes a famous 1970s Chanel No. 5 advertisement that features a portrait of Catherine Deneuve gazing straight out of the picture at the reader. Williamson suggests that this 'mirror-image technique' encourages the reader to momentarily identify with Ms Deneuve. At the same time, the presence of a bottle of Chanel No. 5 in the corner of this ad is key to how it works to sell the product. 'Correlative sign work' is involved. The sense of 'French chic' that Deneuve represents to us carries over to the bottle of perfume.

But it is not enough just to analyse the assembly of signifiers in the ad in order to fully understand how advertisements work. In addition, Williamson argues, attention to the knowledge that viewers bring to the reading the advertisement is required. Many readers will know that Ms Deneuve is an international film star. She has a particular image (chic, sophisticated, French) that is very different from other film stars who advertise perfume. Williamson contrasts the very different signifieds associated with the American actress, Margaux Hemingway who featured in a series of advertisements for Babe perfume. Hemingway strikes a contrasting figure – active, tomboyish, youthful, exuberant – through the signifiers used in Babe advertisements depicting her practising karate, etc. Film stars stand in a system of differences and contrasts with one another, which is how they each cultivate their distinctive image. Williamson goes on to show how much advertising depends upon the reader's mobilisation of three 'referent systems'. This is our general cultural knowledge linked to our notions of 'nature', 'magic' and 'time'. Butter advertisements trade on the naturalness of the product; vodka advertisements on the impossibly exotic things that might happen to you once you start drinking the product; wholemeal bread ads draw upon nostalgic notions about how bread was once made. Williamson's book deserves close attention by students of cultural studies as a richly illustrated training manual for doing semiotic analysis.

Signs are organised into systems which convey meaning; these systems are often called codes in structuralist and semiotic approaches (Fiske and Hartley, 1978: 59). One of the areas where such codes have been most studied is advertising (see, most importantly, Williamson, 1978), which forms the topic of this section.

It is important to recognise the range of different types of advertising in contemporary societies. A useful categorisation of five different types has been suggested by Dyer (1982) who distinguishes between 'informational', 'simple', 'compound', 'complex' and 'sophisticated' advertisements.

*Informational* advertisements are like the classified advertisements found in newspapers. They are often brief and small, and may contain very little elaboration of the basic message. *Simple* advertisements are larger than informational advertisements, but they still contain relatively precise and clear information about a particular product or service. There is some degree of encouragement to buy the product. Many advertisements in the free local newspapers in Britain are of this type.

In *compound* advertisements there is more encouragement, which may be of a subtle kind. Pictures are more persuasive and facts may be contained in the copy that accompanies the advertisement. The picture is often 'glossy' and it is the intention of the advertiser that the reader will associate the product with the whole impression created by the picture. Advertisements in the magazines associated with newspapers are often of this kind. In *complex* advertisements the background takes over and the product merges into it. It is sometimes difficult to see precisely what is being sold. The whole image conveys a message of status, wealth and power. *Sophisticated* advertisements move beyond such complex advertisements and they often

contain an attempt to draw upon hidden feelings through subtle associations. A deep-seated psychological appeal is often made.

## A semiotic analysis of a sophisticated advertisement

A humorous semiotic analysis of a sophisticated advertisement (for the cigarette Silk Cut) is contained in the extract from David Lodge's (1989) novel *Nice Work*. In this novel a university lecturer in English, Robyn Penrose, has been detailed to 'shadow' an industrialist, Vic Wilcox, with the aim of encouraging greater mutual understanding between academia and business. Much of the humour in the novel revolves around the interaction between the two main characters who represent very different worlds. We conclude this section with this fictional but generally sound example of semiotic analysis in action.

# 4.3 Ethnography

Semiotics has been a very important method within cultural studies. However, like content and thematic analysis, it is very much a method for analysing cultural texts as relatively discrete entities. It is commonplace to contrast the study of culture as text with the study of lived experience. Here, cultural studies has drawn upon the classic anthropological technique of ethnography, but as we shall see, has adapted it to its own ends. In this section we consider the contributions of ethnographic method to cultural studies through a discussion of two influential studies: Paul Willis's (1977) *Learning to Labour* and Janice Radway's (1984) *Reading the Romance*.

A primary aim of ethnography since the days when Bronislaw Malinowki (1884–1942) first articulated the canons of modern fieldwork has been to articulate the 'native's point of view'. This has usually involved a period of prolonged immersion in a fieldwork setting. Malinowki spent several years on the Trobriand Islands (now part of Papua New Guinea) living among the islanders in order to understand and describe their activities, including such apparently odd ceremonies as

## Box 4.1

### Semiotic analysis of a Silk Cut ad

A typical instance of this was the furious argument they had about the Silk Cut advertisement. They were returning in his car from visiting a foundry in Derby that had been taken over by asset-strippers who were selling off an automatic core moulder Wilcox was interested in, though it had turned out to be too old-fashioned for his purpose. Every few miles, it seemed, they passed the same huge poster on roadside hoardings, a photographic depiction of a rippling expanse of purple silk in which there was a single slit, as if the material had been slashed with a razor. There were no words on the advertisement, except for the Government Health Warning about smoking. This ubiquitous image, flashing past at regular intervals, both irritated and intrigued Robyn, and she began to do her semiotic stuff on the deep structure hidden beneath its bland surface.

It was in the first instance a kind of riddle. That is to say, in order to decode it, you had to know that there was a brand of cigarettes called Silk Cut. The poster was the iconic representation of a missing name, like a rebus. But the icon was also a metaphor. The shimmering silk, with its voluptuous curves and sensuous texture, obviously symbolized the female body, and the elliptical slit, fore-grounded by a lighter colour showing through, was still more obviously a vagina. The advert thus appealed to both sensual and

sadistic impulses, the desire to mutilate as well as penetrate the female body.

Vic Wilcox spluttered with outraged derision as she expounded this interpretation. He smoked a different brand, himself, but it was as if he felt his whole philosophy of life was threatened by Robyn's analysis of the advert. 'You must have a twisted mind to see all that in a perfectly harmless bit of cloth,' he said.

'What's the point of it, then?' Robyn challenged him. 'Why use cloth to advertise cigarettes?'

'Well, that's the name of 'em, isn't it? Silk Cut. It's a picture of the name. Nothing more or less.'

'Suppose they'd used a picture of a roll of silk cut in half – would that do just as well?'

'I suppose so. Yes, why not?'

'Because it would look like a penis cut in half, that's why.'

He forced a laugh to cover his embarrassment. 'Why can't you people take things at their face value?'

'What people are you referring to?'

'Highbrows. Intellectuals. You're always trying to find hidden meanings in things. Why? A cigarette is a cigarette. A piece of silk is a piece of silk. Why not leave it at that?'

'When they're represented they acquire additional meanings,' said Robyn. 'Signs are never innocent. Semiotics teaches us that.'

'Semi-what?'

'Semiotics. The study of signs.'

'It teaches us to have dirty minds, if you ask me.'

'Why d'you think the wretched cigarettes were called Silk Cut in the first place?'

'I dunno. It's just a name, as good as any other.'

' "Cut" has something to do with the tobacco, doesn't it? The way the tobacco leaf is cut. Like "Player's Navy Cut" – my uncle Walter used to smoke them.'

'Well, what if he does?' Vic said warily.

'But silk has nothing to do with tobacco. It's a metaphor, a metaphor that means something like, "smooth as silk". Somebody in an advertising agency dreamt up the name "Silk Cut" to suggest a cigarette that wouldn't give you a sore throat or a hacking cough or lung cancer. But after a while the public got used to the name, the word "Silk" ceased to signify, so they decided to have an advertising campaign to give the brand a high profile again. Some bright spark at the agency came up with the idea of rippling silk with a cut in it. The original metaphor is now represented literally. But new metaphorical connotations accrue – sexual ones. Whether they were consciously intended or not doesn't really matter. It's a good example of the perpetual sliding of the signified under the signifier, actually.'

Wilcox chewed on this for a while, then said, 'Why do women smoke them, then, eh?' His triumphant expression showed

## Box 4.1 (continued)

that he thought this was a knock-down argument. 'If smoking Silk Cut is a form of aggravated rape, as you try to make out, how come women smoke 'em too?'

'Many women are masochistic by temperament,' said Robyn. 'They've learned what's expected of them in a patriarchial society.'

'Ha!' Wilcox exclaimed, tossing back his head. 'I might have known you'd have some daft answer.'

'I don't know why you're so worked up,' said Robyn. 'It's not as if you smoke Silk Cut yourself.'

'No, I smoke Marlboros. Funnily enough, I smoke them because I like the taste.'

'They are the ones that have the lone cowboy ads, aren't they?'

'I suppose that makes me a repressed homosexual, does it?'

'No, it's a very straightforword metonymic message.'

'Metowhat?'

'Metonymic. One of the fundamental tools of semiotics is the distinction between metaphor and metonymy. D'you want me to explain it to you?'

'It'll pass the time,' he said.

'Metaphor is a figure of speech based on similarity, whereas metonymy is based on contiguity. In metaphor you substitute something like the thing you mean for the thing itself, whereas in metonymy you substitute some attribute or cause or effect of the thing for the thing itself.'

'I don't understand a word you're saying.'

'Well, take one of your moulds. The bottom bit is called the drag because it's dragged across the floor and the top bit is called the cope because it covers the bottom bit.'

'I told you that.'

'Yes, I know. What you didn't tell me was that "drag" is a metonymy and "cope" is a metaphor.'

Vic grunted. 'What difference does it make?'

'It's just a question of understanding how language works. I thought you were interested in how things work.'

'I don't see what it's got to do with cigarettes.'

'In the case of the Silk Cut poster, the picture signifies the female body metaphorically: the slit in the silk is like a vagina – '

Vic flinched at the word. 'So you say.'

'All holes, hollow spaces, fissures and folds represent the female genitals.'

'Prove it.'

'Freud proved it, by his successful analysis of dreams,' said Robyn. 'But the Marlboro ads don't use any metaphors. That's probably why you smoke them, actually.'

'What do you mean?' he said suspiciously.

'You don't have any sympathy with the metaphorical way of looking at things. A cigarette is a cigarette as far as you are concerned.'

'Right.'

'The Marlboro ad doesn't disturb that naïve faith in the stability of the signified. It establishes a metonymic connection – completely spurious of course, but realistically plausible – between smoking that brand and the healthy, heroic, outdoor life of the cowboy. Buy the cigarette and you buy the life-style, or the fantasy of living it.'

'Rubbish!' said Wilcox. 'I hate the country and the open air. I'm scared to go in a field with a cow in it.'

'Well then, maybe it's the solitariness of the cowboy in the ads that appeals to you. Self-reliant, independent, very macho.'

'I've never heard such a lot of balls in all my life,' said Vic Wilcox, which was strong language coming from him.

'Balls – now that's an interesting expression . . .' Robyn mused.

'Oh no!' he groaned.

'When you say a man "has balls", approvingly, it's a metonymy, whereas if you say something is a "lot of balls", or "a balls-up", it's a sort of metaphor. The metonymy attributes value to the testicles whereas the metaphor uses them to degrade something else.'

'I can't take any more of this,' said Vic. 'D'you mind if I smoke? Just a plain, ordinary cigarette?'

'If I can have Radio Three on,' said Robyn.

(Lodge, 1989)

exchanging kula shells. Malinowski emphasised the importance of living among a group of people in order to come to appreciate the logic and rationale of their customs and practices, an element of ethnography now known as participant observation. Later, as the traditional topic matter for anthropology fast disappeared as part of a process now glossed as globalisation, anthropologists began to study their own societies. Sociologists had early taken their lead from anthropologists (for example, the Chicago School of the 1920s) and could also draw upon the model of the nineteenth century 'urban explorers' (Mayhew, Booth, Rowntree). Outside the university system the Mass Observation projects of the 1930s and 1940s produced a number of studies of aspects of everyday life in Britain using ordinary people as observers and informants. Ethnography enjoyed a major revival in the hands of the so-called Second Chicago School of Sociology in the immediate post-Second World War period. One of its most gifted exponents expressed the key features of the approach thus:

> Any group of persons – prisoners, primitives, pilots or patients – develop a life of their own that becomes meaningful, reasonable and normal once you get close to it ... a good way to learn about any of these worlds is to submit oneself in the company of the members to the daily round of petty contingencies to which they are subject.
>
> (Goffman, 1961: ix-x)

So when the Birmingham School (CCCS – p. 241) first began to use ethnographic methods in cultural studies in the 1970s, there was a rich tradition to draw upon.

*Learning to Labour* by Paul Willis (1977) is a controversial early application of ethnographic methods by an investigator trained at CCCS in its early 1970s heyday. Willis is interested in the transition from school to work and specifically in the question of how it is that working-class kids come to choose the worst jobs in the labour market. As memorably expressed in the book's opening lines:

> The difficult thing to explain about how middle-class kids get middle-class jobs is why others let them. The difficult thing to explain about how

> working-class kids get working class jobs is how they let themselves.
>
> (Willis 1977: 1)

They are not forced or duped into taking low-paid work with poor long-term prospects. They make a choice. Willis's study attempts to understand and explain the choice they make. He uses the methods of participant observation, interviews, groups discussions and case study work. He concentrates on one group of 12 boys at a secondary modern he calls Hammertown Boys School. He has some smaller groups both from this school and neighbouring schools to serve as points of comparison. The school's intake is entirely working class and Hammertown has the reputation of being a 'good' school. The main focus of Willis's research was on the group of 12 boys. He spent a great deal of time with them as a participant observer, both in class (sitting with the pupils) and outside of it. This provided opportunities for individual interviews and group discussions, and allowed him the opportunity to become closely acquainted with the boys over their last two years at school. Willis was also interested in how they dealt with the world of work, and followed the boys into their first jobs after leaving school. In the workplace Willis spent short periods of time with each of the 12 boys and with some of the boys in the control groups. He also interviewed the boys and did some further interviews with their foremen, managers and shop stewards.

The boys develop an oppositional culture. They quite consciously reject the school's authority structures through many minor acts of defiance. They despise those conformist pupils who do their homework and play things by the school's rules. They – the 'lads' – feel superior to those pupils they call 'ear'oles'. The lads frequently come into conflict with teachers over how they dress (they prefer the style of the latest youth subculture, not school uniform). They drink. They smoke as soon as they are through the school gates. They brag about their sexual conquests. They do as little school work as they can. They show up while the register is taken then manage to 'wag off' their classes, often finding other places and activities within the school to occupy their time when they are not simply 'dossing'. 'Having a laff' and fighting are major

## Box 4.2

### 'Having a laff'

**'Even communists laff' (Joey)**

The space won from the school and its rules by the informal group is used for the shaping and development of particular cultural skills principally devoted to 'having a laff'. The 'laff' is a multifaceted implement of extraordinary importance in the counter-school culture. As we saw before, the ability to produce it is one of the defining characteristics of being one of 'the lads' – 'We can make them laff, they can't make us laff'. But it is also used in many other contexts: to defeat boredom and fear, to overcome hardship and problems – as a way out of almost anything. In many respects the 'laff' is the privileged instrument of the informal, as the command is of the formal. Certainly 'the lads' understand the special importance of the 'laff':

[In an individual discussion]

Joey  I think fuckin' laffing is the most important thing in fuckin' everything. Nothing ever stops me laffing (...) I remember once, there was me, John, and this other kid, right, and these two kids cum up and bashed me for some fuckin' reason or another. John and this other kid were away, off (...) I tried to give 'em one, but I kept fuckin' coppin' it ... so I ran off, and as I ran off, I scooped a handful of fuckin' snow up, and put it right over me face, and I was laffing me bollocks off. They kept saying 'You can't fuckin' laff'. I should have been scared but I was fuckin' laffing (...)

PW  What is it about having a laugh, (...) why is it so important?

Joey  (...) I don't know why I want to laff, I dunno why it's so fuckin' important. It just is (...) I think it's just a good gift, that's all, because you can get out of any situation. If you can laff, if you can make yourself laff, I mean really convincingly, it can get you out of millions of things (...) You'd go fuckin' berserk if you didn't have a laff occasionally.

Key to transcript symbols:

...  Pause

(...)  Material edited out
(Willis, 1977: 29)

preoccupations. In addition there is a lot of sexism and racism evident in the lads' talk among themselves.

When it comes to seeking a job, the lads choose those forms of heavy manual labour that pay reasonably well in the short term but which do not offer 'prospects'. Willis's main point is that the oppositional culture of the school actually prepares them for this type of work and seals their fate. It provides a context in which these occupations are positively valued, undertaken with pride as a symbol of one's adult masculinity. This is one of the ways how the class structure reproduces itself.

Willis secures his interpretation of the lads' conduct by quoting extensively from individual and group interviews. He is able to depict the attitudes and points of view of the lads by presenting verbatim transcripts in

the text. Consider the fragment shown in Box 4.2 in which Willis develops the theme of humour as an instrument to subvert the authority of the school.

This is a common device in ethnography but its use is not as unproblematic as first seems. Willis has been criticised for not paying sufficient attention to the intricacies of interpreting some of his data. For example, he seems to take the lads' dislike of the authority of teachers as evidence of a general opposition to authority in general. The issue here is how particular pieces of the lads' talk are interpreted as evidence of a broader analytic theme, a very common problem in any ethnographic analysis. More generally, Willis is said to develop 'over-rapport' with the lads so that much of the book reads as almost a celebration of what they think and do. Willis seems ready to find in the lads' behaviour and attitudes traces of authentic working-class culture, yet the ear'oles, who are no less working class, are denied that voice (Hammersley and Atkinson, 1983; Bessett and Gualtieri, 2002). Ethnography has been derided in some academic circles as 'merely descriptive'. But cultural description and analysis turns out to be a rather more complex process than is often thought.

Cultural studies uses ethnographic methods in order to access people's lived experience. That lived experience includes experience of texts traditionally considered the province of specialists in the humanities. Janice Radway's (1987) examination of how women read romance novels offers a novel ethnographic approach to the study of popular fiction. It also links to the new directions cultural studies took towards audiences in the 1970s and 1980s.

Studies of romance fiction prior to Radway adopted textualist methods. They undertook a thematic analysis of popular romantic fiction, concluding that they reinforced and perpetuated prevailing patriarchal attitudes, practices and institutions. Women's pleasure ultimately came down to pleasing men. Such approaches, in Stuart Hall's distinction, concentrated on the encoding of cultural texts in isolation from how these texts were decoded by their audiences. Radway seeks to remedy this inattention by addressing not only how readers interpret texts but also how they make use of them in their everyday lives.

To follow through this approach Radway carried out ethnographic interviews with a group of avid romantic novel readers in 'Smithton', a city in a Midwestern state of the USA. She was directed to 'Dot Evans', a 48-year-old bookshop worker who was regularly consulted by a large network of women who were heavy consumers of romances. Dot's knowledgeability about romance novels was well known. In fact she developed a newsletter to comment on the qualities of new romantic fiction. She became so successful that publishers began to ask her to read manuscripts for them. Radway's research activity consisted of:

➤ approximately 60 hours of interviews with Dot over an eight-month period and observation of Dot's interactions with bookshop customers;

➤ group and individual interviews with 16 regular customers;

➤ a lengthy questionnaire given to 42 customers.

Radway (1983: 57) reports that the demographic profile of her sample seemed to match what information she could glean from the market analysis obtained from somewhat secretive publishing houses. Around two-thirds of her sample were aged between 25 and 50. The Smithton group were particularly avid romance readers: half of them read between four to 16 romances a month while 40 per cent read more than 20. Asked why they read romances, the overwhelming response was 'escape' or 'relaxation' ('its an escape'; 'it offers me a small vacation from everyday life'). A big part of the attraction of the books was their fantasy element, how they contrasted with the humdrum concerns of the women's ordinary life. In particular, 'the heroine is frequently treated as they themselves would most like to be loved' (Radway 1983: 60). Dot spoke for many romance readers when she told Radway that romance reading amounts to a ' "declaration of independence" from the social roles of wife and mother' (Radway 1983: 60–1). In this time out from family obligations women are afforded an opportunity for emotional reconstitution.

Discovering that many of her sample knew each other and thus made up a loose social network, Radway deployed the literary critic Stanley Fish's notion of 'interpretive communities'. This is the idea that the meaning of a text is neither produced by its author nor by the reader acting on their own. Rather, readers from the same social grouping will make sense of a text in much the same way, in accordance with much the same standards. Radway found that the Smithton romance readers made up an interpretive community with shared standards about what constituted a 'good' and 'bad' romantic novel: for example, a good novel will have no obscenity or explicit sex; no serious abuse of the heroine; and is likely to correspond to a narrative structure in which misunderstandings and misrepresentations are finally cleared away as the hero's apparent indifference toward the heroine is revealed as only hesitancy on his part about declaring his love and need for her. Fish made the point that culture fills people's heads in finely detailed ways. By taking an eth-

**Figure 4.3** A selection of popular romantic fiction.

nographic approach in her research Radway was able to discover an interpretive community of romance readers who 'join forces symbolically and in a mediated way in the privacy of their individual homes and in the culturally devalued sphere of leisure activity' (Radway 1987: 212).

## 4.4 Conclusion

This chapter has sketched some of the leading methods used by researchers in cultural studies. The aim has been not to provide a comprehensive and detailed guide but rather to give an indication of some of the popular and distinctive ways of working in this field. We hope that the discussion will encourage readers to undertake some research of their own. The good news is that neither huge resources nor expensive equipment are required. Some kinds of work in cultural studies require no more than a text (a magazine, a film, a CD, a book) and an analytical and critical inclination. For other kinds of work the reader may need to draw more extensively on established social science methods (interviews, ethnography, content analysis). The

further reading below offers a good guide to concepts and methods.

A useful exercise is to take a text and to interrogate it with ideas drawn from a particular theory or theorist. This might then generate research questions like the following.

➤ What insight might semiotics offer into anti-globalisation demonstrations?

➤ How would Walter Benjamin respond to the Internet?

➤ In what respects could the latest Rolling Stones tour be regarded as a postmodern phenomenon?

➤ What light could Georg Simmel cast on the attractions of shopping malls?

➤ How might Richard Hoggart rewrite *The Uses of Literacy* at the beginning of the twenty-first century?

Attempting to apply the ideas of a theorist or perspective to a cultural phenomenon should give the reader a surer sense of its potential and shortcomings. What does the theory or theorist illuminate? What gets overlooked? It should also sensitise one to questions of method. Which research methods would provide the evidence to support or question a particular interpretation? Some careful thought needs to be given to the selection of the theory/theorist used to mobilise analysis of any given phenomenon (which theory or theorist would *you* choose to analyse the Lottery?).

> ## Recap
>
> ➤ No single method is *the* method of cultural studies.
>
> ➤ Research in cultural studies coalesces around investigations of texts and investigations of lived experience.
>
> ➤ Textual methods seek to isolate the key components of the messages communicated by the text.
>
> ➤ Methods for investigating lived experience draw upon anthropological and sociological traditions of ethnography.

# Further reading

Perrti Alasuutari's *Researching Culture: Qualitative Method and Cultural Studies* (1995) is a bold attempt to cover a range of methods of analysis relevant to the practice of cultural studies. Jim McGuigan's edited collection *Cultural Methodologies* (1997) contains some influential contributions. Several recent publications outline the current state of the art: Mimi White and James Schwoch's edited collection *Questions of Method in Cultural Studies* (2006); Paula Saukko's book *Doing Research in Cultural Studies* (2003); and *The Practice of Cultural Studies* (2004), co-written by Richard Johnson, Deborah Chambers, Parvati Raghuram and Estella Tincknell. A good guide for students beginning a project in cultural studies is Jane Stokes's *How to do Media and Cultural Studies* (2003).

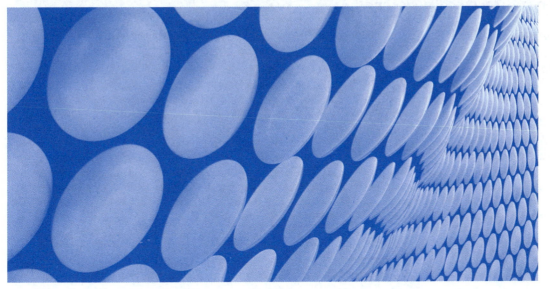

# Chapter 5

# Topographies of culture: geography, meaning and power

## 5.0 Introduction

One increasingly important aspect of cultural studies is what can be called the geographies (or, indeed, topographies) of culture: the ways in which matters of meaning are bound up with spaces, places and land-scapes. One sign of this is that the language of cultural studies is full of spatial metaphors. Chapter 1 of this book, for example, understands culture in terms of 'fields', 'maps' and 'boundaries'. You will also find that cultural studies is full of talk of 'margins', 'borders' and 'networks'. Yet there is more to this than just language since there is also a sense that culture – particularly when it is understood as something that is plural, frag-mented and contested – cannot be understood outside the spaces that it marks out (like national boundaries or gang territories), the places that it makes meaningful

(perhaps the Statue of Liberty or your favourite coffee shop), the landscapes that it creates (from 'England's green and pleasant land' to the suburban shopping mall), and the networks that connect people together (such as virtual communities of gamers on the Internet). What this chapter aims to do is to use a variety of examples, both historical and contemporary, to show the ways in which issues of culture and meaning are geographical. It does this through a dis-cussion which shows how a 'new' cultural geography developed in the late 1980s concerned with the connec-tions between representations of places at a variety of scales from the local to the global and relationships of power. It then goes on to show how this focus on rep-resentation, although still useful and fundamental to geography's place in cultural studies, has a series of limitations. Firstly, in terms of discussions of mobility

## Defining concept 5.1

### Space, place and landscape

#### Space

Considering space means considering the ways in which, in 'reality' or 'representation', the distribution of things and activities, the formation of boundaries and patterns of movements are both culturally produced and part of the construction of culture. The spaces that we inhabit, whether they are the sacred and profane spaces of an African village or of Wall Street, are intimately bound up with the ways in which we live out our lives.

#### Place

Considering place means considering the ways in which particular locations are important in the making of a cultural world. Our understandings of the world are tied closely to the ways in which we construct and contest the meanings of particular, often named, places. For example, the ways in which certain meanings of 'home' are used to support specific understandings of how families should work, or how positive or negative understandings of 'New York' capture the different political and economic relations between the USA and other parts of the world.

#### Landscape

Considering landscape means considering how both an area and the look of that area are laden with meaning. 'Reality' and 'representation' are not easily separated here and the object of study can be a city skyline or a country scene in oils. What is at issue is the ways in which areas and representations of them are part of our cultural worlds. This means that the Los Angeles' skyline can be read as an assertion of the power of big money and that depictions of certain sorts of rural landscapes have been made to represent a particular notion of Englishness.

and movement which show how particular cultural forms are created in the relationships between places, rather than just in places. Secondly, through discussions of performativity which demonstrate how identities are continually being made and remade through performances in particular spaces. Thirdly, through a recognition that cultural studies (and cultural geography) needs to take account of the materiality of objects, technologies and the natural world. If all this is new to you it is worth starting with some basic principles of cultural geography.

Figure 5.1 is a sign from a university campus in east London. It is on a small piece of fenced off and immaculately kept grass next to the Law faculty. It says, 'This grassed area is consecrated ground. It is not to be used for any purpose.' This tiny portion of the earth's surface has been given specific meanings. The plot of land, now part of a university, has been given meaning by being made sacred. In fact, it is part of the cemetery of the Congregation of Spanish and Portuguese Jews, the larger portion of which lies behind a screen of pine trees on the other side of the path passing the sign. The land does have a purpose. It was for burying the dead

of a particular social and cultural group. It is very unlikely that anyone will be buried there now, but the sacred meanings given to that space mean that 'It is not to be used for any [other] purpose.' This little piece of land can, therefore, begin to tell us about how social and cultural groups give meaning to space (through, for example, the rituals of consecration) and how the making of these spaces are part of the definition of social groups and their cultural identities – in this case, a set of Jewish people living in the East End of London but part of much wider national and international religious communities. Thinking about other such spaces can lead us to seeing how social and political conflicts can be played out as cultural conflicts over spaces and their definitions. Thus, during the Second World War, the Nazis in Poland desecrated Jewish gravestones by using them as paving stones and building materials. Indeed, the desecration of Jewish graves and cemeteries continues to be used as a way to attack Jewish people in places as far apart as France and New Zealand. Therefore, this little space raises important questions of who has the power to make meaning and to craft their own spaces and places through which to define

**Figure 5.1** University campus sign.

identities. These are the questions that cultural geography aims to deal with, and we can investigate them further by seeing how cultural geography has developed in ways that put these issues of meaning, power and space right at the heart of what it does.

## Learning objectives

- ➤ To understand the relationship between 'cultural studies' and 'cultural geography'.
- ➤ To see how meanings are given to spaces, places and landscapes through power-laden processes of representation
- ➤ To understand how the centrality of representation has been questioned within cultural geography, and to understand the subsequent interest in the cultural geographies of mobility, performativity and materiality.

# 5.1 What is cultural geography?

There have been different versions of a sub-discipline called 'cultural geography' and many discussions about what it should be and how it should be studied (for general texts see, Crang, 1998; Anderson and Gale, 1993; and Mitchell, 2000). One of the most important sets of arguments was made in the 1980s and discussed what the future of cultural geography should be in relation to the work of the influential American geographer Carl Ortwin Sauer. Sauer studied cultural geography in a particular way. As he put it, 'There is a strictly geographical way of thinking of culture; namely, as the impress of the works of man [sic] upon the area' (Sauer, 1967: 326). What he understood by cultural geography was a matter of the ways in which, particularly in rural areas, people shaped the landscape through field patterns, hedgerows and distinct types of houses, barns and bridges. What he was interested in was the interaction between humans and nature that produced a particular landscape. For him this was material (what mattered were things in the landscape such as crops, trees, and buildings), regional, and tended to be focused on rural traditions since that was where he felt these distinctive regional landscapes could best be seen. This, for Sauer, gave cultural geography a particular emphasis. As he said: 'We are not concerned in geography with the energy, customs, or beliefs of man but with man's record upon the landscape' (Sauer, 1967: 342).

At first the rethinking of cultural geography was not heavily critical of Carl Sauer. Peter Jackson's (1980) 'A plea for cultural geography' argued that geography could learn a lot from anthropology, but also argued that both Sauer's cultural geography and the work of anthropologists had a strong basis in fieldwork and started from the relationships between nature and culture. Jackson thought that Sauer's idea that appraisals of natural resources were part of a set of cultural meanings, and not simply a matter of economic rationalities, offered a way of understanding the importance of culture in material life. At the same time, Denis Cosgrove (1983) was arguing for a radical cultural geography, but again this was one that would combine Karl Marx's concerns for the relationship between nature and culture, and the primary significance of material life, with that of Carl Sauer. Sauer would bring to Marx a more careful understanding of the cultural landscape. Marx would provide Sauer with a stronger definition of class and the inequalities involved in the exploitation of nature.

Despite these early statements the direction in which cultural geography was moving was away from Sauer's vision of what the subject should be. In 1987, Denis Cosgrove and Peter Jackson set out what they took to be the 'New directions in cultural geography'. They argued that it should be:

➤ contemporary as well as historical;

➤ concerned with space as well as landscape;

➤ urban as well as rural;

➤ concerned with relations of domination and resistance;

➤ assertive of the centrality of culture to human life;

➤ concerned with 'representation' as much as 'reality'.

They explicitly stated that cultural geography should not be 'rural and antiquarian', and that it should not be concerned with 'physical artefacts' or 'cultural areas'. A

'new' cultural geography was being constructed against one that, in the process, became 'old'. Cosgrove and Jackson (1987) turned against what they saw as Sauer's conservative anti-modernism, his celebration of the rural and traditional against change and modernity, and his notion that culture somehow existed as an entity independent of particular people (what was called a 'super-organic' notion of culture, see Duncan, 1980). This is especially clear in the first few chapters of Peter Jackson's (1989) *Maps of Meaning*, one of the first textbooks of the 'new cultural geography'. Jackson (1989: 9) castigated Sauer as 'deficient' and argued that 'Cultural geography is in urgent need of reappraisal; its conception of culture is badly outdated and its interest in the physical expression of culture in the landscape is unnecessarily limited.' Jackson rejected Sauer's vision in favour of an analysis that owed much to the 'cultural politics' of Raymond Williams, the Birmingham **Centre for Contemporary Cultural Studies** (p. 241) and the new anthropology.

This alternative version of cultural geography had three basic positions:

1 'Culture' is the meanings that are made by people through social interaction and social relations. Cultural geography is the study of how those meanings relate to questions of space, place and landscape.

2 Those processes of making the cultural meanings of space, place and landscape are matters of power and resistance. Cultural geographers have to concern themselves with who has the power to make those meanings, the ways in which they are challenged, and the effectiveness of those challenges.

3 Those meanings are made through processes of 'representation'. Cultural geographers should study how spaces, places and landscapes are represented in different media such as writing, painting, music, film and photography.

As will be shown later, this emphasis on representation has been questioned. Indeed, the 'new' cultural geography is now not so new. However, from the late 1980s onwards studies of representation formed the basis for a huge range of work that pursued questions of meaning and power through the investigation of spaces, places and landscapes. In what follows we will look at some of that work in relation to landscape, national identity and Orientalism, before seeing how some of these assumptions have come to be questioned in terms of mobility, performance and a return, albeit in a different form, to questions of material culture and nature. Before getting into all that it is worth setting out how this form of cultural geography works with the example of placenames.

## 5.2 Placenames: interaction, power and representation

The first position set out above – that 'culture' is the meanings that are made by people through social interaction and social relations – suggests that the naming of places is a matter of people giving meaning to them by naming them in ways which are shaped by their interaction. Allan Pred's (1990a) research on everyday placenames in nineteenth-century Stockholm illustrates this very nicely. His aim was to recover what he saw as the 'lost words' of nineteenth-century Stockholm – words for places, people, things and activities that are now no longer used – because he saw these words (these meanings) as the keys to the cultural lives of the past. In recovering these lost words he is recovering lost lives and, as he puts it, 'lost worlds'. Box

5.1 contains some of the Stockholm placenames that were used in the late nineteenth century when the city was undergoing a transformative period of intensive industrialisation, urbanisation and modernisation which saw huge areas being torn down and rebuilt. One problem that the city's inhabitants faced, many of them new migrants from the countryside, was simply finding their way around. So Pred sees the placenames that he has recovered, and which were being used by Stockholm's new working class, as part of a 'folk' or 'popular' geography which helped people navigate a rapidly changing city. These names had, Pred notes, certain characteristics: they were local, they were based around the everyday activities of the city's working people, and they were often part of a rude, earthy popular culture. So pubs and cafes were named after the origins or characteristics of those who owned or ran them; or after their characteristics, however unpleasant (who would want to have their meals in *Döden i grytan* or *Brakskiten*? – see Box 5.1). The workhouse for those who had no other work took a name that suggested it was a routine part of the lives of Stockholm's poor, and the names of the areas in which they lived suggested the conditions of their everyday lives. Finally, the comic names for military barracks, the haunts of the rich, and the monument to the king suggest the rude humour of this hard existence. In each case it is evident that names and meanings are being made for places as part of the everyday interactions between people.

## Box 5.1

### Stockholm's Folk Geography

**Pubs and cafés:**

*Fosbergs or Karlbergskan* [Karlberg's wife]

*Ryskan* – The Russian Woman

*Halta Lotta's* – Lame Lotta's

*Glaskalles* – Glass Karlsson's, a reference to his dependence on a glass tube for urinating.

*Futten* – The Shabby Place

*Döden i grytan* – Death in the Pot

*Brakskiten* – The Loud Fart

**Places, public buildings and monuments:**

Military housing – *Korvkasern* – sausage barracks

Workhouse – *Träffen* – the meeting place

An obelisk to King Oscar II – *Kungens tandpetare* – the King's toothpick

*Svältholmen* – Starvation Islet – for a very poor part of the city

*Snobbrännen* – the Snobgutter – for the *Kungsträdgården* – a promenade in the Royal Gardens

(from Pred, 1990a)

Yet there is more to this than just 'social interaction'. The second position of the new cultural geography states that the processes of making the cultural meanings of space, place and landscape are matters of power and resistance As Peter Jackson (1989: ix) states, culture 'is a domain, no less than the political or the economic in which social relations of dominance and subordination are negotiated and resisted, where meanings are not just imposed but contested'. Culture is a contested domain in which different social groups try to define and express meanings, and struggle to impose them on the world, and therefore on other social groups, as the meanings that will count. Placenames are no exception. Indeed, they are a very clear example of this. Giving a place a name is an act of claiming ownership, of defining what that place is, who it belongs to, and what it means. It is important who gets to define the name. This is perhaps most evident in circumstances of colonialism where one group appropriates the land from another and, as part of the process, renames places in a new language with new meanings. As a result, the white settler colonies of the Americas, Australia, New Zealand and southern Africa, are full of European placenames: New York, Melbourne, Wellington, and Johannesburg (Berg and Kearns, 1996; Cohen and Kliot, 1992). Yet it can also be the case where one political regime succeeds another, as in Berlin (Azaryahu, 1986), or where nationalist movements take the opportunity to impose particular meanings on the landscape through placenames (Yeoh, 1996). In nineteenth-century Stockholm the official (rather than popular) response to the need to rename the streets of the changing city was to establish a list of official street names that were increasingly enforced across the city from 1885 onwards as part of a concerted effort to police, clean and regulate the new city. These names fell into six categories:

➤ patriotic and historical names,

➤ nordic mythology,

➤ famous places near the city,

➤ the southern provinces,

➤ the northern provinces,

➤ famous swedish authors,

➤ prominent men within technology and engineering.

As Moaz Azaryahu (1996: 312) has argued, thinking about Berlin, 'commemorative street names, and their officially ordained meanings in particular, are instrumental in substantiating the ruling sociopolitical order and its particular "theory of the world" in the cityscape'. The 'theory of the world' that is evident in Stockholm is a nationalist one. It is also one that is imbued with the middle-class ideas and values of history, progress, high culture and the power of science and technology. The aim was to impose this set of official class-based meanings, and this theory of how the world works, on the cityscape and in the process to obscure the names and meanings of the local, popular and rude culture of working-class Stockholm (Pred, 1992b). Placenaming is therefore a matter of the cultural politics of place.

These examples demonstrate that the names themselves matter as much as who gets to impose them. The third position outlined above is that meanings are made through processes of 'representation'. Each placename represents a place in a particular way, emphasising certain things and obscuring others. Every representation comes from a particular position and works towards particular purposes. It matters, therefore, whether those islands in the Pacific get called 'Aoteroa' (the land of the long white cloud) or 'New Zealand'. It matters whether you say 'Derry' or 'Londonderry' to talk about that city in Northern Ireland, or is it Ulster, the Six Counties or the North? A placename is a representation of a place just as much as a painting, a photograph or a story about that place. What is significant here is the multiplicity of representations. There are many, many competing versions of a place, and it is not simply the case (as it may have seemed for Stockholm) that they are simply opposed to each other, or that one inevitably wins out over the others. Ireland is a good example here. There is certainly a history of colonial placenaming by the British, and of nationalist renaming after independence in the 1920s (for example, Queen's County became County Laois). There is also conflict over naming (Derry or Londonderry?). However, local placenames can connect different sorts of people together as well as divide them as Catherine Nash's (1999) work on the campaign to preserve the names of Townlands in Northern Ireland shows.

Townlands are very small administrative units that cover Ireland. They were under threat in Northern Ireland in the early 1970s because of the Post Office's attempt to get people to use postcodes (like zipcodes) rather than townland names in the addressing and delivery of letters. The campaign to preserve them was both rural and urban, and it involved both Protestant and Catholic communities, and Irish as well as English speakers. The loss of these names was felt very strongly. As one campaigner put it: 'A generation of children are growing up who have never used their townland names in their addresses. A fundamental element in our identity is being lost' (quoted in Nash, 1999: 469). Yet the identities involved were not simple and singular ones. Another activist suggested that these placenames were representations that could indicate complex and shared histories of people in that place:

[T]ownlands help tell the story of the settlement of Ireland from the Celtic peoples who established townlands, through the Norse, Normans, English, Scots and others who have settled in Ireland and left their mark on the landscape. Although predominantly Celtic, townland names bear the distinctive influence of the different peoples who have become part of the Irish fabric. The continued use of townlands and their acceptance as their own by all sections of the community in Ulster makes them a unique and priceless element of our cultural heritage … If we are seeking to heal the wounds that divide our society and to illustrate the richness of what we share, then townlands have a crucial role to play. For they are not only part of a past which we all share but are a living part of the present too.'

(Tony Canavan, Development Officer for the Federation of Local Studies, quoted in Nash, 1999: 472)

There was in the successful Townlands Campaign a recognition of the meanings of placenames being made through social interaction in place, of the politics involved in the struggle for their continued existence, and in the power of these names as representations of places that could unite as well as divide. In what follows we will see these foundations of the new cultural geography at work with many other forms of representation, power and interaction, starting with landscape depictions.

## 5.3 Landscape representation

Jim Duncan, in the *Dictionary of Human Geography* (2000: 703), argues that:

shared meanings are based on representations of the world. Representations not only reflect reality, but they help to constitute reality. People make sense of their worlds and are positioned within social worlds through representations. Some representations are imposed on them from the outside but these are also contested by representations generated from within the culture.

Much of this should now be familiar. Meanings are made through representations, and the contestation over meanings is pursued through competing representations. What is new, and quite difficult to grasp, is that it does not help us very much to simply oppose 'representation' to 'reality', and to ask which representations most closely reflect reality. Without getting too philosophical here, it is certainly the case that we cannot apprehend reality except through representations. So we do not really have a basis for using 'reality' to judge representations in terms of 'bias' or 'distortion of the truth'. It is, therefore, more productive to ask what sorts of 'realities' representations construct and to ask not how far a representation deviates from the truth, but what position the representation is constructed from and what version of the world does it represent. It is on this basis that we can then see how the processes of power – of positioning, imposition and contestation in Duncan's discussion – work out in particular circumstances. Of course, these questions of representation can be addressed to any subject area – representations of men and women, representations of 'race', representations of progress – what we are interested in here are specifically geographical representations. The first of these is representations of landscape.

When discussing landscape what comes most readily to mind is a visual depiction of a certain sort: a land-

**Figure 5.2** Thomas Gainsborough (1748) *Mr and Mrs Andrews.*
(Source: The National Gallery, London.)

scape painting constructed according to the conventions of the 'picturesque' (see Figure 5.2). Indeed, this has become so familiar as a way of depicting landscape that it becomes hard to see these as particular conventions of representation. The characteristics of this sort of depiction are an elevated and distanced viewpoint from which the landscape is seen; the framing of the scene by trees or rocky outcrops; and the organisation of the image into foreground, mid-ground and background by interlocking planes or bands of light, which produces a zig-zag path between the foreground details and the distant horizon (Nash, 2005). These conventions became very important in the depiction of English landscape in the eighteenth and nineteenth centuries and they did so because they constructed a view of the land from a particular position: that of the landowner.

A closer look at Figure 5.2 shows what is going on here. The painting is Thomas Gainsborough's *Mr and Mrs Andrews*, produced in 1748 as both a portrait to celebrate the wedding of Robert Andrews and his new bride Frances and a landscape painting of their estate, the Auburies at Bulmer in Essex. The context for interpreting the painting is the overwhelming importance of land in eighteenth-century England. Land was seen as the foundation of individual and national economic prosperity within a pre-industrial economy. All wealth was seen to come from the land. Land was, therefore,

the foundation of political power within the nation. Only property owners could vote, and parliament was predominantly made up of landowners. It was also seen as the foundation of identity. People like Mr and Mrs Andrews were defined by their relationship to their land and what they did with it. This 'theory of the world' based on the primacy of land and the power of landowners was served by the conventions of picturesque landscape painting. Firstly, the distanced view of the landscape provided by the elevated and removed viewpoint of the picturesque depiction exactly matched the justification that landowners gave for their right to rule and for the inability of others to do so. Eighteenth-century English gentlemen argued that only landowners had the sufficient independence of income (which came from owning land) to effectively govern in the interests of all. Merchants and particularly working people lacked this distanced, objective view. Only landowners could 'both govern impartially and see landscape with a proper distance', the rest of the population 'were thought to be too close to the land to see it "properly", and too caught up in making their own living to consider the good of society as a whole' (Nash, 2005: 159). Secondly, the landscape is presented in its interlocking bands, as a framed and well-organised scene. Eighteenth-century viewers with a keen eye for agricultural techniques would have spotted the neatness of the wheatsheafs and hawthorn hedges, and

## Key influence 5.1

### Edward W. Said (1935–2003)

Edward Said was born in Jerusalem in 1935 and educated in Cairo. Like millions of other Palestinians his family became part of the Palestinian diaspora after the foundation of the State of Israel in 1948. He completed his education in the United States of America, at Princeton and Harvard universities. As Professor of Comparative Literature at Columbia University he has published work on nineteenth- and twentieth-century literature and music, and on the politics and culture of the Palestinians. He has also been an outspoken critic of both Israeli and Palestinian political leaders. He died in 2003.

Said's book *Orientalism* (1978) has had an enormous impact on cultural studies (and on many of the disciplines that contribute to it). It offered a way of understanding the 'politics of **representation**' (p. 43) in texts and images which connected their words and pictures to issues of **power** (p. 64) and domination. Drawing on the work of **Michel Foucault** (p. 20), and combining it with close attention to a range of texts, Said offered a reading of 'The West's' representa-

tions of 'The East' – in novels, poems, scientific texts and academic monographs – which implicated the written word in the practices of imperialism. He argued that the version of the East which was created within this **discourse** (p. 21) was one that was created for the West. It was both a romanticised view of what the West lacked – spirituality, exoticism – and an image that justified the West's imperial domination of the East by portraying it as weak and degenerate. This pioneering work has been followed by a range of similar studies – on other sorts of texts and other places – and has been an important part of the development of a body of postcolonial theory and of other studies which connect language and power. Much of this has also involved criticisms of Said for the ways in which he dealt with power, agency and gender (see pp. 122–5).

Said's other work has attempted to publicise and analyse the plight of the Palestinians. This has been done through historical and political writings (some of which use ideas of 'Orientalism' to understand the

history of Palestine); through attempts to show how they have been misrepresented in a range of texts and images; and through the production of alternative images which offer another view. For example, Said's *After the Last Sky: Palestinian Lives* (1986), which combines his text with photographs by Jean Mohr, is an attempt to evoke and represent the experience of a people who have been displaced and dispossessed. As such it offers an attempt to avoid the discourses that Said set out in *Orientalism* and a corrective to their more recent counterparts.

### Further reading

Said, E.W. (1978) *Orientalism*, Harmondsworth: Penguin.

Said, E.W. (1995) *The Politics of Dispossession*, London: Vintage.

Said, E.W. (1999) *Out of Place: A Memoir* (London, Granta).

Sprinker, M. (ed.) (1992) *Edward Said: A Critical Reader*, Cambridge, MA: Blackwell.

---

would have recognised agricultural improvements such as the five-bar gate and the new breeds of sheep. This was well kept land justifying the power of the landowners.

There is, however, something missing. This a painting of land and landowners which has no room for those that worked the land:

> [T]he means of production are taken for granted: the crop of wheat, the venerable oak, fat sheep, wild partridges and everything else are appropriated by the landowner who stands complacently in front of these accumulated assets. The picture extols the

present and prospective satisfactions of landownership and attendant possessions, offering a life of contented ease, a comely wife, fine clothes, broad acres, a bounteous harvest, an obedient hound at heel and the promise of good shooting ahead.

> (Prince, 1988: 103)

This is a painting about property and, as John Berger has argued, even the material with which it was made plays a part here. As he puts it, 'among the pleasures their portrait gave to Mr and Mrs Andrews, was the pleasure of seeing themselves depicted as landowners and this pleasure was enhanced by the ability of oil paint to render their land in all its substantiality.' (Berger, 1972: 108). Oil paint made things look solid, substantial and real even if that was only achieved through daubing oily pigment onto canvas. The representation made the land substantial and real. Therefore, in form, content, and medium this mode of landscape representation presented the world of the landowners and their power in eighteenth-century England. The representation gave it reality.

However, as it stands this argument is a little too simple. First, it is important to situate paintings such as *Mr and Mrs Andrews* within the range of forms of landscape depiction in eighteenth-century England, and as they changed over time. As John Barrell (1980) has shown, doing so demonstrates that it was not simply the case of the dominance of landowners and the picturesque, but of a range of attempts from quite different positions to resolve the contradictions of depicting working people within a changing agricultural landscape. He argues that there were landscape representations, such as the poetry of John Clare, that sought to give the rural poor and dispossessed a place in the landscape. Secondly, there was a continual and increasing challenge to the political ideology of land and landownership from the growing towns and cities. This represented landowners not in terms of independence and objectivity, but in terms of corruption and selfishness. In contrast, the towns, which were claiming the right to be represented in parliament, presented themselves as places of order, progress, and prosperity. In each instance, for city as well as countryside, the battle for political legitimacy was a war of representations (Arscott *et al.*, 1988; Williams, 1973a). Thirdly, this is not just about class. While *Mr and Mrs Andrews* can be divided into two halves, with the possessors on one side and what is possessed on the other, there is a debate about where the line should be drawn. As Gillian Rose (1993) has pointed out Mrs Andrews was both possessor and possession. Eighteenth-century England's property laws meant that, following her marriage, the new Mrs Andrews passed control of all her property to her husband. Indeed, she herself had become her husband's property. Rose sees her as seated and fixed at the foot of the (family) tree, and as part of the landscape that is ordered and viewed by the con-

ventions of the picturesque. The power relations here are ones of gender as well as class. Finally, the history of this form of landscape representation is not simply confined to England. The imperial and colonial engagement of England with the rest of the world in the eighteenth and nineteenth centuries meant that the conventions of the picturesque were used as part of the representation and settlement of land overseas. The distanced and ordered view of landscapes in the Americas, Africa, Asia and the Pacific were important in their possession by European travellers, soldiers and settlers (Nash, 2005). These new settings also brought new ambivalences and contradictions (Quilley, 2003).

These historical debates over the interpretation of eighteenth-century landscape painting have strong contemporary resonances too. This period and this form of representation were crucial in establishing a set of meanings for the English countryside that still endure. The idealised, chocolate box view of a serene, peaceful and orderly rural landscape and society is summarised as 'the rural idyll'. As Keith Halfacree (1996: 51) puts it, this is the representation of 'a particular type of rural land, rooted in the past of the large country house and widely celebrated as "our" national heritage. Physically, "real" England consists of small villages joined by narrow lanes and set amongst small fields where cows lazily graze away the day. Socially, it is a tranquil landscape of social stability and community, where people know not just their next door neighbours but everyone else in the village ... The countryside is perceived as unchanging, and as an escape from the urban industrial society, characterized by tension, strife, pollution and general misery.' It is, as he says, 'profoundly conservative', and this version of the countryside has been used to defend it against the perceived threats from New Age Travellers and from urban liberals ('townies') seeking to impose a fox hunting ban and to establish rights of access for all over the claims of property owners.

It is, however, important to remember that the process of representation and interpretation continues as different positions are taken in contests to make meaning. *Mr and Mrs Andrews* has also been used to challenge the rule of property. The *Guardian* cartoonist Steve Bell redrew it in 1992 with Margaret Thatcher and John Major as the happy couple, and a sign saying

**Figure 5.3** Yinka Shonibare (1998) *Mr and Mrs Andrews without their heads.* (Source: The National Gallery of Canada.)

'Trespassers will be shot' on the tree. More recently, the artist Yinka Shonibare has reworked this group as *Mr and Mrs Andrews without their heads* (1998) (Figure 5.3). Here the couple are disconnected from their landscape. They are headless and propertyless: aristocrats after the revolution. Instead the artist seeks to depict the connections between England and the rest of the world by dressing the figures in the sort of printed cloth that was a product of a world made through imperial networks: cotton produced in India, dyed in Europe and sold in Africa. As part of the same group of works which saw Shonibare dress the statue on top of the Tate Gallery in London (originally funded by money from sugar plantations) in batik, this art work is an attempt to change the meanings of *Mr and Mrs Andrews* by re-presenting and challenging the notions of property, identity and legitimacy through which it was structured by removing all the conventions of the picturesque. As one commentator has put it this is a form of sly post-colonial revenge.

## 5.4 National identity

All of these forms of representation raise the question of the relationship between geography and identity, one of the key concerns of cultural studies. If we define identity as 'a sense of self that encompasses who people think they are, and how other people regard them'

(Blunt *et al.*, 2003: 72) then there is a similar relationship between self-definition and the imposed definitions of others as in the discussion of representation. This means that identities are always social constructions rather than simply matters for the individual. It also means that contestation over different versions of identity are power struggles. In this chapter we will see many ways in which identities have geographies, but the most obvious involves identities which are constructed in relation to places. People identify with places. They say that they are Los Angelenos, Parisians, or Paulistanos. They also construct their identities at the level of neighbourhoods within cities, or even particular streets. And in many very significant ways our identities are defined both by ourselves and for us in claims or attributions of national identity.

One very influential framework for understanding national identity is Benedict Anderson's (1983) idea of 'imagined communities'. Anderson's starting point was the wars in the 1970s between Cambodia, Vietnam and China. He wanted to understand why all these Marxist-socialist (or communist) states were fighting against each other as nation-states. He also looked at Eastern Europe – and remember that this was before the fall of the Soviet Union – and concluded that it was only the presence of the Red Army that was preventing armed conflict between the state-socialist nation-states in the region. As he put it, and history has proved him right, 'Who can be confident that Yugoslavia and Albania will not one day come to blows?' (1983: 12). Any idea that nationalism would disappear seemed to him to be an illusion and he set out to study it. His approach is to say that nations are 'cultural artefacts' that we create in our collective imaginations. This does not mean that they are simply illusions. Instead they have a huge power as deep attachments for which people are willing to fight and die, as very many bloody wars have shown.

Anderson's (1983: 15) definition of the nation is a political community that is 'imagined as both inherently limited and sovereign'. Firstly, 'It is *imagined* because the members of even the smallest nation will never know most of their fellow-members, meet them, or even hear of them, yet in the minds of each lives the image of their communion.' Secondly, it is imagined as *limited* because not even the largest nation imagines that it could include all of humankind. Unlike empires or religions of conversion (such as Christianity and Islam) the nation always imagines itself as one political community existing in a world of nations, all similar but different. Finally, the nation is imagined as *sovereign*. It is the central principle of nationalism that the nation should determine its own destiny, and to do so each nation should have its own state. Thus the ideal political form is seen to be the nation-state, and the world should be made up of a patchwork of nation-states, again similar but different. The deep attachments formed come from imagining these limited and sovereign entities as *communities* – what Anderson terms 'a deep horizontal comradeship' where internal divisions are much less important than being different from other nations – and understanding them in a language of primordial attachments and national destiny. In the words of a current football chant: 'I'm England till I die, I'm England till I die. I know I am. I'm sure I am. I'm England till I die.'

Significantly, these imagined communities are imagined to be rooted in place. The imagining of a nation as a community also imagines it in relation to a particular, and particularly meaningful, part of the world: the homeland. This is imagined as a territory with specific borders and boundaries, so representations on maps become very important. It is also imagined as a certain sort of landscape with distinctive national characteristics. This can be seen in Keith Halfacree's discussion of the Englishness of 'the rural idyll.' Indeed, Stephen

Daniels (1993: 5) has argued that 'Landscapes ... provide visible shape; they picture the nation.' For example, he shows that John Constable's *The Hay-Wain* (1821) (Figure 5.4) has been seen as the definitive representation of an English national landscape. Looking at this picture was to look directly at England. In 1916 it was used in a *Country Life* article to illustrate the 'Green and Pleasant Land' for which men were dying, and in 1929 it was redrawn for a *Daily Express* cartoon by Sydney Stube to protest against the brash 'American' commercial development of the English countryside with petrol stations and the sort of metal advertising boards that are now seen as quaint relics from a more innocent age. As Daniels points out, each of these representations was using the notion of the English countryside as a way of constructing a version of national identity from a particular position and for particular political purposes.

Nationalism is, therefore, always a matter of cultural politics. Culture matters to nationalists because for them primary political identities – which nation you belong to – are defined in cultural terms. Therefore, nationalist movements devote much attention to symbolic struggles over space. They devise placenames to inscribe their theory of the world into the landscape. They use public monuments and memorials to give meaning to space and to 'transform neutral places into ideologically charged sites' (Whelan, 2002: 508). This is often done in opposition to colonial rule. For example, we can see the construction of an ideologically-charged landscape in colonial Dublin, and its subsequent destruction after the end of formal imperial rule from London. Before Irish independence in 1922 the monumental landscape of Dublin included statues of the English monarchs William III, George I, George II and Queen Victoria; of the military commanders Lord Nelson and Duke of Wellington; and a range of the English aristocrats who had governed the island for the British. As a writer in *The Nation* put it in 1843, 'We have statues to William the Dutchman, to the four Georges – all either German by birth or German by feeling – to Nelson, a great admiral but an Englishman, while not a single statue of any of the many celebrated Irishmen whom their country should honour adorns a street or square of our beautiful metropolis' (quoted in Whelan, 2002: 512). Wellington was born in Ireland but

**Figure 5.4** John Constable (1821) *The Hay-Wain.* (Source: The National Gallery, London.)

he is famous for saying that being born in a stable did not make one a horse! Even with the addition of statues of Irish cultural and political figures such as Oliver Goldsmith and Edmund Burke this was still 'a landscape of colonial power.' (Whelan, 2002: 521).

The War of Independence fought against the British from 1919–21 ended with a treaty that partitioned Ireland (separating Ulster from the rest) and sparked a civil war that pitted different nationalist political parties against each other in a battle to control Ireland's future and the type of nationalism that would shape it. During and after this there were attempts to create a new national identity through Dublin's symbolic landscape. New statues and monuments were erected in Dublin to nationalist leaders such as Charles Stewart Parnell, Daniel O'Connell and James Larkin. It also meant the destruction of the old landscape of power. The statue of William III was blown up in 1928, and that of George II was similarly destroyed in 1937 the day after the coronation of George VI. Finally, the fiftieth anniversary of the Easter Rising of 1916 saw Dublin's Nelson's column toppled by another republican bomb. In each case a message was being sent to the British about their continued presence on the island of Ireland. More quietly, the large statue of Queen Victoria (which James Joyce called the *Auld Bitch*) was removed from the front of the Irish parliament in 1948,

the year that Ireland left the Commonwealth. It was eventually rescued from a museum overflow store in County Offaly and given to the Australians in their bicentennial year. It now stands outside the restored Queen Victoria Building in Sydney.

There are two stories here. One is the cultural battle for national determination waged in terms of control over the symbolic space of monuments and memorials. The other is the ways in which these nationalist meanings are themselves part of symbolic battles over the meanings of nationalism that relate to the sorts of political and social divisions – of class, gender and ethnicity – that are obscured, but never removed, within the 'imagined community' (for example, Bell, 1999; Leitner and Kang, 1999; MacDonald, 1995; and Sidorov, 2000). Nations may imagine themselves as 'communities', but like all communities they are full of differences which work their way out through varied ideas of what the nation should be and who should get to define it. For example, in early twentieth-century Ireland women found themselves in a contradictory position in relation to nationalist politics (Nash, 1993). On the one hand they were central to nationalist images of Ireland. Paintings such as Paul Henry's *The Potato Diggers* depicted the peasant women of the west of Ireland as part of a distinctive Irish landscape (Figure 5.5), and as the key to a set of

**Figure 5.5** Paul Henry (1912) *The Potato Diggers.* (Source: The National Gallery of Ireland.)

moral values that connected that landscape to the nation through the values of the family and motherhood. Yet this meant that women were marginalised in terms of political participation in the nation. Ireland's 1937 Constitution guaranteed 'to protect the family … as the necessary basis of social order and as indispensable to the Welfare of the Nation and the State' and promised to 'ensure that mothers shall not be obliged by economic necessity to engage in labour to the neglect of their duties in the home'. This version of nationalism fixed women in the home as wives and mothers, denied them the rights and responsibilities of full citizenship – such as sitting on juries – and prevented them working in civil service occupations. Nationalism's imagined community was constructed to include different members on a differential basis. Similar questions are raised in relation to Englishness and 'race'. In 2000 the Parekh Report from the anti-racist Runnymede Trust argued, that: 'To be English, as the term is in practice used, is to be white. Britishness is not ideal, but at least it appears acceptable, particularly when suitably qualified – Black British, Indian British, British Muslim and so on' (2000: 38). This question of whether blackness and brownness and

Englishness are mutually exclusive (Gilroy, 1987) was understood using Anderson's terminology. There was a recognition (also present in the work of artists such as Yinka Shonibare and Ingrid Pollard, see Kinsman 1995) that the meanings of Englishness, including those of the 'rural idyll', were problematic in terms of 'race'. As the Parekh Report put it, provoking a storm of controversy, 'A state is not only a territorial and political entity, but also an 'imagined community'. A genuinely multicultural Britain urgently needs to reimagine itself' (Runnymede Trust, 2000: 15).

## 5.5 Discourses of Orientalism

Thinking through these representations of places (indeed, all representations) requires concepts that allow the grouping together of those that work in similar ways, and which deal with the regularities and differences in the relations between meaning, power and representation across different media and different contexts. A concept that seeks to do that is the idea of 'discourse' associated with the French social theorist Michel Foucault. This enables us to speak of a discourse of 'the rural idyll' that links together eighteenth-century oil paintings, early twentieth-century magazine articles, and twenty-first-century advertisements for country homes. Discourses can be defined as:

> the frameworks that define the possibilities for knowledge. As such, a discourse exists as a set of 'rules' (formal or informal, acknowledged or unacknowledged) which determine the sorts of statements that can be made. These 'rules' determine what the criteria for truth are, what sorts of things can be talked about, and what sorts of things can be said about them.
>
> (Blunt *et al.*, 2003: 11)

Foucault himself used this idea to talk about the changing forms of knowledge that were at work in discussing medicine, madness, criminal justice and sexuality. In doing so he was always interested in the connection between these forms of knowledge and relationships of power. Foucault's basic view of knowledge had some distinctive characteristics. Firstly, he did

## Defining concept 5.2

### Essentialism and difference

Essentialism is the doctrine that ascribes a fixed property or 'essence' as universal to a particular category of people. To propose that women are good childcarers because they are women, or that black people are good at sports because they are black, or that Jews are good at arguing because they are Jews – all because 'they are like that' – is to engage in essentialist thinking. Stereotyping any cultural grouping works along essentialist lines.

In cultural studies there is a wariness of essentialist reasoning for at least four reasons:

1 Proposing supposedly 'essential' characteristics often simply involves the reproduction of the prejudices of one group about another – essentialist reasoning imposes a partial set of judgements grounded in the situation and interests of one social group upon another.

2 Essentialist accounts of persons and activities as 'typical' usually involve enormous over-generalisation which ignores the differences between the members of a category (are *all* women really like that? or *all* black people?).

3 It follows that essentialist reasoning cannot explain why these differences within a category exist in the first place.

4 Essentialist doctrines are especially pernicious when they postulate the presence of essential characteristics as a matter of biology and genetic inheritance.

The alternative to essentialism is some form of social constructionist account. The prototypical view here is summed up in Simone de Beauvoir's statement: 'one is not born a woman; one becomes one'. Social constructionism emphasises the part played by social learning in the acquisition of supposedly 'essential' characteristics. It can be regarded as a more realistic point of view that is better equipped to do justice to the diversity of experiences encountered by persons within a category. Constructionism does not have it all its own way, however. Some would maintain that 'black music' has a core that only 'black' people can fully appreciate because of their shared origins and experiences of oppression.

Cultural studies tends towards a valorisation of differences and a corresponding recognition of the plurality of identities to which persons can lay claim. Some of these identities arise from the increasing scale and complexity of modern societies (class, occupation, education, race, gender, regional and national identities). Others derive from the emergence of new social movements (**feminism** (p. 82), gay rights, black struggles, environmentalism) and create the social basis for **identity** (p. 142) politics. The celebration of difference brings difficulties of its own. The relations between groups are power relations that mark off who is to be included and excluded. They are often accompanied by valuations of relative worth made in the context of material interests. The policy of 'separate development' in apartheid South Africa was not simply about maintaining cultural differences. Also, the plurality of identities available can make for some strange alliances: for example, **bell hooks** (p. 141) (1991: 59) observes that 'sexism has always been a political stance mediating racial domination, enabling white men and black men to share a common sensibility about sex roles and the importance of male domination'. Rights to difference, it seems, can only be sustained within an agreed framework of rights and provision universal to all members of a society.

### Further reading

Grossberg, L. (1996) 'Identity and cultural studies: is that all there is?', in S. Hall and P. du Gay (eds) *Questions of Cultural Identity*, London: Sage.

Sarup, M. (1996) *Identity, Culture and the Postmodern World*, Edinburgh: Edinburgh University Press.

not believe in any ultimate truth, but argued that there are systems of knowledge (discourses) produced by multiple authors which organise, rather than correspond to, what is out there in the world. This means that 'truth' is internal to these discourses, and differs between them. What was 'true' for the sixteenth-century view of madness, nature or sexuality was very different from what was 'true' for the nineteenth-century view. Each discourse has its own rules for ordering and judging statements about the world. Secondly, Foucault argued that the relationship between power and knowledge was a very close one (he used the term power/knowledge to show just how inseparable they are, see Foucault, 1980). As he put it, 'there is no power relation without the correlative constitution of a field of knowledge, nor any knowledge that does not presuppose and constitute at the same time power relations' (Foucault, 1977: 27). Power and knowledge are not separate, with one judged bad and the other good. They depend upon each other. You need knowledge to exert power, good or bad. And with power comes knowledge. This understanding of discourse as regimes of power/knowledge means that this is not just about words (the everyday meaning of discourse). For Foucault it was important that discourses worked through particular institutions and spaces. For example, he saw the modern hospital and the modern prison – which separated the sick and the bad from the rest of society – as particular manifestations of regimes of power/knowledge in the areas of medicine and criminal justice.

As well as understanding how discourses operate from certain spaces such as the court room or the hospital, cultural geographers and others have been interested in how representations of places, territories and landscapes can be thought of in terms of discourse. The most well-known and influential (and therefore most criticised) version of this is **Edward Said**'s argument that representations of 'the East' made by 'the West' are organised as a discourse he calls 'Orientalism'. Said was Professor of Comparative Literature at Columbia University in New York and a politically active Palestinian in exile. His work was both an intellectual and political project to demonstrate the implications of the ways in which the West has represented the East. His book *Orientalism* (1978) was primarily based on nineteenth-century textual representations of North Africa and the Middle East from English and French sources. His aim was to show how these representations divided the world up into 'East' and 'West', Orient and Occident, and gave each very different characteristics. The problem was what he called 'geographical essentialism', and he argued that 'the notion that there are geographical spaces with indigenous, radically 'different' inhabitants who can be defined on the basis of some religion, culture or racial essence proper to that geographical space is . . . a highly debateable idea' (Said, 1978: 322). For Said, following Foucault, the divisions seen in the world are a product of these discourses. As he said, 'the Orient is not an inert fact of nature. It is not merely *there*, just as the Occident is not just *there* either. . . . [B]oth geographical and cultural entities ... such as locales, regions, geographical sectors as 'Orient' and 'Occident' are man-made' (1978: 4–5). What was important was the question of who had the power to make these geographical entities and identities through representation. Said set out to describe the 'rules' of the discourse of Orientalism and to show how this form of knowledge was connected to power.

Firstly, as we have already seen, Said argued that this discourse makes sense of the world, and makes statements about it, based on a binary division of it into 'West' and 'East': Orientalism *dichotomises*. It then assumes that the West or, more usually, the East can be spoken of in general terms: 'One could speak in Europe of an Oriental personality, an Oriental atmosphere, an Oriental tale, Oriental despotism, or an Oriental mode of production, and be understood' (1978: 31–32). Orientalism allowed statements to be made about the absolute differences between Orientals and Occidentals. For example, as Lord Cromer – England's representative in Egypt – put it in 1908, 'Want of accuracy, which easily degenerates into untruthfulness, is in fact the main characteristic of the Oriental mind. ... [Whereas] The European is a close reasoner; his statements of fact are devoid of any ambiguity' (quoted in Said, 1978: 38). Such statements serve to 'strip humanity down to ... ruthless cultural and racial essences' (1978: 36). So Orientalism *essentialises*. Finally, East and West are always being compared. While the Orient may have positive characteristics as well as negative ones – as 'a place of romance, exotic beings, haunting memories and landscapes, remarkable experiences' (1978: 1) – there is no doubt that the future lies with the West. Therefore, Orientalism *hierarchises* (or creates hierarchies). As Said argued, it is through this discourse that the West creates an identity for itself in opposition to the essentialised characteristics of its Oriental 'Other' (see Box 5.2). In the process these geographical essentialisms severely limit what those on either side of the division can be, and what sorts of relationships can be formed between them.

Said's aim was to demonstrate the connections between the discourse of Orientalism and Western imperial power over the East. Again, following Foucault

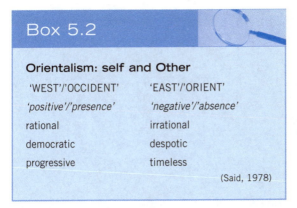

**Box 5.2**

**Orientalism: self and Other**

| 'WEST'/'OCCIDENT' | 'EAST'/'ORIENT' |
|---|---|
| 'positive'/'presence' | 'negative'/'absence' |
| rational | irrational |
| democratic | despotic |
| progressive | timeless |

(Said, 1978)

he sought to show how this discourse was embedded in institutions and practices. As well as a way of thinking about the East which could be found in pictures, poetry and prose, Orientalism was an academic discipline for those who studied the East, and, from the late eighteenth century, 'the corporate institution for dealing with the Orient … by making statements about it, authorizing views of it, describing it, by teaching it, settling it, ruling over it: in short, Orientalism as a Western style for dominating, restructuring, and having authority over the Orient' (Said, 1978: 3). For Said, Orientalism as a form of knowledge was intimately bound up with the process of imperialism. The 'rules' of the discourse enabled imperial rule. For example, when Napoleon invaded Egypt in 1798 as a way of putting the British empire in India under pressure, he not only sought to take military possession of the country, but to take intellectual possession of it too. The full-scale academy that accompanied him published their work between 1809 and 1828 as the 23 huge volumes of the *Description de l'Egypte*. This was not so much the practical forms of knowledge required by empire – such as a mapping of the land invaded – but Said argued that it sought to organise knowledge of Egypt in European terms: 'to make out of every observable detail a generalisation and out of every generalisation an immutable law about the Oriental nature, temperament, mentality, custom, or type' (Said, 1978: 86). (See also Godlewska, 1995.) The aim was to establish in discourse the regular characteristics of the Orient through which it could be ruled.

Said primarily restricted his analysis to eighteenth- and nineteenth-century textual representations of the Middle East produced by the English and the French.

His few comments on American representations have been taken much further by Donald Little in his book *American Orientalism* (2003) to argue that very similar images of Arabs appear in twentieth-century popular culture – in films such as *Jewel of the Nile* (1984), cartoons such as Disney's *Aladdin* (1992), and magazines like the *National Geographic* (see also Shaheen, 2003) – and in policy documents which have shaped US foreign policy in the Middle East. Indeed, in some quarters 'Orientalism' seems alive and well. Sir John Keegan, the military historian and Defence Editor of the *Daily Telegraph*, offered the following analysis of the 'war against terror' in Afghanistan in October 2001:

> Westerners fight face to face, in stand-up battle, and go on until one side or the other gives in …
> Orientals, by contrast, shrink from pitched battle, which they often deride as a sort of game, preferring ambush, surprise, treachery and deceit as the best way to overcome an enemy. … This war belongs within the much larger spectrum of a far older conflict between settled, creative productive Westerners and predatory, destructive Orientals … It is no good pretending that the peoples of the desert and the empty spaces exist on the same level of civilisation as those that farm and manufacture. They do not.

> (Quoted in Driver, 2003 p. 131)

Indeed, Derek Gregory (2004) has shown the full range of Orientalist imagery and ideas that have underpinned recent Western interventions in Afghanistan and Iraq, and Israeli policy in Palestine. It is clear that the sorts of essentialisms (including geographical essentialisms) that Said was keen to challenge are still present in influential views of the world. For example, Harvard professor Samuel Huntington's analysis of the post-Cold War world order portrayed it in terms of a 'Clash of Civilizations' (see Figure 5.6). The old ideological battlelines between capitalism and communism would be replaced by conflicts between civilizations understood as 'cultural entities', particularly between what he saw as 'Western Civilization' and 'Islamic Civilization' (Huntington, 1993). While this may be a view endorsed by fundamentalists on both sides it is clearly essentialist. It represents changing, differentiated and contested sets of ideas and institutions – such

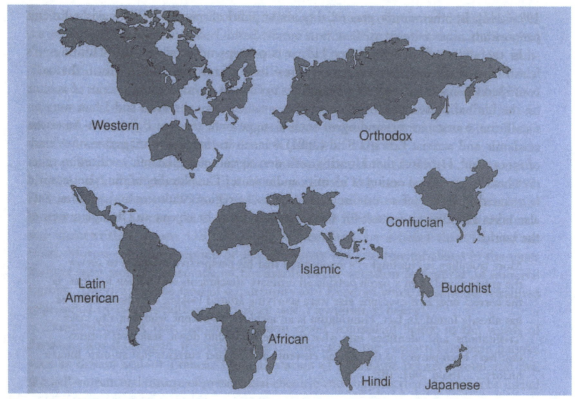

**Figure 5.6** The world according to Samuel Huntington. (Source: *Foreign Affairs*, 72(3), © the Council on Foreign Relations, Inc.)

as liberalism, democracy, and Islam – as singular, coherent and unchanging entities in eternal conflict to the death. As Said put it in an essay published just before his death (objecting both to American fundamentalism and its Islamic counterpart): 'The terrible conflicts that herd people under falsely unifying rubrics like "America", "The West" or "Islam" and invent collective identities for large numbers of individuals who are actually quite diverse, cannot remain as potent as they are, and must be opposed' (Said, 2003).

Yet Said's analysis of Orientalism has not gone unquestioned. Some have argued that he overstates the degree to which the West had a negative view of the East, arguing that Orientalism was also a celebration of the Orient (MacKenzie, 1995). Others have questioned the degree to which Orientalist scholarship can be seen to directly contribute to the making of empire, arguing, for example, that the strong tradition of German Orientalism never found expression in imperial power (Irwin, 2006). What the most telling criticisms point to is the degree to which Said presented Orientalism as a

single discourse that can be traced over the centuries, taking in an expansive 'Orient' which was represented in all sorts of different media, and which had many varied relationships with a similarly differentiated 'Occident'. This is both a political and an intellectual point. Politically, the argument is that Said's 'monolithic' Orientalism leaves little room for people of the East to represent themselves, and to represent the West. A more differentiated notion of Orientalism gives scope for self-representation and resistance. Intellectually, the move has been not simply to define representations as 'Orientalist', but to specify what sort of Orientalism is involved, and how specific representations are connected to relations of power (Driver, 1992). Much attention has, for example, been paid to the question of gender and Orientalism, seeking to determine the ways in which women produced representations of the East that were different to those produced by men (Lewis, 1996).

Overall, Said's book was one of the first attempts to generate a post-colonial critique of colonial discourse which really highlighted the relationships between knowledge and power in the representation of places. Although this has subsequently been developed in much more complex ways by others (Bhabha, 1994; Spivak, 1990 and Young, 2001) it does not detract from the importance of Said's work in raising the question. It is also important not to confuse Said's analysis of the way in which Orientalism constructs the world with his own view of the geography of culture. He did not think of the world as dichotomised, essentialised and hierarchised. Instead, he argued that 'cultures are hybrid and heterogenous and . . . cultures and civilizations are so interrelated and interdependent as to beggar any unitary or simply delineated description of their individuality' (Said, 1995b: 349). Putting questions of hybridity, mobility and heterogeneity at the centre of the interpretation of culture offers quite a different view of cultural geography than we have seen so far. It also begins to question a view of culture based on the question of representation.

## 5.6 Mobility, hybridity and heterogeneity

So far what has been considered are the representations that try to fix the meanings of landscapes, places and territories. But geography is also about mobility, the movement across space and between places. One influential form of geographical representation is travel writing. This has often been analysed as part of colonial discourses, in ways that are similar to interpretations of Orientalism (see Blunt, 1994; Duncan and Gregory, 1999; McEwan, 1996; Mills, 1991). There has also been attention to the critical representations of European places produced by travellers from other parts of the world (Burton, 1996 and 1998). As with Orientalism, interpretations have moved away from 'monolithic' identifications of travel writing with imperial power to a more nuanced sense of the different modes of representation produced by different sorts of travellers travelling in different places under different conditions. This is part of a broader development of a notion of 'cultures of travel' or 'travelling cultures' that tries to understand movement itself as the subject matter of cultural studies. Thinking this through is the starting point for developing a quite different geography of culture that is one of networks, webs and journeys rather than of places, territories and fixed positions.

The anthropologist James Clifford has argued that anthropology (and it is also true of geography) has been far more concerned with 'dwelling' (being in place) than with 'travelling'. There has been a tendency to see what stays put as normal, and what moves as peculiar. This, he says, means that a whole series of

## Defining concept 5.3

### Globalisation–hybridity

Globalisation describes the process of gradually intermeshing world economies, politics and cultures into a global system. While some commentators argue that a world trade system has been in operation since ancient times, the contemporary world is marked by a greater and faster flow of goods, images and communications than ever before. The trade routes that have linked Africa, Asia and Europe for hundreds, if not thousands of years, cannot compare with the present volume and speed of interactions and flows.

The growth of a world system is usually associated with the rise of capitalism in the fifteenth and sixteenth centuries. The capitalist mode of production spread with the expansion of European powers into the Americas and later Asia and Africa. Capitalism undercut earlier forms of economic relations, for example, the non-money economies of North and South America. However, while European empires linked far-flung parts of the globe, their economies were characterised by the import of raw materials from the colonies by the European powers and the export of manufactured goods in the opposite direction. Thus, the European empires marked the beginnings rather than the establishment of a world system. Two periods of what David Harvey has called 'time-space compression' saw an acceleration of this process. The first occurred at the turn of the twentieth century. New technologies like telegraph, telephone, rail and steam ships permitted speedier flows of goods and faster communications. The volume of world trade grew rapidly until it

## Defining concept 5.3 (continued)

was stalled by the First World War. The inter-war period was one of pro-tectionism, but since 1945, world trade has increased to the point where the concept of a global system seems plausible.

The debate about globalisation has fallen into two broad camps: pro-ponents of hyperglobalisation and the globalisation sceptics (Perraton *et al.*, 1997). The proponents of hyperglob-alisation maintain that a world system now operates and that national and regional economies are both subject to the global economy. Such is the **hegemony** (p. 73) of the world system that there is little that national gov-ernments or regional bodies (like the European Union) can do to protect themselves from the ups and downs of international financial markets and trade cycles. Globalisation sceptics argue that the volume of world trade was, in fact, not much greater at the end of the twentieth century than it was in 1913 (Glyn and Sutcliffe, 1992). Perraton criticises both these positions as too simplistic, because they posit an idealised version of a perfect global market. Instead, Perraton argues that globalisation is a process. It is not that nation–states or regional trade blocs have no power, but that their power is now dependent on their place in a developing, but unequal global system.

Globalisation affects culture as well as trade. In fact, rather than one global system there are different pro-cesses of globalisation occurring at the same time. The world system has facilitated the global distribution of Hollywood's films and North American television. Chinese, Indian, American and European cooking is available in most of the world's large cities. International communications are now more widely available. A three-minute telephone call betwen London and New York cost $244.65

in 1930 (1990 cost equivalent); in 1996 it was possible to ring London from the United States for 30 cents a minute. While it is possible to point to large-scale population movements in the past – for example, the volun-tary (migration) and enforced (the slave trade) movement of people to the Americas – low-cost air travel has meant that contacts between distant cultures have increased in frequency. Cities like Los Angeles are made up of a patchwork of different cultures from around the world.

The speed and frequency of inter-national contact have led to a phenomenon which has been called, variously, *mestizo* culture or hybridity. *Mestizo* culture referred originally to the mixture of cultures, African, Native American and European, found in South America. It has been used by Gloria Anzaldúa and Cherie Moraga to describe the permeable and shifting identities that come into being in the human and cultural border traffic between the USA (particularly the state of California) and Mexico. Anzaldúa writes of 'the new *mestiza*' (literally 'mixed woman') as on the border between two cultures. The new *mestiza* is not defined by an essen-tialist **identity** (p. 142), but by *una lucha de fronteras* (a struggle of borders). This mapping of bound-aries has much in common with comparable postcolonial projects, fictional and theoretical, which have attempted to engage with the inten-sifying pace of global interactions. Salman Rushdie's *The Satanic Verses* (see Chapter 6), for example, charts the metamorphoses that occur in the process of migration from the Indian subcontinent to the former imperial centre, a process that creates, in the words of the postcolo-nial critic, Homi Bhabha, a kind of third space of cultural hybridity:

For me the importance of hybridity is not to be able to trace two original moments from which the third emerges, rather hybridity to me is the 'third space' which enables other positions to emerge. This third space displaces the histories that constitute it, and sets up new structures of authority, new political initiatives, which are inadequately understood through received wisdom.

(Bhabha, 1990: 211)

Paul Gilroy's concept of the 'Black Atlantic' (see p. 131) constitutes a similar attempt to think outside the fixed and misleading boundary lines of nation–states and to create a space in which a double consciousness that is both inside and outside modernity can be thought. The point here is not, of course, to say that the new *mestiza*, Bhabha's hybridity, or Gilroy's development of du Bois's double consciousness delineate the same space. It is rather to suggest that current conditions create the same kinds of problems for mean-ingful narratives in different parts of the globe. Gloria Anzaldúa, between Mexico and California, tackles similar kinds of disclocation as (albeit in a very different way) Salman Rushdie between Bombay (now Mumbai) and London. They all give examples of new identities which, although created by the new global capitalism, are resistant to its logic.

### Further reading

Harvey, D. (1990) *The Condition of Postmodernity*, Oxford: Blackwell.

Featherstone, M. (1996) *Undoing Culture: Globalization, Postmodernism and Identity*, London: Sage.

activities, meanings, and relationships have been missed, or seen as marginal. In contrast, acknowledging that London's Heathrow Airport expects to develop an annual throughput of 40 million passengers, more than the population of the world's largest city (Tokyo: 35.5 million people in 2006), begins to show what is missed by ignoring what Clifford (1992: 100) calls the 'wider world of intercultural import-export'. This would involve interpreting different *practices of travel*. There are lots of different forms of mobility, from the deadly boat journeys taken by African migrants seeking to enter Europe to the first-class air travel of the world's business elite. Different forms of travel are produced by the unequal access to forms of mobility and they affect how the journey is experienced and the meanings that are given to travel and the places that are travelled from, through and to. Indeed, the differences are so great that some have questioned whether 'travel' is the appropriate term for any but the most privileged forms of movement (Wolff, 1993). The second issue that is raised is what happens when people move. Mary Louise

Pratt (1992: 4) has argued that mobility takes the traveller into a *contact zone*: 'social spaces where disparate cultures meet, clash, and grapple with each other, often in highly asymmetrical relations of domination and subordination.' Understanding the cultural processes of these contact zones has meant trying to develop ideas able to comprehend the complex cultural forms created when different systems of meaning meet within unequal relations of power (see Box 5.3).

As the example of language shows, the meeting of cultural meanings leaves both sides changed as something new is produced. Pratt avoids ideas of 'acculturation' (the gaining of a culture) or 'deculturation' (the loss of a culture) and uses the term 'transculturation' to capture this two-way process. Others have talked about 'hybridisation': the production of something that is both made up of the elements that meet, yet different from them too. The significance of these hybrid cultural forms is that they do not conform to self/Other binary structure characteristic of colonial discourse and Orientalism (Bhabha, 1994). This means that they can at times work to subvert or disrupt colonial power in various ways. For example, Figure 5.7 shows a Yoruba carving from the contact zone of the British empire in Nigeria in the 1930s. It is a representation of an English District Officer, said to be Mr B. J. A. Matthews. It is certainly a hybrid. The use of a Yoruba technique to represent a colonial official produces a hybridised Afro-European object. However, it is not clear whether this representation of the man with the pen, pipe and pith helmet is a celebration, an incorporation into Yoruba ways of doing things, or a critique of imperial bureaucracy.

We also have to think carefully about where the contact zone is. The process of imperialism meant that British culture was made hybrid in fundamental ways. In fact, since Britain itself was a product of empire we can say that there never was a British culture that was not hybrid. A simple example is the humble cup of tea. This came to be a sign of Britishness in the eighteenth century, but was made of leaves from China, India or Sri Lanka, sweetened with sugar from Caribbean plantations worked by African slave labour. Again, it is a hybrid that renders notions of an essentialised and localised 'Britishness' or 'Englishness' very problematic (Hall, 1992a).

## Box 5.2

### Contact languages

In the contact zone various languages known as pidgins and creoles are devised for communication between speakers of different languages. Tok Pisin is one of the three national languages of Papua New Guinea. Note that words may be from different languages, they may preserve sounds, or they may be composites which convey the meaning:

| | |
|---|---|
| bedroom | rum slip |
| book | buk |
| coast | nambis |
| cloth | lap lap |
| dictionary | buk bilong painim mining |
| dish cloth | hap laplap bilong wasim plet |
| look for | painim |
| piece | hap (also means half, place and area) |
| plate | plet |
| voyage | wokabaut long sip |
| wash | wasim |

Source: www.tok-pisin.com

**Figure 5.7** Yoruba Carving, 1930s. Thought to be District Officer B.J.A. Matthews. (Source: Pitt Rivers Museum, Oxford.)

Thinking about mobility, contact zones and hybridisations means considering the geographies of movement that shape cultural forms. Just as with travel, there are different ways in which different people are positioned in relation to these flows of other people, things and ideas. Extending the example of tea to think further about food and drink reveals different ways in which this proliferation of hybrids, mobilities and flows can be conceptualised. Tea shows that producers and consumers of foodstuffs across the world are part of a globalised food system. It is a familiar sight in European and American supermarkets to see papaya from Jamaica, green beans from Kenya, and bananas from Ecuador. Food has a geography that is global, but it is produced and consumed locally and there are particular patterns of mobility that are shaped by cultural, political and economic relationships. The question is how people respond to these geographies, and what meanings they hold.

Food is obviously important for sustenance and nourishment, but as well as carrying energy and vitamins it also carries meanings. These might be personal memories of childhood or of good or bad times. Yet, like all meanings these are social and cultural and not just individual. As Uma Narayan puts it:

> Thinking about food has much to reveal about how we understand our personal and collective identities. Seemingly simple acts of eating are flavoured with complicated and sometimes contradictory cultural meanings. Thinking about food can help reveal the rich and messy textures of our attempts at self-understanding, as well as our interesting and problematic understandings of our relationship to social Others.
>
> (Quoted in Bell and Valentine, 1997: 2)

The meanings that are made for foods are made by a whole range of people. There are those who want to encourage the consumption of particular foods by making them trendy, healthy, exotic or fun. There are also those who want to stop consumption of other foods by giving them meanings that stress how they are unethical, unhealthy or associated with the wrong people, places or tastes. Whatever is eaten, wherever it is eaten, and whoever it is eaten with says something about the diners. Eating always involves making interpretations of meanings and choices about identity.

In terms of the cultural geographies of food the question is how identities are made within global food networks. What is evident is that there are a whole series of responses to the problem. One concern is that people's diets and tastes are becoming globally homogenised (and that means Americanised) because of the dominance of global foods such as the McDonald's Big Mac and Coca-Cola. Since there are more than 30,000 McDonald's restaurants in 119 countries, and since the Coca-Cola Corporation sold over $8 billion worth of soft drinks worldwide in 2005 it is unsurprising that these have been a target of concern for those worried about the effects of globalisation. However, looking more closely at the ways in which people make their identities in relation to such global foods reveals that they do so in very different ways. The meanings of a Big Mac and a Coke are different in different places. On the one hand, they have had very positive connotations in certain contexts. For example, in Moscow when the first McDonald's opened after the fall of the Soviet Union people queued for hours to sample what they saw as the taste of democracy and freedom. Also, Marie Gillespie (1995) found that among young British-Asians in Southall fast food carried with it connotations of progress, modernity and freedom. Elsewhere the same food and drink has very negative connotations. There are the campaigns of environmentalists and anti-fast food and anti-globalisation protestors (for example www.mcspotlight.org and www.killercoke.com). The Indian Parliament banned Coca-Cola from its cafeterias in 2004 because of reports of its damaging environmental effects, and a charity-business selling a drink called Mecca-Cola has been set up to encourage Muslims to reject the materialist capitalism of Coke, and to channel the profits from its Islamic soft drink to supporting the Palestinian cause. As Alison James has noted '[t]he homogenizing of food across the globe through the fast food revolution has not … produced a comparable set of homogenized identities' (1996: 84).

At the opposite end of the spectrum from these global corporations are the campaigns for *local* food. For example, the 'slow food movement' which started in Italy in 1986 'promotes gastronomic culture, develops taste education, conserves agricultural biodiversity and protects traditional foods at risk of extinction' (www.slowfood.com). Here it is the local and distinctive that matters both because of the environmental and social benefits of reducing food miles (the distance travelled from farm to plate) and because the 'local' brings with it a range of meanings associated with quality, authenticity and wholesomeness. This is evident in the rise of farmers' markets in many towns and cities, where consumers buy directly from producers, and in campaigns to preserve specialist food producers and retailers. Yet there are also concerns about who can afford to buy the foods that are marketed in this way. Prices at farmers' markets are high, and the main market for such foods is certainly a middle-class one. It is also evident that consumers are not encouraged to find their own 'local' and stick to it: only eating the local produce of Tuscany, Kent or the Napa Valley. What is more evident in this turn to the local (and in many of the cookbooks, magazines and TV programmes that

promote it) is the setting out of an array of distinctive local gastronomic cultures from which the knowledgeable consumer can pick as they choose. The identity that is constructed is what can be called 'cosmopolitan'.

Cosmopolitan consumers make their identities in relation to *local* food, but they do so in a global marketplace. They have the resources to pick and choose between different local traditions in a global food provisioning system. Doing so has often been seen as problematic in exactly the way in which representations of the exotic and foreign are seen as problematic. The cultural critic bell hooks (1992) has described this as a process of 'Eating the Other' in which cultures are simplified, essentialised and consumed by the privileged. Jon May (1996a) has shown how gentrifiers in parts of London appropriate the cultures that they find around them via the search for 'a little taste of something more exotic'. In the process the danger is that this sort of culinary neo-imperialism creates a static mosaic of 'authentic' and unchanging gastronomic traditions each of which is localised to a particular place, region or country. Italian food, Chinese food, Thai food, Indian food become separate, fixed and sealed off cultural entities which are to be preserved as authentic. However, ideas of mobility and hybridity soon make it clear that this cannot be the case. The cultural geography of food is both a complex process of movement and mixing, and, at the same time, people trying to impose certain meanings on this complexity, including ideas about where food comes from.

It does not take much thought about food to see the mixtures at work, and to see that these mixtures are of many different kinds. There are the developments of fusion food, particularly in California and Australia, which blend Asian, European and American techniques and flavours, and which are seen as inventive, exciting and multicultural. On the other hand there are other mixtures – such as the Chicken Tikka Pizza or the Hungarian Cornish pasty – which some see as illegitimate and even inedible. But it also soon becomes evident that mixing is not something rare and strange. First, there are gastronomic cultures that are defined by mixture. The 'Creole' cuisine of Louisiana mixes French, American and African ingredients and techniques in dishes such as gumbo. Indeed, all the cuisines of the Caribbean are a product of 'creolisation'. For example, Jamaica's national dish – ackee and saltfish – combines the fruit of a West African tree now grown in the Caribbean with the North Atlantic salt cod originally imported to feed slaves on plantations. Taking this further shows that any assertion of purity in the origins of food is just that, an assertion. Think about potatoes – a staple of the Northern European diet – originally coming from the Americas. Think about chillies – a fundamental part of cuisines as diverse as those of Thailand, India, Lebanon and Italy – again, coming from the Americas. Think about aubergines (eggplant) which came from China, or the Chinese noodles that became 'Italian' pasta. It is within this complex cultural geography of movements and mixtures, and of assertions about purity and authenticity, that people are making their identities. As Ian Cook and Phil Crang say:

> [I]magined and performed representations about 'origins', 'destinations' and forms of 'travel' surround these networks' various flows; [and] … consumers (and other actors in food commodity systems) find themselves socially and culturally positioned, and socially and culturally position themselves, not so much through placed locations as in terms of their entanglements with those flows and representations.
>
> (Cook and Crang, 1996: 138)

As with all forms of representation, all forms of 'travel', and all forms of identity construction people are positioned differently and both get to make meanings for themselves and have to negotiate the meanings that are made by others. This is done in different ways by those who celebrate or denounce global fast food, those who choose local food, the cosmopolitans and the fusion fanatics. The sorts of choices that are being made are well illustrated by thinking about migrants who use food to negotiate their position in ways that combine the local and the global.

In a world whose history and geography is one of mobility and hybridity it is not easily to define foods or the people who eat them as either located or displaced. There is a need for ways to understand the cultures of those 'who may be dispersed across geographical boundaries and may have connections to several places they call "home"?' (Dwyer, 1999: 291) These are people who are part of transnational groups defined by their

links to multiple places, a geography that is often described using the term 'diaspora'. This means 'scattering through' and was originally applied to the situation of Jewish people driven from the Holy Land since the eighth century BC and setting up home in many other places. The term is now applied to many diasporas – the Indian diaspora, the Chinese diaspora, the Irish diaspora, the Armenian diaspora – to understand their connections across global space and the significance of their multiple local identifications. For example, Paul Gilroy (1993b and 1997) uses the term 'the Black Atlantic diaspora' to describe a social formation that was produced by transatlantic slavery and subsequent migrations, and which links people in North and South America, the Caribbean, Europe and Africa. He argues that this cultural formation should be understood in terms of both roots (the local identifications that people make) and routes (the connections that link them together and mean that their identities cannot be defined in terms of a single location). Gilroy has thought about this in terms of the music of the Black Atlantic, but food is equally important. Think, for example, of people with Jamaican connections eating ackee and salt fish in Brixton (London) or Flatbush (New York).

All diasporic cultures negotiate the relationships between several places thought of as 'home'. Diasporic cultures are, therefore, not fixed and singular but mobile and hybrid, although also dealing with difficult notions of origins and authenticity. Once again, it is apparent that different diasporas have different geographies and different relationships of power within them and in relation to the rest of the world. For example, poor Somalian refugees in London are very differently positioned than Hong Kong businessmen in Vancouver (Mitchell, 1997). However, food is part of these cultural negotiations of roots and routes. For example, Irish women in Coventry, England, see food and food preparation as an important way of maintaining and making Irish identities in the diaspora (Kneafsey and Cox, 2002). Cooking Irish recipes such as corned beef and cabbage (also the traditional Irish-American St Patrick's day meal), colcannon, or boxty; buying Irish foods such as sodabread or Irish butter; and using Irish brands such as Tayto crisps, Barry's tea or Denny's sausages (often sent over by relatives still in Ireland) are ways of maintaining a connection to Ireland and Irishness.

## Key influence 5.2

### Paul Gilroy (1956–)

Paul Gilroy is a black British cultural analyst. The main focus of his work has been on the cultural politics of 'race'.

Gilroy studied as a postgraduate at the **Centre for Contemporary Cultural Studies** (CCCS) (p. 241) at the University of Brimingham. He worked for the greater London Council in the 1980s before lecturing at Essex University and then Goldsmiths College. Following a joint appointment as professor in the African-American studies and sociology departments at Yale University, he became Anthony Giddens Professor of Social Theory at the London School of Economics in 2005.

Gilroy's early work on race and culture appeared in contributions to the edited collection from CCCS, *The Empire Strikes Back* (1982). In *There Ain't No Black in the Union Jack* (1987) he carried out a multilayered analysis which emphasised the complexity and centrality of interactions and struggles around race, class and nation in contemporary Britain. He was critical of cutlural studies' general lack of consideration of 'race' but more importantly suggested that concern with this arena would have to transform cultural studies itself. He paid particular attention to the nature and importance of 'black expressive culture', especially in music, which, while appealing to many whites, articulated core concerns of the black diaspora, especially in some anti-capitalist themes. If this work is contextualised by capitalism, in his more recent work Gilroy has taken on conceptions of **modernity** (p. 295). In *The Black Atlantic* (1993) he argued for the integration of the experience of black people into conceptualisations of modernity, but perhaps more significantly emphasised the **hybridity** (p. 125) of cultures as they interact and develop to form new connections and patterns. This emphasis on new connections and the re-thinking of the work of major black writers led Gilroy to what he called a position of 'anti-anti-essentialism'. For example, in discussions of 'black music' it has been maintained that such categories should be rejected as there is no 'essence' to black music in either racial or musical terms. Gilroy accepts this critique of essentialism but argues that it is possible to trace the interconnections in 'black identity' in social and cultural terms. As with his earlier works, many of the examples discussed come from the area of music. His more recent work defends multiculturalism against criticisms framed by the strident political language of the post 9/11 world.

Gilroy's influence has been in rethinking aspects of cultural studies from within. His arguments tend towards suggestions for the transformation of the approach to take account of ever more complex connections of **identity** (p. 142) formation in **modernity** (p. 295). This is in many respects a working out of the implications of **poststructuralist** (p. 17) critiques of fixed identities and characterisations.

### Further reading

Gilroy, P. (1987) *'There Ain't No Black in the Union Jack: The Cultural Politics of Race and Nation'*, London: Hutchinson.

Gilroy, P. (1993) *The Black Atlantic: Modernity and Double Consciousness*, London: Verso.

Gilroy, P. (2004) *After Empire: Melancholia or Convivial Culture?*, London: Routledge.

Gilroy, P. (2007) *Black Britain: A Photographic History*, London: Saqi Books.

These foods carried meanings of goodness and wholesomeness, which differentiated them from English foods, but they also invoked memories of bad times as well as good ones. Yet in almost every meal these 'Irish' ingredients and foods would be combined with other ingredients and foods. What is created is a cuisine that cannot simply be called either Irish or English: it is *diasporic*. This point can, of course, be multiplied for all diasporas. Think of how Indian or Chinese cooking is changed around their diasporas. But it also has implications for those who do not think of themselves as part of a diaspora. Avtar Brah (1996) has argued that instead of making a distinction between those who have moved and those who have stayed put ('diasporians' and 'natives') we should recognise that the existence of diasporic populations in a society means that everyone inhabits 'diaspora space' and has to face the cultural issues that involves. Although a slightly flippant example, given the problems of racism that are also involved in these spaces, it is telling that chicken tikka massala, an 'Indian' dish that has no direct equivalent in India, is often described as England's new national dish.

# 5.7 Performing identities

Another problem with a cultural geography that is defined in terms of the representation of spaces, places and landscapes is that it misses not only issues of mobility and hybridity, but that the focus on representation misses all the other practices (like eating) through which people engage with the world and through which meanings are made. Cultural geographers are increasingly interested in questions of emotion and affect; in neglected senses such as smell, taste and hearing; in theatre and dance; and in everyday movements, gestures and practices. This has opened up new sorts of source material. For example, the investigation of 'geographies of music' has sought to give prominence to sound as a signifying practice rather than texts and visual images (Smith, 1994 and 1997). This approaches familiar questions of identity (Valentine, 1995), nationalism (Kong, 1995), and the local and the global (Kong, 1996; Wall, 2000; and Feld, 2000) through the production and consumption of music. It also opens up the question of different methods for studying music that cannot rely on the thinking about it as 'text'. More fundamentally, there has been the development of what is called 'non-representational theory' which aims to avoid seeing everything as a representation to be read and decoded for its hidden meanings (Thrift, 2000 and 2004). This stresses forms of embodied knowledge (how what is 'known' is worked into our bodily movements, for example, ways of moving through a crowded city or learning to drive a car) and it takes seriously the notion that the world is continually in process rather than interpreting cultural artefacts in terms of pre-existing structures of meaning. This is often difficult, challenging and experimental work, but one area in which it has had a very strong impact is by making the idea of *performance* central to the study of cultural geography. Through this questions of embodiment, embodied knowledge and the world as a process can be connected to the ideas of meaning, space and power that have already been explored.

It is evident that people's identities are produced through ongoing and active relationships to other people and places. It can be said that people make choices of how to 'perform' their identities depending on where they are and who they are with. In part, people are in control of those performances, and actively construct their identities through those performances and the props (clothes, hair, make-up) that support them. However, it is also the case that these performances are also shaped (consciously and unconsciously) by the expectations of other people and by the settings in which the performances take place. These expectations are individual: people are expected to maintain some continuity of personality. They are also social and cultural: there are expectations in terms of roles – son, employee, friend; in terms of matters of gender, sexuality, class and 'race'; and these are worked into particular geographical settings: the expectations are different at home or at work; in church or in the sports arena. All in all, and this gets at the idea of the world in process, identities are not something that pre-exist what people do, they *are* what they *do*. Identities are made in action. There are, however, quite different ways of understanding this.

Some discussions of performance treat it very directly as 'theatre'. The sociologist Erving Goffman (1959) argued that social interactions should be thought about as dramatic performances in which the 'actors' attempt to maintain a sense of self-identity and control in the interaction. For Goffman, the nature of the space of the performance was crucial to this. For example, he talked about 'front regions' – such as a hotel dining room – where the 'actor' (perhaps a waiter) was overtly on stage, and 'back regions' – such as the hotel kitchen – where the waiter's performance (in relation to the diners if not the kitchen staff) could be stepped down. Goffman's ideas on the performance of identity have provided a rich resource for researchers who want to study the nature of service work. For example Robin Leidner (1993) investigated working in McDonald's restaurants in order to understand how people deal with the 'depersonalisation' involved in such settings where workers have to perform 'scripts' devised for them by their employers. As McDonald's says, 'We want to treat each customer as an individual, in sixty seconds or less.' What Leidner found was that people used various strategies to evade the threat to self-expression, authenticity and personal integrity that this work posed. Some simply quit, others adopted a conformist work persona that they shed as soon as they clocked out, hammed up the performance to demonstrate that it was a performance, or delivered the script in an over-routinised, almost robotic manner to stress the constraints being placed upon them. Working in the different setting of a theme restaurant he calls 'Smoky Joe's', Phil Crang (1994) used participant observation to demonstrate the multiple strategies required of workers who are asked to do 'emotional work' as part of their job. He shows how workers drew on the resources provided by the different spaces of the restaurant to manage a job which required presenting a seemingly natural and spontaneous expression of personality (see also McDowell and Court, 1994; and McDowell, 1995 and 1997).

One of the questions that has been raised about Goffman's work and the uses made of it is the extent to which he understands identity in terms of an authentic sense of self that is revealed and concealed by the artful and conscious use of a series of masks, costumes and scripts. Other theories of performance offer the more radical suggestion that there is nothing there but the performance of identity. In particular, Judith Butler (1990 and 1993) has argued in series of books about gender and sexuality that they should be understood in terms of performativity. Drawing on Foucault's idea of discourse Butler argues that identities are made by the constant reiteration of discourses of gender and sexuality. As Gregson and Rose (2000: 437) put it: 'Butler certainly does not work with any notion of a social agent existing prior to its production through enacted discourse. Instead, she argues that the "doing" of discourse cites already established formations of knowledge and it is this citation which produces social subjects.'

Butler's aim is to destabilise any naturalisation of sexual identities. Heterosexual identities are performances just as much as queer identities are. The only difference is that the normalisation of the discourses of heterosexuality has rendered those performances and repeated citations invisible. Thus, for Butler, gender becomes a cultural performance: It is 'a stylized repetition of acts. The effect of gender is produced through the stylization of the body, and, hence must be understood as the mundane way in which bodily gestures, movements, and styles of various kinds constitute *the illusion* of an abiding gendered self' (Butler, 1990: 140–1). What are taken to be the differences between men and women are, for Butler, the effects of the disci-

plining of a multiplicity of bodies into a binary division based on performative styles. However, since these identities and divisions have to be constantly performed in order for them continue to exist there is always the room for 'slippage' where the performance is less than successful, or the potential for transgression where what is taken as natural is revealed as performance. For example, Bell, Binnie, Cream and Valentine (1994: 36) argue that the sight of two gay skinheads kissing in public destabilises a whole series of expectations: 'By behaving in this way the gay skinhead can disrupt or destabilise not only a masculine identity but heterosexual space. Can you ever be sure again that you can read the identity of others or the identity of a space?' (see also Nelson, 1999).

This last point is an important one. Taking the notion of performance seriously means acknowledging the processual nature of the world. For geographers this has meant arguing that all spaces – long seen to be social or cultural constructions – should be reconceptualised as performed and, therefore, as ongoing and never completed processes. This means that spaces are not just stages on which performances take place, they are themselves performative. As Gregson and Rose say:

> We want to argue that it is not only social actors that are produced by power, but the spaces in which they perform ... [W]e maintain that performances do not take place in already existing locations: the City, the bank, the franchise restaurant, the straight street. These 'stages' do not preexist their performances, waiting in some sense to be mapped out by performances; rather, specific performances bring these spaces into being.
>
> (Gregson and Rose, 2000: 442)

Such a view of the world enables political interventions into the performance of identity and the critique and reconstruction of those performative spaces. A good example of this refers to disruptions of notions of Mexican/American identities in the performance art of Guillermo Gómez-Peña and his collaborator Roberto Sifuentes. Their *Temple of Confessions* premiered in Arizona as a cross between a pseudo-anthropological diorama (as in US natural history museums) and a version of the religious dioramas found in Latin American churches. The two artists exhibited themselves in plexiglass boxes with Sifuentes as 'El Pre-Columbian Vato' (a holy historical gang member) and Gómez-Peña as 'San Pocho Atlaneca' ('a hyper-exoticised curio shop shaman for spiritual tourists') (Gómez-Peña 2000: 37). What lay behind these artful creations was a sense of the regulatory discourses which governed the performance of Mexican identity in the USA. As Gómez-Peña put it, 'In the American imagination, Mexicans are allowed to occupy two different but strangely complementary spaces: we are either unnecessarily violent, hypersexual, cannibalistic and highly infectious; or innocent, 'natural,' ritualistic and shamanic. Both stereotypes are equally colonizing' (Gómez-Peña's performance diaries 1997). The artists' invitation to the gallery visitors to confess to these living saints their intercultural sins produced an outpouring of fears and desires:

> The range of confessions went from extreme violence and racism toward Mexicans and other people of color, to expressions of incommensurable tenderness and solidarity with us or with the cause we were perceived to represent. Some confessions were filled with guilt, some with archetypal American fears of cultural, political, or sexual invasion, or of violence, rape, and disease. Others were fantasies about escaping one's race or ethnicity and wanting to be Mexican or Indian ... People invited us to join them in acting out hardcore sexual fantasies, or expressed their desire to hurt or even to kill us.
>
> (Gómez-Peña 2000: 40)

This work was then developed using digital technologies to explore the 'visual and performative representations of the new mythical Mexican and Chicano of the '90s'. A now-inactive *Temple of Confessions* website was set up and the 20,000 hits were used to create a range of 'ethno-cyborgs' such as 'CyberVato' (a robo-gang member) (Figure 5.8) and 'El Mad Mex' (a transgender Tex-Mex shaman on a custom-made lowrider wheelchair). These were to be a set of racialised and sexualised performances based on the audience's fears and desires, what the artists called 'an army of Mexican Frankensteins ready to rebel against their Anglo creators' (Gómez-Peña 2000: 49).

The artists then toured their creations as a performance piece where live audiences were encouraged to interact with them. The artists and audience were actively performing the relationships between power, fantasy, fear and identity between Mexicans and Americans. The audience were 'instructed that they can feed us, touch us, smell us, massage us, braid our hair, take us for walks on dog leashes, or point prop weapons at us to experience the feeling of shooting at a real, live Mexican ... We try to comply obediently with whatever interactions audience members may choose to initiate, unless they are simply too dangerous or personally invasive' (Gómez-Peña 2000: 55). Visitors were invited to dress up themselves, making and performing a 'temporary ethnic identity'. Audience responses (see **reconstruction.eserver.org/BReviews/revElMex.htm**) show how shocking these events might be. There were people shouting, crying, breaking down, and acting out fantasies of sex and violence. Overall, the artists' intention was to use performative notions of identity to

11 CyberVato Prototype #27.

**Figure 5.8** CyberVato. (Source: G. Gómez-Peña (2000).)

reveal the power relations involved in the ascription and adoption of particular geographical essentialisms. Engaging with questions of power and representation, but also going beyond them, this demonstrated how such geographical identities are matters of emotion and affect, embodied knowledge, and an on-going open-ended process.

## 5.8 Living in a material world

The final problem with the new cultural geography's focus on representation is that it does not pay enough attention to the material world of things and nature. The cultural geography of Carl Sauer had been very concerned with the material artefacts which made up the cultural landscape (barns, housing types, hedges, crops, domesticated animals), and therefore with human interactions with nature (for example, Kniffen, 1965). Turning away from that, involved an emphasis on questions of representation, symbolism and meaning. However, the rejection of the 'old' cultural geography involved, in terms of questions of materiality, throwing the baby out with the bathwater. Therefore, it took a long time for cultural geographers to being to think about material objects again. Inevitably this has not involved a return to work on things like rural building types. Instead, the sources of inspiration have come from archaeology, anthropology, and science and technology studies.

In each case what is of interest are the meaningful relationships between people and objects. This is a matter of what objects mean to people, but also what people do with those objects. In terms of meanings this is a matter of seeing how objects are part of meaningful relationships between people. For example, Figure 5.7, the Yoruba sculpture of Mr B.J.A Matthews (p. 128), shows how objects work to make meaning within the contact zone. The anthropologist Nicholas Thomas (1991) describes these as 'entangled objects' to which people have given new meanings in the process of incorporating them into their ways of life and forms of identity. He demonstrates how the islanders of the Pacific appropriated European objects. So European guns became part of local politics and gift giving, and were changed in the process though local techniques of wood-working and inlaying (Figure 5.9). But he also demonstrates how the islanders' objects – such as weapons, cloth and tools – were appropriated by Europeans (Figure 5.10). This also changed their meanings by incorporating them into cultures of collecting and the practices of science which themselves were part of the local politics and gift-giving practices of Europeans. However, this is not simply a matter for cross-cultural objects. Arjun Appadurai (1986) uses the term *The Social Life of Things* to signal the need to trace the 'biographies' of even the most everyday objects to show how their appropriations, uses and meanings change over time and space.

There are several sorts of geography involved here. The cultural appropriations of objects are made in specific contexts and involve the making of the meaning of places and with it the making of identities. One clear example is home decoration and DIY. The many home makeover programmes on TV and the vast home improvements industry signal the increasing importance of this intersection of place, material culture and identity. Once again, the material and sym-

**Figure 5.9** A European gun with inlaid shell decoration from the western Solomon Islands. (Source: The Australian Museum.)

**Figure 5.10** Joseph Banks with part of his collection of Pacific objects. (Source: National Maritime Museum.)

bolic choices made may be personal but they always exist in social, cultural and political contexts. For example, the design historian Judith Attfield studied changes in the London suburb of Cockfosters in the 1980s as part of a particular cultural politics of domestic space. She argued that Margaret Thatcher's notion of a property-owning democracy based on the values of the private homeowner was performed through material changes to domestic space:

> Increased accessibility to home ownership gave rise to a particular aesthetic of privatization through the personalisation of the façade and the front door in particular. Privately-owned property could thus be readily distinguished from public housing on estates once entirely council-owned. The introduction of particular features such as pseudo-Georgian doors, bay windows, closed-in front porches, coach lamps and heraldic features such as eagles and lions became common upgrading signifiers.
>
> (Attfield, 2000: 203)

People were appropriating their homes – as they bought them from the council – in order to express and perform their new identities in public through the transformation of 'private' (and privatised!) space. Indeed, as Alison Clarke (2001) shows in an ethnographic study of home-making, the ideal, or transforming, home then becomes something that the inhabitants have to live up to.

There are also geographies of mobility involved here, and much of the work on the social life of things has involved showing how and why things have moved and how their meanings have changed in the process. One important shift is from non-commodity to commodity forms – the way things become entities that can be bought and sold – and how their meanings and geographies are changed in the process (Jackson, 1999). For example, Michael Redclift (2004) has investigated how *chicle* collected from the sapodilla tree in Yucatan Mexico became commodified as chewing gum in the early twentieth century (and in the process became heavily associated with America), and then was decommodified as other ways of making gum from hydrocarbons were found. An important argument here is that the commodity form allows the social relations of production, and the relationship between the producer and consumer, to be ignored by consumers. The commodified object does not carry with it the stories and meanings of all those who have been part of its life. Indeed, the new meanings that it has been given, through advertising for example, may further obscure these relationships (what is called the 'commodity fetish'). This can be countered by efforts to make and show other meanings for things. As Ian Cook *et al.* (2000) have shown, Shelley Sacks' artwork *Exchange Values* seeks to demonstrate to consumers what the usually mute banana means to those whose livelihoods depend upon them. The gallery space contains a pile of 10,000 bananas and 26 wall-mounted pieces which each incorporate the dried, cured and stitched banana skins from a single grower on St Lucia and a set of headphones. Sacks traced and visited each grower and asked what they wanted to say to those who bought their bananas. Their voices can be heard on the headphones speaking directly to the visitor. This is Vitalis Emmanuel:

> *What* is money? I've been working for 50 years, and 30 years ago I used to get up at 6 in the morning

and go to bed at 8 at night and earn that much money. And I could feed my children! Now I still work the exact same hours. I get up at 6 o'clock in the morning, and I, and I earn that much money. And I can't feed my children. So where are these guys? Where are these guys who are deciding what money is? This can't be my work – this money – 'cause I don the same work! The same banana. The same ground. So you tell me, *what is money?* I haven't been to school. I don't know what these guys are doing. *Where are they?* Tell me, *who are these guys? How can they decide what money is? There must be people there, where you come from, who are deciding what money is!*

(Quoted in Cook *et al.*, 2000: 339)

The aim is to emphasise the connections that the commodity obscures, and to demonstrate what it means to buy and eat a banana in the context of falling prices due to the World Trade Organization ending (at the prompting of the US government) preferential pricing in the European Union for former colonies. This installation shows the social life of the banana and how it stitches together a whole world of people. Ian Cook estimates that buying five bananas in an English supermarket mobilises a network of 50,000 people (see also Cook, 2004). He also asks whether this installation does not simply counter the 'commodity fetish' by revealing these connections but whether it seeks to beat it by working the same sort of magic: 'Like the magic of the commodity fethish? The magic that disconnects? By attaching stories to things on sale? Stories that are absolutely nothing like the ones these farmers can tell you? The adventures of "Bananaman"! Or the female version. Miss Chiquita. With fruit on her head! Singing!! Like Carmen Miranda!!! What's that all about!?' (Cook *et al.*, 2000: 342).

As is perhaps evident, the shift to materiality means that the ground of cultural geography and cultural studies is no longer as clearly defined as it might once have been. Talking about material objects as cultural objects cannot simply stop with their meanings. It also needs to consider their materiality in terms of the economic processes that they are part of, the connections that they make between people and places, and the effects that they have (for example, those madeover

houses that become entities that shape their inhabitants lives). This is even more evident in the ways in which cultural geography has begun to reconsider the natural world through the lens of science and technology studies. There are clearly a whole series of important questions about the meanings of nature and how they have changed over time. It is possible to trace different metaphors of nature – the book, the body, the machine, the economy – which lead to different environmental values and different orientations towards nature which range from reverence to exploitation (Livingstone, 1995 and Smith, 1990). There is also a very extensive body of work that has discussed the meanings of nature (or the 'cultures of nature') in terms of gender, 'race', class, and disability, showing how processes of 'naturalisation' have shaped the relationships of power between people, and between people and nature (Anderson, 2000). Yet what is intriguing about nature, and the cultural studies of nature, is that it cannot just be about meaning (and representation). It also needs to recognise the materiality of nature and its effects on people. This is tricky stuff and is not intended to suggest some sort of 'environmental determinism'. What matters is the place of natural and technological objects in our social and cultural worlds.

There are two sides to this. Firstly, how people use objects to make a social order. Secondly, how people use a social order to make the natural world. In terms of the first, Bruno Latour (1987) and the other proponents of what is called Actor Network Theory such as Michel Callon and John Law argue that objects and technologies are a crucial and active part of our world. They are both natural and cultural and need to be understood as such (they would say 'symmetrically'). This is neatly summed up by Takashi Harada with reference to Latour and Callon talking about baboons:

Their suggestion is that baboons manage a social structure *more or less without materials*, whereas people delegate social relations into material (and we might add spatial) form. This process tends to hold social relations in place and allows them to extend across time and space, and also, one might add, tends to hold people together. This material and spatial ordering of the 'social', then, helps us to make ourselves.

(Harada, 2000: 205–6)

The argument is that societies (and cultures) are not just made up of things that are conventionally considered as social or cultural, but of things from across the nature-culture divide which are thought of as part of the object world or the natural world. For example, Simon Naylor (2000) argues that the material properties of the tin can, when properly cared for, allowed the extension of the networks of the British Empire out across the world since it was then possible to preserve food in time and move it across space in new ways. This means, therefore, that if we want our world to hold together we have to engage in what John Law (1987) calls 'heterogenous engineering' that is both social and cultural: imperial heterogenous engineers had to work on the mechanics of making tin cans airtight, the social relations of the ships that carried them, and on the cultural meanings of long-dead animal flesh encased in metal (John Law, 1986 and 2002). It also means that objects (and not just people) can be thought of as having 'agency' – they act in the world, and shape the world. For example, Chris Philo and Eric Laurier discussing Bruno Latour's book *Aramis* on a failed French public transport system note that:

> It is blinkered social scientists whom he [Latour] urges to extend their notion of agency beyond human activity, because other things impinging on the human world act, and act to assist in the shaping of that world. They have names, they solidify networks, they stabilise and constitute power relations; we delegate to them, we enlist them in our projects, we have expectations of them, we invest in them. In turn they act back on us, they carry their own expectations of humans, their own programmings of humans: how long can they allow us to get on and off the train? How quickly must an Aramis car come to a halt so as not to hurt its passengers?
>
> (Laurier and Philo, 1999: 1061)

Indeed, Latour goes so far as to give voice to Aramis – the transport system complains about not being brought into the world – and parodies himself in the figure of the sociologist who 'had long conversations with electric staplers ... [and] noted the degree of politeness, laziness, violence, or nastiness of all the automatic door openers he came across, going so far as to tip them, which usually left them quite indifferent.' (Latour quoted in Laurier and Philo, 1999: 1057–8). Instead of a divide between nature and culture, Actor Network Theory sees the proliferation of hybrids and cyborgs for whom that divide makes no sense (see also Haraway, 1991, and Whatmore, 1999)

This demand for symmetry means that we also need to understand how the material world is made sense of using the social order. Questioning the divide between culture and nature also means questioning the role of science as the way in which the truth about nature can be established. There can be no separate domain of pure knowledge about nature. This has set the stage for what are known as the 'science wars' (paralleling the 'culture wars' (Mitchell, 2000)) between those who defend the integrity of science and those who are seen to be attacking it (Sokal and Bricmont, 1999, and Latour, 1999). One important intervention has been to show the ways in which the production of scientific truth (and therefore the ordering of the natural world) is inevitably bound up with social and cultural meanings. The argument is that scientific knowledge must always be social and cultural since it is always a matter of agreement between people on what is considered to be true. Moreover, what they are discussing are 'quasi-objects' produced by machines, techniques and practices that are both social and natural (more 'heterogenous engineering') such as the vacuum in an air pump or the traces of high-energy particles in a bubble chamber. This is shown very nicely by Steven Shapin's work on the Royal Society in the 1660s. He argues that their new empirical science (the 'Scientific Revolution') of the laboratory and the experimental demonstration could only work if people trusted the witnesses to those experiments and demonstrations. In particular, he argues that those who were trusted (and remember the discussion of landscape and objectivity earlier in this chapter) were adult men with landed property. Their independent wealth meant they had no need to curry favour, and could be depended upon to tell the truth of what they saw demonstrated to them. There was no natural knowledge, and no ordering of nature, without putting the social order to work. As Shapin puts it: 'This is a story about the gentlemanly constitution of scientific truth. I concentrate upon the role of gentle cultural practices in the making of factual knowledge. I argue that preexisting gentlemanly practices provided working solutions to the problems of credibility and trust which presented themselves at the core of the new empirical science of seventeenth-century England' (Shapin, 1994: xxi, see also Demerrit, 2001). Overall, therefore, nature and culture are inseparable in both the making of social and cultural formations through technological and natural objects and the ordering of nature through science that can only work through social and cultural forms.

## 5.9 Conclusion

In many ways what has happened to cultural geography mirrors broader developments in cultural studies. The development of a notion of cultural politics in the 1980s gave new impetus to a range of studies that focused on questions of representation and power in all areas concerned with culture. The sorts of interpretations made of landscape, national identity and Orientalism in cultural geography had parallels in other areas of cultural studies which were, for example, more concerned with literary texts or with sociological categories. Indeed, this convergence was reinforced by the adoption of a geographical language and a renewed sense of the importance of questions of space and place, across cultural studies. These studies of the politics of representation have, however, been increasingly challenged as the way in which to study culture. Those who judge this focus on territory, place and landscape as too static have encouraged a focus on mobility and movement which brings with it questions of hybridity and mixture. Again, these are concerns that are shared across cultural studies, often prompted by post-colonial thinking. Those who judged questions of representation to be too concerned with closed-off and finished formations of power and knowledge have encouraged a focus on performance and the world-in-process. This, drawing on Judith Butler, has animated studies of identity across cultural studies, provoking both excitement and criticism. Finally, in what is, at least in part, a return to some of the concerns of Carl Sauer and the Berkeley School, cultural geographers

have moved back from the world of signs and symbols to re-engage with the material world, and to re-investigate the complex relationships between culture and nature. Again, this has drawn on older traditions of the study of material culture, from archaeology and anthropology, but also engages with a new concern with objects which runs throughout cultural studies. Indeed, in the case of nature there is an increasing concern that this is where some of the new frontiers of understanding ourselves and our relationships of power, knowledge and meaning must lie.

### Recap

➤ Cultural geography is an important part of cultural studies.

➤ Cultural geography demonstrates how spaces, places and landscapes, and their representations, are laden with meanings within varied relationships of power and resistance.

➤ New ways of doing cultural geography have seen a move away from deconstructing representations to considering cultures of mobility, performativity and material culture.

## Further reading

Different sorts of introduction to cultural geography are provided by: Peter Jackson (1989) *Maps of Meaning: An Introduction to Cultural Geography* (Unwin Hyman, London) who provides a perspective based on the Birmingham Centre for Contemporary Cultural Studies; Don Mitchell (2000) *Cultural Geography: A Critical Introduction* (Blackwell, Oxford) who gives a Marxist reading; and Pam Shurmer-Smith and Kevin Hannam (1994) *Worlds of Desire, Realms of Power: A Cultural Geography* (Edward Arnold, London) who come from a more poststructuralist direction. For a range of perspectives on different aspects of cultural geography's subject matter, see Kay Anderson, Mona Domosh, Steve Pile and Nigel Thrift (eds) (2003) *The Handbook of Cultural Geography* (Sage, London) and for a guide to doing research in the field, see Alison Blunt, Pyrs Gruffudd, Jon May, Miles Ogborn and David Pinder (eds) (2003) *Cultural Geography in Practice* (Hodder Arnold, London).

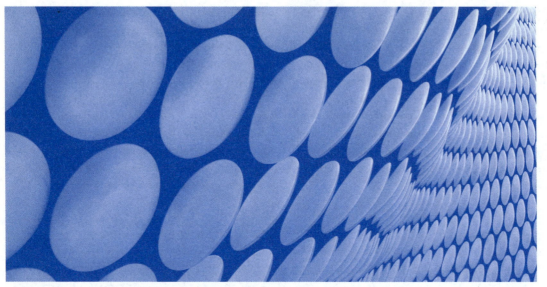

Chapter 6

# Politics and culture

## 6.0 Introduction

A key way in which cultural studies has been influential is in its transformations of the ideas of what is 'political'. Indeed, many of those who want to use the term 'cultural politics' for their work on culture would argue that 'everything is political'. By this they mean that everything is a matter of contested power relations. **bell hooks** (p. 141) argues that 'Vigilant insistence that cultural studies be linked to a progressive radical cultural politics will ensure that it is a location that enables critical intervention' (hooks, 1991: 9). This means a move away from more conventional notions of what is 'political' – the realm of parliaments, political parties, international relations, state institutions, bureaucracies, trade unions and so on – and broadens out the field of study to include the politics of art and literature, the politics of gender and race, and the politics of everyday life.

In this chapter we focus specifically on the relation-ship between politics and culture. We acknowledge that it is still important to retain something of the conventional sense of politics as a particular set of arenas in which certain strong claims to legitimacy and power are made. What we want to do is to understand formal politics through the lens provided by the expanded notion of politics that we provide, which includes what is sometimes called 'informal politics' (Painter, 1995). This focus offers a sense of the particularity and peculiarity of formal politics as a set of arenas of power relations, and as a set of arenas that operate in terms of some quite particular cultural practices and products. In the end we hope that this serves not to maintain it as a privileged arena of power but to show how it claims that privilege. Thus, this chapter looks at the way that the arena of formal politics is made through culture and, more generally, at the politics of culture.

## Learning objectives

➤ To learn about the role of culture in the formal politics of states, parties and bureaucracies as well as in the arena of informal politics.

➤ To see how there has been a shift towards a politics of identity.

➤ To understand the ideas of performativity and transgression and their potential as cultural practices that can challenge formal political power.

➤ To appreciate the importance of symbols and representation in establishing political legitimacy.

# 6.1 Cultural politics and political culture

## From politics to cultural politics

The success of cultural studies since the 1970s and the transformation of older disciplines such as geography, sociology and English literature in the same period have been based upon an understanding of politics that goes way beyond the confines of the conventional delimitation of it in terms of legislative bodies, states and diplomacy. Politics now is as much about textual politics or sexual politics as it is about elections and

## Key influence 6.1

### bell hooks (1952–)

bell hooks's work explores the cultural politics of race and gender. In a series of books she has written on racism, television, literature, feminism and postmodernism. Her work considers topics such as black subjectivity, whiteness, community and utopian longing.

hooks was born in Kentucky and teaches in New York. In 1981 she published *Ain't I a Woman: Black Women and Feminism*, a major contribution to feminist debates. She has published *Black Looks* (1992) and *Art on My Mind* (1995) on visual representation. She has also written on education in *Teaching to Transgress* (1994). Her work is an example of a move in the 1980s and 1990s towards the study of our subjective understandings of culture and politics. Readers of her books will notice that the copyright is in the name of Gloria Watkins, not bell hooks. Although she uses autobiographical experiences to insert her own subjectivity into essays on culture and politics, bell hooks is a pseudonym. Thus, in essays like 'The chitlin circuit: on black community' she

writes about her own childhood in another persona. At the end of *Yearning: Race. Gender, and Cultural Politics* (1991), in a piece subtitled, 'no not talking back, just talking to myself', Gloria Watkins interviews bell hooks about her work. Watkins asks her why she chose to do the interview and she replies:

> for me these are two parts of a whole self that is composed of many parts. And as you know in many parts of my life I am such a serious person. To be contemplative in these times is to be seriously serious and I have to take a break now and then to balance things. So I indulge the playful in me. That me that in a very childlike way loves play, drama and spectacle. Of course there is a way that play is very serious for me. It is a form of ritual.
> (hooks, 1991: 221)

Through her double persona, hooks is able to show the gap between how **identities** (p. 142) are defined, for example by categories like gender and race, and how they are per-

formed. She demonstrates the difference between representing one's experience and analysing it as part of cultural studies. Her interest in the fragmented self has much in common with postmodern culture, but at the same time she is critical of **postmodernism** (p. 295) for absorbing many of the insights of African-American cultural politics, but still not recognising the importance of black culture. Her work demonstrates that concepts like postmodernism are contested. There is, in other words, a politics of postmodernism.

bell hooks's work is an example of the importance of critical writing on the cultural politics of race and gender to cultural studies.

### Further reading

hooks, bell (1982) *Ain't I a Woman*, London: Pluto.

hooks, bell (1991) *Yearning: Race, Gender and Cultural Politics*, London: Turnaround.

hooks, bell (2006) *Outlaw Culture* (new edition), London: Routledge.

## Defining concept 6.1

### Identity

Identity is about how we define who we are. Literally, both identity and the self mean 'the same as'. In cultural theory identity is used to describe the consciousness of self found in the modern individual. The modern self is understood to be autonomous and self-critical. The German philosopher G.W.F. Hegel saw individualism, the right to criticism and autonomy of action as the three main character-istics of modern subjectivity. This self-reflexive aspect of identity means that, in the modern age, identity is understood to be a project. It is not fixed. The autobiographical thinking that characterises modern identity creates a coherent sense of a past identity, but that identity has to be sustained in the present and remade in the future. The constant remaking of identity reveals that the sense of self is to some extent an illusion, because the making of the self requires a constant interaction with the not-self or non-identity: the external world.

In modern Western societies, certain identities have been privileged over others. Men have been privileged over women. White Europeans have been privileged over non-whites. Certain modes of sexual behaviour have defined normal against deviant sexual identities. 'Identity politics' is the term used to describe the emergence into the political arena of identities other than those of white, European, heterosexual men. The assertion of alternative identities has followed a number of different strategies which Jonathan Dollimore (1991) divides into four types of 'reverse discourses': (1) the assertion of a positive identity as normal and natural as the domi-nant 'norm'; (2) the assertion of a negative identity, which is abnormal, but can be explained and assimilated by recourse to legitimating (for example, medical or scientific) dis-courses; (3) the assertion of a different identity as more natural and normal than the dominant norm; (4) the strategy of transgression, where the very categories that define what is normal and abnormal are subverted. The first of these four can be described as essentialist strategies. They assert oppositional identity as essentially unchangeable. An example would be the cultural move-ment known as 'negritude' which emerged at the end of the French Empire. One of its leading pro-ponents, Leopold Senghor (1993: 30) argued that African culture is 'more sensitive to the external world, to the material aspect of beings and things'. However, the result of such strategies is often anti-essentialist. An assertive African culture will in fact change the nature of both African and European identities. The fourth reverse discourse is explicitly anti-essentialist. **Identity** (p. 132) is understood to be performative, not based on any essential character-istics, but rather is a performance based on cultural expectations. Dollimore's example of an anti-essen-tialist identity is Oscar Wilde, who famously argued for the primacy of culture in his statement that 'life imi-tates art'.

One of the most interesting develop-ments in identity politics emerging from this insight has been queer poli-tics. This has developed from lesbian and gay politics; but queer politics resists the division of sexuality into a binary opposition of essentialist homosexual or heterosexual identi-ties. Instead, Judith Butler (1993) argues that identities are the prod-ucts of the **discourses** (p. 21) that define sexuality. We perform mascu-linity or femininity, homosexuality or heterosexuality according to a script already written as the cultural con-ventions of our society. In this view, identities are cultural constructions rather than pre-set.

The concept of identity politics has been subject to criticism from a number of different perspectives. Some Marxists have argued that a focus on identity gives a fragmented perspective and detracts from the need for a universal message of emancipation (Hobsbawm, 1996). Critics of queer politics have argued that the idea that we can perform identity downplays the powerful social forces that make us who we are and over which we have little control. While the performative element in sexuality makes it particularly appro-priate to this approach, it may be less apt for identities constructed by class, 'race' or disability.

### Further reading

Hall, S. and du Gay, P. (eds) (1996) *Questions of Cultural Identity*, London: Sage.

Dollimore, J. (1991) *Sexual Dissidence: Augustine to Wilde, Freud to Foucault*, Oxford: Oxford University Press.

Du Gay, P. Evans, J. and Redman P. (2000) *The Identity Reader*, London: Sage party activism. This change is based on a set of understandings of the world, many of which owe a lot to the work of **Michel Foucault** (p. 20) and other broadly **poststructuralist** (p. 17) authors, who think about it in terms of 'power' and 'power relations'. While an interest in power relations is also shared by some **Marxist**

## Defining concept 6.2

### Colonialism and postcolonialism

There are a bewildering number of terms that refer to the history of colonialism. These include: imperialism, colonialism, neocolonialism and postcolonialism. Of these, imperialism is the broadest. It describes the domination of one society by another. Thus, we can talk of French or American imperialism in terms of the sphere of control that each country exercises over other parts of the world. Colonialism describes more direct control by settlement and military subjugation. Examples are the Spanish colonisation of South America or the British colonisation of India. In practice, however, the terms 'imperialism' and 'colonialism' are often used interchangeably.

Neocolonialism and postcolonialism refer to the period after decolonisation and the end of formal colonial rule. Most North and South American states gained independence in the nineteenth century. In the decades after the Second World War, nations in Africa and Asia assumed control over their affairs. Neocolonialism refers to the continuing control of such countries (sometimes referred to as the 'Third World') by imperial powers through military, political and economic means, despite their formal independence. Neocolonialism is characterised by domination of former colonies' economies by large transnational corporations and their dependence on the export of natural resources and the import of manufactured goods.

Postcolonial theory, by contrast, is a catch-all term for the theories that

have analysed at least four distinct areas: (1) imperial cultures; (2) the cultures of resistance that opposed imperialism; (3) the cultures of decolonised states; (4) the relationship between First World metropolitan and Third World (sometimes called peripheral) cultures. Postcolonial theory now finds its origins in those intellectuals who were the champions of the national liberation movements that fought for independence, for example: Frantz Fanon, C.L.R. James and Amil Cabral. However, the first example of what is now called postcolonial criticism was **Edward Said**'s (p. 115) Orientalism (1978). Said used a combination of **Gramscian Marxism** (p. 38) and **Foucauldian discourse** (p. 21) theory to identify a colonial discourse, Orientalism that denied and misrepresented Eastern and particularly Arabic culture. Subsequent theorists have also used poststructuralism and psychoanalysis to analyse imperial cultures. However, equal emphasis is now given to the problems of understanding colonised cultures. Gayatri Spivak has questioned the ability of finding the voice of the 'subaltern' when, of necessity, that voice is heard through the academic discourses of Western metropolitan culture (Spivak, 1993). Homi Bhabha has attempted to understand the stereotyping that occurs in colonial discourse, for example 'racial' stereotyping, in relation to psychoanalytic theory. He argues that the need to repeat a 'racial' insult indicates an uncon

scious ambivalence in the mind of the coloniser. Repetition demonstrates the need to continually remake the relationship of dominance between the coloniser and the colonised (Bhabha, 1994). Postcolonial literature describes writing that has emerged in the aftermath of decolonisation. It reflects on the colonial period, as in the Nigerian novelist Chinua Achebe's Things Fall Apart; it criticises the impact of neocolonialism, as in the novels of the Kenyan writer Ngugi wa'Thiongo; or, as in novels like Salman Rushdie's **The Satanic Verses** (see p. 172), it explores the increasingly interrelated cultures of the First and Third Worlds, in this case between India and Britain. These kinds of relationships mean that there are strong theoretical commonalities between postcolonial theory and some strands of postmodern theory.

### Further reading

Chrisman, L. and Williams, P. (eds) (1993) Colonial Discourse and Postcolonial Theory, Hemel Hempstead: Harvester Wheatsheaf.

Barker, F., Hulme, P. and Iverson, M. (1994) Colonial Discourse/Postcolonial Theory, Manchester: Manchester University Press.

Loomba, A., Kaul, S. and Bunzi, M (2005) Postcolonial Studies and Beyond, North Carolina: Duke University Press.

(p. 65) theorists, **Marx's** (p. 66) understanding of power as class power, where one class rules another or as the power of capitalism to transform lives and landscapes, has been modified and rendered more complex by Marxist and poststructuralist political theorists confronted with the social transformations of the twentieth century. Now, for example, thinking in a broadly poststructuralist vein, authors like Glenn Jordan and Chris Weedon can say things like the following:

> In this book we make a scandalous claim: *everything* in social and cultural life is fundamentally to do with *power*. Power is at the centre of cultural politics. It is integral to culture. *All signifying practices – that is, all practices that have meaning – involve relations of power.*
>
> (Jordan and Weedon, 1994: 11, emphasis in original)

**Power** (p. 64) has become a (if not *the*) key term in cultural studies and is used in the interpretation of the whole range of cultural practices and products. So, if we take 'politics' as the realm of power relations in general, then 'politics' has expanded its definition to cover all social and cultural relations, not just those of class. We now hear, among other things, of the politics of masculinity, queer politics, the politics of vision and the politics of identity (Sinfield, 2005; Nochlin, 1991b; Keith and Pile, 1993).

Understanding the controversial issue of **identity** (p. 142) politics and its importance at the start of the twenty-first century means thinking about the context in which French poststructuralists and European Marxists have developed their theories. It means thinking about why this new definition of power might have made sense to people working to understand their social and cultural worlds both inside and outside academia. While this is clearly a complicated question, and not one to which we should expect to find a single answer, we would argue that it is bound up with a whole series of 'new social movements', most prominently the women's liberation movements, anti-racist movements, lesbian and gay liberation movements, peace, green and anti-globalisation movements. All of these, in various ways, began to bring into the realm of 'politics' issues that were not previously considered as

political. One key example is the feminist slogan 'the personal is political' which sought to put a whole range of questions about personal identity, personal lives and personal conduct onto an explicitly political agenda. In turn, these new political movements have been responded to in various ways by new political ideologies – of the 'New Left' and the 'New Right' – which have also challenged conventional definitions of politics, though in quite different ways. We would also want to argue that the context for these changes in the definitions of politics is a massive shift in geopolitical organisation which involves both the globalisation of the world's economy and transitions from 'industrial' to 'postindustrial', from 'socialist' to 'postsocialist', from 'modern' to 'postmodern' and from 'colonial' to 'postcolonial'. These changes have entailed the transformation of lives, formal politics and broader power relations for most of the world's population.

It is important to stress therefore that, alongside a broadening of many political agendas (academic and non-academic) towards what we might call 'cultural politics', there has also been a series of transformations in formal politics. In part these are a matter of what is happening 'on the ground'. It is also a matter of how these changes are being interpreted by researchers. In considering changes 'on the ground' we need to take seriously a whole series of fundamental political reorganisations as a connected series of scales. For the historian Eric Hobsbawm, for example, 'The history of the twenty years after 1973 is that of a world which has lost its bearings and slid into instability and crisis' (Hobsbawm, 1994: 403). One key arena of formal politics that has been thrown into confusion is the nation-state:

> As the transnational economy established its grip on the world, it undermined a major, and since 1945, virtually universal, institution: the territorial nation-state, since such a state could no longer control more than a diminishing part of its affairs. Organizations whose field of action was effectively bounded by the frontiers of their territory, like trade unions, parliaments and national public broadcasting systems, therefore lost, as organizations not so bounded, like transnational firms, the international currency market and the

globalized media and communications of the satellite era, gained.

(Hobsbawm, 1994: 424)

Other commentators have also noted these changes, arguing that 'Politically ... things are falling apart' (Ó Tuathail and Luke, 1994: 384). They point to: the collapse of the Soviet Union; the unpredictable outcomes of German reunification; the difficulties experienced by the new European Union; the end of nation-states like Czechoslovakia and the creation of new ones like Macedonia; the end of the Warsaw Pact, but the expansion of its adversary, NATO; the corruption brought to light in the governments of established industrialised democracies like Japan, Italy and France; the contradiction between the USA's attempts to maintain security across the globe and the anarchy in its inner cities (Ó Tuathail and Luke, 1994: 381–4).

The changing nature and declining power of the nation-state has inaugurated a period in which attention has shifted both to the global and to the local scale. Global concerns such as environmental issues are now commonly politicised alongside, and often in relation to, more local concerns (like motorway building or pipe-laying). New political alliances have developed as arguments over sovereignty in the new Europe are worked out. New political forces have emerged as local grievances over resources boil over into racial tension. New state forms are made as health and welfare services are privatised and we learn to live with the chaotic fragmentation of 'community care'. A new politics of identity has been crucial to these developments. In the late twentieth century and early twenty-first century, as Hobsbawm points out, the discourse of nationalism has moved from the state to 'identity groups':

human ensembles to which a person could 'belong', unequivocally and beyond uncertainty. ... Most of these for obvious reasons, appealed to a common 'ethnicity', although other groups of people seeking collective separatism used the same nationalist language (as when homosexual activists spoke of 'the queer nation').

(Hobsbawm, 1994: 428)

These related processes of political fragmentation and universalisation that form the combination of the local and the global have been increasingly conducted through the expanding realm of the international media. Politics is now as much a matter of opinion polls, sound bites and spin doctors as party organisation, activists and militants. The amount of information that people have is massively increased and previously separated places are brought crashing together by new communications technologies.

In response to these issues, people who study 'politics' are changing too. In the most general sense there is a broadening of political analysis which is evident in the development and use of terms such as 'governance' which seeks to expand what might be included in the remit of formal politics to include all forms of regulation, control and guidance. A more specific example would be the development of a 'new critical geopolitics'. Its practitioners and promoters have tried to shake off the old association of geopolitics with analyses of comparative state power which sought to help states win trade wars and real wars with each other. Instead they seek a 'cultural turn' towards a very broad notion of geopolitical power and, along with it, a critical stance. This has involved taking that expanded notion of power developed within cultural studies – as textual, as gendered, as visual – and applying it to an arena of traditional political debate. In the new critical geopolitics, questions of formal and informal politics are being brought together in fruitful ways which enable, among other things, an understanding of the complex cultural, political and economic phenomena of globalisation. In these analyses questions of writing, visual representation and identity are as much a part of the analysis of global political arrangements as warfare, international relations and uneven economic development, and, more importantly, they alter the ways in which we understand these issues. In many ways it is this agenda that we want to address here.

Our concern with culture and politics (or cultural politics) is, therefore, not just the understanding of culture as political. Those themes are addressed elsewhere in the book as they are the very stuff of cultural studies. We mainly want to address how formal politics – the world of political parties, parliaments, bureaucracies, state formation, protest movements and the rest are cultural: how they are arenas of contested meaning rather than places of privileged sanctity and power. To do all this we first need to introduce some of the concepts that are most useful in the discussion of cultural politics.

## Legitimation, representation and performance

The rest of this chapter will look at examples of cultural politics that are concerned with legitimation, **representation** (p. 43) and performance. By legitimation we mean the way in which individuals and groups present themselves as the authentic and lawful holders of power. All but the most brutal forms of government rule through a mixture of coercion (rule by force and violence) and consent (rule by voluntary agreement – see **hegemony**, p. 73). In order to rule with some measure of consent, the government of a constitutional state must establish its legitimacy in the eyes of the ruled. Culture is a key factor in securing the legitimacy of governments. Historically, the original legitimating claim to the right to rule in many societies is the claim to divine right. According to this claim, the ruler is appointed by divine power (God or the gods) to represent the interests of the people. Religion furnishes the authority by which rulers secure the consent of the ruled. Government is legitimated by using the religious culture of the society. Later in this chapter we shall see how culture is used to legitimate various forms of rule through literature, dress and architecture.

**Representation** (p. 43) can mean two different things in relation to politics and culture respectively. Political representation refers to the way in which rulers claim to represent the people over whom they rule. Political representation may be democratic, where political representatives seek a mandate from their electorate to represent them in an assembly (like the British Parliament or the American Congress), or undemocratic. However, representation has a different but connected meaning in the context of culture, where it means 'a symbol or image, or the process of presenting to the eye or mind' (Williams, 1983b: 269). These two meanings come together in the context of cultural politics. A political representative (whether democratic or authoritarian) must represent themselves and their principles, convictions and opinions as the image of those whom they claim to represent. Thus,

to continue the example of divine right given above, this kind of government involved the appropriation of religious imagery in order to represent the ruler as symbolising divine authority. The Queen of England, for example, is also head of the Church of England and has the title *Fidei Defensor* (Defender of the Faith). 'F.D.' is imprinted on all British coins. The government of a state which claims to rule by divine right is represented through symbolism and imagery as the proper and lawful servants of divine power.

Often politics is conducted through and against symbolism and imagery, rather than through rational debate or physical conflict. This is as true for those who resist as for those who uphold power. In a state where rule was legitimated by divine power, intervention by or against the rulers normally also took its authority from religion. In this kind of a conflict, each side needed to legitimate itself as the proper, lawful defender of religion and the conflict was often cultural as well as openly violent. During the Civil War in England (1642–47) both sides claimed to represent the same religion. Radical Protestants accused Catholics of idolatry – the worship of false idols. Members of the Parliamentary forces destroyed figures and paintings in churches because they had associations with the Roman Catholic Church. Another example is the native Amerindians who were forcibly converted to Christianity by the Spanish conquerors of South America. However, when they were permitted to decorate the insides of churches they combined Christian and native imagery in their paintings, in a way that transformed both their own culture and the nature of Roman Catholicism in Latin America. Many religious festivals in the continent which claim Christian legitimacy can be traced back to earlier pre-Conquest religious rites (Martin, 1989). Political interventions are thus made through culture and by culture.

We would argue that, in all these cases, claims to legitimacy and battles over representation are a matter of performance. Politics is always a performance because however much each side claims to represent the truth, in the debate each participant must perform a role through which they enact their position. The concept of performance or performativity is a useful one in the study of cultural politics, because it emphasises the ways in which particular political positions, whether positions of power or resistance, have to be continually made and remade. The idea that politics must be performed inevitably questions any claim to permanent legitimacy. Legitimacy has to be made through a performance that accrues to itself the trappings of power. That performance will often disguise the fact that the positions held are as much the products of debate and conflict as those that oppose them. Broadly speaking, legitimacy is secured by disguising the performative element of politics. Oppositional political movements may seek to establish an alternative form of legitimacy; but, even if this is the ultimate goal, they must first reveal the extent to which power is a performance.

In the rest of the chapter we discuss both conventional and unconventional forms of political activity as performances. First, however, we examine some of the political theories that form a background to this approach. We begin with the work of Niccolo Machiavelli (1469–1527), who was one of the first people to question the idea that political legitimacy is performed and not granted by divine sanction. He suggested that politics can be detached from religion and should be thought of as an 'autonomous science' (Gramsci, 1971: 136). In *The Prince* (1513) he argued that religion might be used by a ruler for political ends. He suggested that it could be a way of gaining legitimacy and of making rulers 'representative'. Machiavelli's ideas were both useful and threatening to forms of government that legitimated themselves through religion. The idea that religion could be used politically undermines its claims to absolute authority and opens up a much wider space for a politics of culture. It is through Machiavelli that politics starts to get a bad name as trickery or hypocrisy.

This broadening of politics was taken further by **Antonio Gramsci** (p. 38) – an important figure in the development of cultural studies. He was a great admirer of Machiavelli's interventionist stance but argued for an understanding of politics that would take into account the whole culture and philosophy of a period (Gramsci, 1971: 140). This meant moving away from just thinking about the rulers and the ruled. Instead he understood politics as a 'war of position', a much more general conflict in which politics is fought out in all the institutions of civil society – religion, the media, entertainment. He

argued that culture can act to fortify the state, and later on we will look at some of the cultural formations that perform this function: the culture of the British Parliament, of bureaucracy and of imperial and military monuments. Those influenced by Gramsci have also stressed how political opposition, or resistance, is also a matter of cultural politics. For example, **E.P. Thompson** (p. 66) has stressed the role of culture in making classes. As he says, 'class-consciousness is the way in which ... experiences are handled in cultural terms: embodied in traditions, value-systems, ideas and institutional forms' (Thompson, 1968: 9). He has shown how what were often crude and brutal customs, like the sale of wives and the tradition of 'rough music' (the use of loud raucous music to punish those who were felt to have transgressed the rules of a community), can be understood as examples of ways in which ordinary people could take back through the performance of rituals some of the power denied to them by society. Thus, the wife sale could be a form of divorce, as well as an act of misogynist male power, while rough music could be 'a property of a society in which justice is not wholly delegated or bureaucratised, but is enacted by and within the community' (Thompson, 1991: 530).

By picking up on these issues of power, identity and performance we might broaden the analysis still further. **Michel Foucault** (p. 20) helps us argue that politics is a matter of **power** (p. 64) relations and that 'power is everywhere ... because it comes from everywhere' (Foucault, 1984b: 93). Such insights, taken up by gender politics, lesbian and gay politics, queer politics and the politics of cultural, ethnic or religious identity, have produced creative forms of political protest (some of these tactics will be described later in the chapter) which play upon the idea of performance to throw both the legitimacy of governments and the legitimacy of identity into doubt. For example, queer politics and queer theory have developed from within the lesbian and gay movement. They emerge from gay and lesbian studies but rather than focusing on questions of homosexuality, the scope is widened. They refuse **essentialist** (p. 121) hetero- or same-sex identities, which exclude, for example, bisexual men and women. So the social and political movement Queer Nation had no patience with exclusions of this kind. Embracing many

147

communities of sexual dissidents, it promoted a discursive strategy to create an innovative paradigm for thinking about sexuality (Bristow, 1997: 217). While it no longer exists, this short-lived organisation made a lasting impression on sexual identity politics. By using the word 'queer' in their name and slogan it is credited with starting the process of reclaiming the word 'queer' from its previous pejorative use and laying the foundations for the acceptability of the representation of 'queer culture' in mass culture.

Queer theory, a term first used by Teresa de Lauretis in 1990, proposes that we do not have fixed identities that determine who we are. Indeed, it is argued that it is meaningless to talk in general about 'women' or 'men' or any other group. Identities consist of so many

elements that to assume that people can be seen collectively on the basis of one shared characteristic is wrong. Queer theory provides a political critique of anything that falls into normative and deviant categories, particularly sexual activities and identities. It is argued that all categories of normative and deviant sexualities are social constructs and it proposes that we deliberately challenge all notions of fixed identity. Recent developments have seen queer theory explore the ways in which sexuality, subjectivity and sociality have been discursively produced in various historical and cultural contexts (Sullivan, 2003). The 'queer theorist' **Judith Butler** (below) has argued that questions of identity are governed by legitimating and 'juridical' discourses. Here juridical means not just relating to the law, but to

## Key influence 6.2

### Judith Butler (1956–)

During the 1990s Judith Butler became one of the most influential writers in feminism and lesbian and gay studies. Her work combines cultural criticism, philosophy and political ideas. She is one of the leading proponents of queer theory.

Judith Butler is Professor of Rhetoric and Comparative Literature at the University of California at Berkeley. Her book *Gender Trouble: Feminism and the Subversion of Identity* (1990) proposed a radical critique of many of the assumptions of second-wave **feminism** (p. 82). Butler challenged the distinction between sex and gender that formed the basis for many earlier analyses of women's subordination. She argued that the idea of sex is culturally constructed. There are no pre-existing biological characteristics which we do not already come to with a set of cultural expectations: 'sex will be shown to have been gender all along' (1990: 8). Instead, Butler develops what she calls a performative theory of identity. Against the

normative stigmatisation of gay and lesbian identities as unnatural, she argues that heterosexuality is as much a performance of cultural conventions as homosexuality. In her influential essay 'Imitation and gender insubordination' (1993) she uses the example of the male drag artist. His (or her) performance is enabled by the conventional nature of heterosexual femininity, which is itself a performance of certain expectations of what is natural. The theory of performativity argues that there is no original sexual identity, only a constantly repeated imitation of an idea of an original. Butler develops these ideas further and responds to some of her critics in *Bodies that Matter: On the Discursive Limits of 'Sex'* (1993). In another book, *Excitable Speech: A Politics of the Performative* (1997), she tackles the question of censorship and 'hate-speech'. Other work has led her to apply some of her ideas to political questions like the status of gays in the American military and

racism. In 2004, she published a collection of writings on war's impact on language and thought entitled *Precarious Life: Powers of Violence and Mourning*.

Butler's work is an example of the growing importance of feminist and lesbian and gay perspectives in cultural studies over the last two decades.

### Further reading

Abelove, H., Barale, M.A. and Halperin, D.M. (eds) (1993) *The Lesbian and Gay Studies Reader*, London: Routledge (contains Judith Butler, 'Imitation and gender insubordination', as well as many other useful essays).

Diamond, E. (ed.) (1996) *Performance and Cultural Politics*, London: Routledge.

Salih, S (2002) *Judith Butler*, London: Routledge.

## Key influence 6.3

### Julia Kristeva (1941–)

Julia Kristeva is a Bulgarian critic and philosopher who has lived in France since 1966. Her work explores the relationship between language, literature and psychoanalysis.

In England and the USA, Kristeva is usually identified with French feminism, which includes theorists such as Hélène Cixous, Luce Irigaray and Monique Wittig. Educated in Marxist and formalist theory in Bulgaria, Kristeva was instrumental in introducing the work of Mikhail Bakhtin to the West. Her writings on transgression (see the collection *Desire in Language*, 1980) are strongly influenced by his work. In Paris she worked closely with the French **structuralist** (p. 17) critic **Roland Barthes** (p. 96). Like Barthes, she became critical of structuralism. In 1970 she joined the editorial board of the influential **poststructuralist** (p. 17) journal *Tel Quel*. With other French intellectuals of the time, she was much affected by the uprising of May 1968,

the fall-out from which led to a disillusionment with orthodox Marxism and a search for new forms of political organisation. In 1974 she published *Revolution in Poetic Language* (1984), a book that combined linguistic and psychoanalytic theory with an analysis of literary texts. In it Kristeva argues for a micropolitics of identity, to be effected through a psychoanalytic understanding of the subject rather than conventional political struggle. In the same year she also published *About Chinese Women* (1977), a book that reflects the influence of Maoism on the Left in the 1970s and the search for an alternative model to the Soviet Union. Her exploration of the constructions of femininity continued in her study of the Virgin Mary, 'Stabat mater' (1986) and in her influential essay 'Women's time' (1981). Her research into the construction of subjectivity has continued in books like *Powers of*

*Horror: An Essay on Abjection* (1982). She has also written about the representation of time in the works of Marcel Proust.

Kristeva's work has had most impact in feminist and literary theory, but her work on transgression has also been influential in cultural politics. In particular, her interest in psychoanalysis has been important in relation to identity politics. Her work in the area of linguistics and on the construction of the subject has important implications for cultural history.

### Further reading

The best introduction to Kristeva's work up until 1982 is Toril Moi (ed.) (1986) *The Kristeva Reader*, Oxford: Blackwell.

Kristeva, J. (1982) *Powers of Horror: An Essay on Abjection*, New York: Columbia UP.

McAfee, N. (2004) *Julia Kristeva*, London; Routledge.

processes of 'limitation, prohibition, regulation, control and even "protection" of individuals' (Butler, 1990: 2). Her critique argues that there is no such thing as a legitimate gender identity, that what we understand to be masculinity and femininity are, in fact, performances conditioned by society: 'there is no gender identity behind the expressions of gender; that identity is performatively constituted by the very "expressions" that are said to be its results' (Butler, 1990: 25). Queer politics, by performing transgressive sexual identities (which can range from drag queens to two lesbian mothers bringing up their children together), can challenge the naturalness of heterosexuality. So, performance is the thing – it makes new transgressive political identities and in doing so it unmakes and unmasks identities that were pretending not to be performances.

The concept of transgression is an important one here. It involves an overturning of the 'proper' order of things. This is described by **Mikhail Bakhtin** (p. 00) as the 'carnivalesque', referring to the brief period of anarchy that occurs during carnivals: 'a world of excess where all is mixed, hybrid, ritually degraded and defiled' (Stallybrass and White, 1986: 8). It turns the world upside down. At carnival, kings become fools and fools become kings. What lies behind carnival is not just disorder, but a conception of an alternative order. The French feminist Julia Kristeva writes that **transgression** (p. 170) of 'linguistic, logical and social codes within the carnivalesque only exists and succeeds ... because it accepts *another law*' (Kristeva, 1986: 41). In this sense, transgressive performances oppose or challenge the legitimacy and representativeness of the ruling law, suggesting that another set of values is possible. We will look further at the concept of transgression (and some of its limits) later in this chapter.

We have now identified some of the ways in which both the culture of politics and the politics of culture might be analysed. The next section will take up some of these themes to look at some of the ways in which political structures can be understood as cultural through notions of representation, performance and identity. The examples include: the use of cultural representations to make political interventions (discussing Benjamin Disraeli's novel, *Sybil*); the performance of parliamentary identities in late twentieth-century and early twenty-first-century Britain; the cultural politics of bureaucratic performances, identities and ethics; and monuments as political statements that transform space and meaning. The final section of this chapter will look in more detail at cultures of resistance and the limits of the concept of transgression.

# 6.2 Cultures of political power

## The cultural politics of democracy in nineteenth-century Britain

Any period of political change will inevitably also be a time of cultural change. Cultural studies is interested in such periods and an interest in cultural politics means an interest in the ways that cultural change is characterised by conflict and struggle. The politics of nineteenth-century Britain were characterised by the demand for suffrage by the majority of the population who did not have the vote. Two major Acts of Parliament extended the vote. The Reform Bill of 1832 increased the electorate from 220,000 to 670,000 men in a population of 14 million. The Reform Bill of 1867 extended the franchise to all male householders in the boroughs, leaving voteless lodgers and workers outside the parliamentary boroughs. Women were denied the vote until 1920.

The struggle for democratisation produced major shifts in cultural politics. The debate was characterised by two contrasting forms of legitimacy: on the one

hand, the old symbols of authority – the monarchy, the Church and the aristocracy; on the other, the democratic principle that only the votes of the people can legitimate a government. According to the critic Catherine Gallagher, the struggle over legitimacy was not just about the 'politics of representation': who represented whom. It also included a cultural conflict about 'the representation of politics' (Gallagher, 1985: 188). One of the arenas of conflict was the novel – in particular, the 'industrial' or 'condition of England' novels of Charles Dickens, Elizabeth Gaskell, Benjamin Disraeli and George Eliot.

One of these novelists, Benjamin Disraeli, was himself a Member of Parliament who later, as prime minister (and in response to extreme pressure from extra-parliamentary agitation), introduced the second Reform Bill in 1867. One of the reasons that Disraeli chose to write political novels when, as a politician, he had access to far more conventional outlets for his opinions, demonstrates an understanding of politics in modern societies that comes closer to Gramsci's war of position than to simplistic notions of rulers and ruled. Disraeli's novels can be seen as a form of complex intervention, designed not just to make a particular political point, but to negotiate the process of cultural change in such a way that elements of his beliefs and principles (which were fundamentally anti-democratic) could be maintained.

As many critics have pointed out, much of the pleasure of Disraeli's novel *Sybil* (1845), what **Raymond Williams** (p. 3) calls his 'likeable panache' (Williams, 1963: 108), is in the way in which Disraeli appears to undermine his own case, exposing the illegitimacy of the aristocrats he advocates as political representatives (see Box 6.1). English lords are revealed to be from families that have bought their right to titles and in numerous passages are shown to be no more discriminating of cultural value than the working-class Disraeli thinks they should represent. The attitude of both classes to drinking is shown to be remarkably similar. First, in high society: "'I rather like bad wine," said Mrs Mountchesney; "one gets so bored with good wine"' (Disraeli, 1845: 3); and later during a riot, when the ironically titled 'Bishop' and his followers break into the cellars of Mowbray Castle:

## Box 6.1

### Industrial Novels: *Sybil, or the Two Nations* by Benjamin Disraeli

*Sybil* is the second book of a trilogy of three novels: *Coningsby, Sybil* and *Tancred*. Charles Egremont, an aristocrat and Member of Parliament, meets and falls in love with Sybil Gerard in the ruins of Marney Abbey. Sybil is the daughter of the Chartist leader Walter Gerard and through her Egremont discovers the difference between England's two nations, the rich and the poor. It is revealed that the estate belonging to Egremont's elder brother, Lord Marney, was taken from Sybil's family during the reign of Henry VIII. Thus, the novel represents the current demands for political reform in terms of the cause of a disenfranchised aristocracy. It describes Chartist political agitation and Egremont's attempts to secure reform through Parliament. The political activities of the Chartists end in riots which leave Sybil's father, Lord Marney, and Egremont's rival for Sybil's hand, Stephen Morley, dead. The way is then open for Sybil, the rightful heir to the Marney estate, to marry its new owner, Egremont, and in that marriage to make one nation out of two. The term 'one-nation Tories' is still used to describe the left wing of the British Conservative Party.

According to Raymond Williams, other 'Condition of England' (or 'Industrial') novels are:

➤ *Mary Barton* (1848) and *North and South* (1855) by Elizabeth Gaskell

➤ *Hard Times* (1854) by Charles Dickens

➤ *Alton Locke* (1850) by Charles Kingsley

➤ *Felix Holt* (1866) by George Eliot.

---

[T]he Bishop himself, seated on the ground and leaning against an arch, the long perspective of the cellars full of rapacious figures brandishing bottles and torches, alternately quaffed some old Port and some Madeira of many voyages, and was making up his mind to their relative merits.

(Disraeli, 1845: 411)

By criticising both sides equally, Disraeli successfully represents a society in which all cultural values have become illegitimate. Under these circumstances, his solution is not a democratic one, but a symbolic one in which he unites both upper and working classes in the figure of the novel's heroine, Sybil. Sybil is at once a working-class activist and, it turns out, from a family descended from the original Anglo-Saxon aristocracy. In addition, as a Roman Catholic she represents the older form of Christianity in England and as a woman can be taken to stand for the monarchy in the shape of the young Queen Victoria. Having represented Victorian England as without values, the character of Sybil brings together those marginalised by that society (the industrialised working class, Roman Catholics and, when represented as a 'Hebrew Maiden' by her association with the Virgin Mary, Jews (Gallagher, 1985: 213)) with a legitimate ruling class, Church and state. She thus performs the symbolic work of uniting a fragmented political culture which has lost its legitimacy. Catherine Gallagher argues that this results in the 'exclusion of politics from the novel, even in the work of a writer who was above all a political man and who believed that politics, like literature, provided the best hope for reconciling facts and values' (Gallagher, 1985: 217–18). However, this can only be accounted an exclusion of politics if politics only involves the narrow definition of the politics of political institutions. In terms of the wider definition of cultural politics, *Sybil* counts as an important intervention because, in the context of a conflict over political rights, the novel intervened in the way that politics was represented, creating new symbols of political legitimacy out of that conflict. In the nineteenth century 'the politics of culture' were:

one very significant component within a larger ideological battle between the gentry, with its allies in the intelligentsia, and the industrial middle-class, a battle that was handily won by the gentry. Their ideological victory, it seems, contributed to the decline of England as an industrial power.

(Gallagher, 1985: 267)

In fact, it is very difficult to judge the success or failure of an intervention in cultural politics, because the relationships between a particular debate and such material factors as economic growth or decline are very difficult to measure. What can be said is that the conflicts and disputes that characterise cultural politics are a crucial part of cultural studies, while their outcomes become debates in competing accounts of cultural history. What can also be said is that such cultural interventions are a matter of the representation and performance of political identities.

## Performing identities in conventional politics

Conventional politics, that is the politics of governments and political parties, appears at first to be least open to a discussion of cultural politics. Closer examination, however, reveals that conventional politics are constructed by and through culture. For example, one important way that conventional politics establishes its cultural legitimacy is through the impression of continuity. The rituals and traditions of the British Parliament give an impression of stability and longevity that contributes to the sense that it is a legitimate institution. The often-made claim that this Parliament is the 'mother of all Parliaments' is an example of how legitimacy is established through the representation of the British Parliament as the origin of parliamentary democracy. Such commonly known facts about the debating chamber as that the distance between the two sides is the length of two swords – so that no one may be harmed for speaking their opinions – signify a tradition of free debate that stretches back into distant history.

Our analysis of the cultural politics of the British Parliament, however, is interested in how the representation of tradition is sustained and performed – in other words, how tradition has to be made and remade. One example that demonstrates the cultural politics of what we have been calling formal politics would be the way that politicians dress. Politicians' dress codes can be seen as evidence that the role of parliamentary politician is not something to which individuals are born, but something they have to *perform*. The advantages of the theory of performativity here are that it allows an

understanding of conventional and non-conventional political activity that relates the question of **identity** (p. 142) to political practice. In the case of conventional identities it allows what appears to be normal and natural to be seen as culturally constructed.

Male members of the Conservative Party, for example, commonly wear business suits when they are in London, but are often filmed wearing tweed jackets when they give interviews in their constituencies at the weekends. These two 'uniforms' allow the politician to perform a particular role which signifies something about the kind of politics they represent. The business suit is commonly worn by men who work in the City of London and might be seen to signify a knowledge and control of financial matters. The tweed jacket, on the other hand, has associations of a more leisured, rural, upper-class life. The two dress codes indicate the different aspects of the male MP's life. During the week he is an efficient worker in London; at the weekend he leads a more leisured existence in his rural constituency (though not one that precludes television interviews if the matter is important enough). At the same time the codes bring together two perhaps contradictory elements of Conservative political philosophy: a belief in finance capitalism and in the traditions of rural England.

In 2007 the leader of the Conservative Party is David Cameron, who is the first Eton-educated leader since the early 1960s. He is from an establishment family background, and is a member of the exclusive Mayfair gentleman's club White's. Despite his obviously privileged background away from work Cameron has sought to use clothes to project and perform a down to earth image to widen his appeal and appear classless rather than the upper-crust figure his background might suggest. (see Figure 6.1). However, just like the male leaders of the Conservative party before him his work uniform is still the formal 'city' suit (see Figure 6.2). This adds weight to our suggestion above that the role of parliamentary politician is not something to which individuals are born, but something they have to perform.

It is easy for such codes to become naturalised as the normal dress for politicians, so that they go unquestioned. The fact that the performance of being a politician is enacted through dress codes only becomes

Figure 6.1 The performance of the 'down to earth'. (Source: Corbis.)

Figure 6.2 The performance of financial control. (Source: Corbis.)

apparent when they are transgressed in a public way. One example of transgression in the sphere of conventional parliamentary politics occurred in November 1981 when the leader of the Labour Party, Michael Foot, attended the ceremony at the Cenotaph in London to commemorate those who died in the two world wars (see Figure 6.3). The formal dress expected on such an occasion was described by the *Daily Express* as that worn by the Prime Minister, Margaret Thatcher, the leader of the Liberal Party, David Steel, and Princess Diana:

> Mrs Thatcher wore a smart tailored black topcoat with matching hat, handbag and shoes. David Steel was in black morning suit. The Princess of Wales wore a smart black coat with a white lace collar and a black hat with a plume feather.
>
> (*Daily Express*, 9 November 1981)

By contrast, Michael Foot is claimed by the *Express*

to have 'angered millions of television viewers yesterday. He turned up for the solemn Cenotaph Remembrance Day ceremony in a donkey jacket, plaid tie and dirty shoes'. The multiple nature of Mr Foot's transgression is indicated by the readers who, the *Daily Express* claims, phoned in to complain:

> Reader Mrs Margaret Tully of Bettesford, Nottinghamshire said: 'Foot looked like he had come out of Steptoe's yard.'

> RAF veteran Robert Brookes of Brockham, Surrey said: 'Foot came as though he had just been dragged through a hedge. His dress, manner and behaviour was a direct insult to our war dead.'

> Mrs Linda Caine, of Toton, Notts, said: 'I expected him to be carrying a Right to Work placard. I blame his wife. No self-respecting wife would let her husband go out like that. I just can't get over it. Even his shoes were mucky.'

The objections chosen for the article indicate certain expectations of the leader of Her Majesty's Opposition. Mrs Tully's reference to 'Steptoe's yard' alludes to a popular television situation comedy about a scrap dealer and his son. Her contribution suggests that, at least during formal, ritualised public appearances, Foot should dress according to the dress codes of the upper,

**Figure 6.3** Michael Foot at the Cenotaph.
(Source: PA News Ltd.)

Reagan' (then President of the United States and a former Hollywood film star) how he would advise Mr Foot and produced a mocked-up photograph of the result. Nor should Foot be seen to be an innocent player in the politics of performance. He is criticised in *The Times* for looking as if he had just returned from walking his dog on Hampstead Heath; but Hampstead, where Foot lives, is a part of London with a reputation for bohemianism and middle-class radicalism. His dress and actions, while described by the *Daily Telegraph* as having 'all the reverent dignity of a tramp bending down to inspect a cigarette end', could be seen as signifying Julia Kristeva's definition of the carnivalesque as the acceptance of 'another law' (see p. 149 above), which creates the dialogue or debate of cultural politics. Here, the other law is the radical political tradition in which Foot usually wishes to place himself, signified by a more informal mode of dress that recalls protest demonstrations (Foot was renowned for his involvement in the Campaign for Nuclear Disarmament). This comes into conflict with the rituals of Remembrance Sunday, which often recalls national pride in military victories as well as commemoration of the dead.

One aspect of Foot's transgression that is interesting for the student of culture is the way in which it does not matter exactly what Mr Foot was wearing. The versions of his dress change from paper to paper. The 'donkey jacket' becomes a 'green donkey jacket' in the *Daily Telegraph*, a 'duffel coat' in the *Mirror*, and in the *Times* the shoes become 'sneakers', while the 'plaid' (*Express*) or 'check' (*Mirror*) tie becomes 'paisley'. What is important are not the details themselves, but that his dress places him outside the codes that stabilise the significance of his position as representative of authority (the dress codes of class), loyalty (religion and patriotism) and masculinity (the gendered roles of husband and wife). We can see from these examples that conventional political identities are performed within sharply defined cultural boundaries and that these boundaries are shaped by the broader contexts of political debate. Cultural expectations are a key determinant of political identities and thus culture itself is an enormously powerful factor in limiting the terrain on which traditional politics is conducted.

not the working class. Robert Brookes' complaint refers to the fact that Foot did not appear to bow when he placed his wreath or join in the hymns. This articulates an expectation that he will pay tribute to the religious elements and patriotic elements of Remembrance Sunday. Mrs Caine asks that his appearance should reflect a family background where the traditional gender roles of husband and wife are sustained. If Mr Foot and his wife did occupy these roles, it is suggested by Mrs Caine, the transgression would never have occurred.

The *Daily Express* is not usually sympathetic to the Labour Party, and its criticisms are in turn criticised as 'petty' by left-leaning papers like the *Daily Mirror* and the *Guardian*. However, even the more sympathetic papers emphasise the importance of appearance for a politician. There is a recognition on all sides that performativity is an important part of the way in which politics is conducted. On 10 November 1981, the *Daily Express* asked the consultant who 'groomed Ronald

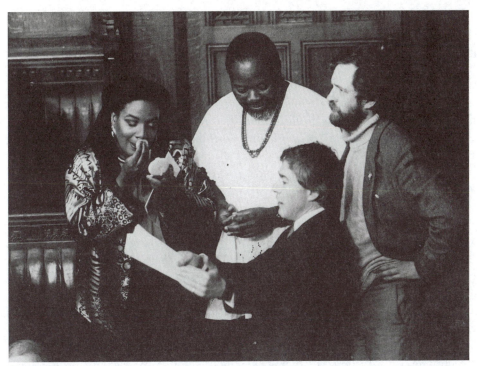

**Figure 6.4** Diane Abbott and Bernie Grant, who also transgressed convention by not wearing the traditional jacket and tie. (Source: PA News Ltd.)

These limitations become more obvious when social groups enter Parliament that, for reasons of culture and background, cannot lay claim to the traditions of formal politics. When the first four black MPs entered Parliament in 1987, newspaper coverage paid great attention to putative differences between the culture of Parliamentary tradition and that of the new representatives. Many papers commented on the fact that the first black woman MP, Diane Abbott (see Figure 6.4) sat in the seat formerly occupied by Enoch Powell, who had made inflammatory speeches advocating the repatriation of non-whites:

> Where he sat, cadaverous and grimly mocking, sits now dusky Diane Abbott (Lab. Hackney N.). As if to emphasise that times have changed, she took out a make up case and sensuously painted her lips. For the rest she and her coloured colleagues listened decorously, no doubt amazed by the ceremonious mysteries and ancestral mumbo-jumbo of what they have invaded and challenged.
>
> (*Daily Mail*, 26 June 1987)

The satirical tone that is commonly used in parliamentary sketches here employs the language of 'racial' stereotypes ('mysteries', 'mumbo-jumbo') to describe the traditions of Parliament. This upset or inversion, however, maintains the idea of cultural conflict in the words 'invaded and challenged', which reproduce some of the discourse of Enoch Powell's anti-immigration speeches. The limits of the concept of performativity to understand political identities are also glimpsed here. While the concept works well to deconstruct codes that legitimate power, in the case of social groups that have historically been labelled as illegitimate it is not enough to argue that they can perform an oppositional identity. For those who have to compete with the way they are identified by restrictive definitions of 'race' and 'gender', the room to 'perform' can be severely circumscribed.

It is in this context that it is interesting that three newspapers chose to emphasise Abbott's make-up, which was mentioned by the *Guardian* and the *Express* as well as the *Mail* in their reporting of the Queen's Speech. The limited room allowed Abbott is shown by the way that three journalists concentrate on not just her appearance but the way in which she herself makes up that appearance. In the context of her symbolic position as the first black woman MP, the way that she constructs her self, her identity – in other words, the mechanics of Abbott's performance in terms of her gender and 'race' – becomes the focus of discussion. The racist overtones of this focus are most clear in the quotation from the *Mail* above, but the implication underlies all the reports that, because she is black and a woman, she will not be able to perform the role of MP as naturally as a white woman or man.

It is now more than 20 years since Diane Abbott was first elected to parliament on 11 June 1987 and she remained the only black woman in the House until the election of Oona King in 1997. In 2007, along with Dawn Butler, they remain the only three black women ever elected to Parliament. To date, no Asian woman has ever been elected. The position of ethnic minority women in British politics is as negligible as ever. The *Guardian* reported this 20-year anniversary thus,

> Twenty years ago today, history was made. On June 11 1987 a feisty, garrulous, perpetually late and infectiously high-spirited Diane Abbott became the first black woman to be elected as a member of the House of Commons. Yet you could almost as easily say that history stopped too, because since then just two others have followed her … what I most remember about her is a huge loud laugh that got everyone else grinning. She was, and is, a cheerer-upper. She was never the cautious, quietly hard-working type.
>
> (*Guardian*, 11 June 2007)

In many ways little seems to have changed; the emphasis is still upon Abbott's performance of restrictive definitions of race and gender, rather than on her performance of the role of MP. The examples of Michael Foot and Diane Abbott demonstrate how transgression can both be empowering in its challenge to legitimacy and how 'another law' can be quickly marginalised as frivolous or disrespectful.

We have shown, therefore, that political identities must be performed, and that different types of performances carry different meanings. Yet, so far this has all been conducted in terms of the most visible political 'actors' – parliamentary politicians. The next section looks at a different site of political power, one that is, as we say, 'behind the scenes'. This is the world of the bureaucrats. The aim here is to show that the apparently dehumanising, routine and supposedly invisible forms of social organisation which characterise bureaucracy also involve cultural meaning and performance in the structuring and legitimating of power relations.

# Bureaucracy as culture

## Introducing bureaucracy

Most discussions of bureaucracy begin with the work of the sociologist **Max Weber** (p. 158) (see Weber, 1967). He argued that what he called the 'characteristics of bureaucracy', or 'modern officialdom', could be set apart from the ways in which other forms of rule operated. For example, they are different from older monarchical states where the administration was an extension of the king's household run by patronage and tradition. In this sense Weber is one of those thinkers discussed above (see p. 147), who are interested in analysing the complexities of the relationship between rulers and ruled. By separating out these characteristics Weber hoped to understand bureaucracy (see Box 6.2).

What Weber presents us with is a bureaucratic system in which full-time, salaried, trained, qualified, appointed and finely graded staff, with job security, career prospects and pension rights, operate according to sets of written and rational rules to make administrative decisions within specific areas of official competence which are carefully demarcated to separate them from each other, from their home lives and from the public. It is a rationally organised and objective system whose calculable rules operate 'without regard for persons' rather than on the basis of doling out personal favours or on the basis of tradition. Weber suggests that the reasons for its success (as measured by its dramatic historical development and geographical spread alongside capitalist economic relations; see Lefort, 1986) can be understood as the same as the reasons for the success of machines in arenas where things had previously been produced without them. As he said:

## Max Weber's bureaucratic ideal type

1 'There is a principle of fixed and official jurisdictional areas, which are generally ordered by rules, that is, by laws or administrative regulations ... Permanent and public office authority, with fixed jurisdiction, is not the historical rule but rather the exception.'

2 'The principles of office hierarchy and levels of graded authority mean a firmly ordered system of super- and subordination in which there is a supervision of the lower offices by the higher ones.'

3 'The management of the modern office is based upon written documents ("the files"), which are preserved in their original or draught form ... In principle, the modern organisation of the civil service separates the bureau from the private domicile of the official, and, in general bureaucracy segregates official activity as something distinct from the sphere of public life.'

4 'Office management ... usually presupposes thorough and expert training.'

5 '[O]fficial activity demands the full working capacity of the official ...'

6 'The management of the office follows general rules, which are more or less stable, more or less exhaustive, and which can be learned. Knowledge of these rules represents a special technical learning which the officials possess.'

Weber (1967: 196–8)

---

The decisive reason for the advance of bureaucratic organisation has always been its purely technical superiority over any other form of organisation. ... Precision, speed, unambiguity, knowledge of the files, continuity, discretion, unity, strict subordination, redirection of friction and of material and personal costs – these are raised to the optimum point in the strictly bureaucratic administration.

(Weber, 1967: 214)

What all this suggests is that bureaucracy is somehow outside the sphere of culture. It operates in a world of cold, hard economic and political realities which do not admit the claims of meaning, feeling and intersubjective interpretation that come within the reach of what we call the cultural. Weber's analysis suggests that older forms of rule – operating according to ancient religious traditions or the whims of despotic emperors – were 'cultural' (see the discussion of divine right above). He notes that they were coupled with educational systems designed to produce 'the cultivated man' whose criteria for acceptability for governing was 'the possession of "more" cultural quality' (Weber, 1967: 243). Rationalised bureaucracy is very different:

Its specific nature ... develops the more perfectly the more the bureaucracy is 'dehumanised', the more completely it succeeds in eliminating from official business love, hatred, and all purely personal, irrational, and emotional elements which escape calculation. This is the specific nature of bureaucracy and it is appraised as its special virtue.

(Weber, 1967: 243)

Instead of seeking those with 'cultural quality' (whatever that may mean), bureaucracy is tied to educational systems that produce technical experts or 'the "specialist type of man"' (Weber, 1967: 243). Thus, as bureaucratic forms develop, there also develops a series of conflicts between these specialists and those who had previously ruled on a different – 'cultural' – basis: 'This fight is determined by the irresistibly expanding bureaucratisation of all public and private relations of authority and by the ever-increasing importance of expert and specialised knowledge. This fight intrudes into all intimate cultural questions' (Weber, 1967: 243).

We can see that bureaucracy, for Weber, has crucial implications for 'cultural questions', but is not presented as being 'cultural' itself. It is this last assumption that we want to question here and the reason for setting out Weber's thinking on bureaucracy in so much detail is to show that many of the issues we want to develop can be found lurking in Weber's own texts. The first is that for bureaucracy to be successful it is not merely a technical administrative matter – like Parliamentary identities it must be *performed*. The various 'eliminations' and 'separations' that Weber refers to must be performed for the publics that legitimate its authority.

That issue will be taken up below by considering how bureaucratic office buildings perform bureaucracy in different ways. This performance is, however, also a matter for the bureaucrats themselves and here it connects to issues of identity and power which will be investigated by considering how the bureaucratic persona is gendered. Weber was aware of the 'produc-

## Key influence 6.4

### Max Weber (1864–1920)

Born in Erfurt, Central Germany, the son of a lawyer and National Liberal politician, Weber was schooled in Berlin before studying law and history at the universities of Heidelberg, Berlin and Gottingen. Following spells of military training and work in criminal law courts he returned to university to specialise in economic history. He obtained a doctorate in 1888 and completed a post-doctoral habilitation thesis in 1891 that allowed him to pursue an academic career. He married Marianne Schnitger in 1893. Marianne became an influential figure in the German feminist movement. In 1896 Weber was appointed professor of economics at Heidelberg University, where he settled for the rest of his life. However, his father's death in 1897 provoked the onset of a depressive illness, which led to lengthy sick-leaves from his post.

By 1903 Weber felt well enough to resume some academic work. His 1904 visit to the USA influenced his famed *The Protestant Ethic and the Spirit of Capitalism* (1904–05). Around this time he began to reorient his intellectual interests in the direction of sociology and the 'cultural sciences'. He emphasised the centrality of the meanings that people attach to objects and activities, defining culture as the 'finite segment of the infinity of the world process, a

segment on which human beings confer meaning and significance'.

According to Weber rationalisation is the master trend accounting for the broad development of Western societies. More and more spheres of life were being wrested from the influence of the incalculable, the whimsical, the magical, and the non-standardised, and brought under rational control. The application of instrumental rationality was facilitated by the emergence of modern science, by systematic forms of accountancy and law, but above all by bureaucracy as the dominant form of social organisation. Weber saw rationalisation as a relentless process. He saw the future in bleak terms as an 'iron cage' in which human individuality would be increasingly circumscribed:

No one knows who will live in this cage in the future, or whether at the end of this tremendous development entirely new prophets will arise, or there will be a great rebirth of old ideas and ideals, or, if neither, mechanized petrification, embellished with a sort of convulsive self-importance. For of this last stage of cultural development, it might truly be said: 'Specialists without spirit, sensualists without heart; this nullity imagines it has attained a

level of civilization never before achieved'.

(Weber, 1930: 182).

Weber held that facts and values occupied radically different domains, and that science and politics were distinct spheres of activity. But he was not afraid to become involved in practical action and political activity (for example, at the outbreak of World War One he took up the post of Director of Army Hospitals, Heidelberg; later, he became a critic of Germany's war policies and was a delegate to the Versailles peace conference).

Weber's analyses of the impact of rationality on the cultural features of modern societies have been enormously influential on subsequent theorists. Weber's methodological writings, which deal with questions about how cultures and societies can be investigated in a principled manner, have a contemporary relevance in light of their stress on the unavoidably partial and fragmentary character of cultural and scientific knowledge.

### Further reading

Poggi, G. (2006) *Weber: A Short Introduction*, Cambridge: Polity.

Whimster, S. (ed.) (2003) *The Essential Weber: A Reader*, London: Routledge.

tion' of different sorts of ruling men but he did not follow up the implications of that. Finally, we briefly consider how the bureaucratic structures and the bureaucratic personas constructed within them are ethically problematic. Again this is something that Weber was aware of in his discussion of the difficulties of dismantling a bureaucracy but which he did not take further. So, bring on the performing bureaucrats.

## Bureaucracy and the performance of power

The French social theorist Henri Lefebvre understood modern societies as shaped by a process of 'bureaucratisation through space' which subjected social life to increasing regulation and surveillance (Gregory, 1994: 401; see also Foucault, 1977; Dandeker, 1990; and Giddens, 1985). This is coupled with a heightened 'bureaucratisation of space' whereby each administrative system 'maps out its own territory, stakes it out and signposts it' (Lefebvre, 1991b: 387). While these ideas are useful for understanding how states administer societies, they can also be turned towards understanding bureaucracy itself. One of the implications of Weber's work is that bureaucracies involve tight internal surveillance, and that the putting into place of these forms of surveillance means a careful attention to organising space within bureaucratic offices (Giddens, 1984). This, then, is a matter of how best to regulate the flows of people, papers and ideas within an office to get the job done: 'bureaucratisation through space' in the bureaucratic office. Where should departments be located? Which offices should be open plan, which private? What are the 'correct channels' for people and files to go through? More interesting perhaps is the 'bureaucratisation of space' within bureaucracy. While the mapping and staking out of territory and the erection of signposts is a useful metaphor for the division of administrative responsibilities between ministries or departments – separating education and employment, home and foreign, agriculture and industry – it is also inscribed onto bureaucratic space. These signposts exist in the form of the offices that the bureaucracy inhabits.

There are several points that can be made about the sorts of buildings that bureaucrats occupy in terms of how they are part of a culture of bureaucracy. Firstly, simply as separate buildings they make statements about the nature of bureaucracy. Their separation from each other, from the homes of the bureaucrats, from Parliament or other centres of power, is not merely a question of efficiency but is a demonstration – a performance – of the autonomy of the bureaucrats and bureaucratic processes housed within them from 'political' influences which might question whether they really function 'without regard for persons'. Secondly, the architecture is important in this performance too. The way the buildings look makes statements about what goes on inside. Some of this is about various representations of the functions of the ministries (for example, bulls' heads on the Ministry of Agriculture, Food and Fisheries) and these small signs help to make these more than just anonymous office blocks. However, the primary role is to 'perform' the legitimate authority of bureaucracy, and this is not so easily done with such specific symbols. The solid, geometrical, well-built, large, clean buildings with their imposing entrances and uniform, regularly spaced windows speak of the importance, solidity, rationality and efficient impersonality of bureaucracy. These are all the characteristics that give it legitimacy as a way of ruling. The buildings themselves demonstrate the 'precision, speed, unambiguity, knowledge of the files, continuity, discretion, unity, strict subordination [and] efficiency' that Weber saw as characteristic of bureaucracy. What we want to add is that this is a matter of cultural politics in that it is *performed*: not only must it be done, it must be seen to be done.

It might, however, be argued that, just as state forms are changing in the twenty-first century, then so are forms of bureaucracy and the ways in which their presence is performed. Some of these issues are raised in relation to MI6 (see Box 6.3). Previously, the British security services were part of a national bureaucracy at the centre of a worldwide empire. As a secret organisation, MI6 saw itself as playing a discreet role – no one was supposed to know where its headquarters were – and was happy for its public image to be represented by fictional agents, like James Bond, who was a heroic but human figure, carrying out Britain's purpose in a hostile world. The new building fits in with the new **postmodern** (p. 299) architecture of the City of

## Box 6.3

### MI6 and the architectural performance of power

None of these interpretations of bureaucratic buildings can be static. The forms that they take are always changing. The question is whether these changes are significant ones and how we might interpret them. For example, this building on the South Bank of the River Thames at Vauxhall, into which MI6 (part of the British government's secret service) recently moved, raises some interesting questions

How does it differ from the traditional architecture of bureaucracy? Is this part of a shift from 'modernism' to 'postmodernism'?

What does it say about a government department that it is housed in something reminiscent of a postmodern version of a Babylonian temple? What relations of authority are being performed here?

The M16 building.

London (which, as a centre of finance, is one of Britain's last claims to international leadership), announcing itself as part of the new transnational world. It represents the new business of intelligence, which involves high-tech surveillance techniques like satellites (James Bond specialised in small, pocket-sized gadgets) and Britain's new role within international organisations like NATO and the United Nations, and the more complex interaction of diplomacy, military might and economic aid that structures interventions in the new multipolar or globalised world described earlier. Thus, looking at this building in relation to the geopolitical situation within which it operates shows how questions of representation and **symbolism** (p. 214) are inseparable from those of political power and the ways in which it is always changing.

Bureaucracies, however, are not simply a matter of offices; they are also about bureaucrats. These issues of performance can be widened in order to understand

the culture of bureaucracy in similar terms to those we have used for parliamentary identities, addressing them in terms of issues of identity and, particularly, gendered identity.

### Bureaucracy and identity

In part, questions of **identity** (p. 142) within bureaucracy can be understood in the terms used above. The mapping and signposting of territories goes on as much within offices as it does between them. The signalling of hierarchies with more and more elaborate and graded office spaces, office furniture, and the rituals and ceremonies of super- and subordination are very much part of our common currency of jokes about what bureaucrats are like. Yet these issues of identity run much deeper than which sort of wastepaper bin a Grade 5 civil servant has. As Claude Lefort (1986) has argued, 'Bureaucracy loves bureaucrats just as much as bureaucrats love bureaucracy' (1986: 108) and one reason for this situation is that bureaucratic society forms 'a concrete milieu from which each individual derives his own identity' (1986: 113). Indeed, as in all workplaces there is a complex process by which the organisational culture shapes the identities that are available to workers. As Paul du Gay (1996) has shown for the retailing sector, changes in organisational forms (often away from 'bureaucratic' or 'authoritarian' modes towards ones associated with 'flexibility' and 'enterprise') mean that new identities arise which are adopted, resisted and negotiated by workers and managers. We need to understand organisations and identities at the same time. That Lefort does so in terms of class means that he has not investigated the arena in which this has been most dramatically demonstrated: gender.

Anne Witz and Mike Savage (1992) have challenged the idea that what Weber presents is the general form of bureaucratic organisation. Instead, they argue that it is just one 'historically and spatially specific form of organising' (1992: 3) among many. Moreover, their argument is that each of these organisational forms can be seen to 'rest upon particular gendered foundations' (1992: 3) and, as a result, the gender relations upon which Weber's model depends can be uncovered. Instead of being a matter of technical efficiency, bureaucracy is seen to be a matter of social relations and power relations. They show how hierarchies within bureaucracies have been gendered: how the employment of women within subordinate, often clerical, offices was essential to guaranteeing meritocratic career structures for male bureaucrats. Moreover, they show how these careers were also dependent on having a wife at home to do all the work necessary to send the bureaucrat back to the office, day after day, clean, fed, rested and ready for work. This all means that Weber's notions of the bureaucratic career need to be understood as gendered. It also means that we have to think carefully about what this gendering of bureaucracy means for Weber's sense of the objectivity and rationality of such organisational forms.

Let us go back to what Weber calls bureaucracy's 'specific nature' and 'special virtue', the elimination 'from official business [of] love, hatred, and all purely personal, irrational, and emotional elements which escape calculation' (Weber, 1967: 243). What Weber refers to as a process whereby bureaucracy becomes 'dehumanised' has been seen by those interested in gender as the construction of a particular form of masculinity which is built upon its exclusion of the personal, the sexual and the feminine. Rational administration can only exist if those characteristics constructed as 'masculine' and mental – distance, objectivity and reason – are given precedence over those characteristics constructed as feminine and bodily – closeness, compassion and emotion. The imagined bureaucrat is the dark-suited man with the tightly rolled umbrella and the briefcase. However, this cannot be a simple separation of the 'masculine' and the 'feminine'. First, the 'male' sphere of rational, objective reason and action can only exist if a space is made for it by a whole load of other work being done. This work is gendered feminine. As Savage and Witz argue, women are 'housekeeping' in the office as well as at home. 'They are facilitating, cleaning, tidying, bolstering, soothing, smoothing over, sustaining … relieving men of having to bother with the messy, untidy, unpredictable bodily mode of existence' (Savage and Witz, 1992: 23). Gender is there right at the root of bureaucracy. Second, men cannot so easily escape the body and sexuality. As we have already seen in relation to parliamentary identities, the supposedly asexual and unbodily identity is one that has to be performed constantly using suits, ties, postures and briefcases. Here is Malcolm Young talking about policemen's bodies:

> To walk into a pub function room as I have often done during the ten years I was collecting fieldnotes and to see two or three hundred detectives in their 'uniform' of modern suit and tie, neat haircut, and the fashionable moustache of the times, is to be visibly reminded that there is a narrow symbolic range of bodily correctness within which all policemen can properly operate.
>
> (Young, 1991: 83)

As with Parliament, entry into organisations like the police is restricted by cultural factors which are built into bureaucratic forms of organisation. Indeed, even when perfectly performed it is not actually an asexual identity but a particular mode of sexuality that is constantly used to gain and maintain power within the organisational setting. Michael Roper (1994), discussing businessmen, has argued that the bureaucratic life is a vividly emotional one where bonds and divisions between men – young and old – animate working lives via a struggle to maintain a sufficiently masculine identity: an identity that, it must be noted, is assertively heterosexual (men who desire women) while operating through homosocial (men who work with men and exclude women from the world of work) relationships.

In thinking about why all this is the case, we clearly need to situate it within the cultural struggles for power which are the stuff of cultural politics. There are gendered power struggles in the office within which identities are a weapon. As much as in the sphere of formal politics, this involves bids for legitimacy to civil society (or the public) within which the connected performances of masculinity and objectivity are crucial. However, legitimation is not simply a one-way street. Thomas Osbourne (1994) stresses that those involved in bureaucracy also have to convince themselves that they are fit to rule. He suggests that the question that we need to ask is: 'What do those who rule have to do to *themselves* in order to be able to rule?' In answering this question in terms of the development of a civil service in Britain through the Northcote-Trevelyan Report of 1854, he shows how competitive examinations were used for the first time to legitimate the authority of the bureaucracy by developing a sense of vocational unity, an attachment to a wider public (who could take the exams if they wanted, and might even pass if they had a classical education) and a particular mode of masculinity (which Osbourne calls 'muscular liberalism') which made them feel fit to govern. As Lord Ashley put it in 1844: 'we must have nobler, deeper, sterner stuff; less of refinement and more of truth; more of the inward and less of the outward gentleman; a rigid sense of duty and not a delicate sense of honour' (quoted in Osbourne, 1994: 306). That the rooting of this in the classics bound it to a particular class and that the examination system had been first developed in British India as part of a racialised bureaucratic system stresses that class, race and gender are again bound together in these issues of bureaucratic identity.

What are the costs of this masculinisation of bureaucratic identity? Certainly for women it presents a crucial problem in terms of the ways that they can operate within such organisations. As Savage and Witz say, they have to perform a particularly problematic identity, one that is gendered but not sexualised: they 'must behave like men but not be men and behave unlike women and yet be women' (Savage and Witz, 1992: 53). There are also what we might think of as costs to men (although we must also bear in mind the benefits they stand to gain as men from the process) through the circumscribed forms of life that are connected to bureaucratic success. Finally, we need to think about the ethical costs of masculinised bureaucratic systems which emphasise objectivity, rationality and efficiency above all else.

## Bureaucracy and ethics

In his investigations of the Holocaust the sociologist Zygmunt Bauman (1989) had begun to question the ethics of bureaucracy and to stress the ways in which it is able to silence morality. Again, his argument runs against Weber's since for Bauman bureaucracy is not neutral, it is positively dangerous. He argues that the meticulous functional division of labour and the replacement of moral responsibility by a purely technical responsibility (getting the job done efficiently) distances bureaucrats from the final products of the bureaucratic processes of which they are a part. They become concerned only to carry out the orders that come from above, believing that this absolves them of moral responsibility for their actions. This means that they only pay attention to how smoothly their part of the process operates rather than considering the final outcomes and their responsibility for them. They become insulated from the results of their actions via the structure of bureaucracy and, as a result, they can operate in a language of rational and technical efficiency which only concerns itself with seemingly neutral measures of efficiency and with rational input–output equations. What is being dealt with – and in the case that Bauman is concerned to investigate it is people being transported to death camps and then killed on a huge scale – becomes less important than that the process operates efficiently and cost-effectively. Bauman's argument is, therefore, that these processes bring with them a 'dehumanisation of the objects of bureaucratic action' (Bauman, 1989: 102). In the bureaucrats' forms, ledgers, graphs and accounts, people become units to be processed, no different from pig iron or potatoes, and not 'potential subjects of moral demands' (Bauman, 1989: 103). For Bauman, bureaucracy, in its pursuit of rationality and efficiency, silences morality. As a result he can point to the bureaucrats whose actions moved millions of Jews through the railway system to their deaths in Germany and Poland and argue that 'bureaucracy made the Holocaust. And it made it in its own image' (Bauman, 1989: 105). He also enables us to ask difficult ethical questions about seemingly neutral rational and technical processes.

It should now be clear that bureaucracy needs to be understood as cultural, as part of the world of cultural politics. It involves questions of performance, identity and ethics which cannot simply be understood as matters of technical rationality. That this is also true of other arenas of state activity, particularly warfare, now needs to be explored.

## Performing state power

Having explored the question of the performance of power in relation to parliamentary politics and bureaucratic administration, we want to argue that it is useful in understanding how states (political entities which claim rights to violence, taxation and administration over specific territories) display their power in order to claim authority and legitimacy. In particular it will be concerned with the ways in which the culture of politics is crucial to understanding how states manage to legitimate their extensive use of violence. This will also mean showing how partial these performances are, particularly in terms of gender, and how restrictive they are in terms of the identities that they offer and the moralities that they suggest. Finally, it will mean thinking about how these cultural claims to power are challenged.

One excellent starting point for a discussion of what we might call the connections between 'state formation' (the making of state power) and 'cultural politics' is the work of Peter Corrigan and Derek Sayer:

States, if the pun be forgiven, *state*; the arcane

**Figure 6.5** The Victoria Monument, London.

rituals of a court of law, the formulae of royal assent to an Act of Parliament, visits of school inspectors, are all statements. They define, in great detail, acceptable forms and images of social activity and individual and collective identity; they regulate ... much – very much, by the twentieth century – of social life. Indeed, in this sense 'the State' never stops talking.

(Corrigan and Sayer, 1985: 3)

In other words, states have to assert their legitimacy, and one place where the state keeps on and on at us about this is in the city streets. Its insistent voice can be 'heard', or rather its statements can be seen, in the monuments that it erects and maintains (including the bureaucratic buildings discussed above). These monuments give meaning to certain, and carefully selected, groups, institutions, people, places and events. In the process they also *make* those groups, institutions, people and so on by marking them as important and defining them in certain ways. So, 'the state' states by making and marking space with monuments, but what is it saying?

## Monuments and the marking of centres

Political power, as we keep stressing in this chapter, must be performed. In order for it to be sustained this must be a credible performance (Scott, 1990). This is partly achieved by the various props that can be used in the performance. As the anthropologist Clifford Geertz has it, elites 'justify their existence and order their actions in terms of a collection of stories, ceremonies, insignia, formalities, and appurtenances that they have either inherited or, in more revolutionary situations, invented' (Geertz,1983b: 124). All these trappings of rule serve to mark where these elites are as the centre, symbolising it as the place where the power lies and symbolising the people there as the powerful. Even despotic monarchs, including those who claim divine authority, had to perform that authority. Geertz works through several examples of royal progresses (journeys made by monarchs around the territories that they claim) – Queen Elizabeth I in sixteenth-century

England, Hayam Wuruk in fourteenth-century Java and Mulay Hasan in nineteenth-century Morocco – to show how they all try to perform political power by presenting themselves as symbolically central. This is also the way in which many monuments work. The Victoria monument – erected between 1908 and 1911 as a memorial to the Queen – stands in front of Buckingham Palace, at the end of the Mall and at a point where several major roads meet (see Figure 6.5). Along with the Palace it is part of the marking of the symbolic centre of the nation through the monarchy (at least since the nineteenth century), showing in its grandeur and mass of symbolic figures the importance and moral virtues that the state associates with its symbolic head. The ways in which this symbolism is gendered is crucial. The figure on the side of monument facing Buckingham Palace (balancing the statue of Victoria on the other side) is a woman suckling an infant. Victoria is the 'mother' of the nation. It also marks this place as the centre of Empire. Each of the gates through which we must pass to approach the monument has its gateposts inscribed with the name of an imperial dominion: South Africa, West Africa,

**Figure 6.6** Statue of Gunnery on Admiralty Arch, London.

**Figure 6.7** Monument to Edith Cavell.

Australia, Canada, the Malay States and so on. Thus, the nation and the empire are seen to have the same centre. This is not Parliament, the war office or the colonial office, but the monarchy and, more specifically, Queen (and Empress) Victoria. This symbolic marking is a statement about **power** (p. 64), monarchy, nation and empire which presents a particular version of how they are related.

## Monuments as partial performances

In interpreting monuments, as with all cultural artefacts, we need to be aware of the partiality of the statements that they make (see also the discussion of buildings on p. 160). They are constructed by certain groups, people or institutions for certain purposes and, like all symbol- or meaning-laden objects, they present particular views of how things are. Thus, the Victoria monument tried to legitimate Britain's imperial power.

Indeed, if we can reveal the partiality of these statements we can diffuse some of the power that rests in making a partial world-view seem like the way that the world *really* is. There are plenty of examples of readings of monuments that seek to reveal their partiality by uncovering the ways in which their symbolism is shaped by class, race, gender and sexuality: for example, David Harvey's reading of the Sacré Coeur in Paris as an anti-revolutionary symbol of conservative Catholic Monarchism (Harvey, 1985a), or Marina Warner's understanding of New York's Statue of Liberty as the taming of a powerful female symbol of revolutionary change into a staid and matronly figure (Warner, 1985). Two brief examples will suffice here. They both concern the ways in which gender was used by the early twentieth-century British state to discuss warfare.

Admiralty Arch, built in 1910, stands at the other end of the Mall from the Victoria monument and is the entrance to it from Trafalgar Square. The concave (Mall) side has two allegorical statues on either end. One represents 'gunnery', the other 'navigation'. The statue shown in Figure 6.6 is 'gunnery'. As you can see, the practice of firing missiles from or at ships at sea is represented by a woman. More importantly, the destructive power of the British Navy is represented by a maternal figure: a mother who cradles a cannon in her arms as if it were a baby. By presenting gunnery as a mother, the statue makes a statement about warfare as a natural action, and of the navy as a protecting force rather than an aggressive institution built upon violence. It also makes statements about women's roles within the nation-state which reinforce the partial role given to them as carers for and mothers of the nation rather than the other political roles they might adopt. Women, who are supposedly unlucky aboard ship, are excellent material for partial statements about what those warships do.

A monument erected to Edith Cavell (1865–1915) stands near Trafalgar Square in London. It is one of the few statues to a woman in the city. Edith Cavell was a nurse who trained in England and moved to Belgium in 1906 to help establish a training school for nurses. When war broke out in 1914 her school became a Red Cross hospital treating both Allied and German prisoners. As the British and French forces were pushed back late that year, it became a place where Allied soldiers trying to escape sought refuge. Edith Cavell helped them. For this she was arrested, held in solitary confinement, tried by a German court martial on the basis of her written confession, and sentenced to death. She was shot at 2 a.m. on 12 October 1915. She rapidly became a martyr. She also became a symbol of the inhumanity of the enemy. They were presented as people who would not only execute a woman but a woman for whom, as the *Dictionary of National Biography* puts it, 'Charity and the desire to aid the distressed were the mainsprings of her life.' The monument (see Figure 6.7) presents her in a particular way, which again connects warfare, gender and the nation-state.

Edith Cavell is presented as a particular sort of woman, a figure that Klaus Theweleit (talking about the cultural politics of German masculine militarism in the early twentieth century) has called the 'white nurse'. This is a male image of the perfect woman: so perfect that no woman can ever live up to it. These are 'sisters' and 'disinfected sweethearts' who are, for these soldiers, 'the essential embodiment of their recoiling from all erotic, threatening sexuality' (Theweleit, 1987: 125–6) and whose purity is symbolised by the white uniform. They share with mothers 'a loving, caring side [that] is posed in opposition to a cold, distantly heroic side' (Theweleit, 1987: 104). This image was used by both the British and the Germans in the World War One (and before and since) to spur soldiers on and to justify the punishing (and killing) of women whose political and military actions made them 'impure'. It is within this gendered cultural politics of warfare that Edith Cavell has to be understood. For the Germans she was a spy, an evil woman whose position as a nurse made her crime all the worse. She had to be shot. For the British her death meant that she could be presented as a martyred 'white nurse' and her image used to demonise the German enemy for their inhumanity. Propaganda pictures showed a nurse in white uniform lying dead while a black-cloaked skeleton played the piano behind her. The legend read: 'The murder of Miss Cavell inspires German "*Kultur*".'

The monument, designed by Sir George Frampton, participates in this form of representation. Her pose captures the two sides that Theweleit talks about: she is presented as both caring and distantly heroic. The monument carries the words 'Humanity', 'Devotion', 'Sacrifice' and 'Fortitude' and the inscription 'Faithful unto Death' which repeat this dualistic message. Most importantly, the whiteness of the stone chosen for her statue works to make her into a 'white nurse'. It performs this gendered identity. The statue's whiteness is set off by the grey granite background much more dramatically than it would be by the sky. She is memorialised here as a 'white nurse'. It is, however, worth pointing out that, as with the example of Michael Foot's clothes above, what is important is not so much what she actually wore, but how she was represented. In fact, most photographs of her show her in the dark suit that she wore as director of the training school rather than in a nurse's uniform. This, then, is a monument not so much to a real woman as to an image of the 'white nurse'. It is also a monument that stresses how Edith Cavell is less important than the values and moralities that she might inspire in the nation. Instead of topping a pedestal, she is backed and overshadowed by a grey stone block bearing the words 'For King and Country' and the pronouncement 'Patriotism is not enough I must have no hatred or bitterness for anyone', a statement that claims the moral high ground for a moralised British patriotism by opposing it to the supposedly 'blind' patriotism of the Germans. Finally, the monument is capped by an allegorical woman and baby. The baby is protected by the maternal figure while she also gazes into the distance.

We want to read this monument as a public statement about the connection of the 'white nurse' and mother to the nation. The memorial to Edith Cavell operates as a connected set of symbols which work to justify patriotism and the wars fought in its name through the presentation of certain sorts of female figures (nurses and mothers, both real and allegorical) and the virtues that they, and therefore the nation, are said to stand for. It presents a very partial view of what warfare might mean and, like the statue of gunnery, this statement by the state severely circumscribes the political positions that women can adopt in relation to the nation, the state and warfare.

## Challenging monuments

We have argued that states are continually performing their power in attempts to claim authority and legitimacy. Yet this does not go unchallenged. Monuments are also the sites of **resistance** (p. 170) to the meanings that they try to fix, and this resistance may come from various quarters, conservative and radical. Indeed, it is the power of monuments as symbols that sets them up as sites where challenges to authority can strike at what the powerful hold most dear. Two examples will illustrate this argument before we move onto more general questions of the cultural politics of resistance.

In 1871 the column erected in the Place Vendôme as a monument to the European and imperial victories of Napoléon's Grand Army was pulled to the ground and its destroyers danced among the rubble (see Figure 6.8). The context was the Paris Commune and its revolt against hierarchy. In the aftermath of the disastrous French defeat in the Franco-Prussian war, many Parisians revolted and took over the city. In part this was a workers' revolt, many of them women; in part it was a massive 'rent strike'; in part it was a revolt of the city against the provinces; in part it was a battle over who had the right to define what sort of city Paris should be. Since 1850 Paris had been transformed by the state and capital into a place for the display of state

power and into a playground for financial speculators (Harvey, 1985b). It would now be transformed some more. The largely leaderless protesters declared Paris an autonomous commune. This political transformation only lasted 73 days and ended in much bloodshed, but as an opposing army massed at Versailles the communards set about transforming the social organisation of the city. Part of this was an attack on the **symbolism** (p. 214) of the prior regime, on its monumental statements. As one Commune decree stated:

The Commune of Paris:

Considering that the imperial column at the Place Vendôme is a monument to barbarism, a symbol of brute force and glory, an affirmation of militarism, a negation of international law, a permanent insult to the vanquished by the victors, a perpetual assault on one of the three great principles of the French Republic, Fraternity, it is thereby decreed:

Article One: The column at the Place Vendôme will be abolished.

(Quoted in Ross, 1988: 5)

This 'refusal of the dominant organisation of social space and the supposed neutrality of monuments' (Ross, 1988: 39) was understood by both the commu-

**Figure 6.8** *The Toppling of the Vendôme Column* (1871) by unknown artist. (Source: reproduced by permission of the Musée Carnavalet, Paris.)

**Figure 6.9** *The americanisation of the Toppling of the Statue of Saddam Hussein.* (Source: Reuters/CORBIS.)

nards and the anti-communards as a blow to the heart of the powerful. The poet Catulle Mendès, an observer and opponent of the Commune, wrote:

> the Vendôme column is France, yes, the France of yesteryear, the France that we no longer are, alas! It's really about Napoléon, all this, it's about our victories, superb fathers moving across the world, planting the tricoloured flag whose staff is made of a branch of the tree of liberty.
>
> (Quoted in Ross, 1988: 5–6)

It may have been a symbolic gesture of resistance but its target was evidently a good one. A more contemporary example of symbolic resistance can be seen in the toppling of the giant statue of Saddam Hussein in Firdos Square in Baghdad in April 2003, (see Figure 6.9). However, resistance here is circumscribed, as it is located within the context of the spread of US neo-imperialism since the events of 9/11 in 2001 (the attacks on the Twin Towers in New York and the Pentagon in Washington). This symbolic gesture of resistance is therefore as much a celebration of US imperialism and military might as it is a form of resistance symbolising the Iraqis' dissatisfaction with Saddam Hussein's regime (see Figure 6.10). The *Guardian* reported the event thus:

> Removing this visible sign of a quarter-century of dictatorship from Baghdad yesterday was a highly symbolic act, but so was the manner of its removal: a metaphor for the ongoing debate about who will

**Figure 6.10** *The Toppling of the Statue of Saddam Hussein.* (Source: Reuters/CORBIS.)

really be in charge of the new political order. When it came to toppling Saddam's statue, the Iraqis were soon elbowed out of the way. US armoured vehicles are like Swiss army knives, fitted with gadgets that are useful in all kinds of predicaments, so long as you can find the right one in a hurry ... A jib with a hook and chain on the end slowly extended up to Saddam's chest. A soldier climbed up the jib, hooked the chain around Saddam's neck, and produced a US flag, which he draped over the Iraqi leader's head. ... This was exactly the sort of triumphalism that had caused so much trouble when troops hoisted the stars and stripes over Umm Qasr in the early days of the war: completely off-message. It's supposed to be a war of liberation, not of conquest. The US flag duly came down and

... Finally, the crowd was ushered back, the armoured vehicle slowly reversed and the chain tightened. With more grace than he ever displayed in power, Saddam Hussein made his final bow.

(The *Guardian,* 10 April 2003)

Indeed, it is in exactly this way (if rather less dramatic) that contemporary protesters choose to protest by occupying symbolic spaces in the city. In Britain they may try to get through the police cordon and iron gates into Downing Street, where the Prime Minister occupies Number 10, or they may try to climb onto the roof of or even invade the Houses of Parliament (see below). In countries of the former Soviet bloc, protestors were quick to pull down statues of Marx and Lenin after the 'revolutions' of 1989. In either place people are challenging the partial versions that such spaces or monuments present, and they are seeking to use some of the symbolic power of these monuments – the way that they mark a centre – to promote their cause. It is to a fuller consideration of these cultures of resistance that we now turn.

# 6.3 Cultures of resistance

## Performing identities in unconventional politics

The idea of cultures of **resistance** (p. 170) brings us back to the concept of transgression. Julia Kristeva's view of the carnivalesque suggests that its transgressions actually equalise the **power** (p. 64) relations between the official law and that which challenges it:

Carnivalesque discourse breaks through the laws of a language censored by grammar and semantics and at the same time, is a social and political protest. There is no equivalence, but rather identity between challenging official linguistic codes and challenging official law.

(Quoted in Stallybrass and White, 1986: 201)

But this optimism is modified by Peter Stallybrass and Allon White: 'Only a challenge to the hierarchy of *sites* of discourse, which usually comes from groups and classes "situated" by the dominant in low or marginal positions, carries the promise of politically transformative power' (1986: 201). This section gives some examples of political protest, which are also performances that challenge political power in an attempt to transform it.

During periods of military dictatorship, women activists in Argentina and Chile used various types of symbolism as part of their protests in an attempt 'not just to get women to participate more in traditional politics but to find new ways of engaging in politics' (Waylen, 1992: 311). According to Georgina Waylen, this invokes a particular form of the carnivalesque: 'carrying photographs of their children and cut-out images of missing people, covering their hair with kerchiefs embroidered with their names and using silence' and involves the 'concept of the spectacle ... expressing the oppositional culture of the oppressed'. This oppositional culture invokes Kristeva's 'another law', so that two political positions then enter into dialogue with one another. Kristeva describes this 'dialogism' as not 'the freedom to say anything', but as a kind of 'dramatic banter' (Kristeva, 1986: 41). One example of *dramatic* banter was seen in protests against the new consumerism in Chile, from which many women were excluded:

On Saturday afternoons (the busiest time), women would abandon full trolleys, blocking the supermarket checkouts, with a note on each one saying: 'It's a pity we can't afford to buy because we don't have any money.' These protests were carefully organized to receive the maximum amount of coverage from the opposition media and were seen as a symbolic act sabotaging consumption, and challenging and subverting ... a dominant image of the Pinochet government ... its success in promoting wealth and economic prosperity.

(Waylen, 1992: 312)

## Defining concept 6.3

### Resistance and transgression

One of **Foucault**'s (p. 20) fundamental messages was that power always brings forth opposition and resistance to its effects. **Power** (p. 64) will seek to contain and control such resistances, often by incorporation through the working of **hegemony** (p. 73). Resistance is a kind of 'counter-power' always likely to surface in response to power's expression. Resistance takes many forms ranging from micropolitical gestures of contempt and alienation in the classroom to full-scale social and political revolutions.

Transgression involves exceeding the 'acceptable' boundaries set by established customs, hierarchies and rules. Cultural studies first appropriated the notion from Bakhtin's (1984) writings on carnival – predominantly pre-industrial events such as fairs, popular feasts and wakes, processions and the like. The 'world upside down' (WUD) (Stallybrass and White, 1986) created in carnival links the inversion of hierarchy (kings become paupers, criminals make laws, men dress as women) with a 'grotesque realism' towards the human body which is depicted as bulky, protuberant, its orifices open and its lower regions (belly, buttocks, genitals, feet) ruling its upper parts (head, reason). The significance of carnival, according to Bakhtin, is that it is a **ritual** (p. 214) occasion where transgressive desires can be temporarily voiced and vented, established hierarchies momentarily inverted and forbidden pleasures briefly indulged. For Bakhtin the notion of carnival refers not only to a ritual occasion but also to a 'mode of understanding ... a cultural analytic' which draws attention to the cultural

significance of symbolic inversions and transgressions (Stallybrass and White, 1986: 6, 183ff).

Cultural studies has used the pioneering ideas of Bakhtin and Foucault to explore the organised ways that subordinate and marginalised groups resist the imposition of dominant meanings (expressed via the dominant **ideology** – p. 35). Oppositional tendencies can make for cultural creativity. Youth subcultures are sometimes seen as structured environments for the expression of beliefs and attitudes that run counter to the adult world's. Often the opposition runs no deeper than the adoption of particular clothing styles and musical tastes. Thus the resolutions they represent to the 'contradictions' that young people encounter are only 'magical' or 'imaginary' resolutions – giving rise to the notion of 'resistance through rituals' (Hall and Jefferson, 1976). Yet these symbolic resistances give real opportunities for personal expression that close down again once young people make the transition to the demands of work, marriage and family.

Cultures are not just creative; they are also 'contested terrains', sites of struggle. The dominant ideology is not simply or inevitably reproduced. **Stuart Hall**'s (p. 55) (1980) important essay 'Encoding/decoding' suggested that the encodings of TV programme makers might not go on to be straightforwardly decoded by the television audience. The variable social situations of the audience need to be taken into account. The encoded text may carry the dominant ideology. This would be the 'preferred reading' of it, but viewing that text is a 'negotiation' between it and the viewer, and other

('against the grain') readings might emerge. Hall's theory was empirically tested by Morley's (1980) study of the audience for the *Nationwide* television news programme. Morley found that some groups made a dominant decoding of the programme (managers, apprentices). Others presented a negotiated decoding, inflecting the programme makers' message with elements drawn from their own social position (university students, trade union officials). Two groups (shop stewards, black further education students) offered an oppositional decoding that directly contested many of the programme's encoded claims and assumptions. This group simply refused to accept the dominant ideology as it worked through the programme. Hall and Morley show that it is necessary to adopt a more active and differentiated conception of the audience, who draw on their own cultural experience when viewing television, to understand fully the dynamics of reception.

In cultural studies the notions of transgression and resistance serve to underline the embodied and agentic characteristics of persons and the creative and contested dimensions of culture.

### Further reading

Bakhtin, M. (1984) *Rabelais and His World*, Bloomington, IN: Indiana University Press (orig. 1968).

Jenkins, C. (2003) *Transgression*, London: Routledge.

Morley, D. (1980) *The 'Nationwide' Audience*, London: BFI.

Stallybrass, P. and White, A. (1986) *The Politics and Poetics of Transgression*, London: Methuen.

An even starker example of the use of culture to make a political statement was the use of the Chilean national dance, the Cueca, by Chilean women whose relatives had disappeared. The Cueca is usually performed by a man and a woman. Wives of political prisoners who 'disappeared' during the Pinochet dictatorship (1973–89) danced the Cueca alone in public, to make the point about how the regime's repression had destroyed the families and the national culture it was claiming to preserve. The protest was publicised worldwide through *arpilleras*, stitched pictures of the dance and by the popular musician Sting in his song 'They danced alone'.

The Cueca was also appropriated as a form of protest by gay men in Chile, who danced together to protest against the regime's family policy which denied the legitimacy of gay relationships. The political group Outrage has organised similar forms of public protest in London. Kiss-ins and public marriage ceremonies between lesbians and gay men have been used by Outrage to attract maximum press attention to laws that discriminated against same-sex relationships. The carnivalesque has been used to great effect by lesbian and gay movements internationally. In San Francisco, USA, and in Sydney, Australia, gay and lesbian carnivals have appropriated the traditional forms of cross-dressing, satirical floats and parodic styles as a way of asserting the diversity of lifestyles that exist in those cities. These 'performances' are political and cultural both in their subversion of the expected norms of public behaviour and in their skilful use of the media to announce the presence of lesbian and gay men on the political scene.

Some of the limitations of using **identity** (p. 142) as a form of protest are exemplified in the case of *Las Madres* (the Mothers) of the Plaza de Mayo in Argentina. They were a group of women whose relatives had 'disappeared' during the 'dirty war' conducted by the military regime against those who opposed it. The women protested silently in the main square, the Plaza de Mayo, in Buenos Aires. The protest can be interpreted in two ways. Firstly, staying within the military regime's version of gender relations, they were protesting as mothers, because mothers are naturally concerned about the family. A second view, however, which takes into account notions of performativity,

suggest that the women's use of motherhood was *strategic*. They used the fact that the military government believed that women's place was in the home to protest in a way that the military found difficult to suppress: as mothers who cared about their families. This strategy was successful even after the end of the dictatorship, because it allowed them to 'act as a political conscience, resisting the tendencies to reconstruct periods of military rule as times of stability or economic growth' (Jaquette, 1994: 224).

If we return to the debate about **transgression** (p. 169) which introduced this section, we can understand the Mothers' challenge to the military regime as introducing the kind of dialogue described by Kristeva. However, as Stallybrass and White suggest, the two sides of the dialogue are not equal: the women's roles as mothers were imposed by the official culture, and this limited the part that they were able to play in public politics. Nonetheless, and despite the fact that the women did not entirely reject a traditional view of motherhood, they were able to use that conventional role and to politicise it: 'the politicization of motherhood breaks down the rigid boundary of public and private' (Jaquette, 1994: 224). While the protest cannot be said to have transformed political power, it created a space in which a dialogue about justice and events that the military government wanted to suppress could take place. Stallybrass and White suggest that it makes little sense to argue about the 'intrinsic' radicalism or conservatism of the carnivalesque: 'The most that can be said ... is that ... given the presence of sharpened political antagonism, it may often act as *catalyst* and *site of actual and symbolic struggle*' (Stallybrass and White, 1986: 14).

Cultures of **resistance** (p. 169) are, thus, most effective when they involve the symbolic performance of some kind of cultural conflict. An example that brought together (and into conflict) conventional and unconventional identities in politics was the protest organised in the House of Lords by a group of women on 2 February 1988 against Clause 28 of the Local Government Act 1988. Clause 28 was a wide-ranging and ill-defined clause introduced to prevent the 'promotion of homosexuality' by local councils. When the vote for the clause was announced, three women abseiled down into the chamber, supported by shouts from the public gallery. This transgression introduced 'another law' by subverting a passive version of femininity. In press coverage, the act was described as 'SAS-style' (*Daily Mail*, 3 February 1988), 'commando-style' (*Daily Telegraph*, 3 February 1988) and a 'Tarzan raid' (*Daily Mirror*, 3 February 1988). The women's unconventional behaviour was contrasted with the 'legitimate' conventions of the House of Lords. Peers were described as 'startled' (*Telegraph*) and as 'watching in disbelief' (*Mail*). The women temporarily created a carnivalesque atmosphere, upsetting the authority of the chamber. Unruly scenes followed: 'They descended into the chamber, and were met by three House of Lords ushers – all retired naval warrant officers' (*Guardian*), 'Parliament's most distinguished official, Black Rod, grabbed one of the women' (*Mirror*). The carnivalesque unleashes laughter, so that the conflicts appear to border on the farcical. One Tory MP, Dame Elaine Kellet-Bowman, commented: 'One chap almost lost his trousers in the melee' (*Mirror*). The actual conflict, which the *Telegraph* reported as quite violent, is represented in the press as a symbolic battle between the forces of order and disorder.

The debate or dialogue that emerges out of the protest revolved around the sense of exclusion from the formal political process felt by the women. This was articulated by one of the women, Stella Blair, as follows: 'I think they probably have never seen anything like it before. We planned it in the morning. We felt it was time we had our say. It is all right for them to have a say about us but we should have a right to answer these things' (*Guardian*). The protest was successful in so far as it reveals the conventions of the House of Lords to be as far removed from any version of what is 'normal' as the lifestyles of the women. However, the transgressive or carnivalesque situation that the protest brought about only achieved the stated aim of 'answering' the conventional legislative process in so far as the women's points of view as well as their actions were articulated. The protest, like the supermarket protests of Chilean feminists, was timed for maximum press coverage; but this meant that it was dependent on how the press represented it. While the *Guardian* printed the fullest justification of the women's position, less sympathetic papers gave more attention to the protestors' shouted 'abuse', representing them as rude and inarticulate. As

we shall see in the final section, there are always limits to transgression.

## The limits of transgression: *The Satanic Verses*

In 1981, as well as his prize-winning novel, *Midnight's Children*, Salman Rushdie published a short story in the *London Review of Books*, 'The Prophet's Hair'. The story describes an event which also occurs in the novel, the theft of a holy relic, a hair of the Prophet Mohammed, from the shrine at Hazratbal in Kashmir. The disappearance of the hair sets off a series of events which, seven years later, was to move from the world of fiction into real life: processions through the streets of 'endless, ululating crocodiles of lamentation … riots … political ramifications and … men whose entire careers hung upon this single lost hair'. The effect of the hair on the rich moneylender who finds it is equally familiar. He abandons his liberal Western values and imposes a new tyrannical regime on his family. All books in the house are burnt except the Koran. Prayers five times a day become mandatory and his daughter and wife are forced into purdah. In a manner that is characteristic of all Rushdie's prose, the tale combines elements of the contemporary short story with elements of the fairy tale or parable. It contains a thief who could have come from the *Arabian Nights*, yet whose sons are modern Islamic fundamentalists, denied a pilgrimage to Mecca because their father has smashed their legs at birth to give them an income as beggars. To use a term introduced earlier, it is 'carnivalesque'. Indeed, **Bakhtin** originally introduced his concept of the carnivalesque in relation to literature (Bakhtin, 1981). The narrative of 'The Prophet's Hair' deliberately transgresses cultural conventions: the magic and the modern, the secular and the sacred, the political and the traditional clash and reinterpret one another.

On 26 September 1988, Rushdie's carnivalesque novel *The Satanic Verses* was published. Its transgressive qualities had rapid consequences. On 5 October it was banned in India. On 14 January 1989 the book was burned during demonstrations in Bradford, England. In February seven people were killed in rioting in Pakistan and India; and on 14 February, the head of state of Iran, Ayatollah Khomeini, proclaimed a *fatwa* on Rushdie. Shortly afterwards, a price of £1.5 million was put on his life (Appignanesi and Maitland, 1989). 'The Prophet's hair' demonstrates that the issues that caused this storm of protest were not new to Rushdie's work. What, then, was the relationship between the transgressive cultural artefact, the novel, and the politics in which it became embroiled?

Rushdie's two most successful novels before *The Satanic Verses* were deliberately transgressive in their criticism of the post-independence governments of India and Pakistan. He has also been consistently critical of racism in England, where he has lived since he was 14. His use of the novel form to parody claims to political legitimacy is continued in *The Satanic Verses,* but the novel goes further in an attempt to represent international cultural conflict. Its subject matter is the effects of **globalisation** (p. 125), where different cultures are brought into contact with one another through migration and the increasingly powerful international culture industries (see p. 62). The central idea of the novel is the way in which things that are considered sacred in one culture are treated irreverently when they come into contact with another culture. In Rushdie's words, it is about 'migration, metamorphosis, divided selves, love, death, London and Bombay' (Appignanesi and Maitland, 1989: 44). It suggests that transgression, sacrilege and blasphemy are part and parcel of the **postmodern** (p. 295) world.

One example of this is the novel's use of language. The narrator makes a case for the reuse of insults by those who have been insulted. He cites the term 'black', which was reappropriated by the Civil Rights Movement in the USA as a proud self-definition (another example would be the use of the terms 'gay' or 'queer', which have been reappropriated by the lesbian and gay movements). In *The Satanic Verses*, the name 'Mahound', an insulting reference to the Prophet Mohammed, is given to one of the characters. The narrator's argument is that it is possible to reappropriate this name, as part of a reinterpretation of myth in the context of the modern world. The novel, then, should act as a free space where different and conflicting positions are in dialogue. In an interview, Rushdie wrote 'in writing *The Satanic Verses*, I wrote from the assump-

tion that I was, and am a free man' (*Independent on Sunday*, 4 February 1990).

As is now well known, the fate of the novel and its author did not exemplify freedom. The Ayatollah's *fatwa* forced Rushdie into hiding. *The Satanic Verses*, far from being a free space, quickly became a political football, representing for some the epitome of liberal values and the rights of the individual to free speech, and for others a gross insult to the Islamic faith. Despite the text's attempt to reflect on how cultures represent themselves, Rushdie was even accused of racism in his representation of African characters (Mazrui, 1989).

The case of *The Satanic Verses* demonstrates an aspect of cultural politics that has already been touched on in this chapter: the importance of not just representation and performance, but also of reception. While the novel is transgressive and is about transgression, that transgression is limited by how it has been received. The novel was originally banned in India as a result of protests by a Muslim MP, Syed Shahabuddin. The Congress Party, then in power, became worried about the Muslim vote at the next election. Despite the fact that Shahabuddin proclaimed that he had not read the book, the novel started to signify a crisis between state and religion (Spivak, 1990: 50). When the Ayatollah Khomeini pronounced the *fatwa* in the context of the Iranian revolution, the meaning of that crisis widened to include the relationship between the 'West' and the Islamic world. This does not mean that the transgressions that the text is interested in are irrelevant. Despite not having read it, Shahabuddin shows a good understanding of the subject matter: 'your book only serves to define what has gone wrong with the Western civilisation – it has lost all sense of distinction between the sacred and the profane' (Appignanesi and Maitland, 1989: 47). Rather, it is an example of how the relationship between a text and its audience, whether they had read it or simply heard about it within a religious, national or other political discourse, is, as Gayatri Spivak describes it, 'transactional' (Spivak, 1990: 50).

In this context, the intentions of the author become irrelevant to how the text is understood, but in so far as the author was seen to be responsible for the text, Rushdie became implicated in the crisis. The consequences were as ironic as any novel. Rushdie was now protected by the security forces of the British state, which he had long criticised. He continued his support for the reform and modernisation of Britain's political structures and traditions, but he was forced to speak only through the establishment media, the BBC and major newspapers. Where he once spoke in solidarity with the British Asian community, he was now seen by many (but by no means all) to speak against it.

In the tragi-comic finale of 'The Prophet's Hair', all but one member of the moneylender's family are dead, and she has gone mad, while the fairy-tale thief's religious sons have been miraculously cured of their disabilities. It appears to be the perfect ending of an Islamic morality tale, where the virtuous are rewarded and the wicked get their just deserts. It is comparable with a thriller filmed in Pakistan which ended with a fictional Rushdie being struck down by Allah. But the tale can also be read in another way. The violent ending seems extreme and unnecessary and it is notable that the sons, rather than welcoming the restoration of their limbs and the opportunity of making a pilgrimage to Mecca, complain instead that their earnings have been reduced by 75 per cent. The tale and the case of *The Satanic Verses* illustrate that although transgression creates another law, it rarely replaces the ruling law. Instead it creates dialogue, debate and an arena in which conflict can be represented. If this arena is described as the carnivalesque, then, as we have already seen, the transgressions that take place are not always revolutionary or subversive. The politics of carnival is often characterised by nostalgia, uncritical populism, and the demonisation of weaker social groups, such as women, ethnic and religious minorities, or those who 'don't belong'. There is complicity with and a failure to get rid of the official dominant culture (Stallybrass and White, 1986: 19). *The Satanic Verses* affair illustrates many of these problems, not least the difficulty of defining what is the official or ruling law and what can be counted as oppositional culture. These problems are, however, the very meat and drink of cultural politics.

## 6.4 Conclusion

An expanded notion of politics has led to an increasing interest in the role of culture in a world where conventional political boundaries are breaking down. This chapter has shown the importance of culture in the politics of identity, social organisation, architecture and literary texts as well as in formal politics. The politics of nations, states and governments are conducted on a terrain that is created and circumscribed through culture. Apparently small things like dress, language and the organisation of an office can be the site of meaning where important battles are fought out. One instance that we have emphasised as an example of the politics of identity is that of gender. In conventional politics, bureaucracy, struggles over issues of consumption (in the case of women's protests in supermarkets in Chile) and battles over the right of the silenced to be heard (in the case of *Las Madres* in Argentina), gender plays a vital role. The danger with such an approach is that it is used to argue that everything is politics, or, following the introduction, that everything is about power. We hope that the examples in this chapter show that cultural politics is not just about expanding the notion of politics to include culture, but about making that notion more sophisticated, and showing that formal politics also has an important cultural dimension. While this is sometimes a case of demonstrating that areas like the personal are indeed political, it is also about showing that dialogues, debates, disputes and outright conflict cannot be easily categorised in terms of two rational positions. The case of *The Satanic Verses* shows that one political 'message' can be transformed and made illegitimate when it is taken out of its cultural context. Representation and performance are very much of the moment. What in one time and place is subversive (even revolutionary) politics can, when used in a new context, become precisely the opposite. An efficient and productive form of social organisation in one sphere can become a means of mass destruction in another. Symbols that announce peace in one society can mean hatred and war in another. This is why notions of resistance and transgression, while essential to our understanding of the relationship between culture and power, are slippery at best. During the carnival you do not know who is wearing what mask.

## Recap

➤ Both formal and informal politics are conducted to some extent through culture.

➤ An important site of contestation in cultural politics is around questions of identity.

➤ The concept of performance or performativity is key to understanding cultural politics.

➤ Cultural politics describes a shifting, transient arena in which meanings are constantly in dispute.

## Further reading

For a general discussion of the field of cultural politics which deals with class, race and gender, see Glenn Jordan and Chris Weedon, *Cultural Politics: Class, Gender, Race and the Postmodern World* (1994). The specific themes of performance and identity politics in relation to race, gender and sexuality are taken further in bell hooks, *Yearning: Race, Gender and Cultural Politics* (1991) and Alan Sinfield, *Cultural Politics, Queer Reading* (2005). For the culture of bureaucracies a good starting point is Mike Savage and Anne Witz, *Gender and Bureaucracy* (1992) and the cultural politics of monuments are introduced in terms of gender, and with lots of good examples, in Marina Warner, *Monuments and Maidens: The Allegory of the Female Form* (1985). The debates over transgression and resistance are well covered by Peter Stallybrass and Allon White, *The Politics and Poetics of Transgression* (1986) and by Chris Jenks in *Transgression* (2003). For those interested in current debates in Britain over national identity, they should look at the The Runnymede Trust's website **www.runnymedetrust.org/**

# Chapter 7

# The postmodernisation of everyday life: consumption and information technologies

## 7.0 Introduction

Chapters 2 and 10 consider the meaning and application of ideas of postmodernism in our understanding of visual imagery and semiotics. The concept of 'postmodernism' has its foundations in European philosophy and American architecture, and refers to a rejecting of what is viewed as 'modernist' philosophy, aesthetic and artistic forms. Postmodernism is therefore a philosophical and theoretical position, which rejects what it views as 'modernist' thought. Here a distinction can be drawn between this idea of 'postmodernism' and the idea of 'postmodernity'.

Postmodernity more specifically can be understood as a social development and a shift into a new historical period (or epoch), which is different to that which was frequently referred to as 'modernity'. Characteristics of this new historical period are that we have witnessed a shift away from a production-based society towards one based primarily around patterns of consumption,

as well as the rise in importance of information, and media for its mass dissemination, such as the mass media and new information communication technologies (ICTs).

Consequently, this chapter focuses on the interconnected subjects of consumption and ICTs, and their role in the transformation of our everyday lives and culture. First, we begin by providing a definition of 'consumption' and its relationship to the process of production. The chapter then considers some key theories of consumption, such as the importance of Karl Marx, the work of Frankfurt School authors such as Theodor Adorno, and the theories of other authors such as Thorstein Veblen, Georg Simmel and Pierre Bourdieu. This then leads into a consideration of consumer society and the argument that consumption has become the primary defining characteristic of contemporary society and culture.

The next part of the chapter deals with issues surrounding new media forms and ICTs. We begin by considering the importance of 'information' within contemporary society and the importance and meaning of new media and ICTs. We then go on to consider the culture of ICTs, considering the social and cultural significance of these under the six headings (proposed by Flew, 2002) of digit[al]isation, convergence, interactivity, virtual reality, globalisation and networks. The chapter next considers the social and cultural consequences of an information society, before finally considering the location and impact of ICTs in everyday life and culture.

## Learning objectives

➤ To understand the meaning and social and cultural significance of consumption.
➤ To learn key theories of consumption and consumer society.
➤ To understand the social and cultural significance of information and new ICTs.
➤ To reflect on the impact of new ICTs on social and cultural patterns.

# 7.1 Consumption

## Defining consumption

The word 'consume' dates from the fourteenth century and was used to mean something that was 'used up' or 'destroyed'; such as to be consumed by fire. Similarly, the term 'consumption' came into usage in the sixteenth century to refer to any disease that causes 'wasting away' such as TB (tuberculosis) (Aldridge, 2003). Hence, 'consumption' is most often seen as an end point and the direct opposite of 'production', which is seen as the (often more important) process of 'creation', rather than destruction.

However, Lury (1996: 1) suggests that consumption needs to be understood as part of a wider 'material culture'. 'Material culture' is the term given to the study of 'person–thing' relationships. That is to say, the study of material culture is the study of objects and how these are used. Hence, Lury (following Warde 1990, 1992) suggests that consumption, rather than the outcome

(and antithesis) of production, needs to be understood as a constituent part of a continuing process and cycle of various forms of both production and consumption. As Lury writes:

> The identification of consumer culture as a specific form of material culture helps ensure that it is studied in relation to interlinking *cycles* of production and consumption or reappropriation. The consumption that is referenced via consumer culture can, through the lens of material culture, be seen as conversion, or, more precisely, 'the manner in which people convert things to ends of their own'. (Strathern, 1994: Lucy, 1996:3)

Hence, Lury (1996) suggests that consumer objects should be seen to have a social life of their own. That is to say, consumer goods will have changing and different meanings throughout their lifespan, depending on who is viewing or using them and in what context they are located. Consumer goods are therefore (to varying degrees) *polysemic* – open to multiple readings and meanings. People will use consumer goods in different ways and they will have different meanings for different people.

This in many respects is a development of the **Birmingham School** (p. 241) argument, such as that of Hebdige (1979), which suggests that subcultures engage in a process of 'bricolage', whereby they draw on existing consumer goods, but redefine and combine these to develop a distinct style to mark themselves out from the general public and as a form of social subversion and resistance (see Chapter 9). However, authors such as Lury and Warde extend this idea to suggest that it is not just subcultures, but most (if not all) consumers who engage in this act of (re)defining the meaning of consumer goods, and it also reconceives this as an everyday (often mundane) act, rather than necessarily an act of social resistance.

Important links can also be drawn between consumption and processes of communication (see Chapter 2). This can be illustrated in the way Barthes (1957) viewed clothing and fashion as a form of language, communicating meanings which are read (or consumed) by others. Hence, consumption can be understood in a similar way to processes communication, where cycles of meanings (both intended and not) are communicated and consumed through and via consumer goods, and interpreted, re-interpreted and invested with meanings by others.

## Theories of consumption

Stephen Miles (1998) provides a good overview of some of the key theories on consumption, and begins by suggesting that the origins of theories of consumption can be traced back to the work of **Karl Marx** (p. 66). Marx was concerned with how society was divided between those who had money and power (the bourgeoisie) and those who did not (the proletariat); where the basis of this distinction was fundamentally located within the nature and form of the economy, and in particular, social groups' relationship to the 'means of production'.

Hence, Marx's interest was primarily focused upon the process of production (rather than consumption) and its role in shaping the nature of society and culture. However, Marx does present a significant contribution to our understanding of consumption in his discussion of 'commodification' and 'commodity fetishism'. In particular, Marx (1963: 183) wrote of commodity fetishism:

> the mystery of the commodity form ... consists in the fact that in it the social character of men's labour appears to them as ... a social natural quality of the labour product itself, and that consequently the relation of the producers to the sum total of their labour is presented to them as a social relation, existing not between themselves, but between the products of the labour ... a definite social relation between men ... assumes, in their eyes, the fantastic form of a relation between things.

This is what Marx (1963: 183) calls 'fetishism which attaches itself to the products of labour as soon as they are produced as commodities, and which is therefore inseparable from the product of commodities'. That is to say, in a capitalist system the production of a commodity seems 'natural', and hence, the real social processes behind it are hidden, such as the labour and exploitation taken to make it. The consumer object itself exists as a desirable (fetishised) item apparently disconnected from the social relations behind and embedded within it.

Marx also distinguishes between the exchange and use value of commodities. The 'exchange value' relates to the economic value a commodity can command on the market, while the 'use value' refers to the value derived only from the practical usefulness of the commodity. For Marx, the exchange value will always dominate in a capitalist system, as the production, marketing and consumption of commodities will always exceed and take precedence over people's real needs.

Furthermore, Marx is also key in inspiring others' theorisations and considerations of consumption, such as the work of **The Frankfurt School** (p. 75), which included writers such as Theodor Adorno (p. 75) and Herbert Marcuse. However, the argument of the Frankfurt School is complicated, because though it offers a criticism of traditional Marxist theory, it is evident that the School itself is proposing a variation of Marxism. Where it differs most notably from Marxism is the attempt to move away from an economic deterministic model, which sees the economy as the sole factor shaping the nature of society. In particular, it develops a consideration and critique of contemporary culture and the culture industry.

On arriving in the USA, having left Germany after the Nazi rise to power in 1930s, Adorno wrote extensively on popular music and the culture industry he saw operating in the USA. He suggested that cultural goods 'are produced for the market and aimed at the market' (Adorno 1991: 34). That is to say, for Adorno, what dominates and dictates the production of cultural goods is the production of economic capital (profit). What primarily drives and shapes popular cultural industries is not artistic freedom and creativity, but rather profit margins and exploiting the market. The Frankfurt School suggests that cultural products therefore become formulaic and standardised, as the industry continues to churn out similar products that have proven sales success, but involve minimal innovation – such as the almost constant stream of 'manufactured' 'boy' and 'girl' pop groups produced by the contemporary pop music industry.

In this system of cultural production, differences in films or music are not so much a reflection of creativity or artistic expression, but rather a method of ensuring that no section of the market is under-exploited, which ensures that '[s]omething is provided for all so that none may escape' (Adorno and Horkheimer, 1972 [1999]: 123). However, this capitalism profiteering 'disguises itself as the object of enjoyment' (Adorno, 1991: 34). It is the entertainment and enjoyment that popular culture offers which Adorno suggests provides a release and escape for people, taking their minds off their exploitation and allowing capitalism to run smoothly.

The Frankfurt School's reading of popular culture has been extensively criticised (see Longhurst, 2007a), most notably as a form of cultural elitism, where high culture (such as 'serious' art and music) is seen to be valued over more 'popular' forms (such as pop music). However, it is vital to realise that Adorno and his colleagues were not cultural snobs but rather neo-Marxists. What Adorno is advocating is that art and culture can potentially be liberating, freeing and an expression of human creativity, but the opportunities for this are stripped away by the capitalist pursuit for profit.

The consideration of consumption is also developed significantly by the work of Thorstein Veblen and Georg Simmel (p. 271).

Veblen (1934 [1899]) discussed the new emergent American *nouveaux riches* (newly rich) of the late nineteenth century. These were a 'leisure class' of newly rich (middle-class) individuals, who copied and mimicked the consumption patterns of the social upper classes. However, the higher social groupings continually update their consumer patterns to stay one step ahead of these newly rich individuals, who likewise try their best to keep up with new tastes and fashions – to distinguish themselves from those (socially) below them. Hence, Veblen identifies how this pursuit (and ultimately display) of culture was mobilised by the American leisure classes to demonstrate social distinction and rank, based upon displays of 'taste'. Therefore, Veblen identifies a complex and elaborate social hierarchy based around consumer patterns and choices.

Georg Simmel provides an important discussion of the role of monetary-exchange and argues that this is at the heart of modernity (modern life). This is important as it recognises that consumption is not incidental, but that monetary-exchange plays an important role in

people's lives. Elsewhere, Simmel (1957 [1904]) also provides a consideration of fashion, where he argues that in an increasingly mass consumer orientated society, fashion provides a source of self-expression and exemplifies a dual tension between both affiliation and differentiation.

Other more contemporary key writers on consumption include Peter Saunders (1981) and Pierre Bourdieu (1984).

Saunders (1981) is particularly important in his assertions that social class has lost its significance in the face of increased consumption in contemporary society, and that it is access to consumer goods that is the chief social division and hierarchy in contemporary society.

The work of Pierre Bourdieu, and in particular *Distinction* (1984), is commonly viewed as one of the most significant and influential contributions to the theoretical consideration of consumption. In *Distinction* Bourdieu provides a complex and impressive sociological study of cultural consumption and the role of culture in contemporary society. The work is based on a large survey carried out in France in 1963 and 1967–68, with a total of 1217 respondents. In this survey, people were asked to specify their preferences in a range of things, such as their personal tastes in music, art, theatre, home decor, social pastimes, literature and so on. They also responded to questions regarding their knowledge about these arts. Drawing on this empirical material Bourdieu identifies a link between cultural practices and social origins and shows how cultural tastes and preferences correspond to a person's education level and social class. In other words, people learn how to consume culture and this education is differentiated by social class (Jenkins, 2002).

A key concept used in *Distinction*, is that of **cultural capital** (see p. 259) for further elaboration and use of this term), this is the cultural knowledge and understanding that people accumulate through their up-bringing (or socialisation) and their educational experience. The term 'cultural capital' is used because, like money (or economic capital) our cultural knowledge can be translated into resources such as wealth, power and status. Children are socialised into the culture that corresponds to their social class and this set of cultural experiences, attitudes, values and beliefs represents a form of cultural capital that equips people for their life in society. According to Bourdieu class-based cultural advantages are passed on from parents to children; cultural capital acts as the linchpin of distinction as cultural hierarchies correspond to social ones.

Bourdieu's work is important because he shows how cultural preference or 'taste' is an acquired cultural skill. Through his skilful use of the survey data he demonstrates that this cultural competence is used to legitimate differences between different social groups, for 'taste classifies, and it classifies the classifier' (Bourdieu, 1984:6). Hence, for Bourdieu people's cultural taste is predominantly a marker of social class, consumption is related to class cultures.

A significant contribution to our understanding of consumption is also provided by Michel de Certeau (1984), and others who have drawn on his work such as Henry Jenkins (1992) and John Fiske (1989a, 1989b, 1993). In particular, the work of de Certeau and his followers provides a useful counter-argument to the wholly negative attitude towards consumption expressed by Adorno and his Frankfurt School colleagues.

These authors do not deny that capitalism and popular culture are exploitative, but they argue that popular culture and consumption also provide people with the tools to fight back and resist. For de Certeau (1984) everyday life is a site of 'guerrilla warfare', where in common practices, such as in conversations, shopping and leisure, people engage in small acts of subversion and resistance. De Certeau suggests that this resistance may not lead to wide-scale upheaval of the existing social order, but it does constitute a way of 'ordinary people' getting by in their everyday lives and 'making do' with the objects that capitalism sells them.

Jenkins (1992) borrowing the idea of 'textual poaching' from de Certeau, suggests fans of cult-television shows such as *Doctor Who* and *Star Trek*, will take elements (poach) from these texts (such as characters and storylines) and use these to create new texts, such as stories, art or poetry, which is then consumed by themselves and other. This not only helps break down the production/consumption distinction, but

also demonstrates the creativity and (relative) power of some consumers.

Fiske (1989a: 23) suggests that 'popular culture ... is contradictory to the core', and that while artefacts of popular culture are manufactured and sold in a capitalist market economy for profit, these are then incorporated into the everyday lives of consumers, who construct their own meanings and uses of these. Fiske suggests therefore, that popular culture provides a fertile ground for resistance. For instance, Fiske (1989b) offers the example that though shopping malls may be designed as sites of consumption, this is often subverted by youths who frequent the malls, not to consume, but just to hang out and sometimes engage in deviant behaviour.

Similarities can be drawn between this argument (of authors such as de Certeau, Fiske and Jenkins) and the work of Birmingham School authors such as Dick Hebdige (1979) on subcultures, as on the face of it, both arguments appear to be advocating an understanding of how individuals or groups appropriate and use consumer goods in individual subversive ways. However, the key difference between these two arguments is that for the Birmingham School authors the resistance of youth subcultures was ultimately impotent and ineffective. The Birmingham School suggest youth rebellion constituted 'imagery solutions' to their social situations, but ultimately did little to change these for 'real'. This can be seen most notably in Paul Willis' *Learning to Labour* (1977). In this Willis suggests that working class boys will seek to rebel and fight back against the education system and school authorities, but ultimately this rebellion will see them fail to gain an adequate education and qualifications, and therefore will help prevent their social mobility. By contrast, the work of authors such as de Certeau, Fiske and Jenkins provide a much more positive reading of resistance, and suggest that individuals and groups can disrupt or even undermine social power relations, and significantly, this is a position towards which Willis moves in his later work. In particular, in 1990 Willis suggests that in everyday life there are numerous ways people challenge dominant power relations, and that the powerful are always being challenged and undermined by the powerless (Inglis and Hughson 2003).

However, all of these theories (and more) illustrate the importance of consumption in cultural studies, which reflects the increasing importance of consumption in contemporary society and culture. In particular, some have suggested that consumption has now become the dominant social and cultural force within contemporary society, and it is to this idea of a 'consumer society' that we now turn.

## The consumer society

Many theorists have argued that consumption has become the central concern of contemporary society, and that we are entering into a new epoch (historical period), based upon the construction of self-identity through consumer goods.

Lash and Urry (1987: 2) suggest that **Marx** (p. 66) and Engels set out a useful consideration of *organised capitalism* in the 'Manifesto of the Communist Party' towards the end of the nineteenth century. That is to say, capitalist society was very organised and structured, with a set (and fairly rigid) class hierarchy, where people had fewer options and life choices. However, Lash and Urry argue there has been a steady move towards what they call *disorganised capitalism*.

This move to disorganised capitalism, Lash and Urry (1987: 5–7) argue, has been caused and is characterised by certain key developments in the nature of capitalist societies. First, there has been a decline in primary industries (like extraction industries such as coal mining) and secondary (manufacturing) industries, and a move towards a greater emphasis on the tertiary (service) sector. Consequently, people are employed in a wider range of jobs, with different working patterns and different kinds of lives. Linked to this, there has been a decline in the 'traditional' working classes, and a rapid growth in a more affluent (white collar, service sector) working class. This has also resulted in a decline in the power of the working classes – primarily because people are now employed in different kinds of jobs, so they tend to feel less solidarity or commonality with other workers.

Lash and Urry (1987) suggest that the most significant change in disorganised capitalism has been the rapid growth of the 'service class' (and decline of the traditional working class) in most capitalist western societies from the 1960s onwards. As they state:

Old-style occupational communities have been undermined by the atomization of the worker; by higher wages and consumerism; by reduced work time; by individual mobility and changed residence patterns; and by the increased availability of highly differentiated consumer goods.

(Lash and Urry, 1987: 228).

Crucially, this 'new' service class is a class not of producers, but a class of consumers. Moreover, due to the decline of many traditional social indicators, such as location and social class (due to increased social and geographic mobility) individual identities become more or less fixed, and more based upon 'lifestyles' choices. These lifestyles are purchased ready-made through the huge amount of diverse consumer products and mass media sources available in a consumer society.

Bauman (1998: 22) suggests then that 'ours is a consumer society'. He suggests that all societies are consumer societies, to a greater or lesser extent, but there is something 'profound and fundamental' about the nature of contemporary consumer society that makes it distinct from all other societies (1998: 24).

Most significantly, Bauman argues that all prior societies have been primarily producer societies. Before an individual could fully participate in society they had to be a producer of goods or at least part of the production process, and social order and hierarchies were based upon an individual's position within the production process. However, in 'our' (consumer) society an individual 'needs to be a consumer first, before one can think of becoming anything in particular' (1998: 26). According to Bauman, it is consumption that defines who we are and who we can be. Bauman suggests that in this postmodern (or as he prefers to call it 'liquid modern') consumer society, the certainties and our key identifiers of modernity, such as employment, class and locality become less set and stable. We live in a constantly shifting and fluid society, where set identities become less useful to us. Therefore our identities likewise become fluid, flexible and based increasingly on consumer choices, which can be easily swapped or adapted to meet our changing needs and circumstances.

As with Saunders (1981), Bauman states that it is therefore our ability to consume, which shapes and influences our identity and social status. In particular, Bauman (1997) uses the terms the 'tourist' and the 'vagabond' as metaphors to describe the extent to which people can participate in this consumer society. Most people are like 'tourists'. For the 'tourist' consumer life is about never staying in any one place for too long, it is always temporary, and they are on a never-ending journey of consumption and endless reinvention. It is an endless journey, as consumer desires are never fulfilled – as consumer desires do not desire fulfilment and completion, but rather 'desire desires desire' (Bauman, 1998: 25). Hence, these are desires that can never be met or fulfilled.

At the other end of this continuum is what Bauman calls the 'vagabond'. Vagabonds are the people excluded from consumer culture. The vagabond also moves from place to place but not because of desire, but because they are not welcome anywhere. They are the excluded, those who cannot participate in consumer society, so they are not welcome anywhere. In a society where the ability to consume is the measure of social success, being poor is increasingly a 'crime' (1987: 43). For instance, shopping malls, which Goss (1993) sees as contemporary 'machines for shopping', not only exclude the poor in economic terms, but also physically – regularly ejecting people who do not (or cannot) shop or those who do not 'fit in' (such as the homeless).

However, it is important to recognise that not everyone agrees with Bauman's arguments, and in particular several authors have questioned the idea that our identities become totally fluid and based solely upon consumer goods. For instance, Warde (1994, 1996) suggests identities are not necessarily constructed simply by what we buy, but rather that other factors such as nationality, ethnicity, occupation and family continue to play important roles in shaping our identities. Furthermore, Warde suggests that many (if not most) consumer goods are selected with little impact on an individual's identity, and Campbell (1996) suggests, that rather than consumer items being selected to construct an identity, it is more likely that items are selected on the basis of whether they 'fit' with our *existing* identities and lifestyles.

A more useful way forward maybe is to see (certain) consumer goods as 'resources' drawn on by consumers in their construction of their identities and their social interactions. This is an argument forwarded by Abercrombie and Longhurst (1998) who suggest that we live in an increasingly performative society, where individuals will draw on consumer goods and mass media resources (such as television and music) in their social performances and interactions. Similarly, Matt Hills (2002) provides a consideration of the 'performative consumption' of cult-media fans. Unlike Bauman who suggests that individuals use consumer goods to define themselves, Hills suggests that the fans he studied use their fan interests as a means of expressing their own (existing) personalities. For instance, Hills uses the example of Henderson's (1997) discussion of a Japanese Elvis impersonator, Mori Yasumasa. Henderson suggests that this and other impersonators are not simply trying to *be*, or even seeking to accurately replicate, Elvis, but rather they are using 'Elvis as a platform for their own personality' (Henderson, 1997: 251-252, cited in Hills, 2002: 165). Hence, again, consumption can be seen as a 'resource' for identity production and social performances, rather than constituting 'ready-made' identities consumers buy 'off the shelf'.

However, it is undeniable that consumption is more important today in our everyday lives than ever before in history. In particular, consumer society has developed with, been supported by, and likewise helped support, a rise in and an increased reliance on mass media and ICTs – and it is to the social and cultural significance of these we now turn

# 7.2 The information society

Though the term 'technology' is one many tend only to associate with very contemporary culture, it is evident that there exists a very long historical relationship between technology and culture. The ability to craft and use tools, construct dwellings, the invention of the wheel and gunpowder, along with an almost endless list of historical and ancient technologies have significantly shaped human culture. In more modern times, **Karl Marx** (p. 66) argued that the 'mode of production', in other words the technologies of production (such as factories) within a society, were crucial in shaping the social relations and culture within that particular society. In particular, Marx was concerned with how the industrial revolution had brought into being the modern capitalist era. Likewise, Heidegger (1977) expands upon the work of Marx, but suggests that the techniques and knowledge associated with technologies also play a significant role in shaping the nature of society and culture.

However, as we have seen, there are those who suggest that we have now moved beyond the industrial modern society, which was considered by Marx, towards a more **postmodern** (p. 295) era. And, once again, it is suggested that technologies have played a key and responsible role in ushering in this new (post-modern) epoch – but in this case it is new media and new ICTs which are seen to have had (and continue to play) an influential role in shaping the contemporary nature of society and culture.

However, again it is important that we do not see the mass media and ICTs as necessarily very contemporary and existing solely within a postmodern era. For instance, the ability to commutate at a distance, and almost instantaneously, dates back to at least the early 1800s and invention of the telegram, if arguably not before this, such as in the form of signals and beacons, which have been used for many centuries. Likewise, the invention of the printing press in the fifteenth century constituted a significant development in mass communication, and in more modern times, the telephone (invented in the mid- to late-nineteenth century) has had an important impact on reducing the sense of time and distance, and seen significant cultural developments around its use.

However, from around the late 1950s and 1960s the idea began to emerge that we were shifting into a new historical period, characterised by new forms of society and culture based around new ICTs and the importance of the transfer and ownership of information and knowledge. In particular, the Austrian Economist Fritz Machlup in 1958 suggested that we were witnessing a shift towards a 'new economy', based around 'knowledge industries'. Similarly, a few years later Peter Drucker (1968) noted the shift in employment trends away from 'manual' labour towards 'knowledge work'. From this point on, theories of a new 'information society' began to grow and develop, most notably with

the rise of several new technologies in the 1990s, such as the advent of the Internet.

# New information communication technologies

It is evident that there has been a rapid development and growth in both new media forms and new ICTs (such as DVDs, digital and HD television, the Internet, mobile telephones, video gaming and computing) over the past two or three decades. However, asking 'What is new about new technologies?' proves problematic. Most technologies constitute a slow and gradual development over a very long history. For instance, Blu-Ray Discs and HD-DVD may constitute relatively new media technology forms, but in terms of their development they are a small step away from DVDs, which in turn developed from CDs, which replaced tape and vinyl, and before them phonograph cylinders and music boxes. Technology tends to move forward in small steps, rather than great leaps.

ICTs also enter different countries and regions at different times, making it difficult to define one piece of technology as necessarily 'new'. For instance, in many rapidly developing nations (such as those in East Asia) technologies such as the Internet are entering many people's homes at the same time as television – making both of these technologies 'new' for many people there. Also a lot of new technologies are 'recombinant', simply combining existing media forms into new media – such as the Internet, which consists mainly of written text, pictures and video, all of which predate the World Wide Web (Flew 2002). Even the idea of *hypertexts* (texts made up of multiple textual parts, which allow the user to move in different tangents from one text to another) is not particularly new, as in 1945 Vannevar Bush discussed the idea of 'computational machines' that would 'allow users to create ancillary "thought trails" through documents' (Flew 2002: 15).

Therefore, the question of 'What is "new" about new technologies?' Livingstone (1999: 60) suggests should be rephrased to ask 'What is "new" about these technologies *for society*?' (emphasis in original, cited in Flew 2002: 10). In other words, what impact or role do these technologies play in helping shape, or how are they located within, social and cultural patterns and practices?

# The culture of new information communication technologies

In considering the social and cultural significance of new technologies, Flew (2002) suggests six key (interrelated) aspects of new media and ICTs – those of digit[al]isation, convergence, interactivity, virtual reality, globalisation and networks.

However, as with the ideas of certain media and technologies being necessarily 'new', it is also questionable to what extent these six factors constitute 'new' or radically different departures from cultures and practices that pre-date the idea of an information age. A problem with many considerations of new media and ICTs is their emphasis on change and new possibilities (and/or new limitations) rather than on progression and continuity – and therefore this section also considers the limitations of these (so-called) 'new' developments.

First, it is suggested that there is increasingly a 'digtalsation' of society and culture. That is to say, there is occurring a major shift away from analogue technologies, towards the storage, delivery and reception of information in digital forms – which is the storage and delivery of information in binary (zero and ones) code. For example, Chapter 10 highlights the importance of digitalisation in photography (p. 301).

The simplest illustration of the difference between analogue and digital technology is the radio. With analogue radios, information is carried on radio waves, which either modulate (vary up and down) in strength (AM radio) or in frequency (FM radio). However, there is only a limited range of frequency or strength variations that can be used to carry information. Digital radio, though still using modulation, sends information in binary code, which has a much greater possible variation/combination and can therefore carry significantly more information – allowing for (in this case) better quality of sound and a wider choice of radio stations.

However, digitalisation constitutes only a relatively small advance in technology, which generally allows for better quality and more choice of media forms; but significantly, it does not radically change the nature of these media forms. It is also evident that we have had

'digital' forms of technology for a considerable amount of time. For instance, signal beacons could be considered as a form of digital media as they convey a message in binary code (as the beacon is either off or on). Therefore it is questionable whether digitalisation is necessarily 'new' or has had (or will have) any significant impact on cultural forms.

Second, there has also been a 'convergence' of technology, on several levels. There has been a convergence at the level of functionality – as increasingly new ICTs perform multiple functions and services. For instance, many mobile telephones can now be used to play music, take pictures, play video games, send emails and surf the World Wide Web, as well as making telephone calls. Likewise, there has been a convergence of media forms and types. For instance, music, television and film have been linked for some time, but increasingly media forms are becoming ever more intertwined and interdependent. For instance, it is possible to see a blurring and convergence in many aspects of film and video gaming. Over the previous decade or so we have seen numerous examples of both films based on games and games based on films. Early examples of films based on games themes and narratives include *Mario Bros.* (1993) and *Street Fighter* (1994), but in recent years these have become more numerate with examples such as the *Tomb Raider* films (2001, 2003) and most recently *Doom* (2005) and *DoA: Dead or Alive* (2006). Similarly, most major films now have digital game tie-ins, such as game versions of *Batman Begins* (film and game 2005) and *Pirates of the Caribbean: Dead Man's Chest* (film and game 2006).

However, there is also evidence of a blurring in the structure and content of films and games. As Yates and Littleton (2001: 109) wrote 'gaming technologies and the gaming industry are growing at a rapid pace and are converging with existing media production – most notably film and video'. Many video games are becoming more 'cinematic' (and not just those based on films) featuring filmatic styles and narratives, such as the *Max Payne* (2001, 2003) games that borrow heavily from film noir in their style and employ filmatic elements, such as 'bullet time' slow motion, as seen in films such as *The Matrix* (1999) (Howells, 2002). Likewise, it has been suggested that some contemporary films are becoming increasingly game-like in their style. For instance, certain films rather than being character or narrative driven are based upon the visual and spectacular, and are often episodic, mimicking digital game levels and styles, and frequently employ computer generated imagery (CGI) (Bryce and Rutter, 2002). Similarly in recent years we have seen numerous examples of other cross-overs and convergences between different media forms, formats and styles. A good example of this is the film *300* (2007), which not only looks visually like a video game, but also follows a similar narrative structure, with short narrative-linking scenes between key battles and even 'level bosses'.

There has also been a convergence and a monopolisation of companies controlling these technologies, with a few companies and individuals dominating world technology and media. For instance, Rupert Murdoch owner of Sky Television also owns the UK newspapers the *Sun*, the *News of the World*, and *The Times*, as well as the international broadcasting Fox network, 20th Century Fox film and Harper–Collins publishers, amongst numerous other media companies. Likewise, Ted Turner controls CNN, Warner Brothers film, Warner music, Time magazine, AOL and numerous other media companies. However, the convergence of both technology and media formats could be seen as capitalist businesses simply trying to expand the reach of their production and increase their products' saleability, which is not particularly new. Likewise, the idea of monopolisation predates even capitalism.

A third key feature of many new technologies is 'interactivity'. Many new media forms and ICTs claim to provide their users with greater levels of interactivity or user-control. For instance, the World Wide Web has an almost infinite number of links and pathways through it. The idea being that the user 'surfs' their way through this medium in the way that they want to – as the Microsoft Windows advertisement proclaims 'Where do you want to go today?' Likewise, video games give their players multiple choices and options, such as taking control of a football team, either as a player or a manager, or shooting your way through levels of zombies. Digital television also allows the viewer several choices such as key information to support the programme they are watching (by pressing their remote control 'red button'), or greater control,

Figure 7.1 The MySpace web site is a recent example of new interactive technology.

such as watching a football match from numerous different angles.

However, it is important that the levels of control over new technologies are not overstated. Palmer (2003: 160) suggests that new technologies are frequently introduced and sold to the market using the rhetoric of their increased 'user-control', such as the first Sony VCRs which promised the ability to 'master time, memory and circumstance'. However, a user's control is still severely restricted by not only the limitations of technology, but also the aims of the designers and manufacturers, and the ideologies behind these. For instance, most new media forms continue to include the same biases as old media forms, such as being constructed from the perspective of the 'male gaze'. For example video games that tend most frequently to involve male characters and protagonists, and when women do feature they are frequently both objectified and sexualised (Yates and Littleton, 2001). This provides gamers with limited choices over what characters they can play and what direction they wish to take the gaming narrative in.

It is evident, however, that new media and new ICTs do provide many new opportunities for (certain degrees of) user control and interaction. This is particularly notable in relation to the Internet. Though many of the most popular Internet sites continue to be those created and controlled by large capitalist and/or (old) media corporations such as the BBC, CNN and Microsoft, the Internet allows users to create their own content, have a large degree of choice over what they see and the ability to interact with people all around the world. In particular, social networking sites such as MySpace, Classmates and YouTube as well as individual's own 'blogs' (short for 'web-logs', which are online diaries), allow users to easily create their own profiles, pages and/or online contents, which others can view, and act as a means of interaction, social networking and meeting people (either online or off). This has led some to suggest that the Internet has now evolved into what is sometimes referred to as the 'Web 2.0'. This evolution is supported by changes and developments in technology and the structure of the Internet, but also refers to the more 'interactive' and 'user-controlled' nature of the web; incorporating many more social networking sites, blogs, wikis (websites that allows users to edit and add to contents, such as online encyclopaedias like Wikipedia) and similar. In particular, the importance, influence and growing frequency of 'user' created online content on the web, led *Time* magazine in December 2006 to vote 'you' (the everyday users of the web) their 'person of the year'; the award given to who they see as the most influential person in the world for that year. As *Time* magazine wrote:

> The 'Great Man' theory of history is usually attributed to the Scottish philosopher Thomas Carlyle, who wrote that 'the history of the world is but the biography of great men'. He believed that it is the few, the powerful and the famous who shape our collective destiny as a species. That theory took a serious beating this year.

> To be sure, there are individuals we could blame for the many painful and disturbing things that happened in 2006. The conflict in Iraq only got bloodier and more entrenched. A vicious skirmish erupted between Israel and Lebanon. A war dragged on in Sudan. A tin-pot dictator in North Korea got the Bomb, and the President of Iran wants to go nuclear too. Meanwhile nobody fixed global warming, and Sony didn't make enough PlayStation3s.

> But look at 2006 through a different lens and you'll see another story, one that isn't about conflict or

> great men. It's a story about community and collaboration on a scale never seen before. It's about the cosmic compendium of knowledge Wikipedia and the million-channel people's network YouTube and the online metropolis MySpace. It's about the many wresting power from the few and helping one another for nothing and how that will not only change the world, but also change the way the world changes.

> The tool that makes this possible is the World Wide Web. Not the Web that Tim Berners-Lee hacked together (15 years ago, according to Wikipedia) as a way for scientists to share research. It's not even the overhyped dotcom Web of the late 1990s. The new Web is a very different thing. It's a tool for bringing together the small contributions of millions of people and making them matter. Silicon Valley consultants call it Web 2.0, as if it were a new version of some old software. But it's really a revolution.

> And we are so ready for it. We're ready to balance our diet of predigested news with raw feeds from Baghdad and Boston and Beijing. You can learn more about how Americans live just by looking at the backgrounds of YouTube videos – those rumpled bedrooms and toy-strewn basement rec rooms – than you could from 1,000 hours of network television.

> And we didn't just watch, we also worked. Like crazy. We made Facebook profiles and Second Life avatars and reviewed books at Amazon and recorded podcasts. We blogged about our candidates losing and wrote songs about getting dumped. We camcordered bombing runs and built open-source software.

> America loves its solitary geniuses – its Einsteins, its Edisons, its Jobses – but those lonely dreamers may have to learn to play with others. Car companies are running open design contests. Reuters is carrying blog postings alongside its regular news feed. Microsoft is working overtime to fend off user-created Linux. We're looking at an explosion of productivity and innovation, and it's

just getting started, as millions of minds that would otherwise have drowned in obscurity get backhauled into the global intellectual economy.

Who are these people? Seriously, who actually sits down after a long day at work and says, I'm not going to watch *Lost* tonight. I'm going to turn on my computer and make a movie starring my pet iguana? I'm going to mash up 50 Cent's vocals with Queen's instrumentals? I'm going to blog about my state of mind or the state of the nation or the *steak-frites* at the new bistro down the street? Who has that time and that energy and that passion?

The answer is, you do. And for seizing the reins of the global media, for founding and framing the new digital democracy, for working for nothing and beating the pros at their own game, TIME's Person of the Year for 2006 is you.

*Time* Magazine, December 2006.

New ICTs also increase the opportunity for individuals to modify or change content and media forms created by others. For instance, many video gamers will engage in what is referred to as 'modding'. Modding (short for modifying) is where individuals either edit the existing content of a game and/or create new and additional content. Sometimes gaming codes (programmes) are left 'open' by games designers, which allow users easy access to these and hence encourages modding, while other games are 'hacked' into by modders. A 'hack' (in relation to ICTs) is the 'breaking-into' of a (usually commercial) program. Hacking, and hackers, have been discussed by several authors such as Taylor (1999) and Kirkpatrick (2004). In particular, adopting a critical theory perspective, Kirkpatrick suggests that multinational media and capitalist corporations utilise ICTs to mass produce and standardised products, and in the process deskill both the producers (such as computer programmers) and users of these. Kirkpatrick therefore suggests that hacking is part of a **hegemonic** (p. 73) struggle over the control and use of ICTs; where hackers seek not necessarily to achieve specific goal or ends, but rather to undermine power relations through disruptive and anarchic means. However, again, it is important that the fre-

quency and impact of both hacking and modding are not overstated, as these will be activities engaged in by only a very small minority of ICT users.

Fourth, a concept often associated with new ICTs is that of 'virtual reality' (VR). Virtual reality is the idea of occupying spaces or personas outside of the 'real world'. The idea of a virtual reality has existed since the 1960s; however, it is the rise of the Internet and video gaming, particularly in the 1990s, that led many to begin to explore these ideas further (Flew, 2002). For instance, Turkle (1995) argues that the Internet has allowed people to play with their identities and personas; providing a new opportunity to project their fantasies and ideas into this virtual reality. Similarities here can be drawn with the concepts of cyborgism (such as the work of **Donna Haraway** – p. 233). The 'cyborg' constitutes the intersection between machines and humans, such as the implanting of mechanical technologies into the human body, but more importantly raises the idea of blurring identities, where the boundaries between humans and machines becomes less fixed and more malleable. These are ideas that have been also been explored both in science fiction films such as *The Matrix* trilogy (1999, 2003 and 2003) and *eXistenZ* (1999) and to a certain extent also in writings on **cyberpunk** (p. 188) (such as the work of William Gibson). Cyberpunk stories, set in (dystopian) futures, tell of a blurring between the 'real' and the 'unreal' as 'cyborgs' (human-machine hybrids) stretch the boundaries of our known world and the possibilities within this.

Though contemporary technologies have not reached the levels of human/machine integration outlined in literature (such as cyberpunk) and cinematic fictional accounts, contemporary video gaming does provide gamers with the opportunity to play out 'alternative' lives and realities. For instance, one of the biggest phenomena in video gaming in recent years has been the rapid growth and popularity of Massively Multiplayer Online Role Playing Games (MMORPGs), such as *World of Warcraft*, *EverQuest*, and *Lineage*. These games allow the player to create characters ('avatars') that they control, and to play out adventures in an online world inhabited by other players from all over the ('real') world. Games often allow characters to develop careers, not just as warriors or wizards but also

## Defining concept 7.1

### Cyberpunk

In her essay, 'A cyborg manifesto' (Haraway, 1991), Donna Haraway outlines the blurring of new technologies into 'real' world identities within an increasingly postmodern world as developments that pave the way for two possible futures: a terrifying vision of social control, or new emancipatory possibilities. This opposition operates a dialectic between determinate and conditional futures. Where a determinate future promises fixed and controlled identities, an alternative, and perhaps equally frightening, prospect is the lack of any unified identity at all. In particular, postmodern 'cyborg fictions' explore the kinds of identities needed to live in the new world (McCracken, 1997). They attempt to think through the problem of the self in a context where the cultural boundaries are constantly shifting.

Some of the ideas are explored in a science fiction movement which emerged in the 1980s: cyberpunk. Cyberpunk has been described by Fredric Jameson as 'a new type of science fiction ... which is fully as much an expression of transnational corporate realities as it is of global paranoia itself' (Jameson, 1991: 3). The fictional world of the best-known proponent of cyberpunk, William Gibson, describes a geo-political system, characterised by weak nation-states and dominant transnationals. But, though inspired by the development of new technologies like virtual reality, personal computers and the Internet, Gibson's narratives focus as much on the social contradictions thrown up by technology as the machinery itself. On the one hand, cyberpunk is resolutely post-humanist. It delights in the transformation of what is meant by being human: Gibson's characters employ genetic engineering, drugs and advanced forms of surgery to transform themselves. On the other hand, the cyberworld is peopled with the descendants of postwar counter-cultures who represent a persistent romanticism.

Gibson's style is influenced by hard-boiled detective fiction. A consequence is that the most marked aspect of his world is a sense of lack or unfulfilled potential. His novels and short stories explore the forms of hybrid, 'cyber' consciousness that arise from the employment of new technologies as a means of domination. His most famous contribution to the genre is the idea of 'jacking in'. Using a jack into their central nervous system, his characters are able to plug themselves directly into the 'matrix' (an enhanced form of the Internet) and explore a virtual world of information, described as: 'A graphic representation of data abstracted from the banks of every computer in the human system. Unthinkable complexity. Lines of light ranged in the nonspace of the mind, clusters and constellations of data. Like city lights, receding' (Gibson, 1986: 67). The matrix acts as a metaphor for the kinds of cultural collisions and re-inventions of the self made possible by new technologies.

professions such as dancers, miners or doctors; some games also allow players to own vehicles, pets and property (such as houses and shops) and even to get married. These games have proved hugely popular with many players, with the *EverQuest* frequently referred to by gamers as 'EverCrack', due to its 'addictive' qualities. Nick Yee, who runs a research website (the Daedalous Project) on MMORPGs, suggests that nearly 19 per cent of over 2900 gamers who completed his online survey stated they play MMORPGs over 30 hours per week and over 40 per cent in excess of 20 hours per week. In January 2007 the number of players of *World of Warcraft* exceeded eight million – greater than the population of New York City, and even some countries such as Bulgaria and Israel.

Turkle and Haraway, in their consideration of online identities, adopt a similar perspective to that of **Baudrillard** (p. 299) suggesting that new media ICTs offer a blurring between the 'real' and 'unreal'. However, distinctions between what is 'virtual' and what is 'real' are problematic. For instance, Murray and Jenkins (n.d.: 2) suggest that many digital games contain a level of 'immersion', which involves 'being transported to another place, of losing our sense of reality and extending ourselves into a seemingly limitless, enclosing, other realm'. However, video gamers, as with the users of any other ICTs, are not 'transported to another world' but rather are physically and socially located. All technologies (both 'new' and 'old') are used and located in certain psychical locations, which can have important social consequences. For instance, it has been noted the propensity for video and computer games machines to be located within certain 'male' household spaces, such as male siblings' bedrooms, and hence are restricted to many women (Green, 2001). As Shields (1996: 3) argues 'it is essential to treat telecommunications and computer-mediated communications networks as *local* phenomena, as well as global networks ... [and] embedded within locally specific routines of daily schedules and the 'place-ballets' of individuals' (emphasis in original).

Another online 'gaming' phenomenon has been *SecondLife* (launched in 2000). In *SecondLife* you create an avatar (or 'av' for short) with the idea that you live out a second (online) life. There are no 'missions' or set objectives in this game, but rather you can buy property, clothing and accessories, get tattoos and piercings, furnish your home, modify the way your avatar looks, and interact with other 'residents' of *SecondLife*. You can even get a job, or employ other 'residents', and there is a fluctuating exchange rate (as with currencies in real life) between Linden dollars (the game's currency) and 'real' US dollars, which allows you to buy currency in the game, or exchange money you earn in the game for real cash. Though 2700 Linden dollars are only worth about 10 US dollars, this does give the opportunity for people to easily buy and sell *SecondLife* items with real (or 'first life' as it is called in *SecondLife*) money. In particular, *SecondLife* has generated a thriving 'real life' economy around it. *BusinessWeek* magazine devoted a recent cover story to Ailian Graef (whose online avatar is called 'Anshe Chung'), who earns hundreds of thousands of (actual) dollars as *SecondLife*'s biggest real-estate mogul and has become the game's first 'real life' millionaire through the game (Newitz, 2006).

Furthermore, films and television shows (including those by the BBC) have been premiered in *SecondLife*, people from around the world are holding work-based conferences, and both unsigned pop bands and major recording artists are performing and selling their music, all in this 'virtual' world. At Montana State University, architect lecturer Terry Beaubois taught a class to distance learning students using *SecondLife* (Newitz, 2006).

This therefore demonstrates not just the links between 'virtual' and 'real' life, but rather the importance of understanding the use of new (and old) ICTs as *part* of everyday life and culture. Media audience and users of ICTs bring their physical, psychological and social selves to what they watch and interact with, and factors such as personal interests, knowledge, gender, ethnicity and age, will all greatly affect what and how technology is used and experienced. Likewise, the role and use of ICTs will have numerous physical and 'real' consequences for the people that use them: for example, people arranging to meet friends via email, someone having nightmares from playing a violent video game, or having back- or eye-strain from using a computer for too long. All these may be fairly mundane, but they clearly illustrate that new ICTs need to be understood, not necessarily as 'virtual' (and therefore existing outside of social and cultural life) but rather as 'real' cultural and everyday items with 'real' consequences. (The everyday use and consumption of technology is consider further, later in this chapter.)

Fifth, another concept closely linked to the rise of new media technologies is that of globalisation. **Globalisation** (p. 125) is often seen to have helped create, and in turn has been greatly extended by, the rise of the mass media and ICTs – such as telegraph communications, the telephone and television, and now new media technologies such as the Internet and satellite television, which some have argued has led to the 'death of distance' (Cairncross, 1998) or what McLuhan (1964) referred to as the 'global village'.

This argument suggests that the mass media and ICTs have helped reduce a sense of distance and time, allowing people to communicate globally almost instantaneously and also that therefore people's identities have become less based upon location, space and time. For instance, Ian Taylor (1995) argued that due to the rise in media technologies, football supporters were now increasingly likely to form sporting allegiances at the 'level of the imagination'. That is to say, rather than connecting with sport on the basis of location or family tradition, 'traditionally the main influences' media technologies (such as television and the internet) allow individuals to form sporting affiliations on the basis of

## Defining concept 7.2

### Network society

Manuel Castells in his three-volume work *The Information Age: Economy, Society and Culture* (1996, 1997, 1998) argues that since the 1980s a new type of economy and society has developed. Though Castells was not the first person to suggest that ICTs have changed the nature of global life (for instance, a similar argument was made by Nora and Minc in the book *Computerization of Society* in 1980) Castells is the person most commonly associated with this argument.

Castells argues that while societies remain capitalist in nature, what has changed is a shift away from an 'industrial mode of development' towards an 'informational mode of development'. At the centre of this informational mode of development are networks, and Castells terms the development of this new social structure as a 'network society'. Though social networks have existed in 'other times and spaces' Castells (1996: 469) argues that 'the new information technology paradigm provides the material basis for its pervasive expansion throughout the entire social structure'.

Information becomes the basis of economic activity, it is both the resources and the product of new technologies (Flew 2002) and ICTs have an increasing influence and impact on our everyday lives. Consequently network society, Castells suggests, has led to a transformation in the nature of work, where structures, organisations and individuals need to be flexible. In an information-based society, changes happen quickly and frequently, therefore for businesses, organisations and individuals to survive they must also be able to adapt and change quickly. Hence, labour has become less standardised, and more flexible, and the working classes have become 'de-massified'. As labour becomes fragmented, diverse and flexible, social class identities and commonalities become less apparent, and social inequalities become increasingly based around inclusion or exclusion from global networks.

Castells also suggests that there has been a transformation of social power and communities in the network society. Nation-states become less relevant and important as economies, media and electronic communication become increasingly global. Castells emphasises the importance of new social movements, and communities become 'elective' communities – communities we join because we want to, rather than those attributed to us by society.

Castells (1997: 321) argues that politics becomes a 'race for audience ratings' and politics competes with the entertainment industries to get our attention. Power for Castells increasingly exists within information networks, but this power is organised around certain 'spaces of flows'. That is to say, certain places become hubs, nodes or links within this global network: certain cities, like London, Paris and New York, Castells suggests, are 'global cities', points or links within a global network. As too are places such as 'Silicon Valley' in California where much of the world's computer industry is largely based (these Castells refers to as 'technopoles'). People also form cultural links within this network society. Hence, power is less located within the hands of political leaders, but more based in the cultural, economic and information flows of a networked society.

The spread and rapid increase in access to information can have posi-tive consequences, but it can also have negative ones as well. Castells, like many others, warns about the rise of a surveillance society, where information is increasingly gathered and stored on ordinary individuals. However, unlike many other writers on surveillance society, Castells (1997: 299–303) argues that we should be less concerned with 'big brother' and more worried about 'little sister'. Castells suggests that the global networks society may have reduced the power and influence of nation-states, but what are rising in importance and power are privately owned corporations, which increasingly monitor, observe and record our behaviour.

However, by way of critique of the idea of a 'network society' it could be argued that there is nothing particularly new about Castells' arguments. For instance, numerous other authors (such as Elias) consider the importance of social networks as the basis of social structure. May (2002) also points to that fact that authors such as Castells greatly exaggerate the impact of new technologies on society, which still remains capitalist and has changed little in its fundamental nature in recent decades.

Castells has also been criticised for being over-deterministic. For instance, Calhoun (2000) argues that Castells sees network society as inevitable and unavoidable, that there are no alternatives, and that the power of information and globality will continue and increase. This ignores other possibilities of how society could or should develop, and fails to recognise that the future is not written for us: societies do not necessarily have to develop in the way Castells believes they will continue to.

more personal factors, such as ethnicity or personal choice, with clubs located anywhere in the world. For example someone who is English of Irish Catholic descent, following Glasgow Celtic football club because of its association with Irish Catholicism

However, as illustrated elsewhere in this book (p. 125) globalisation is not a particularly new phenomenon and has a very long history, dating back to the period of European colonialism, if not before this. For instance, Mennell (1990: 359) suggests that globalisation is a 'very long-term process' that has existed for as long as the human race. Likewise, the idea that a sense of identity and community may be formed at the 'level of the imagination' rather than on locality is also not a new phenomenon. For instance, Bauman (2001) suggests that since modern times, and the decline of small-scale relatively isolated rural communities, all communities have become imagined, and not necessarily based upon locality, space or time.

Finally, Flew (2002) identifies 'networks' as a key feature of new media and ICTs. Networks involve the ability to carry large quantities of information to a series of interconnected points. Networks involve technological links, such as the Internet, but they also involve links between people – such as people communicating via text messages or Internet chat rooms, or voting in television polls, by telephone, text or remote control voting. In particular, new media and ICTs, Castells suggests (1996, 1997, 1998), have allowed the development of a 'network society', where social connections and communications are less hierarchical or linear, but more web-like and multidirectional – as information flows quickly in all different directions.

However, again it is questionable whether there is anything significantly different or new about the idea of a network society (and, in particular, see p. 190 for a critique of these ideas).

## Consequences of an information society

Both the level of impact new technologies have had on society and culture, and the degree to which these changes can be seen as either positive or negative, are also highly debated issues. For instance, Ithiel de Sola Pool (1983) suggested that new ICTs would allow a

much greater freedom of publishing and authorship, which would transform social and political life, leading to new democratic freedoms – throwing off the shackles of censorship and the hierarchies and ideologies of existing media forms (such as television). This emancipatory nature of new ICTs and new media forms is echoed by numerous other authors such as George Gilder (1990), Jonathan Emord (1991) and Nicolas Negroponte (1995). Though probably the most often used theorisation of the possible 'positive' consequences of media technologies has been the application of Marshall McLuhan.

McLuhan (1964) suggested that media forms could be divided into 'hot', which are closed, unidirectional, consisting of a complete message (such as television), and 'cool' forms, which are open, multidirectional, interactive and require engagement (such as books). In particular, he suggested that cool media forms extended human capabilities and allowed us to escape previous limitations, such as those placed upon us by time and distance (May, 2002). Though many of McLuhan's examples of 'cool' media tend to be 'older' media forms (such as comic books) his writings have been applied by other authors (such as Mark Poster, 1990) to new ICTs, such as the Internet, which are seen as new 'cool' media forms that allow for radical and diverse (non-hierarchical) modes and lines of communication.

However, conversely there are numerous authors who point towards what they see as the negative (even dystopian) consequences of new ICTs and media, and the new information-based society they suggest these have led to. One of the most cited considerations of the possible negative consequences of a new information age is that of Neil Postman. Postman (1993) suggests that contemporary society can be seen as 'Technopoly'; that is to say, a society dominated and controlled through new technological forms. This society is a society dominated by a blind faith in science and technology, yet without any purpose or meaning. This is 'progress without limits', where we are producing increasingly vast quantities of information, but without any means of evaluating this. The prime example of this is the computer, which Postman sees as undermining education. The computer has merely increased our reliance upon it, which perpetuates the creation of more and more information, but under-mines and replaces group learning, cooperation and social reasonability. As Postman wrote: 'Technopoly is a state of culture. It is also a state of mind. It consists in the deification [becoming a god] of technology, which means that the culture seeks its authorization in technology, finds its satisfactions in technology, and takes its orders from technology' (1993: 71). Furthermore, the Hollywood film industry, in films such as *The Terminator* and *The Matrix*, as well as science fiction writers like Philip K. Dick, have for many decades provided a vision of dystopian futures where our reliance on machines and technology leads to the human race's subjugation to, or at least conflict, with technologies.

New ICTs, such as the Internet, have also been criti-cised as both a consequence and contributor to the individualisation of society. As Rob Shields (1996: 5) argues:

Technology is often viewed as a source of *separation*. In allowing interaction at a distance, first the telegraph, then the telephone and now the computer have negated the limitations of physical presence. Conversations are held with distant and absent others. Nonetheless, the local and the copresent remain privileged. There is an all too easy tendency to contrast the here and now with the distant (emphasis in original).

In particular, this is a criticism often levelled at video gaming, which has been seen by many (particularly within the mass media) as an anti-social and isolating activity, producing a generation of passive 'mouse potatoes' (Kline *et al.*, 2003).

New ICTs have also been extensively criticised for what is seen as their key role in the proliferation of consumer culture. For instance, Webster (1995: 95) argues that 'information developments are central to the spread of consumerism since they provide the means by which people are persuaded by corporate capitalism that it is both a desirable and an inevitable way of life' (cited in Miles 1998: 75). Furthermore, following on from **Baudrillard** (p. 301) (1998), Oh and Arditi suggest that the Internet helps both create and satisfy an endless stream of con-sumer desires:

Take the first point Baudrillard raises in *The Consumer Society* (1998), the profusion of goods. With the Internet, this profusion attains a new dimension: it denotes not just an abundance but limitless possibility. The Internet gives the impression that everything is attainable ... the magical effect of this hyperabundance takes on a new dimension in which any need can be invented and immediately satisfied ... [where] shoppers are taken even deeper by their very own desires into the labyrinth of consumerism (2000: 83).

However, a limitation of both these negative and positive reading of new ICTs is that both sides of the argument provide a *technological deterministic* argu-ment (Flew 2002). That is to say, both sides of this argument tend to see technology as driving and bringing about social and cultural change (either for better or for worse). This can be challenged on two levels. First, it could be argued that the degree to which new ICTs have changed the nature of society has been greatly over-exaggerated. In particular, May (2002) sug-gests that even though we have witnessed a rapid rise in information-based technologies and occupations, these have not had a radical or fundamental affect on the nature of society. Fundamentally, we still live in a capi-talist society based upon the ownership of property; it is simply that some of that this has become 'intellec-tual' (rather than physical) property. It is also the case that the mass media (even in 'new media' arenas, such as the Internet) continues to be dominated by tra-ditional media corporations and business, while laws governing these are still largely dictated by nation-states. Furthermore, as we have seen above in relation to the six elements of new media and new ICTs Flew (2002) identifies (those of digitalisation, convergence, interactivity, virtual reality, globalisation and net-works) none of these need necessarily be seen a 'new' phenomenon.

Second, what technological deterministic arguments also fail to see is that it is most commonly society and culture that determine technology changes and advances, and not the other way round. In particular, Flew (2002) offers two examples that appear to chal-lenge the technological deterministic argument – those of the gas powered refrigerator and the QWERTY keyboard. The gas powered refrigerator developed alongside its electric counterparts, but failed to secure a market simply because the manufacturers of these lacked the promotional power of the electric companies. The QWERTY keyboard, a key component of modern computing, developed as a means of slowing down typists on early typewriters, whose typing speed was seizing up the keys. Hence, the nature (and failure and success) of these technologies, as well as countless others, have been shaped by the cultures that surround them. It is crucial then that we consider technology, not as merely shaping culture, but as cultural objects themselves that are shaped and interact with other cultural and social processes – and in particular, it is to the location and use of technology in everyday life and culture that we now turn.

## Technology and everyday life

As highlighted above, one of the chief criticisms levelled at many new ICTs and media is that these are frequently seen as isolating and individualising for their users. For instance, criticism often aimed at video gaming is that it is an anti-social and isolating activity, and similar comments have been made in respect of the Internet, as they were about television and other media forms and technologies before them.

A key limitation with many considerations of the social implications of ICTs and new media is that these tend to focus either on 'macro' societal explanations or the 'effects' of these on an individualistic level. (The previous section has already considered some of the perceived consequences of new ICTs and media forms on the nature of contemporary society.) However, in turn there also exists a body of literature on media 'effects', which focuses on the perceived impact of media forms on individuals. For example, a large proportion of the literature on video games has focused upon the apparent effect high levels of in-game violence has on (individual) gamers.

It is evident that violence or violent themes and/or action are present in a large proportion of video games, with some of the most successful and popular games such as the *Grand Theft Auto* series or *God of War* involving high levels of violent content. Games such as

*America's Army* are now being used for military training and recruitment. As with past concerns over violent content in films such as Sam Raimi's *Evil Dead* and Stanley Kubrik's *A Clockwork Orange* in the 1970s and 80s, there are now growing concerns that violence in video games could lead to aggression within their players (Rutter and Bryce, 2006) (see also Chapter 2). In particular, authors such as Dill and Dill (1998) have suggested that violence in video games could potentially be more damaging than that seen in television and film, due to the 'interactive' nature of gaming. As Emes (1997) argues, while television viewers are (largely) passive, video games often require that players actively direct the (in-game) aggression, and hence the aggression/violence is more 'participatory'.

However, the relationship between violent games and increased levels of aggression (as with violence on television) is far from conclusive. In particular, such research has been heavily criticised for its often inconsistent methodologies and small and unrepresentative sample groups. It has also been challenged for overestimating the ability of games to influence the specific attitudes and behaviour of individuals and/or groups, and for seeing gamers as passive and vulnerable to representations of violence within games (Bryce and Rutter, 2003: 4).

Moreover, what 'media effects' studies frequently fail to do, is locate the gamer or audience member within a wider social and cultural context. However, it is important that we consider technology as cultural objects, which are used and located in people's cultural activities and everyday lives.

Green (2001) suggests that to date there is little empirical research on the role of new ICTs in everyday practices. However, key work on the everyday use of new technology has been undertaken by Roger Silverstone and colleagues (and most notably Leslie Haddon) who have written on the 'domestication' of technologies. This is defined as the 'social processes at work when new ICTs entered the home' (Haddon 2004: 4). In other words, the social relationship people have to ICTs, and the meaning they place upon these, when they enter into their homes. This work therefore provides a missing element to research that focuses on the impact of technology on society or individuals, by considering the social and cultural nature of technologies.

The work of Silverstone and his colleagues has considered not just computers and new ICTs, but also more mundane ('older') technologies such as the use of telephones. In particular, the use and placement of telephones within the home can tell us a lot about the social and everyday uses of technologies. For instance, people will have very different attitudes and uses of the telephone. For some (frequently younger) people the telephone might offer an escape from family life and a connection to friendship networks, while the placement of the telephone within a 'family' space of the home (such as a hallway or living room) can be used as a mechanism of control by certain individuals (particularly parents). Likewise individuals will have different attitudes and usage patterns towards other ICTs, such as video games machines, VCRs and computers, and often these will be shaped by gender and age, as well as other social and cultural factors. For instance, Gray (1992) suggests that many women chose not to learn how to work VCRs to avoid the programming of these becoming another household chore and responsibility of theirs. Also, Haddon (2004: 60) suggest that many women remain 'less comfortable' with new technologies, often seeing these as 'men's' and often not wanting to enter into a situation where they would be 'novices' to more knowledgeable male family members or friends.

Similarly, Lally (2002) considers the 'ownership' of computers within our homes. She suggests that as technologies are incorporated into the rhythms and locations of our everyday lives, we appropriate these technologies and attach our individual means and uses to these. However, in turn these objects also appropriate other objects, by 'fitting-in' and interacting with other objects within spaces, and also appropriate us (their users) and have an impact on our everyday lives and identities.

There exists a quite extensive literature on the use and reception of television. For instance, Chapter 2 highlights the work of **Stuart Hall** (p. 55) on television and media audiences. However, there also exists a literature on television viewing habits and patterns within households and everyday social patterns. For instance, Morley's (1980, 1986) work on television audiences is important as it not only considers the audience's reception and interactions with their tele-

vision, but also seeks to locate this particular piece of technology within an understanding of its place and use within the everyday workings of the household and family. In particular, one notable finding of this research was the control of the television by male members of the household, and in particular, their monopolisation and control of the television remote control – hence providing them with the final control/veto over what is (and is not) watched (Morley, 1986).

As well as the gendered and structured nature of technologies within households, studies of the everyday use of technology also alert us to the potentially 'sociable' nature of these and the social interactions that utilise and surround them. It is evident that new technologies can extend the possibilities of communication between individuals and social groups. In particular, there has been considerable discussion and debate about the possibility of online or 'virtual' communities. For instance, Rheingold (1994) sees the Internet as offering a renewed sense of community participation, activity and democracy. And in contrast to more technological deterministic accounts, Rheingold emphasises the importance of personal choice and voluntary participation in these communities (Flew, 2002).

This (online) sense of community may be about forming new affiliations or may represent, for some, a strengthening of 'older' social links. For instance, Mitra's (2000) consideration of (ethnically) Indian users of the Internet, suggests that this can provide for some people an important link between them and their ethnic community and identity. This is particularly apparent with geographically mobile individuals who may live outside of their home country and culture.

However, it is important to recognise that the Internet is in itself a cultural text, which is not just passively consumed by its users, but created and recreated by a significant proportion of them. Though many individuals may simply draw on the Internet as a source of information, many others will actively contribute to its structure and contents. For instance, many Internet users will frequently construct their own websites, newsgroups, mailing lists or discussion sites, or actively contribute to those that already exist.

Hence, Internet communities often involve *active* participation within this culture, and this is particularly the case of many fan online mailing lists and news-groups, which usually contain a limited number of contributors and users, further increasing the sense of coherence and community for these members. For example, Hills (2002: 180) suggests that Internet fan communities (and in particular he discusses the con-tributors to *alt.tv.X-Files*) need to be viewed as a 'community of imagination'. As he argues: 'this is a community which, rather than merely imagining itself as coexistent in empty clocked time, constitutes itself precisely through a common affective engagement, and thereby through a common respect for a specific poten-tial space' (Hills, 2002: 180).

However, it is important not to fall into the all too easy trap of trying to emphasise the positive aspects of the Internet as a means of stimulating and enabling community links, as it is evident that not all communi-ties are 'good'. Just as the Internet may give access to a sense of community and help reinforce cultural identi-ties for the ethically Indian (Mitra, 2000) or *X-Files* fans (Hills, 2002), it can also do the same for racists, mis-ogynists, criminals and various other deviant groups or individuals. It has been noted that the anonymity of the Internet allows for high levels of bullying and threats to be made against individuals and, in particular, Jessica Valenti (editor of Feministing.org) writing in the *Guardian* newspaper notes how this is frequently directed at women on the Internet:

> While no one can deny that men experience abuse online, the sheer vitriol directed at women has become impossible to ignore. Extreme instances of stalking, death threats and hate speech are now prevalent, as well as the everyday harassment women have traditionally faced in the outside world ... It's all very far from the utopian ideals that greeted the dawn of the web ... Most disturbing is how accepted this is. When women are harassed on the street, it is considered inappropriate. Online, though, sexual harassment is not only tolerated – it's often lauded. Blog threads or forums where women are attacked attract hundreds of comments, and their traffic rockets.
>
> (2007: 16)

In particular, Valenti discusses several editors and contributors to 'women friendly' or 'feminist' websites (including herself) who have received threats of rape, murder and violence against them, via the Internet. As well as bringing people together, the Internet (and other new technologies) also helps to isolate them as victims.

However, of the communities (both 'good' and 'bad') that do exist online, it is apparent that these can be carried on *off* line too. For instance, it is evident that in many cases online communities consist of the same members as those also present in 'offline' communities (Clerc, 2000). Friends, or people who have met in face-to-face situations, may use the Internet as a way of communicating and extending their social interaction. Likewise, people who make new friends and acquain-tances online may then later meet in a 'face-to-face' (rather than interface-to-interface) setting.

It is also apparent that not all new media and ICTs are used alone. For instance, though video gaming has often been criticised as an anti-social and isolating activity, this wholly negative attitude towards gaming has been questioned by many. For instance, Colwell and Payne (2000) in their study of over 200 London school children, found no evidence to suggest that those who regularly played video games had fewer friends, and research undertaken for the Interactive Software Federation of Europe (2005) suggests that 55 per cent of gamers play with others. Likewise, many other ICTs and new media technologies will be used by groups of individuals together (in-person), such as families sitting down to watch a DVD, or a group of friends surfing the Internet for information on their favourite bands, or similar.

However, even if an ICT is used by a lone indi-vidual, this does not necessarily mean this is a socially isolating activity. ICTs, such as televisions, computers, video game machines and in particular (and obvi-ously) telephones, can frequently be drawn upon as a source and resource for social interaction and conver-sation between family members and friends. These interactions can then also carry on away from the technologies themselves. For instance, several authors such as Haddon (2004) and Crawford and Rutter (2007) highlight how video game players will discuss games away from the gaming screen. As Haddon (2004: 74) writes:

interviews with British youth revealed that many of the boys were playing these [video games] in isolation. But they also talked about games at school. They swapped games. They compared notes as regard tactics. And they passed on information about ways to cheat or get round problems.

Similarly, information gained for other ICTs, such as from telephone conversations or from television pro-grammes, can then be used as a resource for social interactions, such as further conversation around gossip we have just learnt or a television programme we have just seen. It is therefore important that we try to move away from ideas of ICTs and media forms as necessarily 'good' or 'bad', towards an understanding and consideration of their everyday cultural uses and meanings.

## Defining concept 7.3

### Everyday Life

Gardiner (2000: 2) in his book *Critiques of Everyday Life* refers to 'everyday life' as 'the largely taken-for-granted world that remains clandestine, yet constitutes what Lefebvre (1991a) calls the 'common ground' or 'connective tissues' of all conceivable human thoughts and activities'. That is to say, the everyday routines, habits and mundane patterns, including our 'ordinary' consumption, which underlies and links together our lived experiences. In particular, the term 'everyday life' is most commonly used to describe our world and practices outside of work and education, and most frequently those that take place within the home (Haddon, 2004).

However, though the everyday consists of the relatively mundane, it is frequently 'the most overlooked and misunderstood aspect of social existence' (Gardiner, 2000: 1). The origins of sociology lay in a consideration of 'systems' and 'macro'-processes, such as the work of Comte, Durkheim and Marx. By the late nineteenth century a more 'micro' approach was developed through the work of social thinkers such as Max Weber and later George Herbert Mead, and from this, the interpretive turn of the post-war era, which saw the birth of a number of approaches including ethnomethod-ology, phenomenology and symbolic interactionism. Though these micro approaches provided an important foundation for the study of the everyday, Gardiner (2000: 5) suggests that these continue to adhere to 'the pretence of objectivity' and 'scholarly detachment' – viewing everyday life as relatively homogenous and attempting to impose order and structures on often highly complex social patterns.

However, in the past couple of decades there has been an increased interest and awareness in the everyday and patterns of mundane consumption (such as eating, cooking, using the telephone or watching television). In particular, Lefebvre was one of the first writers to argue that the everyday was important and should not be taken for granted. However, when published (in French) in the 1940s his work was largely ignored by English-speaking academia until quite recently. Lefebvre, applying a Neo-Marxist ideology in *Critiques of Everyday Life* (1991a), highlights everyday life as a site of repression and social control – recog-nising that dominant power relations operate not just in formal social institutions such as the workplace or educational system.

However, other authors have highlighted the everyday as a site of social resistance. In particular, authors such as Bakhtin (1984a) and de Certeau (1984) suggest that everyday practices are not fully engulfed by 'false consciousness', nor can the panoptic gaze peer into every aspect of our lives, but rather everyday life can provide the opportunity for liberation and resistance. Though de Certeau recognised social life as constraining and oppressive, where individuals are largely 'marginalised' and have little say or control over factors such as market forces, he suggested everyday life was extremely complex and mul-tifaceted; allowing room for manoeuvre and individuality. Where grandnarratives tend to strip away the mundane, seeking some hidden and deeper truth or meaning, for de Certeau this stripping away of the everyday hides what is truly important; as it is only at the level of the everyday that we can understand how social relations are experienced and lived out.

# 7.3 Conclusion

In this chapter we have highlighted and considered specifically two key aspects of contemporary (post-modern) society and culture – the importance of consumption and new technologies in shaping our lives and culture. The chapter begins by considering the definition and meaning of the term 'consumption'. In particular, drawing on the work of Lury and Warde we argue that consumption needs to be understood, not as the end-point of the process of production, but rather as part of an on-going cycle of processes of production and consumption, as consumer objects live out a life of their own and are constantly invested with meaning and (re)interpreted by others. In this chapter we also highlighted some key and important theorisations of consumption. We noted the important contribution Marx makes to the study of consumption, particularly in his influence upon other authors such as those working with the Frankfurt School. Also amongst those highlighted here is the work of Veblen and Bourdieu, who highlight the role of consumption as a mark of social distinction, and de Certeau, Fiske and Jenkins who consider the role of consumption as a resource for social resistance. Finally, this first main section concludes by considering the argument that we now live in a consumer society, where consumption becomes seen as the most important factor in shaping the nature of contemporary society and social and cultural relations within it.

In the second main section of this chapter we considered the idea of an 'Information Society' and that new ICTs have become ever more influential in shaping our society, culture and interpersonal relations. Here, drawing on categories offered by Flew (2002), we considered the social importance and influences of new ICTs, and in particular their role in digitalisation, convergence, interactivity, virtual reality, globalisation and networks in society and culture. Though it is evident that new ICTs are important social and cultural artefacts and influences, this section also provides some warning against overstating the importance or impact of new ICTs on society and cultures, and suggests that many of these (so-called) new processes, may not necessarily be that new or fundamentally different from older technologies, media forms, and what has gone before.

This is also an argument emphasised in the consideration of the *Consequences of an Information Society*, which follows. Here we considered the counter-arguments that new technologies have had either a positive or negative impact on society, but argue that both sides probably overstate their argument, and review the impact new technologies have on society. In particular, we argued that it is more important to consider the location and use of new ICTs within patterns of everyday life and culture, and consequently this chapter finished with a consideration of how new media and ICTs are located within people's social and culture networks and practices at a more mundane and everyday level.

## Recap

➤ Consumption is not the end-point of processes of production, but rather part of a complex cycle of production and consumption.

➤ Consumption now plays a very important role in shaping our social and cultural lives.

➤ Likewise, new ICTs have become ever more influential in shaping our society, culture and interpersonal relations.

➤ However, it is important that we do not see new technologies as radically different from older technologies or media forms, and necessarily deterministic in shaping our social lives and culture.

## Further reading

There are several good textbooks on consumption, but a pick of some of the best include Alan Aldridge *Consumption* (2003), Celia Lury *Consumer Culture* (1996), and Steven Miles *Consumerism – As a Way of Life* (1998). For books on new media and new technologies, Terry Flew *New Media* (2002) provides a good introduction. Considering in more detail the location of new technologies in everyday life, look to the work of Elaine Lally *At Home with Computer* (2002) and Leslie Haddon *Information and Communication Technologies in Everyday Life: A Concise Introduction and Research Guide* (2004). Finally, a good introductory book on video gaming is Jason Rutter and Jo Bryce's edited collection *Understanding Digital Games* (2006).

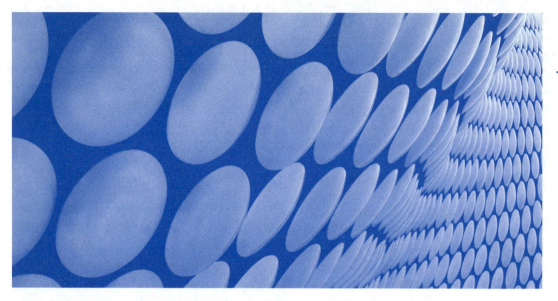

# Chapter 8

# Cultured bodies

## 8.0 Introduction

The idea that the human body is a cultural object might initially strike us as absurd. After all, our bodies are most decidedly a part of nature, subject to natural processes such as growth and decay, hunger and illness and so forth, all of which daily remind us of our connection to a realm outside culture and society. While the human body consists of an indisputable natural substratum, cultural studies takes seriously the notion its appearance, condition and activity are culturally shaped. We do not have to look far for illustration of this fundamental theme.

In the film *Big* (dir. Penny Marshall, 1988) Tom Hanks plays the part of a 13-year-old boy who is granted his wish to become – overnight – an adult. Much of the humour of the film turns around the amusing consequences of a 'grown man' behaving like an 'adolescent'. Although he has the body of an adult, he still has many childish interests and attitudes. When he brings a girlfriend back to his apartment, instead of

the expected seduction scene he coaxes her into joining him on his oversized trampoline. His tastes and desires, his ways of moving and talking, his concerns and gestures, his thoughts and feelings are all incongruous with the grown man's body he now inhabits. (Yet precisely because this grown-up has such a childish imagination, he readily finds well-paid work as an adviser to a toy manufacturing company.) The film clearly shows how our notions of personhood are tied to our bodies. Who and what we are taken to be is very much bound up with the looks and movements of our body. In possessing a body of a given age and gender we are culturally expected to be a certain kind of person, and it can be a source of considerable surprise, annoyance or amusement when these expectations are breached.

Just as the human body has become a compelling focus of popular concern in contemporary Western societies – as is witnessed by the mass media's preoccupations with sex, sport, stars and diet – so too have cultural studies come to take increasing interest in the body as a key site for the playing out of social and cultural difference. Among the key reasons for the upsurge of academic interest in the body are Foucault, feminism, and the growth of consumer culture. Foucault drew attention to the practices, discourses and technologies through which power is imprinted or 'inscribed' on the human body. A common argument in much feminist thought is that women's embodied experience is a significant but often overlooked starting point for analysis. Finally the growth of consumer culture, especially since the end of the Second World War, has accelerated the commodification of the human body, creating ever more finely graded status hierarchies based around the costuming and display of embodied **difference** (p. 216).

Six broad aspects of the cultural shaping of human bodies are charted in this chapter. It begins with a consideration of the *social construction* of human corporeality. It is followed by a review of a notion fundamental to a fully cultural understanding of the body, Mauss's concept of *body techniques*. Next, the chapter examines the cultural *regulation* of the human body, with particular reference to the works of Elias and Foucault to show how cultural values are 'inscribed' on the body. The chapter then reviews some issues of *representation*, considering how embodied states are depicted with particular reference to fashion, femininity and masculinity. The following section considers some aspects of the body as *a medium of expression and transgression* – a vehicle for the realisation of personal preferences, some of which may run against widely held cultural standards. The last section of the chapter examines developments in technoculture around the *figure of the cyborg* , which is widely believed to presage the end of the human body as we know it.

## Learning objectives

➤ To appreciate the sense in which the human body is socially constructed.

➤ To understand the cultural shaping of body techniques.

➤ To learn how forms of power are 'inscribed' on the human body and how the body is 'civilised' by cultural codes.

➤ To understand the place of the body in the construction of femininity and masculinity.

➤ To grasp the varying ways in which the body is a medium of cultural expression and a key site for transgressing cultural beliefs.

➤ To perceive the potential of new technologies to challenge conventional beliefs about the coherence of the human body.

# 8.1 The social construction of corporeality

The most general feature of the studies examined in this chapter is that they adopt a *constructionist* approach to the human body. They identify a range of social and cultural influences that shape the appearance and activity of our bodies. A constructionist approach, as we shall see, can take many forms but what they all have in common is an opposition to simplified **essentialist** (p. 121) explanations, i.e. explanations of bodily appearance and activity that assign sole or major significance to biological factors (such as the gender or ethnic categorisation of the person).

Discussions of the human body in cultural studies often also refer to the related terms 'mind' and 'self'. What are the differences and relations between these notions? A place to begin is the material human body as evolutionary biology might consider it. It is now widely accepted that *homo sapiens* emerged from a long process of evolution. The precise point when recognisably modern humans appeared is still a matter of dispute among specialists, although it does seem that they were present in Europe by 35,000 years ago. At least five specific features of the bodies of humans distinguish humans as a species:

1 *The capacity for binocular vision*. Certain aspects of how we interact with the world arise from humans' capacity for vision. Most social encounters begin with an assessment, however fleeting, of the appearance of the other. Consequently blind persons experience very obvious handicaps in their interaction with others. Most generally vision serves as the coordinator of the senses: an awareness of our body in its own right is crucially tied to vision, to our capacity to scan and thus monitor many areas of our own bodies.

2 *The audio-vocalic system*. The throat, mouth and ears are coordinated with the brain and the central nervous system to enable us to speak. The use of language is our fundamental symbolic capacity (see Chapter 2).

3 *Bipedalism*. We walk upright. Even in the West's automobile-dominated culture, walking remains the basic way of moving around in our world. Bipedalism also enhances the way that our vision works.

4 *Hands*. The fingers and opposing thumb of the human hand permit the manipulation of objects in a precise and careful way. Tool use involves complex bodily coordination focused around the skilled use of the hands. The physical environment is more malleable to the will of humans, as tool-using creatures. This capacity is thought to have contributed to the development of sociality by providing a basis for cooperation arising from the need to coordinate tool-using activities.

5 *Expressive capacity*. Humans have a capacity for greater gestural complexity than other primates. The faces of humans, for example, can express a wide range of emotions and some embodied gestures, notably laughter, appear to be unique to humans.

These five features frame the kinds of activity in which humans can engage. They are species-specific capacities that all healthy adult human can mobilise, irrespective of time or place. The distinctive slant of cultural studies is to approach the body as an acultur-

ated state that varies across cultures and through history. Thus, cultural studies emphasises that the body is not merely a material entity, biological datum or physiological fact but is, in a real and significant sense, a social construction.

*Mind* is the capacity for reasoned thought and reflection, carried out by the brain but not reducible to it. At least since Descartes' famous dictum 'I think therefore I am', a radical split between body and mind has been widely accepted. The mind is regarded as dwelling in a human body but remains somehow distinct from it. The mind–body split is often linked to a number of further contrasts:

| mind | body |
|------|------|
| private | public |
| inner | outer |
| culture | nature |
| reason | passion |

This schema gives prominence to mind in defining the person. The body is seen, at best, as the mind's vehicle and, at worst, as driven by desires and appetites that need the mind's restraining influence, guidance and command. However, this dualism is misleading, pushing mind and body too far apart. Body and mind are better thought of as interdependent, not as separate entities. People's mundane competence in making sense of talk and human expressions is an embodied and deeply cultural capacity.

If mind is the rational faculty, the capacity for thought and reflection, then *self* (or self-identity) refers to who and what the person is. According to the philosopher and social psychologist George Herbert Mead (1934), the distinctive quality of the self is that it can be an object to itself: as selves, we can reflect upon what we have done, contemplate alternative scenarios and choose between alternative lines of action. According to Mead:

> We can distinguish very definitely between the self and the body. The self has the characteristic that it can be an object to itself, and that characteristic distinguishes it from other objects and from the body. It is perfectly true that the eye can see the foot, but it does not see the body as a whole. We

cannot see our backs; we can feel certain portions of them, if we are agile, but we cannot get an experience of our whole body.

(Mead, 1934: 136)

Sociologists like Goffman (Smith, 2006) have proposed that any person has a 'multiplicity of selves', some relatively enduring, like those premised on occupational roles (e.g. a shop assistant self), while others may be fleeting, as when we tease a friend about her dress sense (e.g. a teasing self).

For constructionism, it is important to understand that the human body straddles the realms of nature and culture. The functioning of the material body must obey natural processes – we all have to sleep and eat, for example – but how sleeping, eating and any other bodily activity actually occurs is inescapably framed by social and cultural factors. Consider the pervasive significance of age and gender in the treatment of human bodies (already touched upon above in the filmic example of *Big*). Except for transsexuals, the assignment of 'male' or 'female' is a categorisation that is exhaustive of the population and lifelong in duration. The engendering of bodies – the attribution of culturally conventional correlates of sex to produce the qualities recognised as 'masculinity' and 'femininity' – begins almost immediately as what arrives in the world as a dimorphically classifiable organism is rapidly transformed into such eminently social constructions as a 'little boy' or 'little girl'. Age is, in many societies, no less significant. At every stage of the life course there are expected forms of behaviour and culturally defined and approved experiences. Shakespeare gave canonical form to this idea with his notion of the 'seven ages of man' (Jacques' speech in *As You Like It*, ii. vii. 135ff.). Gender, usually in tandem with age, provides two of the deepest determinants of the cultural shaping of the human body.

A parallel distinction is between the body as an object and as a subject. We *have* bodies and we also *are* bodies (cf. Berger and Luckmann, 1966). My body is an object that others can categorise and which I can own or possess (according to Simmel (1950: 322), the body is my 'first "property"'). Or my body can be seen as a subject, the physical embodiment of a self, the seat of subjectivity, the 'I'. Our bodies are vehicles of our exist-

ence as individuals. Our being in the world, our agency as humans is grounded in our embodied state and we know that our eventual fate is to age and die.

In cultural studies this contrast has led some theorists to argue for a distinction between 'the body' and 'embodiment' – between the objectified bodies we have and the embodied beings we are (Hayles, 1992; Turner, 1992). In this chapter some studies (e.g. Foucault, Elias) tend to emphasise external constraints on the body, while others (e.g. Theweleit, Wacquant) tend to stress the experiential dimensions of embodiment (although, as we shall see, there are often intricate relations between the two).

## 8.2 Techniques of the body

Very obviously, the body is the means or instrument for carrying out all the practical actions through which persons engage the world. Accordingly, the notion of body techniques (or 'techniques of the body') is a pivotal concept.

## Mauss's identification of body techniques

In a 1934 lecture the French anthropologist Marcel Mauss (1872–1950) devised the concept of 'body techniques' to describe 'the ways in which from society to society men [sic] know how to use their bodies' (Mauss, 1979: 97). There is no 'natural' form to bodily actions, no pan-human, precultural, universal or inherent shape to actions such as walking, swimming, spitting, digging, marching, even staring or giving birth (see Box 8.1). Rather, bodily actions are historically and culturally variable. They are acquired skills that arise because we belong to specific cultural groups. According to Mauss, the human body is a 'natural instrument', in other words, our 'first and most natural technical means'. When we engage the material world, for example when we drink, we employ 'a series of assembled actions, [which are] assembled for the individual not by himself alone but by all his education, by the whole society to which he belongs, in the place he occupies in it' (Mauss,

## Box 8.1

### Mauss's budget of body techniques

1 Techniques of birth and obstetrics
   (a) positions for giving birth
   (b) care of the mother and infant

2 Techniques of infancy
   (a) rearing and feeding the child
   (b) weaning
   (c) the weaned child

3 Techniques of adolescence
   (a) initiation rituals

4 Techniques of adult life
   (a) techniques of sleep
   (b) waking: techniques of rest

(c) techniques of activity, of movement:
   (i) walking
   (ii) running
   (iii) dancing
   (iv) jumping
   (v) climbing
   (vi) descent
   (vii) swimming
   (viii) pushing, pulling, lifting

(d) techniques of care of the body:
   (i) rubbing, washing, soaping
   (ii) care of the mouth
   (iii) hygiene in the needs of nature

(e) consumption techniques:
   (i) eating
   (ii) drinking

(f) sexual techniques

(Based on Mauss's 'biographical list of body techniques', 1979)

1979: 104, 105). Sometimes the individual's society may not provide the relevant technique. Mauss tells how he taught a little girl with bronchial problems in a remote part of France how to spit. At four *sous* per spit, she proved to be an adept learner!

Having established the cultural shaping of body techniques, Mauss then goes on to identify topics worth further investigation. Among these are gender and age differences, the effects of training, and the transmission and acquisition of these techniques. Body techniques vary quite conspicuously according to gender and age. For example, women deliver weak punches (at least they did in the France of Mauss's day!) in part because they usually clasp their thumbs inside their fingers; women throw differently from men (see Young, 1980, below); children can squat with ease while most adult Westerners cannot. Body techniques can also be more efficiently executed as a result of training or cultivation: dexterity as a trained accomplishment is a key notion here. Finally Mauss argues for close observation of socialisation practices in order to discover how these techniques are acquired. Holding a baby or applying make-up are body techniques acquired through processes of informal and explicit instruction. Even fighting, sometimes regarded as a 'natural' human activity, requires the learning of particular techniques

of the body (Downey, 2007). Mauss's groundbreaking work encourages the analysis of 'the details of *in situ* interaction and practice' (Crossley, 2007: 93).

## Young: 'Throwing like a girl'

The notion of body techniques is designed to bring some order to a large collection of Mauss's miscellaneous observations about human actions and has thus helped to legitimate an area of inquiry. However, Mauss himself never went beyond his own observations as an anthropologist, sportsman and soldier. What, more concretely, might a more systematic analysis of techniques of the body include? As an illustration of what is involved, we can consider Iris Marion Young's 1980 paper 'Throwing like a girl' (see also Crossley, 1995). Though not explicitly mentioned (the theoretical basis of Young's study is the phenomenology of Merleau-Ponty and the feminism of de Beauvoir), her analysis usefully illuminates Mauss's thinking about body techniques. Young is interested in those gender differences in bodily existence and movement described in the vernacular as throwing like a girl ('girl' is intendedly ironic), running like a girl, climbing like a girl, hitting like a girl and so forth. She focuses on ordinary purposive action and deliberately excludes expressly sexual uses of the body and also non-task-oriented activity, such as dance. Young picks out features of feminine existence that she sees as produced by the structures and conditions that women face in a particular society, not some mysterious quality assigned to all biological females everywhere. Consequently, there will be exceptions to the patterns that she identifies. This does not invalidate her analysis; rather, it is to be expected that some women will manage to escape or transcend the typical conditions that women face in any society.

Young identifies differences in Western industrial societies in how women 'hold' themselves (comportment), their manner of moving (motility) and their relation to space (spatiality) which are more limited and circumscribed than the corresponding behaviours of men. Beginning with how girls throw differently from boys, she writes:

> girls do not bring their whole bodies into the motion as much as the boys. They do not reach back, twist, move backward, step and lean forward. Rather the girls tend to remain relatively immobile except for their arms, and even the arm is not extended as far as it could be.
>
> (Young, 1980: 142)

Feminine comportment and movement is characteristically marked by a failure to use the body's full potential range of motion. Some examples:

> Women are generally not as open with their bodies as men in their gait and stride. Typically, the masculine stride is longer proportional to a man's body than is the feminine stride to a woman's. The man typically swings his arms in a more open and loose fashion than does a woman and typically has more up and down rhythm in his step. Though we now wear pants more than we used to, and consequently do not have to restrict our sitting postures because of dress, women still tend to sit with their legs relatively close together and their arms across their bodies. When simply standing or leaning, men tend to keep their feet further apart than do women, and we also tend more to keep our hands and arms touching or shielding our bodies. A final indicative difference is the way each carries books or parcels; girls and women most often carry

books embraced to their chests, while boys and men swing them along their sides.

> (Young, 1980: 142)

Many of the differences between men and women in the performance of tasks such as lifting and carrying heavy things are not due to simple strength variations. Women often lack ready technique and easeful engagement with such physical tasks which comes quite readily to many men. Women will often lift things using their arms and shoulders rather than also bringing the power of their legs to the task. Young portrays these limits on feminine motility as an 'inhibited intentionality' (1980: 145) and draws on the ideas of the phenomenologist Maurice Merleau-Ponty, who maintains that the primary locus of human beings in the world is not mind or consciousness but rather the body orienting itself to its surroundings. Through approaching, grasping and appropriating these surroundings the body realises its intentions. But currently dominant forms of feminine motility serve to restrict and inhibit the realisation of women's intentionality.

The origins of these characteristic features of feminine comportment and movement are not innate. They derive from women's situation in a sexist, patriarchal society. In such a society women are 'physically handicapped', according to Young: 'as lived bodies we are not open and unambiguous transcendences which move out to master a world that belongs to us, a world constituted by our own intentions and projections' (1980: 152). This embodied dimension of women's subordination is rooted in the way that women live and experience their bodies as subjects, vehicles of their own intentionality, but also as an object to be looked at as a mere body, appraised only in terms of its appearance. What Young's study brings to light is taken-for-granted aspects of the engendering of body techniques in modern societies. Does it matter that women cannot throw? Young says yes. A lack of confidence about bodily capacities may infuse other areas of women's lives, evident, for example, as doubts about intellectual or managerial capability. But if feminine comportment and movement are culturally shaped, then they are also open to cultural transformation: there is nothing ingrained in the 'nature' of women that decrees that they must always throw like girls.

## Goffman: body idiom and body gloss

In emphasising the cultural basis of embodied action, Mauss's notion of body techniques tends to look to the biographical and historical origins of these techniques. Indirectly Young extends Mauss's concept (she does not expressly refer to it) in showing some important gender differences in the lived experience of how men and women carry themselves and move. But how are body techniques enacted in the actual situations of everyday life? Here the sociology of Erving Goffman (1922–82) can help us to appreciate how body techniques feature in ordinary interaction (see Crossley, 1995).

Goffman noticed that a special set of cultural understandings obtains whenever people are in the physical presence of each other. He called this the 'interaction order'. In situations of co-presence (social encounters), such as when we are engaged in a conversation with a friend or are travelling on public transport, we have a pressing practical need to acquire information about others, about their status and identity, mood and orientation towards us and so forth. Some of this information is given verbally by what people say to us, but other information is 'given off' or exuded by non-verbal conduct: their facial expressions, the stance they adopt, the disposition of their limbs, the tone of their speech. The cultural meaning of these gestures is not so much a language (the popular phrase 'non-verbal language' is at best a metaphorical usage) as an idiom: a standardised mode of expression. Hence the concept 'body idiom', which describes 'dress, bearing, movements and position, sound level, physical gestures such as waving or saluting, facial gestures and broad emotional expressions' (Goffman, 1963a: 33). There is no time out from body idiom in any social encounter, for although 'an individual can stop talking, he cannot stop communicating through body idiom; he must say either the right thing or the wrong thing. He cannot say nothing' (Goffman, 1963a: 35). Some elements of body idiom can be employed by the person to provide a gloss or explanation or critical comment on an untoward feature of the immediate social situation. Waiting on a street to meet someone, the person may scan the surrounds or glance ostentatiously at a wristwatch in order to graphically display an innocent intent to passers-by.

A pedestrian on a crossing may shake a head or wag a finger at a motorist who has only just managed to stop. These acts of 'body gloss' (Goffman, 1971: 125) are gestures that broadcast to anyone who witnesses them our attitude towards some real or potentially threatening act. In another influential study Goffman (1963b) investigated the vicissitudes facing those who have some physical attribute or handicap (anything from a nervous tic to paraplegia to a visible ethnic identity) that acts as a 'stigma', that is, which disqualifies persons from full social acceptance in their encounters with others. Our gender is also marked in face-to-face conduct. Goffman (1979) analysed features of 'gender displays', the culturally conventional expressions of sex-class membership that are ordinarily available to us 'at a glance'. Gender displays are the taken-for-granted ways of conducting ourselves in the presence of others; 'sitting' in a feminine way or 'taking charge' in a manner that bespeaks of 'masculinity'. These gender displays are social constructions, i.e. not innate but rather the product of the acquisition of cultural knowledge and skills. In Goffman's perspective, then, the human body is the prime instrument of face-to-face interaction, an expressive entity capable of complex and nuanced communicative activity. Although the body was never a major analytic focus of Goffman's inquiries, his studies have proved a rich resource for constructionist analyses of embodiment.

As an illustration of this potential, consider how Goffman's focus on the specifics of interaction can serve to develop Mauss's notion of body techniques (Crossley, 1995). Take the example of walking. Mauss (1979: 100, 102) recognises that different groups acculturate a characteristic gait and posture in their members. He mentions the loose-jointed, hip-rolling *onioni* gait of Maori women; he notes how as a small boy he was schooled to walk with his hands closed not open; he speculates about how American cinema is influencing French women's style of walking in the early 1930s. Goffman takes this constructionist stance as his starting point for investigating how walking figures in face-to-face situations, such as making one's way down a busy city street (see Box 8.2) or shopping mall. He shows how walking involves a range of cultural understandings about types of persons who may have to be managed or avoided (beggars, market

## Box 8.2

### Marshall Berman: the modern city and the embodied experience of the pedestrian

In the middle of the nineteenth century Baron Haussmann's reconstruction of the centre of Paris created new wide boulevards which attracted a big increase in pedestrian and vehicular traffic. Berman draws on the observations of the poet Charles Baudelaire to describe the change in the pace of life that ensued:

> the life of the boulevards, more radiant and exciting than urban life had ever been, was also more risky and frightening for the multitudes of men and women who moved on foot.

This, then, was the setting for Baudelaire's primal modern scene: 'I was crossing the boulevard, in a great hurry, in the midst of a moving chaos, with death galloping at me from every side.' The archetypal modern man, as we see him here, is a pedestrian thrown into the maelstrom of modern city traffic, a man alone contending against an agglomeration of mass and energy that is heavy, fast and lethal. The burgeoning street and boulevard traffic knows no spatial or temporal bounds, spills over into every urban space, imposes its tempo on everybody's time, transforms the whole modern environment into a 'moving chaos'. The chaos here lies not in the movers themselves – the individual walkers or drivers, each of whom may be pursuing the most efficient route for himself – but in their interaction, in the totality of their movements in a common space. This makes the boulevard a perfect symbol of capitalism's inner contradictions: rationality in each individual capitalist unit, leading to anarchic irrationality in the social system that brings all these units together.

The man in the modern street, thrown into this maelstrom, is driven back to his own resources – often on resources he never knew he had – and forced to stretch them desperately in order to survive. In order to cross the moving chaos, he must attune and adapt himself to its moves, must learn to not merely keep up with it but to stay at least one step ahead. He must become adept at *soubresauts* [jolting movements] and *mouvements brusques* [sudden moves], at sudden, abrupt, jagged twists and shifts – and not only with his legs and his body, but with his mind and his sensibility as well.

Baudelaire shows how modern city life forces these new moves on everyone; but he shows, too, how in doing this it also paradoxically enforces new modes of freedom. A man who knows how to move in and around and through the traffic can go anywhere, down any of the endless urban corridors where traffic itself is free to go. This mobility opens up a great wealth of new experiences and activities for the urban masses.

(Berman, 1983: 159–60)

researchers, pamphleteers), those to whom special care must be exercised (the frail, persons with white canes or guide dogs, toddlers), those who can be turned to for reliable directions (traffic wardens, police), those who want us to stop and listen and watch (buskers, mime artists), those who look likely to threaten our persons and property. In walking down a street we must constantly monitor our own bodies and those of others in order to avoid collisions – less complicated when we are a 'single' (i.e. a solitary walker) than if we are a 'with' (accompanied by others with whom we must coordinate our progress). This involves scanning upcoming pedestrians but doing so in an unobtrusive and non-threatening way. Goffman calls this the norm of 'civil inattention' (see p. 291). The orderliness of many public places depends upon people following this rule (Smith, 2006). The actions Goffman describes are body techniques at the micro level of everyday social interaction.

Goffman's conceptual apparatus thus provides the basis for an analysis of the *exercise* or *performance* of body techniques. In addition, it shows how a rigid mind-body dualism cannot be sustained. Mind is implicated in interactional conduct that is unavoidably mediated through the human body. Ordinary practices such as those required to get down the street without mishap involve the coordination of practical intelligence and embodied skills. In examining the exercise of body techniques we can come to see that mind and self are not ghosts in the machine of the body, resident in the upper portion of the skull, which somehow lie 'behind' action. Rather, mind and self are better understood as encoded in the ordinary enactment of body techniques.

## 8.3 Culture as control: the regulation and restraint of human bodies

One of the simplest ways to conceive of culture's impact on the body is to consider the early socialisation of infants and small children. In the West a primary concern of adult carers is instilling such basic skills as the bodily management of eating, elimination and the expression of the emotions. But beyond childhood socialisation there continues to be a wide range of regulations and restraints on the bodies of persons, some set in law, others in custom and convention. Two of the most important analysts of culture's supervisory impact on the human body are **Michel Foucault** (1926–84) (p. 20) and Norbert Elias (1897–1990). Foucault shows how bodies are disciplined by power operating through discourses that are institutionalised (in modern society by bureaucratic organisations – hospitals, prisons, asylums – but also by more diffusely located forms, e.g. discourses about sexuality). Elias identifies a 'civilising process', a long historical transformation that is marked by significant changes in manners, and specifically how people regard their own and others' embodied actions. This section will review their contributions to the understanding of the body and illustrate their usefulness with reference to the topic of diet.

## Power, discourse and the body: Foucault

Michel Foucault's singular intellectual project explores the shifting and contested relations between power, knowledge and the human body. Most generally Foucault attempts to produce historically grounded analyses ('genealogies') of the discourses that organise social arrangements and practices. By 'discourse' Foucault intended not simply a specialist language that described the world. He stressed that **discourse** (p. 21)

was itself part of the broader phenomenon of **power** (p. 64) and thus deeply implicated in how social arrangements were formed as such. His most influential studies were of the discourses of punishment, madness, medicine and sexuality (Foucault 1973, 1975, 1977, 1984b).

Foucault (1977) draws a contrast between the *sovereign power* that rulers exercised over their subjects in medieval times and its gradual replacement in the modern period by *disciplinary power*. In a study of the development of the modern prison system, Foucault shows how those who contravened the monarch's law and wishes were often publicly punished by methods that directly assaulted the body of the wrongdoer (whipping, branding, the pillory, torture, dismemberment and execution). Foucault's *Discipline and Punish* opens with a gruesome account of the 1757 execution in Paris of Damiens the regicide, which graphically details the difficulties the executioner faces in exercising his craft. Before his life is extinguished, Damiens is burnt, dismembered, drawn and quartered. The spectacle of public punishment, Foucault argues, awesomely dramatises and reinforces the sovereign's authority and right to rule.

Since the eighteenth century this 'gloomy festival of punishment' (Foucault, 1977: 8) has given way to forms of imprisonment as the major method of punishing offenders. Foucault follows the description of the execution of Damiens with an extract from the rules governing inmate conduct in a Paris prison for young offenders. The rules tell how prisoners are expected to rise at a specified hour early in the morning and work nine hours each day. The rules specify that prisoners must rise, dress and make their beds between the first and second drum-roll every morning. They state how long religious instruction will take, when and where they may wash and receive their first ration of bread, how they will assemble before being allowed to eat dinner and so forth. What these illustrations portray are two very different penal styles. The body of the wrongdoer remains central, only that body is now incarcerated rather than mutilated. The focus of reform is now the 'soul' of the prisoner's body made 'docile' by the prison regimen. The objective of punishment changes from displaying the dreadful consequences of contravening the sovereign's will to instilling discipline in the offender. The aim is to ensure that bodies and

## Box 8.3

### Foucault: the body of the condemned

The disappearance of public execution marks therefore the decline of the spectacle; but it also marks a slackening of the hold on the body. In 1787, in an address to the Society for Promoting Political Enquiries, Benjamin Rush remarked: 'I can only hope that the time is not far away when gallows, pillory, scaffold, flogging and wheel will, in the history of punishment, be regarded as the marks of the barbarity of centuries and of countries and as proofs of the feeble influence of reason and religion over the human mind'. Indeed, sixty years later, Van Meenen, opening the second penitentiary congress, in Brussels, recalled the time of his childhood as of a past age: 'I have seen the ground strewn with wheels, gibbets, gallows, pillories; I have seen hideously stretched skeletons on wheels' (*Annales de la Charité*, 329, 30). Branding had been abolished in England (1834) and in France (1832); in 1820, England no longer dared to apply the full punishment reserved for traitors (Thistlewood was not quartered). Only flogging still remained in a number of penal systems (Russia, England, Prussia). But, generally speaking, punitive practices had become more reticent. One no longer touched the body, or at least as little as possible, and then only to reach something other than the body itself. It might be objected that imprisonment, confinement, forced labour, penal servitude, prohibition from entering certain areas, deportation – which have

occupied so important a place in modern penal systems – are 'physical' penalties: unlike fines, for example, they directly affect the body. But the punishment-body relation is not the same as it was in the torture during public executions. The body now serves as an instrument or intermediary: if one intervenes upon it to prison it, or to make it work, it is in order to deprive the individuals of a liberty that is regarded both as a right and as property. The body, according to this penalty, is caught up in a system of constraints and privations, obligations and prohibitions. Physical pain, the pain of the body itself, is no longer the constituent element of the penalty. From being an art of unbearable sensations punishment has become an economy of suspended rights. If it is still necessary for the law to reach and manipulate the body of the convict, it will beat a distance, in the proper way, according to strict rules, and with a much 'higher' aim. As a result of this new restraint, a whole army of technicians took over from the executioner, the immediate anatomist of pain: warder, doctors, chaplains, psychiatrists, psychologists, educationalists; by their very presence near the prisoner, they sing the praises that the law needs: they reassure it that the body and pain are not the ultimate objects of its punitive action. Today a doctor must watch over those condemned to death, right up to the last moment – thus juxtaposing

himself as the agent to welfare, as the alleviator of pain, with the official whose task it is to end life. This is worth thinking about. When the moment of execution approaches, the patients are injected with tranquillizers. A utopia of judicial reticence: take away life, but prevent the patient from feeling it; deprive the prisoner of all rights, but do not inflict pain; impose penalties free of all pain. Recourse to psychopharmacology and to various physiological 'disconnectors', even if it is temporary, is a logical consequence of this 'non-corporal' penalty.

The modern rituals of execution attest to this double process: the disappearance of the spectacle and the elimination of pain. The same movement has affected the various European legal systems, each at its own rate: the same death for all – the execution no longer bears the specific mark of the crime or the social status of the criminal; a death that lasts only a moment – no torture must be added to it in advance, no further actions performed upon the corpse; an execution that affects life rather than the body. There are no longer any of those long processes in which death was both retarded by calculated interruptions and multiplied by a series of successive attacks. There are no longer any of those combinations of tortures that were organised for the killing of regicides, or of the kind advocated, at the beginning of the eighteenth century, by the anonymous author of *Hanging not*

▶

## Box 8.3 (continued)

*Punishment Enough* (1701), by which the condemned man would be broken on the wheel, then flogged until he fainted, then hung up with chains, then finally left to die slowly of hunger. There are no longer any of those executions in which the condemned man was dragged along on a hurdle (to prevent his head smashing against the cobble-stones), in which his belly was opened up, his entrails quickly ripped out, so that he had time to see them, with his own eyes, being thrown on the fire; in which he was finally decapitated and his body quartered. The reduction of these 'thousand deaths' to strict capital punishment defines a whole new morality concerning the act of punishing.

(Foucault, 1977: 9–11)

souls function in a uniform and regular way in the interests of the smooth functioning of the prison. Thus the modern prison regulates its inmates by a regimen that precisely stipulates when eating and sleeping, work and instruction may take place. In this way standardised and uniform inmate conduct can be secured.

Foucault strongly opposed any simple theories of historical progress and emphasised instead the discontinuity, complexity and fragility of many historical changes. Thus he recognised that developments in the treatment of offenders often proceeded unevenly in actual societies as struggles occurred around attempts to supplant one form of domination with another. For example, the removal from public view of execution and other forms of punishment between 1760 and 1840 was not a single event in several European societies but is better understood, Foucault suggests, as a series of advances and retreats. In times of unrest, governments reintroduced more punitive measures. Moreover the treatment of offenders was also influenced by changes occurring outside the juridical system. Foucault emphasised the part played in this process by the emergence of the new sciences of criminology, modern medicine and psychiatry which sought to understand and control the human body by making it an object of knowledge. *Disciplinary power* had its basis in the knowledge and technologies produced by these new sciences. The modern prison and the juridical system it served used disciplinary power exercised through prison governors, probation officers, psychiatrists and the like.

The work of these officials involved examining and assessing people as cases. The officials interview and observe, analyse and classify, write and file reports, all in the name of designing the most appropriate regimen of punishment and reform of the offender. At the back of such exercises of disciplinary power is the process of *normalisation*. The aim of examination and assessment is to determine the nature and extent of the offender's deviation from the norm and to devise the most efficacious means of remedying their criminal behaviour and restoring them to normal, conforming conduct. A further extension of disciplinary power is found in the new methods of *surveillance* incorporated in the design of prison buildings. The 'panopticon', a building designed by Jeremy Bentham, the nineteenth-century utilitarian philosopher, epitomised this new trend for Foucault (see Figures 8.1 and 8.2). The panopticon was a circular building constructed around a central axis that allowed the guards to observe prisoners while themselves remaining unobserved. The point of this design was to induce in inmates the belief that they were under constant surveillance, irrespective of whether this was always actually the case (see also pp. 283–4). The panopticon design influenced the construction of prisons built in Britain from the early nineteenth century. Foucault's additional point is that these processes have been generalised beyond the precincts of the prison.

Thus, the panopticon comes to stand as a metaphor for many leading features of modern society. Other bureaucratic organisations are also in the business of surveillance. The police force and security companies patrol public places and oversee private property. Schools and colleges monitor the education and accreditation of the population. Public health authorities and social service agencies keep extensive

# PANOPTICON;

OR,

# THE INSPECTION-HOUSE:

CONTAINING THE

## IDEA OF A NEW PRINCIPLE OF CONSTRUCTION

APPLICABLE TO

## ANY SORT OF ESTABLISHMENT, IN WHICH PERSONS OF ANY DESCRIPTION ARE TO BE KEPT UNDER INSPECTION;

AND IN PARTICULAR TO

## PENITENTIARY-HOUSES,

| PRISONS, | POOR-HOUSES, | LAZARETTOS, |
| HOUSES OF INDUSTRY, | MANUFACTORIES, | HOSPITALS, |
| WORK-HOUSES, | MAD-HOUSES, | AND SCHOOLS: |

WITH

## A PLAN OF MANAGEMENT

ADAPTED TO THE PRINCIPLE:

## IN A SERIES OF LETTERS,

WRITTEN IN THE YEAR 1787, FROM CRECHEFF IN WHITE RUSSIA,
TO A FRIEND IN ENGLAND.

## BY JEREMY BENTHAM,

OF LINCOLN'S INN, ESQUIRE.

DUBLIN, PRINTED: LONDON, REPRINTED; AND SOLD BY T. PAYNE,
AT THE MEWS GATE, 1791.

**Figure 8.1** Title page of Jeremy Bentham's *Panopticon* (1791).

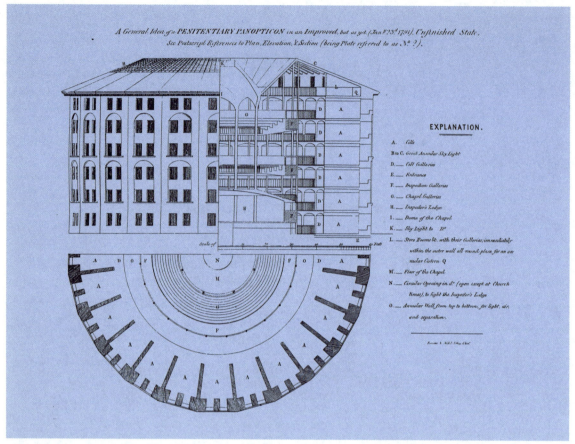

**Figure 8.2** Plan of the Panopticon. (Source: *The Works of Jeremy Bentham*, ed. Bowring, Vol. IV, 1843: 172–3.)

records on citizens' uptake of services. Government revenue offices check whether we have paid our taxes. All these forms of surveillance have been powerfully aided by advances in computing and video technology. These technological advances have enlarged the opportunities for overseeing and controlling the conduct of individuals and extended the range, scope and ease with which personal information can be acquired.

Foucault's early work considers the relation of body to power and knowledge and focuses on techniques of domination. Thus in his study of the development of modern medicine Foucault (1973) showed how changes in medical technologies (the stethoscope, the microscope, laboratory testing) and in medical practices (the physical examination, the post-mortem), together with the development of disciplines such as anatomy, radiology and surgery and the institutionali-

sation of the hospital and the consulting room, served to subject the patient's body to unprecedented medical power. In this process the consultation with a physician came to resemble not so much a puzzle-solving encounter as a confessional in which the secrets of the body would be disclosed (Armstrong, 1983). In his later work on sexuality (Foucault, 1984b) there is a shift towards *techniques of the self* as Foucault became interested in how subjectivity is constituted through discourse. Techniques of the self are the ways that individuals can form and transform themselves by monitoring their bodies, souls, thoughts and conduct. This should not be seen as a piece of southern Californian lifestyle exported to the rest of the world! Foucault shows that a 'culture of self', an intense preoccupation of self with self, was a feature of a number of societies beginning with the early Greek states.

According to Foucault, **power** (p. 64) (or power/knowledge, as he sometimes terms it, to emphasise how each conditions and transforms the other) is not to be understood in conventional political senses as something to be 'held' by special groups, 'won' or 'exercised' over others – power is not simply about securing one's own will over that of others. Rather, power is dispersed in a society and works in capillary fashion through discourses. Wherever there is power there will be **resistance** (p. 170) to that power, often based in local or disqualified discourses. Further, Foucault argues that power should not be simply seen as essentially repressive in character. It can also be 'productive'.

A good example of the positive and productive conception of power is Foucault's discussion of 'bio-power'. This refers to disciplinary power over life as it affects both individual bodies and social bodies (entire populations). Sexual discourses are prime concerns for understanding the operation of bio-power for they connect both to conceptions of individuality and pleasure and to the management of populations (in the shape of birth statistics, contraceptive practices, sexually transmitted disease, longevity, and the community's general level of health). Unlike the Victorians, in the late twentieth century we are 'free' to talk about sex – more, compelled to talk about sex almost incessantly. Discourses about sexuality are produced by newspapers, magazines, films, health workers and so forth. In this way sexual discourses extend the hold of their power over our selves and bodies. Sexual discourses, internalised by the self, are no less effective than the more repressive orders and regimes that formerly imposed their demands on the self. When power is seen as dispersed through a multiplicity of discourses it becomes difficult to narrowly identify the operation of power with sectional interests. So sexual freedom cannot be identified with sexual indulgence – that would be to fall under the sway of a sexual discourse that recommends repression. For Foucault the self must come to see such discourses for what they are (often devices that extract guilt, confession, renunciation from the self and result in a loss of self) and attempt to reach an informed decision that strikes a balance between continence and pleasure.

# Civilising the body: Elias

In *The Civilizing Process* (Elias, 1978) the German sociologist Norbert Elias analyses a long historical process through which people acquired an increasing capacity to control the expression of their emotions and other embodied acts. What is now taken as 'proper' and 'civilised' behaviour is the outcome of a wide range of social processes, which resulted in the redefinition of standards of propriety and repugnance (in the direction of greater refinement and polish). Accompanying these changes was a reconceptualisation of the nature of human nature, of what human beings were expected to be – especially as this was manifest in their embodied actions.

Elias's evidence to document these changes came from many sources. He drew upon books of manners such as the 1530 volume by Erasmus of Rotterdam, *On Civility in Children*, but also used the evidence of literature, paintings and drawings. He initially focused on the manners of the medieval upper classes in Europe. In a discussion rich in vivid historical illustration, Elias charts the characteristics of acceptable conduct in well-to-do circles. Table manners involved eating with one's fingers or perhaps a spoon; forks did not appear in daily use until the sixteenth century. People served themselves from a common pot and used the tablecloth to wipe their greasy fingers (though not their noses!). The 'natural functions' were often carried out in the public company of others and spoken of without shame or embarrassment; Erasmus advises that, 'It is impolite to greet someone who is urinating or defecating' (Elias, 1978: 130). It is only in later centuries that these become private matters sequestered from public view and incurring shame and repugnance. In medieval times people used their fingers to blow their noses. Handkerchiefs were only adopted in the seventeenth century by the upper classes. The habit of spitting was commonplace and the convention was to tread on the sputum. The spittoon came later (and persisted in many public places in Europe until the twentieth century).

Sharing beds in inns with persons of the same sex was commonplace. People were advised to be modest when undressing, to bow to their social superiors in the choice of the side of the bed to be slept in and when to go to bed, and to lie straight and still. It was common for people to sleep naked, but the bedroom did not then have the modern connotation of privacy and intimacy. The sight of naked humans, in bed or at public bath-houses, was an everyday occurrence. Correspondingly, Elias (1978: 177–8, 214) suggests that in the Middle Ages sexuality was marked by an absence of modern notions of shame and obscenity. One illustration of this is the custom (varying between classes and countries) of wedding guests undressing the bride and groom so that they could be 'laid together' on the marital bed. (Elias also acknowledges that there was a good deal of sexual violence within marriage.) Furthermore, medieval society was itself marked by much aggressiveness and cruelty towards both humans and animals: 'Rapine, battle, hunting of men and animals... for the mighty and strong these formed part of the pleasures of life' (Elias, 1978: 193). Medieval people were more volatile and fiercer when roused than is found to be acceptable in the twenty-first century.

From the fifteenth century on, changes took place that brought manners increasingly in line with modern standards. Elias emphasised that he did not wish to endorse the positive modern standards against the 'inadequate' customs of the past. His primary task was description and explanation. He saw the civilising process as having no beginning or end. How did the transformation come about? Not for material reasons: for example, the rich had special cutlery for Lent that was simply considered unnecessary at other times of the year. Nor did it come about because of greater concern for health and hygiene or respect for one's fellows and social superiors – these reasons, Elias demonstrates, were very much retrospective justifications for changes after they had occurred (see Mennell, 1989: 45–7). The key factor, for Elias, arises from changes in the social composition of the upper class occurring in the late Middle Ages. A fundamentally warrior class became transformed into a court society. The new aristocracy came from diverse social backgrounds and were politically organised around the court. Thus the new upper-class courtiers found themselves in the close company of others in the court, others upon whom they were dependent for patronage, favour, advancement, etc. It became important to monitor one's own conduct and observe carefully that

of the people on whom one's prospects depended. Living closely with such significant others made for 'stricter control of impulses and emotions ... first imposed by those of high social rank on their social inferiors or, at most, their social equals' (Elias, 1978: 137). But court society was highly competitive. What was first imposed (e.g. Brunswick Court Regulations of 1589 stated: 'Let no-one, whoever he may be ... foul the staircases, corridors, or closets with urine or other filth, but go to suitable, prescribed places for such relief' (Elias, 1978: 131)) soon became a matter of self-restraint. Elias emphasized how over time an internal dynamic built around the *interdependencies* of court society made for increasingly refined standards. These standards in turn spread downwards through the social structure as the socially striving bourgeoisie sought to emulate their superiors.

Elias (1982) went on to further situate these changes in a long process of state formation centring on a monopoly mechanism in which territorial expansion was linked to the concentration in single hands of the means of administration, taxation and violence. Elias offered a complex account of 'the historical development of human bodies' (Shilling, 2003: ch. 6) that for some commentators is more historically nuanced than Foucault's view. Some of these differences can be further illuminated through two contrasting studies of the cultural practice of eating.

## Eating: a disciplined or a civilised cultural practice?

Eating and drinking are plainly learnt, culturally shaped activities, as observation of small children at mealtimes readily attests. The consumption of food and drink is also a generic cultural practice: 'Of everything which people have in common, the most common is that they must eat and drink' (Simmel, 1994). What we eat, how and how often are influenced more by cultural than biological factors. The contributions of a Foucauldian and an Eliasian approach to this cultural practice can be appreciated by comparing two studies by Bryan Turner (1991) and Stephen Mennell (1991). Turner (1991) offers a Foucauldian examination of the discourses that have arisen around the notion of a healthy diet, while Mennell (1991) presents an Eliasian investigation of the civilising of the appetite for food and drink.

The inscription of power on the body can be seen in the dietary advice directed at particular populations of a society. Foucault (1973, 1977) recognised the disciplining function of institutional diets in prisons, workhouses, armies and asylums. Popular literature on dietary advice has a long history. Around the early eighteenth century, advice on 'diaetetick management' became fashionable among the professional and upper classes in Britain seeking to sustain good health. A key figure in the promotion of this discourse was George Cheyne, a Scottish physician who wrote several books recommending the psychological and physical benefits of regular sleep, moderate exercise, temperance and a diet high in milk and vegetables. Cheyne conceived the human body in mechanistic terms as a fluid-filled hydraulic system. He combined his medically based advice with Christian principles, attracting the endorsement of the influential founder of Methodism, John Wesley. For Cheyne, according to Turner:

> Lack of exercise, a surplus of food, intoxicating drinks and urban life-styles were particularly threatening to the health standards of the upper classes, especially among 'the Rich, the Lazy, the Luxurious, and the Unactive' [Cheyne 1733]. The availability and abundance of strong drinks among the elite enraged their passions to 'Quarrels, Murder, and Blasphemy' [Cheyne 1724]. Changes in eating habits and fashions in cuisine stimulated the appetites of the upper classes in ways which were contrary to nature and which interfered with the natural process of digestion. . . . Cheyne [1733] lamented that 'When Mankind was simple, plain, honest and frugal, there were few or no diseases. Temperance, Exercise, Hunting, Labour and Industry kept the Juices Sweet and the Solids brac'd.'
>
> (Turner 1991: 162)

This discourse was not relevant to the working classes who in the eighteenth century still encountered starvation periodically. Only with the establishment of capitalism in the nineteenth century did a distinct dietary discourse targeted at the labouring classes emerge. This was a discourse founded on scientific

principles of modern dietetics. It sought to establish the minimum amount of protein and calories necessary to sustain the physical efficiency of the working body, which was essential for the productivity of capitalist enterprises. Thus, thermodynamic images of the human body replaced the earlier hydraulic portraits. Unlike the eighteenth-century discourse it was bereft of religious justifications. However, moral connotations still figured in the new discourse. Rowntree in his famous survey of York in 1899 found that the working class was underfed and that the artisan class could only manage to meet his minimum nutritional standards provided there was no 'wasteful expenditure on drink'. Sobriety came to be justified not in divine terms but by the demands of the prudent housekeeping needed to sustain physical efficiency. In the late twentieth century dietetic discourses become secularised. But moral elements have not disappeared, as is evidenced by the endorsement of very particular conceptions of the body's shape and appearance in discourses surrounding contemporary fitness enthusiasms (step classes, fitness videos, running, bodysculpture and the like).

Medical and scientific discourses on diet, however, represent but one set of constraints on the appetite. According to Mennell medical discourses 'are only small parts of the complex history of appetite and its control in European society' (1991: 127). To begin with, appetite is not quite the same as hunger. Hunger is physiological, a bodily grounded drive, while appetite is psychological, an inclination and desire to eat that is itself culturally shaped. Accepted present-day standards of eating – what we eat, how quickly food is consumed, when we eat – involve a considerable degree of self-control. In medieval Europe rather different patterns of eating obtained. The popular conception of the banquet was a predominantly upper-class phenomenon but variants were to be found throughout society. Even among the aristocracy, however, such indulgent events were interspersed by significant spells of frugal living. In the Middle Ages an oscillating pattern of fasting and feasting was widespread. This pattern parallels Elias's description of medieval people as emotionally more volatile than moderns, as more likely to fluctuate between extremes in the expression of their feelings. Changes in eating patterns thus reflect the civilising process writ small.

213

The fasting/feasting pattern arose from pervasive uncertainties about food supply. Famines were regular occurrences in the Middle Ages, as were fires, epidemics, wars and vagrancy, and the interacting effects of these led to recurrent 'steeples' of mortality which often cut across social class differences. Food scarcity was a real threat until well into the eighteenth century. The perception of the threat of food scarcity, especially by the lower levels of society, per-sisted through to the nineteenth century. Fasting was required of the medieval good Catholic by the Church on at least three days a week and, although it did not involve total abstinence, it was expected that people would eat only a small simple meal, usually in the evening. Sumptuary laws, which specified what could be eaten by particular categories of person as well as what they could wear, were common through Eurtope and elsewhere up to the late Middle Ages,

## Defining concept 8.1

### Ritual and symbolism

We live, in Victor Turner's (1967) celebrated phrase, in 'a forest of symbols'. Objects in our environment – things, people, activities – make sense to us in terms of their meanings. We act toward objects on the basis of the meanings that these objects have for us. These meanings are conventional, learned as part of socialisation (the process of acquiring cultural knowledge and competence) and, importantly, these meanings are shared. In some versions of semiotics, the favoured method in cultural studies for interpreting meanings, it is suggested that a distinction can be made between signs and symbols. The relationship of a sign to what it signifies is that of a part to a whole (i.e. is *metonymic*), as the word 'apple' is to a certain kind of fruit. The relationship of a symbol to what it stands for is an arbitrary similarity (i.e. is *metaphoric*), as the apple proffered by Eve in the Garden of Eden symbolises 'worldly knowledge'.

The sharing of symbols (wearing your team's colours on the way to a match) breeds social solidarity – a sense of belonging to a group, and confirms social identity – a sense of who and what you are (a Blackburn Rovers supporter, perhaps). **Symbolism** has been examined in cultural studies in a variety of ways, perhaps most memorably with respect to youth subcultures. Since the 1950s a succession of youth subcultures have used diverse symbols – long hair, cropped hair, quiffed hair, spiky hair, beads, safety pins, all kinds of thoroughly distinctive clothing styles – to convey their distance from conventional society and thereby to challenge its **hegemony** (p. 73) (Hebdige, 1979). Often the symbolism involves bricoleur logic: something intelligible in one context is re-contextualised in another, as in the Ted's appropriation of the Edwardian gentleman's jacket ('drapes'). Sometimes structural similarities (or 'homological relations') can be discerned between different elements of a subculture's chosen symbols. Willis (1978) suggests a homology between motorbike boys' fascination for the speed and hardness of the motorcycle and their liking for late 1950s rock 'n' roll.

Rituals involve a standardised sequence of acts and utterances 'of a symbolic character which draws the attention of participants to objects of thought and feeling which they hold to be of special significance' (Lukes, 1975). The form of the sequence is more or less invariant and the acts must be enacted – the fundamental rule being no performance, no ritual. Religious ritual involves acts and attitudes of respect and reverence toward some sacred object (something that is placed beyond the everyday profane world and regarded with awe) but all rituals direct people towards things symbolically significant to them. Political rituals, such as Cenotaph ceremonies, May Day parades or street demonstrations, are believed to build social solidarity among participants and reaffirm shared values. To the extent that the western world is witnessing a decline in organised religion and a corresponding rise in the importance of individualistic ideologies, the individual person is coming to be regarded as a minor deity (Goffman, 1967), normally to be accorded deference in the shape of polite acts and other interaction rituals.

#### Further reading

Hebdige, D. (1979) *Subculture: The Meaning of Style*, London: Methuen.

Leach, E. (1976) *Culture and Communication*, Cambridge: Cambridge University Press.

Lukes, S. (1975) 'Political ritual and social integration', *Sociology* 9(2), May, 289–308.

partly in order to restrict conspicuous consumption. Medical opinion, which tended to recommend moderation in eating, was another source of external constraint on people's desires to indulge their appetites.

The fasting/feasting pattern eventually gave way to a modern self-controlled pattern from the eighteenth century on. 'The civilizing of appetite' says Mennell (1991: 141) was linked to 'the increasing security, regularity, reliability and variety of food supplies' that accompanied the commercialisation and industrialisation of European society. The extension of trade, the growth of the economy, divisions of labour and processes of state formation all contributed to the abolition of endemic food scarcity in Europe. Feasting, involving the conspicuous consumption of large quantities of food, became less of a status symbol. In its place the qualitative possibilities opened by the developing gastronomic arts helped to instill a new spirit of moderation. The old distinctions between foodstuffs consumed at banquets and those suitable for everyday eating disappeared. The food of the wealthy increasingly resembled the food eaten by other members of society. The growing interdependence characteristic of modern societies contributed to a levelling out of the kinds of foods eaten by the different classes and thus to an extension of the self-controls over appetite. In addition, Mennell argues that obesity and anorexia nervosa are best understood as disturbances in the normal patterns of self-control over appetite expected in prosperous Western societies (anorexia in particular seems to be largely confined to modern societies where the supply of foodstuffs is not at issue). The historical shaping and constraint of the appetite is thus a complex affair best understood, Mennell suggests, as 'one more example of a long-term civilizing process' (1991: 152).

The dietic discourses sketched by Turner have certainly been influential in shaping patterns of eating. A Foucauldian perspective highlights how human bodies are constituted by power mediated through particular kinds of discourse. Mennell's Eliasian perspective, however, provides a method for exploring in more detail the links between discourse and cultural practice, demonstrating how the cultural patterning of the appetite is shaped by a range of social interdependen-

cies. An Eliasian perspective thus shows us how particular discourses are established in relation to shifting sets of social interdependencies.

# 8.4 Representations of embodiment

This section addresses how the human body is represented in everyday life, popular culture and the mass media. Beginning with an examination of the phenomenon of fashion, it then reviews studies of the representation of femininity and masculinity and concludes with a consideration of some of the debates around pornography in order to illustrate the issue of the effects of bodily representations and the limits of representation.

## Fashion

The adornment of the human body by a variety of methods (clothing, make-up, jewellery, accessories, tattooing, scarification, etc.) expresses fundamental dimensions of cultural identification and social participation – of who and what we consider ourselves to be. Stylistic changes and preferences in adornment are often described as fashion, but it is hard to define the term precisely and generally. To begin with, it is best thought of in relation to its opposite, the outmoded. The basic pattern involves cultural forms which enjoy a 'temporary acceptance and respectability only to be replaced by others more abreast of the times' (Blumer, 1968). Thus fashion can be distinguished from custom, which refers to established and fixed forms of belief and conduct. In traditional societies where customs are slow to change, fashion is an alien notion. Yet fashion itself has a customary basis. It exemplifies a dual tension, as Georg Simmel (1957) recognised long ago, between differentiation and affiliation. On the one hand, the fashionable individual wants to stand out from the crowd and appear special. On the other hand, by dressing in a certain style the individual is displaying a kinship with other similarly fashionable persons. The anthropologist Edward Sapir neatly refined this idea in stating that 'fashion is custom in the guise of departure from custom' (1931: 140).

Since fashion is always responsive to what is considered 'up to the minute', it is a sharp indicator of the so-called 'spirit of the times', a telling reflection of the here and now. Fashion, of course, is not a phenomenon confined to adornment. It occurs in a wide variety of fields including architecture, drama, household furnishing, literature and the theories and methods of the natural and social sciences. Sometimes a fashion can be responsive to changes in other spheres of life, as in the link between young people's clothes and pop music. Since this chapter is concerned with the cultural bases of the body, our concern will be restricted to its adornment.

A celebrated theory of the purpose of clothing was advanced in a number of works by the historian of costume James Laver (see, for example, 1946, 1950). Clothing, he suggested, is motivated by three basic principles: utility, hierarchy and attraction (or seduction). Very simply, clothes can serve a useful purpose (a sunhat to protect the head, a macintosh to keep the wearer dry in the rain), or they can distinguish us in social status terms (suits and ties rather than jeans and t-shirts), or they are designed for purposes of sexual attraction. Laver's own assumption about the prevalence of these principles (that modern clothing is little concerned with utility, that men's clothing turns on the hierarchical principle while women's is based on the seduction principle) looks somewhat absurd nowadays and probably was never meant to be taken too literally. But it is easy to see how close these principles stand to the much more seriously advanced contentions of functionalist sociologists (Barber and Lobel, 1952) who argue that clothes have a *utilitarian function* (all clothes may be more or less useful), a *symbolic function* (all clothes may be more or less indicative of the wearer's social status) and an *aesthetic function* (all clothes may be more or less attractive).

A key feature of fashion is a 'rapid and continual changing of styles' (Wilson, 1985). Fashion is intimately connected to **modernity** (p. 295). In particular, it reflects and is made possible by two characteristic aspects of modernity: (a) the sense of perpetual change generated, especially by advertising and the mass media; (b) the wide range of choice of consumer goods which gives people alternatives and control over their self-presentation. The point can be made conversely.

Fashion is exclusively a significant feature of societies with a more or less open class system where the elite can mark itself off from neighbouring classes by wearing costume and insignia that are not institutionalised signifiers of rank but which are seen as stylish and distinctive. The fashions of the elite, so the theory goes (Simmel, 1957; Veblen, 1934), will trickle down to the other classes. When other classes copy these fashions, the elite will adopt a new one. This theory explains why fashion is a recurring process and also explains why it is absent in caste and other traditional societies because social position is rigidly enforced (so in classical China the mandarins were required to wear ankle-length gowns; in pre-revolutionary France only the aristocracy were allowed to wear silk).

Trickle-down theory may have validly explained fashion in nineteenth-century urban industrial societies but is not adequate to explain the complexities of the fashion process in the twenty-first century. Fashion increasingly seems to work as a bottom-up rather than a top-down process. Lower groups, especially youth subcultures, actively construct their own styles or seek out the styles of higher classes rather than passively absorb what comes down from above. Alternatively, what may be at work is a 'trickle-across' process that works from minority group to mainstream consumption. Some writers have argued that it is more profitable to regard fashion as a sign system like language (Barthes, 1985) or that it *is* a language (Lurie, 1992) with its own grammar and syntax. Attempts to specify in detail the language of clothing have not been conspicuously successful and the idea seems at best metaphorical: after all, clothing cannot communicate anything like the complexity or rich imagery possible in a spoken or written language.

Another view is that not just fashions but *fashion* itself is changing in late modern or **postmodern** (p. 295) society. Commentators such as Fred Davis (1992) argue that the weakening of the formerly tight tie of status and occupation to clothing suggests that the signifier-signified link in contemporary clothing is becoming increasingly loose or under-coded. With the growing diversity of subcultural and retro styles, fashions can now not merely be followed but knowingly *played with* by the wearer. Knowledge of the identity and mood of the wearer and the context in which clothes are worn become pivotal to an adequate understanding of their meaning. The plasticity and productivity of these meanings cannot be underestimated:

> The systems of meaning within which ... practices of looking [at clothes], buying and even just daydreaming take place are constantly regenerating themselves. What we buy and consequently wear or display in some public fashion in turn creates new images, new, sometimes unintended constellations of meaning. In a sense we become media forms ourselves, the physical body is transformed into a compact portable 'walkman'.
>
> (McRobbie, 1989: xi)

Clothing and fashion are nowadays better regarded as aesthetic than as communicative codes, i.e. codes that express ideas and feelings that are often difficult to directly express rather than straightforward indicators of social standing and moral worth. This leads Davis (1992) to propose that modern fashions are fuelled by *identity ambivalence*. Our identities are not cut and dried but subject to all kinds of dislocations, pressures and contradictions, which we express through the clothes we wear. Among the **identity** (p. 142) ambivalences expressed through clothing are the following:

| | | |
|---|---|---|
| youth | vs | age |
| masculinity | vs | femininity |
| work | vs | play |
| revelation | vs | concealment |
| licence | vs | constraint |
| conformity | vs | rebellion |

Items of clothing can encode these tensions, highlighting one or other pole. Postmodern theorists go one step further than Davis. They suggest that stylistic variability and the stress on individual diversity in people's clothing means that fashion ultimately signifies nothing (socially). Whether such a dramatic cultural shift in fashion has actually been accomplished is, however, an open question. Some commentators, like Tseëlon (1995) are sceptical, pointing to the real constraints on people's choice of clothing, from workplace dress codes to the 'fashion police'.

Alongside these developments has been the revival of some of the earliest forms of adornment: body painting, ornaments, scarring, tattooing, and the like, which are associated with very distinct personal and social meanings. Among some cultures the marking of the body has long held established ritual significance, often marking the transition from one state to another. In many traditional African societies, for example, scarification of the cheeks or forehead symbolises the passage to adult malehood. Circumcision is a religiously justified form of body modification long practised by Jews and other groups. Men in military occupations often bear tattoos which proclaim their membership of a regiment, ship, etc. Pierced ears have become a mainstream form now widely accepted for both sexes in Europe and America and other styles, such as pierced nostrils, no longer have the shock value that punks could once count upon. Other forms of 'non-mainstream body modification' such as branding, cutting and scarring the skin and genital piercing (Myers, 1992) are becoming more commonplace. The motives for engaging in non-mainstream body modification are varied, including sexual enhancement, displaying trust and loyalty towards a significant other, aesthetic value, group affiliation and sheer shock value. Underlying these diverse motives is a more general function of body modification and ornamentation. These practices serve to 'socialise' the body, bringing certain biological aspects of the person into the social realm, converting a raw and mute body into an active communicator of symbolic significance. This function is present even in these minority pursuits:

> As surely as the Suya highlight the importance of hearing by wearing large wooden discs in their earlobes, so the genital piercers in contemporary American society celebrate their sexual potency by sporting a Prince Albert in the head of the penis or a silver heart on a labia piercing.
>
> (Myers, 1992: 299)

These forms of adornment, along with clothing more generally, serve to link biological body to social being and underscore the point that the body is considerably more than a biological entity. They also raise questions about where the body ends. With our skin or with our clothes, jewellery, make-up? What is the status of our bodily products and emissions? We can 'donate' our blood, eggs and sperm which medical technology

**Figure 8.3** Body piercing and Celtic tattoos (the subject is Irish, hence the tattoos show membership of a Celtic group).

can preserve for long periods of time. The boundaries of the human body are not unambiguous. These questions become all the more pressing in light of developments in bio-engineering and computing technologies that promise to take the figure of the cyborg out of science fiction and into lived cultures.

# Gender difference and representations of femininity

Gender is often regarded as a cultural overlay to the anatomically founded differences between the sexes. Sex refers to biological differences between males and females while gender refers to the culturally specific ways of thinking, acting and feeling. Femininity and masculinity are thus gender terms, referring to the ways of thinking, acting and feeling considered appropriate in a society for females or males. Sometimes the relation between biology and culture is thought of in additive terms (Connell, 1987) – culture rounds out and amplifies the dimorphism that nature provides so that, for example, a propensity towards care of infants is linked to the biological capacity to breastfeed.

Such an essentialist view is difficult to sustain. To begin with, there seems to be no reliable way of apportioning accurate values to the biological and the cultural. Second, they seem to be predicated on assumptions implicit in the natural attitude of Western societies towards sexual difference, namely that there

are two and only two sexes, that male or female are the only possible categories to which individuals can be assigned, that this determination is made on the basis of possession of a penis or vagina, that assignment to either male or female categories is lifelong and cannot be retrospectively altered after the person's death (Garfinkel, 1967: 122–6). A further reason for questioning the additive conception of the relation of biology and culture is that there seems to be considerable variability in acceptable forms of femininity and masculinity. For example, the North American Indian practice of *berdache*, which allows anatomical males to engage in 'women's work', dress like women and move in women's circles, gainsays any doctrine of a natural dimorphism of the sexes. Rather, it seems that cultural definition actually plays a major part in the constitution of gendered bodies, as we saw earlier in Young's (1980) discussion of 'throwing like a girl'. Gender difference is so closely bound up with the workings of cultural definitions and interactional practices (Connell, 1987; Goffman, 1977, 1979) that essentialist views positing some biological feature that is shared by all men or all women and which can account for how people think, act or believe seems absurd.

In large-scale societies it is inevitable that there will be a range of femininities and masculinities to be found. However, some will be preferred over others – an idea that Connell (1987: 183–8) captures with his concepts of 'hegemonic masculinity' and 'emphasized femininity'. These notions articulate the culturally dominant gender codes that movies, advertising and so on both draw upon and help to construct. Also, it is important to distinguish between the versions of femininity and masculinity presented in dominant discourses and people's actual lived experiences, which may well be significantly at variance with these. Black sportsmen may display hegemonic masculinity but that may not be enough to give them social authority in all the situations they encounter. In contemporary Western culture, femininity – or at least emphasised femininity – seems to be very much more a representational and self-presentational matter than is masculinity. It is said that men act, while women appear (Berger, 1972) – women trade on their 'looks', men on their 'presence'. Contemporary discourses of femininity are not seamless ideological webs but rather contain ambiguities and contradictions within them. Tseëlon's (1995) examination of how heterosexual women present themselves in everyday life explores five paradoxes through which culturally dominant beliefs and expectations about women's personal appearance can be understood:

➤ *The modesty paradox* – women are constructed as seduction, ever to be punished for it.

➤ *The duplicity paradox* – women are constructed as artifice, then marginalised for lacking essence and authenticity.

➤ *The visibility paradox* – women are constructed as a spectacle, yet are culturally invisible.

➤ *The beauty paradox* – women embody ugliness while signifying beauty.

➤ *The death paradox* – women signify death as well as the defence against it.

Contemporary femininity is constructed; it is in Tseëlon's term a kind of 'masque', in which women each work out their own relation to these paradoxes. Consider just one example from this list, the beauty paradox. The looks of the human body are very much more important for women than for men: attractiveness matters much more to how women are regarded and regard themselves. While men also express concerns about their appearance, it is much less consequential for them (indeed, men who pay too much attention to their looks are likely to be dubbed 'effeminate'). Female beauty, it is felt, is an ideal state that can be attained by only a few and then for only a short period of the lifespan. So many women work hard to stave off the threat of ugliness by means of cosmetics, diet regimes, plastic surgery, injections, liposuction and the like. But attractiveness itself can become a kind of stigma, a discrediting attribute, since female beauty is a temporary state to be transgressed by even the most beautiful woman. Furthermore, it implies that her bare and uncontrolled body is unacceptable, something requiring intervention and disguise. The cultural valorisation of youthful beauty means that the ageing process urgently brings women up against what may be seen as 'ugliness'. If women attempt to contest ageing too vigorously they encourage unkind comments about their refusal to

'gracefully' yield to the years. Such reasoning is very much a cultural, not natural logic and the standards thereby invoked are not universal but culturally specific. Very different logics and standards seem to apply to men.

Popular awareness of these issues is becoming more developed through a variety of actions, including the banning of excessively thin models from published advertising in countries like Spain and cosmetics company Dove's Campaign for Real Beauty. Notwithstanding the commercial interests involved, the internet popularity of its *Evolution* (2005) film points to the emergence of a cultural politics openly questioning hegemonic conceptions of women's beauty.

## Representations of masculinity

One element of hegemonic masculinity involves bodily displays of aggression and violence. This is often regarded as facilitated, if not actually caused, by male musculature and chromosomal heritage. Studies of the cultural and social dimensions of violent behaviour suggest that these biological endowments are, at best, enabling devices and that there is a complex cultural context mediating aggressive acts from the interpersonal (e.g. assault) to the institutionalised (e.g. wars). But since actual displays of interpersonal violence are often frowned upon, it is the potential for aggressive action that is critical – a potential that is often translated into the stance, posture and muscle tensions of the male body. Among teenage working-class boys, for example, a certain amount of pushing and punching, playfully framed, can function as a signifier of friendship.

Sometimes this aggressive behaviour can be institutionalised, for example in fascist ideologies. Klaus Theweleit's (1989) extraordinary study of the inner experience of German fascism explores the doctrine's appeal to many different kinds of men. The study is premised on the assumption that fascism itself was a distinct culture created by and for its adherents and which cannot be properly understood as a culture if it is reduced to other factors (e.g. class interest, character structure). Theweleit draws mainly on the novels and memoirs of the Freikorps, a right-wing militia which flourished in 1920s Germany whose ideology and activities foreshadowed the later ascendancy of the Nazis. Theweleit portrays some significant cultural features of the Freikorps, centring upon the organisation's conceptions of masculinity. The military culture of the Freikorps exalted war and maintained that only through battle could men's wholeness be fully attained. These beliefs about masculinity are well captured in the words of a popular Freikorps writer:

> These are the figures of steel whose eagle eyes dart between whirling propellers to pierce the cloud; who dare the hellish crossing through fields of roaring craters, gripped in the chaos of tank engines; who squat for days behind blazing machine-guns, who crouched against banks ranged high with corpses, surrounded, half-parched, only one step ahead of certain death. These are the best of the modern battlefield, men relentlessly saturated with the spirit of battle, men whose urgent wanting discharges itself in a single concentrated and determined release of energy. . . . Tomorrow, the phenomenon now manifesting itself in battle will be the axis around which life whirls ever faster. A thousand sweeping deeds will arch across their great cities as they stride down asphalt streets, supple predators straining with energy. They will be the architects building on the ruined foundations of the world.
>
> (quoted in Theweleit, 1989: 160–2)

This warrior mentality sharply polarises bodily characteristics along gender lines. Women are regarded as soft, fluid, a subversive source of pleasure or pain who must be contained, a negative 'other' to be hived off from authentic masculine existence. Men therefore need to police the boundaries of their bodies carefully, and through drills and exercises develop a machine-like, organised and hard body that can resist merger or fusion with others, that is reliably autonomous and subservient only to the correct political leader. In this belief system the rapture of combat is extolled and killing comes to be seen as a means of affirming a man's wholeness, a way of asserting the coherence of his body and self by invading the bodily boundaries of the other. Whilst Theweleit presents an extreme case, many

contemporary military cultures have incorporated elements of this world-view.

The movie industry, now just a century old, has proved to be a potent source of representations of masculinity. Arguably, there is a greater range of masculinities on offer in popular film than femininities – that the models of masculinity represented by the roles played by James Dean, Sean Connery and James Stewart, for example, are more diverse than those acted by comparable cinematic icons of femininity such as Marilyn Monroe and Madonna (but note Burchill's (1986) survey). One very influential role model and mythic resource for dominant conceptions of masculinity is *film noir*. A genre of Hollywood film whose classics originally appeared between 1940 and 1955, *film noir* was popularised by Humphrey Bogart's detective roles taken from Raymond Chandler's and Dashiell Hammett's novels. Its conventions include a compromised protagonist and a *femme fatale* with whom he becomes involved. The action takes place in urban locations with predominantly night-time settings. *Film noir* often used the techniques of the voice-over and the flashback. Its distinct visual style includes the use of chiascuro effects, low-key lighting, high or low camera angles, skewed framing and strongly contained, claustrophobic close-ups.

The 'tough' hero of *film noir* is usually a flawed character, sometimes neurotic, alienated or shabby, but with a number of redeeming qualities which become evident as the plot unfolds. Many commentators suggest that he is an attractive, but certainly not a sterling model of masculinity. The standard representation of the tough hero was described by one commentator in 1947 as follows:

> He is unattached, uncared-for and irregularly shaven. His dress is slovenly. His home is a hall bedroom, and his place of business is a hole in the wall in a rundown office building. He makes a meagre living doing perilous and unpleasant work which condemns him to a solitary life. The love of women and the companionship of men are denied him. He has no discernible ideal to sustain him – neither ambition, nor loyalty, nor even a lust for wealth. His aim in life, the goal to which he moves and the hope which sustains him, is the unravelling

of obscure crimes, the final solution of which affords him little or no satisfaction. ... His missions carry him into situations of extreme danger. He is subject to terrible physical outrages, which he suffers with a dreary fortitude. He holds human life cheap, including his own. ... In all history I doubt there has been a hero whose life was so unenviable and whose aspirations had so low a ceiling.

(John Houseman, cited in Krutnik, 1991: 89)

How is such a difficult and discordant conception of masculinity to be interpreted? From a psychoanalytic point of view this can be seen as a form of turning in on oneself, an inversion or narcissism. These characteristics achieved wide popularity first in the 1940s but they continue to be glamourised. There is frequent intertextual use of *noir* elements in mainstream movies, which can be seen as 'some kind of crisis of confidence within the contemporary regimentation of male-dominated culture' (Krutnik, 1991: 91).

Noir may be one of the cultural origins of the so-called 'crisis of masculinity'. This is an often vague term used to refer to the decline of traditional male authority in the household; changes in the jobs market, which have favoured women in recent decades; the decline of educational attainment by boys relative to girls; increasing levels of suicide among young men; the threat to traditional male values and attitudes represented by feminist ideologies and their practical implementation in the regulation of marriage, divorce and workplace relations. Cultural responses to this 'crisis' (whose existence has been contested) are said to include 'laddism', apparently promoted by magazines aimed at young men such as *Loaded* and *Nuts*. Second, it needs to be emphasised that male bodily power is evident in many, very much more mundane settings, such as angling on a river or canal bank. Anglers are overwhelmingly male, which is testimony to the unequal rights that men and women have to occupy public space; it involves embodied skills (control, patience, sensitivity to the elements); and it involves moments of excitement – 'action' – which are themselves strongly gendered (Morgan, 1993). Since male power is so highly pervasive a cultural feature it is easy to overlook more mundane features of its representation.

# Representing sexuality

The representation of the human body, in particular by the modern representational technologies of photography and film, has stimulated a range of debates about the limits of acceptable images of the human body. These technologies can picture the human body's pleasures, pains and degradations. Even before digital technologies massively expanded the availability and circulation of images of the human body, there has been a great deal of debate about images of sex and violence. Here we focus on some of the issues raised by sexual representations, and in particular how human sexuality is pictured.

At the outset it is important to offer some definitions and draw some distinctions, however provisional they may seem. First, there is the distinction between *erotica* and *pornography*. Erotica has its roots in the Greek word for love and generally connotes a diffuse source of sexual stimulation. Many would regard Rodin's 'The Kiss' as an erotic sculpture. Pornography, however, pushes sexual explicitness to the extreme. It is a form of representation that graphically depicts sexuality in order to stimulate its consumer. Pornographic magazines and films have long excited controversy because they are seen, variously, as offensive or harmful. Thus it is also necessary to distinguish between *offence* and *harm*. What persons and groups find offensive varies and is a matter of taste and moral conviction: you may well find offensive the cartoons that children watch on TV. But it is a different matter entirely to hold that these cartoons are harmful. When we claim that some object or arrangement is harmful we are maintaining that it has measurable deleterious effects on people's attitudes and behaviour. Manifestly, there are many sexualised images that give offence to individuals or groups. But to claim that pornography is harmful is to propose that negative, anti-social consequences (e.g. increases in sexual offences towards women and children) can be proven to follow from its existence and consumption.

Three kinds of evidence have been drawn upon to investigate the harmful effects of pornography on its predominantly male consumers. *Anecdotal* evidence draws on connections deemed to exist between an individual's consumption of pornography and the commission of a sexual offence. An offender charged by a court may seek to mitigate the offence by blaming his predilection for pornography. However, this evidence proves nothing beyond the individual case; it cannot be used to support generalisations of a stable relation between pornography and sexual violence. To do that it is necessary to employ much larger samples. One such source of large-scale data is found in *criminal statistics*. Criminologists have attempted to find patterns in the availability of pornography in a society and changes in the commission of sexual offences by examining cross-cultural evidence. Thus far the evidence has been ambiguous or contradictory and no clear patterns have emerged. An apparently more promising line of research has involved testing people in psychological laboratories to measure changes in their personality as a consequence of exposure to large amounts of pornographic imagery (see Linz and Malamuth, 1993, for a summary review). A number of experimental studies have found that significant shifts in men's personalities in the direction of greater tolerance of violence towards women have been detected. However, there remain doubts about extending the findings of this research beyond the psychological laboratory to the everyday sexual cultures in which pornography figures.

A range of feminist positions in cultural studies use all three kinds of evidence about pornography's harmful effects. Anti-porn feminists have used the experimental research in particular to provide scientific legitimation for attempts to change the law (e.g. the Minneapolis ordinance promoted by Catherine MacKinnon and Andrea Dworkin) to eliminate some of the prevalent forms of pornography. Dworkin (1983) has taken the debate about anti-social effects one step further by proposing that, by its very nature, pornography *is* violence towards women in an insidious form. In contrast, anti-censorship feminists (e.g. Assiter and Carol, 1993) have emphasised the ambiguity of the research and pointed to the historical connection of the repression of pornography and the disvaluing of women's rights. It seems that societies that allow pornography to flourish also offer laws and customs that best preserve the collective interests of women.

Cross-cutting both these positions are feminist critiques of pornography as a representational genre.

Feminists have proposed that the form and content of much current pornographic imagery is founded upon overwhelmingly phallocentric premises. In much pornography the male gaze (see p. 281) rules: women are portrayed as sex objects designed only to satisfy male sexual desire. Questions about gender relations inevitably arise since pornography can be regarded as a mirror of wider power relations in society. This has led to a debate about the possibility of a 'feminist erotica' (Myers, 1982) or an 'erotica for women' (Semple, 1988). More is involved than simply replacing naked female models with males (attempts to do this have not been very successful commercially and seem to attract a large unintended audience of gay males). Erotica for women tends to adopt a different form and content than pornography aimed at heterosexual men. Among the candidates for inclusion are popular romantic fiction (Radway, 1987) and the production of lesbian pornography by lesbians themselves. One of the themes that has emerged from these debates is the issue of pleasure, and women's sexual pleasure in particular (Kaplan, 1983). Pornography is an avowedly transgressive genre that is a potent source of fantasy. This dimension of the debate is advanced by some feminist and gay theories that endeavour to reclaim at least a part of sexuality for the private sphere. In this view the pleasures of the body are individual concerns outside the public realm. Further, it is suggested that the enticements of the forbidden, the danger and excitement associated with certain kinds of sexual practice, are civil liberties not to be given up lightly. From this point of view, legal attempts to circumscribe transgressive sexual practices, such as the Spanner trial of 1990–1 where gay men were prosecuted under the law of assault for engaging in mutually consenting sadomasochistic activities, stand as an important incursion into personal freedom and the rights of the citizen.

This last position is often linked to arguments about the vagaries of interpreting sexually explicit material. There may be a personal aspect to these interpretive matters (whatever turns you on). But there is also a pervasive social dimension: Clark Gable's cinematic kisses are seen as only 'staged' kisses, whereas it is difficult to extend the fictional frame fully to hard-core pornography – the sex itself seems always to be 'real' sex, not an imaginary, theatrical version. It appears that hardcore trades on certain documentary conventions which could never enter the minds of the audience for *Gone With the Wind*. What this underlines is that the distinguishing features of pornography do not merely concern graphicness of depiction of sexual organs and activities (if that were true, gynaecology and urinary-genital medicine textbooks could be categorised as pornographic). Rather, pornography has to be understood as a 'regime of representation', a genre assembled out of certain combinations of camera angles and lighting, bodily postures, apparel, footwear and the like (see Kaite, 1995, for a semiotic analysis). Mainstream pornography is a genre that turns sex into a spectacle in which the male gaze predominates. It is a discourse where male desire has triumphed over representational form (Williams, 1990). While these images in themselves do not cause sexual violence, it is widely felt that they powerfully shape the sexual basis of gender relations.

Many of these debates predate the Internet, which circulates pornographic images on an unprecedented scale. The flow of Internet pornography is outside the control of nation-states though many issue severe penalties to their citizens who frequent sites devoted to depictions of minors. The Internet has helped internationalise the porn industry, aided by major hotel chains that offer X-rated movies to their guests. Alongside this familiar story of capitalist market expansion has been a rise in small peer-to-peer networks devoted to producing and sharing sexually explicit materials. These networks open the possibility of more diverse and less exploitative forms of sexual representation. Katrien Jacobs (2004) describes some of these networks operating according to the logic of the gift rather than the profit motives of capitalist enterprise. Drawing on Foucault, she suggests that the Internet is a contested and somewhat disorderly public space in which power is diffusely distributed. She writes: 'The Internet creates consumers, artists and activists who are eager to operate the viewing contexts of porn spaces. Porn consumers are citizens of small places and 'other spaces', engaged in multiple lines of communication' (Jacobs 2004: 80). The Internet has helped to increase the profits of the mainstream porn industry, it has also promoted the development of alternative forms of production and exchange of sexual materials, and with that alternative conceptions of the producers and consumers of porn.

# 8.5 The body as medium of expression and transgression

In our logocentric world, the communication and expression conveyed through language is often valued over communication and expression mediated through the body. This section picks up some of the themes of the earlier discussion of body techniques. We consider some of the ways in which the body is a medium of expression, its techniques serving as a vehicle for our being-in-the-world. A closely related theme is how the body can also serve as a medium of **transgression**. This section explores the themes of bodily expression and transgression under five headings: the emotional body, the sporting body, body arts, the fit body and the symbolism of body building.

## The emotional body

The cultural shaping of the body's emotions is built into their expression. Arlie Hochschild (1983) speaks of the 'feeling rules' specific to cultures and subcultures which specify the kind and level of emotional expression appropriate to any situation. We feel happy at parties and sad at funerals in part because we are meant to – we are conforming to the locally relevant feeling rule. From this it follows that persons are capable of 'managing' their emotions, and this emotion management, this control over the expression of embodied feelings, is a key part of what it is to be regarded as a competent adult. Among the Inuit of northern Canada, for example, any show of strong emotion by adults is frowned upon; only very small children are allowed to behave in that way. So when an anthropological fieldworker vigorously remonstrated visiting Western fishermen who were taking advantage of the Inuit's generosity, she found herself shunned by the very people she was attempting to defend (Briggs, 1970). The Inuit could neither comprehend nor accept what they saw as her 'childish' outburst.

Emotion management is part of our daily lives. Some emotions such as shame or embarrassment are eminently social in character: they are elicited by the real or imagined responses of others. Embarrassment minimally seems to involve the projection of one's self as a given kind of person (a competent driver, a reliable colleague, a trustworthy friend) that the facts of a situation then come to contradict (we dent the car's bumper while parking, we make a foolish mistake in our work, we disclose personal information to the 'wrong' person). Some categories of person are required to be particularly skilful in the management of emotions. Hochschild (1983) examines the training and working techniques of flight attendants for a big US airline. Part of their working personality involves being continually courteous and smiling in their dealings with passengers, no matter how they are actually feeling. Flight attendants receive schooling in these techniques by the company, techniques that are then refined on the job, for example, in coping with difficult or demanding passengers – attendants call them 'irates' ('a noun born of experience', as Hochschild observes). The control of one's own emotions in this manner often paves the way to the successful management of the feelings of others.

## The sporting body

In increasingly sedentary contemporary societies, sporting activities, whether undertaken professionally or recreationally, are a major form of physical engagement in the world, especially for men. The 'disciplining' that practice and training in a sport involves can be regarded in Foucauldian terms as producing 'docile bodies' (Hargreaves, 1986) but such a view overlooks the care, attention to detail and enthusiasm that sportspeople bring to their sports activities . In this section we consider a study of the culture of professional boxing based on its author's four years of participant observation in a gym in Chicago (Wacquant, 1995, 2004). This study takes up a key Bourdieusian concept, **cultural capital** (p. 259), concentrating on one sub-type, the notion of 'bodily capital'.

Boxers, like dancers, strongly identify with their bodies: they *are* their bodies, and they clearly see their skill at using their bodies for pugilistic purposes as an asset that can be translated into worldly success. Boxers thus own a certain 'bodily capital' – bodies of a certain size, shape, and condition – that they seek through training practices to convert into 'pugilistic capital'.

This is 'a set of abilities and tendencies liable to produce value [i.e. recognition, titles, financial rewards] in the field of professional boxing' (Wacquant, 1995: 66–7). Bodily capital is thus closely interrelated with the bodily labours undertaken in the gym and the regimens that extend beyond the gym to the rest of the boxer's way of life.

Bodily labour is undertaken by a fighter who, as an untrained novice, has a certain height and weight, deportment and motility, facial shape and skin tone, all of which are noticed by the trainer in assessing the novice's potential as a boxer. These characteristics define but do not determine the likely future of the novice. The gym is a kind of factory for retooling, refurbishing and restructuring the novice's body into a fighting machine. A trainer is quoted as saying 'I like creatin' a monster, jus' to see what you can create . . . like the master Frankenstein: I created a monster, I got a fighter, I created a good fighter, same difference' (Wacquant, 1995: 70). The boxer's bodily labour is much the same the world over: running, skipping, punch-bag work, callisthenics, sparring and shadow boxing. The result of such repeated and intense training is to change the boxer's physique but also to change his 'body sense', his awareness of his own body and how it stands to the world. The development of this physique and body sense comes about also by what the boxer does *not* do, the pleasures deliberately forgone. Wacquant speaks of the 'trinity of pugilistic sacrifice': food, sociability and sex (in that order). Boxers need to pay close attention to their diet in order that they can make the weight of the class in which they plan to compete. The training is physically demanding, often requiring an exacting routine of early morning runs and strenuous workouts that make a social life difficult. Near a fight, trainers will insist that their charges abstain from sexual activity in the belief that if they do not, they will lose their edge, their sharpness. One fighter says of these sacrifices: 'You're in jail when you're trainin', it's like doin' time, you know' (Wacquant, 1995: 82). Body and self become so immersed in the sport of boxing that the risks – which most commonly involve not brain damage or broken noses but chronic pain from deformations of the hands – are minimised by the boxer as the desire to fight grows. Wacquant's study is a sustained demonstration of Bourdieu's notion that 'the body is in the social world but the social world is in the body' (Bourdieu and Wacquant, 1992).

## Body arts

It is not to the physical object that the body may be compared, but rather the work of art.
(Maurice Merleau-Ponty, quoted in Benthall, 1975: 5)

Embodied capacities, particularly those located in the hands and eyes, are central to the production of artistic objects such as paintings and music. These skills are often the product of long periods of patient cultivation. In this section we briefly review some of the cultural significances of dance, an activity where the artistic product is quite literally inscribed on the body, where the movements of the body serve as expressive and aesthetic vehicles.

There is an initial distinction to be drawn between *performance dance* (a ballet performance, Ginger Rogers and Fred Astaire musicals, dancing competition programmes on television) to be watched and *social dance* (in clubs, dance-halls and, since rave, even open fields) in which one participates. The distinction echoes but does not exactly reflect the earlier discussion of culture in the sense of elevated artistic standards and culture as a whole way of life, the means through which a sense of 'we-ness' is assembled. Performance dance is usually approached as a source of artistic contemplation and enjoyment while social dance is part of the lived experience of members of a group. Performance dance itself has 'high' and 'popular' forms (consider the very different appeals of Ballet Rambert and Riverdance). Ballet, for example, attracts a predominantly female audience from professional and semi-professional backgrounds (Novack, 1993; Sherlock, 1993). Feminists have argued that classical forms of ballet employ costume, movements and narrative structures that reproduce nineteenth-century dimorphic gender stereotypes of female passivity and male dominance.

Cultural studies has tended to focus on social dance and to consider its subcultural location and functions. Thus dance in black popular culture is seen as a form of

resistance to cultural hegemony; for many non-white and white young people, dance is a form of escapism, instrumental in the construction of fantasy (Ward, 1993). Willis (1978) argues that bikers' dance is 'homological', directly extending other themes and attitudes in the subculture, while Hebdige (1979) sees pogoing as another element of punk 'bricolage'. Dance is certainly linked to sexual pursuit in many youth subcultures but that is only part of its significance for members, males no less than females, who often consider competence in a particular dance style as a key subcultural emblem (e.g. Teds and jiving). According to **Angela McRobbie** (p. 249), dance's subcultural significance has to be seen in relation to other subcultural elements such as music, fashion, graphic design and drugs. Writing of rave, she observes:

What image of femininity, for example, is being pursued as female ravers strip down and sweat out? Dance is where girls were always found in subcultures. It was their only entitlement. Now in rave it becomes the motivating force for the entire subculture. This gives girls a new found confidence and a prominence. Bra tops, leggings and trainers provide a basic (aerobic) wardrobe. In rave (and in the club culture with which it often overlaps) girls are highly sexual in their dress and appearance, with sixties TV stars like Emma Peel as their style models. The tension in rave for girls comes, it seems, from remaining in control, and at the same time losing themselves in dance and music. Abandon in dance must now, post-AIDS, be balanced by caution and the exercise of control in sex. One solution might lie in cultivating a hypersexual appearance which is, however, symbolically sealed or 'closed off' through the dummy, the whistle, or the ice lolly.... The communality of the massive rave crowd is balanced by the singularity of the person. Subcultural style is in this instance a metaphor for sexual protection.
(McRobbie, 1993: 419–20)

But dance styles themselves are not irrevocably tied to given subcultures. Frith (1983) shows how disco started in black clubs in Detroit and New York, and was then taken up by young people more widely in Europe and North America before finally being appropriated by urban gay populations. Dance, then, is a **hybrid** (p. 125) activity carrying a variety of subcultural significances that may change over time.

## Discoursing the fit body

While the body has probably always been a major focus of care and concern, that attention has intensified since the 1970s in Europe and North America mainly due to the big upsurge of interest in physical fitness. The marathon boom has peaked and declined but runners are now an established feature of the urban landscape. There has been a rapid expansion in the numbers of gyms, often lavishly reconfigured as health clubs which symbolise not so much a hobby or pastime as a lifestyle choice. 'Working out' is no longer the province of a minority of sports enthusiasts but embraces a significant proportion of the population. 'Celebrities' market their own fitness DVDs and exercise programmes. Personal trainers are no longer the sole preserve of wealthy clients. For a fee, they will design a customised exercise and diet programme and supervise the anticipated physical metamorphosis of their charges. At the back of this is a scientific rhetoric based on research studies that trumpet the merits of regular exercise in reducing the risk of cardiovascular disease, cancer and a host of other conditions. Only exercise, goes the constant refrain, and you will live longer and live better. It is as if the body has become a work of art, an object of special cultivation, a project in its own right. Of course it is only in affluent Western societies, which have significant sections of the population who enjoy high levels of health and longevity and ample discretionary time, that such body projects can flourish.

Fitness concerns chime in with Lasch's (1980) thesis about the emergence of the narcissist personality type which is highly self-conscious, constantly monitoring the body for signs of decay, perpetually afraid of the advancing years and the certain prospect of death, who wants to be liked but who is unable to sustain friendships and who treats the self as a marketable commodity. This broad line of theorising is taken further by Featherstone (1991) in his writing on consumer culture. Consumer culture fully emerges in the early twentieth century as production is dramatically increased in Western economies and as advertising comes to assume a prominent place in securing a market for the proliferation of consumer goods. Traditional values are eroded as advertising in particular advances consumer culture values:

> Certain themes, infinitely revisable, infinitely combinable, recur within advertising and consumer culture imagery: youth, beauty, energy, fitness, movement, freedom, romance, exotica, luxury, enjoyment, fun. Yet whatever the promise in the imagery, consumer culture demands from its recipients a wide-awake, energetic, calculating, maximising approach to life – it has no place for the settled, the habitual or the humdrum.
>
> (Featherstone, 1991: 174)

The preponderance of visual images in consumer culture heightens the significance of the body's appearance. The 'look' of the body, its demeanour, clothing and adornment came to assume an importance that it did not have in the nineteenth century when the idols of production (Lowenthal, 1961) held sway, or in earlier times when Christianity vilified the human body by subjecting it to ascetic regimes in order to cultivate the soul. The massive impact of Hollywood cinema throughout most of the twentieth century reinforced the importance of 'looking good'. Fitness and slimness became linked to attractiveness and worthiness as a person.

These changes are crystallised by Featherstone (1991) in the notion of 'the performing self' which emphasises the current importance of display and impression management. Nineteenth-century conceptions of 'character' involved ideas of duty, work, honour, reputation and integrity, to be achieved through industry, thrift and sobriety. These beliefs come to look outmoded by the middle of the twentieth century with the ascendance of the notion of the 'personality' that is judged by its charm, fascination and its ability to be found attractive and likeable by others. This in turn could be achieved by a proper balance of good conversation and flawless manners, appropriate clothing, energy and poise. The need to produce a consistent performance every time calls for a disciplining and rationalising of the spirit of the kind epitomised by the flight attendants studied by Hochschild (1983) (see

p. 224 above). Gone is the older recognition of the possibility of a discrepancy between inner self and outward appearance and conduct, and between self and body. For the performing self, impression management is all. The body is taken as emblematic of the soul.

The enormous explosion of interest in diet and exercise programmes, epitomised by developments such as the increase in health clubs and gymnasia, the ubiquity of runners on city streets and mountain bikers in the countryside, the growth of health food shops and the commercial success of companies such as Nike, point to the emergence of a concern for health as a good to be obtained through individual achievement rather than acquiescence to medical regimes. This amounts to a contemporary 'cult of the perfect body' (Edgley and Brissett, 1990; Edgley 2006), a quest for an ideal that is now firmly entrenched in popular culture. The perfect body

> is slender, fit and glowing. It does not smoke. If it drinks, it does so in moderation. It carefully regulates its diet in terms of calories, carbohydrates, fats, salts and sugars. It exercises regularly and intensely. It showers (not bathes) frequently. It engages only in safe sex. It sleeps regular hours. It has the correct amount of body fat. … It has flexibility. … It has proper muscle strength. … It has appropriate aerobic capacity. … In short the perfect body is one that is biochemically, physiologically and autonomically balanced. Moreover, it is one that does not allow toxic substances and activities to disturb its inner harmony. It is wrapped in a protective membrane around itself. It is, in a word, 'healthy'.
>
> (Edgley and Brissett, 1990: 261–2)

Often, however, the quest for the perfect body is accompanied by an intolerance towards those who are sedentary, who eat the 'wrong' foods and drink to excess, who smoke and who engage in other unhealthy habits. Individuals are sorted by healthist discourses into saints and sinners. This zealous underside to healthist ideologies has been termed a perspective of 'health fascism' and its exponents 'health nazis'. Health nazis are critical of the lifestyle of what they derisively label 'couch potatoes' whom they regard as 'an inferior class of people, certainly unfit, undependable, ineffi-

cient and probably unclean in mind as well as body' (Edgley and Brissett, 1990: 263). These attitudes no longer obtain only in the private spheres of home and leisure but increasingly come to figure in the public domains. Consider the growing restrictions on smoking in public and work places. In some corporate cultures there is evidence that smoking is seen as a real handicap to career advancement. 'Passive smoking' has emerged as a health problem trumpeted on cigarette packet labels but also figuring as a basis for litigation. There is a similarity between the new health fascism and Puritan ethics: just as suffering, self-sacrifice and denial paved the way to a proper relationship with God in the Protestant ethic, so too there is a conviction among health nazis that physical deprivation and forsaking the easy pleasures will ennoble the spirit. The 'me generation' of the 1960s and 1970s which sought salvation through reforming the self (consciousness-raising, therapy) has given way in the 1980s and 1990s to a 'no generation' obsessed with improving the body. Of course, these beliefs are not distributed equally through societies; in the West they are first the province of the professional middle classes (though by no means exclusive to them). The rise of these ideologies and the evidence of the increasing fashionability of running, aerobics and working out in the gym seems to be linked to the emergence of **postmodern** (p. 295) culture.

According to Barry Glassner (1990), current fitness enthusiasms are best understood as a quest for postmodern selfhood. Modernist discourse from the nineteenth century through to the 1950s proposed that exercise and sound diet could help combat the ills of affluence and thereby build a better society. Fitness was thus positively implicated in progressivist convictions concerning national regeneration and social improvement. Contemporary fitness concerns have a different character. They can be seen as responses of persons who seek regeneration in the face of the assaults of an increasingly technological, affluent society. Risks to health and personal wellbeing, it is contended, can best be managed by exercise and diet which will produce stronger, healthier people better able to cope with the daily stresses of life. Thus 'fitness' now connotes not merely an exercise regime but a whole range of lifestyle choices bearing on the physical and mental wellbeing of the individual. At the heart of current fitness concerns lies the individual – notions of the consequential improvement of the collectivity have dwindled into insignificance.

Furthermore fitness, this health-conscious complex of exercise and diet, is most appropriately regarded as a postmodern activity. It comprises a 'pastiche, a borrowing from diverse imagery, styles, and traditions, including both "high" and "low", mundane and special, and past, present and future, wherever these seem usable; a form of contentless quotation' (Glassner, 1990: 217). Step classes will be anathema to those who dislike contemporary pop music, even though workouts may be accompanied occasionally by the nostalgic references of 1950s rock 'n' roll numbers like 'Blue Suede Shoes'. There are tie-ins between diets and exercise programmes (cereal manufacturers who offer their consumers a special offer on the latest celebrity DVD). Fitness imagery and equipment have the properties of *simulacra*, representations that are more copies of other images than they are reproductions of real-world originals. The models who appear in fitness videos are themselves simulacra, unobtainable ideals carefully constructed through make-up, pose and lighting (see Figure 8.4). The shifting ideal of the fit body is in keeping with postmodernism's borrowings and adaptations. The androgenous figures of the 1970s have been replaced by the more substantial and transparently gendered figures of the 1980s and 1990s. Voluptuous female body shapes once again became fashionable, as did muscles for men (and increasingly for women). (In this process the role of media imagery such as provided by *Baywatch* or the *Terminator* movies should not be underestimated.) A similar process is at work in the development of exercise equipment: exercise bicycles were once modelled after their road counterparts (for which they were mere substitutes); now their appearance owes much to motorcycle design and many of their riders would never dream of pedalling on a road.

What makes contemporary fitness discourses decidedly postmodern, according to Glassner, is that they propose to undo some longstanding dualities:

➤ *Male and female.* Fitness as an avenue of female empowerment has been – contentiously – advocated by Jane Fonda and others. The new fitness movements differ from their predecessors in that their recommendations apply equally to women as to

**Figure 8.4** Training videos for the postmodern self?

men: women are urged to undertake the same forms and intensity of exercise as men and to follow the same dietary recommendations.

➤ *Inside and outside.* The (outer) appearance of health has come to be seen as no less important than the (inner) actuality – so much so that the decision to have plastic surgery can be justified in terms of a concern for health and fitness. Once clearly distinguishable notions of 'health' and 'vanity' become interchangeable.

➤ *Work and leisure.* Modernism brought us labour-saving machines, the postmodern health club labour-*making* devices. Leisure becomes something to be worked at, while many work organisations offer fitness programmes and on-site gymnasia to their employees. Keeping the employee in shape is not so far removed from keeping the business in shape. The modernist divide between work and leisure has clearly narrowed.

➤ *Mortality and immortality.* Postmodern fitness discourses obviously cannot promise immortality, but they do point a way to a postponement of mortality. Through exercise and the right diet, it is claimed, a longer life and a more active life can be obtained.

Whatever other uncertainties and contradictions it faces, the postmodern self finds a compelling sense of security in its well-conditioned body.

## Bodybuilding: comic-book masculinity and transgressive femininity?

Contemporary fitness discourses have also served to redefine conceptions of masculinity and femininity, and in particular the desirable looks of the human body. Television soap operas offer currently popular images of masculinity and femininity. These images are, of course, subject to modification and change, perhaps more so in respect of desirable female than male body shapes. In recent years there have been some contradictory shifts. On the one hand, top fashion magazines like *Vogue* have increasingly featured anorexic-like female figures ('heroin chic'). On the other hand, a more solid and muscular build has been popularised by the likes of Madonna and Linda Hamilton (in *Terminator 2*). In this latter trend the sport of bodybuilding has begun to impact on circles outside its own subculture. It is therefore worth examining the conceptions of masculinity and femininity found in bodybuilding since this is an activity that exemplifies an extreme preoccupation with gender issues and the appearance of the body.

The statuary of ancient Greece and Rome provide evidence of some long-term stabilities in Western standards of the desirable appearance of the male body. It seems that men have long desired muscles and have regarded a visibly developed musculature as emblematic of masculinity. A muscular physique in many societies is indicative of warrior competence or employment in a physical occupation (and may therefore also carry the stigma of low class position), although in contemporary Western societies it is more likely to suggest involvement in fitness pursuits. Muscles come to be seen as an accomplishment, not natural endowments but cultured products. They are achievements, the outcome of time and effort put into their cultivation (Dyer, 1989). The sport of bodybuilding emerged in Europe and North America in the 1930s and 1940s as men used weight training and dietary techniques to increase the size and definition of their muscles and achieve desirable physical proportions. In appearance male bodybuilders seem to portray a magnified version of the idealised male body. A key element of the culture of top bodybuilders has been described as 'comic-book masculinity' (Klein, 1994). This can be seen in the chronically hyperbolic discourses of bodybuilding that employ mechanistic terms to describe the techniques of body sculpting. Klein suggests that bodybuilding culture plays with fascistic imagery, exhibits homophobic and misogynist tendencies and embraces a view of masculinity closely resembling that of comic-book superheroes, and incomplete superheroes at that – Superman without his feminine, Clark Kent side. For Klein the hypermasculinity of bodybuilding subculture represents a triumph of form over function since it is only the appearance of masculinity that is sought, not its enactment. And this appearance can itself be a tenuous accomplishment, a costly body project. Bodybuilders get sore backsides and acne from the steroid injections, drugs and diet; they have calloused hands; they ache all the time from training; and they drastically restrict their diet prior to a competition. As one bodybuilder put it (quoted in Fussell, 1991: 153), 'this is about *looking* good, not feeling good'.

Other interpretations of bodybuilding are less judgemental of the culture. They depart from 'emic' concerns with the experience of the lived body – with embodiment rather than with Klein's 'etic' discourse-oriented focus on the objective body. Monaghan (2001)

## Box 8.4

### Kathy Acker: building a body

I am in the gym. I am beginning to work out. I either say the name 'bench press', then walk over to it, or simply walk over to it. Then, I might picture the number of my first weight; I probably, since I usually begin with the same warm-up weight, just place the appropriate weights on the bar. Lifting this bar off its rests, then down to my lower chest, I count '1'. I am visualizing this bar, making sure it touches my chest at the right spot, placing it back on its rests. '2'. I repeat the same exact motions. '3' . . . After twelve repetitions, I count off thirty seconds while increasing my weights. '1' . . . The identical process begins again only this time I finish at '10' . . . All these repetitions end only when I finish my work-out. On counting: each number equals one inhalation and one exhalation. If I stop my counting or in any other way lose focus, I risk dropping or otherwise mishandling a weight and so damaging my body.

In this world of the continual repetition of a minimal number of elements, in this aural labyrinth, it is easy to lose one's way. When all is repetition rather than the production of meaning, every path resembles every other path.

Every day, in the gym, I repeat the same controlled gestures with the same weights, the same reps . . . The same breath patterns. But now and then, wandering within the labyrinths

of my body, I come upon something. Something I can know because knowledge depends on difference. An unexpected event. For though I am only repeating certain gestures during certain time spans, my body, being material, is never the same; my body is controlled by change and by chance.

For instance, yesterday, I worked chest. Usually I easily bench press the bar plus sixty pounds for six reps. Yesterday, unexpectedly, I barely managed to lift this weight at the sixth rep. I looked for a reason. Sleep? Diet? Both were usual. Emotional or work stress? No more than usual. The weather? Not good enough. My unexpected failure at the sixth rep was allowing me to see, as if through a window, not to any outside, but inside my own body, to its workings. I was being permitted to glimpse the laws that control my body, those of change or chance, laws that are barely, if at all, knowable.

By trying to control, to shape, my body through the calculated tools and methods of bodybuilding, and time and again, in following these methods, failing to do so, I am able to meet that which cannot be finally controlled and known: the body.

In this meeting lies the fascination, if not the purpose, of bodybuilding. To come face to face with chaos, with my own failure or a form of death.

Canetti describes the architecture of

a typical house in the geographical labyrinth of Marrakesh. The house's insides are cool, dark. Few, if any, windows look out into the street. For the entire construction of this house, windows, etc., is directed inward, to the central courtyard where only openness to the sun exists.

Such an architecture is a mirror of the body: When I reduce verbal language to minimal meaning, to repetition, I close the body's outer windows. Meaning approaches breath as I bodybuild, as I begin to move through the body's labyrinths, to meet, if only for a second, that which my consciousness ordinarily cannot see. Heidegger: 'The being-there of historical man means: to be posited as the breach into which the preponderant power of being bursts in its appearing, in order that this breach itself should shatter against being'.

In our culture, we simultaneously fetishize and disdain the athlete, a worker in the body. For we still live under the sign of Descartes. This sign is also the sign of patriarchy. As long as we continue to regard the body, that which is subject to change, chance, and death, as disgusting and inimical, so long shall we continue to regard our own selves as dangerous others.

has argued that bodybuilders themselves develop a complex understanding of the symbolism and aesthetics of excessive muscularity. Bodybuilders' own standards of appreciation involve an inversion of the wider society's generally hostile attitudes and appraisals. In Monaghan's 'ethnophysiology thesis', bodybuilders identify different types of excessive muscularity, each of which can be understood as aesthetically pleasing in its own terms. They speak of fellow bodybuilders as for example, 'Oxo cubes' or 'panthers', clearly distinguishing different kinds of excessive muscularity. Bodybuilders themselves do not think of the symbolism of their bodies in Klein's terms. Instead, they invoke their own transgressive aesthetics of the muscular body.

Bodybuilding competitions for women have an even more recent – and controversial – history, dating from the late 1970s. The sight of elite female bodybuilders strikes many people as even more shocking than their male colleagues. The author of a book of photographs writes:

> The images on these pages are as powerful as the women they depict, and many will find both to be threatening. No wonder. The association of women and muscles developed to this degree is unprecedented in history. These images press hard against every notion of femininity with which we are familiar. Here is the female form remade and reconsidered.
>
> The idea of men with muscles is easily accepted. It requires no new concept or category to do so. . . . The muscular female physique is something else; it doesn't fit with most people's idea of the norm. Muscular women are a contradiction to, even an attack on, our sense of reality.
>
> (Dobbins, 1994)

Just as the comic-book masculinity of male bodybuilding culture represents an exaggerated stereotype of conventional conceptions, so too female bodybuilding seems to occupy a clearly transgressive position, challenging conventional discourses of the female body in an overt way.

For some commentators (e.g. Bartky, 1988) the Amazon femininity encoded in the appearance of female bodybuilders clearly establishes the body as a site of cultural resistance. Others are less sanguine about the sport's potential for resistance. Bordo (1988) concentrates on the experiences rather than the appearance of female bodybuilders and argues that, with their emphasis on diet and exercise as techniques to achieve bodily perfection, they can be grouped with anorexics and bulimics. Like anorexics they perceive their body as an alien object constantly at risk of running out of control and therefore needing to be disciplined. Like anorexics they get a kick out of being completely in charge of their bodies. But female bodybuilders do not seem to have escaped patriarchal standards of beauty. In comparison to anorexics the standards by which they judge themselves are different (wanting to be muscular rather than thin) but the means (diet, exercise) are the same, as are their motivations (again, variable conceptions of what it is to look good, particularly as framed by 'the male gaze' – see p. 281). There are ironies and contradictions in the current practice of bodybuilding by women. The clearly coded messages of masculinity connoted by muscularity are muted by other aspects of their appearance that are hyper-feminine: the use of hairstyles and make-up, breast implants, and posing styles that are linked to the graceful movements of dance and so forth. In this way female bodybuilding is 'made safe' for participants and onlookers (Mansfield and McGinn, 1993). (See also the 1985 film, *Pumping Iron 2: The Women*.) Female bodybuilders are playing the beauty game by different rules but it is still a beauty game. Until the subculture changes, it will remain an insurrectionary rather than truly transformational practice (Guthrie and Castelnuovo, 1992).

## 8.6 Cyborgism, fragmentation and the end of the body?

As the studies considered in the above two sections indicate, the human body is increasingly coming to be treated not as a unitary whole but as a differentiated entity requiring specialised treatment. Consumer culture fragments the body into a series of body parts to be maintained through diet, cosmetics, exercise, vitamins. Fashion, advertising and pornography all give testimony to the ever more fragmented ways in which the body is conceptualised and treated. There are a wide range of cosmetics to be applied to the many different parts of the body: mouth, hair, skin, eyes, lips, teeth, legs, feet – and products and applications continue to diversify. Health care is provided by medical specialisms which divide the body up into regions and functions. For many health-care purposes the person is not an ailing body but a set of symptoms to be assessed in terms of what is signified by the evidence of X-rays, blood pressures, blood tests, scans and invasive techniques. The fragmentation of the human body into a collection of body parts can be regarded as implicated in the larger process of fragmentation in the contemporary world which postmodern theory in particular addresses.

The concept of the cybernetic organism or 'cyborg' is another challenge to conventional essentialist understandings of the human body. The term was coined in 1960 by two American astrophysicists, Manfred Clynes and Nathan Kline, to describe the 'artefact organism' that might be developed to meet the very different environments that would be encountered in space travel. The cyborg was originally conceived as a neurophysiologically modified human body that could withstand the demands of space journeys. Science fiction movies such as *Blade Runner* (dir. Ridley Scott, 1982), *Robocop* (dir. Paul Verhoeven, 1985) and *The Terminator* (dir. James Cameron, 1985) have popularised the cyborg concept. The reality, however, is not as remote as might seem. The cyborg combination of the mechanical with the human is already with us, evident in the extensive use of simple prosthetic devices such as spectacles, bicycles and skateboards. It is also apparent in the wide acceptance of cosmetic surgery, biotechnological devices like pacemakers, the use of vaccination to programme the immune system to destroy viruses and advances in genetic engineering (Featherstone and Burrows, 1995). These developments give rise to questions about where the human ends and the machine begins. They question our conventional understandings about the embodied basis of human identity.

These ideas sit easily with some postmodern theses postulating the disappearance of the natural body

(Kroker and Kroker, 1988). Postmodern culture 'invades' the body. This 'panic body' is so fully inscribed by cultural rhetorics of postmodernity, so completely interpellated by its ideologies that no 'natural' residue can be discerned. For Arthur and MariLouise Kroker:

> *Semiotically*, the body is tattooed, a floating sign processed through the double imperatives of the cultural politics of advanced capitalism: the *exteriorization* of all the body organs as the key telemetry of a system that depends on the *outering* of the body's functions (computers as the externalization of memory; *in vitro* fertilization as the ablation of the womb; Sony Walkmans as ablated ears; computer-generated imagery as *virtual perspective* of the hypermodern kind; body scanners as the intensive care unit of the exteriorization of the central nervous system); and the *interiorization* of ersatz subjectivity as a prepackaged ideological receptor for the pulsations of the desiring-machine of the fashion scene.
>
> (Kroker and Kroker, 1988)

For the Krokers, it is consistent with the conditions of postmodernity that the body is disappearing into a kaleidoscope of changing signs.

Some of these questions have been explored in science fiction. For example, *Blade Runner* thematises the role of memory in guaranteeing the individual's biographical continuity by giving 'replicants' a 'memory implant' (Landsberg, 1995). The genre of cyberpunk (see also p. 188) has posed questions about the integrity of the human body in an especially pointed form. Cyberpunk suggests that the invasive nature of cyborgism combined with the expansive aspects of cyberspace thoroughly relativise conventional conceptions of the body. Case, the protagonist of William Gibson's *Neuromancer* (1986), views his body as 'meat' and talks of 'escaping the prison of his own flesh' through 'jacking in' to cyberspace. Elsewhere in Gibson and the works of cyberpunk there is consideration of the nature of immortality (Wintermute in *Neuromancer*), the implications of various prosthetic and bionic aids (e.g. Case's internal organs have been surgically adjusted to modify his drug-taking habits) and the blurring of categories produced by **hybrid** (p. 125) species such as dogpeople. Our ordinary notions of the body and embodiment are thoroughly problematicised in cyberpunk. The 'meat' component (or 'wetware') is often regarded as something to be transcended through drugs, surgery, genetic manipulation and cruising cyberspace. Yet the human – or perhaps 'posthuman' – body is always there in some shape to fix subjectivity and **identity** (p. 142) (Bukatman, 1993).

The productivity of the cyborg notion has also been appropriated by feminist writers who see it as a route out of dimorphic gender relations towards new possi-

bilities of human being (McCracken, 1997). The germinal text for cyberfeminism is Donna Haraway's 1985 essay 'A manifesto for cyborgs' (reprinted as 'The cyborg manifesto' in Haraway, 1991). The hybrid status of the cyborg, part machine and part organism, presents an effective metaphor for exploring the diverse relationships between humans and technologies: she sees the cyborg as 'an imaginative resource suggesting some very fruitful couplings' (Haraway, 1991: 150). The importance of the cyborg figure emerges from the leakiness and potential imminent breakdown of two once

## Key influence 8.1

### Donna J. Haraway (1944–)

'Once upon a time,' writes Donna Haraway in the introduction to *Simians, Cyborgs and Women* (1991), 'the author was a proper, US socialist-feminist, white, female hominid biologist, who became a historian of science to write about modern Western accounts of monkeys, apes, and women.' In the following decade her work broadened to explore the potential opened by 'cyborg feminism', a notion first introduced in her celebrated 1985 essay, 'A Manifesto for Cyborgs'. Haraway's essay established her place as a leading theorist of 'technoculture', of the complex interdependencies between humans and technologies. Her career has crossed several disciplinary boundaries. She studied English, biology and philosophy as an undergraduate at Colorado College and went on to complete a Yale doctorate that spanned philosophy, history of science and biology. Now a professor in the History of Consciousness Board at the University of California, Santa Cruz, she is internationally renowned for her distinctive analyses of the relations between culture, nature and technoscience.

Haraway's cyborg manifesto is an intricately woven text that is premised on the belief that the cyborg, 'a hybrid of machine and organism', is now 'a creature of social reality as well as a creature of fiction'. Scientific and technological developments are making the old distinctions between humans and machines and humans and animals increasingly untenable. Haraway therefore has some sympathy for postmodern theorists who likewise suggest that established dualisms are breaking down. But she is also enough of a materialist to stress the importance of the ways in which technologies are used. It is imperative, therefore, for feminism and cultural studies to reject anti-science metaphysics. New technologies offer the potential to transcend the old determinations of class and gender.

Haraway endorses the advocacy by feminists of partial, situated knowledges as against the usual canons of scientific objectivity. Such situated knowledges can enable the enquirer to escape the 'god-tricks' of totalising objectivity on the one hand and thoroughgoing relativism on the other. In

acknowledging the socially constructed character of scientific knowledge she shows how science studies needs cultural studies. But she insists also on recognising the obstinacy of nature. For Haraway nature is a trickster or coyote with a constant capacity to surprise humankind.

Haraway's writing is intentionally lively, ironic and playful. In form and content it seeks to disrupt the reader's taken-for-granted assumptions about the boundaries marking off such fundamental categories as 'nature', 'culture', 'humans' and animals. The stylistics of Haraway's texts match her characterisation of her work as 'an argument for pleasure in the confusion of boundaries and for responsibility in their construction'.

### Further reading

Haraway, D. (1991) *Simians, Cyborgs and Women: The Reinvention of Nature*, London: Free Association Books.

Haraway, D. (2003) *The Haraway Reader*, London: Routledge.

robust distinctions: between humans and animals (language, tool use, social behaviour can all be possessed in some measure by other primates) and between machines and humans (bio-engineering, computerised expert systems). As the boundaries of the different parts of the world become more permeable, the established dualisms (mind/body, culture/nature, truth/illusion, civilised/primitive, active/passive, etc.) cease to hold the relevance they once did. Humans are immersed in the world, producing their humanness in relationships with each other and with objects. We exercise in the gym, play sports in specialist shoes and contact people by mobile phone. These routine interactions with machines and technologies draw us into increasingly international technocultural networks. Haraway argues that humans might be better thought of as nodes, as intersections of a multiplicity of networks rather than independent monads. There is an important sense in which, Haraway claims, we are all cyborgs now (later acknowledging that the precise constituency of 'we' in a world riven with inequalities is an open question).

For Haraway the cyborg notion refers not to Frankenstein figures or swimmers or runners built on steroids and hormones but to the hybrid networks that arise from the incorporation of humans into technologies designed to facilitate human projects. The enormous impact of technoscience ('the informatics of domination') on the home, the market, the workplace, the school and the hospital offers the potential to override the old determinations of class, race and gender and establish new modes of human being. In the postmodern world, identities, relationships and categories are up for grabs. Transformation and reconstruction increasingly centre on the emergent social relations of science and technology. Haraway suggests that the fluidity and openness presented by cyborg imagery is a helpful guide for understanding the immense implications of these changes. She sees the cyborg as a significant oppositional figure that transgresses boundaries and which is capable of suggesting new modes of gendered being and new forms of politics. Haraway

urges us to embrace the new technologies rather than turn away from them in the manner of some New Age ideologies – hence her declamation 'I would rather be a cyborg than a goddess' (1991: 181).

Haraway's work, and texts on designer babies, genetic foods and human-animal contacts, including *Modest_Witness@Second_Millenium.FemaleMan©_Meets_Oncomouse*[TM] (Haraway, 1997), are hugely controversial. For example, there is some scepticism that gender can be readily dissolved or constructed anew by technological developments when many bio-technologies continue to construct women in essentialist terms (as 'reproductive', 'womb', 'maternal', etc.), thereby perpetuating conventional gender associations (Balsamo, 1995; Hayles, 1992). Cyborg imagery may effect a thorough dislocation of our easy notions that closely tie the body and the natural; dislodging the body from established cultural discourses may prove more difficult.

## 8.7 Conclusion

This chapter has reviewed some contributions to cultural studies of the body. The chapter has sought to examine some of the diverse ways in which human corporeality is best understood in non-essentialist, cultural terms. The constructionist stance employed does not deny the biological dimensions of the material body but does serve to underline the limitations of such explanations in accounting for the enormous variety of corporeal beliefs and practices. Essentialising explanations cannot do justice to the cross-cultural variety of body techniques or their historical evolution through transformations in forms of power or developments in the civilising process. Likewise, consideration of issues of the body's representation, its expressive modalities and the impact of technoculture cannot be easily accommodated within explanations couched only in biological terms. Cultural studies of the body is a large field to work. Bodies are likely to be 'in' in cultural studies for some time to come.

## Recap

This chapter has:

➤ introduced the fundamental concepts and theories in constructionist accounts of the body – techniques of the body, forms of power/knowledge, the civilising process;

➤ considered aspects of the debates around the representation of the human body and its use as an instrument of expression and transgression;

➤ examined the impact of modernity, postmodernity and technoculture on conceptions of human embodiment.

# Further reading

The principal works of Michel Foucault on the body – *The Birth of the Clinic* (1975), *Discipline and Punish* (1977) and the three-volume series on *The History of Sexuality*, *The Use of Pleasure* (1986) and *The Care of the Self* (1990), are challenging reading. In sociology the seminal text, Bryan S.

Turner's *The Body and Society* (1984)) blends the analytic concerns of Parsons and Weber with those of Foucault. Anthropological interest is much older; see the very useful collection edited by Ted Polhemus, *Social Aspects of the Human Body* (1978). In addition, Horace Miner's satirical analysis of the body ritual of one very well known tribe, 'Body ritual among the Nacirema' (1956 and widely reprinted) is still an illuminating read. Michel Feher *et al.*'s 1,600-page, three-volume *Fragments for a History of the Human Body* (1989) is an important resource. Postmodern interests in the body are well represented by contributions to Arthur and MariLouise Kroker's edited collection, *Body Invaders: Sexuality and the Postmodern Condition* (1988). A historically wide-ranging photographic compendium of images of the human body is William A. Ewing's *The Body: Photoworks of the Human Form* (1994). There is much to debate concerning both the material accomplishment and representation of the female body in Bill Dobbins' *The Women: Photographs of the Top Female Bodybuilders* (1994). Many aspects of the debates around body projects and body modification are covered in Nick Crossley's *Reflexive Embodiment in Contemporary Society* (2006).

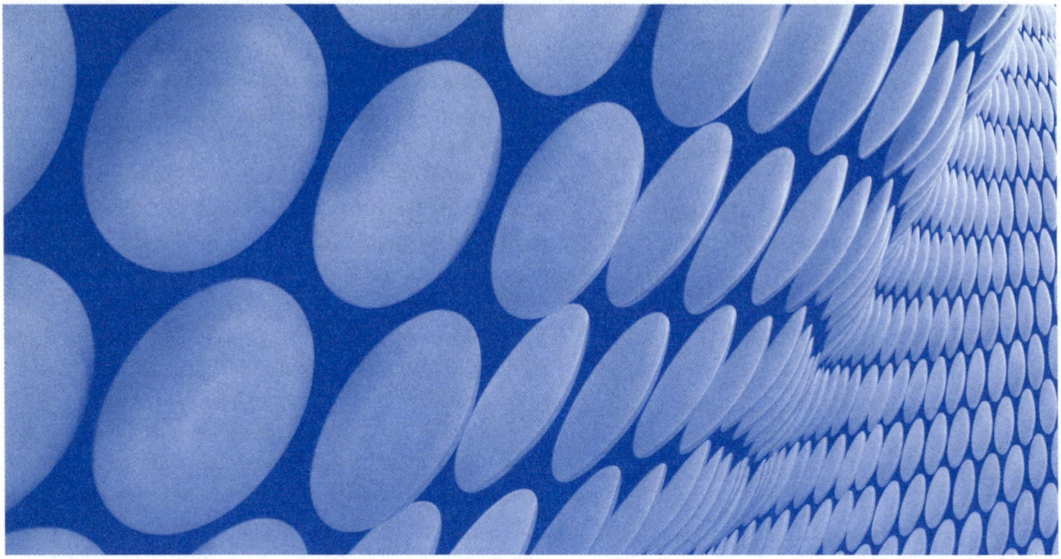

Chapter 9

# Subcultures, postsubcultures and fans

## 9.0 Introduction

In this chapter we are concerned with subcultures, which in broad terms are often defined as subgroups of a wider culture. A significant proportion of the chapter is devoted to the exegesis of the way in which the idea of subculture was developed and used in research at the Birmingham Centre for Contemporary Cultural Studies during the 1970s which, despite the numerous criticisms that have been made of this body of work, remains very influential as the reference point for many contemporary approaches that often have to define their approach against that developed at Birmingham (for example, Macdonald, 2001). This literature concentrates overwhelmingly on young people so that what is normally being examined are youth subcultures. While this particular emphasis is followed in much of the chapter, we also explore the relevance of the idea to subcultures less tied to age. This is done in a later part of the chapter through discussions of fans, which also points to the significance of identity and performance in ordinary life (see also Longhurst, 2007b).

### Learning objectives

- To familiarise readers with the main contours of the approach to the study of youth subcultures developed at the Birmingham Centre for Contemporary Cultural Studies.
- To examine the critique of the Birmingham approach.
- To consider recent studies of youth and fan cultures.

# 9.1 Power, divisions, interpretation and change

In the course of this chapter we shall consider four important themes. Firstly, subcultures, we shall suggest, are intimately connected to issues of **power** (p. 64) and struggle. Thus, one of the most important approaches to subcultures, developed at the **Centre for Contemporary Cultural Studies** (p. 241) at the University of Birmingham during the 1970s, conceptualises and analyses youth subcultures in terms of opposition to, and incorporation in, dominant culture. Each youth subculture seeks to mark itself off from the dominant culture while simultaneously also accommodating certain aspects of it.

Secondly, as the concept of subculture divides wider forms of culture into smaller units, which may exist in relationships of opposition to wider cultures, the concept potentially allows consideration of the division of culture. One of the most important criticisms made of the idea of culture is that it tends to lead to the bringing together of disparate components to produce an over-simplified description of a phenomenon that is actually very complex. For example, familiar formulations like the 'American way of life', British values or 'European culture' seem to obliterate some important distinctions. In Chapter 1 we examined the way in which cultures are actually built up out of forms of cultural struggle and argued that they should never be taken at face value, as cultures are actually divided. Many different writers have utilised the concept of subculture in attempts to overcome such problems. Thus, we can examine how American culture can contain subcultures based on hot-rod car enthusiasm (Moorhouse, 1991), *Star Trek* fans (Bacon-Smith, 1992; Jenkins, 1992; Tulloch and Jenkins, 1995; Penley, 1992), soap opera fans (Harrington and Bielby, 1995) and *Simpsons* fans (Gray 2006) in addition to the more often considered youth subcultural groups. Moreover, as well as facilitating examination of cultural divisions, the concept of subculture also aids analysis of how culture is fragmenting. Are there more and more subcultures and does this mean that it is now impossible to separate subcultures from the 'mainstream'?

The third theme running through the chapter concerns interpretation. Chapter 1 examined some of the general issues, but a discussion of subcultures concretises some of the dilemmas involved. For instance, influential accounts of subcultures, such as that produced by Hebdige (1979), read or decode subcultures using the tools of **semiotics** (p. 29). As we shall see, Hebdige's interpretation of punk is controversial. However, the general point is that different interpretations can be offered of the meaning of any subculture. Moreover, such readings or interpretations tend to neglect the meaning of the subculture for its participants (Widdicombe and Wooffitt, 1995; Muggleton, 1997: Muggleton 2000). This difficulty is compounded by the fact that youth and other subcultures are often highly visible in the mass media, where their members are often stereotyped as folk devils who provoke moral panic (Cohen, 1973). However, there are other forms of representation that require interrogation. For example, we all 'know' that *Star Trek* fans are 'nerdish' men who are 'personally inadequate'. It is therefore surprising to read studies (for example, Bacon-Smith, 1992; Jenkins, 1992) that point to the importance of this series in the lives of 'normal' women.

A fourth theme addressed by the chapter is the argument that suggests that because of the way that society and culture is changing, it is no longer possible or useful to deploy the concept of subculture. There are various positions with respect to this debate, which are reviewed below. This will entail consideration of ideas of postmodern subcultures or postsubculture and tribes (or neo-tribes), as well as the evolving literature on fans.

At this point it may be illuminating to pause and reflect on your own enthusiasms and activities: do you belong to a group that you think of as a subculture? Would you class yourself as a fan of any form of culture (music, television, sport and so on), and how important are these activities in your everyday life? Do you collect things? Do you discuss your interests with others? Do you get depressed when your team loses? It might be useful to use the material discussed in this chapter to analyse these experiences but also, perhaps more importantly, to evaluate that material in the light of your own experience.

# 9.2 Folk devils, moral panics and subcultures

Stanley Cohen's *Folk Devils and Moral Panics* (1973) introduces a number of important and still salient ideas concerning the way in which subcultures (and fans, enthusiasts and marginalised groups) are represented in the press and visual media. This section examines this work in some detail, before considering some more recent discussions of the nature of moral panic.

## Stanley Cohen: *Folk Devils and Moral Panics*

Stanley Cohen developed and expanded upon the work of American writers such as Howard Becker (1963), who emphasised the way in which deviants and deviance are created by the way in which they are labelled as such by powerful agencies of social control. Cohen moved away from a focus on the nature and values of deviant subcultures and the explanation of their deviance. Instead, he emphasised the *reaction* of various official bodies and the media (especially the press) to relatively small-scale disturbances that took place at English seaside towns between 1964 and 1966, which created a moral panic in society around the folk devils of mods and rockers. This moral panic is a central aspect in the development of a control culture. The specific moral panics examined by Cohen and the folk devils around which they centred are now part of history. However, his ideas and approach have continued to be highly influential and used in analysis of more recent issues (see, for example, Critcher, 2006).

Cohen spends little time describing what actually occurred in the towns. Indeed most of the description that he does provide comes towards the end of his book rather than at the beginning. Rather, he begins with what he calls 'The Inventory', which emphasises the media reporting of the clashes of mods and rockers. Cohen argues that the media reporting systematically exaggerated and distorted the events, maintained that they would inevitably happen again, therefore predicting future occurrences of the same type, and used mods and rockers in a symbolic way. According to

Cohen, there are 'three processes in such symbolization: a word (mod) becomes symbolic of a certain status (delinquent or deviant); objects (hairstyle, clothing) symbolize the word; the objects themselves become symbolic of the status (and the emotions attached to the status)' (Cohen, 1973: 40).

Cohen develops his analysis through a detailed examination of the reaction to the seaside events. He first discusses what was thought about the mods and rockers and follows this with a consideration of what was proposed should be done about them. He argues that there were three themes running through the first dimension of reaction (Cohen, 1973: 51):

1 'Orientation': 'the emotional and intellectual standpoint from which the deviance is evaluated'.

2 'Images': 'opinions about that nature of the deviants and their behaviour'.

3 'Causation': 'opinions about the causes of the behaviour'.

There were two main themes running through orientation. Firstly, there were those whose spoke as if what had occurred was akin to a natural disaster. For example, there was talk of towns being 'wrecked'. Secondly, many statements saw what had occurred as presaging worse developments. They were prophecies of doom. Likewise, two recurring themes ran through the images: that young people were affluent and bored. In terms of causation, mods and rockers were seen as indicators of social decline. 'The aspects of the social malaise most commonly mentioned were: the decline in religious beliefs, the absence of a sense of purpose, the influence of the do-gooders' approach and the coddling by the welfare state' (Cohen, 1973: 62). The behaviour of the young people was often seen as a kind of disease. Through these processes from, in Cohen's view, relatively trivial occurrences, a moral panic was generated.

The generation of a moral panic in turn produces opinions and actions to do 'something about it'. Cohen (1973: 77) discusses these responses through three further categories: '(i) Sensitisation; (ii) the Societal Control Culture; (iii) Exploitation'. He argues that the process of sensitisation involves far more attention being taken of acts of 'hooliganism', the description of such acts in terms of mods and rockers when previously they may have been described as acts of other young people, and the expansion of the symbolisation process described above.

The reaction of the 'Societal Control Culture' is a particularly important part of Cohen's analysis. He examines three main agents of social control – the police, the courts and local 'action groups' – suggesting that three common elements were of particular importance in the actions of these institutions: diffusion, escalation and innovation. Reaction diffused away from the original point of occurrence to other institutions. Thus, for example:

in response to the Mods and Rockers, involvement diffused (not, of course, in a straight line) from the local police force, to collaboration with neighbouring forces, to regional collaboration, to co-ordination activity at Scotland Yard and the Home Office and to the involvement of Parliament and the legislature.

(Cohen, 1973: 86)

Furthermore, this process involved escalation of the perceived seriousness of the problem. Innovation involved the introduction, or ideas for introduction, of new methods of social control to deal with the perceived problem. Cohen discusses the actions of the different components of the control culture in some detail, before considering the exploitation of the phenomenon much more briefly. For example, consumer goods such as sunglasses were advertised using mod imagery. Cohen sees a 'flow' taking place of the kind shown here:

(i) *Initial deviance* leading to:
(ii) the *inventory* and
(iii) *sensitization* which feed back on each other so as to produce:
(iv) an *over-estimation* of the deviance which leads to:
(v) an *escalation* of the control culture.

(Cohen, 1973: 143)

In the final chapter of his book, Cohen considers the development of the subcultures of the mods and rockers although, as he subsequently recognised (1987: ii–iii), his analysis here was not particularly innovative, owing a lot to the earlier work of Downes (1966) who, drawing on the American subcultural literature, had

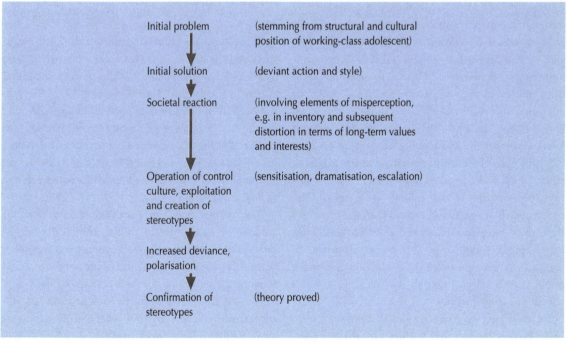

**Figure 9.1** Deviance amplification. (Source: Cohen, 1973: 199.)

239

argued that 'The English "corner boy" successfully traverses the humiliations of school and job allocation by his re-affirmation of traditional working-class values' (1966: 258). As Cohen says, 'It is quite true that the book was more a study of moral panics than of folk devils. Influenced by labelling theory, I wanted to study reaction; the actors themselves just flitted across the screen' (1987: iii). The discussion of the generation and nature of subcultures was taken forward in the work carried out at the Birmingham Centre for Contemporary Cultural Studies (see below).

The sort of approach that Cohen elaborated, which is represented in Figure 9.1 (p. 239), has been hugely influential.

## Moral panic updated

The idea of a moral panic has passed into everyday speech and examples of the process described by Cohen seem to occur at regular intervals. All sorts of groups from football hooligans and striking workers to single mothers, drug users and asylum seekers seem to be labelled as folk devils and to generate moral panics. (You may wish to consider other contemporary examples of your own.) In accord with the rather pessimistic tone of Cohen's work, these panics are seen by some commentators as strategies on the part of those in power to create diversions from 'real issues'. Thus, the idea of blaming 'asylum seekers' for delinquency and for taking up public services is used to divert attention from more 'important' issues such as causes of migration and political oppression in other countries. However, one problem with this point of view is that it is not clear that the wider public actually agrees with the definitions of these groups that are contained in the tabloid press. Indeed, Cohen himself found that significant proportions of the public were much less concerned about mods and rockers than the press hysteria would have led the commentator to believe. Thus these representations may be more important to members of the control culture than to the wider public, which does not mean that they are any less effective or consequential.

Furthermore, it can be suggested that various groups have become more sophisticated in their understanding and use of the idea of a moral panic since

Cohen's original analysis. For example, in discussion of the development and reaction to rave culture in Britain, Sarah Thornton (1994, 1995) argues that, in part due to the way that he focused his attention on national and local newspapers, Cohen misses the way in which moral panic is both a marketing strategy and something sought by potential 'folk devils' (see also Angela McRobbie, 1994). Thus many such groups would actually welcome negative tabloid coverage as it can promote the group and music more widely. As Thornton argues:

> Although negative reporting is disparaged, it is subject to anticipation, even aspiration. Affirmative tabloid coverage, on the other hand, is the kiss of death. Cultural studies and sociologies of moral panic have tended to position youth cultures as innocent victims of negative stigmatization. But mass media understanding is often a goal, not just an effect of youth's cultural pursuits. Moral panic is therefore a form of routinized hype orchestrated by the culture industries that target the market. Moralizing denunciations are, to quote one music monthly, a 'priceless PR campaign'. They render a subculture attractively subversive as no other promotional ploy can.
>
> (Thornton, 1994: 184)

Subcultures are as much generated by music magazines and the music press (which are themselves parts of multinational companies) as they are by subcultural adherents themselves (Thornton, 1994, 1995). They do not exist in some pure state ready to be exploited and demonised. Furthermore, most fanzines tended to appear after the tabloid moral panic rather than before it (1994: 185). They were thus heavily nostalgic for the supposed pure rave scene which had existed prior to tabloid exploitation!

The points made by Thornton should alert the student of moral panics to the complexity of the relation between subcultures, the media and societal or control culture reaction. While the idea of moral panic remains a useful tool, it should perhaps be used carefully in the context of thorough analysis, especially in a context where differentiated sources of information are available through electronic media.

Having considered some of the early material that

looked at the way in which subcultures are developed and the values that they express, as well as the importance of media reaction to them, it is now possible to consider the way in which the influential discussion of subculture at the **Birmingham Centre for Contemporary Cultural Studies** inflected these ideas in particular, distinctive and influential ways.

# 9.3 Youth subcultures in British cultural studies

Much research on subculture, which has focused on youth subcultures, draws on the two most important meanings of culture outlined in Chapter 1: firstly, that which uses culture to refer to the works and practices of artistic and intellectual activity. In this sense, music or

## Key influence 9.1

### The Centre for Contemporary Cultural Studies (CCCS)

Also known as the Birmingham Centre for Contemporary Cultural Studies or the 'Birmingham School', the Centre was the key site for the development of cultural studies. Birmingham is now less influential as cultural studies has expanded to become an international activity.

The Centre was founded by Richard Hoggart in 1964 initially within the English Department. Hoggart was the first director, with Stuart Hall as his deputy. Hall became director in 1968 when Hoggart left to work at UNESCO. Hall led the Centre through its most productive period before leaving in 1979. He was succeeded by his own deputy, Richard Johnson. In the wake of upheavals in the Social Sciences and Arts at the University of Birmingham, the Centre became the Department of Cultural Studies and the activity has since become part of the Sociology Department.

Founded in many ways to develop the approach formulated by Hoggart in *The Uses of Literacy* (1958), the Centre rapidly made its mark through its Stencilled Occasional Papers Series which included papers on topics as diverse as women domestic servants, the Kray twins and the theory of Karl Marx. It also produced

its own journal, *Working Papers in Cultural Studies*. These were the sites for the first publication of many of the Centre's best-known writers whose ideas later appeared in book form. By the 1970s, the Centre's activities were contextualised by a **Gramscian** (p. 38) Marxist emphasis on the role of culture in **resistance** (p. 178) and **hegemonic** (p. 73) domination. This informed the analyses in collective texts such as *Resistance through Rituals* (1976), *Policing the Crisis* (1978), *On Ideology* (1977) and *Working-Class Culture* (1979). The Marxist emphasis on class was contested by feminists at the Centre in *Women take Issue* (1978) and its relative inattention to 'race' in *The Empire Strikes Back* (1982). The work of Richard Johnson led to a more historical approach in *Making Histories* (1982). Writers associated with the Centre through this period include Stuart Hall, Paul Willis, Dick Hebdige, Angela McRobbie, Iain Chambers and Paul Gilroy. There are many others. The upheavals of the 1980s and the expansion of cultural studies made Birmingham less important, although it continued to publish a journal, *Cultural Studies from Birmingham*, and books.

The Centre's attention to youth culture, news, ideology, race, cultural politics and gender in ways that took popular culture seriously from within an academic Marxist approach was the key moment in the formation of the cultural studies approach. Authors once associated with the Centre continue to fill some of the most senior and influential positions in academic cultural studies. However, the points of view developed at Birmingham (the over-unified idea of a 'school' is very misleading) are now only a part of the much wider activity of cultural studies.

#### Further reading

Hall, S. and Jefferson, T. (eds) (1976) *Resistance through Rituals: Youth Subcultures in Post-war Britain*, London: Hutchinson.

Hall, S., Critcher, C., Jefferson, T., Clarke, J. and Roberts, B. (1978) *Policing the Crisis: Mugging, the State and Law and Order*, London: Macmillan.

Hall, S., Hobson, D., Lowe, A. and Willis, P. (eds) (1980) *Culture, Media, Language*, London: Hutchinson.

a painting is a form of culture, where college work, for example, is not. At times, this definition of culture involves a judgement of value. Thus, certain forms of writing, such as by Dickens or Shakespeare, are held to be proper 'culture' and works by writers such as Jeffrey Archer or Dan Brown to be trash. As we have shown, the second sense of culture is rather different, referring to the idea of culture as a 'way of life'. This more inclusive definition can be found in problematic expressions such as 'the American way of life' or 'British culture'. Both of these definitions fed into the development of what has become known as British Cultural Studies (Turner, 1990) in the **Centre for Contemporary Cultural Studies** (CCCS) at the University of Birmingham where many of the most important studies of youth subcultures have been carried out.

## Resistance through Rituals: the general approach

The cornerstone paper which outlines many of the concepts and themes pursued in the work from Birmingham is 'Subcultures, cultures and class' (Clarke *et al.*, 1976) in the collection *Resistance through Rituals* (Hall and Jefferson, 1976). Some key definitions are set out in this paper.

There are *seven* concepts introduced in this paper which need to be considered in some detail: culture, **hegemony** (p. 73), dominant culture, dominant ideology, class culture, subculture and parent culture. All of these are used extensively in CCCS work and in much of the subsequent literature on subcultures.

The definition of culture produced within this tradition explains that:

> we understand the word culture to refer to that level at which social groups develop distinct patterns of life, and give *expressive form* to their social and material life experience. Culture is the way, the forms, in which groups 'handle' the raw material of their social and material existence.
>
> (Clarke *et al.*, 1976: 10)

There are three aspects of social life identified in this definition: social experience, social groups and patterns of life. In their view, social groups develop distinct patterns of life, based on their own social experiences, in relation to other social groups and forms of experience. Culture is both a level or area of society (distinct from the economic or political) and the forms in which the raw material of social experience is handled.

We shall explore the particular way in which hegemony (p. 73) is subsequently used in this essay below. Clarke *et al.* further argue that there is a dominant culture which connects to the dominant class. However, they do not actually identify the content of this dominant culture, nor likewise do they explicate the specific content of the dominant **ideology** (p. 35), nor provide much detail on the conceptualisation of this concept, which is further discussed in Chapter 3.

The argument of Clarke *et al.* rests on Marxist premises, which is reflected in their assertion that classes are 'the most fundamental social groups'. This generates the further assumption that cultures are fundamentally class cultures. Subcultures are 'sub-sets – smaller, more localised and differentiated structures, within one or other of the larger cultural networks'. Subcultures in this approach have to be seen in a class context. Finally, the paper elucidated the concept of parent culture. Thus, there was a working-class parent culture which generated other distinguishable subcultures, as discussion of the East End working class shows (see Cohen 1980, below)

The analysis in the paper and, despite some differences of emphasis, in the CCCS tradition, is based around the study of the 'double articulation of youth subcultures'. Youth subcultures are connected, first, to their parent culture (in the case of working-class youth subcultures, this is to working-class culture), and second, to the dominant culture.

After outlining their general approach and some of their key concepts, Clarke *et al.* examine some of the different dimensions of the debate on youth and youth culture that had emerged since the Second World War. In what was a common mode of exposition in work from CCCS, the discussion seeks to outline and then recontextualise everyday debates and common sense. They begin by identifying the factors that had been thought in earlier literature to be responsible for the generation of the new youth culture. These included: firstly, affluence in that society in general, and young people in particular, had more money to spend; secondly, the spread of mass communication, especially television; thirdly, social dislocation brought on by the Second World War; fourthly, educational changes which produced more extensive participation; and finally, the emergence of new styles and fashions.

These factors in themselves were to be understood in the wider context of debate about social change since the war. There were three key terms in this debate: affluence, consensus and embourgeoisement. The new affluence, apparent agreement on politics and the decline of political dispute were, in the eyes of many commentators, leading the working class to adopt middle-class values and practices. Class was thought to be becoming less important in society. Clarke *et al.* recognise that there was evidence for the existence of some aspects of this idea. There had been a rise in living standards, although the established pattern of social inequality remained, and party politics did seem to be based on substantial agreement, with the two main parties between them gathering a very high proportion of the total votes cast in elections. The actual evidence for embourgeoisement was much less convincing, although there did appear to be some shifts in the values of more affluent workers. Despite this, class and social inequalities had not disappeared.

Clarke *et al.* are critical of the American deviance literature for its relative neglect of class. They also suggest that the beginnings of a more satisfactory approach to the study of youth subcultures had begun to be developed in Britain by Mike Brake and Graham Murdock, who had taken class seriously. The fault of these approaches was that, in attempting to see subcultures as engaged in collective 'problem-solving', these authors had accepted the idea of a problem 'too unproblematically'. They did not accord sufficient weight to aspects of class culture and class socialisation. The most sophisticated precursor to the *Resistance through Rituals* approach, which greatly influenced Clarke *et al.*, was a paper by Phil Cohen (1980, first published in 1972 in the CCCS journal *Working Papers in Cultural Studies*) which examined the nature of youth subcultures in the East End of London in the 1960s.

# Phil Cohen: working-class youth subcultures in East London

Phil Cohen (1980) argued that, after the Second World War from the 1950s onwards, the East End working-class community was disrupted by three factors: firstly, migration out of the area to new towns such as Harlow, Stevenage and Basildon; secondly, the redevelopment of housing involving the building of new tower blocks which were patterned on a middle-class nuclear family model that destroyed the communal spaces and the patterns of female support characteristic of the East End; and thirdly, a series of economic changes, which led to a 'polarization of the labour force' (Cohen, 1980: 80) between specialised, 'high tech', well-paid jobs and dead-end, unskilled labour.

One outcome of this process of dislocation was the development of youth subcultures, like teds, mods and skinheads, which opposed the working-class parent culture. In Cohen's (1980: 82) view, 'the internal conflicts of the parent culture came to be worked out in terms of generational conflict'. Furthermore Cohen argued that youth subcultures 'express and resolve, albeit "magically", the contradictions which remain hidden or unresolved in the parent culture' (1980: 82). Subcultures are ways of dealing with the difficulties that structural transformations in society have produced in the parent culture to which they belong. Following the pattern of the polarisation of the workforce between an upward or downward option, Cohen argues that youth subcultures can express such routes in a variety of different ways. Hence:

[M]ods, parkas, skinheads, crombies are a succession of subcultures which all correspond to the same parent culture and which attempt to work out, through a system of transformations, the basic problematic or contradiction which is inserted in the subculture by the parent culture.

(Cohen, 1980: 83)

This sort of approach was represented diagrammatically by Clarke *et al.* (1976), as shown in Figure 9.2. Cohen argued that there were upward (for example, mod) and downward (for example, skinhead)

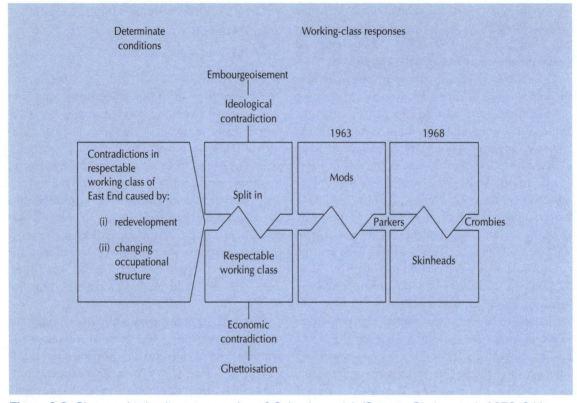

**Figure 9.2** Class and subcultures: a version of Cohen's model. (Source: Clarke *et al.*, 1976: 34.)

responses to these conditions which attempted to resolve structural problems in an ideological fashion.

## Ideology and hegemony

Clarke *et al.* (1976) identified a number of problems with Cohen's article, including the historical specificity of the analysis, the precise way in which the structural conditions affected the subcultural adherents, the causes of the upward and downward solutions and so on. However, they were concerned to build upon Cohen's approach which was therefore a crucial influence on their arguments. In particular they wanted to emphasise the idea that subcultures represented an ideological or, in a phrase influenced by the work on **ideology** (p. 36) of the French Marxist Louis Althusser (1971), an 'imaginary relation' to their real conditions of life.

Clarke *et al.* explore in some detail structural and class changes and the relations between dominant and

parent cultures which produce subcultures. The working class had been affected by changes in employment patterns and housing which affected the nature of the working-class family and the way in which it could act to protect the working class from the power of the dominant class. The generation of subcultures was also located in the changing patterns of **hegemony** (p. 73).

We have discussed this concept in other places (p. 72); but it is important to pay attention to the specific way in which this concept is used in this approach. Clarke *et al.* argue that:

Gramsci used the term 'hegemony' to refer to the moment when a ruling class is able, not only to coerce a subordinate class to conform to its interests, but to exert a 'hegemony' or 'total social authority' over subordinate classes. This involves the exercise of a special kind of power – the power to frame alternatives and contain opportunities, to win and shape consent, so that the granting of

## Box 9.1

### Some readings and pictures of subcultures

Thus the 'Teddy Boy' expropriation of an upper-class style of dress 'covers' the gap between largely manual, unskilled, near-lumpen real careers and life-chances, and the 'all-dressed-up-and-nowhere-to-go' experience of Saturday evening. Thus, in the expropriation and fetishisation of consumption and style itself, the 'Mods' cover for the gap between the never-ending-weekend and Monday's resumption of boring, dead-end work. Thus, in the resurrection of an archetypal and 'symbolic'(but, in fact, anachronistic) form of working-class dress, in the displaced focussing on the football match and the 'occupation' of the football 'ends', Skinheads reassert, but 'imaginarily', the values of a class, the essence of a style, a kind of 'fan-ship' to which few working-class adults any longer subscribe: they 're-present' a sense of territory and locality which the planners and speculators are rapidly destroying: they 'declare' as alive and well a game which is being commercialised, professionalised and spectacularised. 'Skins Rule, OK.'

Clarke et al. (1976: 48)

A young teddy boy, 1955. (Source: Getty Images.)

*right:* A skinhead, 1980. (Source: Getty Images.)

*left:* A mod on his scooter, 1964. (Source: Getty Images.)

## Box 9.2

### Structures, cultures and biographies

*Structures* are the set of socially-organised positions and experiences of the class in relation to the major institutions and structures. These positions generate a set of common relations and experiences from which meaningful actions – individual and collective – are constructed.

*Cultures* are the range of socially-organised and patterned responses to these basic material and social conditions. Though cultures form, for each group, a set of traditions – lines of action inherited from the past – they must always be collectively constructed anew in each generation.

*Biographies* are the 'careers' of particular individuals through these structures and cultures – the means by which individual identities and life-histories are constructed out of collective experiences. Biographies recognise the element of individuation in the paths which individual lives take through collective structures and cultures, but they must not be conceived as either wholly individual or free-floating.

(Clarke *et al.*, 1976: 57)

legitimacy to the dominant classes appears not only 'spontaneous' but natural and normal.

(Clarke *et al.*, 1976: 38)

Furthermore, such hegemony 'works through ideology, but it does not consist of false ideas, perceptions, or definitions. It works primarily by inserting the subordinate class into the key institutions and structures which support the power and social authority of the dominant order' (Clarke *et al.*, 1976: 39). Hegemony is not consistent in that at some points the dominant class is dominant without the aid of hegemony. Hence, at times 'economic crisis' and 'unemployment' do the job just as well. Furthermore, at other points the dominant class will be overthrown and by definition hegemony does not exist. In sum, 'the idea of "permanent class hegemony" or of "permanent incorporation" must be ditched' (1976: 41).

Within the context of such patterns of domination the working class had won space for themselves, where they often developed their own forms and ways of life. Subcultures do the same sort of thing, winning space for young working-class people. 'They "solve", but in an imaginary way, problems which at the concrete material level remain unresolved' (Clarke *et al.*, 1976: 47–8).

Clarke *et al.* apply this idea to three subcultures in the passage reproduced in Box 9.1. Furthermore, 'In organising their response to these experiences, working-class youth subcultures take some things principally from the located "parent" culture: but they apply and transform them to the situations and experiences characteristic of their distinctive group-life and generational experience' (1976: 53).

## Structures, cultures and biographies

Three key terms are used by the authors of this article to summarise their approach: *structures, cultures* and *biographies*. The definitions given by Clarke *et al.* (1976: 57) of these are detailed in Box 9.2.

These can be used as keywords to remember the theory and approach developed in *Resistance through Rituals*. The essay by Clarke *et al.* concludes with a rather dated section on the counter-culture and a discussion of the reaction to youth which considers the idea of moral panic introduced above. The book also contains a number of discussions of specific subcultures – teds, mods and skinheads – and elaborations of some of the key concepts such as style. It also includes some significant criticisms of the approach. However, before these difficulties are discussed it is important to consider some of the other most important work that emanated from CCCS in this period.

# 9.4 Three classic studies from the Birmingham Centre for Contemporary Cultural Studies

In this section we examine three studies which have been very influential exemplars of the CCCS approach: *Learning to Labour* (Willis, 1977), *Profane Culture* (Willis, 1978) and *Subculture: The Meaning of Style* (Hebdige, 1979).

## Paul Willis: *Learning to Labour*

*Learning to Labour* has achieved the status of a classic text. Its title and subtitle – *How Working Class Kids Get Working Class Jobs* – summarise its content clearly. Working in the context of a discussion of how school prepares young people for different slots in the labour market and therefore ensures the continued reproduction of a division of labour in contemporary capitalist society, Willis demonstrates the continuities between the culture of a group of secondary school working-class rebels and the culture of their subsequent employment.

Willis's study mainly focuses on a group of 12 boys in a school that he calls Hammertown Boys. He identifies the different components of the culture of the boys whom he terms 'lads'. The lads oppose the authority of the school and they reject the conformist attitudes of those boys who follow the accepted ethic of the school who they call 'ear 'oles' or 'lobes', defining themselves as a group with an oppositional stance. One of the greatest sins that one of the 'lads' can commit is to 'grass' to the school authorities. The 'lads' attempt to get out of as much work as possible and to miss school if they can. At school they are concerned to 'have a laff', enjoying their own culture in the context of the school. This can involve goading teachers, bending the rules to see how far they can go and so on. They try to bring excitement into what in other ways may be boring lives and this can occur through expressions of 'hard' masculinity and in fighting. On one hand, women are treated as sex objects, and the lads will attempt to see 'how far they can go'; on the other, a steady girlfriend will be looked upon as a future wife to service domestic needs. In the often reported and continuing double standard of sexual behaviour, women who are sexually active will be derided. The 'lads' were also racist in behaviour and beliefs, expressing hatred of Pakistanis and Jamaicans, and reported being involved in 'paki bashing'.

Willis argues that the main contours of this culture, despite bringing the 'lads' into conflict with the school authorities, actually prepared them for incorporation in forms of repetitive, heavy industrial work on the factory shop floor. This was also based around forms of masculinity, practical joking, getting away with what you can, sexual bragging and so on. So in adopting what in some ways can be seen as an oppositional culture (to the school), or in ways opposing the dominant culture of their experience, by drawing on the resources of their working-class (male) parent culture the 'lads' were actually preparing themselves for the world of manual labour. In lots of ways this aids the reproduction of established patterns of exploitation. The culture of opposition actually suited the dominant culture.

## Paul Willis: *Profane Culture*

In *Profane Culture*, which reports on research carried out before that discussed in *Learning to Labour*, Willis (1978) examined various dimensions of the lives of two youth subcultural groups in the late 1960s: the motorbike boys and hippies. While these examples are rather dated, it is the nature of the link that Willis makes between different aspects of the lifestyle of these groups that has resonated through work on subcultures. Thus, for example, Willis argued that the musical preferences of these groups were intimately connected to the nature of their lives. The motorbike boys' preference for early rock'n'roll in a 45rpm single format and the hippies' like of album-based progressive rock was no accident. Rock'n'roll music matched the restlessness and mobility of the motorbike boys' lives:

the suppression of structured time in the music, its ability to stop, start and be faded, matches the motor-bike boys' restless concrete life style. As we have seen, it is no accident that the boys preferred singles, nor is it an accident that the rock 'n' roll form is the most suited to singles and its modern technology (fading, etc.). Both the music and its 'singles' form are supremely relevant to the style of the bike culture.

(Willis, 1978: 77)

Willis mounts a similar sort of argument about the homologous relationships between different aspects of a youth subculture for the hippies (see especially Willis, 1978: 168–9). In Hebdige's words (1979: 113) this expresses: 'the symbolic fit between the values and life-styles of a group, its subjective experience and the musical forms it uses to express or reinforce its focal concerns'. This means that subcultures are structured in that different aspects of the lifestyle of the subculture fit together to form a whole. So there is a homology between an 'alternative value system', 'hallucinogenic drugs' and progressive rock for the hippie subculture. Subcultures express a response to a set of conditions and the different aspects of the subculture are tied together into structured, relatively coherent wholes. The introduction of this concept, which was also used by Clarke *et al.*, was a very significant innovation on Willis's part.

## Dick Hebdige: *Subculture: The Meaning of Style*

Hebdige (1979) developed the reading of the styles of subcultural groups using the tools of the **structuralist** (p. 17) and **semiotic** (p. 29) approaches discussed in Chapter 2. In particular, he focused on the different dimensions of the style of subcultural groups. Using the general definition of culture proposed by Clarke *et al.* (1976), Hebdige argued that the styles expressed by different subcultures are a response to social conditions and experiences. Furthermore, according to Hebdige, such styles often encode an opposition to the dominant or **hegemonic** (p. 73) forms of culture associated with dominant groups. Such challenges are often indirect and can involve the utilisation and transformation of forms of culture that were previously the property of dominant groups. In engaging in such practices, sub-cultural members act as *bricoleurs* engaging in a process

of *bricolage*, responding to the world around them by improvising in a structured fashion, creating meanings that are different from those of the dominant culture or dominant groups. As Hebdige says about the teddy boy's style:

> In this way the teddy boy's theft and transformation of the Edwardian style revived in the early 1950s by Saville Row for wealthy young men about town can be construed as an act of bricolage.

(Hebdige, 1979: 104)

Hebdige argues that subcultures often **resist** (p. 170) the dominant social order, though indirectly and in symbolic ways. However, he also argues that forms of subcultural expression are often incorporated into the dominant social order through two main routes. Firstly, there is the commodity form which involves 'the con-version of subcultural signs (dress, music, etc.) into mass-produced objects'. Secondly is the 'labelling" and re-definition of deviant behaviour by dominant groups – the police, the media, the judiciary' (Hebdige, 1979: 94) in a process of ideological incorporation.

This sort of account of the ways in which subcul-tural groups produce new and resistant meanings which are then bought off or incorporated by the capi-talist system is now relatively familiar. It entails the notion that there is some kind of sphere where 'authentic' meanings are produced which are then cor-rupted. However, Thornton (1994, 1995), as discussed above, problematises this aspect of Hebdige's work, showing how media images are involved in subcultures from their inception.

## 9.5 Youth subcultures and gender

One of the most important problems with the litera-ture discussed in this chapter so far is its almost exclusive focus on boys or men. This myopia was first challenged from within the CCCS approach by **Angela McRobbie** (p. 249) and Jenny Garber who asked four main questions:

(1) Are girls really absent from the main post-war

subcultures? Or are they present but invisible? (2) Where present and visible, were their roles the same, but more marginal, than boys; or were they different? (3) Whether marginal or different, is the position of girls specific to the subcultural option; or do their roles reflect the more general social-subordination of women in the central areas of mainstream culture – home, work, school, leisure? (4) If subcultural options are not readily available to girls, what are the different but complementary ways in which girls organise their cultural life? And are these, in their own terms, subcultural in form?

(McRobbie and Garber, 1976: 211)

In response to (1) they argued that, at least partly because of the male bias of previous investigations, it was difficult to answer the question they had set. As the men who had studied subcultures had not looked at the possible participation of girls in them, girls' invisibility tended to be a self-fulfilling prophecy. In pursuing questions (2) and (3) they looked in more detail at the parts that women have played in three subcultures. Firstly, in the rocker, greaser or motorbike subculture as described by Willis, women were subordinate. They were passengers on the motorbikes – they did not control them. Secondly, they considered the mod girls of the early 1960s, whom they see as prominent within

## Key influence 9.2

### Angela McRobbie (1951–)

Angela McRobbie is a British cultural analyst. She combines the study of different dimensions of youth culture with commentary on developments in cultural theory and politics.

McRobbie studied as a postgraduate at the **Centre for Contemporary Cultural Studies** (CCCS) (p. 241) at the University of Birmingham. She lectured in London before moving to Loughborough University. She is currently Professor of Communications at Goldsmith's, University of London.

McRobbie's most well-known work centres on the analysis of gender in youth culture. She was critical of the 'malestream' nature of work carried out at CCCS on youth subcultures, emphasising the need to critique work by such as Paul Willis and Dick Hebdige for its lack of attention to gender, and the partial nature of its consideration of women. Moreover, she argued for the need to analyse the nature of the cultural life of young women, to see if this is structured in different ways to that of boys. This approach resulted in papers on the culture of femininity, romance, pop music and teenybop culture, the

teenage magazine *Jackie* and so on. These earlier researches can be found collected in *Feminism and Youth Culture* (1991). McRobbie developed this approach and the entailed research and argument through the 1980s. She wrote influentially on the importance of dance in female youth culture and pointed to the developing informal economy of second-hand markets in a paper in her own edited collection *Zoot Suits and Second-hand Dresses* (1989). Cultural change in gender roles (as well as her own position as a parent) led to reconsideration of some of her earlier arguments. She has analysed rave culture and the opportunity that it provides for new roles for young women as well as discussing the shift to the centrality of pop in magazines for young girls such as *Just Seventeen*. These concerns were connected to the influence and evaluation of debates about **postmodernism** (p. 295) in theory and culture which are to be found in *Postmodernism and Popular Culture* (1994). She has also commented on debates in left cultural politics,

especially around the concept of 'New Times'. She continues to work on gender, popular culture and the culture industries.

McRobbie's essays have had a large impact on the consideration of youth culture. She has been at the forefront of arguments emphasising the importance of taking gender into account and for the need to examine the works of male writers for the versions of masculinity they contain.

#### Further reading

McRobbie's work has appeared in essay form. Excellent collections now exist:

McRobbie, A. (1991) *Feminism and Youth Culture*, Basingstoke: Macmillan.

McRobbie, A. (1994) *Postmodernism and Popular Culture*, London; Routledge.

McRobbie, A. (ed.) (1989) *Zoot Suits and Second-hand Dresses*, Basingstoke: Macmillan.

the mod subculture. Thirdly, they examined hippie culture, identifying two particular confining roles for women: the earth mother and the pre-Raphaelite fragile lady.

McRobbie and Garber argued that the places for women in the subcultures so far described were related to their wider social roles. They also suggested that girls tended to organise their cultural life differently to boys, forming a more home-based, romantic or 'teenybop' culture. This point and others made by McRobbie were developed in a subsequent critique of the male-dominated nature of research on subcultures (McRobbie, 1980) which argued that there are two main approaches that can be taken to previous male-dominated writing on subcultures. Firstly, such accounts can be dismissed, or accepted as applicable only to boys, and attention placed on the different nature of girls' culture. Secondly, previous accounts, such as those by Willis (1977) and Hebdige (1979), can be read 'against the grain' to see what they can offer for the analysis of masculinity, both in the nature of the subcultures and the writing on them.

In developing her points about the different nature of girls' culture, McRobbie argues that the street is a potentially dangerous place for girls:

younger girls tend to stay indoors or to congregate in youth clubs; those with literally nowhere else to go but the street frequently become pregnant within a year and disappear back into the home to be absorbed by childcare and domestic labour.

(McRobbie, 1980: 47)

McRobbie argued that the use of drink and drugs can induce the same sort of perils: 'it is clear from my recent research, for example, that girls are reluctant to drink precisely because of the sexual dangers of drunkenness' (1980: 47).

# The teenybop culture of romance

McRobbie suggested that the working-class girls she studied tended to form a teenybop culture based around romance. These girls spent more time in the home, at least partly because of the dangerous nature of public places, like the street. Frith (1983) added three

other aspects to this when he argued: that girls are more subject to parental control and discipline than boys are; that girls are often expected to carry out work in the home, in a way that boys are not, a point that was illustrated graphically by McRobbie (1978) when she pointed out that girls were expected to perform large amounts of work in the home for very little financial recompense; and, finally, that girls spend more time at home getting ready to go out than boys do.

This form of girls' subculture identified in the 1970s consisted of the following features:

1 The centrality of the home and often of the bedroom. Girls tended to get together with other girls and listen to records by their favourite artists in each other's bedrooms.

2 Girls formed a *teenybop* culture, where there was a romantic attachment to one star or group. There is a history of different stars and groups that have filled such a role.

3 When girls did go out, it was most likely to be a youth club.

4 Dance was important to girls in ways that it was not for boys. McRobbie (1984, 1993) has continued to stress the importance of dance to girls.

5 For the girls in McRobbie's study, the relationship with a *best friend* was very important and they valued this more than their relationships with boys.

6 The idea of romance was very important. Many of the girls, despite at times showing a 'realistic' appreciation of some aspects of marriage, place great stress on the idea of romance and the romantic attachment to one boy. This can be related to the continued existence of a sexual double standard, where girls could easily become known as 'slags' if they went out with several boys (see the discussion of *Learning to Labour*, Willis 1977, above).

7 McRobbie argued that the girls she studied stressed some dominant ideas of femininity in an exaggerated fashion. This may form part of a culture that opposed the perceived school ethic of responsibility, hard work and seriousness. The girls spent much time talking about boys and wanted to bend the school rules about dress and make-up in as fashionable a direction as possible. McRobbie argued that

this culture, while it may oppose official culture in some ways, reinforces the culture of romance and the idea of femininity which is a part of this. This parallels the argument advanced by Willis (1977) concerning the way in which the exaggeration of masculinity among working-class boys, in opposition to school norms, suited them for manual labour.

Various writers have identified some problems with this idea of the teenybop culture of romance. Firstly, McRobbie may have underestimated the participation and seriousness of the commitment of some girls to 'deviant' subcultural groups (for example, Smith, 1978). Secondly, Cowie and Lees (1981) found that girls had a more realistic appraisal of the potential problems in marriage than McRobbie found in her group. Cowie and Lees found far more emphasis on having a good time before marriage. Thirdly, Cowie and Lees (1981) suggested that McRobbie's work tended to isolate a discrete female youth subculture, over-integrating and separating it from the relations between men and women which existed in society more widely. Relatedly, they argued that too much emphasis is placed on the **resistance** (p. 170) entailed in the culture of femininity. Fourthly, McRobbie's work concentrated mainly on white working-class girls, and more evidence is needed about black and middle-class girls for comparison. Furthermore, it might be that some of this work is now rather dated. This point can be considered through an examination of some of McRobbie's more recent work.

## Pop music, rave culture and gender

In her earlier work, McRobbie had drawn attention to the role of magazines like *Jackie* in the culture of romance. In reconsidering this argument, McRobbie (1991) demonstrated the difference between contemporary magazines like *Just Seventeen* and *Jackie*. Romance has drastically declined in importance and pop and fashion are central, leading to a greater emphasis on image and the pop star. McRobbie argues that, 'It is pop rather than romance which now operates as a kind of conceptual umbrella giving a sense of identity to these productions' (1991: 168). In such girls' magazines:

there is an overwhelming interest in personal information. The magazines increasingly play the role of publicist for the various bands who fall into the teenybopper camp. In return their pages are filled with glossy pictures and they can claim to have a direct line to the stars. This makes for cheap and easy copy. Three pages can be covered in a flash with the help of a transatlantic telephone call, a tape-recorder and a selection of publicity shots often provided by the record company.

(McRobbie, 1991: 169)

In McRobbie's view, pop music is more important to girls now than it was in the 1970s. However, girls are not only involved with pop music of the teenybop type, and McRobbie has also drawn attention to their participation in rave culture. She argued that such culture can be connected to drastic changes in femininity over recent years in Britain, which have opened up the possibility of new roles for women, suggesting that 'girls both black and white have been "unhinged" from their traditional gender position while the gender and class destiny of their male counterparts has remained more stable' (McRobbie, 1993: 408). McRobbie suggests that white middle-class women are increasing their participation in traditional professions like medicine and that black working-class girls are more likely to go into higher and further education than their male peers. Moreover, McRobbie reiterates some of the points already made about the changing nature of girls' magazines, but develops her arguments about dance. She points to the continuity of rave culture with earlier cultures in that 'dance is where girls were always found in subcultures. It was their only entitlement.' However, 'in rave it becomes the motivating force for the entire subculture' (McRobbie, 1993: 419). The centrality of dance allows a far more important place for girls within such contemporary subcultures. However, in continuity with earlier work, McRobbie still sees the danger of these occasions for girls, even if at this later date it is as a parent rather than as a sociological observer.

## 9.6 Youth subcultures and race

The most significant consideration of 'race' from within the **Centre for Contemporary Cultural Studies** (p. 241) had come in the collectively authored *Policing the Crisis* (Hall *et al.,* 1978). This considered media construction of 'mugging' in the context of the re-patterning of hegemony in Britain. More specifically in the context of consideration of subcultures, Hebdige (1979) had stressed the centrality of black culture and the black presence in Britain in the generation of the style of white subcultures. Hebdige's interest was in the effects of black culture on white youth. 'Race' was reconsidered in *The Empire Strikes Back* (Centre for Contemporary Cultural Studies, 1982). This collection of articles examined the place of race in the political problems of British capitalism in the 1970s; explored and criticised representations, theories and investigations of race in mainstream sociology; examined representations of black criminality; and considered the challenge presented to white feminism by black women and the political experience of Asian women in Britain. The predominant tone of the volume was a critique of what had gone before and the **ideological** (p. 35) or 'common-sensical' images of race that had informed so-called scientific research.

Some of these themes were further developed by **Paul Gilroy** (p. 131) (1987) which built upon the discussions of the earlier collective CCCS volume. Again, this book criticised a great deal of established work, and sought to explore the relations between race and class in contemporary Britain. It examines a number of different dimensions of black expressive culture and includes extensive discussions of black music (see also Hebdige, 1987). In more recent work, Gilroy (e.g. 1993b) continued to emphasise the nature of black culture in the contemporary world, in developing an alternative account of the nature of **modernity** (p. 131) (see further, Chapter 5).

For present purposes, it is important to note that there was relatively little discussion of subculture in this predominantly critical and reframing literature. There had been studies, from outside the CCCS tradition, of black subcultures in Bristol in the work of

Ken Pryce (1979), but one of the important studies influenced by this critique re-examined the idea of racial identity in contemporary Birmingham, although his primary emphasis was on white youth.

## Simon Jones's *Black Culture, White Youth*: new identities in multiracial cities

Simon Jones's (1988) book on *Black Culture, White Youth* falls into two relatively discrete parts. In the first he presents an overview of the development of reggae and its connection to forms of culture in Britain and Jamaica. However, it is the second half of the book, which contains an ethnography of black and white youth in Birmingham, that is of greater interest. Jones discusses the formation of identity in a multiracial area of the city of Birmingham in the English Midlands. Thus many white boys had adopted forms of culture that would in more conventional analyses be seen as black. In particular, 'Black' language was used to express opposition to authority on the part of white children (1988: 149).

Reggae was adopted by the young white people growing up in this environment, and Jones shows how different themes from Jamaican music were adapted by young white men and women (see also Jeater, 1992). Thus, he maintains that:

Black music generally and Jamaican music in particular have functioned as transmitters of oppositional values and liberating pleasures to different generations of whites for nearly three decades. They have consistently supplied white youth with the raw material for their own distinctive forms of cultural expression. Through the political discourses of Rastafari, reggae has provided young whites with a collective language and symbolism of rebellion that has proved resonant to their own predicaments and to their experiences of distinct, but related, forms of oppression.

(Jones, 1988: 231)

However, Jones recognises contradictions that existed around these modes of appropriation. Thus, 'powerful feelings of attraction to black culture could easily coexist with perceptions of that culture as threatening and with resentment and fear of black people' (Jones, 1988: 216).

Jones suggests that new forms of 'racial' identity are being formed in parts of Birmingham and other inner-city metropolitan areas. He ends his book with a quotation from one of the people he studied which captures this. He says:

[in Jo-Jo's] eloquent conclusion is captured both the reality of the new 'England' that is already emerging, as well as the hope that such an England might itself not be 'recognisable as the same nation it has been', or perhaps, one day, 'as a nation at all':

Its like, I love this place ... there's no place like home ... Balsall Heath is the centre of the melting-pot, man, 'cos all I ever see when I go out is half-Arab, half-Pakistani, half-Jamaican, half-Scottish, half-Irish, I know 'cos I am [half-Scottish-Irish] ... Who am I? ... Tell me? Who do I belong to? They criticise me, the good old England. Alright then, where do I belong? ... you know, I was brought up with blacks, Pakistanis, Africans, Asians, everything, you name it ... Who do I belong to? I'm just a broad person. The earth is mine. You know, 'we was not born in England, we was not born in Jamaica' . .. we was born **here** man! It's our right! That's the way I see it ... That's the way I deal with it.

(Jones, 1988: 239–40)

Jones's discussion resonates with those **postmodernist** (p. 295) arguments, outlined at other points in this book, that suggest that there has been a 'decentring' of our **identities** (p. 142) in contemporary culture. For example, it has been suggested by a number of writers that we no longer have the same attachments to place as earlier generations. This might be the result of living in a society where, in some respects, it is easier to see what is happening on the other side of the world through television coverage than it is to observe events at the other end of the street.

In an introductory discussion of the idea, Hall (1992b) distinguishes three concepts of identity: 'Enlightenment', 'sociological' and 'post-modern'. The 'Enlightenment' concept rested on the idea of the existence of an essential core to identity which was born

with the individual and unfolded through his or her life. The sociological concept argued that a coherent identity is formed in relations with others and thus develops and changes over time. The postmodern subject is thought to have no fixed or essential identity. In postmodern societies identities have become 'dislocated'. The emphasis on identity shifts the focus on the CCCS approach from class to more diffuse sources of social belonging.

# 9.7 The Birmingham Centre for Contemporary Cultural Studies and youth subcultures: a general critique

At this point it is necessary to consider some of the main points made against the CCCS approach to youth subcultures. In a very useful overall critique, Gary Clarke (1990) makes a number of specific criticisms of work from CCCS:

1  Much of this writing is imprecise on the nature of the 'structural location' of subcultures and the nature of the problem solving involved in the subculture.

2  There is relatively little explanation of where the different subcultural styles actually come from. For example, why does one working-class subculture adopt the foppish sartorial style of the Edwardian era, while another caricatures the boots and braces dress of the factory worker?

3  There is a rigidity in the analysis, as the subcultures that are identified tend to be 'essentialist and non-contradictory', meaning that there is little attention paid to variations of style and commitment within different subcultures. In part this is a consequence of the tendency for these analyses to start from subcultures and work backwards to class situations and contradictions. This leads to a kind of 'freezing' of distinct subcultures.

4  There is a lack of attention to the way in which individuals move in and out of subcultures. Thus, Clarke

(1990: 82–3) argues that Phil Cohen 'classifies Crombies and parkas as distinct subcultures, but surely the only "problem" which distinguished them from skins and mods respectively was the need to keep warm'.

5 There is a dichotomy between subcultures and the rest of young people, who are in the mainstream.

Clarke identifies *three* important consequences that stem from these criticisms. Firstly, there is the lack of consideration of 'subcultural flux and dynamic nature of styles' (1990: 84). Secondly, there is the separation of subcultures from the rest of society which is incorporated into a 'consensus' or dominant social relations. Thirdly, a 'vague concept of style' is elevated 'to the status of an objective category' (Clarke, 1990: 84).

Stanley Cohen (1987) used the introduction to a new edition of *Folk Devils and Moral Panics* to develop a critique of the CCCS approach, which had become influential since his book was originally published. Cohen organised his critique with respect to the Birmingham keywords of structure, culture and biography.

With respect to structure, Cohen argues that in much recent work on subculture there is an 'over-facile drift to historicism' (1987: viii). By this phrase Cohen suggests that there is too much contextualisation and overemphasis on historical development within the Birmingham work, which often involves the particular emphasis of one historical variable at the expense of a variety of others. He argues that often 'a single and one-dimensional historical trend is picked out – commercialization, repression, bourgeoisification, destruction of community, erosion of leisure values – and then projected onto a present (often by the same sociologist's own admission) which is much more complicated, contradictory or ambiguous' (1987: viii-ix).

Moving on to consider the area of culture, Cohen (1987: x) characterises the Birmingham approach to style in terms of two dominant themes, which should come as no surprise by this stage:

1 Style 'is essentially a type of **resistance** (p. 170) to subordination'.

2 '[T]he form taken by this resistance is somehow symbolic or magical, in the sense of not being an actual, successful solution to whatever is the problem.'

Cohen makes a number of points against this approach. Firstly, he maintains that it is over-simplistic to decode styles only in terms of resistance and opposition. In his view, styles may be both reactionary and indeed inconsistent. Thus, some aspects may be oppositional and others reactionary. Secondly, he suggests that the development of style is often seen as somehow internal to a group. Commercialisation comes later. In fact, as we have seen, there are much more intimate relations between the development of subcultures and commercial activities. Thirdly, Cohen argues that too often the activities of subcultural adherents are understood or interpreted in the context of traditions of English working-class resistance to dominance. Thus, Cohen (1987: xiii) maintains that 'where we are really being directed is towards the "profound line of historical continuity" between today's delinquents and their "equivalents" in the past'. This leads to the fourth issue of whether subcultural members are 'aware' of what they are doing, whether they are doing it intentionally, or would see it in the same terms as the analyst. Cohen's point is that these theories, especially Hebdige (1979), play down the meaning of style and subcultures to those who are a part of it. He contends that 'it is hard to say which is the more sociologically incredible: a theory which postulates cultural dummies who give homologous meaning to all artefacts surrounding them or a theory which suggests that individual meanings do not matter at all' (Cohen, 1987: xv). Finally, Cohen raises a number of issues concerning the methods and results of the readings performed by the likes of Hebdige (1979). He poses the question of why we should believe the interpretations offered of these subcultures and to what extent there is any rigour in the way in which they have been arrived at. A graphic example of this point can be seen in the extract from Cohen in Box 9.3 which criticises Hebdige's reading of the symbolism of the swastika.

## Box 9.3

### Stanley Cohen's critique of Hebdige's reading of the symbolism of the swastika

Let me conclude this section by giving an example of the dangers of searching the forest of symbols without such a method – or indeed any method. This is the example often used by Hebdige and other theorists of punk: the wearing of the swastika emblem. Time and time again, we are assured that although this symbol is 'on one level' intended to outrage and shock, it is really being employed in a meta-language: the wearers are ironically distancing themselves from the very message that the symbol is usually intended to convey. Displaying a swastika (or singing lyrics like 'Belsen was a gas') shows how symbols are stripped from their natural context, exploited for empty effect, displayed through mockery, distancing, irony, parody, inversion.

But how are we to know this? We are never told much about the 'thing': when, how, where, by whom or in what context it is worn. We do not know what, if any, difference exists between indigenous and sociological explanations. We are given no clue about how these particular actors manage the complicated business of distancing and irony. In the end, there is no basis

whatsoever for choosing between this particular sort of interpretation and any others: say, that for many or most of the kids walking around with swastikas on their jackets, the dominant context is simply conformity, blind ignorance or knee-jerk racism.

Something more of an answer is needed to such questions than simply quoting Genet or Breton. Nor does it help much to have Hebdige's admission (about a similar equation) that such interpretations are not open to being tested by standard sociological procedures: 'Though it is undeniably there in the social structure, it is there as an immanence, as a submerged possibility, as an existential option; and one cannot verify an existential option scientifically – you either see it or you don't.'

Well, in the swastika example, I don't. And, moreover, when Hebdige does defend this particular interpretation of punk, he does it not by any existential leap but by a good old-fashioned positivist appeal to evidence: punks, we are told, 'were not generally sympathetic to the parties of the extreme right' and showed 'widespread support for the anti-Fascist movement'.

These statements certainly constitute evidence, not immanence – though not particularly good evidence and going right against widespread findings about the racism and support for restrictive immigration policies among substantial sections of working-class youth.

I do not want to judge one reading against the other nor to detract from the considerable interest and value of this new decoding work. We need to be more sceptical though of the exquisite aesthetics which tell us about things being fictional and real, absent and present, caricatures and re-assertions. This language might indeed help by framing a meaning to the otherwise meaningless; but this help seems limited when we are drawn to saying about skinhead attacks on Pakistani immigrants: 'Every time the boot went in, a contradiction was concealed, glossed over or made to disappear'. It seems to me – to borrow from the language of contradictions – that both a lot more and a lot less was going on. Time indeed to leave the forest of symbols; and ' . . . shudder back thankfully into the light of the social day'.

(Cohen, 1987: xvii–xviii)

Cohen also examines the issue of biography. He suggests that the Birmingham approach tends to focus too much on the spectacular and not enough on everyday deviance or 'ordinary' working-class activities. Furthermore, the boundaries around subcultures are often drawn in far too tight a manner. Cohen maintains that they are actually much looser and that people drift in and out of them over time and indeed at one point in time. Moreover, can the theory explain why one individual becomes involved in a subculture and others do not?

In this vein, Clarke argues that there is a need to

study what all categories of youth are doing, rather than just subcultures:

> It is true that most youths do not enter into subcultures in the elite form described in the literature, but large numbers do draw on particular elements of subcultural style and create their own meanings and uses of them.
>
> (Clarke, 1990: 92)

Furthermore, he suggests that there are important differences in the early 1980s from the situation described in the 1960s and 1970s by the classic writers from Birmingham. Thus, there was the combination of styles involved in movements like punk and two-tone, and the argument that 'new wave' broke the 'distinction between "teenyboppers" and youth' based around the distinction between LPs and singles. Thus, Clarke's general conclusion is that:

> what is required is an analysis of the activities of all youths to locate continuities and discontinuities in culture and social relations and to discover the meaning these activities have for the youths themselves.
>
> (Clarke, 1990: 95)

Some later literature which has attempted to take up this challenge is analysed in the next section.

## 9.8 Aspects of youth culture

Willis *et al.* (1990) argue that as human beings we are symbolically creative, saying that 'we argue for symbolic creativity as an integral ("ordinary") part of the human condition, not as the inanimate peaks (popular or remote) rising above the mists' (Willis *et al.*, 1990: 6). Being symbolically creative involves work of a **symbolic** (p. 214) kind, which is:

> the application of human capacities to and through, on and with symbolic resources and raw materials (collections of signs and symbols – for instance, the language as we inherit it as well as texts, songs, films, images and artefacts of all kinds) to produce meanings.
>
> (Willis *et al.*, 1990: 10)

The basic elements of symbolic work include language and the active body, and symbolic creativity involves the 'production of *new* ... meanings intrinsically attached to feelings, to energy, to excitement and psychic movement' (Willis *et al.*, 1990: 11). A number of different products are produced through symbolic work and symbolic creativity. These include our own individual identities, the location of those identities in a wider social context and the notion that we have the capacity to change things in some respect. Thus, in a general sense, Willis *et al.* argue that:

> In a way the spectacular subcultures of the 1950s and 60s prefigured some of the general shifts we are claiming for the contemporary situation. They defined themselves very early and gained their very spectacle from seeking visible identities and styles outside or against work and working respectabilities. Now the idea of a spectacular subculture is strictly impossible because all style and taste cultures, to some degree or another, express something of a general trend to find and make identity outside the realm of work.
>
> (Willis *et al.*, 1990: 16)

However, it does seem to be the case that some subcultures are rather more spectacular than others.

Willis's book explores the symbolic creativity of young people across a number of different dimensions, including television, VCR and microcomputer use, relationships to film, advertising, and magazines and engagements with fashion, pub culture, street culture, sport and romance. Perhaps for current purposes one of its most important points is the attempt to break down the barriers between subcultures and other young people. The idea that people are in general more creative has been linked to the development of new forms of consumer expression and the idea of a postmodern society.

Therefore, in addressing a number of the issues that have arisen in the theorisation and empirical use of the concepts of subculture, writers like Willis have argued that the concept of subculture should no longer be used and that the 'space' that it fills in the examination of culture of young people should be replaced by another concept (see also Hesmondhalgh, 2005). The reasons given by these writers vary in their emphases, but key points are: (1) that social and cultural life has frag-mented so that it is no longer possible to find the clearly isolatable forms of subculture; and (2) that the spec-tacular processes deployed by youth subcultures have become more generalised and thus it is no longer poss-ible to locate and identify clear subcultural groupings.

Both of these aspects are discussed by Chaney, who suggests that 'The idea of subculture is redundant because the type of investment that the notion of sub-culture labelled is becoming more general, and therefore the varieties of modes of symbolization and involvement are more common in everyday life' (2004: 37). An important and influential line of thinking in this respect can be found in the work of Andy Bennett (for example, 1999), who argues that the idea of sub-culture is 'deeply problematic in that it imposes rigid lines of division over forms of sociation which may, in effect, be rather more fleeting, and in many cases more arbitrary than the concept of subculture, with its con-notations of coherence and solidarity allows for' (1999: 603).

This sort of argument, which emphasises fragmen-tation, fluidity and the increasing lack of distinctiveness of what were often seen as separable subcultural groups, has sometimes been supplemented by another type of argument, which maintains that a key problem of the Birmingham approach to subcultures was that, under the influence of Hebdige, it became increasingly concerned with the decoding of the meaning of subcul-tures as texts and less concerned with the voices and views of those who form them (see, for example, Widdicombe and Wooffitt 1995; Muggleton 2000). These general concerns have led to a range of argu-ments and concepts that are able, it can be suggested, potentially to supersede that of subculture.

In this debate three broad positions can be identified:

1  That which argues that the concept of subculture is redundant and therefore that it needs to be replaced.

2  That which wishes to retain some aspects of the sub-culture concept but to consider the way in which subcultures have in some sense been 'postmod-ernised'.

3  That which suggests that the term 'subculture' can be deployed but only in reference to groups that

retain such key features of subcultures as examined by writers such as those associated with the Birmingham Centre for Contemporary Cultural Studies.

While these positions often shade into each other, it is possible to see how studies discussed in the subse-quent parts of this chapter represent them.

The idea that the concept of subculture needs to be replaced has led to the formulation and deployment of several related concepts (see Hodkinson 2002: 19–24; Bennett and Kahn-Harris, 2004: 11–14). The key ideas to have been suggested and deployed here are tribe and neo-tribe, lifestyle (Miles 2000) and scene. The idea of tribe is, in the main, derived from the work of the French sociologist Michel Maffesoli (1996). This emphasises that in an increasingly consumerist society, groupings are related through consumerist practices. Groups may therefore exist that are more fluid, in the sense that their commitment may shift depending on consumer choices and consumer change. This concept is related to that of lifestyle, which has become popu-larised in everyday life as depicting the way in which a series of consumer choices become crystallised into a form of life that has some consistency and which can be related to some social basis (even if it is only those who share a particular postcode). As Hodkinson (2002) points out, another related term – *Bunde* – was intro-duced into this debate by Hetherington (1992), which follows many of these emphases while suggesting that groups may have more solidity and substance. In many ways these concepts recognise the significance of the social changes concerning consumerism, fluidity of commitment and the fragmentation of society into numerous niches that are the hallmarks of the ideas that have been grouped under the heading of postmod-ernist thinking. A slightly different approach has picked up on the idea of scene as used in everyday speech to examine the production and consumption of music (initially) in a specific locality (see Bennett and Peterson, 2004).

The second broad trend in contemporary thinking on subcultures also picks up on some key aspects of the first position, but seeks to retain rather more of the subculture heritage. Thus, in arguing for a post-subcul-tural or postmodern subcultural position, Muggleton examines the extent to which 'subculturalists may be expected to display a number of "postmodern" characteristics, some of which have an affinity with certain countercultural sensibilities' (2000: 52). The broad set of 'ideal-typical traits' identified by Muggleton are discussed as to the extent to which the (post-) subculturalists whom he examines exhibit the features that he has described in these postmodernist ways. In so doing, he perhaps retains more ways of thinking about subcultures than he might have expected and might be represented by the first strand of thinking discussed above.

The third position continues to deploy the idea of subculture, while restricting its use to particular subcultures that do (relatively) deploy the forms of coherence that approximate those discussed in the earlier Birmingham literature. Hodkinson's (2002) examination of the Goth subculture is a good example of this.

While, therefore, there are different positions advanced here and, as Muggleton and Weinzerel (2003: 6) point out, 'some of this confusion can .... be alleviated if we recognise that different concepts can be used to abstract different aspects of social reality', it is important to examine the findings of different studies which, in various ways, have sought to advance the debate on subculture.

## Some key studies of recent subcultures

In many ways, the study of subcultures was revitalised by the development of dance and rave culture (as in the work of Thornton introduced above). For example, Rietveld (1993) examined a number of different dimensions of rave culture in the north of England in the late 1980s. The account given of this form of culture is not dissimilar from that of the CCCS writers. For example, Rietveld argues with respect to rave culture that:

> Not only the lack of finance, but also the intensive dancing and the use of the drug Ecstasy determined the style. It makes a person sweat, so baggy cotton clothing is the most comfortable to wear. Make up is useless in those circumstances, because it would

simply 'wash' off in a short time. The euphoria caused by the excitement of the rave events, the excessive body movement and drug use all interfere with a person's sense of balance: high heels are therefore definitely 'out of order' from a raver's point of view.

> (Rietveld, 1993: 53)

This is very close to the sort of homology argument used by Willis which continues therefore to be influential. However, other work on rave culture was more critical of the Birmingham approach. We have already considered the work of Thornton (1994, 1995) in relation to moral panic and the role of media in the creation of youth subcultures, but she also, in direct criticism and the working out of her own analysis, makes an important contribution to the analysis of more contemporary youth culture. Thornton argues that what she calls 'club cultures' are 'taste cultures' (1995: 3).

Thornton (1995) argues that the definition of and approach represented by the Birmingham Centre is empirically unworkable in sociological terms. This is important, as it suggests the need for more empirical work on youth from a different perspective. As outlined above, as it developed the Birmingham approach was more concerned with the reading of subcultures as texts than with in-depth investigation of the views of the participants themselves. However, it is significant that these views are themselves often relatively neglected in Thornton's study, and only in more recent work (e.g. Muggleton, 2000; Hodkinson, 2002) have they have been considered at greater length.

Secondly, Thornton points to the significance of divisions within the working of a subculture, rather than focusing on the relationship between subculture and dominant culture, or on the youth subculture and the 'parent' culture. This means that she considers how cultural hierarchies or oppositions work within the subcultural group. These distinctions are complex, but revolve around issues such as the authentic versus the phoney, the hip versus the mainstream and the underground versus the mass media.

Thirdly, Thornton shows that the club culture worked around the possession and deployment of what (following Bourdieu) she terms 'subcultural capital',

## Defining concept 9.1

### Cultural capital and habitus

The concepts of cultural capital and habitus, developed by the French sociologist Pierre Bourdieu (1930–2002), have become increasingly influential in cultural studies.

Initially best known in Britain and the English-speaking world through his work on education, Bourdieu's book *Distinction* (1984, orig. 1979) represented an important potential bridge between those in the social sciences concerned with class inequality and domination, and the developing emphasis on culture in a number of disciplines, including cultural studies.

Bourdieu's central innovation was to coin the concept of cultural capital, which he used in tandem with the more familiar idea of economic capital. Thus, in discussing the ways in which classes seek distinction from each other, Bourdieu pointed out that some groups, while high in economic capital, are low in cultural capital. Hence businesspeople may be well paid and own shares in their company but they may not be able to appreciate or understand fine art or classical literature. On the other hand, there are some groups that are high in cultural capital but relatively low in economic capital, university lecturers for instance. Cultural capital, like economic capital, is a resource to be drawn upon in the pursuit of power. Cultural capital is not secondary to economic capital in general, as each may be important in different contexts. *Distinction* used survey data to map some of the complexities of the relations between different sectors of the French middle class. This has inspired theoretical refinement of the concept as well as further empirical work in a number of countries. Increased attention to the cultural significance of consumption has been influenced by Bourdieu. One clear implication of Bourdieu's work is that distinctions between a variety of groups may be based on differences in capitals. For example, Thornton (1995) argues that subcultural groups mobilise subcultural capital, through the notion of 'hipness', to create their own distinction. It is important to possess or have knowledge of the hip dance record and to be wearing the right clothes.

Bourdieu, in addition to a range of other conceptual innovations, developed the concept of habitus to refer to the way in which different social groups classify the world and view it. Rather than arguing that a particular class position carries with it a specific ideology, Bourdieu points to the way in which groups have habituated ways of seeing or a disposition to classify the world. Groups inhabit a particular cultural space. Again, this emphasis on classification has been influential especially as it echoes and connects to the centrality of such ideas in social anthropology, which itself has been important to some variants of cultural studies.

Bourdieu's reliance on survey data, and his inattention to the aspects of culture shared across social classes and groups, may be criticised, but his concepts and approach are likely to become more influential in the future as more empirical work is done.

### Further reading

Jenkins, R. (1994) *Pierre Bourdieu*, London: Routledge.

Bourdieu, P. (1990) *In Other Words: Essays towards a reflexive sociology*, Cambridge: Polity.

---

which is represented through the idea of being 'hip' – that is, culturally aware and on the cutting edge of developments and knowledge that are prized within the subculture – which may be valueless outside it. Different forms of media are critical to the circulation of subcultural capital. These might be flyers for particular events or the fanzines produced by those who are particularly committed to the subculture. In this way, Thornton developed the idea that media are critical to subcultures. Thus, in a world were various forms of media have become increasingly important (Abercrombie and Longhurst, 1998), there are still forms of subculture, but they have become increasingly mediatised.

Thornton examined the relationships within the broad area of dance culture and pointed to its media-centred nature, but also to its internal divisions. Different aspects of these developments have been picked up by further studies.

Some themes concerning postmodernism and the study of youth culture were addressed by Redhead (1990; see also Redhead, 1993, 1995, 1997, and Redhead *et al.*, 1997) who places a particular emphasis on the examination of the relationships between music and subcultures. Redhead criticises the idea of a neat fit between different elements of youth subculture, which are entailed in the concept of homology used by Willis (1978). He also suggests that it is problematic to see music as the straightforward expression of a subcultural community. For example, it is often difficult to specify what the community is of which music is an expression. Furthermore, the subcultures and communities from which music is often held to issue or which put it to use, do not simply exist, but have to be examined within language and communication. They are, in important senses, constructed within writing about them or, in other terms, discursively constructed.

Redhead considers whether there was a clear fit between music and subcultural use in the way identified by the Birmingham writers, or whether there has been a change in the articulation of music with subcultures in the period since punk rock in the late 1970s. In some accounts **postmodernism** (p. 295) in pop has developed through the 1980s, leading to the break-up of the forms of association identified by earlier writers. However, Redhead argues that in many respects pop music has always possessed some of those features that are characteristic of postmodernism. For example, he maintains that pop music has broken barriers between high and popular culture at different points. In common with theories of postmodernism, he argues that the best way to understand contemporary pop music is not through some of the conventional 'oppositions' which have often been used to study it, like those between 'rock and pop', 'authentic and synthetic', 'true and false' and 'high and low', but through the distinction and relationship between the local and the **global** (p. 125). Thus 'world musics' are affecting local music making in a number of complex and diverse ways.

Muggleton (2000) sought further to evaluate the extent to which subcultural adherents had been affected by the development of forms of postmodernist culture. He found that the subculturalists had not moved completely to the postmodernised position. As he says:

We can, I feel, grant a qualified acknowledgement of a postmodern sensibility. Subculturalists are

postmodern in that they demonstrate a fragmented, heterogeneous and individualistic stylistic identification. This is a liminal sensibility that manifests itself as an expression of freedom from structure, control and restraint, ensuring that stasis is rejected in favour of movement and fluidity. Yet there is no evidence here of some of the more excessive postmodern claims. Informants did not rapidly discard a whole series of discrete styles. Nor did they regard themselves as an ironic parody, celebrating their own lack of authenticity and the superficiality of an image saturated culture.

(Muggleton, 2000: 158)

Muggleton draws attention to the way in which the subculturalists whom he studied wished to retain (and promote) key aspects of their individuality, partly through music, while also expressing some aspects of commitment to belonging to a recognisable group.

In another detailed piece of research, Hodkinson (2002) examined the Goth subculture in late 1990s Britain. This extended discussion argues for the continuing value of the concept of subculture as applied to those groups that exhibit the relative coherence of features such as those combined in Goth. Thus, although there is significant internal variation in, for example, modes of dress within the subculture (as he clearly shows), there are also clear commonalities and patterns. In reworking the idea of subculture, Hodkinson shows how it can be retained 'to capture the relatively substantive, clearly bounded form taken by certain elective cultural groupings' (2002: 9). He considers the criteria of 'identity, commitment, consistent distinctiveness and autonomy' and argues that 'each of them should be regarded as a contributory feature which, taken cumulatively with the others, increases the appropriateness of the term subculture' (2002: 29). Music is a part of this subculture and Hodkinson discusses its importance in a number of places. It remains an important aspect of the subcultural package.

Andy Bennett's (2000) work represents a third study that has considered in some detail a number of groupings. After developing the sort of critique of the Birmingham approach to subculture considered above, Bennett argues that it is important to examine the local experience of youth groups with popular music. The local is a space where different forms of culture are brought together and new syntheses created that involve creativity on the ground. This does not mean that the culture or subculture is locally bounded, but that it is lived out in localities that are connected to other places and translocal processes (as is also discussed at some length by Hodkinson, 2002), which is facilitated by the increasing availability of computers and the Internet.

Bennett includes four case studies in his book that show the significance of the processing of different influences in particular contexts: dance music; Bhangra; hip-hop in Newcastle in the north-east of England and Frankfurt in Germany; and the live music of the Pink Floyd tribute band the Benwell Floyd, again in Newcastle. Bennett's conclusion is important in that he argues that: 'Aspects of popular culture, such as music and style, in addition to being understood as global cultural forms, assume particularised "everyday" meanings which respond to the differing local contexts in which they are appropriated and which frame their incorporation into forms of social action' (2000: 197). This is significant in two ways: firstly, because it suggests the importance of the local consumption of global products and secondly, because it links music to other forms of popular culture. Thus, while subculture remains a useful concept in some respects (especially in analyses such as those of Muggleton and Hodkinson), it directs attention to wider production and consumption processes and how they are lived out.

Hollands suggests that there has been a shift in youth culture in the sense that 'going out', especially on a Friday or Saturday night, to the centre of a large city (in his analysis, Newcastle-upon-Tyne in the north-east of England) has become a central aspect of culture for young people between 16 and 30. In response to economic change which means that young people are less likely to be employed, get married and start families, going out often in a group has become less of a 'rite of passage' from childhood to adulthood, which is then curtailed, but more an ongoing part of the everyday. The meeting of friends (often in mixed groups for more middle-class young people) is an important part of this process. Going out, in Hollands' words, is 'a permanent fraternisation ritual' (1995: 41).

The work examined in this section on more contemporary youth culture has demonstrated some of the ways in which analysis has moved beyond the Birmingham approach. It can be argued that there is less concern with the spectacular. Moreover, there is a break with some of the more simple oppositions between the subcultural and the mainstream in a way that reduces the influence of Marxist theories of power and opposition to hegemony. Furthermore, there is an increased concern with the empirical investigation of subcultures and less with the 'decoding' of their inner meanings. Finally, there is a move away from the examination of youth to a more expanded notion of what is happening in people's cultural lives more widely. One way forward from this sort of work is to reconsider a rather different approach to the study of subculture.

## 9.9 Rethinking subcultures: interactions and networks

The American interactionist authors Gary Fine and Sherryl Kleinman (1979) argue that the concept of subculture needs to be rethought within a framework derived from sociological approaches that emphasise interaction. In the main, by implication their approach is critical of the sort of work associated with the CCCS which placed emphasis on the structural aspects of society, like class. They argue that the concept of subculture had previously been used in a confused and unclear fashion. They identify four conceptual problems with this literature, which concern: firstly, subculture and subsociety; secondly, the referent; thirdly, subculture as a homogeneous and static system; and finally, the value orientation in subcultural research.

With respect to the first point, they argue that because of the way in which subcultures have been structurally defined 'as aggregate of persons' they have often been treated as a subdivision of society, as what they call a subsociety. However, in contemporary societies which allow movement between different groups and which have a number of different belief systems, it is difficult to see subsociety and subculture as the same thing. As Fine and Kleinman explain:

> Thus, all members of the age category 13–21 might, according to a 'structural' conceptualization, be considered part of the youth subculture. However, it is clear that many of the persons within that age cohort do not share common cultural values and behaviors.
>
> (Fine and Kleinman, 1979: 3)

On this basis Fine and Kleinman argue that it is important to distinguish between subsocieties and subcultures.

Concerning the second issue, they argue that the concept of subculture is often used without a referent – 'a clearly defined population which shares cultural knowledge' (1979: 4). Thus, as they explain:

> Although researchers identify the subculture to which the group 'belongs' (such as the delinquent subculture), they have no way of knowing the extent to which the cultures of the gangs overlap, the extent to which the particular gang examined is representative of all gangs in the population segment, and the degree of interrelatedness among the cultures of the gangs under study.
>
> (Fine and Kleinman, 1979: 4).

The third point is more familiar in that Fine and Kleinman argue that the study of subcultures tends to treat them as if they were both homogeneous – more or less as if all members of the group were the same and all shared exactly the same beliefs and practices – and unchanging. In fact what should be kept in view is the *fluidity* of subcultures. Finally, they argue that through the *selectivity* of the way in which the subculture is discussed or *read*, the representation of it often becomes little more than a caricature. There is a tendency to focus on the central themes of the subculture at the expense of the complex interplay of different cultural aspects which may be a part of the subculture.

Fine and Kleinman argue that there is a better way to understand subcultures, proposing that 'the conceptualization of the subculture construct within an interactionist framework will provide a more adequate account of subcultural variation, cultural change, and the diffusion of cultural elements' (1979: 8). They argue

that subculture should be used to refer to an interacting group. On first sight this would seem to produce rather small subcultures. However, Fine and Kleinman argue that subcultures exist beyond immediate groups because of the way in which cultural patterns are diffused in contemporary societies. The network that results from the diffusion of cultural elements is then the referent which did not exist in most earlier writing. Subcultures start from group cultures:

> Cultural forms are created through the individual or collective manipulation of symbols. From its point of creation, the cultural form is communicated to others, and diffused outward from the individual's own interaction partners. The transmission of culture is therefore a product of interaction. The diffusion may remain quite limited unless the information reaches wider audiences via the mass media.
>
> (Fine and Kleinman, 1979: 9)

Fine and Kleinman identify four mechanisms by which communication can occur. Firstly, individuals may be members of a number of different groups; secondly, there may be other interconnections which do not involve group membership as such but which are based on 'weak ties', casual conversations with acquaintances and so on; thirdly, some individuals or groups perform what Fine and Kleinman refer to as structural roles, in linking groups that may not otherwise be in contact and providing cultural information (drug dealers, for example); and fourthly, there may be media diffusion as when certain films or television programmes influence cultures in the wider sense.

This approach also emphasises the need for analysis to concern itself with what they call the 'affective' dimension of subcultures (Fine and Kleinman, 1979: 12). People need to be seen as involved in choices about culture and the extent of the identification with the culture needs to be considered and researched. These are important points which need to be recognised in contemporary work on subcultures. Indeed, they have been echoed, if in an indirect way, in work that has begun to explore the subcultures or groupings of television and pop music fans (for example, Lewis, 1992; Aizlewood, 1994; Roberts, 1994) and enthusiasts and hobbyists (for example, Bishop and Hoggett, 1986;

Moorhouse, 1991). It can be suggested that attention to contemporary cultural life has to pay greater attention to actual processes of interaction, the role of the media in the construction of the network (as Thornton's (1995) study maintains in relation to club cultures), and the importance of 'affect' (Grossberg, 1992) or pleasure.

A good example of a study that has taken the agenda of examining contemporary relative media use forward is that by Laughey (2006). He demonstrates how fluidity of commitment by young people to different forms of music is played out in personal terms as well as a range of public performances. This captures the way in which music flows through contemporary life in a range of interacting ways. Laughey's work is based on detailed research on young people in the north-west of England.

In accord with the sorts of criticisms considered above, Laughey argues against the ways in which music use has been situated within approaches that deploy the idea of youth subculture. In addition, Laughey demonstrates how such theories have emphasised generational conflict and separation rather than influence and continuity. Moreover, he argues that there are subtle shifts in musical taste within a generally wide-ranging set of tastes:

> Two types of narratives about music tastes and performances that accorded to different timeframes will thus be substantiated: narratives that are embedded – frequently in family contexts – through memories facilitated by (domestic) music experiences; and narratives that are radically contextualised (Ang, 1996) – frequently in peer group contexts – in immediate relation to the whims of music fashions.
>
> (Laughey, 2006: p. 5)

Laughey explores the complex dynamics between the personal tastes and the public performances of a range of musically based practices. An important part of this discussion is where he shows the different positions that are taken up by young people with respect to music and related cultural activities. He discusses these positions along two particular dimensions: firstly, the degree of involvement with music, which he divides into causal and intensive; and secondly whether the tastes and practices are inclusive or exclusive. Combining these dimensions produces four positions: drifters (inclusive and casual consumers), surfers (exclusive and casual consumers), exchangers (inclusive and intensive users) and clubbers (exclusive and intensive users). The drifters:

> had little awareness of their music consumer and producer practices even though their everyday life contexts regularly featured music within earshot. Music often played a minor role in these young people's everyday lives. Although music would be infrequently purchased or experienced in public contexts where high amounts of financial capital were necessary, its pervasive presence through casual media such as radio perhaps explains drifters' populist tastes and mainstream sensibilities.
>
> (Laughey, 2006: p. 175)

The surfers, despite also being casual in consumption were exclusive in public practices – 'if specific types of music *texts* were immaterial to the pleasures of surfers, specific practices associated with exclusive music *contexts* were of paramount importance' (2006: 177). Exchangers 'tended to invest more significance in mediated than co-present practices. Music texts and technologies would be more important to the everyday lives of exchangers than exclusive music contexts. Whilst exchangers' tastes would often be alternative and specific to particular music genres, their sensibilities leaned towards mainstream public practices of inclusion' (2006: 177). Finally, 'clubbers engaged in intensive media use and exclusive public practices. Being a clubber refers more to a sense of membership in a specific music taste group than to the particular context of clubbing. However, the term is also apt because clubs were mainly perceived as sites for exclusive music consumption and production' (2006: 178).

This typology is important for the attention to a range of different aspects of public and private, meaningful or casual interaction with music and other media. Laughey's work shows in general how an empirical approach based on different theoretical assumptions from those deployed from Birmingham can illuminate the complexity of young people's social and cultural lives. His approach is interactional, in the way that Fine and Kleinman recommend, but also manages to capture dynamics of consumption in ways that resist the rather overgeneralised accounts that directly connect this to postmodernism. Thus his work shows how a theoretically informed, sophisticated study of youth is possible in ways that overcome some of the uses of subcultural theory. Recent studies of fans and audiences can also be taken as examples of this developing approach.

# 9.10 Fans: stereotypes, *Star Trek* and opposition

We all probably have commonsensical images of the fan in our minds and they would perhaps be linked by the idea of some kind of excess of admiration of an activity or star. Moreover, there has been a clear tendency for much writing on fans to suggest that there is something wrong with being a fan. Fans are seen as fanatics (from the origin of the term) and deranged (Jenson, 1992: 9). Jenson maintains that the literature on fans has produced two models of the 'pathological fan'. Firstly, there is the 'obsessed loner', 'who (under the influence of the media) has entered into an intense fantasy relationship with a celebrity figure. These individuals achieve public notoriety by stalking or threatening or killing the celebrity' (Jenson, 1992: 11). Secondly, there is the 'frenzied or hysterical member of a crowd' (1992: 11), shouting at a rock star or misbehaving at a sports match.

Jenson contests this idea that there is something wrong with the fan by contrasting the traits of the fan with those of the high culture or academic 'aficionado'. She argues that many academics form attachments to their favourite writers or theorists which are just as obsessive as those the fan may feel for the pop star. However, the division of the world between fans and non-fans allows those who define themselves as non-fans to suggest that others are abnormal and thus to constitute themselves as the normal or the safe. For Jenson:

> Defining fandom as a deviant activity allows
> (individually) a reassuring, self-aggrandizing stance

to be adopted. It also supports the celebration of particular values – the rational over the emotional, the educated over the uneducated, the subdued over the passionate, the elite over the popular, the mainstream over the margin, the status quo over the alternative.

> (Jenson, 1992: 24)

Characterising fans as 'other' in this way blocks analysis and proper understanding of how people actually interact with the media in contemporary society. Further, writers like Fiske (1992) have suggested that fan activities are actually more like those of 'ordinary' people. Two studies of fans have been particularly influential.

## Fans of *Star Trek*

Camille Bacon-Smith (1992) considers the appropriation and reusing of television texts like *Star Trek*, *Blake's 7* and *The Professionals* as the basis on which to develop new cultural forms. So the women in Bacon-Smith's study do things with such texts. They go to conventions on them, dress up as characters from the shows, write and perform 'filksongs' about them, paint pictures of the characters, and produce music videos about them.

Bacon-Smith devotes much discussion to the types of written text that are produced, utilising the characters and situations from the different series, although again her main focus is on *Star Trek*. Characters and situations from the series are placed in new situations and different 'universes'. New characters are introduced or ones who had only relatively minor roles are developed at much greater length and depth. She examines four main genres of *Star Trek* writing. The first of these is the 'Mary Sue' which entails the introduction of a young woman into the crew of the Enterprise who manages to save the ship and its crew from disaster, but who perishes due to her efforts. This is often the first sort of story written by the developing *Star Trek* fan, and has become a relatively disliked form. The term 'Mary Sue' is often used in a negative sense, the phrase 'it's a bit of a Mary Sue' indicating disapproval.

The second type of writing is the 'lay Spock' (or someone else from the crew). This involves producing a story which entails placing Spock in a heterosexual relationship, for example with Nurse Chapel, who is thought to be attracted to him. The third type of writing is the 'K/S' or 'slash' (see also Penley, 1992) which places Kirk and Spock in a homosexual relationship. This form of writing seems particularly 'transgressive' of the accepted meanings of *Star Trek*. It is suggested that female fans have taken up an affective core of *Star Trek* (the friendship of Kirk and Spock) and inflected it in a rather surprising direction.

The final type is 'Hurt/Comfort' which again often places two of the central characters into a close relationship. One of the characters suffers pain through a terrible injury and the other character is involved in caring and comforting the injured friend. This genre is explained by Bacon-Smith to be particularly controversial among fans due, for example, to the distressing effects that the reading about the severe pain inflicted on a much-liked character can have on them.

These texts are often produced in a collective manner. One individual may be primarily responsible for the initial development of an alternative *Star Trek* universe, but this is then opened up for expansion by others who can fill in gaps and open up new possibilities in the story. In an important sense, the authorship of these stories is shared and is a part of a network in the sense identified by Fine and Kleinman. Their production goes against the stereotype of the lone author at work in creating a product for an industrialised book market.

This subculture is also involved in a form of **resistance** (p. 170), like that described in the CCCS approach. Bacon-Smith describes the way in which the women in her study carve out a 'female-terrorist space' for their activities. One of the things which is significant about Bacon-Smith's book is her characterisation of the women as opposing the dominant male controllers of the more official forms of science fiction fandom. The established male science fiction (SF) conventions are both organised and often disapproving of the activities of the female fans. There is also some insightful material of the intimidation of women in the role-playing sections of the SF conferences. These, on Bacon-Smith's account, are virtually completely male-dominated. Dominant forms which are opposed by the female forms tend to be both individualistic and mas-

culine, although when they are engaged in struggle or are under attack they tend toward associative modes of organisation. This can be seen as a network of interaction which forms a subculture on the basis of which mass-circulated stories and characters are reworked and developed in a way that opposes the control of the wider science fiction culture by men. Henry Jenkins (1992), in another study of *Star Trek*, reinforces these points.

Jenkins emphasises the creativity of fans. He shows how they are involved in the writing of different stories based on the characters from familiar television programmes and, like Bacon-Smith, discusses some of the different genres of these stories. In addition fans indulge in video making, painting, singing and so on. Like a great deal of the writing on fans, Jenkins argues against the ideas that fans are somehow figures of fun, deranged, or isolated (sad and lonely) individuals. They are seen as active and involved in extensive communicative networks forming a subculture that is open to outside influences. The members also engage in a full range of 'normal' activities. Jenkins also shows how technologies like computer networks are facilitating new forms of interaction, adding significant new dimensions of the communication possibilities that were detailed in Fine and Kleinman's earlier article. In sympathy with much other writing on subculture, these fans are seen as engaged in reframing the meanings of a dominant culture; they are not so far away from Hebdige's (1979) youth subcultural *bricoleurs*. However, one of the significant issues that this literature raises is the extent to which all television viewers are becoming as skilled and active in their understanding of television programmes as the fans described by Bacon-Smith and Jenkins. This refers back to the point made by Willis *et al.* (1990) about the essential creativity involved in everyday cultural life. However, as Jenkins (1992) shows through his discussion of the failure of fans to convince the producers of particular programmes to keep them running or not to develop a particular storyline, the fans tend to be in relatively weak positions in a wider sense. Moreover, some more recent work on the fans of daytime television programmes in the USA has taken a rather different view of fandom.

# Fans of daytime soap opera

Harrington and Bielby (1995) examine a different type of fan from that considered by Bacon-Smith (1992), Jenkins (1992) and Penley (1992) in that these are not people who engage in the productive generation of new texts in the concrete sense on the basis of their fan attachments; rather, they suggest that fan feelings and identifications are central in the productive construction of identity. Their approach is 'to question not just what fans *do* but who they *are*' (Harrington and Bielby, 1995: 7). In important respects this lack of 'concrete' production is related to the pleasure that fans find in the already existing texts. As Harrington and Bielby (1995: 21) explain, 'It is *because* female consumers of women's texts – including soaps – find it easier to identify with and find pleasure in the primary narrative that they rarely produce derivative texts.' However, partly because of the derision to which soaps and their fans are subjected, involvement tends to take place within a supportive environment. The increasing identification with the soap and the **identity** (p. 142) of a soap fan is difficult.

As has been argued by Grossberg (1992; see further Longhurst, 2007a: 233–5), the fan forms an affective link to the object of attachment. This is critical to Harrington and Bielby's examination of soap fans, where pleasure in the product is central. This may be an essentially private pleasure, or it may become more public through participation in fan lunches, correspondence, computer bulletin boards and so on. Harrington and Bielby emphasise the pleasure that is involved in these affective connections and suggest that this should be considered in its own sense as a form of love attachment rather than being explained in other terms as a form of struggle and opposition. This does not mean that they ignore struggle and opposition but, as we have argued in general terms, they relocate these ideas in a different framework with an emphasis on spectacle and performativity (see Chapter 6 for discussion of performativity in contemporary politics). They argue:

> Unlike most media theorists who posit a barrier between subject and object, we believe that soap watching (like reading or fantasy gaming) is simultaneously a spectator and participant activity.

It is participatory in that the story and the alternative world do not exist until we consciously and actively engage the text . . .; it is a spectator activity in that we necessarily adopt a bordered position to the fictional world.

> (Harrington and Bielby, 1995: 132)

For Harrington and Bielby (1995: 178–9), 'soap fans' practices are guided by a sense of agency – an awareness of their ability as socially embedded individuals to initiate and control behaviour. Soap fans' viewing choices and practices emerge for a myriad of reasons, including pleasure and experience of emotion. The concept of agency more adequately captures the general process of intentionality that is obscured by a focus on hegemonic resistance'. What fans are or what they do are extensions of their integration and participation in viewing and everyday life. In the conclusion to this chapter we shall build on this important point.

## 9.11  Conclusion

At the outset of this chapter we suggested that attention to subcultures was important through the consideration of three issues: resistance/incorporation; social divisions and fragmentation; and interpretation/representation. The core of the chapter examined the approach developed at the **Centre for Contemporary Cultural Studies** (p. 241) at the University of Birmingham which focused on the way in which the distinctive patterns of life associated with subcultures could be read or interpreted within the frame of their **resistance** (p. 170) or incorporation within dominant culture and their relation to parent culture. This approach was sophisticated and influential. However, the discussion in the subsequent sections suggests that it now seems inadequate as a way of understanding the complexity of contemporary culture.

More recent studies of youth and fans can be interpreted to suggest that what is important is not so much the reading of subcultures for resistance and opposition, but the understanding and gathering of evidence about the activities of a diverse range of groups which point to the meanings of the activities, especially in terms of pleasure, to the people that engage in them.

Further, it may be suggested that these activities concern the performance of self (see Chapter 8).

**Postmodernist** (p. 295) arguments have suggested that society has become both more fragmented and more media saturated. Moreover, **identities** (p. 142) have become more complex. The burden of much of the literature considered in the later sections of this chapter is to support such ideas, despite the framing of some of the fan studies in terms of opposition and resistance. It can be suggested that our sense of self is often constructed in relation to our enthusiasms as well as in the context of family and occupation. Youth subcultures seemed to be a place for resistance and opposition at a particular stage in the life course, where movement from one set of relations in the family was managed in the process of transition to a new set. However, contemporary society offers fewer jobs for life and involves more divorce, family break-up and reconstitution. In such a context, the concern with youth subcultures may have been a starting point, but such study now needs to be reconsidered within the development of the life course, in fragmented and complex ways. Some people may be members of reasonably tight subcultures, for example that around graffiti studied by Macdonald (2001) , but perhaps a better way to look at the complexities of everyday cultural interaction is through networks oiled by media, where complex identities are reconstructed in the performances of everyday life (an argument developed further in Abercrombie and Longhurst, 1998, Crawford 2004, Laughey, 2006 and Longhurst, 2007b).

## Recap

This chapter has considered:

➤ a range of conceptual issues introduced by the concept of subculture;

➤ literature on the concept of moral panic;

➤ the nature and the critique of the approach to the study of youth subcultures developed at the Birmingham Centre for Contemporary Cultural Studies;

➤ the nature of fans and enthusiasts and the developing importance of the concept of identity in this field.

## Further reading

Ken Gelder and Sarah Thornton's *The Subcultures Reader* (2005) contains an excellent selection of papers and extracts on subcultures. Other useful collections include *After Subcultures: Critical Studies in Contemporary Youth* Culture (Bennett and Kahn Harris, 2004) and *The Post-Subcultures Reader* (Muggleton and Weinzierl, 2003). Stuart Hall and Tony Jefferson's *Resistance through Rituals* (1976) is the classic collection from the Centre for Contemporary Cultural Studies. Many of the subsequently influential Birmingham writers such Dick Hebdige (*Subculture*, 1979), Angela McRobbie (*Feminism and Youth Culture: From 'Jackie' to 'Just Seventeen'*, 1991; *Postmodernism and Popular Culture*, 1994) and Paul Willis (*Learning to Labour*, 1977; *Profane Culture*, 1978; Willis *et al.*, *Common Culture: Symbolic Work at Play in the Everyday Cultures of the Young*, 1990) can be found in shorter form in these books. For fans, Lisa Lewis's *The Adoring Audience* (1992) and *Fandom: Identities and Communities in a Mediated* World (Gray, Sandvoss and Harrington, 2007) are good collections. Less academic but also enlightening are the works of Nick Hornby (*Fever Pitch*, 1994; *High Fidelity*, 1995).

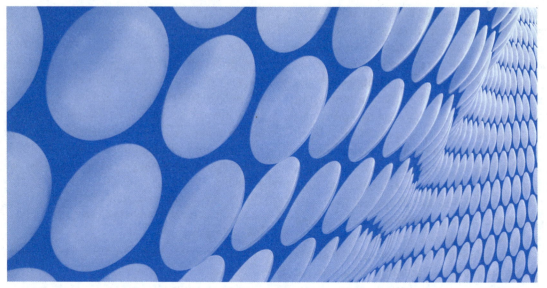

# Visual culture

## 10.0 Introduction

In contemporary Western societies we are surrounded by the products of visual culture: billboard and magazine ads, signs in shops, offices and public places telling us where to go and what not to do, cinema and television, and increasingly on computer screens, mobile phones and other communicative devices. Technological developments, beginning with the printing press, have ensured that we live in times when visual images are instantly available and everywhere present. In this chapter, three overarching themes shape our examination of visual culture. Firstly, a shift from **modernity** to **postmodernity** or late **modernity** (p. 295) informs many of the analyses considered. We shall suggest that forms of visual culture are intimately connected to changes in society – moreover, that such shifts are themselves part of the re-ordering of **power** (p. 64) relations, especially in respect of their gendered dimensions. Secondly, we want to suggest the range of alternative approaches to the study of visual culture

taken by scholars in and around cultural studies. Thirdly, we shall place particular emphasis on the city, for visual culture is intimately linked to urban life. The contemporary city is a key site of social transformation. Cities, which have always been significant centres of science and culture, are now accommodating an increasing proportion of the population. In 1975 some 38 per cent of the world's population lived in cities. This figure is rapidly rising and by 2030 it is estimated that over 60 per cent of the world will live in urban environments (Giddens, 2006: 907). The chapter focuses on the interplay between the city and the visual cultures it sustains, building on the more general forms of representation and visual culture, such as painting and television, examined in other parts of the book (see Chapters 2 and 7).

After a consideration of the ideas of visual culture and visual representation, these three general themes are addressed in this chapter through the examination of a range of aspects of the visual culture of cities, beginning with the ideas advanced in the earlier part of the twentieth century by the work of Simmel and Benjamin. We then consider photography and film as modern representational practices that are widely regarded as outstanding methods for 'capturing' elements of that visual culture. In the next section we consider the important work of **Michel Foucault** (p. 20) on surveillance and the gaze. Work on a different type of gaze is considered in a section on tourism which also examines the application of the concept of postmodernism to this activity. This is followed by an examination of the differences between the glimpse, the gaze, the scan and the glance. The visual culture of cities, especially behaviour in public places and the built environment itself, forms the topic of the next two sections. Finally, some of the ideas first introduced in the earlier sections are reconsidered in the light of suggestions that visual culture is assuming the increasingly simulated forms characteristic of postmodernism. However, first we must address the concept of visual culture.

## Learning objectives

► To understand changes in visual culture as connected to the reordering of power relations.
► To appreciate different ways of studying visual culture.
► To recognise the importance of the changing visual culture of the city.

# 10.1 Visual culture and visual representation

Of all of the senses that humans possess, sight is the most developed. The structure of human eyes and their placement at the front of the head gives human vision some important capabilities. The eyes of humans can detect and resolve fine detail; they are capable of distinguishing a wide range of colours of the spectrum; and their broad area of binocular overlap permits ready appreciation of the depth of visual fields (Passingham, 1982: 36–48). These capabilities are part of the universal biological features assigned to *Homo sapiens* in the evolutionary sequence, distinguishing us from other species. Together they form the biological basis for the primacy accorded to sight among the human senses. 'Seeing comes before words', says John Berger (1972: 7), 'the child looks and recognises before it can speak.' The primacy of vision is evident in many everyday sayings such as: 'seeing is believing', 'If I hadn't seen it with my own eyes, I wouldn't have believed it ', 'if looks could kill', 'it's staring you in the face' (readers might like to furnish further examples of their own). Seeing provides a certainty that no other sense seems capable of affording. It is therefore unsurprising that scientific discourse is replete with visual imagery. Science is based on true 'observations' of the world and seeks objective, 'clear-sighted', unbiased 'views' of its topic-matter.

Although vision is a naturally endowed sense, our ways of looking at things and seeing the world are thoroughly cultured. The biology of vision cannot explain the way that we actually interpret the appearances of the world. Seeing is always cultured seeing. Anthropologists report instances of puzzlement and incomprehension from persons unfamiliar with modern photographic technology when shown photographs of ordinary objects. These persons lack the appropriate cultural codes to grasp what the photographs represent. As cultural beings we are able to 'see' two people walking down the street as 'a mother going shopping with her child' or to 'look at' people embracing at a railway station as 'lovers saying their farewells'. We routinely make sense of the objects, persons and relationships in our cultural environment by looking. Yet this quite ordinary and easily exercised skill is not innate but is acquired through social learning. What we see is always conditioned by what we know – the cultural categories we employ, the common-sense knowledge we possess – provided by our socialisation. The world that we experience is full of appearances, sights that make sense to us, at least as adult members of a culture. Yet we have all encountered situations where the looks of things are not always transparent; our knowledge may be deficient to grasp what is actually going on, or we may sense that something is not quite right, out of place, and infer that a puzzling or untoward event is happening. (Sociologists of everyday life, notably Erving Goffman (see p. 291) have shown the importance of vision in encounters between unacquainted persons in public places.) For the most part, however, our ordinary knowledge of the world is adequate for us to make sense of its appearances. That knowledge and those appearances are subject to constant revision since, as Berger (1972) reminds us, what we know and what we see never stand in a finally settled relation.

This leads us to the influential notion of *visual culture*. Like the notion of culture itself, this term can be usefully understood and analysed as a text and as a way of life. As *text*, the concept of visual culture draws attention to images and the technologies through which images are produced. An image is a representation of the sights or appearances of the world. A drawing, painting or photograph recreates or reproduces a version of the world's appearances, giving material form to what we see. To make an image, a technology however simple (pencils, crayons) or complex (digital cameras) is required. As *way of life*, visual culture points to one dimension of the 'design for living' held by any group of people. Every culture provides its members with an ordinary capacity to decode the looks of things, persons, relationships and so forth that are encountered every day. As adults walking down a city street we will be careful to give that blind person escorted by a guide dog plenty of room to pass; if we are female, we may avoid the importunate behaviours of male workers on a building site by taking another route to our destination. We are able to figure these things out, as we say, 'just by looking'. What such simple acts do not disclose is the considerable social learning lying at the back of these lines of conduct, learning that (as children) may have included being forcibly pulled out of the path of a blind person or that (as adolescent girls) may have involved an embarrassing episode of running the gauntlet of building workers' catcalls.

As a way of life, visual culture suffuses our everyday experience but it also takes more institutionalised forms. Svetlana Alpers (1983) shows how seventeenth-century Holland had a richly developed visual culture which was most obviously marked by the work of the great landscape painters of the era but which itself was embedded in wider arrangements including the development of many optical instruments (camera obscura, telescope, microscope), table linens, tiles and tapestries.

These built up a discriminating vocabulary for interpreting visual representations that many ordinary Dutch people shared. The advent of **modernity** (p. 295) has heightened the significance of the visual. Although the verbal, in both spoken and written forms, is the primary means of communication, Western culture's pervasive concern with the appearance of objects makes it decidedly ocularcentric. Seeing has become the privileged sensorial mode. In such societies issues of representation come to the fore.

Representation generally means one thing standing for another. A portrait painting such as the Mona Lisa can stand for a real woman's appearance and facial expression. The realism of such visual representations is often a matter of debate, and photographic representations are widely felt to more realistically stand for real features of the world than paintings. Cultural studies treats representation as connected to the exercise and disposition of power, and can be linked to patterns of class, capitalism, gender and sexuality. Some of these issues are discussed in later sections of this chapter.

## 10.2 Modernity and visual culture: classic thinkers and themes

In this section we shall consider the influential ideas of two early twentieth-century German theorists, Georg Simmel and Walter Benjamin. Their ideas have provided a benchmark for subsequent analyses of the visual culture of modern cities. In particular, they have done much to rekindle interest in the figure of the *flâneur*, a key metaphor in the appreciation of the visual dimensions of city life.

### Georg Simmel: metropolitan culture and visual interaction

**Georg Simmel** (1858–1918) is now best known as one of the earliest exponents of sociology in late nineteenth-century Germany. He was originally trained as a philosopher and his interests ranged well beyond the narrow confines of a single discipline. Simmel's

## Key influence 10.1

### Georg Simmel (1858–1918)

Georg Simmel was born on 1 March 1858 in the centre of Berlin, a cosmopolitan city in which he spent all but the last four years of his life. His parents had converted from Judaism to Protestantism, a faith Simmel also embraced, albeit weakly. However, others defined him as a Jew and for much of his career Simmel fell victim to the pervasive anti-Semitism in the German university system of the time. He was denied a full-time appointment commensurate with his intellectual stature. When he did finally obtain a salaried post, it was at the university of the border city of Strasbourg, in 1914 – just in time to see the cessation of normal academic activity by the outbreak of the First World War. For most of his life Simmel was dependent upon the fees paid by students who enrolled in his classes and a legacy left by the friend of the family who had brought him up after the death of his parents.

Anti-Semitism is only part of the story. Throughout his life Simmel was no stranger to controversy. He was widely regarded as a brilliant philosopher and sociologist, but also recognised as a maverick intellectual, the possessor of a mind that delved into a range of topics and areas that some felt too wide for his own scholarly good. After initial studies at Berlin University in the fields of history and folk psychology, he settled on philosophy, the discipline that provided an enduring identity for his intellectual interests. In 1881 he was awarded a doctorate by Berlin University. His first thesis (on the psychological and ethnological origins of music) was rejected as unsatisfactory but an earlier, prize-winning essay was allowed to stand in its place. In 1885 he was finally awarded the Habilitation (a higher doctorate that is a prerequisite for university teaching). At the oral defence of his thesis Simmel responded to one of his examiners in a manner that was taken as offhand and sarcastic, and he was sent home for six months 'to ponder how one behaves toward worthy older scholars'. Throughout his career Simmel was not afraid to challenge conventional thinking.

Working for fees only, Simmel quickly established a reputation as a gifted lecturer at Berlin. His classes became attractions for the cultural elite of the city, as well as large numbers of foreign and women students, a following that did not endear Simmel to the state's educational authorities. Simmel's forte was as an essayist. His writings reveal a sharp eye for the universal elements ('forms') underlying the manifestations of cultural phenomena. He was not interested in building a system or inventing a method. Rather, he sought to find 'in each of life's details the totality of its meaning'. His essay on fashion shows how clothing styles can articulate apparently contradictory wishes for difference (e.g. use of clothing to set oneself apart from others) and similarity (e.g. belonging to a group of fashionably costumed persons). His enormously influential essay on cities, 'The metropolis and mental life' (1903), emphasises the emergence of shared dispositions among modern city-dwellers, a distinctive mental set of reserve and calculation. Fashion flourishes in the city because people there often experience themselves as undistinguished and reduced, and see others as a source of unanticipated demands. Fashion, because it is encoded in people's clothing, is compatible with a cool, detached metropolitan outlook but it can also serve as a device whereby people can exaggerate their singularity and thus protect themselves from being overwhelmed or submerged by the demands of city living.

Although Simmel was most at home in the essay format and published regularly in newspapers and periodicals, he also wrote some large 'academic' books, most notably for students of cultural studies *The Philosophy of Money* (1900; the English translation did not appear until 1978). This, Simmel's major treatise on **modernity** (p. 295), traces the diverse impacts of money economies on social and cultural life. Simmel also addressed the massive expansion in the scale and availability of culture in modern life that enormously increased the scope for cultural deformation and domination – 'the tragedy of culture'.

Simmel's impact was felt originally in sociology, where he conceived a distinctive focus for the discipline (investigating the forms of human association) and in philosophy, where he influenced the thinking of **Benjamin** (p. 274) and Lukács. In the English-speaking world since the 1980s there has been a 'Simmel renaissance' as more of his writings have been translated into English. His contemporary relevance for cultural studies lies in his original understanding of the bases of modernity, constructed out of numerous close studies of cultural minutiae.

### Further reading

Frisby, D. and Featherstone, M. (eds) (1997), *Simmel on Culture: Selected Writings*, London: Sage.

Frisby, D. (2002) *Georg Simmel*, London: Routledge.

Weinstein, D. and Weinstein, M. (1993) *Postmodern(ized) Simmel*, London: Routledge.

contribution to our understanding of visual culture and modernity principally stems from his thinking on visual interaction and the distinctive features of metropolitan culture. These analyses in turn have to be located in the context of Simmel's broader theory of **modernity** (p. 295) articulated most fully in *The Philosophy of Money* (1978).

For Simmel, modernity involved 'the modes of experiencing what is ' "new" in "modern" society' (Frisby, 1985: 1). Many of Simmel's observations were sparked off by his experience of the cosmopolitan urban centre of the city of Berlin. Simmel sought to penetrate the 'inner nature' or 'soul' of modernity by contemplating the conditions of existence of its products. What resulted was a form of analysis that was as much aesthetic in character as scientific. Simmel held out the prospect 'of finding in each of life's details the totality of its meaning' (1978: 55); he sought to extract the most general principles from the inspection of cultural minutiae, for example elucidating features of the instrumentality bred by the money economy by reference to the practice of prostitution or the contrasting attitudes of the miser and the spendthrift.

For Simmel, modernity was not to be understood as simply the culture of capitalism or industrial society. Its roots lay further back in history. Modernity's origins are to be found in the advent of a fully monetarised economy rather than in variants of the traditional society/industrial capitalism distinction. For Simmel it is the replacement of seigniorial dues and other forms of barter by money as the principal medium of economic exchange that has far-reaching consequences for modernity. In a complex analysis Simmel shows how money is a highly flexible form of exchange. It can be divided in any number of ways and can be put to any number of purposes. Money, then, is pure instrumentality, completely subservient to the ends to which it is put. In this respect it promotes the calculative outlook so common today. The processes of rationalisation explicated by Weber (see Chapters 1 and 6) have their origins in monetary exchange, which becomes almost synonymous with calculation.

In his classic essay of 1903, 'The metropolis and mental life', Simmel (1971) highlights some social psychological features of the culture of modern cities. Many persons come into fleeting anonymous contact with one another in the modern city, for example travelling on public transport or purchasing goods in a department store. People are removed from the emotional ties and social bonds that once linked them together in smaller communities. Simmel describes a social psychological configuration that seems characteristic of those who live in large urban centres. The urban dweller's mental life is predominantly *intellectualistic* in character. People respond to situations in a rational rather than an emotional manner. The broad orientation of urban dwellers tends to be *calculative*. People's daily life is filled 'with weighing, calculating, enumerating', which reduces 'qualitative values to quantitative terms' (1971: 328). A common stance of urban dwellers is thus the *blasé outlook*, a renunciation of responsiveness, an indifference towards the values that distinguish things. The world of the blasé person is flat, grey and homogenous. Often accompanying this outlook is to be found an attitude of *reserve*. A reserved attitude acts as a protective shield for the urban dweller behind which candid views and heartfelt sentiments can be preserved from scrutiny.

Simmel is contrasting the differences between the *traditional* village or small town and the modern city (Savage and Warde, 1993). Moreover, he maintains that within modern societies it is not easy to sustain a distinction between rural and urban ways of life because the city's influence has ramifications throughout the entirety of society. Further, Simmel does not see the features he describes as simply originating from the ecology and organisation of the modern city. Instead he regards the city as the prime 'seat of the money economy'. The most distant roots of calculativeness, the blasé attitude, reserve, etc. ultimately derive from the advent of fully monetarised systems of exchange.

The features of modern urban culture delineated by Simmel point to the predominance of the visual sense. In public places, for example, it is essential that the calculative, blasé, reserved urban dweller is able to scan the immediate environment for all kinds of practical purposes – finding one's way about, avoiding colliding with others on a busy street, being watchful for potential sources of danger. These everyday interactions were considered by Simmel be the basic material of society. Although it is commonplace to think about society in terms of institutionalised social structures such as political and economic organisations, social classes and the like, these large-scale structures are themselves crystallisations of multitudes of everyday interactions between people (buying tickets, asking the way, dining together, standing in a queue and so forth). Simmel considered a fundamental task for sociology to be the description and analysis of the characteristic features of these forms of interaction.

In a brief fragment, Simmel gave particular attention to sight, for of all of humanity's senses 'the eye has a uniquely sociological function' (Simmel, 1969: 358). Consider first the mutual glance, when two persons catch each other's eyes. In the mutual glance, says Simmel, we find 'the most direct and purest reciprocity that exists anywhere'. Each person gives equally to the encounter. 'The eye cannot take unless at the same time it gives. . . . In the same act in which the observer seeks to know the observed, he surrenders himself to be understood by the observed' (1969: 358). Naturally enough, glances are transitory, gone in the moment they occur. But social interaction as we know it would not be possible if humans did not have the capacity for the mutual glance, since the glance serves as a vehicle for conveying recognition, acknowledgement, understanding, intimacy, shame and so forth.

Simmel draws out further aspects of the sociological significance of the eye. When humans interact the face tends to be the primary focus of visual attention because it is a crucial indicator of mood and intent. People are first known by their countenance, not their acts. Indeed, the human face serves no practical purpose except to tell us about the state of mind of its possessor.

It follows from these observations about glances and faces that the attitude of the blind characteristically differs from that of the deaf. 'For the blind, the other person is actually present only in the alternating periods of his utterance' (1969: 359). This gives the blind 'a peaceful and calm existence' in contrast to the often 'more perplexed, puzzled and worried' (1969: 360) attitude of the deaf. Moreover the visual mode assumes a greater significance in the large city because the person is likely to encounter many people in a relationship of anonymity, a relationship in which all that is available to the person is the appearance of the other. Cities present a range of situations (in cinemas,

theatres, restaurants, buses and trains) where the individual is placed in the company of anonymous others who are only known to the individual through what can be inferred about their appearance. The increased role of 'mere visual impression' (1969: 360) is characteristic of modern, large-scale society. People living in such a society, Simmel concludes, suffer from some of the same perplexity that afflicts the deaf. The increased role of 'mere visual impression' contributes to a widespread sense of estrangement.

Simmel was one of the earliest writers to trace modernity's impact on visual culture. His frequently diffuse, elliptical yet persuasive writings have influenced further studies of the visual dimensions of ordinary city life, including those of Walter Benjamin.

## Walter Benjamin: mechanical reproduction, aura and the Paris arcades

As with Simmel, **Walter Benjamin**'s (p. 274) (1892–1940) writings are wide ranging and challenging, resisting disciplinary classification. He studied a diverse set of topics in an often literary and philosophical style reflecting the influence of progressive artistic movements and the German philosophical tradition. We want to highlight his contribution to debates on **modernity** (p. 295) and visual culture in two main areas. Firstly, Benjamin pointed to the significant transformations effected by the development of new technology (specifically photography and film) for representing visual culture. Secondly, he considered particular aspects of everyday life in the changing cities (particularly Paris) of the nineteenth century.

In his most famous essay, 'The work of art in the age of mechanical reproduction' which was first published in 1936, Benjamin (1970) asks the question of how art is changed or affected in an era when it can easily be reproduced by mechanical means. For film and photography allow a large number of copies to be made of an art work that originally had a single unique existence. He suggests that this process leads to a decline in what he calls the *aura* of the work. Benjamin argues that in previous periods in history the work of art was specifically located in time, space and tradition (churches and chapels, religious ritual, aristocratic patronage and so forth). Such traditions were not unchanging but they did give the work of art a specific and original meaning. Contemporary reproduction techniques (photography, film, CDs, digitised audio recordings, etc.) lift works of art out of tradition and lead to a decline in what he called the aura or unique meaning of the work.

Tradition is particularly important in Benjamin's argument. Tradition mobilises rituals and cultic meanings. Thus, paintings and objects would have possessed a secure meaning arising from their clear anchorage in the religious and cultic practices of particular social groups. In a sense this generates a sense of reverence or power around the object. Within the Christian tradition, for example, art objects located in churches such as the paintings on the walls of the Sistine Chapel in

Rome possess an aura in the tangible sense that they create a space around them. The work of art was then located in tradition and had power due to its presence in that tradition, creating aura. The text was an original in the sense that it existed in a specific physical location and could only be seen and appreciated by visiting that location. The development of mechanical reproduction (photography and film principally) transforms this situation. Presence is replaced by portability. As Benjamin explains: 'for the first time in world history mechanical reproduction emancipates the work of art from its parasitical dependence on ritual. To an ever greater degree the work of art reproduced becomes the work of art designed for reproducibility' (1970: 226).

Benjamin argues that this lifting out, or 'disembedding' (Giddens, 1990), of art from tradition leads to a

## Key influence 10.2

### Walter Benjamin (1892–1940)

Walter Benjamin's work combined a creative **Marxism** (p. 65) with elements of Judaic Messianic theology. He was a close associate of members of the **Frankfurt School** (p. 75). He wrote about modernity, the city, baroque and nineteenth- and twentieth-century literature.

Benjamin was born in Berlin and studied philosophy and literature in Berlin, Freiburg, Munich and Bern. His first and only published book-length study, *The Origin of German Tragic Drama* (1928), failed to secure him an academic job. After the First World War he worked as a freelance critic and translator. In the late 1920s he met Bertolt Brecht whose work he defended and championed. With Brecht he took a more optimistic view of mass culture than members of the Frankfurt School like Theodor Adorno. He argued that the 'mechanical reproduction' of art and culture could be used in a progressive politics as well as be the tool of Fascist

propaganda. In the 1930s, Benjamin moved to Paris to escape the Nazis and there worked on his most ambitious undertaking, *The Arcades Project*, which attempted to read the work of the poet Charles Baudelaire in the context of nineteenth-century capitalism. The unfinished work has proved a rich resource for sociologists and cultural critics writing about the modern city. After the German invasion of France, Benjamin escaped to the Franco-Spanish border, where he committed suicide rather than be handed over to the Nazis. As a consequence, most of his work was published posthumously. Theodor Adorno and Gershon Scholem helped to revive interest in his work after the Second World War and collections of his essays began to appear.

Benjamin's influence in cultural studies has been diffuse. His work on Brecht and Kafka has been important to the understanding of the relation-

ship between modernist art, politics and mass culture. His essays have sparked debates within feminism, postcolonial theory and historical studies. One of his best-known essays is 'Theses on the philosophy of history', which criticised the idea of a linear, causal history. Instead, Benjamin proposed the spatial metaphor of the constellation as the way in which the cultural historian should relate the present to the past.

### Further reading

The best introduction to Benjamin's work are the collections of his essays:

*Illuminations*, London: Fontana (1970).

*Charles Baudelaire: A Lyric Poet in the Era of High Capitalism*, London: Verso (1983).

*Understanding Brecht*, London: New Left Books (1977).

politicisation of art. Since techniques of mechanical reproduction make knowledge of the art work so much more widely available, it can become the subject of contested meaning and implicated in a much more developed sense in wider attempts to justify the exercise of power. Thus, it can be suggested that familiarity with certain films and photographs can provide the basis for attempts to influence the public in particular directions, but that the audience can in fact often find different meanings within those forms. It also leads to the increased importance of what Benjamin calls 'exhibition value' which he traces in the development of photography and film. We will concentrate on the themes introduced by Benjamin on film at this point, as they illustrate some important aspects of Benjamin's theses on aura.

Benjamin argues that the performance of an actor in a play has auratic elements. It is (and remains) a unique performance in the sense that it is socially located in one place – the actor performed his or her part in the particular performance of the play, in *that* place, on *that* night. With the development of film, clear changes occur. The audience might watch the same performance in a number of places (the same film can be watched by audiences in the USA or in France at the same time). Importantly, the notion of performance also changes. The performance of the actor in the film is actually made up of a number of segments edited together long after the actors have finished their work. This suggests a decline in the originality of the work and the authenticity and originality of the performance.

The decline in the aura of the performance, Benjamin maintains, is compensated by the rise of the phenomenon of 'personality' and 'stardom', where actors and performers are stars who generate audience appeal by their special personal qualities. The production of films to be sold on a market, that is as commodities, is facilitated by the fact that a secure demand for them can be generated by the use of stars. One consequence of this arrangement is that the decision by a star as to whether he or she wants to act in a particular film can determine whether that film is made or not. Stars can generate a form of brand loyalty (Lury, 1993) from the public.

In some respects Benjamin viewed such developments rather more positively than several other writers

associated with the **Frankfurt School** (p. 75). He recognised that the wider availability of works of art made possible by processes of mechanical reproduction could lead to a greater democratisation of art. Thus, culture could become part of a progressive political practice in the ways that it was used, by Brecht for example. But Benjamin was also very critical of aspects of these developments. He saw that they could lead to the commodification of art and also to the use of movies and personalities to prop up exploitative and repressive political regimes through propaganda. As he says:

> The cult of the movie star, fostered by the money of the film industry, preserves not the unique aura of the person but the 'spell of the personality', the phoney spell of a commodity. So long as the movie-makers' capital sets the fashion, as a rule no other revolutionary merit can be accredited to today's film than the promotion of a revolutionary criticism of traditional concepts of art.
>
> (1970: 233)

To summarise, Benjamin sees a decline in the aura of art as it becomes reproduced. This reproduction lifts art out of specific and traditional contexts and allows it to be relocated more widely. The work of art loses originality and uniqueness in this process. Furthermore, mass or commodified art tends towards the superficial and the phoney. Surface appeals are made and the public is manipulated by the cult of personality and stars. Some of the key differences between auratic and non-auratic art are indicated in Table 10.1.

| Table 10.1 Auratic and non-auratic art | |
| --- | --- |
| **Auratic art** | **Non-auratic art** |
| Original | Copy |
| Tradition | Modern |
| Ritual | Entertainment |
| Religion | Secular |
| Use | Exchange |
| Distance | Immediacy |
| Whole | Fragmented |

In addition to these important and influential ideas concerning aura and reproduction, in 'The work of art in the age of mechanical reproduction' Benjamin also offers some significant comments on architecture and the ways in which members of the public appropriate buildings. In this discussion he emphasises the role of touch, in that buildings are *used* by people, and sight, in that people perceive images of buildings and the city. Benjamin explores the visual and everyday culture of the city at greater length in his work on Paris in the nineteenth century (Buck-Morss, 1989).

In this work Benjamin explores the relationship between the city as text and as experienced by the people who live, work and play in it. However, Benjamin was not so much interested in the conscious ways in which people use cities as in the ways that they experience them unconsciously, almost without cognition in a straightforward sense. There is in Benjamin's view a sense in which cities may be experienced almost as a dream (Savage and Warde, 1993). There is, then, a relationship between the meanings that are stored up in the city and the associations that they possess and the experience of those meanings for the inhabitant and the visitor. We shall return to these issues in the later sections of this chapter. First, we consider an important form of analysis of the experience of the city, issuing from the idea of the *flâneur*.

## The figure of the flâneur

A number of convergent themes concerning **modernity** (p. 295), visual culture and the city in the thought of Simmel and Benjamin are captured by the figure of the *flâneur*. Simmel's broad analytic stance, it has been suggested, is that of a *flâneur* (Frisby, 1981; but see Weinstein and Weinstein, 1993), the gentleman stroller of the city streets who, in the nineteenth-century French poet and writer Charles Baudelaire's expression, goes 'botanising on the asphalt' (Benjamin, 1983: 36) as he observes the urban spectacle. This interpretation of Simmel itself has its origins in Benjamin's interest in the way in which cities are experienced by people in the course of ordinary work and leisure activities. In essays written in the mid-1930s Benjamin (1983) was led to examine the work of Baudelaire who had earlier popularised the concept of the *flâneur*, drawing attention to this figure who takes an almost voyeuristic pleasure in detachedly watching the doings of fellow city-dwellers.

The recent flourish of interest in the figure of the *flâneur* has several dimensions. It seems that the *flâneur* was a type of person with a real historical existence, as this anonymous description from Paris (1906) shows (adapted from Wilson, 1992: 94–5):

➤ A 'gentleman' who spends most of the day roaming the streets observing the urban spectacle – the fashions in dress and adornment, the buildings, the shops, the books, the novelties and attractions. A kind of voyeur with an endless curiosity for witnessing the ordinary scenes of city life.

➤ His means of support are invisible; there is the suggestion of private wealth (he is possibly a *rentier*) but an apparent absence of family, business or landowning responsibilities.

➤ His interests are primarily aesthetic and he frequents cafés and restaurants where actors, journalists, writers and artists gather.

➤ For the *flâneur* a significant part of the urban spectacle is provided by the behaviour of the lower orders (workers, soldiers, street vendors and street people).

➤ He is a marginal figure, tending to be portrayed as isolated from those he observes, a solitary figure in crowds.

No one knows just how widespread this social type was in Paris and other cities of nineteenth-century Europe. Perhaps most significant is the way the *flâneur* speaks to the new conditions of modernity. *Flânerie* – a leisurely amalgam of strolling, loitering and, importantly, gazing at the urban spectacle – only becomes possible in the social conditions provided by the big cities of industrialising Europe. Thus, the *flâneur* can be considered to typify the experience of modernity's public places.

The *flâneur*, strolling through the city streets and preserving his incognito in the anonymity of the crowd, witnesses a variety of situations which are seen at a safe and detached distance. Watching the world go by lies at the heart of the *flâneur*'s stance: simple observation, not prescription or remedy. Vision is paramount: 'the *flâneur* moves through space and among the people with a viscosity that both enables and privileges vision' (Jenks, 1995: 146). For the *flâneur* the city is not a home but a showplace. The labyrinthine images of metropolitan culture provide an endless source of fascination tinged with mystery. 'This inconspicuous passer-by', says Benjamin, has 'the dignity of the priest and the sense for clues of a detective' (cited in Frisby, 1985: 229–30). In varying degrees *flânerie* is evident in the novels of Charles Dickens (Benjamin specifically identifies *Sketches by Boz*), the documentary reports of the Victorian 'social explorers' like Booth and Mayhew, the 'man in the crowd' of Edgar Allen Poe and Benjamin's (1999) own *Arcades Project*.

Feminists have highlighted the taken-for-granted male associations implicit in the *flâneur* figure. From one point of view the non-existence of the role of *flâneuse* (a female *flâneur*) symbolises women's restricted participation in public places as well as the malestream bias of some of the classical literature on modernity (Wolff, 1985). The freedom to roam was very much a male freedom: the *flâneur*'s licence to watch the city sights is very much the walking embodiment of the 'male gaze' (see below). Other feminists have argued that there is a risk of over-generalising this argument. They point out that women's experiences of urban life, even in the nineteenth century, varied from city to city and from class to class. Thus Elizabeth Wilson (1992) has suggested that it is misleading to claim that women were comprehensively excluded from public spaces in late nineteenth-century England. She maintains that the growth of department stores, tea rooms, railway station buffets, ladies-only dining rooms, public conveniences with female attendants and so forth, made it possible for middle and lower middle-class women to experience public places and thus afforded at least some women the opportunity for *flânerie*. These issues connect to more contemporary studies of behaviour in public places (see section 10.7 below).

# 10.3 Technologies of realism: photography and film

As Benjamin's discussion of aura implies, photography and film are each nineteenth-century technical innovations that have made a major impact on the development and apprehension of the visual cultures of **modernity** (p. 295) and late modernity. In this section we consider how photography and film have promoted a concern with the **realistic** (p. 43) representation of the world, a claim that needs to be approached cautiously and treated critically.

## The development of photography and film

Cameras existed long before photographs did. The camera obscura was in widespread use as a drawing aid by the sixteenth century. However, the ancient Greeks knew the principle on which it was based (light that enters an enclosed space through an aperture or lens throws an inverted image against the facing surface). Photography is a modernist technology. The French inventor, Joseph Niepce, took the world's first genuine photograph in 1826. Early photographs were one-of-a-kind images produced by the action of light on specially treated plates. Through the 1830s the search was on to refine the technique. One of the most influential techniques was daguerreotypy, devised by a colleague of Niepce, Louis Daguerre, who sold his invention to the French government in 1839. The daguerreotype quickly became popular throughout Europe and America but its big drawback was that it could only produce single images. In England the scientist, traveller, linguist and Member of Parliament William Henry Fox Talbot finally perfected the calotype in 1841. The calotype only required an exposure time of a couple of seconds and it was the first system to print multiple copies of positives from a single negative. Indeed, the word 'photography' and the terms 'positive' and 'negative' originated from Talbot's friend, the scientist Sir John Herschel. The commercial possibilities of photography were quickly exploited and soon photographic studios were set up in every town and city, first in Europe and North America, then quickly elsewhere.

For most of the nineteenth century, photography remained largely in the hands of small numbers of technically knowledgeable practitioners. Its popularisation as an everyday practice requiring no special skills came about with the American Max Eastman's marketing of the Kodak box camera in 1888 under the famous slogan, 'You press the button, we do the rest'. The camera was equipped with a roll of film that took 100 pictures. Once the whole film was used, the camera was returned to the factory where the old film was developed and a new one installed. This marked the beginning of the major revolution in the history of photography which was advanced by the introduction of the Brownie box camera at the turn of the century. A simple and cheap camera, unlike the expensive Kodak and its successors, this really put photography into the hands of large sections of society. This 'democratisation' of photography has been advanced by a number of important technical developments this century including the invention of the 35 mm camera (the Leica, 1925), the Polaroid instant camera (by the American Henry Land, 1947), the cartridge Instamatic (1963) and the widespread availability of colour photography from the late 1960s on. Today the act of taking pictures is an accepted part of weddings, christenings, holidays and other occasions of ceremonial significance. We take photos of our families, our friends, our pets, our heroes. In recent years with the advent of digital cameras, and mobile phones capable of taking photos, taking pictures has become even more prevalent. More than ever we use the pictures we make to construct our biography (see Spence and Holland, 1991). Photography is a 'middle-brow art' (Bourdieu et al., 1990). Yet as a mass vernacular practice photography is only a century old.

Film – motion photography – has an even briefer history than still photography. The brothers Louis and Auguste Lumière, who opened the world's first cinema in Paris in 1895, invented the cinematograph. Unlike other competing inventions the cinematograph was portable and this, combined with the energetic entrepreneurial activity of the Lumières, ensured that their machines were installed in every major city of the

world by the century's end. Nowadays, of course, the movie business is the leading entertainment industry on the planet and its impact is felt everywhere. As subsequent history has shown, both motion and still photography can serve diverse purposes – as scientific instruments, as entertainment, as forms of art, as methods of surveillance, for example. As we shall see in our consideration of the documentary photography of city life, these purposes are often complexly interwoven.

## The documentary tradition

The documentary tradition of photography and film emerged in the late nineteenth century in Europe and America as a socially conscious endeavour to depict graphically the actualities of the world. Documentary has a rich and varied history. In the USA a significant early contributor was Jacob Riis whose New York pictures of Lower East Side poverty in *How the Other Half Lives* (1890) had a major impact on public opinion. In the early decades of the twentieth century, Lewis Hines' photographs of industrial working conditions influenced US reform movements and legislation. A generation later, photographers working for the Farm Security Administration assembled an influential collection of pictures. Disseminated through the popular press, especially the new mass-circulation picture magazines like *Life* which employed photo-essay formats, they brought home to wider publics the misery faced by small farmers in the 1930s and the troubles they encountered when migrating to the towns and cities of the west as droughts turned agricultural land into dustbowls. Perhaps the most famous book to describe these dislocations was *Let Us Now Praise Famous Men* (1941) by James Agee and Walker Evans. In Europe, the pictures of Parisian street scenes and café life made by Henri Cartier-Bresson and Brassai reached wide audiences (see Westerbeck and Meyerowitz's (1994) excellent history of street photography). At a time when television was still in its infancy, documentarists found a mass outlet for their work through the new and influential occupation of photojournalism. That documentary found such a ready audience in the 1930s, in both Europe and America, has to be understood as part of wider social currents which showed a new sensitivity to the description of the experiences of the ordinary person and which found expression through such diverse forms as Mass Observation, community studies, phenomenology, folk art, public art, newsreel cinema, photojournalism magazines and soap operas.

One of the first motion pictures ever produced showed workers leaving the Lumières' factory. The Lumières used their new invention to cast new light on many aspects of daily life both at home and abroad. Indeed, they coined the term *documentaires* to describe their short travel films. Although film was quickly exploited by Hollywood for entertainment purposes, its capacity to document ways of life was not neglected. One milestone was Robert Flaherty's account of Eskimo life in *Nanook of the North* (1922). In the Soviet Union aspects of the new society being forged were captured by *Kinopravda* (Film Truth) cinematographers. The ideological potential of documentary was also recognised in Nazi Germany where Leni Riefenstahl's epic documentary *Triumph of the Will*, of the 1934 Nazi Party national rally, lent new dimensions to the propaganda function of film.

It is customary to distinguish documentary from fictional work. Documentary is about reporting, not inventing, whatever is in the world. According to Michael Renov (1986; cited in Winston 1995: 6), 'every documentary issues a "truth claim" of a sort, positing a relationship to history which exceeds the analogical status of its fictional counterpart'. The realist impulse is paramount: documentary pictures and film aim to exhibit the facts of a situation.

> [Documentary] imposes its meaning. It confronts, us, the audience, with empirical evidence of such nature as to render dispute impossible and interpretation superfluous. All emphasis is on the evidence; the facts themselves speak... since just the fact matters, it can be transmitted in any plausible medium. .... The heart of documentary is not form or style or medium, but always content.
>
> (Stott, 1973)

But documentary is also designed to encourage viewers to come to a particular conclusion about how the world is and the way it works. Often what is depicted is the everyday activities and pleasures of ordinary people or the experiences of the suffering and oppressed, who are portrayed in a way that enables the viewer to empathise with their situations. Documentary starts off by avowing merely descriptive concerns, 'telling it like it is'. As one distinguished exponent, Dorothea Lange, put it, 'documentary photography records the social scene of out time. It mirrors the present and documents for the future' (quoted in Ohrn, 1980: 37). Routinely, however, these realist concerns of documentary are linked to persuasive ones. The viewer is asked to take a particular attitude toward what is depicted. For example, John Grierson, the Scottish filmmaker of the 1930s and 1940s who is widely regarded as a pivotal figure in the development of British and North American traditions of documentary film, expressly considered the cinema to be a pulpit and explained that his philosophy was to exploit the observational potential of film in order to construct a picture of reality and thereby to realise cinema's destiny as a social commentator and source of inspiration for social change (Barnouw, 1974).

Documentary thus capitalises upon photography's immense descriptive potential. Photographs provide a precise record of material reality, what is indubitably there in the world. Photography has been described as 'a benchmark of "pictorial fact"' (Snyder and Allen, 1982: 66) arising from the automatism of the process through which photographs are produced (by the machine-generated exposure of light to chemically treated paper) which is said to remove human agency and yield a representation possessing an authenticity and objectivity that easel painting can never obtain. In John Berger's (1989: 96) summary, 'Photographs do not translate from appearances. They quote them.' The camera is, in the famous slogan, 'a mirror with a memory'. These are all powerful claims on behalf of photographic **realism** (p. 43). But they do not support the more exaggerated affirmation that artifice is foreign to photography, nor do they support a hard and fast contrast between documentary (or scientific) and art photography. Art photography emerges around the recognition that photographs are not simply documents but are also aesthetic objects. As Susan Sontag (1979: 85) put it: 'Nobody ever discovered ugliness through photographs. But many, through photographs, have discovered beauty.' Some of the issues at stake are summarised in Table 10.2.

**Table 10.2** Artistic and documentary conceptions of photography

| Art photography | Documentary photography |
| --- | --- |
| The photographer as seer | The photographer as witness |
| Photography as expression | Photography as reportage |
| Theories of imagination and conceptual truth | Theories of empirical truth |
| Affectivity | Information value |
| Symbolism | Realism |

*Source:* adapted from Sekula (1975)

What Table 10.2 sets out are not two distinct types of photograph but rather two dimensions for appraising photographic images. Indeed, the most credible view to take is that documentary is defined by its use; documentary pictures are those that are used in documentary ways (Snyder, 1984). This also allows aesthetic considerations a place in documentary photography: a powerful image is often the most effective way of driving home the facts of some situation. The persuasiveness of documentary is achieved through the artful fusion of descriptive and aesthetic concerns: production decisions about pose, light, composition, lenses, types of film and focus, as well as editing judgements such as cropping and the like, are guided by the photographer's sense of what makes an effective image.

The realism of documentary is thus a professional **ideology** (p. 35). In its most simple form it rests on two questionable assumptions: that the camera takes pictures and never lies, and that the camera faithfully records the world as it appears (Ruby, 1976). Against the first assumption it must be remembered that people, not cameras, take pictures and those pictures are always taken from some point of view that has an arbitrary component. Here 'arbitrary' does not mean happenchance. It means it could have been otherwise – another, different picture could easily have been made. The great French documentarist Henri Cartier-Bresson spoke of this as waiting for the 'decisive moment' to create his arresting pictures of Parisian street life. The second assumption also cannot be accepted without qualification. Photographs do not unambiguously and transparently record reality. The sense that we make of

any photograph depends upon a variety of factors including our cultural and personal knowledge, visual literacy and the picture's place of publication and caption. Such criticisms lead to some further issues.

## Colin MacCabe: the classic realist text

In a much-quoted paper Colin MacCabe (1981) developed a controversial critique of the claims for **realism** (p. 43) in arts like film and photography. He argued that the dominant textual form in contemporary society is the classic realist text. They can range from Disney cartoons to the novels of Dickens, from *Neighbours* to *24* and from *Terminator 3* to 'classics' of British 'realist' cinema such as *Saturday Night and Sunday Morning*. Realism for MacCabe runs much deeper than whether a picture or film corresponds to how things actually are in the world. It is about the *form* of the text. MacCabe thus defines the classic realist text through four main features.

Firstly, the classic realist text consists of a hierarchy of **discourses** (p. 21). At the top of this hierarchy is a discourse that claims adequacy to the real. In the novel this may be the voice of the narrator, or the flow of the (constructed) narrative itself. In more visual forms of the classic realist text the truth will be revealed by what we see on the screen (Hill, 1986). When watching a television programme or a film, we expect the 'truth' to be revealed to us at some point. Furthermore, it is displayed *visually*, normally at the end of the narrative. Thus, at the conclusion of a detective story we expect to find out 'whodunnit'. The central male hero, whose actions lead to the solution of the crime, will often reveal this to us. In many respects the dominant discourse of the display of the truth and the depiction of reality is associated with male activity, which itself structures the narrative (Abercrombie and Longhurst, 1991).

Secondly, the classic realist text promotes relationships of identification, particularly between the hero and the reader or viewer of the text. As readers or viewers we tend to identify with the actions of the hero and his point of view in the narrative, often influencing us in **ideological** (p. 35) ways. The classic realist text does particular work on us as members of an audience, stitching us into the flow of the narrative, and its discourse of the revealing of truth. Thus, to simplify somewhat, in the Sherlock Holmes stories, truth is associated with the actions and knowledge of Holmes, who will reveal that truth to the reader. The actual narrator is Dr Watson, to whom things are communicated by Holmes, and who acts as a mediator to the audience. Watson may sometimes be critical of Holmes, especially when he acts particularly insensitively, but ultimately this discourse will be subsumed beneath that of the scientific revelation of the truth and the real state of affairs.

Thirdly, the classic realist text is closed. It does not reveal a range of options on the truth or reality, then leaving the audience to choose between them. It offers the solution to the range of issues or enigmas raised during the course of the narrative. It is very rare for a popular film or novel to end without a resolution or a conclusion, which ties up all the loose ends. Indeed, it is possible to maintain that one of the pleasures involved in the consumption of the classic realist text is the resolution of the narrative's issues and its characters' fates.

Fourthly, the reader of such texts is essentially passive. The truth or reality will be set out for him or her by the end. This means that when we read or watch classic realist texts we have relatively little work to do. We simply have to be receptive to the text, not actively engage with its presuppositions.

MacCabe is highly critical of the dominance of such classic realist texts and their effects. For MacCabe such texts are ideological, not in the sense that the characters may **represent** (p. 43) racist or sexist stereotypes, although they may indeed do this, but rather because the structure of the text suggests that contradictions or different points of view can be resolved. MacCabe argues that such texts cannot handle or deal with the very real contradictions that exist in a capitalist society without prioritising one particular version of the real. In the course of this process such texts render the reader passive, rather than encouraging them actively to seek out the truth or reality for themselves or in association with others. This is the case even with those texts that attempt to use the realist form to convey a radical or left-wing message. Again, according to MacCabe, a version of the real is displayed to the reader to accept truth as relatively unproblematic. This view gave rise to a debate around political practice and film or television making, which is often known as the *Days of Hope* debate (see Bennett *et al.*, 1981), where MacCabe's positions were disputed by those who saw potential in the realist form for the conveying of radical content, especially in a series such as *Days of Hope* shown on British television, which dramatised the events of the General Strike of 1926. In turn, MacCabe disputes the realist claims of documentary film makers or photographers. MacCabe's essentially Brechtian position was a radical one that suggested that such attempts would be doomed to failure and that the clear alternative was to use more radical forms to disrupt the expectations associated with the classic realist text. MacCabe then suggests that dominant narratives induce passivity and what can be seen as essentially false pleasures.

## Laura Mulvey: the male gaze

MacCabe's description and critique of dominant, realist or narrative cinema chimes with Mulvey's pathbreaking work on the gaze in contemporary Hollywood cinema, as at the core of the classic realist text is the activity and the look of the male hero. Mulvey begins from within the framework of **psychoanalysis** (p. 5), and draws on the work of Freud and Lacan. In particular she explores the sexual aspects of visual pleasures that derive from the watching of narrative cinema of the dominant Hollywood type. She maintains that narrative cinema provides two main forms of pleasure: scopophilia and identification. Scopophilia refers to the sexual pleasure derived from looking. In its extreme form this pleasure becomes voyeuristic – the 'perversion' of scopophilia is to become a 'Peeping Tom'. Scopophilic pleasure depends on a separation of the viewer from that which is being viewed. We are looking in upon a situation or a text. In general, we derive pleasure from 'using another person as an object of sexual stimulation through sight' (Mulvey 1981: 208) and 'subjecting them to a controlling and curious gaze' (Mulvey, 1989:16)

In general, in addition to these pleasures, Mulvey argues that the viewer of a film also derives pleasure from the process of identification. The looking at the screen leads to the identification of the spectator with what appears in front of them. This process of identification tends to break down the distance or separation that is inherent in the scopophilic process outlined above. The boundaries between the self and the film break down. The spectator almost becomes a part of the action in the film. Mulvey suggests therefore that these two processes are intertwined and paradoxical. This can be explained through Mulvey's main concern: the gendered nature of these processes.

Mulvey's contention here is that, 'In a world ordered by sexual imbalance, pleasure in looking has been split between active/male and passive/female. The determining male gaze 'projects its phantasy on to the female figure which is styled accordingly' (1981: 209). Conventional Hollywood cinema displays women to be looked at by men. Men are active within the film itself and in their looking. Women are to be looked at. However, and here Mulvey returns to the paradox outlined above, the display of the woman on the screen tends to interrupt the narrative drive of the development of the film. If spectators become fixated on the image of the woman displayed before them, then they will not be integrated into the narrative flow of the film and will not be sewn into the dominant ideological frame in the way outlined by MacCabe. Mulvey argues that this paradox is resolved in particular ways by conventional cinema. As she says:

> The presence of woman is an indispensable element of spectacle in normal narrative film, yet her visual presence tends to work against the

development of a story line, to freeze the flow of the action in moments of erotic contemplation. This alien presence then has to be integrated into cohesion with the narrative.

(Mulvey, 1981: 209)

This is often done by positioning the woman as the object of the gaze within the narrative itself. Women characters are often looked at by the male characters in the course of the film. The female character may be a showgirl or a scantily dressed prostitute, for example. To use an example from television, the women police officers in *Miami Vice* often seemed to be working undercover as prostitutes, facilitating the display of their bodies for the male spectator. Male spectators derive pleasure from looking (in the scopophilic sense) and are integrated into the narrative through sharing and identifying with the look and the pleasure of the male characters in the narrative itself. The active hero in the film possesses the female character and identification occurs with his action: 'The male protagonist is free to command the stage, a stage of spatial illusion in which he articulates the look and creates the action' (Mulvey, 1981: 211). Through these processes the spectator becomes tied into the film.

Mulvey concludes by suggesting that there are three 'looks' associated with the cinema: first, 'that of the camera as it records the pro-filmic event' (that which is arranged in front of the camera); second, 'that of the audience as it watches the final product'; and, third, 'that of the characters at each other within the screen illusion' (1981: 214). In summary, Mulvey argues that 'the conventions of the narrative film deny the first two and subordinate them to the third' (1981: 214). Pleasure is derived from the male gaze at the female characters but this is incorporated into the narrative of the film itself and we are sewn in. We forget that we are watching a created product, that we are in a cinema and enter the world of the central (male) protagonist. Mulvey is exceptionally critical of this male gaze and of conventional and dominant Hollywood narrative cinema. She contends that 'women, whose image has been continually stolen and used for this [voyeuristic] end, cannot view the decline of the traditional film form with anything more than sentimental regret' (1981: 215). In the name of a more progressive film practice, she intends to destroy the pleasure in dominant cinema.

Mulvey's work is located within a psychoanalytic perspective that has been very influential in film studies. However, her work tends to neglect some issues that have subsequently been raised in both sociology and cultural studies. For example, it can be suggested that her work is over-general in that it neglects the more concrete ways in which different groups of people may react to film in particular ways according to gender, class, ethnicity and so on. Mulvey concentrates on how the cinema constructs male spectator positions. This gives us little inkling as to how audiences actually behave and the very specific pleasures that they derive from cinema. Likewise, she has very monolithic notions of male and female, ignoring the differences that exist, to which cultural studies has increasingly drawn attention. However, one key merit of Mulvey's work has been to provoke debate on these matters. Thus, for example, there has been concern with the concept of female spectatorship (Stacey, 1994: 22) and the extent to which there is a female gaze. As Stacey (1994) suggests, one of the clear fault lines in these arguments has been between those who have adopted a 'film studies' approach and those operating in the domain of cultural studies. Film studies tends to emphasise the nature of the text and how it constructs subject or spectator positions for the viewer. It theoretically examines these issues with little regard for how people actually watch films in a cinema. Cultural studies shares the concern with the analysis of the text, but argues that how texts are produced and consumed are important theoretical and empirical issues. This has led to investigations of real audiences to identify their actual modes of looking and practices derived from cinema attendance (Stacey, 1994).

Despite these problems Mulvey's use of psychoanalysis represents an important influence on wider work that has taken up the idea of the gaze in very different contexts; such as tourism and leisure. We shall address this in section 10.5. However, the extended consideration of the technologies of **realism** (p. 43) in this section has introduced some critical discussion of the dominance of forms of looking, realism and the visual in **modernity** (p. 295). This critical edge is also apparent in the work on the gaze by **Michel Foucault**

(p. 20), which has been a key influence on contemporary discussions of surveillance.

# 10.4 Foucault: the gaze and surveillance

In a number of important studies **Michel Foucault** (p. 20) (1926–84) developed a critique of the way in which the 'gaze' is implicated in the operation of power. Perhaps his most famous book, *Discipline and Punish* (1977), opens with a striking contrast between two forms of punishment. In the first from 1757 Damiens the regicide (someone who kills a king) is tortured and his body literally ripped to pieces in a public spectacle. In Foucault's second example from 80 years later, young prisoners are subject to a regulated regime in which all their activities are structured by processes of inspection (p. 206).

Foucault's essential point here is not that somehow punishment has become less barbaric. Rather, it is to identify how punishment has become less spectacular as a public ritual. It has moved away from destroying the body (see also Chapter 8), to become a process of inspection, classification and surveillance where the aim is to discipline the body in order to affect the soul. It is no accident that the modern prison is known as the penitentiary or the reformatory.

The key principles of the modern prison are condensed in the English philosopher Jeremy Bentham's plans for the panopticon (p. 208). The basic idea here is that individual cells in the prison would be arranged around a central inspection/surveillance tower. This would mean that all the prisoners could potentially be inspected at any time chosen by the guards in the tower. Moreover, because the tower would be fitted with blinds the prisoners would not know when they were being inspected. They could be under constant surveillance or not studied at all. This leads to the internalisation and the normalisation of the idea of being under the gaze of the powerful. It becomes a part of the experience of the prison and punishment. While locked in their cells the prisoners would have time to reflect on their crimes and commit themselves to the process of reform, as the representation of the prisoner in Figure 10.1 shows.

**Figure 10.1** A prisoner in his cell, kneeling at prayer before the central inspection tower. (Source: Foucault, 1977.)

The key points for our purposes here are that this panoptic mechanism constructs the powerless prisoner as a subject of the gaze of the powerful. There are no dark corners where the prisoner can shelter. Punishment is no longer a spectacle, but a form of inspection and surveillance. It is not difficult to see how much everyday life in modern societies approximates to Foucault's account. Thus, it is increasingly the case that as we shop in contemporary Western societies we are under the gaze of cameras that monitor and record our actions. Cameras may be located in police cars checking traffic or on the perimeters of housing developments. Interestingly, surveillance cameras once oversaw only the most exclusive housing – now they are to be found on a wide variety of housing types of different values. Often, we cannot be sure if we are being watched or recorded at any one moment. Of course, for example, surveillance of crowds at football matches may be in the interests of safety, but it also has implications for

civil liberties. It has been suggested that contemporary cities with their extended surveillance systems have become more prison-like. Ideas of the power of the gaze have been applied in diverse ways. One of the more surprising is the analysis of tourism.

# 10.5 Tourism: gazing and postmodernism

The author who has done most to put tourism on the agenda in cultural studies in recent times is John Urry. In his book *The Tourist Gaze* (1990; 2002), Urry identifies a number of key aspects of contemporary tourism. He suggests that travel and tourism are central aspects of contemporary or modern social life. He is also concerned with potential changes in the nature of tourism in the most recent period, and especially as to whether a form of post-tourism is developing. This would be a core aspect of a **postmodern** (p. 295) society or culture. Such developments might also reflect a change from an industrial to a post-industrial society. Hence, Urry makes distinctions between **modern** (p. 295) and postmodern cultures, industrial and postindustrial societies, and mass tourism and post-tourism.

## The tourist gaze

Urry's work is an attempt to understand tourist behaviour, and to provide an insight into the organisation and development of tourist sites. It has been extremely influential. The notion of the gaze rests on the premise that it is a way of looking at the world, which simultaneously forms what is seen and the way of seeing. The gaze is seen to operate through notions of contrast and difference; it is about the departure from the everyday, from routine. There is an emphasis on the visual and visualism as being dominant in tourism. Urry links this to the centrality of the visual to modernity and the proliferation of visual technologies from the camera to television in contemporary society.

Urry (1990: 2–4) identifies several features of the mass tourism of the contemporary period:

➤ Tourism is a leisure activity, occupying a different sphere of life to work.

➤ It involves movement and a stay at a different place to where the tourist normally lives and works.

➤ The tourist will return to their home and work at the end of the trip.

➤ It is a social activity often undertaken by groups ('package holidays') that can be contrasted with more individual and instrumental travel.

➤ Places visited are chosen because of the anticipation of pleasure and the prospect of an experience that contrasts with the normal and everyday.

➤ The gaze of the tourist is directed towards features ('sights') that differ from those normally encountered. This implies greater sensitivity to the visual than normally occurs in everyday life. These features are then reproduced in photographs, postcards and so on.

➤ This tourist gaze is constructed through signs. 'When tourists see two people kissing in Paris what they capture in the gaze is "timeless romantic Paris". When a small village in England is seen, what they gaze upon is the "real olde England"' (Urry, 1990 3).

➤ Tourism generates an 'array of tourist professionals ... who attempt to reproduce ever-new objects of the tourist gaze' (Urry, 1990: 3).

Such tourism developed in the late nineteenth century in the British practice of the mass movement of the working class of an industrial city to a particular seaside resort to which the city was connected by railway. Many visitors to Morecambe on the north-west coast of England came from Bradford in Yorkshire while the industrial working class of Lancashire travelled to Blackpool. It was a mass activity because all the factories in a particular town would close for the same holiday period (a practice that still has residues in many northern towns and cities). The activity would be organised so that people tended to do the same sorts of things and to gaze on the same sights. The decline of the seaside resort from the 1970s onwards has led to a greater range of tourist and leisure experiences, as well as the development of an extensive and increasingly global tourist industry.

A key aspect of Urry's work is his argument that the gaze is central to the tourist experience. Thus he main-

tains that practices of looking, such as the taking of photographs and the purchasing of postcards, are at the core of the tourist activity. Yet despite its centrality, the nature of the gaze is not systematically developed in Urry's book on the topic. However, he does suggest parallels between his notion of the gaze and that of the French theorist **Michel Foucault** (p. 20) introduced in the previous section, in that the gaze is 'socially organised and systematised' (1990: 3). Despite this, he also maintains that, contrary to the ideas of Foucault, 'contemporary societies are developing less on the basis of surveillance and the normalisation of individuals, and more on the basis of the democratisation of the tourist gaze and the spectacle-isation of place' (1990: 156). Thus, he argues that there are in particular two different forms of the gaze: the 'romantic' and the 'collective'. The romantic tourist gaze involves looking at what has been called 'undisturbed natural beauty' (Urry, 1990: 45), the collective gaze involves 'the presence of large numbers of people', and it is the interaction between such large numbers that creates the atmosphere of the tourist place.

Urry has been criticised for his emphasis on the visual, tourism is not confined to visual repertoires of consumption, rather it is characterised by sensuality; it is an embodied experience. Taste, smell, touch, sound are all key to tourism indeed it has been suggested that Urry is in danger of writing the body and pleasure out of tourism (Franklin and Crang 2001; Bagnall, 2003). Urry (1992, 2002) subsequently revised some of these ideas on the gaze. In particular he reiterated his view that in emphasising the gaze he did not want to denigrate or play down other aspects of the tourist experience (smell, temperature and so on). He points out that corporeal movement and forms of pleasure are central to tourism, it is characterized by what he calls 'corporeal travel'. Thus, here he is drawing attention to the way in which tourists encounter other bodies, objects and the physical world multi-sensuously (Urry, 2001). Nevertheless, he argues that it is the visual that is dominant or *organises* this range of experience. The visual environment in which they are carried out transforms more mundane activities like shopping or walking along a street. However, Urry admits that he did not discuss the precise nature of the gaze in enough detail in his book on the topic. He develops this in more

| Table 10.3 Forms of the tourist gaze | |
|---|---|
| Romantic | Solitary<br>Sustained immersion<br>Gaze involving vision, awe, aura |
| Collective | Communal activity<br>Series of brief encounters<br>Gazing at the familiar |
| Spectatorial | Communal activity<br>Series of brief encounters<br>Glancing and collecting different signs |
| Environmental | Collective organisation<br>Sustained and didactic<br>Scanning to survey and inspect |
| Anthropological | Solitary<br>Sustained immersion<br>Scanning and active interpretation |

*Source*: Urry (1992: 22)

detail, first by showing the way in which the concept of the gaze that he employs is derived from and continuous with the work of Foucault, and second by generating some ideal types of different forms of the tourist gaze which obtain in different contexts. This enables Urry to produce the fivefold categorisation of the gaze reproduced in Table 10.3.

More recently, Urry has drawn attention to the way in which tourism vision is increasingly transferred via the media, through his identification of a 'mediatised gaze' (2002:151). This category of gaze is an attempt to capture the way that places made famous in the media-worlds of popular culture become tourist destinations, as people travel to actual places to experience virtual places. Soap operas, such as *Emmerdale*, or films can attract tourists to places where few visited before the location was made visible on the screen (Couldry, 2005). This enables tourism to invent new destinations and has resulted in a growth in 'media pilgrimage' (Couldry, 2005).

Urry's development of a range of ideal types or categories of tourist gaze is an attempt to capture the diversity of tourism and the tourist experience and is in line with his argument that there has been a massive shift from a more or less single tourist gaze in the nineteenth century to a proliferation of countless discourses, forms and embodiments of tourist gazes (Urry 2001). Urry also presents an argument about historical change in visual culture centring on the notion of post-tourism.

## Postmodernism and post-tourism

Urry suggests that there is developing or has developed a form of post-tourism, which is engaged in by the post-tourist. The post-tourist 'does not have to leave his or her house in order to see many of the objects of the tourist gaze, with TV, video, and the internet everything can now be seen, noted, compared and contextualized' (1988: 37). Furthermore, 'the post-tourist is profoundly aware of change and delights in the multitude of choice' (1988: 38). In contrast to the situation where a whole town would go away to the same seaside town at the same time of the year, there is now great and increasing choice of tourist destinations and experiences. Finally, the post-tourist is involved in a game – the game of tourism. As Urry explains:

> the post-tourist is the person who knows that he or she is a tourist, that it is a game, or rather a whole series of games, with multiple texts and no single, authentic tourist experience. The post-tourist knows that he or she will have to queue time and

time again, that there will be 'hassles' over foreign exchange, that the glossy brochure is a piece of pop culture, that the 'authentic' local entertainment is as socially contrived as is the 'ethnic' bar, and that the quaint 'fishing village' preserved in aspic could not survive without the income from tourism.

(1988: 38)

Urry argues that due to social change towards **post-modernism** (p. 295), a post-tourism has developed. This social change is characterised by three general processes: firstly, a change in what we consume; secondly, change in the nature of our identities; and thirdly, the development and increased influence of middle-class social groups. Concerning change in consumption, Urry follows the approach of the French sociologist and philosopher Jean Baudrillard, in arguing that we are living in an age where we consume signs and images rather than real things. These signs and images are copies of an original, but increasingly the idea of what the original actually was is lost. Everything is a copy of something that does not (or did not) exist, or a simulacrum. Urry gives a clear example of this from New Zealand:

A popular nineteenth-century tourist attraction was a set of pink and white terraces rising up above Lake Rotomahana. These were destroyed by volcanic eruptions in 1886 although photographs of them have remained popular ever since. They are a well-known attraction even if they have not existed for a century. Now, however, there is a plan to recreate the physical attraction by running geothermal water over artificially built terraces in an entirely different location, but one close to existing tourist facilities. This set of what might be called themed terraces will look more authentic than the original which is only known about because of the hundred-year-old photographic images.

(Urry, 1990: 146–7)

Secondly, in accord with other writers on postmodernism, Urry maintains that our sense of self, or **identity** (p. 142), is shifting in contemporary society. We are much less rooted in time and space than were people in previous times. Huge numbers of people and

places now get caught up within a more globalised tourism, that is characterised by flows of images and people, and an emerging 'tourist reflexivity' (Urry, 2001, 2003). We are now familiar with many different representations of different cultures and places, due to their availability through the visual media, and the fact that people now travel more, and experience different things. So Urry suggests that we lose our sense of selfhood and became involved in play with different images and different experiences. Paradoxically, this can lead among some groups to the desire for the 'authentic' experience, or the natural, as in the popularity of hill walking among certain social groups.

Thirdly, Urry links these postmodern developments to the influence of the service class (see also Lash and Urry, 1987). These are groups that 'neither own nor individually manage capital, and which cannot because of distinctions of taste be simply regarded as part of the working class' (1987: 40). While it may be suggested that the kind of postmodern tourist practices that Urry labels post-tourist may be confined to this group initially, his point is that because of the increased salience and influence of this group such practices are likely to become more widespread. In fact, one implication of Urry's more recent work with Scott Lash (Lash and Urry, 1994), where they play down the importance of class distinctions in an increasingly reflexive contemporary society, is to suggest that some of these practices have indeed moved out from the service class to other class fractions.

## 10.6 The glimpse, the gaze, the scan and the glance

Other work has developed the idea of the gaze in rather different directions to those pursued by Urry. For example, in work on the differences between television and the cinema, John Ellis (1982) draws a clear distinction between the *gaze* which, following authors like MacCabe and Mulvey, he associates with forms of dominant cinema, and the *glance* which characterises the way that television is viewed. Television is a domestic medium (Morley, 1986) and due to its place in household routines is relatively rarely looked at in the way that films are in the cinema. When watching television we are often doing other things (ironing, playing with children, doing homework, reading the newspaper) and do not give the screen our full attention. It might be argued, therefore, that in contemporary culture we may be glancing as much as gazing. Such a point of view is elaborated by Bernard Sharratt (1989) who distinguishes between four modes of looking which exist in contemporary culture: the glimpse, the gaze, the scan and the glance.

The *glimpse*, according to Sharratt, is 'the elusively incomplete, though not necessarily fleeting, character of the visibility of the divine, of power, even of the sexual' (1989: 39). The glimpse offers us a partial view, perhaps of a representation that is potentially powerful, or something we desire. It is perhaps a characteristic of **power** (p. 64), that something is kept hidden, and therefore made mysterious and threatening.

The *gaze* is a more prolonged form of looking. According to Sharratt, it consists of three 'regimes'. The first, representation, is a regime similar to that identified by MacCabe in his examination of the classic realist text. The idea is that something can be represented in its key or representative forms which convey a sense of reality that is open to all. The second, reproduction implies that something can be completely reproduced, that a full picture can be given. However, there is a clear sense in which this form implies the artificial, as we are often being given copies of something, which suggests some degree of artifice in the reproduction. The third regime of the gaze is the spectatorial, which describes the way in which a spectator may be looking, or gazing, on an actual, rather than a reproduced, landscape.

Sharratt identifies senses of the *scan*, which are concerned with the operation of power in modern societies, in ways derived from the work of Foucault. These can be summarised in terms of 'surveillance', 'supervision', 'oversight' and 'inspection'. Thus in contemporary societies we are often under surveillance, through cameras in shops for example, which may or may not be recording our actions. Such surveillance may be used to supervise and order our behaviour, as when cameras are used in the process of crowd control at say a football match. Furthermore, the scan involves notions of oversight and inspection, in the sense of being looked over and our behaviour or appearance inspected.

The *glance* implies a fleeting or rapid form of looking, where there is a 'rapidation of registration' and a postponement of the glimpse and the gaze: 'a perpetual procrastination (rather than look long at a landscape we take photos for a future scrutiny that never arises)' (Sharratt, 1989: 40). How many of us ever do look at those endless holiday photographs we take, instead we take in tourist sights via the lens of a camera, and subject them to a fleeting glance rather than a detailed inspection.

Through these categories, we can both suggest forms of ways of looking which change historically and identify different ideal types of looking which may be mobilised in the actual analysis of forms of visual culture. Thus, there may be a shift from a dominance of the glimpse in premodern society, where power operated through mystery and keeping aspects of itself hidden. Tantalising glimpses would be given to awe or intrigue the population. Modern power relations are maintained by the forms of surveillance and inspection of the population described in the scan, and visual culture is also characterised by the development of forms of the gaze as in photography and the cinema described above. The glance implies a speed-up of life as images flash before us more rapidly. This is one aspect of what has been termed late or **postmodernity** (p. 295), where we are said to inhabit a media-saturated society. However, in addition to using Sharratt's categories in this way in terms of the historical theme of this chapter, they can also be used in terms of the second in the analysis of forms of visual culture. In particular, it is important to consider forms of looking that do not conform to the gaze as set out by such as Mulvey and Urry, as these may be characteristic of the way in which a number of forms of visual culture are actually appropriated. Thus, some of the analyses of advertising examined in Chapter 4 would seem to imply through their close attention to the advertisements themselves that they are appropriated through a concentrated gaze, when in fact they are more likely to be glanced at. This also raises the important issue of how visual representations are integrated into the relations of everyday interaction, to which issue we now turn.

# 10.7  Visual interaction in public places

The figure of the *flâneur*, we have noted, took pleasure in witnessing the sights afforded by the public places and spaces of the modern city. What facilitates the activity of the *flâneur* is the anonymity of life in the public realm, a feature noted by **Simmel** (p. 271) and many other commentators. Simmel saw this anonymity and the accompanying reserve and blasé attitude as double edged: on the one hand it enlarged the scope of individual freedom beyond what was possible in small-scale rural society, but on the other it created conditions of isolation and social disorganization that impoverished people's existence.

Books with titles like *The Fall of Public Man* (Sennett, 1977) and *The Lonely Crowd* (Reisman *et al.*, 1953) unfavorably contrasted modern city living with rural ways of life. Louis Wirth (1938) famously defined urbanism as a way of life emerging from the large numbers of people living in areas of high density that emphasised social differences. Stanley Milgram (1970), a social psychologist developing Wirth's ideas, suggests that the city's large, dense and heterogenous population creates 'stimulus overload' for the individual. The 'urbanite' adapts to overload by choosing and prioritising. Since urbanites have many more contacts with people than rural-dwellers, they tend to keep these contacts brief and superficial. One filmic example is the splendid scene in *Crocodile Dundee* where Mick, fresh from the Australian Outback, begins the impossible task of greeting everyone he passes on a New York street. Urbanites minimise involvements with unacquainted persons by a range of measures including, for example, giving low priority to the requests or distress of others, assuming an unfriendly countenance when travelling on public transport, or by selecting who to talk to by keeping the answer phone permanently turned on. These methods of dealing with overload can result in an attenuation or withdrawal of the common courtesies, like refusing to give up one's seat to an elderly person or failing to apologise to the person one has just collided with. At worst there is the phenomenon of 'bystander apathy'. Milgram reports incidents where persons have been kidnapped, severely assaulted and even murdered in busy public places because no one would come to the victim's aid. Non-involvement becomes the shield that urbanites use to protect themselves from overload. But the preservation of privacy is something that also requires positive acts from others; they must act towards the self in the same way that self acts towards them for orderly life in public to be sustained. The general orderliness of public places is accomplished through the methods and strategies that people employ when walking down the street, asking directions, buying goods in a shop and so forth. In the accomplishment of this orderliness, ordinary practices of looking and making inferences on the basis of what is seen are central. The rest of this section considers how social organisation and cultural understandings figure in these ordinary practices of looking and making inferences.

## Categoric knowing: appearential and spatial orders

*Public places* can be defined as those sites in a society that are freely accessible to persons (streets, stations and so on) and which can be contrasted with *private places* (such as homes and offices) where access is restricted and which may only be granted by invitation (Goffman, 1963a: 9; Lofland, 1973: 19). Obviously the distinction is not absolute; there are locations, like GPs' waiting rooms or restaurants, that have a hybrid status, semi-public places, and other places like airports which carefully demarcate public places from those that are restricted to various categories of person (people dropping off or collecting friends and relatives gather 'groundside', while passengers, airline personnel and security staff have access to 'airside'). In public places many of the people we encounter will be known to us only in *categoric* terms. We identify them as 'female', 'white', 'elderly', 'walking with a limp', categories that we can glean from visual cues, unlike those we know *personally*, that is those about whose biography we know something – great-aunt Maisie who has been finding it difficult to get around since her fall last year. Again, categoric and personal knowing are merely ends of a continuum.

The **modern** (p. 295) city differs from its pre-modern, pre-industrial counterpart in significant ways. According to Lyn Lofland (1973), public life in cities is made possible through the 'ordering' of urban populations by their appearance and by their spatial location. She suggests that within a city strangers 'know a great deal about one another simply by looking' (Lofland, 1973: 22, emphasis removed). Her thesis is that the pre-industrial city was dominated by appearential ordering: the distinctive costume and insignia worn by people gave visual evidence of social rank and occupation. The pre-modern city was nowhere near as large as its modern equivalent and thus use of public space was mixed. Prisons were built near palaces and rich and poor lived in the same parts of town. Status, legitimated by law and custom, was expressly symbolised in clothing that signified the person's status as craftsperson, entertainer, priest, servant or trader. Public orderliness depended upon the personal appearance of the strangers reliably indexing their standing in society.

In contrast the modern city is dominated by spatial ordering. Considerably larger in area and population than its pre-industrial counterpart, it encompasses a wide range of specialised activities and an extensive division of labour. Activities that commonly occurred in public places, for example the education of children, the elimination of human wastes and the punishment of offenders, are now confined within walled spaces. Persons are sifted and sorted into discrete spaces as urban land use becomes specialised. Residential segregation emerges along class and ethnic lines. Distinct districts develop: working-class estates, middle-class suburbs, Chinatowns, ghettos and enclaves, Italian and gay 'villages', redeveloped docklands. There is also industrial and commercial segregation: industrial estates, malls and out-of-town shopping and entertainment complexes. And there is age segregation, especially at either end of the life cycle: colleges, schools and nurseries keep young people off the streets and away from workplaces for sizeable parts of the day while older people are to be found in residential establishments, sheltered housing and retirement communities.

Moreover, as dress codes become more flexible, costume ceases to be a stable indicator of social status.

People link their clothing choices to their activities rather than their status, often dressing up or down or using clothes to play with social conventions (see also Chapter 8). Where a person stands in the modern city matters more than what he or she wears:

> A homosexual male is a man in a homosexual bar and not necessarily a man in a pink ruffled shirt. A prostitute is a woman standing alone in the 'Tenderloin' and not necessarily a woman in a revealing costume. Elites are persons who can be found in the stores and restaurants which cater to their incredible buying power and not necessarily persons who wear silk. The poor are persons who live in a certain section of town and not necessarily the people who wear the most tattered clothes. ... A university professor is someone who stands facing the students in a university classroom. And the fact that he may look like his students, like a Wall Street lawyer, or like a skid row bum should not be allowed to obscure this simple truth.
>
> (Lofland, 1973: 82–3)

In the modern city, 'who' you are is, for initial purposes at least, very much bound up with 'where' you are. The supplanting of the primacy of appearential ordering by spatial ordering in the modern city is no less a visual phenomenon, discernible to persons simply by looking. Lofland's appearential to spatial thesis articulates a very broad historical trend. She recognises that appearential considerations continue to be important in the modern city and that in given instances people will enhance the reliability of inferences about strangers by bringing to bear their categorical knowledge of places *in combination with* categorical knowledge of appearances. In order to further consider the complexities of such inference making on the basis of observable features of everyday life we need to consider some aspects of the work of Erving Goffman (1922–82), perhaps the pre-eminent scholar of face-to-face interaction, of what transpires when people are in one another's physical presence.

## Unfocused interaction, civil inattention and normal appearances

'Co-present' persons, simply by virtue of their capacity mutually to monitor each other's actions, generate an analytically distinguishable domain that Goffman (1983) calls 'the interaction order'. In other words, whenever we are in the actual presence of others our actions are at least in part shaped by rules and understandings deriving from the demands of interaction. Broadly speaking, these interactional demands or requirements boil down to two: the informational and the ritual (see Figure 10.2). When we interact we must acquire some information about the mood, intentions, trustworthiness, knowledgeability and so forth of others in order to achieve our practical purposes (answering a question, getting an appointment with the dentist, obtaining directions to the cinema that we're having trouble in finding). But we must attend to ritual concerns, that is we need to address the expression and control of our own feelings and those of others, showing respect towards ourself and consideration toward the other (for taking up their time with our queries, for example). Informational and ritual demands are interleaved in interesting ways in actual interaction.

Take the simple act of walking down a moderately busy street. This is an example of what Goffman calls *unfocused interaction* where people simply commingle, information about them becoming observable at a glance in virtue of 'sheer and mere copresence'. Although we may not talk to anyone, we are, none the less, interacting when we walk down the street. We take care so as not to get in their way; we anticipate a way round persons with large shopping bags. We are oriented to the actions of those others. Without giving it much conscious thought we glance at the other, scan their appearance, then quickly look away, if need be adjusting our course. The other does the same. Each person thus succeeds in conveying to the other that neither is a threat. These brief actions – likened by Goffman to passing cars dipping their lights – are instances of the norm of 'civil inattention' (Goffman, 1963a: 83–8) at work. Note that civil inattention is not ignoring someone, giving them non-person treatment, nor is it incivil attention, as occurs when one person pointedly stares at another, for example, the Al Pacino character in the shoe shop scene in *Sea of Love* (dir. Harold Becker). Civil inattention occurs every day on countless occasions in cities throughout the world. It involves an informational element as we acquire some categoric knowledge of the other and it involves a ritual element because the act of turning away our glance as

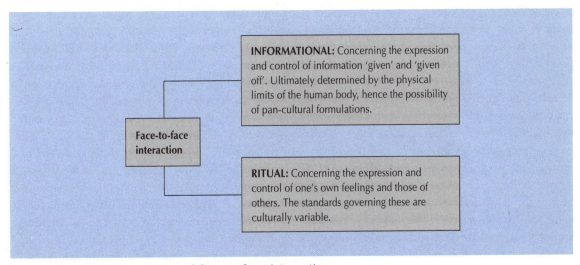

**INFORMATIONAL:** Concerning the expression and control of information 'given' and 'given off'. Ultimately determined by the physical limits of the human body, hence the possibility of pan-cultural formulations.

**Face-to-face interaction**

**RITUAL:** Concerning the expression and control of one's own feelings and those of others. The standards governing these are culturally variable.

**Figure 10.2** Basic dimensions of face-to-face interaction.

soon as it is given is an act of courtesy, a way of not further invading the privacy of the other. As Goffman says, civil inattention 'is perhaps the slightest of inter-personal rituals, yet one that constantly regulates the social intercourse of persons in our society' (1963a: 84). It is one essential prerequisite for trouble-free interaction in public, the cardinal norm through which civility is realised.

Yet interaction in public is not always free of troubles. Sometimes civil inattention can seem more honoured in the breach. As notorious cases like that of Rodney King and the Los Angeles police remind us, public places can be risky sites for the citizenry. They are also sites of routine forms of *public harassment*, 'the abuses, harryings, and annoyances characteristic of public places and uniquely facilitated by communication in public' (Gardner, 1995: 4). Public harassment includes shouted remarks, gratuitous insults and innu-endoes, staring, stalking and the like, which are most commonly (but not exclusively) targeted at women in public. The initiation of this intrusion is based on the observable characteristics of the person – their gender, ethnicity, sexual orientation, physical handicap and so forth.

The relationships or ties between co-present persons are a further observable feature of public places. Goffman distinguishes the 'anonymous relations' occurring between passers-by who know each other only in categoric terms from 'anchored relations', where an element of personal knowing exists. Goffman designates as a *tie-sign* that evidence of the relationship between co-present persons that can be discerned through their 'body placement, posture, gesture, and vocal expression' (1971: 195). Examples of tie-signs include hand-holding and kissing, sharing the same cup or the same bottle of sun-tan lotion, standing close to another or distinctly endeavouring to keep one's distance, wiping another's nose or feeding them with a spoon, addressing a person as 'sir' or 'madam' or replying to them with a term of endearment. Tie-signs such as these, when placed in the context of what we know and have witnessed, enable us to infer the likely anchored or personal relationship between persons: as intimates, servitor and client, parent and child, sales-person and customer, boss and employee, long-married spouses and so forth. While the public realm is some-

times characterised as a world of strangers, the unac-quainted others we encounter are not wholly strange to us. We can readily interpret the tie-signs we witness to form an appraisal of the likely relationship between persons. To be sure, our appraisals are fallible (we all know the adage that appearances can be deceptive), but they are, none the less, adequate for many of our prac-tical purposes. Moreover, these appraisals of relationship depend upon fitting the tie-sign to other features of the context such as time and place, appear-ance, activity, prior knowledge and so forth. Finally, while many tie-signs are accessible to us by merely looking, others depend upon the conversational frag-ments we hear ('Honey, where are my sunglasses?'). The observability of a relationship includes what is more broadly perceivable about it, not just what can be literally seen.

Especially in public places, then, human beings are what Harvey Sacks once called 'inference-making machines' (Sacks, 1992). As members of a society we acquire a body of common-sense cultural knowledge and practical skills that enable us to accomplish the ordinary tasks that face us in our everyday life. In going about our everyday business we will often adopt a stance of easy control that is only made possible because nothing out of the ordinary is happening. We check our immediate surrounds, our *Umwelt* (Goffman, 1971: 252–5), the sphere around us in which sources of alarm, of danger to ourselves reside, to confirm that all is well. The actual size of the indi-vidual's *Umwelt* will vary: on a crowded street this bubble of relevance will only span a metre or two; on an empty street at night we can become concerned at the approach of a stranger hundreds of metres away. In public places especially we will scan our immediate sur-rounds for signs of threat to our person, our property, our privacy and personal well-being. We have a well-developed sense of 'normal appearances', of the world around the individual looking just as we expect it should, portending no threatening or alarming features (Goffman, 1971: 239). As cultural beings interacting in public places we possess not only acquired knowledge but also practical, embodied skills, in short 'experience' in coping with the threats and opportunities that situ-ations can present. One important dimension of experience concerns the looks of normal appearances.

Certain occupations that involve work on the city streets, such as the police, value such experience and describe it in craft-like terms. The policeman's practical problem in conducting work on the streets is to infer criminality from the appearances of persons (Sacks, 1972). The experience required to infer criminality correctly is acquired 'on the beat' by novices from more mature police officers. Part of this experience involves adopting a sceptical attitude to normal appearances, not treating appearances at their face value but rather scrutinising them for evidence of criminal activities that may be accomplished under their guise. An 'incongruity procedure' is employed by the officer in order to warrant further investigation. When something occurs that is at variance with normal appearances, the officer may wish to pursue inquiries. Officers are taught to see persons in behavioural terms, i.e. in terms of the activities in which they are engaged: 'the lovely young lady alighting from a cab is now observable as a call-girl arriving for a session' (Sacks, 1972: 285). The normality of normal appearances is practically defined as 'normal for the place at a time'; trucks that do not normally unload at midnight in this district become objects of suspicion to the officer. There is a 'normal ecology of territories'; persons who 'don't belong' in this place – for example, the apparently poor in a wealthy neighbourhood – may be asked to justify their presence. People who observably treat the police's presence as anything other than normal – giving an officer a 'double look', for instance – may come under scrutiny.

The routine uses of places and objects are seen in terms of favoured misuses: dustbins can contain dead babies, playgrounds attract child molesters, shops are regarded as venues for shoplifting. The police officer's street experience demands a studied attention to normal appearances and what they may conceal.

Of course it is possible to exaggerate the degree of risk, threat and incivility in urban public places and thereby to overlook the rich street life of wide boulevards, pavement cafés, parades, entertainments, sports and games and the like that it is possible to enjoy in many cities. Pleasure and conviviality are no less real features of the apprehension of city life. But both pleasure and risk in public places are underwritten by a taken-for-granted normative ordering, ensembles of cultural understandings that importantly depend upon the visual mediation of our socialised competence.

## 10.8 The city as text

As noted earlier, **Walter Benjamin**'s (p. 274) contribution to the study of visual culture concentrated on the social and cultural life of Paris in the nineteenth century. Paris has been seen as the 'capital of the nineteenth century' crystallizing the key developments of modernity. It was here that the shopping arcades and the *flâneur* originated. The key role of cities like Paris in the development of modern forms of life and visual culture is graphically captured in the work of Marshall

### Box 10.1

**The experience of modernity**

There is a mode of vital experience – experience of space and time, of the self and others, of life's possibilities and perils – that is shared by men and women all over the world today. I will call this body of experience 'modernity'. To be modern is to find ourselves in an environment that promises us adventure, power, joy, growth, transformation of ourselves and the world – and, at the same time, that threatens to destroy everything we have, everything we know, everything we are. Modern environments and experiences cut across all boundaries of geography and ethnicity, of class and nationality, of religion and ideology: in this sense, modernity can be said to unite all mankind. But it is a paradoxical unity, a unity of disunity: it pours us all into a maelstrom of perpetual disintegration and renewal, of struggle and contradiction, of ambiguity and anguish. To be modern is to be part of a universe in which, as Marx said, 'all that is solid melts into air'.

Berman (1983: 15)

Berman (1983). Benjamin and Berman draw our attention to the experience of the city as an environment that increasingly demands to be 'read' by those participating in it.

## Marshall Berman: modernity, modernisation and modernism

Many of the key themes in Berman's work are summed up in the opening paragraph of his book that is reproduced in Box 10.1.

Berman used three key terms in his work: **modernity** (p. 295), which is a form of social experience; modernisation, which is a social process; and modernism, which is a set of visions and values. Berman primarily addresses the relationship between modernisation and modernism, with the link between these two being the experience involved in modernity. Berman sees three phases in modernity: first, from the start of the sixteenth century to the end of the eighteenth, when:

> people are just beginning to experience modern life; they hardly know what has hit them. They grope, desperately but half blindly, for an adequate vocabulary; they have little or no sense of a modern public or community within which their trials and hopes can be shared.
>
> (Berman, 1983: 16–17)

Modern life is new and there is the sense of being bowled over by these new developments. The second phase of modernity begins with the revolutionary wave of the 1780s and 1790s and lasts to the beginning of the twentieth century. Berman argues that after the French Revolution a modern public develops. People realise that they live in the modern age, but can remember what came before. Importantly for Berman, there is a dual tendency in modernity: a sense of adventure combined with a sense of loss and a feeling of insecurity. It is here that the great works of modernist literature and art arise as well as those forms of politics and writing that attempt to confront these dilemmas (notably Marxism).

Many of these changes are contained in Baudelaire's writings from Paris, which address the new forms of modern life in the arcades and the political insurrec-

tions of 1848, and in the subsequent redevelopment of Paris as boulevards were constructed in accord with the plans of Baron Haussmann. The boulevards destroyed old working-class neighbourhoods from where the earlier political protest had arisen, and were constructed to allow the clear and fast movement of troops to put down any future protest. These new roads are also the place of traffic and the dangerous bustle of modernity. 'Thus the life of the boulevards was also more risky and frightening for the multitudes of men and women who moved on foot' (Berman, 1983: 159).

The twentieth century starts a new period of modernity. Here modernisation has become so generalised that it has taken in 'virtually the whole world'. Despite the fact that this is often cited as the period of the greatest achievement of modernism in the arts, which Berman recognises, he also feels that this is the period where modernism loses its way, as the sense of the duality of modernity is overcome. One course was to celebrate modernity as in the Italian futurists and those who would influence the look of cities and architecture for the rest of the twentieth century like Le Corbusier, who celebrates the power of the motor car and the rational redevelopment of the city (Berman, 1983: 166–7) in the direction that will point the way forward to the city of the tower block and the motorway. The other course was to denigrate modernity and seek a return to traditional forms of art and architecture.

The work of critics like Benjamin and Berman suggests that it is possible to interpret cities as texts: to 'read' them as meaningful configurations of visually available signs. At least three aspects of urban physical environments can be interpreted in this way: the architectural displays that a city's buildings provide; the visual features of the built environment that facilitate and constrain people's movement around the city; and the landscape (or cityscape) as condensation of power. We illustrate these different aspects in the following subsections.

## Reading architecture

One way of understanding the city as a text is to examine the implications of the architectural displays of its prominent buildings. The sociologist Keith MacDonald (1989) has interpreted the features of the

## Defining concept 10.1

### Modernity, modernism, postmodernity, postmodernism

These terms are often used in relatively loose and ill-defined ways, leading to much confusion and contestation. Any codification will itself be controversial. Modernity is best thought of as a form of society or experience. For Berman (1983) the key feature is its double-edged nature: change that disrupts the traditional is stimulating but frightening in that old certainties are lost. The sociologist Giddens (1990) argues that modern societies differ from traditional ones in pace and scope of social change, as well as in institutions, like the nation-state. Currently, the idea of modernity is resurgent in social science and the arts as attention has moved away from capitalism and patriarchy as structural concepts. Modernism is most frequently used to characterise a range of activities in the arts and culture (in the more narrow sense) which developed between 1890 and 1930. A key feature was the contestation of **realism** (p. 43) in **representation** (p. 43) and a related focus on form. The role of the artist was emphasised, as was the political nature of art.

Postmodernism is also often used in rather loose ways to refer to a society or experience, particular forms of artistic activity, and a philosophical or theoretical approach. These should be separated analytically. Prefacing modern(ity, ism) with post- implies in some ways that the modern has been superseded, or that new activities are built upon the modern bases. Postmodernity might then refer to a society that still contains some modern aspects (it is not traditional) but which has added or developed a greater role for the mass media of communication (for example, in Baudrillard) or consumption (as in Featherstone, for instance). However, some authors reject this idea, suggesting that the best description is late modernity (Giddens, for example). As a form of artistic activity, postmodernism has been applied to diverse producers in different fields. Rap music or Talking Heads are examples from music. Twin Peaks was seen as a postmodernist television show. It can be suggested that such forms share some of the emphases of modernism, but inflect them in different directions. They are playful, refer to other previous texts, break boundaries between high and popular culture and so on. A problem here is the attempt to apply an overarching term to diverse forms and types. This is particularly paradoxical when the nature of postmodernism as idea or philosophy is considered. A key suggestion here (associated with Lyotard) is that one of the characteristics of postmodernism is the impossibility of 'grand' or 'meta' narratives. Knowledge is both more local, contingent and relative. Postmodernist ideas in theory and philosophy often blur with those associated with **poststructuralism** (p. 17). Meaning is contested, as is the relation between words and things.

Debates over postmodernism were the storm centre of academic life in the social sciences and humanities in the 1980s. Some on the political left saw them as a new irrationalism that fitted well with the rightward drift of Western society and culture. Others emphasised the way in which these ideas allowed those previously marginalised (women, black people, homosexuals and so on) a place from which to speak and contest the domination of even leftist ideas and practices. This connects to contemporary notions of **identity** (p. 142) politics.

### Further reading

Connor, S. (1989) *Postmodernist Culture*, Oxford: Blackwell.

Giddens, A. (1990) *The Consequences of Modernity*, Cambridge: Polity.

Lemert, C. (2005) *Postmodernism Is Not What You Think: Why Globalization Threatens Modernity*, Boulder: Paradigm.

London headquarters of three established professional groups: accountants, lawyers and medical doctors. His study of the Association of Chartered Certified Accountants, the Law Society, and the Royal College of Physicians and the Royal College of Surgeons considers a number of features of the buildings they occupied. The purchase and use of such buildings is a form of conspicuous consumption that forms part of the strategic attempts of these professions to enhance their power. MacDonald examined such factors as the value of the site the building, its size and cost, its materials and interior spaces, and the celebrity rating as assessed by the architectural literature. He suggests that the status claims and desires of professional groups are

**Figure 10.3** The Chartered Accountants' Hall. (Source: MacDonald, 1989: 62.)

reflected in the buildings occupied by the professional organizations of these three groups. Accountants are the 'critical case' in that they were not as successful in their drive for control over the regulation of their profession as lawyers or the older established medical professions had been. This reflected in MacDonald's findings about the site, buildings, and celebrity ratings of the three groups. The Chartered Accountant's Hall does not achieve the same values on these measures as the buildings occupied by the other two profession's London headquarters.

The Westin Bonaventure Hotel in downtown Los Angeles is widely regarded as a classic example of a postmodern building. It has been the subject of analyses by Jean Baudrillard (1988a) and Fredric Jameson (1991).

➤ **Architecture:** the Bonaventure is a building that 'respect(s) the vernacular of the American city' because it does not attempt to impose a 'different, a distinct, an elevated, a new Utopian sign system into the tawdry and commercial sign system of the surrounding city' (Jameson 1991: 39).

➤ **Exterior:** its walls of mirrored glass act as an aggressive shield – like sunglasses that allow the viewer to look out without being seen from the outside (cf. Baudrillard, 1988a).

➤ **Entrances:** 'There are three entrances to the Bonaventure, one from Figueroa and the other two by way of elevated gardens on the other side of the hotel, which is built into the remaining slope of the former Bunker Hill. None of these is anything like the old hotel marquee, or the monumental porte cochere with which the sumptuous buildings of yesteryear were wont to stage your passage from city street to the interior. The entryways of the Bonaventure are, as it were, lateral and rather back-door affairs: the gardens in the back admit you to the sixth floor of the towers, and even there you must walk down one flight to find the elevator by which you gain access to the lobby. Meanwhile, what one is still tempted to think of as the front entry, on Figueroa, admits you, baggage and all, onto the second-story shopping balcony, from which you must take an escalator down to the main registration desk' (Jameson 1991: 39).

➤ **A minicity:** 'the Bonaventure aspires to being a total space, a complete world, a kind of miniature city' (Jameson 1991: 40).

➤ **Escalators and external elevators:** These make visible the visitor's travels around the hotel and downgrade walking as a significant mode of movement: 'Here the narrative stroll has been underscored, symbolized, reified, and replaced by a transportation machine which becomes the allegorical signifier of that older promenade we are no longer allowed to conduct on our own' (Jameson 1991: 42).

➤ **The lobby:** 'can only be characterized as milling confusion, something like the vengeance this space takes on those who still seek to walk through it. Given the absolute symmetry of the four towers, it is quite impossible to get your bearings in this lobby; recently, color coding and directional signals have been added in a pitiful and revealing, rather desperate, attempt to restore the coordinates of an older space.' (Jameson 1991:43).

# Box 10.2

## Important elements of the city

The contents of the city images so far studied, which are referable to physical forms, can conveniently be classified into five types of elements: paths, edges, districts, nodes, and landmarks. These elements may be defined as follows:

1 *Paths* Paths are the channels along which the observer customarily, occasionally, or potentially moves. They may be streets, walkways, transit lines, canals, railroads. For many people, these are the predominant elements in their image. People observe the city while moving through it, and along these paths the other environmental elements are arranged and related.

2 *Edges* Edges are the linear elements not used or considered as paths by the observer. They are the boundaries between two phases, linear breaks in continuity: shores, railroad cuts, edges of development, walls. They are lateral references rather than coordinate axes. Such edges may be barriers, more or less penetrable, which close one region off from another; or they may be seams, lines along which two regions are related and joined together. These edge elements, although probably not as dominant as paths, are for many people important organizing features, particularly in the role of holding together generalized areas, as in the outline of a city by water or wall.

3 *Districts* Districts are the medium-to-large sections of the city, conceived of as having two-dimensional extent, which the observer mentally enters 'inside of,' and which are recognizable as having some common, identifying character. Always identifiable from the inside, they are also used for exterior reference if visible from the outside. Most people structure their city to some extent in this way, with individual differences as to whether paths or districts are the dominant elements. It seems to depend not only upon the individual but also upon the given city.

4 *Nodes* Nodes are points, the strategic spots in a city into which an observer can enter, and which are the intensive foci to and from which he is traveling. They may be primarily junctions, places of a break in transportation, a crossing or convergence of paths, moments of shift from one structure to another. Or the nodes may be simply concentrations, which gain their importance from being the condensation of some use or physical character, as a street-corner hangout or an enclosed square. Some of these concentration nodes are the focus and epitome of a district, over which their influence radiates and of which they stand as a symbol. They may be called cores. Many nodes, of course, partake of the nature of both junctions and concentrations. The concept of node is related to the concept of path, since junctions are typically the convergence of paths, events on the journey. It is similarly related to the concept of district, since cores are typically the intensive foci of districts, their polarizing center. In any event, some nodal points are to be found in almost every image, and in certain cases they may be the dominant feature.

5 *Landmarks* Landmarks are another type of point-reference, but in this case the observer does not enter within them, they are external. They are usually a rather simply defined physical object: building, sign, store, or mountain. Their use involves the singling out of one element from a host of possibilities. Some landmarks are distant ones, typically seen from many angles and distances, over the tops of smaller elements, and used as radial references. They may be within the city or at such a distance that for all practical purposes they symbolize a constant direction. Such are isolated towers, golden domes, great hills. Even a mobile point, like the sun, whose motion is sufficiently slow and regular, may be employed. Other landmarks are primarily local, being visible only in restricted localities and from certain approaches. These are the innumerable signs, store fronts, trees, doorknobs, and other urban detail, which fill in the image of most observers. They are frequently used clues of identity and even of structure, and seem to be increasingly relied upon as a journey becomes more and more familiar.

Lynch (1960: 46–8)

For Jameson, the Bonaventure condenses some key aspects of postmodern culture and life. Jameson's focus on the idea of **postmodern** (p. 295) space and the experience of it is particularly important. For Jameson the confusion engendered by the Bonaventure is symbolic of wider confusions and our inability to locate ourselves in the complexity of the postmodern world. Such claims about postmodernism will be considered further in section 10.9.

## Reading cities: legibility and imageability

We have already shown how critics like **Benjamin** (p. 274) and Berman interpret a city like Paris. Other writers from different disciplinary backgrounds have carried out similar exercises in different ways and using different concepts. One influential case of this can be found in the work of Kevin Lynch (1960) which was used by Jameson (1991) in his work on postmodernism and **postmodernity** (p. 295).

Lynch analyses the nature of inhabitants' experience of three American cities: Boston, Jersey City and Los Angeles. At the heart of his analysis is the concept of *legibility* – 'the ease with which its parts can be recognized and can be organized into a coherent pattern' (1960: 2–3). Also of great importance is the idea of *imageability* – 'that quality in a physical object which gives it a high probability of evoking a strong image in any given observer' (1960: 9). From his three examples, Lynch classifies five different elements of the city which are important in the generation of the experience of the city: paths, edges, districts, nodes and landmarks. Definitions and examples of these are given in the extract from Lynch (1960) in Box 10.2.

Lynch uses the identification of these elements to inform design strategies in the planning of city areas. These elements can also be used as a methodological base for the interpretation of the city in cultural studies. They present an apt set of terms to articulate how people read and use city spaces. Another important aspect of Lynch's work is the emphasis that he places on the inhabitant's experience of the city. Lynch does not simply write as the interpreter or critic, but attempts to mobilise or tap what might be called the experience of the 'audience' for the city. Of course,

there may be many different audiences for the city, divided along lines of class, gender, race and age and so on.

## Reading landscape and power

Sharon Zukin (1991, 1992) suggests that landscape gives a material form to relationships of power. Landscapes can then be interpreted to represent or symbolise the different contours of relationships of power at specific historical moments. Zukin is particularly concerned with the relationships of power that are characteristic of capitalism:

> Asymmetrical power in the visual sense suggests capitalists' great ability to draw from a potential repertoire of images, to develop a succession of real and symbolic landscapes that define every historical period, including postmodernity. This reverses Jameson's dictum that architecture is important to postmodernity because it is the symbol of capitalism. Rather, architecture is important because it is the capital of symbolism.
>
> (Zukin, 1992: 225)

A key aspect of Zukin's work is the emphasis that she places on the nature of the transformation of cities. She examines the nature of the process of *gentrification* which has redeveloped parts of older cities of modernity like London or New York (Zukin, 1989, 1995). Newer cities do not contain the sorts of buildings that can be transformed by this process. Such cities, like Los Angeles, which are emblematic of **postmodernity** (p. 295), are structured around entertainment – they are like a kind of Disney World. In this fashion Zukin raises some crucial issues concerning the contemporary transformation of power and visual culture in the city, which is the subject of the next section.

## 10.9 Visual culture and postmodernity

In this book, and in this chapter, we have suggested that culture can be understood in two main ways: as text and as way of life. In keeping with this distinction, it is possible to argue that contemporary developments in culture can be divided into the movement towards the dominance of postmodernism as a textual form and **postmodernity** (p. 295) as a new way of life. Such an analytic distinction helps to organise a vast range of contemporary debates on contemporary culture.

Interpretations of postmodernism/ity can be summarised quite neatly in discussions of the city and its buildings. Thus in his discussion of the Bonaventure, Jameson examines the nature of this building, the experiences it provokes and its location in a particular city. Charles Jencks (1989), who is the most prominent writer on postmodernism in architecture, maintains that architectural postmodernism involves 'double coding'. He suggests that postmodernism is:

> fundamentally the eclectic mixture of any tradition with that of the immediate past: it is both the continuation of Modernism and its transcendence. Its best works are characteristically doubly-coded and ironic, making a feature of the wide choice, conflict and discontinuity of traditions, because this heterogeneity most captures our pluralism. Its hybrid style is opposed to the minimalism of Late-Modern ideology and all revivals which are based on an exclusive dogma or taste.
>
> (Jencks, 1989: 7)

The following pages explore these issues in more detail.

## Postmodernism and capitalism: Fredric Jameson and David Harvey

In more critical discussions of postmodernism and postmodernity, such processes imply the loss of the sense of historical location, as features from many different historical periods and places are brought together, producing 'flattening' (Jameson, 1991) and 'time-space compression' (Harvey, 1990). This weakening of historicity is one of the four features of postmodernism identified by Jameson (1991: 6–25):

1 *Depthlessness*. The break-down of the depth models characteristic of pre-postmodern societies, such as those between the inside/outside, essence/appear-

ance, authenticity/inauthenticity, signifier/signified, latent/manifest.

2 *Weakening of historicity*. We are no longer able to situate ourselves in historical time as unfolding in a clear and coherent fashion. There has been a weakening of grand or meta-narratives. These developments are represented by the popularity of the 'nostalgia' film which incorporates a notion of 'pastness' or earlier films into an unlocated and vague present.

3 *New emotional tone*. The 'waning of affect' as we no longer seek the depths of human personality or feel separated from our essential self (as in the idea of alienation) but are 'burnt-out'.

4 *Pastiche*. Postmodern culture does not parody other culture with the intention of producing a particular effect but pastiches in a playful manner to no ultimate aim.

These transformations are also taking place in the wider culture of the contemporary period. It has been suggested that postmodernity consists of features that distinguish it from modernity such as those detailed by David Harvey (1990) in Table 10.4.

The kind of changes identified by writers like Harvey and Jameson seem to be furthest advanced in the United States and especially in its cities. If Europe and Paris were the sites of the development of **modernity**, then **postmodernity** (p. 295) is centred in the USA and Los Angeles. The latter contains the predominant 'dream factory' of the contemporary world – Hollywood – but is also at the core of contemporary communications and media developments in the wider sense. Los Angeles is also home to many aspects of US military power (Soja, 1989) and new forms of postmodern building like the Bonaventure. The home of the motor car has been central in the generation of new modes of social interaction, the accommodation of which has transformed other cities.

## Jean Baudrillard: simulacra and hyperreality

In this chapter we have tried to show the range of ways in which culture both as text and as way of life is visually available to its members. Seeing, we have suggested,

**Table 10.4** Fordist modernity versus flexible postmodernity, or the interpenetration of opposed tendencies in capitalist society as a whole

| Fordist modernity | Flexible postmodernity |
|---|---|
| economies of scale/master code/hierarchy homogeneity/detail division of labour | economies of scope/idiolect/anarchy diversity/social division of labour |
| paranoia/alienation/symptom public housing/monopoly capital | schizophrenia/decentring/desire homelessness/entrepreneurialism |
| purpose/design/mastery/determinacy production capital/universalism | play/chance/exhaustion/indeterminacy fictitious capital/localism |
| state power/trade unions state welfarism/metropolis | financial power/individualism neoconservatism/counter-urbanisation |
| ethics/money commodity God the Father/materiality | aesthetics/moneys of account The Holy Ghost/immateriality |
| production/originality/authority blue collar/avant-gardism interest group politics/semantics | reproduction/pastiche/eclecticism white collar/commercialism charismatic politics/rhetoric |
| centralisation/totalisation synthesis/collective bargaining | decentralisation/deconstruction antithesis/local contracts |
| operational management/master code phallic/single task/origin | strategic management/idiolect androgynous/multiple tasks/trace |
| metatheory/narrative/depth mass production/class politics technical-scientific rationality | language games/image/surface small-batch production/social movements/pluralistic otherness |
| utopia/redemptive art/concentration specialised work/collective consumption | heterotopias/spectacle/dispersal flexible worker/symbolic capital |
| function/representation/signified industry/protestant work ethic mechanical reproduction | fiction/self-reference/signifier services/temporary contract electronic reproduction |
| becoming/epistemology/regulation urban renewal/relative space | being/ontology/deregulation urban revitalisation/place |
| state interventionism/industrialisation internationalism/permanence/time | laissez-faire/deindustrialisation geopolitics/ephemerality/space |

*Source*: Harvey (1990: 340–1)

is always cultured seeing and appearances are only real to us in so far as they have cultural significance. All cultures make some of their features visually available but the changes ushered in by modernity magnify this tendency. The writers discussed in the previous section suggest that contemporary shifts in culture and society are leading towards the development of new forms of visual culture of a postmodernist nature. While this is developed upon the foundations of modernity it can be seen to have certain distinctive features. Some of the shifts involved have been characterised by Baudrillard, whose work has already been considered in this chapter as influential on John Urry's analysis of the post-tourist.

Baudrillard criticises the classic **Marxist** (p. 65) ideas of the determination of the **ideological** (p. 35) or cultural superstructure by the economic base and of the distinction between use and exchange value. He suggests that these binary distinctions have been confused or blurred by the proliferation of images and the pronounced roles of the media in contemporary capitalist societies. Jameson's point that depth models are increasingly less central is similar. Moreover, Baudrillard develops an extended critique of the relationship between the sign, as conceptualised within **semiotics** (p. 29) (see Chapter 2), and the referent. Baudrillard (1988: 170) argues that the sign, or the image, moves through the following four stages:

1 It is a reflection of a basic reality.

2 It masks and perverts a basic reality.

3 It masks the *absence* of a basic reality.

4 It bears no relation to any reality whatever: it is its own pure simulacrum.

In the first stage, images or language are seen to represent reality. Thus, for example, natural science suggests that it can capture the nature of the world in language which in many ways corresponds to that world or reflects it as if in a mirror. In the second stage, the sign or language conceals or misrepresents the nature of reality. This is the premise of Marxist theories of ideology (Connor, 1989: 55), where ideology or the 'false consciousness' of the workers serves to misrepresent or conceal the essentially exploitative nature of capitalist society. The image distorts reality in the manner of trick mirrors at a fairground. This situation has developed in the third phase where it is not something real that is masked but the absence of a real. This reaches its zenith in the final stage, where the sign bears no relation to reality at all.

Baudrillard's ideas can be illustrated through consideration of the example of the reporting and media coverage of an election campaign. In stage 1, the election is seen as an independently existing event which is reported in an *objective* way which reflects its *reality*. Certain 'quality' newspapers and public service broadcasting would probably want to argue that their coverage of an election still conforms to this model. The election would exist in this way without the reporting and the reporting does not affect its course. In the stage 2 model, the election is reported in a way that *constructs* it ideologically. For example, there is concealment of core issues and certain aspects are emphasised in a consistent fashion which reflect the interests of powerful groups. Marxists argue that the

mass media do this systematically (see Chapter 2). In stage 3 the election is becoming a media event, for example aspects of actors' behaviour are tailored to the time scale of the media. Speeches are made to hit news bulletin deadlines for prime time and so forth. The election as a real event is becoming an absence. It is often suggested that this process began in Britain with the general election of 1959, which is seen as the first television election.

For Baudrillard the critical point is reached in stage 4. In terms of the election example, the media coverage *is* the election, which does not exist outside its coverage. The most important players are those who select the images and determine the sound bites. Hence, in recent British general election campaigns, the Labour Party 'spin doctors' made sure that no politician made a 'mistake' akin to Michael Foot's choice of coat at the Cenotaph discussed in Chapter 6. In this view it is impossible to conceive of the election outside the media circulation of images. The images are the election.

Baudrillard proposes that we live in a world of simulacra, in *hyperreality* where images desperately try to produce an effect of the real. This view is hugely controversial. For example, Baudrillard's claim that the Gulf War did not happen, seems to neglect the obvious fact that people died in it, or the claim that the election does not exist could seem to neglect the point that people do actually vote. However, the point that it is impossible to think or conceptualise these events outside the media images of them seems plausible. What is also true is that these events are now media events in the extensive nature of the coverage given to them. In the advanced Western world we are now accustomed to 24-hour television and radio news channels that will relay images instantaneously across the globe. In such a context the advancement of media technologies beyond the realms of photography and film is of great significance.

## Digitalisation and the future of representation

In particular, the so-called 'digital revolution' has extended the realms of the hyperreal. Computer techniques which digitise photographic and film images

**Table 10.5** Types of society, modes of pictorial representation and their associated positions

| Traditional society | Autographic (handmade) images | Worshippers |
|---|---|---|
| Modernity | Photographic images | Viewers |
| Postmodernity | Electronic images | Interactive users |

permit an unprecedented enhancement and manipulation of the production of pictorial representations. Digitisation is a process through which a picture is divided in a grid into small picture elements ('pixels'). Each pixel is assigned a number from a code of colours or brightness. By changing the values of the pixels, or by adding or removing them, it becomes possible to change the photograph. As the popular press nowadays often shows us, persons who could not possibly have met can be depicted in a seamless photograph. Movies now contain shots constructed as simulations from angles that no human cameraperson would be capable of filming, affording perspectives that once could only be dreamt. The production of mass-mediated still and moving images is coming to be more a matter of computing proficiency than camera, darkroom or editing skills.

These changes strike at the heart of the notion of photographic causality and the easy conceptions of **realism** (p. 43) they support, severing the necessary tie between photographs and their referents. Digitisation finally puts an end to documentary's 'innocent arrogance of objective fact' by 'removing its claim on the real' (Winston, 1995: 259). When placed alongside such cognate developments as multimedia applications, the growth of the Internet, the emergence of large electronic data banks and virtual reality technologies, it seems that the 'post-photographic' age may have arrived. The broad shifts in the character of visual culture occasioned by these developments are summarised in Table 10.5.

Some consider the changes thus signalled to be as momentous as those postulated by Benjamin's classic essay on mechanical reproduction's implications for the work of art. Digitisation can promote the emergence of new forms of pictorial representation, for example the pop video which exemplifies such key **postmodern** (p. 295) themes as heterogeneity and frag-

mentation. While there is a basis for claiming that digitisation might provide new grounds for perception, claims about the death of photography need to be treated more circumspectly. Such claims rest on an over-simple technological determinism and overlook the dependence of the new technologies on older skills, knowledges and ways of seeing. Continuities coexist with technologically driven ruptures. Moreover, the postmodern world is characteristically an increasingly intertextual one where all kinds of borrowing and pastiche are permissible (Lister, 1997). So the more portentous claims about a post-photographic era are probably premature. As was suggested in the discussion of film and photography as technologies of realism (section 10.3 above), realism has always been properly understood in qualified terms. 'Seeing is believing' is an adage that has long been ironically framed. Digitisation now renders claims about, for example, documentary realism, as transparently **ideological** (p. 35) – it 'destroys the photographic image as evidence of anything except the process of digitisation' (Winston, 1995: 259). If this shifts attention away from the putatively distinctive characteristics of the photographic representation towards the reception and interpretation of these images, then this may be a step in the right direction. Or it may be seen as just another symptom of what Baudrillard has termed 'the triumph of signifying culture'. In these respects, as we have suggested in the course of this chapter, there are different visual regimes connected to forms of society and culture (premodern, modern and postmodern) that are themselves implicated in changing struggles over **power** (p. 64).

## 10.10 Conclusion

We have organised this chapter around three main themes. Firstly, we have shown how visual culture has changed in the shift from modernity to postmodernity. At the beginning of the chapter, we pointed to the significance of the 'classic' writings of Simmel and Benjamin on the visual cultures of modernity and developed this discussion through consideration of photography and film. In the closing sections of the chapter we examined the new visual representations of postmodernity. These shifts are intimately connected to the reordering of power relations. Secondly, we have explored a number of different ways in which visual culture can be studied, using ideas like the classic realist text, the male gaze, surveillance, unfocused interaction, civil inattention and so on. Finally, we have paid particular attention to the city as a key site of social interaction and social transformation. Specifically, we have shown how a number of different dimensions of the city can be interpreted using some of the ideas introduced in the chapter.

## Recap

This chapter has:

➤ illustrated the range of ways in which seeing is always cultured seeing;

➤ shown how the concept of visual culture and the technologies of visual representation are connected to changing relations of power in the growth of cities;

➤ examined the cultural significance of the appearance of ordinary social activity, buildings and places in the contemporary city;

➤ suggested how the modern and postmodern city can be read as texts.

# Further reading

The nature of photographic representation and how it implicates the viewer is critically examined in Susan Sontag's *On Photography* (1979). The arguments advanced in John Berger's *Ways of Seeing* (1972) caused a great deal of controversy when they were first made a quarter of a century ago and they still deserve careful consideration. A wide range of issues arising from the history, forms and technologies of photography are covered in contributions to Liz Wells's *Photography: A Critical Introduction* (2000). Chris Jenks' edited collection *Visual Culture* (1995) contains a number of papers that deal with aspects of the 'visual turn' in contemporary cultural theory. A comprehensive method for explicating 'the grammar of visual design' is set out in Gunther Kress and Theo van Leeuwen's *Reading Images* (Routledge, 1996). Nicholas Mirzoeff's edited book, *The Visual Culture Reader* (Routledge, 2002) is a big collection of key papers. Marita Sturken and Lisa Cartwright's *Practices of Looking: An Introduction to Visual Culture* (Oxford University Press, 2007) offers a comprehensive and interdisciplinary overview of thinking about images.

# Bibliography

Abercrombie, N. (1996) *Television and Society*, Cambridge: Polity.

Abercrombie, N., Hill, S. and Turner, B.S. (1980) *The Dominant Ideology Thesis*, London: Allen & Unwin.

Abercrombie, N., Hill, S. and Turner, B.S. (1984) *The Penguin Dictionary of Sociology*, London: Allen Lane.

Abercrombie, N., Hill, S. and Turner, B.S. (eds) (1990) *Dominant Ideologies*, London: Unwin Hyman.

Abercrombie, N. and Longhurst, B. (1991) *Individualism, Collectivism and Gender in Popular Culture*, Salford Papers in Sociology, no. 12.

Abercrombie, N. and Longhurst, B. (1998) *Audiences: A Sociological Theory of Performance and Imagination*, London: Sage.

Abercrombie, N., Warde, A., Deem, R., Penna, S., Soothill, K., Urry, J. and Walby, S. (2000) *Contemporary British Society*, Cambridge: Polity.

Abelove, H., Barale, M.A. and Halperin, D.M. (eds) (1993) *The Lesbian and Gay Studies Reader*, London: Routledge.

Abu-Lughod, J. (1989) *Before European Hegemony: The World System A.D. 1250–1350*, New York: Oxford University Press.

Achebe, C. (1988) *Hopes and Impediments*, London: Heinemann.

Acker, K. (1993) 'Against ordinary language: the language of the body', in A. and M. Kroker (eds) *The Last Sex: Feminism and Outlaw Bodies*, London: Macmillan, 20–7.

Adorno, T. (1967) *Prisms*, London: Neville Spearman.

Adorno, T. (1991) *The Culture Industry*, London: Routledge.

Adorno, T. and Horkheimer, M. (1972) *Dialectic of Enlightenment*, New York: Continuum (orig. publ. in German, 1947).

Agee, J. and Evans, W. (1941) *Let Us Now Praise Famous Men*, Boston: Houghton Mifflin.

Agnew, J. (1987) *Place and Politics: The Geographical Mediation of State and Society*, London: Allen & Unwin.

Agnew, J. and Duncan, J.S. (eds) (1989) *The Power of Place: Bringing Together Geographical and Sociological Imaginations*, London: Unwin Hyman.

Aizlewood, J. (ed.) (1994) *Love is the Drug*, London: Penguin.

Alasuutari, P. (1995) *Researching Culture: Qualitative Method and Cultural Studies*, London: Sage.

Albrow, M., (1996), *The Global Age*, Cambridge: Polity.

Aldridge, A. (2003) *Consumption*, Oxford: Polity Press.

Alpers, S. (1983) *The Art of Describing: Dutch Art in the Seventeenth Century*, Chicago: University of Chicago Press.

Althusser, L. (1971) 'Ideology and ideological state apparatuses', in L. Althusser (ed.) *Lenin and Philosophy and Other Essays*, London: New Left Books, 121–76.

Amselle, J.-L. (1992) 'Tensions within culture', *Social Dynamics* 18(1), 42–65.

Anderson, B. (1983, 1991) *Imagined Communities: Reflections on the Origin and Spread of Nationalism*, London: Verso.

Anderson, K. (2000) ' "The beast within": race, humanity, and animality,' *Environment and Planning D: Society and Space* 18:3 pp. 301–320.

Anderson, K., Domosh, M., Pile, S. and Thrift, N. (eds) (2003) *The Handbook of Cultural Geography*, London: Sage.

Anderson, K. and Gale, F. (eds) (1993) *Inventing Places: Studies in Cultural Geography*, Melbourne: Longman Chesire.

Anderson, P. (1984) 'Modernity and revolution', *New Left Review* 144, March/April, 96–113.

Ang, I. (1985) *Watching 'Dallas': Soap Opera and the Melodramatic Imagination*, London: Methuen.

Ang, I. (1996) *Living Room Wars: rethinking media audiences for a postmodern world*, London: Routledge.

Anzaldúa, G. (1987) *Borderlands/La Frontera: The New Mestiza*, San Francisco: AnnLute.

Appadurai, A. (ed) (1986) *The Social Life of Things: Commodities in Cultural Perspective*, Cambridge: Cambridge University Press.

Appaduria, A., (1996) *Modernity at Large: Cultural Dimensions in Globalisation*, Minnesota: University of Minnesota Press.

Appignanesi, L. and Maitland, S. (1989) *The Rushdie File*, London: Fourth Estate.

Ardener, E.W. (1974) 'Belief and the problem of women' in J.S. La Fontaine, *The Interpretation of Ritual*, Social Science paperback, London: Tavistock Publications (orig. 1972).

Ardener, S. (1975) (ed.) *Perceiving Women*, New York: Wiley.

Aries, P. (1962) *Centuries of Childhood*, London: Cape.

Armstrong, D. (1983) *Political Anatomy of the Body*, Cambridge: Cambridge University Press.

Armstrong, E. G. (2001) 'Gangsta misogyny: A content analysis of the portrayals of violence against women in rap music, 1987–1993' *Journal of Criminal Justice and Popular Culture* 8(2), 96–126.

Arscott, C., Pollock. G. and Wolff, J. (1988) 'The partial view: the visual representation of the early nineteenth-century industrial city', in J. Wolff and J. Seed (eds) *The Culture of Capital: Art, Power and the Nineteenth-Century Middle Class* (Manchester: Manchester University Press), 191–233.

Ashcroft, B., Griffiths, G. and Tiffin, H. (1989) *The Empire Writes Back: Theory and Practice in Post-Colonial Literatures*, London: Routledge.

Assiter, A. and Carol, A. (eds) (1993) *Bad Girls and Dirty Pictures: The Challenge to Reclaim Feminism*, London: Pluto.

Attfield, J. (2000) *Wild Things: The Material Culture of Everyday Life*, Oxford: Berg.

Aveni, A. (1990) *Empires of Time: Calendars, Clocks and Cultures*, London: I.B. Tauris.

Azaryahu, M. (1986) 'Street names and political identity: the case of East Berlin,' *Journal of Contemporary History*, 21, 581–604.

Azaryahu, M. (1996) 'The power of commemorative street names', *Environment and Planning D: Society and Space* 14, 311–30.

Back, L. (1996) *New Ethnicities and Urban Culture: Racisms and Multiculture in Young Lives*, London: UCL Press.

Bacon-Smith, C. (1992) *Enterprising Women: Television Fandom and the Creation of Popular Myth*, Philadelphia: University of Pennsylvania Press.

Bagnall, G. (2003) 'Performance and performativity at heritage sites', *Museum & Society*, 1(2) 87–103. **http://www.le.ac.uk/ms/m&s/msbagnall.pdf**

Bakhtin, M. (1981) *The Dialogic Imagination*, Austin: University of Texas Press.

Bakhtin, M. (1984a) *Rabelais and His World*, Bloomington, IN: Indiana University Press (orig. 1968).

Bakhtin, M. (1984b) *Problems of Dostoevsky's Poetics*, Manchester: Manchester University Press.

Ball, M. and Smith, G. (1992) *Analyzing Visual Data*, Newbury Park, CA: Sage.

Balsamo, A. (1995) 'Forms of technological embodiment: reading the body in contemporary culture', *Body and Society* 1:3/4, November, 215–37.

Barber, B. and Lobel, S. (1952) ' "Fashion" in women's clothes and the American social system', *Social Forces* 31, 124–31.

Barker, F., Hulme, P. and Iverson, M. (1994) *Colonial Discourse/Postcolonial Theory*, Manchester: Manchester University Press.

Barker, M. (1992) 'Stuart Hall, *Policing the Crisis*', in M. Barker and A. Beezer (eds) *Reading into Cultural Studies*, London: Routledge.

Barnes, T.J. and Duncan, J.S. (eds) (1992) *Writing Worlds: Discourse, Text and Metaphor in the Representation of Landscape*, London: Routledge.

Barnouw, E. (1974) *Documentary: A History of Non-Fiction Film*, New York: Oxford University Press.

Barrell, J. (1980) *The Dark Side of the Landscape: The Rural Poor in English Painting 1730–1840*, Cambridge: Cambridge University Press.

Barthes, R. (1957) 'Histoire et sociologie de vêtement: Quelques observations méthodologiques', *Annales*, 3, 430–441.

Barthes, R. (1973) *Mythologies*, St Albans: Paladin.

Barthes, R. (1977) *Image–Music–Text*, Glasgow: Fontana. (Essays selected and translated by Stephen Heath.)

Barthes, R. (1985) *The Fashion System*, London: Cape (orig. 1967).

Bartky, S. (1988) 'Foucault, femininity and the modernization of patriarchal power', in I. Diamond and L. Quinby (eds) *Feminism and Foucault: Reflections on Resistance*, Boston: Northeastern University Press, 61–86.

Baudrillard, J. (1988a) *America*, London: Verso.

Baudrillard, J. (1988b) 'Simulacra and simulations', in M.

Poster (ed.) *Jean Baudrillard: Selected Writings*, Cambridge: Polity, 166–84.

Bauman, Z. (1987) *Modernity and the Holocaust*, Cambridge: Polity Press.

Bauman, Z. (1989) *Legislators and Interpreters: on modernity, post-modernity and the Intellectuals*, Cambridge: Polity.

Bauman, Z. (1997) *Postmodernity and its Discontents*, Cambridge: Polity Press.

Bauman, Z. (1998) *Work, Consumerism and the New Poor*, Buckingham: Open University Press.

Bauman, Z. (2001) *Community: Seeking Safety in an Insecure World*, Cambridge: Polity Press.

Baxandall, L. and Morawski, S. (eds) (1973) *Marx and Engels on Literature and Art*, New York: International General.

Baxter, P.T.W. (ed.) (1991) *When the Grass is Gone: Development Intervention in African Arid Lands*, Vddevalla: Nordiska Afrikainstitutet.

Beck, U. (2002) 'The cosmopolitan society and its enemies', *Theory, Culture and Society*, 19, 17–44.

Becker, H. (1963) *Outsiders: Studies in the Sociology of Deviance*, New York: The Free Press.

Bell, D. and Valentine, G. (1997) *Consuming Geographies: We Are Where We Eat*, London: Routledge.

Bell, D., Binnie, J., Cream, J. and Valentine, G. (1994) 'All hyped up and no place to go,' *Gender, Place and Culture* 1(1) 31–47.

Bell, J. (1999) 'Redefining national identity in Uzbekistan: symbolic tensions in Tashkent's official public landscape,' *Ecumene* 6(2), 183–213.

Benjamin, W. (1970) *Illuminations*, London: Cape.

Benjamin, W. (1977) *Understanding Brecht*, London: New Left Books.

Benjamin, W. (1983) *Charles Baudelaire: A Lyric Poet in the Era of High Capitalism*, London: Verso.

Benjamin, W. (1999) *The Arcades Project*, Cambridge, MA: The Belknap Press of Harvard University Press.

Bennett, A. (1999) 'Subcultures or neo-tribes? Rethinking the relationship between youth, style and musical taste', *Sociology*, 33, 599–617.

Bennett, A. 2000: *Popular Music and Youth Culture: Music, Identity and Place*. Basingstoke: Macmillian.

Bennett, A. and Kahn-Harris, K. (2004) 'Introduction'. In A. Bennett and K. Kahn-Harris (eds.), *After Subculture: Critical Studies in Contemporary Youth Culture*. Basingstoke: Palgrave Macmillan, 1–18.

Bennett, A. and Peterson, R. A. (eds) (2004) *Music Scenes: Local, Translocal, and Virtual*, Nashville: Vanderbilt University Press.

Bennett, T., Grossberg, L. and Morris, M. (eds) (2005) *New Keywords: A Revised Vocabulary of Culture and Society*, Oxford: Blackwell.

Bennett, T., Martin, G., Mercer, C. and Woollacott, J. (eds) (1981) *Culture, Ideology and Social Process: A Reader*, Milton Keynes: Open University Press.

Benthall, J. (1975) 'A prospectus, as published in *Studio International*, July 1972', in J. Benthall and T. Polhemus (eds) *The Body as a Medium of Expression*, London: Allen Lane, 5–35.

Bereiter, C. and Englemann, S. (1966) 'Teaching disadvantaged children in the preschool', in N. Dittmar (1976) *Sociolinguistics: A Critical Survey of Theory and Application*, London: Edward Arnold.

Berelson, B. (1952) *Content Analysis in Communication Research*, Glencoe, IL: Free Press.

Berg, L.D. and Kearns, R.A. (1996) 'Naming as norming: "race", gender, and the identity politics of naming places in Aotearoa/New Zealand,' *Environment and Planning D: Society and Space*, 14, 99–122.

Berger, J. (1972) *Ways of Seeing*, London: British Broadcasting Corporation and Harmondsworth: Penguin.

Berger, J. (1989) 'Appearances', in J. Berger and J. Mohr (eds) *Another Way of Telling*, Cambridge: Granta.

Berger, P. and Luckmann, T. (1966) *The Social Construction of Reality*, New York: Doubleday.

Berman, M. (1983) *All That Is Solid Melts Into Air: The Experience of Modernity*, London: Verso.

Bernstein, B. (1960) 'Language and social class', *British Journal of Sociology* 11, 271–6.

Bernstein, B. (1961) 'Social class and linguistic development: a theory of social learning', in N. Dittmar (1976) *Sociolinguistics: A Critical Survey of Theory and Application*, London: Edward Arnold.

Bessett, D. and Gualtieri, K. (2002) 'Paul Willis and the scientific imperative: An evaluation of *Learning to Labour*', *Qualitative Sociology* 25(1), 67–82.

Best, S. and Kellner, D. (1991) *Postmodern Theory: Critical Interrogations*, London: Macmillan.

Bhabha, H. (1990) 'The third space', interview with Jonathan Rutherford in J. Rutherford (ed.) *Identity: Community, Culture, Difference*, London: Lawrence & Wishart.

Bhabha, H. (1994) *The Location of Culture*, London: Routledge.

Bird, J., Curtis, B., Putnam, T., Robertson, G. and Tickner, L. (eds) (1993) *Mapping the Futures: Local Cultures, Global Change*, London: Routledge.

Bishop, J. and Hoggett, P. (1986) *Organizing around Enthusiams: Mutal Aid in Leisure*, London: Comedia.

Black, M. (1972) *The Labyrinth of Language*, Harmondsworth: Penguin.

Bloch, E., Lukacs, G., Brecht, B., Benjamin, W. and Adorno, T.W. (1980) *Aesthetics and Politics: Debates between Bloch, Lukacs, Brecht, Benjamin, Adorno*, London:Verso.

Bloch, M. (1991) 'Language, anthropology and cognitive science', *Man* 26(2)183–98.

Blumer, H. (1968) 'Fashion', in *Encyclopaedia of the Social Sciences*, vol. 4, ed. D.L. Sills, New York: Collier-Macmillan, 341–5.

Blunt, A. (1994) *Travel, Gender and Imperialism: Mary Kingsley and West Africa*, New York: Guilford Press.

Blunt, A., Gruffudd, P., May, J., Ogborn, M. and Pinder, D. (eds) (2003) *Cultural Geography in Practice*, London: Arnold.

Blunt, A. and Rose, G. (eds) (1994) *Writing Women and Space: Colonial and Postcolonial Geographies*, New York: Guilford Press.

Bock, G. (1989) 'Women's history and gender history: aspects of an international debate', *Gender and History* 1(1), Spring, 7–30.

Boorstin, D. (1992) *The Image: A Guide to Pseudo Events in America*, New York: Random House.

Bordo, S. (1988) 'Anorexia nervosa: psychopathology as the crystallisation of culture', in I. Diamond and L. Quinby (eds) *Feminism and Foucault: Reflections on Resistance*, Boston: Northeastern University Press, 87–117.

Bourdieu, P. (1984) *Distinction: A Social Critique of the Judgement of Taste*, London: Routledge & Kegan Paul (orig. 1979).

Bourdieu, P. (1990) *In Other Words: Essays Towards a Reflexive Sociology*, Cambridge: Polity.

Bourdieu, P., Boltanski, L., Castel, R. and Chamboredon, J.-C. (1990) *Photography: A Middle-Brow Art*, Cambridge: Polity.

Bourdieu, P. and Passeron, J.C. (1990) *Reproduction in Education, Culture and Society*, London: Sage.

Bourdieu, P. and Wacquant, L. (1992) *An Invitation to Reflexive Sociology*, Cambridge: Polity Press.

Bowring, J. (ed.) (1843) *The Works of Jeremy Bentham*, IV, Edinburgh: William Tait.

Brah, A. (1996) *Cartographies of Diaspora: Contesting Identities*, London: Routledge.

Brannon, R. (1976) 'The male sex role: our culture's blueprint of manhood, and what it's done for us lately', in D. David and R. Brannon (eds) *The Forty-Nine Percent Majority: The Male Sex Role*, Reading, MA: Addison-Wesley.

Briggs, J. (1970) *Never in Anger*, Cambridge, MA: Harvard University Press.

Bristow, J. (1997) *Sexuality*, London: Routledge.

Brunsdon, C. (1991) 'Satellite dishes and landscapes of taste', *New Formations* 15, 23–42. Reprinted in C. Brunsdon (1997) *Screen Tastes: From Soap Opera to Satellite Dishes*, London: Routledge, 148–64.

Bryce, J. and Rutter, J. (2002) 'Spectacle of the deathmatch: character and narrative in first-person shooters', in G. King and T. Krywinska (eds) *Screenplay: Cinema/ Videogames/Interfaces*, London: Wallflower Press.

Bryce, J. and Rutter, J. (2003) 'Gender dynamics and the social and spatial organization of computer gaming', *Leisure Studies*, 22, 1–15.

Buck-Morss, S. (1989) *The Dialectics of Seeing: Walter Benjamin and the Arcades Project*, Cambridge, MA: MIT Press.

Bukatman, S. (1993) *Terminal Identity: The Virtual Subject in Postmodern Science Fiction*, Durham and London: Duke University Press.

Burchill, J. (1986) *Girls on Film*, New York: Pantheon.

Burton, A. (1996) 'A "Pilgrim Reformer" at the heart of empire: Behramji Malabari in late-Victorian London', *Gender and History*, 8, 175–96.

Burton, A. (1998) *At the Heart of the Empire: Indians and the Colonial Encounter in late-Victorian Britain*, Berkeley: University of California Press.

Butler, J. (1990 & 2006)) *Gender Trouble: Feminism and the Subversion of Identity*, London: Routledge.

Butler, J. (1993) *Bodies that Matter: On the Discursive Limits of 'Sex'*, New York: Routledge.

Butler, J. (1997) *Excitable Speech: A Politics of the Performative*, New York: Routledge.

Butler, J. (2004) *Precarious Life: Powers of Violence and Mourning*, London: Verso Press.

Cairncross, F. (1998) T*he Death of Distance: How the Communications Revolution will Change our Lives*, London: Orion.

Caldwell, J.C. (1982) *Theory of Fertility Decline*, London: Academic Press.

Calhoun, C. (2000) 'Resisting globalisation or shaping it?', *Prometheus*, 3, 28–47.

Campbell, B. (1993) *Goliath: Britain's Dangerous Places*, London: Hutchinson.

Campbell, B. (1993) *Unofficial Secrets: Child Sexual Abuse – the Cleveland Case*, London: Virago.

Campbell, C. (1996) 'The meaning of objects and the meaning of actions: A critical note on the sociology of consumption and theories of clothing', *Journal of Material Culture*, 1(1), 93–105.

Carby, H. (1982) 'White woman listen! Black feminism and the boundaries of black sisterhood', in Centre for Contemporary Cultural Studies, *The Empire Strikes Back: Race and Racism in 70s Britain*, London: Hutchinson.

Carlyle, T. (1971) *Selected Writings*, Harmondsworth: Penguin.

Carpentier, A. (1990) *The Kingdom of this World (El Reino de este Mundo)*, London: André Deutsch (orig. 1949).

Carr, E.H. (1964) *What is History?*, Harmondsworth: Penguin.

Carroll, J.B. (1956) *Language, Thought and Reality: Selected Writings of Benjamin Lee Whorf*, Cambridge, MA: MIT Press.

Carter, E., Donald, J. and Squires, J. (eds) (1993) *Space and Place: Theories of Identity and Location*, London: Lawrence & Wishart.

Cashmore, E. (2002) *Beckham*, London: Polity

Castells, M. (1996) *The Rise of Network Society*, Vol. 1. of *The Information Age: Economy, Society and Culture*, Oxford: Blackwell.

Castells, M. (1997) *The Power of Identity*, Vol. 2, of *The Information Age: Economy, Society and Culture*, Oxford: Blackwell.

Castells, M. (1998) *The End of the Millennium*, Vol. 3. of *The Information Age: Economy, Society and Culture*, Oxford: Blackwell.

Centre for Contemporary Cultural Studies (1982) *The Empire Strikes Back: Race and Racism in 70s Britain*, London: Hutchinson.

Chaney, D. (2004) Fragmented culture and subcultures. In A. Bennett and K. Kahn-Harris (eds.), *After Subculture: Critical Studies in Contemporary Youth Culture*. Basingstoke: Palgrave Macmillan, 36–48.

Chrisman, L. and Williams, P. (eds) (1993) *Colonial Discourse and Post-Colonial Theory: A Reader*, Hemel Hempstead: Harvester.

Clark, T.J. (1985) *The Painting of Modern Life: Paris in the Art of Manet and his Followers*, London: Thames & Hudson.

Clarke, A.J. (2001) 'The aesthetics of social aspiration,' in Daniel Miller (ed.) *Home Possessions: Material Culture Behind Closed Doors*, Oxford: Berg, 23–45.

Clarke, G. (1990) 'Defending ski-jumpers: a critique of theories of youth subcultures', in S. Frith and A. Goodwin (eds) *On Record: Rock, Pop, and the Written Word*, London: Routledge, 81–96.

Clarke, J., Hall, S., Jefferson, T. and Roberts, B. (1976) 'Subcultures, cultures and class: a theoretical overview', in S. Hall and T. Jefferson (eds) *Resistance through Rituals: Youth Subcultures in Post-war Britain*, London: Hutchinson, 9–79.

Clerc, S. (2000) 'Estrogen brigade and "big tits" threads: Media fandom on-line and off' in B. Bell and B.M. Kennedy (eds), *The Cybercultures Reader*, London: Routledge.

Clifford, J. (1988) 'On Orientalism', in J. Clifford (ed.) *The Predicament of Culture: Twentieth-Century Ethnography, Literature, and Art*, Cambridge, MA: Harvard University Press.

Clifford, J. (1992) 'Travelling cultures', in L. Grossberg, C. Nelson and P. Treicher (eds) *Cultural Studies*, London: Routledge, 96–116.

Cloke, P., Philo, C. and Sadler, D. (1991) *Approaching Human Geography: An Introduction to Contemporary Theoretical Debates*, London: Paul Chapman.

Cloward, R.A. and Ohlin, L.E. (1960) *Delinquency and Opportunity: A Theory of Delinquent Gangs*, Glencoe, IL: The Free Press.

Cohen, A. (1955) *Delinquent Boys: The Culture of the Gang*, Glencoe, IL: The Free Press.

Cohen, P. (1980) 'Subcultural conflict and working-class community', in S. Hall, D. Hobson, A. Lowe and P. Willis (eds), *Culture, Media, Language: Working Papers in Cultural Studies*, 1972–79, London: Hutchinson, 78–87.

Cohen, S. (1973) *Folk Devils and Moral Panics: The Creation of the Mods and Rockers*, St Albans: Paladin.

Cohen, S. (1985) *Visions of Social Control: Crime, Punishment and Classification*, Oxford: Blackwell.

Cohen, S. (1987) *Folk Devils and Moral Panics: The Creation of the Mods and Rockers*, Oxford: Blackwell (new edn, first published by Martin Robertson, 1980).

Cohen, S. and Kliot, N. (1992) 'Place-names in Israel's ideological struggle over the administered territories,'

*Annals of the Association of American Geographers*, 82, 653–80.

Cole, C. and Denny, H. (1994) 'Visualizing Deviance in post-Reagan America: Magic Johnson, AIDS and the promiscuous world of professional sport', *Critical Sociology*, 20(3), 123–147.

Colley, L. (1992) *Britons: Forging the Nation 1707–1837*, New Haven: Yale University Press.

Collier, J. and Yanagisako, S.J. (eds) (1987) *Gender and Kinship: Essays Towards a Unified Analysis*, Stanford: Stanford University Press.

Collins, R. (1980) 'Weber's last theory of capitalism: a systematization', *American Sociological Review*, 45(6), 925–42.

Colwell, J. and Payne, J. (2000) 'Negative correlates of computer game play in adolescents', *British Journal of Psychology*, 91, 295–310.

Connell, R.W. (1987) *Gender and Power: Society, the Person and Sexual Politics*, Cambridge: Polity.

Connor, S. (1989) *Postmodernist Culture: An Introduction to Theories of the Contemporary*, Oxford: Blackwell.

Cook, I. (2004) 'Follow the thing: papaya', *Antipode* 36 642–64.

Cook, I. and Crang, P. (1996) 'The World on a Plate: Culinary Culture, Displacement and Geographical Knowledges', *Journal of Material Culture*, 1, 131–56.

Cook, I., Crouch, D., Naylor, S. and Ryan, J. (eds) (2000) *Cultural Turns/Geographical Turns: Perspectives on Cultural Geography*, London: Prentice Hall.

Cooke, P. (1989) 'Nation, space, modernity', in R. Peet and N. Thrift (eds) *New Models in Geography: Volume 1*, London: Unwin Hyman, 267–91.

Corrigan, P. and Sayer, D. (1985) *The Great Arch: English State Formation as Cultural Revolution*, Oxford: Blackwell.

Cosgrove, D. (1983) 'Towards a radical cultural geography: problems of theory', *Antipode* 15, 1–11.

Cosgrove, D. (1994) 'Contested global visions: one-world, whole-earth, and the Apollo space photographs', *Annals of the Association of American Geographers*, 84, 270–94.

Cosgrove, D. and Jackson, P. (1987) 'New directions in cultural geography', *Area* 19, 95–101.

Couldry, N. (2005) 'On the Actual Street', in Crouch, D., Jackson, R. and Thompson, F. *The Media and The Tourist Imagination: Converging Culture*. London: Routledge.

Coulter, J. (1979) *The Social Construction of Mind*, London: Macmillan.

Cowie, C. and Lees, S. (1981) 'Slags or drags', *Feminist Review* 9, 17–31.

Cowie, E. (1993) '*Film noir* and women', in J. Copjec (ed.) *Shades of Noir: A Reader*, London: Verso, 121–65.

Crang, M. (1998) *Cultural Geography*, London: Routledge.

Crang, P. (1994) 'It's showtime: on the workplace geographies of display in a restaurant in southeast England', *Environment and Planning D: Society and Space*, 12, 675–704.

Crawford, G. (2004) *Consuming Sport: Fans, Sport and Culture*, London: Routledge.

Crawford, G. and Rutter, J. (2007) 'Playing the game: Performance in digital game audiences' in J. Gray, C. Sandvoss, and C.L. Harrington (eds) *Fandom: Identities and Communities in a Mediated World*, New York University Press.

Critcher, C. (2006) *Moral Panics and the Media*, Maidenhead: Open University Press.

Cross, B. (1993) *It's Not About a Salary . . . Rap, Race and Resistance in Los Angeles*, London: Verso.

Crossley, N. (1995) 'Body techniques, agency and corporeality: on Goffman's *Relations in Public*', *Sociology* 29(1), February, 133–49.

Crossley, N. (2005) *Key Concepts in Critical Social Theory*, London: Sage.

Crossley, N. (2006) *Reflexive Embodiment in Contemporary Society*, Milton Keynes: Open University Press.

Crossley, N. (2007) 'Researching embodiment by way of "body techniques"', *The Sociological Review*, 55 (Supplement 1), 80–94.

Culler, J. (1983) *Barthes*, London: Fontana.

Dandeker, C. (1990) *Surveillance, Power and Modernity: Bureaucracy and Discipline from 1700 to the Present Day*, Cambridge: Polity Press.

Daniels, S. (1993) *Fields of Vision: Landscape Imagery and National Identity in England and the United States*, Cambridge: Polity.

Davidson, A.I. (1986) 'Archaeology, genealogy, ethics', in P.C. Hoy (ed.) *Foucault: A Critical Reader*, Oxford: Blackwell.

Davis, F. (1992) *Fashion, Culture and Identity*, Chicago: University of Chicago Press.

Davis, K. and Moore, W. (1945) 'Some principles of stratification', *American Sociological Review* 10, 242–9.

Davis, L. and Harris, O. (1998) 'Race and ethnicity in US sports media', in L. Wenner (ed) *Mediasport*, London: Routledge.

Davis, M. (1990) *City of Quartz: Excavating the Future in Los Angeles*, London: Verso.

Davis, M. (1993a) 'Who killed LA? A political autopsy', *New Left Review* 197, 3–28.

Davis, M. (1993b) 'Who killed Los Angeles? Part Two: The verdict is given', *New Left Review* 199, 29–54.

de Certeau, M. (1984) *The Practice of Everyday Life*, Berkeley: University of California Press.

Del Valle, T. (1993) (ed.) *Gendered Anthropology*, London: Routledge.

Demeritt, D. (2001) 'The construction of global warming and the politics of science,' *Annals of the Association of American Geographers* 91 (2), p307–37

Derrida, J. (1978) *Writing Difference*, London: Routledge.

de Saussure, F. (1996) *Course in General Linguistics*, London: McGraw-Hill.

de Sola Pool, I. (1983) *Technologies of Freedom*, Cambridge, MA: Harvard University Press.

Diamond, E. (ed.) (1996) *Performance and Cultural Politics*, London: Routledge.

Dicken, P. (2007) *Global Shift: Mapping the Changing Contours of the World Economy*, London: Sage.

Dickens, C. (1970) *Dombey and Son*, Harmondsworth: Penguin (orig. 1848).

Dickens, C. (1969) *Hard Times*, Harmondsworth: Penguin (orig. 1854).

Dill, K. E. and Dill, J. C. (1998) 'Video game violence: a review of the empirical literature', *Aggression and Violent Behaviour*, 3, 407–28.

Disraeli, B. (1981, 1845) *Sybil*, Oxford: World's Classics (orig. 1845).

Dittmar, N. (1976) *Sociolinguistics: A Critical Survey of Theory and Application*, London: Edward Arnold.

Dobbins, B. (1994) *The Women: Photographs of the Top Female Bodybuilders*, foreword by A. Schwarzenegger, New York: Artisan.

Docherty, T. (ed.) (1993) *Postmodernism: A Reader*, Hemel Hempstead: Harvester Wheatsheaf.

Dollimore, J. (1991) *Sexual Dissidence: Augustine to Wilde, Freud to Foucault*, Oxford: Oxford University Press.

Douglas, M. (1966) *Purity and Danger: An Analysis of Concepts of Pollution and Taboo*, London: Routledge & Kegan Paul.

Downes, D. (1966) *The Delinquent Solution: A Study in Subcultural Theory*, London: Routledge & Kegan Paul.

Downey, G. (2007) 'Producing pain: Techniques and technologies in no-holds-barred fighting', *Social Studies of Science* 37(2), 201–26.

Driver, F. (1992) 'Geography's empire: histories of geographical knowledge', *Environment and Planning D: Society and Space*, 10, 23–40.

Driver, F. (2003) 'Editorial: The geopolitics of knowledge and ignorance', *Transactions of the Institute of British Geographers*, 28, 131–2.

Drucker, P. (1968) *The Age of Discontinuity: Guidelines to Our Changing Society*, New York: Harper & Row.

Duberman, M. (1991) 'Distance and desire: English boarding school friendships, 1870–1920' in M.B. Duberman, M. Vicinus and G. Chauncey Jr *Hidden from History: Reclaiming the Gay and Lesbian Past*, Harmondsworth: Penguin, 212–29.

du Gay, P. (1996) *Consumption and Identity at Work*, London: Sage.

du Gay, P., Evans, J. and Redman, P .(2000) *The Identity Reader*, London: Sage.

Dumont, L. (1970) *Homo Hierarchicus: The Caste System and Its Implications*, London: Weidenfeld & Nicolson.

Duncan, J. (2000) 'Representation', in R.J. Johnston, D. Gregory, G. Pratt and M. Watts (eds) (2000) *The Dictionary of Human Geography*, Blackwell: Oxford, 703–5.

Duncan, J. and Gregory, D. (eds) (1999) *Writes of Passage: Reading Travel Writing*, Routledge: London.

Duncan, J. and Ley, D. (eds) (1993) *Place/Culture/Representation*, London: Routledge.

Duncan, J.S. (1980) 'The superorganic in American cultural geography', *Annals of the Association of American Geographers*, 70, 31–98.

Dworkin, A. (1983) *Pornography: Men Possessing Women*, London: The Women's Press.

Dwyer, C. (1999) 'Migrations and diasporas', in P. Cloke, P. Crang and M. Goodwin (eds) *Introducing Human Geography*, London: Arnold, 287–95.

Dyer, G. (1982) *Advertising as Communication*, London: Methuen.

Dyer, R. (1989) 'Don't look now', in A. McRobbie (ed.) *Zoot Suits and Second-Hand Dresses*, London: Macmillan (orig. 1983).

Eagleton, T. (1983) *Literary Theory: An Introduction*, Oxford: Blackwell.

Eagleton, T. (1991) *Ideology: An Introduction*, London: Verso.

Edgley, C. (2006) 'The fit and healthy body: Consumer narratives and the management of postmodern corporeity' in D. Waskul and P. Vaninni (eds) *Body/Embodiment/ Symbolic Interaction and the Sociology of the Body*, London: Ashgate, 231–46.

Edgley, C. and Brissett, D. (1990) 'Health nazis and the cult of the perfect body: some polemical observations', *Symbolic Interaction* 13(2), 257–79.

Edley, N. and Wetherall, M. (1996) 'Masculinity, power and identity', in M. Mac An Ghaill (ed.) *Understanding Masculinities: Social Relations and Cultural Arenas*, Milton Keynes: Open University Press, 97–113.

Elias, N. (1978) *The Civilizing Process, Volume 1: The History of Manners*, Oxford: Blackwell (orig. 1939).

Elias, N. (1982) *The Civilizing Process, Volume 2: State Formation and Civilization*, Oxford: Blackwell.

Eliot, T.S. (1932) *Selected Essays*, London: Faber & Faber.

Ellis, J. (1982) *Visible Fictions*, London: Routledge (rev. edn, 1992).

Emes, C.E. 1997. 'Is Pac Man eating our children? A review of the effects of video games on children', *The Canadian Journal of Psychiatry*, 42, 409–14.

Emord, J.W. (1991) *Freedom, Technology, and the First Amendment*, San Francisco: Pacific Research Institute for Public Policy.

Epstein, B. (2001) 'Anarchism and the anti-globalization movement', *Monthly Review*, 53(4).

Errington, F. and Gewertz, D.B. (1987) *Cultural Alternatives and a Feminist Anthropology: An Analysis of Culturally Constructed Gender Interests in Papua New Guinea*, Cambridge: Cambridge University Press.

Evans, M. (1991) *A Good School: Life at a Girls' Grammar School in the 1950s*, London: The Women's Press.

Evans-Pritchard, E.E. (1939) 'Nuer time-reckoning', *Africa* xii (2), April, 189–216.

Evans-Pritchard, E.E. (1960) *The Nuer*, Oxford: Oxford University Press (orig.1940).

Ewing, W.A. (1994) *The Body: Photoworks of the Human Form*, London: Thames & Hudson.

Evolution film (2005) Available at: http://www.campaignforrealbeauty.com/flat4.asp?id=6909. Last accessed 20 May 2007.

Fanon, F. (1967) *Black Skin, White Masks*, London: MacGibbon & Kee.

Featherstone, M. (1990) 'Global culture: an introduction', *Theory, Culture and Society*, 7, 1–14.

Featherstone, M. (1991) 'The body in consumer culture', in M. Featherstone, M. Hepworth and B.S. Turner (eds) *The Body: Social Process and Cultural Theory*, London: Sage, 170–96 (orig. 1982).

Featherstone, M. (1996) *Undoing Culture: Globalization, Postmodernism and Identity*, London: Sage.

Featherstone, M. and Burrows, R. (1995) 'Cultures of technological embodiment: an introduction', *Body and Society* 1(3–4), November, 1–19.

Feher, M. (1989) 'Introduction', in M. Feher with R. Naddaff and N. Tazi (eds) *Fragments for a History of the Human Body Vol. 1*, New York: Zone, 11–17.

Feld, S. (2000) 'A sweet lullaby for world music', *Public Culture*, 12(1), 145–71.

Felski, R. (1995) *The Gender of Modernity*, Cambridge, MA: Harvard University Press.

Ferraro, G., Trevathan, W. and Levy, J. (1994) *Anthropology: An Applied Perspective*, Minneapolis/St Paul: West.

Fields, B.J. (1990) 'Slavery, race and ideology in the United States of America', *New Left Review* 181, 95–118.

Fine, G.A. and Kleinman, S. (1979) 'Rethinking subculture: an interactionist analysis', *American Journal of Sociology*, 85(1), 1–20.

Firth, R. (1972) 'Verbal and bodily rituals of parting and greeting', in J.S. LaFontaine (ed.) *The Interpretation of Ritual*, London: Tavistock.

Fiske, J. (1987) *Television Culture*, London: Methuen.

Fiske, J. (1989a) *Understanding Popular Culture*, London: Unwin Hyman.

Fiske, J. (1989b) *Reading the Popular*, London: Unwin Hyman

Fiske, J. (1992) 'The cultural economy of fandom', in L. Lewis (ed.) *The Adoring Audience: Fan Culture and Popular Media*, London: Routledge.

Fiske, J. (1993) *Power Plays, Power Works*, London: Verso.

Fiske, J. and Hartley, J. (1978) *Reading Television*, London: Methuen.

Fleming, J. (1992) *Never Give Up*, London: Penguin.

Flew, T. (2002) *New Media*, Melbourne: Oxford University Press.

Foucault, M. (1970) *The Order of Things: An Archaeology of the Human Sciences*, London: Tavistock.

Foucault, M. (1973) *Madness and Civilization: A History of Insanity in the Age of Reason*, New York: Vintage.

Foucault, M. (1975) *The Birth of the Clinic: An Archaeology of Medical Perception*, New York: Vintage.

Foucault, M. (1977) *Discipline and Punish: The Birth of the Prison*, trans. Alan Sheridan, London: Allen Lane.

Foucault, M. (1980) *Power/Knowledge: Selected Interviews and Other Writings* 1972–1977, ed. Colin Gordon, Brighton: Harvester.

Foucault, M. (1984a) *The Foucault Reader*, ed. P. Rabinow, Harmondsworth: Penguin (first published 1978).

Foucault, M. (1984b) *The History of Sexuality, Vol 1*, Harmondsworth: Penguin.

Foucault, M. (1986) *The Use of Pleasure*, Harmondsworth: Penguin.

Foucault, M. (1990) *The Care of the Self*, Harmondsworth: Penguin.

Fox-Genovese, E. (1982) 'Placing women's history in history', *New Left Review* 133, May–June.

Frank, A.W. (1990) 'Bringing bodies back in: a decade review', *Theory, Culture and Society* 7(1), February, 131–62.

Franklin, A. and Crang, M. (2001) 'The trouble with tourism and travel theory?', *Tourist Studies*, 1(1), 5–22.

Frisby, D. (1981) *Sociological Impressionism: A Reassessment of the Social Theory of Georg Simmel*, London: Heinemann.

Frisby, D. (1985) *Fragments of Modernity: Theories of Modernity in the Work of Simmel, Kracauer and Benjamin*, Cambridge: Polity.

Frith, S. (1983) *Sound Effects: Youth, Leisure, and the Politics of Rock*, London: Constable.

Fryer, P. (1984) *Staying Power*, London: Pluto.

Fukuyama, F. (1992), *The End of History and the Last Man*, New York: Free Press.

Fussell, S.W. (1991) *Muscle: Confessions of an Unlikely Bodybuilder*, New York: Poseidon.

Gadamer, H.–G. (1975) *Truth and Method*, London: Sheed & Ward.

Gaisford, J. (ed.) (1981) *Atlas of Man*, London: Marshall Cavendish.

Gallagher, C. (1985) *The Industrial Reformation in English Fiction*, Chicago: University of Chicago Press.

Gardiner, M.E. (2000) *Critiques of Everyday Life*, Routledge: London.

Gardner, C.B. (1995) *Passing By: Gender and Public Harassment*, Berkeley, CA: University of California Press.

Garfinkel, H. (1967) *Studies in Ethnomethodology*, Englewood Cliffs, NJ: Prentice Hall.

Geertz, C. (1983a) *Local Knowledge: Further Essays in Interpretive Anthropology*, New York: Basic Books.

Geertz, C. (1983b) 'Centers, kings and charisma: reflections on the symbolics of power', in *Local Knowledge: Further Essays in Interpretive Anthropology*, New York: Basic Books, 121–46.

Gelder, K. and Thornton, S. (2005) *The Subcultures Reader*, London: Routledge.

Gervais, D. (1993) *Literary Englands*, Cambridge: Cambridge University Press.

Gibson, W. (1986) *Neuromancer*, London: HarperCollins.

Gibson, W. (1993) *Burning Chrome*, London: HarperCollins.

Giddens, A. (1984) *The Constitution of Society*, Cambridge: Polity.

Giddens, A. (1985) *The Nation-State and Violence*, Cambridge: Polity.

Giddens, A. (1989) *Sociology*, Cambridge: Polity.

Giddens, A. (1990) *The Consequences of Modernity*, Cambridge: Polity.

Giddens, A. (1991) *Modernity and Self-identity: Self and Society in the Late-modern Age*, Cambridge: Polity.

Giddens, A. (1993) *Sociology*, Cambridge: Polity.

Giddens, A. (2006) *Sociology*, Cambridge: Polity

Gilder, G. (1990) *Microcosm: The Quantum Revolution in Economics and Technology*, New York: Touchstone.

Gillespie, M. (1995) *Television, Ethnicity and Cultural Change* (Routledge, London)

Gilroy, P. (1987) '*There Ain't No Black in the Union Jack*': *The Cultural Politics of Race and Nation*, London: Hutchinson.

Gilroy, P. (1992) 'Cultural studies and ethnic absolutism', in L. Grossberg, C. Nelson and P. Treicher (eds) *Cultural Studies*, London: Routledge, 187–98.

Gilroy, P. (1993a) *Small Acts: Thoughts on the Politics of Black Cultures*, London: Serpent's Tail.

Gilroy, P. (1993b) *The Black Atlantic: Modernity and Double Consciousness*, London:Verso.

Gilroy, P. (1995) 'Sounds authentic: black music, authenticity and the challenge of a changing same', in S. Lemelle and R.D.G. Kelley (eds) *Imagining Home: Class, Culture and Nationalism in the African Diaspora*, London: Verso, 93–118.

Gilroy, P. (1997) 'Diaspora and the detours of identity,' in K. Woodward (ed.) *Identity and Difference* London: Sage, 299–.343.

Giulianotti, R. and Gerrad, M. (2001) 'Evil genie or pure genius?: The (im)moral football and public career of Paul 'Gazza' Gascoigne in D.L. Andrews and S.J. Jackson (eds) *Sports Stars: The Cultural Politics of Sporting Celebrity*, London: Routledge.

Glaser, B. and Strauss, A. (1971) *Status Passage*, London: Routledge & Kegan Paul.

Glasgow University Media Group (1976) *Bad News*, London: Routledge & Kegan Paul.

Glasgow University Media Group (1980) *More Bad News*, London: Routledge & Kegan Paul.

Glassner, B. (1990) 'Fit for postmodern selfhood', in H. Becker and M. McCall (eds) *Symbolic Interaction and Cultural Studies*, Chicago and London: University of Chicago Press, 215–43.

Global Policy Forum, (2007) Globalization of Culture, **http://www.globalpolicy.org/globaliz/cultural/ index.htm**.

Glyn, A. and Sutcliffe, B. (1992) 'Global but leaderless? The new capitalist order', *Socialist Register*, London: Merlin Press, 79–91.

Godlewska, A. (1995) 'Map, text and image. The mentality of enlightened conquerors: a new look at the *Description de l'Egypte*', *Transactions of the Institute of British Geographers*, 20, 5–28.

Goffman, E. (1959) *The Presentation of Self in Everyday Life*, New York: Doubleday Anchor Books.

Goffman, E. (1961) *Asylums*, New York: Doubleday, Anchor Books.

Goffman, E. (1963a) *Behavior in Public Places: Notes on the Social Organization of Gatherings*, New York: Free Press.

Goffman, E. (1963b) *Stigma: Notes on the Management of Spoiled Identity*, Englewood Cliffs, NJ: Prentice Hall.

Goffman, E. (1967) *Interaction Ritual*, Chicago: Aldine.

Goffman, E. (1971) *Relations in Public: Microstudies of the Public Order*, London: Allen Lane.

Goffman, E. (1974) *Frame Analysis: An Essay on the Organization of Experience*, New York: Harper & Row.

Goffman, E. (1977) 'The arrangement between the sexes', *Theory and Society*, 4, 301–32.

Goffman, E. (1979) *Gender Advertisements*, Basingstoke and London: Macmillan.

Goffman, E. (1981) *Forms of Talk*, Philadelphia: University of Pennsylvania Press.

Goffman, E. (1983) 'The interaction order', *American Sociological Review*, 48, 1–17.

Gómez-Peña, G. (2000) *Dangerous Border Crossings: The Artist Talks Back*, London: Routledge.

Gorham, D. (1978) 'The "Maiden Tribute of Modern Babylon" re-examined: child prostitution and the idea of childhood in late-Victorian England', *Victorian Studies*, 21(3), Spring.

Goss, J. (1993) 'The "magic of the mall": An analysis of form, function and meaning in the contemporary built retail environment' *Annals of the Association of American Geographers*, 83 (1), 18–47.

Gottdeiner, M. (1995) *Postmodern Semiotics*, Oxford: Blackwell.

Gramsci, A. (1971) *Selections from the Prison Notebooks*, London: Lawrence & Wishart.

Gramsci, A. (1985) *Selections from Cultural Writings*, London: Lawrence & Wishart.

Gray, A. (1992) *Video-Playtime: The Gendering of a Leisure Technology*, London, Routledge.

Gray, C.H., Figueroa-Sarriera, H.J. and Mentor, S. (eds) (1995) *The Cyborg Handbook*, London: Routledge.

Gray, J. (2006) *Watching with the Simpsons: Television, Parody and Intertextuality*, London: Routledge.

Gray, J., Sandvoss, C. and Harrington, C. Lee (eds) (2007) *Fandom: Identities and Communities in a Mediated World*, New York: New York University Press.

Green, E. (2001) 'Technology, leisure and everyday practices' in E. Green and A. Adams (eds) *Virtual Gender: Technology, Consumption and Identity*, London: Routledge.

Greenblatt, S. (1988) *Shakespearean Negotiations*, Oxford: Clarendon.

Greenblatt, S. (1989) 'Cultural poetics', in A.H. Veeser (ed.) *The New Historicism*, London: Routledge.

Gregory, D. (1994) *Geographical Imaginations*, Oxford: Blackwell.

Gregory, D. (1995) 'Between the book and the lamp: imaginative geographies of Egypt, 1849–50', *Transactions of the Institute of British Geographers*, 20, 29–57.

Gregory, D. (2004) *The Colonial Present: Afghanistan, Palestine, Iraq* Oxford: Blackwell.

Gregson, N. and Rose, G. (2000) 'Taking Butler elsewhere: performativities, spatialities and subjectivities', *Environment and Planning D: Society and Space*, 18, 433–52.

Grimshaw, A. (ed.) (1992) *The C.L.R. James Reader*, Oxford: Blackwell.

Grossberg, L. (1992) 'Is there a fan in the house? The affective sensibility of fandom', in L. Lewis (ed.) *The Adoring Audience: Fan Culture and Popular Media*, London: Routledge, 50–65.

Grossberg, L., Nelson, C. and Treicher, P. (eds) (1992) *Cultural Studies*, London: Routledge, 187–98.

Gruffudd, P. (1995) 'Remaking Wales: nation-building and the geographical imagination, 1925–50', *Political Geography* 14, 219–39.

Guthrie, S.R. and Castelnuovo, S. (1992) 'Elite women bodybuilders: models of resistance or compliance?', *Play and Culture* 5, 401–8.

Habermas, J. (1987) *The Philosophical Discourse of Modernity*, Cambridge, MA: MITPress.

Haddon, L. (2004) *Information and Communication Technologies in Everyday Life: A Concise Introduction and Research Guide*, Oxford: Berg.

Halberstam, J. and Livingston, I. (eds) (1995) *Posthuman Bodies*, Bloomington and Indianapolis: Indiana University Press.

Halfacree, K. (1996) 'Out of place in the countryside: travellers and the "rural idyll"', *Antipode*, 28, 42–72.

Hall, S. (1980) 'Encoding/decoding' in S. Hall, D. Hobson, A. Lowe and P. Willis (eds) *Culture, Media, Language: Working Papers in Cultural Studies, 1972–79*, London: Hutchinson.

Hall, S. (1991) 'The local and the global: globalization and ethnicity', in A. King (ed.) *Culture, Globalisation and the World System*, London: Macmillan, 19–39.

Hall, S. (1992a) 'Old and new identities, old and new ethnicities,' in A. King (ed.) *Culture, Globalisation and the World System*, Basingstoke: Macmillan, 41–68.

Hall, S. (1992b) 'The question of cultural identity', in S. Hall, D. Held and T. McGrew (eds) *Modernity and its Futures*, Cambridge: Polity Press in association with Blackwell Publishers and The Open University, 273–325.

Hall, S. (1996) 'Introduction: who needs "identity"?', in S. Hall and P. Du Gay (eds) *Questions of Cultural Identity*, London: Sage.

Hall, S., Critcher, C., Jefferson, T., Clarke, J. and Roberts, B. (1978) *Policing the Crisis: Mugging, the State and Law and Order*, London: Macmillan.

Hall, S. and du Gay, P. (eds) (1996) *Questions of Cultural Identity*, London: Sage.

Hall, S. and Jefferson, T. (eds) (1976) *Resistance through Rituals: Youth Subcultures in Post-war Britain*, London: Hutchinson.

Hammersley, M. and Atkinson, P. (1983) *Ethnography: Principles in Practice*, London: Tavistock.

Harada, T. (2000) 'Space, materials, and the "social": in the aftermath of a disaster,' *Environment and Planning D: Society and Space*, 18, 205–12.

Haraway, D. (1989) *Primate Visions: Gender, Race, and Nature in the World of Modern Science*, London: Routledge.

Haraway, D. (1991) *Simians, Cyborgs and Women: The Reinvention of Nature*, London: Free Association Books.

Haraway, D. (1997) *Modest_Witness@Second_Millenium. FemaleMan©_Meets_Oncomouse$^{TM}$: Feminism and Technoscience*, New York and London: Routledge.

Haraway, D. (2003) *The Haraway Reader*, London: Routledge.

Harding, S. (1991) *Whose Science? Whose Knowledge? Thinking from Women's Lives*, Milton Keynes: Open University Press.

Hargreaves, J. (1986) *Sport, Power and Culture*, Cambridge: Polity.

Hargreaves, J. (1994) *Sporting Females: Critical Issues in the History and Sociology of Women's Sport*, London: Routledge.

Harrington, C. L. and Bielby, D.D. (1995) *Soap Fans: Pursuing Pleasure and Making Meaning in Everyday Life*, Philadelphia: Temple University Press.

Hart, N. (1976) *When Marriage Ends: A Study in Status Passage*, London: Tavistock.

Harvey, D. (1982) *The Limits to Capital*, Oxford: Basil Blackwell.

Harvey, D. (1985a) 'Monument and myth: the building of the Basilica of the Sacred Heart', in *Consciousness and the Urban Experience*, Oxford: Blackwell, 221–49.

Harvey, D. (1985b) 'Paris, 1850–1870', in *Consciousness and the Urban Experience*, Oxford: Blackwell, 63–220.

Harvey, D. (1988) *The Urban Experience*, Oxford: Basil Blackwell.

Harvey, D. (1990) *The Condition of Postmodernity*, Oxford: Blackwell.

Hawkes, T. (1977) *Structuralism and Semiotics*, London: Methuen; rpt (1991), London: Routledge.

Hawkins, H. (1990) *Classics and Trash: Tradition and Taboos in High Literature and Popular Modern Genres*, Hemel Hempstead: Harvester Wheatsheaf.

Hayles, N.K. (1992) 'The materiality of informatics', *Configurations*, 1, 147–70.

Hearn, J. (1996) 'Is masculinity dead? A critique of the concept of masculinity/masculinities', in M. Mac An Ghaill (ed.) *Understanding Masculinities: Social Relations and Cultural Arenas*, Milton Keynes: Open University Press, 202–17.

Hebdige, D. (1974) 'Aspects of Style in the Deviant Subcultures of the 1960s', Unpublished MA Thesis, CCCS, Birmingham University. Available as CCCS Stenciled Papers, 20, 21, 24 and 25.

Hebdige, D. (1979) *Subculture: The Meaning of Style*, London: Methuen.

Hebdige, D. (1987) *Cut 'n' Mix: Culture, Identity and Caribbean Music*, London: Methuen.

Hebdige, D. (1988) 'Hiding in the light: Youth surveillance and display', in D. Hebdige, *Hiding in the Light: On Images and Things*, London: Comedia, publ. by Routledge.

Heffernan, M.J. (1991) 'The desert in French orientalist painting during the nineteenth century', *Landscape Research* 16, 37–42.

Heidegger, M. (1977) *The Question Concerning Technology and Other Essays* (trans W. Lovitt), New York: Harper & Row.

Heinemann, M. (1985) 'How Brecht read Shakespeare', in J. Dollimore and A. Sinfield (eds) *Political Shakespeare*, Manchester: Manchester University Press.

Held, D. (1980) *Introduction to Critical Theory*, London: Hutchinson.

Hepworth, M. and Featherstone, M. (1982) *Surviving Middle Age*, Oxford: Blackwell.

Hesmondhalgh, D. (2005) 'Subcultures, scenes or tribes? None of the above', *Journal of Youth Studies*, 8, 21–40.

Hetherington, K. (1992) 'Stonehenge and its festival: spaces of consumption', in R. Shields (ed.), *Lifestyle Shopping: The Subject of Consumption.*, London: Routledge.

Hickerson, N.P. 'Linguistic anthropology' (1980) in Ferraro *et al.* (1994) *Anthropology: An Applied Perspective*, Minneapolis/St Paul: West.

Hill, J. (1986) *Sex, Class and Realism: British Cinema 1956–1963*, London: BFI.

Hills, M. (2002) *Fan Cultures*, London: Routledge.

Hobsbawm, E. (1994) *Age of Extremes: The Short Twentieth Century*, London: Michael Joseph.

Hobsbawm, E. (1996) 'Identity politics and the left', *New Left Review*, 217, 38–47.

Hochschild, A. (1983) *The Managed Heart: Commercialization of Human Feeling*, Berkeley, CA: University of California Press.

Hodkinson, P. (2002) *Goth: Identity, Style and Subculture*. Oxford: Berg.

Hoggart, R. (1958) *The Uses of Literacy*, Harmondsworth: Penguin (orig. 1957).

Hoggart, R. (1988) *A Local Habitation*, London: Chatto & Windus.

Hoggart, R. (1990) *A Sort of Clowning*, London: Chatto & Windus.

Hoggart, R. (1992) *An Imagined Life*, London: Chatto & Windus.

Hoggart, R. (2006) *Mass Media in a Mass Society: Myth and Reality*, London: Continuum.

Hoggett, P. and Bishop, J. (1986) *Organizing Around Enthusiasms: Mutual Aid in Leisure*, London: Comedia.

Hollands, R.G. (1995) *Friday Night, Saturday Night: Youth Cultural Identification in the Post-industrial City*, Newcastle Upon Tyne: Department of Social Policy, University of Newcastle.

Hollis, M. and Lukes, S. (1982) 'Introduction' to M. Hollis and S. Lukes (eds) *Rationality and Relativism*, Oxford: Blackwell.

hooks, bell (1991) *Yearning: Race, Gender and Cultural Politics*, London: Turnaround.

hooks, bell (1992) *Black Looks: Race and Representation*, London: Turnaround.

hooks, bell (2006) *Outlaw Culture*, London: Routledge.

Hornby, N. (1994) *Fever Pitch*, London: Gollancz.

Hornby, N. (1995) *High Fidelity*, London: Gollancz.

Howells, S. A. (2002) 'Watching a game, playing a movie: when media collide', in G. King and T. Krywinska (eds), *Screenplay: Cinema/Video/Interfaces*, London: Wallflower Press.

Huntington, S. (1993) 'The clash of civilisations', *Foreign Affairs*, 72(3) 22–49.

Inglis, F. (1993) *Cultural Studies*, Oxford: Blackwell.

Inglis, D. and Hughson, J. (2003) *Confronting Culture: Sociological Vistas*, Cambridge: Polity Press.

Interactive Software Federaton of Europe (2005) 'Video gamers in Europe – 2005', **http://www.isfe-eu.org** (access date 4 November 2005).

Irwin, R. (2006) *For Lust of Knowing: The Orientalists and their Enemies*, London: Allen Lane.

Jackson, P. (1980) 'A plea for cultural geography', *Area*, 12, 110–13.

Jackson, P. (1989) *Maps of Meaning: An Introduction to Cultural Geography*, London: Unwin Hyman.

Jackson, P. (1999) 'Commodity cultures: the traffic in things,' *Transactions of the Institute of British Geographers*, 24(1), 95–108.

Jacobs, K. (2004) 'Pornography in small places and other spaces', *Cultural Studies,* 18(1), 67–83.

James, A. (1996) 'Cooking the books: global or local

identities in contemporary British food cultures,' in David Howes (ed) (1996) *Cross-Cultural Consumption: Global Markets, Local Realities*, London: Routledge, 77–92.

James, C.L.R. (1980) *The Black Jacobins*, London: Allison & Busby (orig. 1938).

James, C.L.R. (1984) *Selected Writings*, London: Allison & Busby.

Jameson, F. (1981) *The Political Unconscious: Narrative as Socially Symbolic Act*, London: Methuen.

Jameson, F. (1982) 'Progress versus utopia; or, can we imagine the future?', *Science Fiction Studies* 9(2), July, 147–58.

Jameson, F. (1991) *Postmodernism, or, the Cultural Logic of Late Capitalism*, London: Verso.

Jaquette, J. (1994) *The Women's Movement in Latin America: Participation and Democracy*, Oxford: Westview.

Jay, M. (1974) *The Dialectical Imagination: A History of the Frankfurt School and the Institute of Social Research 1923–1950*, London: Heinemann.

Jeater, D. (1992) 'Roast beef and reggae music: the passing of whiteness', *New Formations* (18), 107–121.

Jencks, C. (1989) *What is Postmodernism?*, London: Academy Editions.

Jenkins, H. (1992) *Textual Poachers: Television Fans and Participatory Culture*, New York: Routledge.

Jenkins, R. (1992, 1994) *Pierre Bourdieu*, London: Routledge.

Jenkins, T. (1994) 'Fieldwork and the perception of everyday life', *Man*, 29(2), 433–55.

Jenks, C. (1993) *Culture*, London: Routledge.

Jenks, C. (1995) 'Watching your step: the history and practice of the *flâneur*', in C. Jenks (ed.) *Visual Culture*, London: Routledge, 142–60.

Jenks, C. (ed.) (1995) *Visual Culture*, London: Routledge.

Jenks, C. (2003) *Transgression*, London: Routledge.

Jenson, J. (1992) 'Fandom as pathology: the consequences of characterization', in L. Lewis (ed.) *The Adoring Audience: Fan Culture and Popular Media*, London: Routledge, 9–29.

Johnson, N.C. (1995) 'The renaissance of nationalism', in R.J. Johnston, P.J. Taylor and M.J. Watts (eds) *Geographies of Global Change: Remapping the World in the Late Twentieth Century*, Oxford: Blackwell, 97–110.

Johnson, R. (1986) 'What is cultural studies anyway?', *Social Text* 6, 38–80.

Johnson, R., Chambers, D., Raghuram, P. and Tincknell, E. (2004) *The Practice of Cultural Studies: A Guide to the Practice and Politics of Cultural Studies*, London: Sage.

Johnston, R.J., Gregory, D. and Smith, D.M. (eds) (1994) *The Dictionary of Human Geography*, Oxford: Blackwell.

Joll, J. (1977) *Gramsci*, London: Fontana.

Jones, S. (1988) *Black Culture, White Youth: The Reggae Tradition from JA to UK*, Basingstoke: Macmillan.

Jones, S. (2006) *Antonia Gramsci*, London: Routledge.

Jordan, G. and Weedon, C. (1994) *Cultural Politics: Class, Gender, Race and the Postmodern World*, Oxford: Blackwell.

Kabbani, R. (1986) *Europe's Myths of Orient: Devise and Rule*, London: Macmillan.

Kaite, B. (1995) *Pornography and Difference*, Bloomington, IN: Indiana University Press.

Kamenka, E. (ed.) *The Portable Karl Marx*, Harmondsworth: Penguin.

Kaplan, C. (1983) 'Wild nights: pleasure/sexuality/feminism', in Tony Bennett *et al.* (eds) *Formations of Pleasure*, London: Routledge & Kegan Paul, 15–35.

Kaye, H.J. and McClelland, K. (eds) (1990) *E.P. Thompson: Critical Perspectives*, Oxford: Polity Press.

Keat, R. and Urry, J. (1975) *Social Theory as Science*, London: Routledge & Kegan Paul.

Keith, M. (1990) 'Knowing your place: the imagined geographies of racial subordination', in C. Philo (ed.) *New Words, New Worlds: Reconceptualising Social and Cultural Geography*, Lampeter: SDUC, 178–92.

Keith, M. and Pile, S. (eds) (1993) *Place and the Politics of Identity*, London: Routledge.

Kern, S. (1983) *The Culture of Time and Space*: 1880–1918, London: Harvard.

Kerr, A., Brereton, P., and Kücklich, J. (2005) 'New media – new pleasures?', *International Journal of Cultural Studies*, 8(3), 375–94.

Kinsman, P. (1995) 'Landscape, race and national identity: the photography of Ingrid Pollard', *Area* 27, 300–10.

Kirkpatrick, G. (2004) *Critical Technology: A Social Theory of Personal Computing*, Aldershot: Ashgate.

Klein, A. (1994) *Little Big Men: Bodybuilding Subculture and Gender Construction*, Albany, NY: State University of New York Press.

Kline, S., Dyver-Witherford, N. and De Peuter, G. (2003) *Digital Play: The Interaction of Technology, Culture, and Marketing*, McGill-Queen's University Press.

Kneafsey, M. and Cox R. (2002) 'Food, gender and Irishness: How Irish women in Coventry make home,' *Irish Geography*, 35, 6–15 [available at **www.ucd.ie/gsi/pdf/35-1/food.pdf**].

Kniffen, F.B. (1965) 'Folk housing: key to diffusion', *Annals of the Association of American Geographers*, 55, 549–77.

Kong, L. (1995) 'Music and cultural politics: ideology and resistance in Singapore', *Transactions of the Institute of British Geographers*, 20, 447–59.

Kong, L. (1996) 'Popular music in Singapore: exploring local cultures, global resources, and regional identities,' *Environment and Planning D: Society and Space*, 14(3), 273–92.

Kracauer, S. (1952) 'The challenge of qualitative content analysis' *Public Opinion Quarterly*, 16(4), 635–42.

Kress, G. (1988) *Communication and Culture: An Introduction*, Sydney: University of South Wales Press.

Kress, G. and van Leeuwen, T. (1996) *Reading Images*, London: Routledge.

Kristeva, J. (1982) *Powers of Horror: An Essay on Abjection*, New York: Columbia UP.

Kristeva, J. (1986) *The Kristeva Reader*, Toril Moi (ed.), Oxford: Blackwell.

Kritzman, L.D. (ed.) (1988) *Michel Foucault: Politics, Philosophy, Culture. Interviews and Other Writings 1977–1984*, London: Routledge.

Kroker, A. and Kroker, M. (1988) *Body Invaders: Sexuality and the Postmodern Condition*, Basingstoke: Macmillan.

Krotoski, A. (2004) *Chicks and Joysticks: An Exploration of Women and Gaming*, ELSPA White Paper, website **http://www.elspa.com/about/pr/elspawhitepaper3.pdf**.

Krutnik, F. (1991) *In a Lonely Street: Film Noir, Genre, Masculinity*, London and New York: Routledge.

Labov, W. (1966) *The Social Stratification of English in New York City*, Washington DC: Georgetown University Press.

Labov, W. (1972a) *Sociolinguistic Patterns*, Philadelphia: University of Pennsylvania Press.

Labov, W. (1972b) 'The logic of nonstandard English', in *Language in the Inner City: Studies in the Black English Vernacular*, Oxford: Basil Blackwell, 201–40.

Labov, W. (1973) 'The logic of non-standard English', in N. Keddie (ed.) *Tinker, Tailor . . . The Myth of Cultural Deprivation*, Harmondsworth: Penguin.

Lakoff, R. (1975) *Language and Woman's Place*, New York: Harper & Row.

Lally, E. (2002) *At Home with Computers*, Oxford: Berg.

Landsberg, A. (1995) 'Prosthetic memory: *Total Recall* and *Blade Runner*', *Body and Society* 1(3–4), November, 175–89.

Larrain, J. (1979) *The Concept of Ideology*, London: Hutchinson.

Lasch, C. (1980) *The Culture of Narcissism*, London: Abacus.

Lash, S. and Urry, J. (1987) *The End of Organised Capitalism*, Cambridge: Polity.

Lash, S. and Urry, J. (1994) *Economies of Signs and Space*, London: Sage.

Latour, B. (1987) *Science in Action: How to Follow Scientists and Engineers Through Society*, Cambridge MA: Harvard University Press.

Latour, B. (1993) *We Have Never Been Modern*, Hemel Hempstead: Harvester Wheatsheaf.

Latour, B. (1999) *Pandora's Hope: Essays on the Reality of Science Studies*, Cambridge, MA: Harvard University Press.

Laughey, D. (2006) *Music and Youth Culture*, Edinburgh: Edinburgh University Press.

Laurier, E. and Philo, C. (1999) 'X-morphising: review essay of Bruno Latour's *Aramis, or the Love of Technology*', *Environment and Planning A*, 31, 1047–71.

Laver, J. (1946) *Letter to a Girl on the Future of Clothes*, London: Home and Van Thal.

Laver, J. (1950) *Dress: How and Why Fashions in Men's and Women's Clothes Have Changed During the Past Two Hundred Years*, London: Murray.

Law, J. (1986) 'On the methods of long distance control: vessels, navigation and the Portuguese route to India,' in J. Law (ed) *Power, Action and Belief: A New Sociology of Knowledge*, London: Routledge and Kegan Paul, 234–63.

Law, J. (1987) 'Technology and heterogenous engineering: the case of the Portuguese expansion', in Bijker, W.E., Hugher, T.P. and Pinch, T. (eds) *The Social Construction of Technical Systems: New Directions in the Sociology and History of Technology*, MIT Press: Cambridge, 111–34.

Law, J. (2002) 'Objects and spaces', *Theory, Culture and Society*, 19(5–6), 91–105.

Leach, E. (1970) *Levi-Strauss*, London: Fontana.

Leath, V.M. and Lumpkin, A. (1992) 'An analysis of sportswomen on the covers and in the feature articles of *Women's Sport and Fitness* Magazine, 1975–89', *Journal of Sport and Social Issues*, 16(2), 121–126.

Leavis, F.R. (1962) *The Common Pursuit*, Harmondsworth: Penguin.

Lechner, F. J. and Boli, J. (eds) (2003) *The Globalization Reader*, Oxford: Blackwells.

Leech, G., Deuchar, M. *et al.* (1982) *English Grammar for Today*, in B.V. Street (ed.) (1993) *Literacy in Theory and Practice*, Cambridge: Cambridge University Press.

Lefebvre, H. (1991a) *Critique of Everyday Life: Volume 1, Introduction*, London: Verso.

Lefebvre, H. (1991b) *The Production of Space*, Oxford: Blackwell.

Lefort, C. (1986) *The Political Forms of Modern Society: Bureaucracy, Democracy, Totalitarianism*, Cambridge: Polity.

Leidner, R. (1993) *Fast Food, Fast Talk: Service Work and the Routinization of Everyday Life*, Berkeley: University of California Press.

Leighly, J. (1963) *Land and Life: A Selection from the Writings of Carl Ortwin Sauer*, Berkeley, CA: University of California.

Leitner, H. and Kang, P. (1999) 'Contested urban landscapes of nationalism: the case of Taipei', *Ecumene* 6(2), 214–33.

Lemert, C. (2005) *Postmodernism is Not What you Think: Why Globalization Threatens Modernity*, Boulder: Paradigm.

Leslie, D.A. (1993) 'Femininity, post-Fordism, and the new traditionalism', *Environment and Planning D: Society and Space*, 11, 689–708.

Lévi-Strauss, C. (1966) The *Savage Mind*, London: Weidenfeld & Nicolson.

Levitas, R. (1990) *The Concept of Utopia*, London: Philip Allan.

Lewis, L. (ed.) (1992) *The Adoring Audience: Fan Culture and Popular Media*, London: Routledge.

Lewis, O. (1961) *The Children of Sanchez*, New York: Random House.

Lewis, O. (1966) *La Vida*, New York: Random House.

Lewis, R. (1996) *Gendering Orientalism: Race, Femininity and Representation*, London: Routledge.

Le Wita, B. (1994) *French Bourgeois Culture*, Glasgow: Editions de la Maison des Sciences de l'Homme and Cambridge University Press (orig. 1988).

Ley, D. (1982) 'Rediscovering man's place', *Transactions of the Institute of British Geographers*, 7, 248–53.

Linebaugh, P. (1982) 'All the Atlantic mountains shook', *Labour/Le Travailleur* 10, 87–121.

Linebaugh, P. and Rediker, M. (1990) 'The many-headed Hydra: sailors, slaves and the Atlantic working class in the eighteenth century', *Journal of Historical Sociology*, 3, 225–52.

Linz, D. and Malamuth, N. (1993) *Pornography*, Newbury Park, CA, and London: Sage.

Lister, M. (1997) 'Photography in the age of electronic imaging', in L. Wells (ed.) *Photography: A Critical Introduction*, London: Routledge.

Lister, R. (ed.) (1996) *Charles Murray and the Underclass: The Developing Debate*, London: Institute for Economic Affairs Health and Welfare Unit/*The Sunday Times*.

Little, D. (2003) *American Orientalism: The United States and the Middle East since 1945*, London: I.B. Tauris.

Livingstone, D. (1995) 'The polity of nature: representation, virtue, strategy', *Ecumene*, 2, 353–77.

Livingstone, S. (1999) 'New media, new audiences', *New Media and Society*, (1)1, 59–68.

Lodge, D. (1989) *Nice Work*, London: Penguin.

Lofland, L. H. (1973) *A World of Strangers: Order and Action in Urban Public Space*, New York: Basic.

Longhurst, B. (1995) *Popular Music and Society*, Cambridge: Polity.

Longhurst, B. (2007a) *Popular Music and Society*, Second Edition, Cambridge: Polity.

Longhurst, B. (2007b) *Cultural Change and Ordinary Life*, Buckingham: Open University Press

Loomba, A., Kaul, S. and Bunzi, M. (2005) *Postcolonial Studies and Beyond*, North Carolina: Duke University Press.

Lovell, T. (1980) *Pictures of Reality: Aesthetics, Politics and Pleasure*, London: BFI.

Lowenthal, L. (1961) 'The idols of production and the idols of consumption', in *Literature, Popular Culture and Society*, Englewood Cliffs, NJ: Prentice Hall.

Luhmann, N. (1976) 'The future cannot begin: temporal structures in modern society', *Social Research* 43, 130–52.

Lukes, S. (1974) *Power: A Radical View*, Basingstoke: Macmillan.

Lukes, S. (1975) 'Political ritual and social integration', *Sociology*, 9(2), May, 289–308.

Lukes, S. (ed.) (1986) *Power*, Oxford: Blackwell.

Lukes, S. (2004) *Power: A Radical View*, Basingstoke: Palgrave Macmillan.

Lurie, A. (1992) *The Language of Clothes*, London: Bloomsbury.

Lury, C. (1993) *Cultural Rights: Technology, Legality and Personality*, London: Routledge.

Lury, C. (1996) *Consumer Culture*, Cambridge: Polity Press.

Lynch, K. (1960) *The Image of the City*, Cambridge, MA: MIT Press.

Lyotard, J.–F. (1984) *The Postmodern Condition: A Report on Knowledge*, Manchester: Manchester University Press.

MacCabe, C. (1981) 'Realism and the cinema: notes on some Brechtian theses', in Bennett, T., Boyd-Bowman, S., Mercer, C. and Woollacott, J. (eds) *Popular Television and Film*, London: BFI in association with The Open University Press, 216–35.

MacDonald, G.M. (1995) 'Indonesia's Medan Merdeka: national identity and the built environment', *Antipode*, 27, 270–93.

MacDonald, K.M. (1989) 'Building respectability', *Sociology*, 23, 55–80.

Machlup, F. (1973 [1958]) *The Production and Distribution of Knowledge in the United States*, New Jersey: Princeton University Press.

MacKenzie, J.M. (1995) *Orientalism: History, Theory and the Arts*, Manchester: Manchester University Press.

Maffesoli, M. (1996) *The Time of the Tribes: The Decline of Individualism in Mass Society*. London: Sage.

Mansfield, A. and McGinn, B. (1993) 'Pumping irony: the muscular and the feminine', in S. Scott and D. Morgan (eds) *Body Matters: Essays on the Sociology of the Body*, London: Falmer, 49–68.

Martin, G. (1989) *Journeys Through the Labyrinth*, London: Verso.

Martin, W.B. and Mason, S. (1998) *Transforming the Future: Rethinking Free Time and Work*, Sudbury: Leisure Consultants.

Marx, K. (1951) 'The Eighteenth Brumaire of Louis Bonaparte' in Marx-Engels *Selected Works*, 1, London: Lawrence & Wishart.

Marx, K. (1963) *Selected Writings in Sociology and Social Philosophy*, in T. Bottomore and M. Rubel (eds), Penguin, Harmondsworth.

Marx, K. and Engels, F. (1967) *The Communist Manifesto*, Harmondsworth: Penguin (orig. 1848).

Marx, K. and Engels, F. (1968) *The German Ideology*, Moscow: Progress (orig. 1846).

Massey, D. (1984) *Spatial Divisions of Labour: Social Structures and the Geography of Production*, London: Macmillan.

Massey, D. (1991) 'A global sense of place', *Marxism Today* June, 24–9.

Massey, D. (1994) *Space, Place and Gender*, Minneapolis: University of Minnesota Press.

Matless, D. (1995a) 'Culture run riot? Work in social and cultural geography, 1994', *Progress in Human Geography*, 19, 395–403.

Matless, D. (1995b) '"The art of right living": landscape and citizenship, 1918–39', in S. Pile and N. Thrift (eds) *Mapping the Subject: Geographies of Cultural Transformation*, London: Routledge, 93–122.

Matless, D. (1996) 'New material? Work in social and cultural geography, 1995', *Progress in Human Geography*, 20, 379–91.

Matza, D. (1964) *Delinquency and Drift*, New York: Wiley.

Mauss, M. (1979) 'Body techniques', in *Sociology and Psychology*: Essays, trans. B. Brewster, London: Routledge & Kegan Paul, 95–123.

May, C. (2002) *The Information Society: A Sceptical View*, Cambridge: Polity.

May, J. (1996a) '"A little taste of something more exotic": the imaginative geographies of everyday life,' *Geography*, 81, 57–64.

May, J. (1996b) 'Globalization and the politics of place: place and identity in an inner city London neighbourhood', *Transactions of the Institute of British Geographers*, 21, 194–215.

Mayhew, H. (1968) *London Labour and the London Poor, Volumes 1–4*, New York and London: Dover (orig. 1851–2, 1862).

Mazrui, A.A. (1989) 'Moral dilemmas of the Satanic Verses', *The Black Scholar*, 2(2), 19–32.

McAfee, N. (2004) *Julia Krisveva*, London: Routledge.

McCracken, S. (1997) 'Cyborg fictions: the cultural logic of posthumanism', *Socialist Register*, London: Merlin Press, 288–301.

McCrone, D. (1992) *Understanding Scotland: The Sociology of a Stateless Nation*, London: Routledge.

Macdonald, N. (2001) *The Graffiti Subculture: Youth, Masculinity and Identity in London and New York*, Houndmills, Basingstoke: Palgrave.

McDowell, L. (1994) 'The transformation of cultural geography', in D. Gregory, R. Martin and G. Smith (eds) *Human Geography: Society, Space and Social Science*, London: Macmillan.

McDowell, L. (1995) 'Body work: heterosexual gender performances in city workplaces', in D. Bell and G. Valentine (eds) *Mapping Desire: Geographies of Sexualities*, London: Routledge: 75–95.

McDowell, L. (1997) *Capital Culture: Gender at Work in the City*, Oxford: Blackwell.

McDowell, L. and Court, G. (1994) 'Performing work: bodily representation in merchant banks,' *Environment and Planning D: Society and Space*, 12, 727–50.

McEwan, C. (1996) 'Paradise or pandemonium? West African landscapes in the travel accounts of Victorian women', *Journal of Historical Geography*, 22, 68–83.

McGuigan, J. (1997) *Cultural Methodologies*, London: Sage.

McLellan, D. (1975) *Marx*, London: Fontana.

McLellan, D. (ed.) (1977) *Karl Marx: Selected Writings*, Oxford: Oxford University Press.

McLellan, D. (ed.) (2000) *Karl Marx: Selected Writings*, Oxford: Oxford University Press.

McLellan, D. (2006) *Karl Marx: A Biography*, Basingstoke: Palgrave Macmillan.

McLellan, D. (2007) *Marxism after Marx*, Basingstoke: Palgrave Macmillan.

McLuhan, M (1964) *Understanding Media: The Extensions of Man*, London: Routledge.

McRobbie, A. (1978) 'Working class girls and the culture of femininity', in Women's Studies Group, Centre for Contemporary Cultural Studies, University of Birmingham, *Women Take Issue: Aspects of Women's Subordination*, London: Hutchinson, 96–108.

McRobbie, A. (1980) 'Settling accounts with subcultures: a feminist critique', *Screen Education*, 34, 37–49.

McRobbie, A. (1984) 'Dance and social fantasy', in A. McRobbie and M. Nava (eds), *Gender and Generation*, Basingstoke: Mamillan, 130–61.

McRobbie, A. (ed.) (1989) *Zoot Suits and Second-hand Dresses: An Anthology of Fashion and Music*, Basingstoke: Macmillan.

McRobbie, A. (1991) *Feminism and Youth Culture: From 'Jackie' to 'Just Seventeen'*, Basingstoke: Macmillan.

McRobbie, A. (1993) 'Shut up and dance: youth culture and changing modes of femininity', *Cultural Studies*, 7, 406–26.

McRobbie, A. (1994) *Postmodernism and Popular Culture*, London: Routledge.

McRobbie, A. (2005) *The Uses of Cultural Studies: A Textbook*, London: Sage.

McRobbie, A. and Garber, J. (1976) 'Girls and subcultures: an exploration', in S. Hall and T. Jefferson (eds) *Resistance through Rituals: Youth Subcultures in Post-war Britain*, London: Hutchinson, 209–22.

Mead, G.H. (1934) *Mind, Self and Society: From the Standpoint of a Social Behaviorist*, Chicago: University of Chicago Press.

Mennell, S. (1989) *Norbert Elias: Civilization and the Human Self-Image*, Oxford: Blackwell.

Mennell, S. (1990) 'The globalization of human society as a very long-term social process' in M. Featherstone (eds) *Global Culture: Nationalism, Globalization and Modernity*, London: Sage.

Mennell, S. (1991) 'On the civilizing of appetite', in M. Featherstone, M. Hepworth and B.S. Turner (eds) *The Body: Social Process and Cultural Theory*, London: Sage (orig. 1987).

Meyer, A. (1960) *Caste and Kinship in Central India: A Village and Its Region*, London: Routledge & Kegan Paul.

Middleton, R. (1990) *Studying Popular Music*, Milton Keynes: Open University Press.

Miles, S. (1998) *Consumerism – As a Way of Life*, London: Sage.

Miles, S. (2000) *Youth Lifestyles in a Changing World*. Buckingham: Open University Press.

Miles, R. (1989) *Racism*, London: Routledge.

Milgram, S. (1970) 'The experience of living in cities', *Science*, 167, 1461–8.

Miller, W.D. (1958) 'Lower class culture as a generating milieu of gang delinquency', *Journal of Social Issues*, 15, 5–19.

Mills, S. (1991) *Discourses of Difference: An Analysis of Women's Travel Writing and Colonialism*, London: Routledge.

Miner, H. (1956) 'Body ritual among the Nacirema', *The American Anthropologist*, 58, 503–7.

Mirzoeff, N. (2002) *The Visual Culture Reader*, London: Routledge.

Mitchell, D. (1995) 'There's no such thing as culture: towards a reconceptualisation of the idea of culture in geography', *Transactions of the Institute of British Geographers* 20, 102–16. See also the responses in *Transactions of the Institute of British Geographers* (1996), 21, 572–82.

Mitchell, D. (2000) *Cultural Geography: A Critical Introduction*, Oxford: Blackwell.

Mitchell, J. (1984) *Women: The Longest Revolution, Essays in Feminism, Literature and Psychoanalysis*, London: Virago.

Mitchell, K. (1997) 'Different diasporas and the hype of hybridity', *Environment and Planning D: Society and Space*, 15, 533–53.

Mitchell, T. (1989) 'The world-as-exhibition', *Comparative Studies in Society and History*, 31, 217–36.

Mitra, A. (2000) 'Virtual commonality: Looking for India on the Internet' in B. Bell and B. M. Kennedy (eds), *The Cybercultures Reader*, London: Routledge.

Monaco, J. (1978) 'Celebration', in J. Monaco (ed.), *Celebrity*, New York: Delta.

Monaghan, L. F. (2001) *Bodybuilding, Drugs and Risk*, London & New York: Routledge.

Moore, H. (1993) 'The differences within and the differences between', in T. del Valle, *Gendered Anthropology*, London and New York: Routledge/ European Association of Social Anthropologists.

Moorhouse, H.F. (1991) *Driving Ambitions: An Analysis of the American Hotrod Enthusiasm*, Manchester: Manchester University Press.

Morgan, D. (1993) 'You too can have a body like mine: reflections on the male body and masculinities', in S. Scott and D. Morgan (eds) *Body Matters: Essays on the Sociology of the Body*, London: Falmer, 69–88.

Morgan, G. (1993) 'Frustrated development: local culture and politics in London's Docklands', *Environment and Planning D: Society and Space*, 11, 523–41.

Morley, D. (1980) *The 'Nationwide' Audience*, London: British Film Institute.

Morley, D. (1986) *Family Television: Culture, Power and Domestic Leisure*, London: Comedia.

Morley, D. (1992) *Television, Audiences and Cultural Studies*, London: Routledge.

Morley, D. and Chen, K.-H. (eds) (1996) *Stuart Hall: Critical Dialogues in Cultural Studies*, London: Routledge.

Morley, D. and Robins, K. (1992) 'Techno-orientalism: futures, phobias and foreigners', *New Formations* 16, 136–56.

Morris, M.S. (1996) ' "Tha'lt be like a blush-rose when tha' grows up, my little lass": English cultural and gendered identity in *The Secret Garden*', *Environment and Planning D: Society and Space*, 14, 59–78.

Morris, W. (1986) *News from Nowhere in Three Works by William Morris*, London: Lawrence & Wishart (orig. 1891).

Morton, A.L. (1965) *The People's History of England*, London: Lawrence & Wishart.

Muggleton, D. (1997) 'The post-subculturalist', in S. Redhead with D. Wynne and J. O'Connor (eds) *The Clubcultures Reader: Readings in Popular Cultural Studies*, Oxford: Blackwell, 185–203.

Muggleton, D. (2000) *Inside Subculture: The Postmodern Meaning of Style*, Oxford: Berg.

Muggleton, D. and Weinzierel, R. (eds) (2003) *The Post-Subcultures Reader*, Oxford: Berg.

Mulvey, L. (1981) 'Visual pleasure and narrative cinema', in T. Bennett *et al.* (eds) *Popular Television and Film*, London: British Film Institute, 206–15.

Mulvey, L. (1989) *Visual and Other Pleasures*, London: Macmillan.

Munns, J. and Rajan, G. (eds) (1995) *A Cultural Studies Reader: History, Theory, Practice*, London and New York: Longman.

Murray, J. (1997) *Hamlet on the Holodeck: The Future of Narrative in Cyberspace*, The Free Press.

Murray, J. and H. Jenkins (no date) *Before the Holodeck: Translating Star Trek into Digital Media,* online available at **http://web.mit.edu/21fms/wwww/faculty/henry3/ holodeck.html**

Myers, J. (1992) 'Nonmainstream body modification: genital piercing, branding, burning and cutting', *Journal of Contemporary Ethnography*, 21(3), October, 267–306.

Myers, K. (1982) 'Towards a feminist erotica', *Camerawork*, 24, March, 14–16, 19.

Nash, C. (1993) 'Remapping and renaming: new cartographies of identity, gender and landscape in Ireland', *Feminist Review*, 44, 39–57.

Nash, C. (1996) 'Men again: Irish masculinity, nature and nationhood in the early twentieth century', *Ecumene*, 3, 427–53.

Nash, C. (1999) 'Irish placenames: post-colonial locations,' *Transactions of the Institute of British Geographers*, 24(4), 457–80.

Nash, C. (2005) 'Landscapes,' in P. Cloke, P. Crang and M. Goodwin (eds) *Introducing Human Geographies*, London: Arnold, 156–67.

Naylor, S. (2000) 'Spacing the can: empire, modernity and the globalisation of food,' *Environment and Planning A*, 32, 1625–39.

Negroponte, N. (1995) *Being Digital*, New York, Hodder & Stoughton.

Nelson, C. and Grossberg, L. (eds) (1985) *Marxism and the Interpretation of Culture*, Basingstoke: Macmillan.

Nelson, L. (1999) 'Bodies (and spaces) do matter: the limits of performativity,' *Gender, Place and Culture*, 6(4), 331–53.

Newitz, A. (2006) 'Your SecondLife is ready', *Popular Science*. **http://www.popsci.com/popsci/technology/ 7ba1af8f3812d010vgnvcm1000004eecbccdrcrd.html**

Newsom, D. (2007) *Bridging the Gaps in Global Communication*, Oxford: Blackwell.

Nicholson, L. (1995) 'Interpreting gender', in L. Nicholson and S. Seidman (eds) *Social Postmodernism*, Cambridge: Cambridge University Press.

Nixon, N. (1992) 'Cyberpunk: preparing the ground for

revolution or keeping the boys satisfied?', *Science Fiction Studies*, 19, 219–35.

Nochlin, L. (1991a) 'The imaginary Orient', in L. Nochlin (ed.) *The Politics of Vision: Essays on Nineteenth-Century Art and Society*, London: Thames & Hudson.

Nochlin, L. (1991b) *The Politics of Vision: Essays on Nineteenth-Century Art and Society*, London: Thames & Hudson.

Nora, S. and Minc, A. (1980) *The Computerization of Society*, Cambridge, MA.: MIT Press.

Novack, C. (1993) 'Ballet, gender and cultural power', in H. Thomas (ed.) *Dance, Gender and Culture*, Basingstoke and London: Macmillan, 34–48.

Oh, M. and Arditi, J. (2000) 'Shopping and postmodernism: Consumption, production, identity, and the Internet' in M. Gottdiener (ed.) *New Forms of Consumption: Consumers, Culture and Commodification*, Oxford: Rowman and Littlefield.

Okely, J. (1983) *The Traveller-Gypsies*, Cambridge: Cambridge University Press.

Ó Tuathail, G. and Luke, T.W. (1994) 'Present at the (dis)integration: deterritorialisation and reterritorialisation in the new Wor(l)d order', *Annals of the Association of American Geographers*, 84(3), 381–98.

Ó Tuathail, G. (1996) *Critical Geopolitics: The Politics of Writing Global Space*, London: Routledge.

Ó Tuathail, G. and Dalby, S. (1994) 'Critical geopolitics: unfolding spaces for thought in geography and global politics', *Environment and Planning D: Society and Space*, 12(5), 513–14.

Ohrn, K. (1980) *Dorothea Lange and the Documentary Tradition*, Baton Rouge: Louisiana State University Press.

Ortner, S. (1974) 'Is female to male as nature is to culture?', in M. Rosaldo and L. Lamphere (eds) *Woman, Culture and Society*, Stanford: Stanford University Press.

Osborne, B.S. (1988) 'The iconography of nationhood in Canadian art', in D. Cosgrove and S. Daniels (eds) *The Iconography of Landscape*, Cambridge: Cambridge University Press, 162–78.

Osbourne, T. (1994) 'Bureaucracy as a vocation: governmentality and administration in nineteenth-century Britain', *Journal of Historical Sociology*, 7(13), 289–313.

O'Shaughnessy, M. and Salder, J. (1999) *Media and Society: An Introduction*, Oxford: Oxford University Press.

Painter, J. (1995) *Politics, Geography and 'Political Geography': A Critical Perspective*, London: Edward Arnold.

Palmer, D. (2003) 'The paradox of user control', paper presented to the *Melbourne DAC 2003* conference, 19-25 May, online at **http://hypertext.rmit.edu.au/ dac/papers/ Palmer.pdf**

*Paris Match* (1955) front cover of 'le petit DIOUF', No. 326, 26 juin au 02 juillet 1955. **www.parismatch.com/ unes/recherche.php?texte=25%20juin%201955&search in=tous&separ=AND&auteur_id=0&check_date=false &champs0=25/06/1955&encadrement==&titre_ou_all =titre**, accessed 28 May 2007.

Parker, H. (1974) *View from the Boys: A Sociology of Downtown Adolescents*, London: David and Charles.

Parker, R. and Pollock, G. (1981) *Old Mistresses: Women, Art and Ideology*, London: Pandora.

Parker, R. and Pollock, G. (eds) (1987) *Framing Feminism: Art and the Women's Movement 1970–85*, London: Pandora.

Parkin, D. (1991) *Language is the Essence of Culture*, Group for Debates in Anthropological Theory, Manchester: Department of Social Anthropology, University of Manchester.

Parkin, F. (1973) *Class, Inequality and Political Order*, London: Paladin.

Parkin, F. (1982) *Max Weber*, Chichester: Ellis Horwood.

Parsons, T. (1952) *The Social System*, London: Routledge & Kegan Paul.

Passingham, R.E. (1982) *The Human Primate*, Oxford and San Francisco: W.H. Freeman.

Pateman, C. (1989) *The Disorder of Women: Democracy, Feminism and Political Theory*, Cambridge: Polity.

Patrick, J. (1973) *A Glasgow Gang Observed*, London: Eyre-Methuen.

Pearson, J. (1973) *The Profession of Violence*, London: Panther.

Pearson, R. (1992) 'Gender matters in development', in T. Allen and A. Thomas (eds) *Poverty and Development in the 1990s*, Oxford: OUP, 294.

Penley, C. (1992) 'Feminism, psychoanalysis, and the study of popular culture', in L. Grossberg, C. Nelson and P. Treichler (eds), *Cultural Studies*, London: Routledge.

Perraton, J., Goldblatt, D. and McGrew, A. (1997) 'The globalisation of economic activity', *New Political Economy*, 2, 257–77.

Piercy, M. (1992) *Body of Glass*, Harmondsworth: Penguin (published in the USA by A.A. Knopf under the title *He, She and It*, 1991).

Poggi, G. (2006) *Weber: A Short Introduction*, Cambridge: Polity.

Polhemus, T. (ed.) (1978) *Social Aspects of the Human Body*, Harmondsworth: Penguin.

Poster, M. (1990) *The Mode of Information: Poststructuralism and Social Context*, Cambridge, Polity.

Postman, N. (1986) *Amusing Ourselves to Death: Public Discourse in the Age of Showbusiness*, London: Heinemann.

Postman, N. (1993) *Technopoly: The Surrender of Culture to Technology*, New York: Vintage Books.

Pratt, M.L. (1992) *Imperial Eyes: Travel Writing and Transculturation*, London: Routledge.

Pred, A. (1984) 'Place as historically contingent process: structuration theory and the time geography of becoming places', *Annals of the Association of American Geographers*, 74, 79–97.

Pred, A. (1989) 'The locally spoken word and local struggles', *Environment and Planning D: Society and Space*, 7, 211–34.

Pred, A. (1990a) *Lost Words and Lost Worlds: Modernity and the Language of Everyday Life in Late Nineteenth-Century Stockholm*, Cambridge: Cambridge University Press.

Pred, A. (1990b) 'In other wor(l)ds: fragmented and integrated observations on gendered languages, gendered spaces and local transformation', *Antipode*, 22, 33–52.

Pred, A. (1992a) 'Capitalisms, crises and cultures II: notes on local transformation and everyday cultural struggles', in A. Pred and M.J. Watts (eds) *Reworking Modernity: Capitalisms and Symbolic Dissent*, New Brunswick: Rutgers University Press, 106–17.

Pred, A. (1992b) 'Languages of everyday practice and resistance: Stockholm at the end of the nineteenth century', in A. Pred and M.J. Watts (eds) *Reworking Modernity: Capitalisms and Symbolic Dissent*, New Brunswick: Rutgers University Press, 118–54.

Price, M. and Lewis, M. (1993) 'The reinvention of cultural geography', *Annals of the Association of American Geographers*, 83, 1–17. See also the replies and counter-replies in *AAAG* (1993), 83, 515–22.

Prince, H. (1988) 'Art and agrarian change. 1710–1815,' in D. Cosgrove, and S. Daniels, (eds) *The Iconography of Landscape*, Cambridge: Cambridge University Press, 98–118.

Prior, L. (1988) 'The architecture of the hospital: a study of spatial organisation and medical knowledge', *British Journal of Sociology*, 39, 86–113.

Pryce, K. (1979) *Endless Pressure*, Harmondsworth: Penguin.

Pulgram, E. (1954) 'Phoneme and grapheme', in B. Street (ed.) (1993) *Literacy in Theory and Practice*, Cambridge: Cambridge University Press.

Purvis, T. and Hunt, A. (1993) 'Discourse, ideology, discourse, ideology, discourse, ideology...', *British Journal of Sociology*, 44, 473–99.

Quilley, G. (2003) 'Pastoral plantations: the slave trade and the representation of British colonial landscape in the late eighteenth century,' in G. Quilley and K. Dian Kriz (eds) (2003) *An Economy of Colour: Visual Culture and the Atlantic World, 1660–1830*, Manchester: Manchester University Press, 106–28.

Rabinow, P. (ed.) (1984) *The Foucault Reader*, Harmondsworth: Penguin.

Radway, J.A. (1983) 'Women read the romance: The interaction of text and context', *Feminist Studies* 9(1), 53–78.

Radway, J.A. (1987) *Reading the Romance: Women, Patriarchy, and Popular Literature*, London: Verso.

Rao, R. (1938) *Kanthapura* in B. Ashcroft *et al.* (eds) (1989) *The Empire Writes Back: Theory and Practice in Post-colonial Literatures*, London: Routledge.

Redclift, M. (2004) *Chewing Gum: The Fortunes of Taste*, London: Routledge.

Redhead, S. (1990) *The End-of-the-Century Party: Youth and Pop towards 2000*, Manchester: Manchester University Press.

Redhead, S. (ed.) (1993) *Rave Off: Politics and Deviance in Contemporary Youth Culture*, Aldershot: Avebury.

Redhead, S. (1995) *Unpopular Cultures: The Birth of Law and Popular Culture*, Manchester: Manchester University Press.

Redhead, S. (1997) *Post-Fandom and the Millennial Blues*, London: Routledge.

Redhead, S. with Wynne, D. and O'Connor, J. (eds) (1997) *The Clubcultures Reader: Readings in Popular Cultural Studies*, Oxford: Blackwell.

Rediker, M. (1987) *Between the Devil and the Deep Blue Sea: Merchant Seamen, Pirates, and the Anglo-American Maritime World, 1700–1750*, Cambridge: Cambridge University Press.

Reed, A. (1987) *The Developing World*, London: Bell & Hyman.

Reisman, D. in collaboration with Denney, R. and Glazier, N. (1953) *The Lonely Crowd*, New Haven, CT: Yale University Press.

Relph, E. (1976) *Place and Placelessness*, London: Pion.

Rheingold, H. (1994) *The Virtual Community: Finding Connection in a Computerized World*, London: Secker and Warburg.

Richards, G.D. (1990*) Demons or Resistance: The Early History of Black People in Britain*, Revolutionary Education Development.

Rieff, D. (1992) *Los Angeles: Capital of the Third World*, London: Jonathan Cape.

Rietveld, H. (1993) 'Living the dream', in S. Redhead (ed.) *Rave Off: Politics and Deviance in Contemporary Youth Culture*, Aldershot: Avebury.

Rigby, P. (1985) *Persistent Pastoralists: Nomadic Societies in Transition*, London: Zed.

Robbins, D. (1991) *The Work of Pierre Bourdieu: Recognizing Society*, Milton Keynes: Open University Press.

Robbins, D. (ed.) (1999) *Bourdieu and Culture*, London: Sage.

Roberts, C. (ed.) (1994) *Idle Worship: How Pop Empowers the Weak, Rewards the Faithful and Succours the Needy*, London: HarperCollins.

Roberts, K. (1999) *Leisure in Contemporary Society*, Wallingford: CABI.

Robertson, R. (1992) *Globalisation*, London: Sage.

Robertson, R. (1995) 'Globalisation: time–space and homogeneity–heterogeneity', in M. Featherstone, L. Lash and R. Robertson (eds), *Global Modernities*, 25–44.

Rojek, C. (2001) *Celebrity*, London: Reaktion Books.

Roper, M. (1994) *Masculinity and the British Organisation Man Since 1945*, Oxford: Oxford University Press.

Rose, G. (1988) 'Locality, politics and culture: Poplar in the 1920s', *Environment and Planning D: Society and Space*, 6, 151–68.

Rose, G. (1993) *Feminism and Geography: The Limits of Geographical Knowledge*, Cambridge: Polity.

Rose, T. (1994) *Black Noise: Rap Music and Black Culture in Contemporary America*, Hanover: Wesleyan University Press, University Press of New England.

Ross, K. (1988) *The Emergence of Social Space: Rimbaud and the Paris Commune*, London: Macmillan.

Ruby, J. (1976) 'In a pic's eye: interpretive strategies for deriving meaning and significance from photographs', *Afterimage*, 3(1), 5–7.

Runciman, W.G. (ed.) (1978) *Weber: Selections in Translation*, Cambridge: Cambridge University Press.

Runnymede Trust (2000) *The Future of Multi-Ethnic Britain*, London: Profile Books.

Rutter, J. and Bryce J. (2006) (eds) *Understanding Digital Games*, London: Sage.

Rutter, M. and Madge, N. (1976) *Cycles of Disadvantage*, London: Heinemann.

Sacks, H. (1972) 'Notes on the police assessment of moral character', in D. Sudnow (ed.) *Studies in Social Interaction*, New York: Free Press.

Sacks, H. (1992) 'Lecture 14: The inference-making machine', in *Lectures on Conversation*, vol. 1, ed. G. Jefferson, Oxford: Blackwell, 113–25.

Said, E.W. (1978) *Orientalism*, Harmondsworth: Penguin.

Said, E.W. (1981) *Covering Islam: How the Media and the Experts Determine How We See the Rest of the World*, London: Routledge & Kegan Paul.

Said, E.W. (1986) *After the Last Sky: Palestinian Lives*, London: Faber & Faber.

Said, E.W. (1993a) *Culture and Imperialism*, London: Chatto & Windus.

Said, E.W. (1995a) *The Politics of Dispossession*, London: Vintage.

Said, E.W. (1995b) *Orientalism,* with a new afterword Harmondsworth: Penguin.

Said, E.W. (2003) 'Orientalism 25 years on' *Counterpunch* **www.counterpunch.org/said08052003**

Salih, S. (2002) *Judith Butler*, London: Routledge.

Sapir, E. (1929) 'The status of linguistics as a science', *Language* 5, 207–14, cited in G. Ferraro, (1994) *Cultural Anthropology: An Applied Perspective*, Minneapolis/St Paul: West Publishing Co. 2nd edn.

Sapir, E. (1931) 'Fashion', in E.R.A. Seligman (ed.) *Encyclopaedia of the Social Sciences Volume 6*, New York: Macmillan, 139–44.

Sartre, J-P. (1983) *The Question of Method*, London: Methuen.

Sarup, M. (1996) *Identity, Culture and the Postmodern World*, Edinburgh: Edinburgh University Press.

Sauer, C.O. (1925) 'The morphology of landscape', repr. in J. Leighly (1963) *Land and Life: A Selection from the Writings of Carl Ortwin Sauer*, Berkeley: University of California, 315–50.

Sauer, C.O. (1941) 'The personality of Mexico', repr. in J. Leighly (1963) *Land and Life: A Selection from the Writings of Carl Ortwin Sauer*, Berkeley: University of California, 104–17.

Sauer, C.O. (1967) *Land and Life: A Selection from the Writings of Carl Ortwin Sauer* in J. Leighly (ed.), California: University of California Press.

Saukko, P. (2003) *Doing Research in Cultural Studies: An*

*Introduction to Classical and New Methodological Approaches*, London: Sage.

Saunders, P. (1981) *Social Theory and the Urban Question*, London: Hutchinson.

Savage, M., Bagnall, G. and Longhurst, B. (2005) *Globalization and Belonging*, London: Sage.

Savage, M. and Warde, A. (1993) *Urban Sociology, Capitalism and Modernity*, Basingstoke and London: Macmillan.

Savage, M. and Witz, A. (eds) (1992) *Gender and Bureaucracy*, Oxford: Blackwell.

Schama, S. (1995) *Landscape and Memory*, London: HarperCollins.

Schickel, R. (1985) *Intimate Strangers: The Culture of Celebrity in America*, Chicago: Ivan R. Dee.

Schirato, T. and Yell, S. (2000) *Communication and Culture: An Introduction*, London: Sage.

Schwartz, J.M. (1996) 'The geography lesson: photographs and the construction of imaginative geographies', *Journal of Historical Geography* 22, 16–45.

Scott, J.C. (1990) *Domination and the Arts of Resistance: Hidden Transcripts*, New Haven: Yale University Press.

Scott, J.W. (1986) 'Gender: a useful category of historical analysis', *American Historical Review* 91, 1053–1075.

Sedgwick, E.K. (1985) *Between Men*, Baltimore: Johns Hopkins University Press.

Sekula, A. (1975) 'On the invention of photographic meaning', *Artforum*, 13, 36–45.

Semple, L. (1988) 'Women and erotica', *Spare Rib*, 191, June, 6–10.

Senghor, L. (1993) 'Negritude', in L. Chrisman and P. Williams (eds) *Colonial Discourse and Post-Colonial Theory: A Reader*, Hemel Hempstead: Harvester.

Sennett, R. (1969) 'An introduction', in *Classic Essays on the Culture of Cities*, Englewood Cliffs, NJ: Prentice Hall, 3–19.

Sennett, R. (1977) *The Fall of Public Man*, Cambridge: Cambridge University Press.

Shaheen, J. G. (2003) *Reel Bad Arabs: How Hollywood Vilifies a People*, Gloucestershire: Arris Books.

Shapin, S. (1994) *A Social History of Truth: Civility and Science in Seventeenth-Century England*, Chicago: University of Chicago Press.

Sharratt, B. (1989) 'Communications and image studies: notes after Raymond Williams', *Comparative Criticism*, 11, 29–50.

Sherlock, J. (1993) 'Dance and the culture of the body', in

S. Scott and D. Morgan (eds) *Body Matters: Essays on the Sociology of the Body*, London: Falmer, 35–48.

Shields, R. (1991) *Places on the Margin: Alternative Geographies of Modernity*, London: Routledge.

Shields, R. (1996) 'Virtual spaces, real histories and living bodies' in R. Shields (ed.) *Cultures of Internet*, London: Sage.

Shilling, C. (2003) *The Body and Social Theory*, London: Sage.

Shnukal, A. (1983) 'Blaikman Tok: changing attitudes to Torres Strait Creole', *Australian Aboriginal Studies*, 2, 25–33.

Shukman, A. (ed.) (1988) *Bakhtin School Papers*, Oxford: Russian Poetics in Translation.

Shurmer-Smith, P. and Hannam, K. (1994) *Worlds of Desire, Realms of Power: A Cultural Geography*, London: Edward Arnold.

Sidaway, J.D. (1997) 'The (re)making of the Western "geographical tradition": some missing links', *Area*, 29, 72–80.

Sidorov, D. (2000) 'National monumentalization and the politics of scale: the resurrections of the Cathedral of Christ the Savior in Moscow,' *Annals of the Association of American Geographers*, 90(3) 548–72.

Simmel, G. (1950) *The Sociology of Georg Simmel*, ed. K.H. Wolff, Glencoe: Free Press.

Simmel, G. (1957) 'Fashion', *American Journal of Sociology*, 62(5), 541–58 (orig. 1904).

Simmel, G. (1969) 'Sociology of the senses: visual intereaction', in R.E. Park and E.W. Burgess (eds), *Introduction to the Science of Sociology*, Chicago: University of Chicago Press, 356–61 (orig. 1908).

Simmel, G. (1971) 'The metropolis and mental life', in D.N. Levine (ed.), *Georg Simmel on Individuality and Social Forms*, Chicago: University of Chicago Press, 324–39 (orig. 1903).

Simmel, G. (1978) *The Philosophy of Money*, trans. T. Bottomore and D. Frisby, London: Routledge & Kegan Paul (orig. 1900).

Simmel, G. (1994) 'The sociology of the meal', *Food and Foodways* 5(4), 345–50 (orig. 1910).

Sinfield, A. (2005) *Cultural Politics, Queer Reading*, London: Routledge.

Singer, P. (2000) *Marx: A Very Short Introduction*, Oxford: Oxford Paperbacks.

Skeggs, B. (1997) *Formations of Class and Gender*, London: Sage.

Smith, G. (1996) 'Gender Advertisements revisited: a visual sociology classic?', Electronic Journal of Sociology, 2(1).

Smith, G. (2006) Erving Goffman, London: Routledge.

Smith, L.S. (1978) 'Sexist assumptions and female delinquency: an empirical investigation', in C. Smart and B. Smart (eds) Women, Sexuality and Social Control, London: Routledge & Kegan Paul, 74–88.

Smith, N. (1990) Uneven Development: Nature, Capital and the Production of Space, Oxford: Basil Blackwell.

Smith, S.J. (1994) 'Soundscape,' Area, 26(3), 232–40.

Smith, S.J. (1997) 'Beyond geography's visible worlds: a cultural politics of music', Progress in Human Geography 21(4), 502–29.

Snead, J.A. (1984) 'Repetition as a figure of Black Culture' in H.L. Gates, Jr. (ed.) Black Literature and Literary Theory, London: Methuen.

Snyder, J. (1984) 'Documentary without ontology', Studies in Visual Communication, 10(1), 78–95.

Snyder, J. and Allen, N.H. (1982), 'Photography, vision and representation', in T. Barrow and S. Armitage, (eds) Reading into Photography, Albuquerque: University of New Mexico Press, 61–91 (orig. 1975).

Soja, E.W. (1989) Postmodern Geographies: The Reassertion of Space in Critical Social Theory, London: Verso.

Soja, E.W. (1996) Thirdspace: Journeys to Los Angeles and Other Real-and-Imagined Places, Oxford: Blackwell.

Sokal, A. and Bricmont, J. (1999) Intellectual Impostures, London: Profile.

Sontag, S. (1979) On Photography, Harmondsworth: Penguin.

Sontag, S. (ed.) (1982) A Barthes Reader, London: Cape.

Sorokin, P.A. and Merton, R.K. (1937) 'Social time: a methodological and functional analysis', The American Journal of Sociology, 42, March, 615–29.

Spence, J. and Holland, P. (eds) (1991) Family Snaps: The Meanings of Domestic Photography, London: Virago.

Spencer, P. (1990) Anthropology and the Riddle of the Sphinx: Paradoxes of Change in the Life Cycle, ASA Monograph 28, London: Routledge.

Spender, D. (1982) Invisible Women: The Schooling Scandal, London: Writers & Readers.

Spivak, G.C. (1987) In Other Worlds: Essays in Cultural Politics, New York and London: Methuen.

Spivak, G.C. (1990) 'Reading The Satanic Verses', Third Text 11, Summer, 41–60.

Spivak, G.C. (1990) The Post-Colonial Critic: Interviews, Strategies, Dialogues, London: Routledge.

Spivak, G.C. (1993) 'Can the subaltern speak?', in P. Williams and L. Chrisman (eds) Colonial Discourse and Post-colonial Theory, Hemel Hempstead: Harvester.

Sprinker, M. (ed.) (1992) Edward Said: A Critical Reader, Cambridge, MA: Blackwell.

Stacey, J. (1994) Star Gazing: Hollywood Cinema and Female Spectatorship, London: Routledge.

Stallybrass, P. and White, A. (1986) The Politics and Poetics of Transgression, London: Methuen.

Stephens, G. (1992) 'Interracial dialogue in rap music: call-and-response in a multicultural style', New Formations, 16, 62–79.

Stokes, J. (2003) How to do Media and Cultural Studies, London: Sage.

Storey, J. (1993) An Introductory Guide to Cultural Theory and Popular Culture, Hemel Hempstead: Harvester Wheatsheaf.

Storey, S. (2006) Cultural Theory and Popular Culture: An Introduction, Harlow: Pearson Education.

Stott, W. (1973) Documentary Expression and Thirties America, New York: Oxford University Press.

Strathern, M. (1981) 'Culture in a netbag: the manufacture of a subdiscipline in anthropology', Man(NS), 16(4), 665–88.

Strathern, M. (1987) 'An awkward relationship: the case of feminism and anthropology', Signs, 12(2), 277–95.

Strathern, M. (1988) The Gender of the Gift, Berkeley, CA: University of California Press, 280–93.

Strathern, M. (1994) 'Foreword: The Mirror of Technology' in R. Silverstone and E. Hirsch (eds), Consuming Technologies: Media Information in Domestic Spaces, London: Routledge.

Street, B. (1993) Literacy in Theory and Practice, Cambridge: Cambridge University Press.

Sturken, M. and Cartwright, L. (2007) Practices of Looking: An Introduction to Visual Culture, Oxford: Oxford University Press.

Sullivan, N. (2003) A Critical Introduction to Queer Theory, Edinburgh: Edinburgh University Press.

Tannen, D. (1990) You Just Don't Understand: Women and Men in Conversation, New York: Ballantine.

Tannen, D. (ed.) (1993) Gender and Conversational Interaction, New York and Oxford: Oxford University Press.

Taylor, I. (1991) 'Moral panics, crime and urban policy in Manchester', Sociology Review 1(1), 28–32.

Taylor, I. (1995) 'It's a Whole New Ball Game', Salford Papers in Sociology, Salford: University of Salford.

Taylor, P. (1999) *Hackers: Crime in the Digital Sublime*, London: Routledge.

Tcherkezoff, S. (1993) 'The illusion of dualism in Samoa. "Brothers-and-sisters" are not "men-and- women"' in T. del Valle (ed.) *Gendered Anthropology*, European Association of Social Anthropologists, London and New York: Routledge.

Telles, J.L. (1986) 'Time, rank and social control', *Sociological Inquiry*, 50(2), 171–83.

Theweleit, K. (1987) *Male Fantasies. Volume I: Woman, Floods, Bodies, History*, Cambridge: Polity.

Theweleit, K. (1989) *Male Fantasies, Volume 2. Male Bodies: Psychoanalysing the White Terror*, Minneapolis: University of Minnesota Press (orig. 1978).

Thomas, N. (1991) *Entangled Objects: Exchange, Material Culture and Colonialism in the Pacific*: Cambridge, MA: Harvard University Press.

Thompson, E.P. (1961) 'The long revolution', *New Left Review*, 9, May–June, 24–33.

Thompson, E.P. (1965) 'The Peculiarities of the English' in R. Miliband and J. Saville (eds) *The Socialist Register 1965*, London: Merlin.

Thompson, E.P. (1968) *The Making of the English Working Class*, Harmondsworth: Penguin (orig. 1963).

Thompson, E.P. (1978) *The Poverty of Theory and Other Essays*, London: Merlin.

Thompson, E.P. (1991) *Customs in Common*, London: Merlin.

Thompson, J.B. (1984) *Studies in the Theory of Ideology*, Cambridge: Polity.

Thornton, S. (1994) 'Moral panic, the media and British rave culture', in A. Ross and T. Rose (eds) *Microphone Fiends: Youth Music and Youth Culture*, London: Routledge, 176–92.

Thornton, S. (1995) *Club Cultures: Music, Media and Subcultural Capital*, Cambridge: Polity.

Thrift, N.J. (2000) 'Non-representation theory,' in R.J. Johnston, D. Gregory, G. Pratt and M. Watts (eds) (2000) T*he Dictionary of Human Geography* Fourth Edition, Blackwell: Oxford, 556.

Thrift, N.J. (2004) 'Performance and . . .', *Environment and Planning A*, 35, 2019–24.

*Time* magazine (2006) 'Time's Person of the Year: You', online at **http://www.time.com/time/magazine/article/ 0,9171,1569514,00.html**

Tomlinson, J. (1999) *Globalization and Culture*, Cambridge: Polity Press.

Tomlinson, J. (2006) 'Globalization and culture', paper presented at University of Nottingham Ningbo China (UNNC) Research Seminar Series 2006–2007, co-hosted by the Institute of Asia-Pacific Studies and the Institute of Comparative Cultural Studies; accessed 21 September 2007 at **http://www.nottingham.edu.cn/ resources/documents/A10GZAVA.pdf**.

Tosh, J. (1991) *The Pursuit of History*, London: Longman.

Tseëlon, E. (1995) *The Masque of Femininity: The Presentation of Woman in Everyday Life*, London: Sage.

Tuan, Yi-Fu (1974) 'Space and place: humanistic perspective', *Progress in Geography*, 6, 211–52.

Tuchman, G. (1981) *Cultural Imperialism*, London, Printer Publishers.

Tulloch, J. and Jenkins, H. (1995) *Science Fiction Audiences: Watching 'Doctor Who' and 'Star Trek'*, London: Routledge.

Turkle, S. (1995) *Life on the Screen: Identity in the Age of the Internet*, New York: Simon & Schuster.

Turner, B.S. (1984) *The Body and Society: Explorations in Social Theory*, Oxford: Blackwell.

Turner, B.S. (1991) 'The discourse of diet', in M. Featherstone, M. Hepworth and B.S. Turner (eds) *The Body: Social Process and Cultural Theory*, London: Sage (orig. 1982).

Turner, B.S. (1992) *Regulating Bodies: Essays in Medical Sociology*, London: Routledge.

Turner, B.S. (1994) *Orientalism, Postmodernism and Globalism*, London: Routledge.

Turner, G. (1990) *British Cultural Studies: An Introduction*, London: Unwin Hyman.

Turner, V.W. (1967) *The Forest of Symbols*, Ithaca, NY: Cornell University Press.

Tylor, E. (1871) *Primitive Culture*, London: John Murray.

Urry, J. (1988) 'Cultural change and contemporary holiday-making', *Theory, Culture and Society* 5(1), 35–55.

Urry, J. (1990) *The Tourist Gaze*, London: Sage.

Urry, J. (1992) 'The tourist gaze and the environment', *Theory, Culture and Society*, 9(3), 1–26.

Urry, J. (1995) *Consuming Spaces*, London: Routledge.

Urry, J. (2000) *Sociology beyond Societies*, London: Routledge.

Urry, J. (2001) 'Globalising the Tourist Gaze', published by the Department of Sociology, Lancaster University, Lancaster LA1 4YN, UK, at **http:// www.comp.lancs.ac.uk/sociology/papers/Urry-Globalising-the-Tourist-Gaze.pdf**

Urry, J. (2002) *The Tourist Gaze*, London: Sage.

Urry, J. (2003) *Global complexity*, Cambridge: Polity.

Valenti, J. (2007) 'How the Web became a Sexist's Paradise', *The Guardian, G2*, 16–17 (6 May 2007).

Valentine, C. (1968) *Culture and Poverty*, Chicago: University of Chicago Press.

Valentine, G. (1995) 'Creating transgressive space: the music of kd lang,' *Transactions of the Institute of British Geographers*, 20, 474–85.

van Dijk, T.A. (1991) *Racism and the Press*, London: Routledge.

van Gennep, A. (1960) *The Rites of Passage*, Chicago: University of Chicago Press (orig. 1908).

van Zoonen, L. (1994) *Feminist Media Studies*, Sage, London.

Veblen, T. (1934) *The Theory of the Leisure Class*, New York: Modern Library (orig. 1899).

Venturi, R., Scott Brown, D. and Izenour, S. (1977) *Learning From Las Vegas*, rev. edn, Cambridge, MA: MIT Press.

Volosinov, V.N. (1973) *Marxism and the Philosophy of Language*, London: Seminar Press (orig. 1929 and 1930).

Wacquant, L.J.D. (1995) 'Pugs at work: bodily capital and bodily labour among professional boxers', *Body & Society*, 1(1), March, 65–94.

Wacquant, L. (2004) *Body and Soul: Notebooks of an Apprentice Boxer*, New York: Oxford University Press.

Walkowitz, J. (1992) *City of Dreadful Delight: Narratives of Sexual Danger in Late-Victorian London*, London: Virago.

Wall, M. (2000) 'The popular and geography: music and racialized identities in Aotearoa/New Zealand,' in I. Cook, D. Crouch, S. Naylor and J. Ryan (eds) *Cultural Turns/Geographical Turns: Perspectives on Cultural Geography*, London: Prentice Hall, 75–87.

Wallerstein, I.M. (1974) *The Modern World-System*, New York: Academic Press.

Walvin, J. (1982) *A Child's World: A Social History of English Childhood 1800–1914*, Harmondsworth: Penguin.

Walvin, J. (1997) *Fruits of Empire: Exotic Pleasures and British Taste, 1660–1800*, Basingstoke: Macmillan.

Ward, A.H. (1993) 'Dancing in the dark: rationalism and the neglect of social dance', in H. Thomas (ed.) *Dance, Gender and Culture*, Basingstoke and London: Macmillan, 16–33.

Warde, A. (1990) 'Introduction to the sociology of consumption', *Sociology*, 24, 1–4.

Warde, A. (1992) 'Notes on the relationship between production and consumption' in R. Burrows and C. Marsh (eds), *Consumption and Class: Divisions and Change*, London: Macmillan.

Warde, A. (1994) 'Consumption, identity-formation and uncertainty', *Sociology*, 28(4), 877–898.

Warde, A. (1996) 'The future of the sociology of consumption' in S. Edgell, K. Hetherington and A. Warde (eds), *Consumption Matters*, Oxford: Blackwell.

Warner, M. (1985) *Monuments and Maidens: The Allegory of the Female Form*, London: Picador.

Watt, I. (1963) *The Rise of the Novel: Studies in Defoe, Richardson and Fielding*, Harmondsworth: Penguin (orig. 1957).

Waylen, G. (1992) 'Rethinking women's political participation and protest: Chile 1970–1990', in *Political Studies XL(2)*, June, 299–314.

Weber, E. (1976) *Peasants into Frenchmen: The Modernisation of Rural France, 1870–1914*, Stanford: Stanford University Press.

Weber, M. (1930) *The Protestant Ethic and the Spirit of Capitalism*, London: Allen & Unwin.

Weber, M. (1967) 'Bureaucracy', in H.H. Gerth and C. Wright Mills (eds) *From Max Weber: Essays in Sociology*, Routledge & Kegan Paul.

Weber, M. (1978) 'Classes, status groups and parties', in W.G. Runciman (ed.) *Max Weber: Selections in Translation*, Cambridge: Cambridge University Press, 43–56 (orig. 1922).

Webster, F. (1995) *Theories of the Information Society*, London: Routledge.

Weedon, C., Tolson, A. and Mort, F. (1980) 'Theories of language and subjectivity', in *Culture, Media, Language*, London: Unwin Hyman.

Weeks, J. (1981) *Sex, Politics and Society*, Essex: Longman.

Weiner, J. (1991) *Language is the Essence of Culture*, Group for Debates in Anthropological Theory, Department of Social Anthropology, University of Manchester.

Weinstein, D. and Weinstein, M. (1993) *Postmodern(ized) Simmel*, London: Routledge.

Wells, L. (ed.) (2000) *Photography: A Critical Introduction*, London: Routledge.

Wernick, A. (1991) *Promotional Culture: Advertising, Ideology and Symbolic Expression*, London: Sage.

West, C. and Fenstermaker, S. (1995) 'Doing difference', *Gender and Society* 9(1), 8–37.

Westerbeck, C. and Meyerowitz, J. (1994) *Bystander: A History of Street Photography*, London: Thames & Hudson.

Westwood, S. (1984) *All Day, Every Day: Factory and Family in the Making of Women's Lives*, London: Pluto.

Wetherell, M. and Potter, J. (1992) *Mapping the Language of Racism: Discourse and the Legitimation of Exploitation*, Hemel Hempstead: Harvester Wheatsheaf.

Whatmore, S. (1999) 'Hybrid geographies: rethinking the "human" in human geography,' in D. Massey, J. Allen, and P. Sarre, (eds) *Human Geography Today*, Cambridge: Polity Press, 24–39.

Whelan, Y. (2002) 'The construction and destruction of a colonial landscape: monuments to British monarchs in Dublin before and after Independence', *Journal of Historical Geography*, 28(4), 508–33.

Whelehan, I. (2000) *Over Loaded: Popular Culture and the Future of Feminism*, London: The Women's Press.

Whimster, S. (ed.) (2003) *The Essential Weber: A Reader*, London: Routledge.

White, H. (1973) *Metahistory: The Historical Imagination in Nineteenth Century Europe*, Baltimore, MD and London: John Hopkins Press.

White, M. and Schwoch, J. (2006) *Questions of Method in Cultural Studies*, Oxford: Blackwell.

Widdicombe, S. and Wooffitt, R. (1995) *The Language of Youth Subcultures: Social Identity in Action*, Hemel Hempstead: Harvester Wheatsheaf.

Willet, J. (ed.) (1978) *Brecht on Theatre*, London: Methuen.

Williams, D. (1975) 'The brides of Christ', in S. Ardener (ed.) *Perceiving Women*, London: Dent.

Williams, L. (1990) *Hard Core: Power, Pleasure, and the 'Frenzy of the Visible'*, London: Pandora.

Williams, R. (1963) *Culture and Society 1780–1950*, Harmondsworth: Penguin (orig. 1958).

Williams, R. (1965) *The Long Revolution*, Harmondsworth: Penguin (orig. 1961).

Williams, R. (1973a) *The Country and the City*, London: Hogarth.

Williams, R. (1973b) 'Base and superstructure in Marxist cultural theory', *New Left Review*, 82, 3–16.

Williams, R. (1974) *Television: Technology and Cultural Form*, Glasgow: Fontana/Collins.

Williams, R. (1977) *Marxism and Literature*, Oxford: Oxford University Press.

Williams, R. (1983a) 'Culture', in D. McLellan (ed.) *Marx: The First Hundred Years*, London: Fontana, 15–55.

Williams, R. (1983b) *Keywords: A Vocabulary of Culture and Society*, London: Fontana.

Williamson, J. (1978) *Decoding Advertisements: Ideology and Meaning in Advertising*, London: Marion Boyars.

Willis, P. (1977) *Learning to Labour: How Working Class Kids Get Working Class Jobs*, Farnborough: Saxon House.

Willis, P. (1978) *Profane Culture*, London: Routledge & Kegan Paul.

Willis, P. with Jones, S., Canaan, J. and Hurd, G. (1990) *Common Culture: Symbolic Work at Play in the Everyday Cultures of the Young*, Milton Keynes: Open University Press.

Wilson, E. (1985) *Adorned in Dreams: Fashion and Modernity*, London: Virago.

Wilson, E. (1992) 'The invisible flâneur', *New Left Review* 191, 90–110.

Wilson, W.J. (ed.) (1993) *The Ghetto Underclass: Social Science Perspectives*, Newbury Park: Sage.

Winston, B. (1995) *Claiming the Real: The Griersonian Documentary and its Legitimations*, London: British Film Institute.

Wirth, L. (1938) 'Urbanism as a way of life', *American Journal of Sociology*, 44, 1–24.

Wittgenstein, L. (1981) *Tractatus logico-philosophicus*, London: Routledge & Kegan Paul (orig. 1921).

Witz, A. and Savage, M. (1992) 'The gender of organisations', in M. Savage and A. Witz (eds) *Gender and Bureaucracy*, Oxford: Blackwell, 3–62.

Wolfe, T. (1983) *From Bauhaus to Our House*, London: Abacus.

Wolff, J. (1981) *The Social Production of Art*, London: Macmillan.

Wolff, J. (1985) 'The invisible *flâneuse:* women and the literature of modernity', *Theory, Culture and Society* 2(3), 37–46.

Wolff, J. (1993) 'On the road again: metaphors of travel in cultural criticism', *Cultural Studies*, 7, 224–39.

Woolf, V. (1964) *Mrs Dalloway*, Harmondsworth: Penguin.

World Bank (2007) *World Development Indicators 2007 (WDI)*. The World Bank.

Wright, W. (1975) *Sixguns and Society*, Berkeley, CA: University of California Press.

Yates, S. J. and Littleton, K. L. (2001) "Understanding computer game culture: A situated approach", in E. Green and A. Adams (eds) *Virtual Gender: Technology,*

*Consumption and Identity*. London: Routledge, 103–123.

Yee, N. (2006) *The Daedalus Project*, website **http://www.nickyee.com/daedalus**

Yeoh, B.S.A. (1992) 'Street names in colonial Singapore', *The Geographical Review*, 82, 312–22.

Yeoh, B.S.A. (1996) 'Street-naming and nation-building: toponymic inscriptions of nationhood in Singapore', *Area*, 28, 298–307.

Young, I.M. (1980) 'Throwing like a girl: a phenomenology of feminine body comportent, motility and spatiality', *Human Studies*, 3, 137–56; reprinted in I.M. Young (1990) *Throwing Like a Girl and Other Essays in Feminist Philosophy and Social Theory*, Bloomington, IN: Indiana University Press.

Young, M. (1991) *An Inside Job: Policing and Police Culture in Britain*, Oxford: Clarendon.

Young, R.J. (2001) *Postcolonialism: An Historical Introduction*, Oxford: Blackwell.

Zerubavel, E. (1979) *Patterns of Time in Hospital Life: A Sociological Perspective*, Chicago: Chicago University Press.

Zerubavel, E. (1982) *Hidden Rhythms: Schedules and Calendars in Social Life*, Chicago: Chicago University Press.

Zukin, S. (1989) *Loft Living: Culture and Capital in Urban Change*, New Brunswick, NJ: Rutgers University Press.

Zukin, S. (1991) *Landscapes of Power: From Detroit to Disney World*, Berkeley and Los Angeles: University of California Press.

Zukin, S. (1992) 'Postmodern urban landscapes: mapping culture and power', in S. Lash and J. Friedman (eds) *Modernity and Identity*, Oxford: Blackwell, 221–47.

Zukin, S. (1995) *The Cultures of Cities*, Oxford: Blackwell.

# Index